Abolition and Antislavery

Abolition and Antislavery

A Historical Encyclopedia of the American Mosaic

Peter Hinks and John McKivigan, Editors

 GREENWOOD™

An Imprint of ABC-CLIO, LLC
Santa Barbara, California • Denver, Colorado

Library of Congress Cataloging-in-Publication Data

Abolition and antislavery : a historical encyclopedia of the American mosaic / Peter Hinks and John McKivigan, editors.

    pages cm

Includes bibliographical references and index.

ISBN 978-1-61069-827-6 (alk. paper) — ISBN 978-1-61069-828-3 (eISBN)

1. Antislavery movements—United States—Encyclopedias. 2. Abolitionists—United States—History—19th century—Encyclopedias. I. Hinks, Peter P., editor. II. McKivigan, John R., 1949– editor.

  E449.A148   2015

  326'.80922—dc23

  [B]   2015005610

ISBN: 978-1-61069-827-6
EISBN: 978-1-61069-828-3

19   18   17   16   15   1   2   3   4   5

This book is also available on the World Wide Web as an eBook.
Visit www.abc-clio.com for details.

Greenwood
An Imprint of ABC-CLIO, LLC

ABC-CLIO, LLC
130 Cremona Drive, P.O. Box 1911
Santa Barbara, California 93116-1911

This book is printed on acid-free paper ∞

Manufactured in the United States of America

Contents

List of Entries, vii

List of Primary Documents, xi

Preface, xiii

Introduction, xv

Chronology, xxi

The Encyclopedia, 1

Primary Documents, 373

Selected Bibliography, 413

Index, 421

About the Editors, 447

List of Entries

Abolitionist Women
Adams, John Quincy
Africa Squadron
African American Communities
Allen, Richard
American and Foreign Anti-Slavery
    Society (AFASS)
American Anti-Slavery Society
    (AASS)
American Colonization Society
American Convention of Abolition
    Societies
American Missionary Association
    (AMA)
Amistad
Antislavery Evangelical Protestantism
Antislavery Journalism in the United
    States and Great Britain
Anti-Slavery Society
Antislavery Songs
Atlantic Slave Trade and British
    Abolition

Bailey, Gamaliel
Benezet, Anthony
Birney, James Gillespie (1792–1857)
Bleeding Kansas
British Slavery, Abolition of
Burned-Over District

Burns, Anthony
Burritt, Elihu

Canada, Antislavery in
Chase, Salmon P.
Child, Lydia Maria
Clay, Cassius
Clay, Henry
Come-Outerism
Commonwealth v. Aves (1836)
Compromise of 1850
Confiscation Acts (1861, 1862)
Congregationalism and Antislavery
Congressional Debate on Ending
    U.S. Atlantic Slave Trade
Contrabands
Crandall, Prudence
Creole Affair (1841)

Declaration of Independence (1776)
Delany, Martin Robison (1812–1885)
Democratic Party and Antislavery
Douglass, Frederick (1818–1895)

Equiano, Olaudah

Federalists and Antislavery
Field Order No. 15
Finney, Charles Grandison (1792–1875)

First Great Awakening and
 Antislavery
Fitzhugh, George
Foster, Abby Kelley (1811–1887)
Free Produce Movement
Freedmen's Aid Societies
Freedmen's Bureau
Freedom Suits in North America
Freemasonry and Antislavery
Fugitive Slave Law (1850)

Gabriel's Conspiracy (1800)
Garnet, Henry Highland (1815–1882)
Garrison, William Lloyd
Garrisonians
German Coast (Louisiana)
 Insurrection of 1811
Germantown Antislavery Petition
 (1688)
Gradual Emancipation
Grimké, Angelina
Grimké, Charlotte Forten

Haitian Revolution
Hall, Prince
Helper, Hinton
Higher Law and Antislavery
Hiring-Out and Challenges to Slavery

Immediate Emancipation
Internal Slave Trade and Antislavery

Jefferson, Thomas and Antislavery
Jerry Rescue (1851)

King, Boston

Lane Seminary Debates (1834)
Liberia

Liberty Party
Lincoln, Abraham
Literature and Abolition
Lord Dunmore's Proclamation
Lovejoy, Elijah (1802–1837)
Lundy, Benjamin

Manumission
Memorialization of Antislavery and
 Abolition
Mexican War and Antislavery
Missouri Compromise (1820)
Mott, Lucretia Coffin
Myers, Stephen (1800–1870) and
 Myers, Harriet (1807–1865)

New England Antislavery Society
 (NEASS)
New York Committee of Vigilance
New York Manumission Society
 (NYMS)
Northwest Ordinance (1787)

Parker, John Percial
Paul, Nathaniel
Pennsylvania Abolition Society (PAS)
Phillips, Wendell
Port Royal (South Carolina)
Postal Campaign (1835)

Quakers and Antislavery
Quok Walker Decision (1783)

Radical Republicans
Reconstruction Acts in the United
 States (1867–1868)
Republicanism and Antislavery
Ruggles, David
Rush, Benjamin

Secession Crisis and Abolitionists
Secret Six
Slave Narratives
Slave Power Argument
Smith, Gerrit
Smith, James McCune
Somerset Decision (1772)
Spooner, Lysander
Stowe, Harriet Beecher

Tappan, Arthur
Tappan, Lewis
Texas, Annexation of (1845)
Thirteenth Amendment (1865)
Truth, Sojourner
Tubman, Harriet
Turner, Nat

Uncle Tom's Cabin (1852)
Underground Railroad

Unitarianism and Antislavery
United States, Antislavery in
U.S. Constitution and
    Antislavery
U.S. South, Antislavery in

Vesey's Conspiracy (1822)
Violence and Nonviolence in
    American Abolitionism

Walker, David
Washington, D.C., Compensated
    Emancipation in
Weld, Theodore Dwight
West Indies Emancipation Day
    Celebration
Whig Party and Antislavery
Wilberforce, William
Women's Antislavery
    Societies

List of Primary Documents

Excerpts from *A Narrative of the Uncommon Sufferings, and Surprizing Deliverance of Briton Hammon*, 373

Excerpt from *The Interesting Narrative of the Life of Olaudah Equiano* (1789), 378

Excerpts from *The Confessions of Nat Turner* (1831), 381

The *Liberator* (1831), 388

An Appeal in Favor of That Class of Americans Called Africans (1833), 389

"A Positive Good" (1837), 393

Excerpt from *Narrative of the Life of Frederick Douglass* (1845), 397

Excerpt from *Uncle Tom's Cabin* (1852), 402

Excerpts from *Cannibals All! or Slaves without Masters* (1857), 404

Excerpt from *The Impending Crisis* (1857), 407

Emancipation Proclamation (1863), 410

Thirteenth Amendment (1865), 412

Preface

While the earliest expressions of American antislavery may have only comprised one or a few isolated voices, the antislavery most commonly reviewed in this encyclopedia will be that animated by a systematic and ardent opposition to slavery and intended to mobilize large numbers of people to attack and end the institution. A wide variety of people and organizations motivated religiously, secularly, or otherwise nurtured and extended this antislavery. Its growth was by no means the work exclusively or even principally of an intellectual elite; the force of all, from the lowly and unlearned to the privileged and prominent, must be represented in this encyclopedia if it is to comprehend accurately the scope of antislavery. Sometimes the American antislavery movement was feeble or nonexistent, but pressure from an extra-national force such as the British or world opinion would insert an important antislavery presence. This encyclopedia will detail all of these critical events and others concerning antislavery in America.

While movements to abolish slavery have involved a complex aggregation of social, political, economic, and cultural forces, the actual act of abolition itself was largely state sponsored through legislative or juridical decision. For example, the ending of slavery in the North of the United States during and after the Revolutionary War was largely a legislative, juridical, and elite process with relatively little popular mobilization. While the coalescing of an organized social movement around antislavery might often precede the act of abolition, the actual definitive steps toward abolition and the passage of it may be isolated as a distinct phenomenon meriting a separate category for abolition itself. A vigorous, organized antislavery movement existed in the United States well before definitive steps toward the abolition of slavery were taken in the South. Abolition acts were often passed—and modified—in the face of significant opposition to them from slaveholders and their supporters.

This encyclopedia will also pay attention to the numerous, powerful, and articulate figures who opposed abolition and argued for the innate inferiority of the subjugated and/or their unfitness for freedom. The abolitionists had constantly to respond to these arguments and to undermine pervasive beliefs in the eighteenth and early nineteenth centuries that people of African descent were naturally fit for enslavement. Thinking about race played a vital part in the movement toward—or away from—abolition. Not all abolitionists endorsed principles of racial equality and controversies over race persisted from the time of emancipation to modern times.

The unfolding of emancipation entailed very different processes, expectations, and conflicts from those that preceded abolition. In sum, abolition was involved with organizing and mobilizing for or against the continuation of legal slavery within a society while emancipation was much more concerned with the economic and social consequences of that abolition—most commonly with the regulation and control of the freedmen's labor and with their political status. While these latter concerns about the consequences of abolition were certainly expressed during the struggles over abolition, they were marshalled either to defend or to attack the institution. After the passing of the abolition struggle, these concerns over consequences and regulation ignited severe struggles in the U.S. South. The unfolding of freedom continues long after the movement toward and the act of ending. Thus, in this encyclopedia, emancipation and abolition—while evidently related—are explored as two separate and discrete processes.

However, slaves well might begin becoming free by taking decisive steps toward destroying the legal institution of slavery before formal abolition and emancipation: such measures characterized the actions of slaves in the American North during the American Revolution and in the South during the Civil War. And flight, resistance, and rebellion, which did not contribute directly to the overthrow of slavery, were an integral part of an emerging, organized antislavery movement in the eighteenth and nineteenth centuries. Black rebels were crucial agents of antislavery both for the dramatic evidence they gave of enduring black autonomy and the keen problems they posed for the maintenance of the Southern slaveholding regimes. Moreover, the outcome of emancipation disappointed many of the former American enslaved who witnessed the replacement of slavery by new forms of labor exploitation and economic dependence and who had their aspirations for democracy and social equality checked and crushed.

This encyclopedia thus summarizes the history of American antislavery, abolition, and emancipation. Its entries are organized alphabetically and contain cross-references following each entry. Most entries conclude with a section entitled "Further Readings" which lists additional works—both print and electronic—which the reader may consult to explore the entry's topic further. A bibliography, which includes a number of the most important works written on this broad history, has also been compiled. Finally, a timeline is included to afford a chronological overview of the history of these movements and events.

Introduction

The rise of antislavery and the abolition to which it led from the eighteenth through the twentieth centuries represents one of the great intellectual and social revolutions in the history of the world. Historically, the institution of slavery was often linked with a well-ordered society and the regulation of the irrational and the bestial. Aristotle, the ancient world's foremost commentator on slavery, likened the slave to a dumb instrument guided by the superior moral and intellectual faculties of the master. Jewish, Christian, and Islamic tenets and practices all sanctioned slavery. Judaism developed in a world pervaded by slavery, and the institution continued vital among the Jews as punishment for crime, debt, and capture in war. The first books of Hebrew Scripture are replete with information on the regulation of slaves, both Jewish and outsider, within Jewish society. Nowhere is slavery deplored in Christian Scripture. In a world infused with sinning, government and slavery are ordained by God as key institutions for regulating this unavoidable human propensity to evil. As the Apostle Paul admonished: "Slaves, obey your human masters in everything. . . . Masters, treat your slaves justly and fairly, realizing that you too have a Master in heaven" (Colossians, 3:22, 4:1). Slavery was present throughout the Koran, and numerous rules structured the proper Islamic relationship between master and slave. Unlike Christianity, Islam explicitly sanctioned the manumission of faithful slaves as an act of benevolence by the master and such individual freeing was common in the Islamic world, especially as an act of sacrifice and contrition during the annual observance of Ramadan. But the legitimacy of slavery was in no way challenged by such actions, and it thrived throughout Muslim lands. By the early eighteenth century as slavery thrived in the Atlantic world and beyond, slavery continued to be accepted near axiomatically as necessary, useful, and thoroughly in accord with Judaism, Christianity, and Islam.

Yet from the early 1700s, slavery came increasingly to be viewed as the agent of evil in the world, the very quintessence of sin as some called it, and the chief repository of all that was socially, politically, and especially economically archaic, stagnant, and inefficient. By the formal conclusion of World War I with the signing of the Treaty of Versailles, legal slavery had been eliminated in most of the world.

This transformation was launched most importantly in the Atlantic world where slavery thrived since European powers began colonizing it in the early sixteenth century. Some Catholic clerics in New Spain and Brazil in the sixteenth and seventeenth centuries like Bartolomé de las Casas and Tomas de Mercado attacked the horrendous enslavement of indigenous peoples in New Spain and Brazil and soon the cruelty of the slave trade. But none of these largely lone critics condemned the Atlantic slave trade or slavery per se, arguing instead that they should be regulated justly and that the slaves should be catechized and baptized.

The mounting of an ultimately successful attack on the Atlantic slave trade and on slavery itself would be the project largely of the English Atlantic world. The first attacks from this realm would issue from geographical and social obscurity. A meeting of Quakers in the Germantown section of Philadelphia in 1688 first raised the questions that would preoccupy the rising antislavery movement of the eighteenth century: Who among the Quakers and other whites of the Pennsylvania colony would tolerate being "handled"—forcibly transported under horrid conditions and then sold for life like beasts—as the Africans are? Do Christians have liberty to engage in such brutal practices? Do we have any more right to enslave these people than the Turks do, or the Africans might, us? Other Quakers in Philadelphia, New Jersey, Rhode Island, and Massachusetts would follow this first thrust over the ensuing years. Distinctive Quaker doctrines renouncing worldliness, ostentation, and all forms of violence and coercion and proclaiming devotion to the voice of God within the individual through the "inner light" contributed to sparking this early antislavery. Slavery was condemned as founded on dominance, self-aggrandizement, and greed. By 1758, the Philadelphia Meeting began prodding its members to renounce slavery and prepare their slaves for emancipation. The repercussions from this momentous step would resonate over the coming years, far beyond Pennsylvania. By 1774, when the Philadelphia Meeting forbade any further buying or selling of slaves among its members upon penalty of disownment, even broader international attention would be drawn to the movement.

No one would contribute more to this broadening, international appeal than would Anthony Benezet. A Philadelphia Quaker, Benezet published in 1762 *A Short Account of That Part of Africa Inhabited by the Negroes*. In conjunction with emerging Quaker antislavery organizations, *A Short Account* would prove instrumental in bringing key British politicians to support and work for the abolition of Britain's involvement in the Atlantic slave trade and ultimately in West Indian slavery. However, far more so than prior Quaker advocates, Benezet stressed the moral and intellectual equivalence of black African with white Anglo-American as well as Africans' identical capacity for improvement. What prevented them from manifesting this natural impulse to autonomy and improvement, he argued, were the restrictions and debasements placed upon them by slavery, nurturing them in ignorance, demoralization, and moral corruption. Thus human custom and laws—the social environment, not the predeterminations of God and nature—were responsible for creating the impression of their unfathomable difference from white Europeans, crushing the spirit of the Africans and alienating them so grossly from God.

Slavery itself, not simply the slave trade, was the most reprehensible of sinning, and Quakers and all other slaveholders must disavow this evil by preparing their slaves for freedom and reorganizing their societies so, upon their emancipation, they may be included as equals. Benezet's widely disseminated work influenced numerous other American antislavery authors, including Benjamin Rush and Samuel Hopkins and by the early 1770s, he was corresponding with the influential British reformer, Granville Sharp. In 1787, Sharp helped organize the Quaker-dominated Society for Effecting the Abolition of the Slave Trade and played a pivotal role in drawing the influential Anglicans William Wilberforce, Thomas Clarkson, and James Ramsey into the antislavery movement by the late 1780s. These men orchestrated the political machinery leading to Great Britain's momentous abolition of its participation in the Atlantic slave trade in 1808.

Yet concurrent with the Quakers' attack in North America on slavery was the far more secular speculations of moral philosophers and political economists in France, England, and Scotland. Central to these arguments were fundamental shifts in conceptions of the nature of humans and of their relationship to society. As if to trumpet the end of feudalism in northwestern Europe and its notions of fixed social orders intricately bound to each other through a myriad of mutual obligations, John Locke in the late seventeenth century identified the essence of the human individual to be in their endowment by nature with liberty, a liberty one could not alienate without ceasing to be human. This liberty, responsibly exercised in one's own self-interest, legitimated contracts executed between individuals and between individuals and the state. Locke, more fully than any political philosopher preceding him, newly associated freedom with mobility and individual autonomy rather than with its more traditional connotation—the right to be a recognized and actively participating member of a community from which one derived security and existential meaning. For Locke, slavery was a fundamentally unnatural condition in which the individual all but ceased to be human by relinquishing the liberty essential to identity. Asserting that this would be all but intolerable for Christian Europeans, Locke allowed, however, for the legitimate enslavement of non-Christian war captives and thus conveniently sanctioned the proliferating African slavery of the New World.

The *philosophes* of the French Enlightenment, enrapt by Locke's vision of human freedom, augmented it by championing the application of this individual liberty to society as a whole to generate an enormous increase in the material and political well-being of a society. The liberation of the individual to exercise his quintessentially human faculty of reason free from the constraints of traditions and coercive laws and to identify and condemn outmoded institutions and belief systems was critical to the envisioned social advance. For Montesquieu, Voltaire, Diderot, and Rousseau, no institution corrupted a society and its capacity for improvement more thoroughly than did slavery, although for Voltaire the Catholic Church was at the very least a close second. Slavery dispirited the enslaved, rendering them an inefficient and uncooperative producer. By not being citizens, slaves could not serve the public good and became eternal enemies against which society had to waste energies in vigilance. Masters were damaged as well, for slavery nurtured in them a contempt for labor and a love of indolence, luxury, and tyranny. All of these values contrasted with those promoted by a free society in which reason, enterprise, and efficiency were extolled and human happiness pursued. While none of them finally attacked New World slavery outright, and Montesquieu even speculated that slaves might be necessary in tropical environments where Europeans faltered and sickened, their formidable arguments assaulted and derided the institution of slavery and contributed further to establishing its immorality and dehumanization.

Adam Smith and Frances Hutcheson, respectively, late eighteenth-century Scottish political economist and moral philosopher, pushed the secular antislavery of the *philosophes* even farther in a utilitarian direction. While they sought to create moral and materially abundant societies, they argued uncharacteristically that such societies would be achieved most readily by an unleashed pursuit of self-interest. Historically, the pursuit of self-interest had been firmly associated with all that destroyed virtuous republican government, promoted sinning, and led to the concentration of power in the hands of a corrupt few. It was to be countered and even renounced if social justice and harmony were to be realized. But Smith, Hutcheson, and other contemporary Scottish philosophers boldly asserted that, rather than corrupting the good society, the pursuit of self-interest was the very engine of the advance of society and morality. Self-interest was the very core of human motivation and rather than being suppressed, it should be harnessed, enlightened, and rendered useful and productive. Maximizing individual freedom rather than diminishing it was the key to a healthy and prosperous communitas. As the antithesis of freedom, slavery promoted not only tyranny and civic alienation but also a stagnant economy incapable of encouraging or satisfying the material needs of its members except through coercion.

Strengthening this mounting antislavery of the eighteenth century was the vehement and irrepressible opposition of the enslaved themselves. From slave revolts in Hispaniola during the early Spanish occupation of the sixteenth century through the Maroon Wars in Jamaica in the mid-eighteenth century and the Saint Domingue rebellion later in the century and ensuing Caribbean uprisings in the early decades of the nineteenth, the resistance of the slaves was central to the construction of a widespread and viable antislavery. Rebellions of Africans onboard ships carrying them to slavery in the New World were not uncommon from the onset of the Atlantic slave trade in the late fifteenth century. This long history of shipboard uprisings and colonial rebellions made the frank reality all too clear to the Europeans that Africans were not passive before their subjugators, that they hated their enslavement, and that they were willing to die to free themselves from it. The fierce restiveness of the slaves mandated the brutal regimens characteristic of colonial slavery through the eighteenth century for their overlords fully recognized that the enslaved would rise successfully against them otherwise.

It was not until the great revolt in Saint Domingue in the 1790s—publicized vividly throughout the Atlantic world in newspapers, essays, and lurid lithographs—that the broader white populace in the centers of colonial power began to appreciate the vehemence of slave opposition. While on the one hand a cool strategic decision to preserve colonial power, the revolutionary decision of France's General Assembly to abolish slavery in its colonies in 1794 was integrally bound up with a significant portion of the Assembly's support for the Saint Dominguan slaves' own quest for liberty and equality. Over the ensuing decades, many antislavery advocates would hold high the bloody example of Saint Domingue as an irrefragable argument for the evil of slavery and tens of thousands throughout the Atlantic world would hear those arguments. Similarly, slave rebellions in Demerara, Jamaica, Barbados, and elsewhere in the Caribbean between 1800 and 1830 strengthened popular resolve in England to abolish slavery in the British West Indies in the 1830s.

These three forces—evangelicalism, moral economy, and slave rebellion—of emerging antislavery in the eighteenth century would ideologically undergird the great struggles in Britain to abolish its involvement with the Atlantic slave trade and colonial slavery as well as that of other nations over the ensuing years. Britain's role would be instrumental in prompting or forcing antislavery and abolition on resistant nations in the Atlantic world from the Congress of Vienna in 1815 forward as would be their role in realms well beyond that world in the second half of the nineteenth century and after. These agreements, however, were often compromised in practice. Treaties with Brazil and Spain to end their involvement in the nineteenth-century slave trade were routinely violated and efforts by the British, other colonial powers, or regional powers themselves to emancipate slaves gradually or outlaw slavery altogether in the Arabic world and in the Horn of Africa and sub-Saharan Africa proved largely futile well into the twentieth century. The League of Nations and later the United Nations would proclaim a world free of slavery as a foundation of their principles of human rights. Yet slavery would be renewed with an unusually brutal vigor during World War II and would persist, in ways both official and anomalous, into the second half of the twentieth century. Indeed, after the three forces identified earlier aided the destruction of slavery in the United States by 1865, a brutal regimen of segregation and discrimination would be steadily installed in the South over the years after the war that would itself not be fully eliminated until a century later.

Chronology

1441   Portuguese sailors kidnap Africans from the northwest coast of the continent, bringing them to Europe to work as slaves in the sugar factories in Portugal and on the Atlantic Islands it controlled off the African coast; from these beginnings spring the Atlantic slave trade.

1498   To ensure order and stability in the new Spanish settlements in America, Christopher Columbus sanctions employment of *repartimientos*, allotments of Native peoples, usually a tribal leader and his people, to work in the mines or on the lands of a Spanish master.

1542   The Spanish Crown promulgates the New Laws, which ban Indian slavery and undermine the *encomienda* system in the colonies of Spanish America.

1561   Bartolomé de Las Casas completes his *Historia de las Indias* (*The History of the Indies*), in which he criticizes the Spanish for their cruel treatment of Native peoples and declares, in contradiction to his earlier writings, that Africans deserve the same right of self-determination that he seeks for indigenous.

1619   Africans are landed at the Jamestown Colony in Virginia.

1688   Englishwoman Aphra Behn publishes *Oroonoko, or the Royal Slave*, the supposedly true story of an African prince tricked into slavery; because she graphically depicts the prince's torture and execution by Europeans without referring to the racial denigration of Africans common of the era, Behn is often considered an early abolitionist.

               Quakers in Germantown, Pennsylvania, sign the Germantown Antislavery Petition, which is believed to be the first public protest against slavery in British North America.

1689	English political philosopher John Locke publishes his influential *Second Treatise of Government*, in which he describes his reasons for opposing slavery.
1693	George Keith, a Pennsylvania Quaker, issues an "Exhortation and Caution to Friends Concerning Buying or Keeping of Negroes," one of the first antislavery tracts published in colonial America.
1700	Samuel Sewall of Boston publishes "The Selling of Joseph," an early antislavery tract written in America.
1701	Thomas Bray establishes the Society for the Propagation of the Gospel to spread Christianity in Britain's North American colonies.
1711	Richard Steele publishes an imaginative reworking of the tale of "Inkle and Yarico" in issue no. 11 of the *Spectator;* because the periodical was frequently reprinted throughout Great Britain and North America, the tale became one of the best-known and most compelling antislavery narratives of the eighteenth century.
1739	The Stono Rebellion, one of the largest slave uprisings in colonial America, erupts in South Carolina.
1748	Montesquieu publishes *The Spirit of the Laws*, in which he declares slavery to be "not good by its nature."
1751	Slavery is formally legalized in the colony of Georgia, thus overthrowing the attempts made since 1732 by the Georgia Trustees, the colony's proprietors, to restrict the spread of slavery.
1754	John Woolman of Pennsylvania publishes an essay entitled "Some Considerations on the Keeping of Negroes."
1761	At their Yearly Meeting in London, the Quakers agree to disown any slave dealers among their members.
1762	Anthony Benezet publishes *A Short Account of That Part of Africa, Inhabited by the Negroes, and the Manner by Which the Slave-Trade Is Carried On*, which vividly illustrated the devastating effects of the slave trade upon West African peoples and societies.
1769	Granville Sharp publishes *A Representation of the Injustice and Dangerous Tendency of Tolerating Slavery*, in which he challenges a master's property rights in slaves.
1772	British chief justice William Murray, Earl of Mansfield, renders a decision in the *Somerset* case, declaring that a slave, once brought

to England, was free; the decision is instrumental in ending slavery in Great Britain.

1774   At their Yearly Meeting in Philadelphia, American Quakers implement a plan for the eventual emancipation of all slaves owned by Quakers.

1775   Thomas Paine publishes "African Slavery in America," a pamphlet attacking both the slave trade and the institution of slavery.

Anthony Benezet becomes the first president of the Society for the Relief of Free Negroes Unlawfully Held in Bondage, which in 1784 is renamed the Pennsylvania Abolition Society.

Lord Dunmore, the last royal governor of Virginia, issues a controversial decree declaring martial law and promising freedom to all slaves who left their rebel masters to fight for the Crown.

1776   Abolitionist Samuel Hopkins publishes *A Dialogue Concerning the Slavery of the Africans.*

Adam Smith publishes *The Wealth of Nations*, in which he decries both the moral and economic cost of slavery.

1777   The Vermont State Constitution explicitly abolishes slavery within the state.

1779   Publication of the first edition of the *Olney Hymns*, containing "Amazing Grace," by John Newton, a former slave trader who may have used an old African American melody for the hymn.

1780   The Pennsylvania legislature enacts the first state gradual abolition law.

1783   The Massachusetts Supreme Court, in *Commonwealth of Massachusetts v. Jennison* (known as the *Quock Walker* Decision), pronounces slavery has no standing in the Massachusetts Constitution, thus making Massachusetts the first state to deny its citizens property rights in slaves.

1784   Rhode Island enacts a gradual emancipation law, but continues the slave trade.

Connecticut enacts a gradual emancipation law.

1785   In his *Notes on the State of Virginia*, Thomas Jefferson condemns the institution of slavery, but argues that emancipation should be accompanied by the removal of blacks to a separate colony.

The New York Manumission Society is founded in New York City.

1786   British abolitionist Thomas Clarkson publishes his influential essay entitled, "An Essay on the Slavery and Commerce of the Human Species, Particularly the African."

1787   The new U.S. Constitution counts three-fifths of all slaves for purposes of representation in Congress, a clause that greatly increases the political power of the South.

British abolitionists settle a community of freed slaves in Sierra Leone on the west coast of Africa.

Granville Sharp and Thomas Clarkson found the Society for the Abandonment of the Slave Trade.

Former slave Ottobah Cugoano, one of the first free Africans in Britain to publicly oppose slavery, publishes *Thoughts and Sentiments on the Evil and Wicked Traffic of Slavery and Commerce of Human Species*.

Congress passes the Northwest Ordinance, which prohibits slavery in the territory west of the Appalachians and north of the Ohio River.

1788   Jacques-Pierre Brissot and Étienne Clavière found the *Société des Amis des Noirs*, which calls for an immediate end to the slave trade and the gradual and uncompensated abolition of slavery.

Englishwoman Hannah More publishes "Slavery: A Poem," the first of a series of antislavery verses by which she sought to persuade Parliament to abolish the slave trade.

1789   Former slave and abolitionist Olaudah Equiano publishes his popular autobiography, *The Interesting Narrative of the Life of Olaudah Equiano, or Gustavus Vassa, the African*.

1790s   The Free Produce Movement, which boycotted produce made by slave labor in hopes of thereby undermining the economic viability of the slave system, begins among Quaker groups and continues in some form until the end of slavery in the 1860s.

1790   Founding of the Connecticut Society for the Promotion of Freedom and Persons Holden in Bondage; among the founders are such clergymen as Levi Hart and Jonathan Edwards, Jr.

Benjamin Franklin publishes a major antislavery essay in the *Federal Gazette*.

1791   The Haitian Revolution, which resulted in the abolition of slavery and the achievement of the independence of Haiti (in 1804), begins in the French West Indian colony of Saint Domingue (present-day Haiti).

Jonathan Edwards, Jr., publishes *The Injustice and Impolicy of the Slave-Trade, and of the Slavery of the Africans.*

1793   The U.S. Congress passes the first Fugitive Slave Act, mandating the return of runaway slaves to their legal owners.

Abolitionist Samuel Hopkins publishes *A Discourse upon the Slave Trade.*

1794   Lobbied by the American Convention of Abolition Societies, Congress passes the first American anti-slave trade law, which bans Americans from trading captured Africans to foreign traders.

The French National Convention recognizes the end of slavery in the colony of Saint Domingue and abolishes slavery in the other French Caribbean colonies.

Former slave Richard Allen founds the African Methodist Episcopal Church in Philadelphia.

1794–1836   The American Convention of Abolition Societies meets sporadically during these years, bringing together local abolition societies from around the United States to discuss and coordinate abolitionist tactics and strategies.

1795   The Pointe Coupée Rebellion erupts in Louisiana.

1796   St. George Tucker publishes *A Dissertation on Slavery: With a Proposal for the Gradual Abolition of It, in the State of Virginia,* the only serious proposal to end slavery to be written by a Southerner in this period.

1799   U.S. Congress receives one of the first African American petitions calling for an end to the domestic slave trade and consideration of a plan for gradual abolition.

The New York legislature enacts a gradual abolition law.

1800   A slave conspiracy known as Gabriel's Rebellion is foiled in Richmond, Virginia.

1804   New Jersey passes a gradual emancipation act.

1806   The Virginia legislature amends the state's Manumission Act of 1782 by requiring liberated bondpeople to leave Virginia or face re-enslavement.

1808   With the first day of the new year, both Great Britain and the United States officially cease involvement in the Atlantic slave trade.

1811	The German Coast Slave Insurrection erupts in Louisiana.
1816	American Colonization Society, which advocates sending African Americans, both slave and free, to Africa, is founded.
1820	Congress passes the Missouri Compromise prohibiting slavery north of the southern border of the new state of Missouri.
1822	Slave conspiracy of Denmark Vesey, perhaps the largest in U.S. history, is foiled in Charleston, South Carolina.
	The American Colonization Society, acting with federal assistance, establishes the colony of Liberia on the west coast of Africa for the resettlement on that continent of African Americans.
1823	Major slave rebellion erupts in Demerara, sending shock waves throughout the British slaveholding colonies in the Caribbean.
	Chile bans slavery, the first of the new South American republics to do so.
	The Society for the Amelioration and Gradual Abolition of Slavery is founded in Great Britain.
1824	Elizabeth Heyrick anonymously publishes the pamphlet "Immediate, Not Gradual Emancipation."
1827	America's first African American newspaper, *Freedom's Journal* is founded.
1828	Moses Elias Levy, the most prominent Jewish abolitionist in the United States, publishes his "Plan for the Abolition of Slavery."
	Abolitionist Benjamin Lundy begins publication of his newspaper, the *Genius of Universal Emancipation*.
1829	Mexico abolishes slavery.
1831	Mary Prince, a former West Indian slave, publishes her autobiography, *The History of Mary Prince, A West Indian Slave, Related by Herself.*
	William Lloyd Garrison begins publishing the *Liberator*, an abolitionist newspaper, in Boston.
	Before it is crushed, Nat Turner's Rebellion leads to the death of sixty whites in Southampton County, Virginia.
1832	The New England Anti-Slavery Society is founded in Boston.
	The racially integrated Boston Female Anti-Slavery Society is formed.

1833	American writer Lydia Maria Child publishes *An Appeal in Favor of That Class of Americans Called Africans.*
	Lucretia Mott and other women, both white and black, form the Philadelphia Female Anti-Slavery Society.
	The American Anti-Slavery Society is founded in Philadelphia; the group favors the immediate emancipation of American slaves.
1834	Pursuant to the passage of the Abolition of Slavery Bill a year earlier, slavery is abolished throughout the British Empire. Slaves over the age of six in the British West Indies are apprenticed to their masters for a term of four to six years as the final stage in the abolition of slavery in the region.
1835	An extensive postal campaign by the American Anti-Slavery Society uses the postal system to send abolitionist literature throughout the country and especially into the South.
	Alexis de Tocqueville, a French traveler in the United States of the 1830s, publishes his *Democracy in America*, in which he calls slavery "evil."
1836	Southern members of the House of Representatives force the passage of the Gag Rule, barring petitions relating to slavery from being read in the House.
	Isaac Knapp of Boston publishes the first abolitionist songbook, *Songs of the Free, and Hymns of Christian Freedom*, compiled by Maria Weston Chapman.
	In its decision on *Commonwealth v. Aves*, the Massachusetts Supreme Court sets an important precedent by declaring that slavery cannot exist in Massachusetts except as it is regulated by the U.S. Constitution; thus, any slave brought to the state was immediately freed and the only slaves that could exist in Massachusetts were fugitive slaves whose return was mandated by the federal Fugitive Slave Act.
	The New York Committee of Vigilance, one of the most radical African American abolition societies in the United States, is founded.
1837	The Anti-Slavery Society of American Women holds its first meeting in New York.

An angry mob in Alton, Illinois, murders abolitionist publisher Elijah P. Lovejoy as he attempts to prevent the destruction of his press.

The Hibernian Anti-Slavery Society is established in Dublin by Irish Quakers.

1838   David Ruggles publishes the first black magazine in the United States, the *Mirror of Liberty*.

Apprenticeship is abolished in the British West Indies, thus effectively ending slavery in the region.

1839   The British and Foreign Anti-Slavery Society, which aimed to abolish slavery and the slave trade worldwide without the use of force, is founded.

Abolitionists Theodore Dwight Weld, Angelina Grimké Weld, and Sarah Grimké publish their antislavery pamphlet, "American Slavery as It Is: Testimony of a Thousand Witnesses."

Joseph Cinque, a West African so named by the Spanish who held him captive, won international notoriety when he led a slave mutiny on the slave ship *Amistad* in 1839; the ship is intercepted by the American navy and taken to New London, Connecticut, in August.

1840   Brothers Lewis and Arthur Tappan found the American and Foreign Anti-Slavery Society.

The World Anti-Slavery Convention is convened in London by the British and Foreign Anti-Slavery Society; large delegations from France and the United States are in attendance.

The antislavery Liberty Party is formed.

1841   Former president John Quincy Adams delivers final arguments before the Supreme Court in defense of the thirty-four African American captives from the *Amistad*. The U.S. Supreme Court rules that the *Amistad* captives were never legally slaves and are thus free to return to Africa.

A slave insurrection erupts aboard the *Creole*, an American trading vessel carrying tobacco and slaves to New Orleans.

1842   The Anglo-American Webster-Ashburton Treaty establishes the Africa Squadron, an American naval squadron charged with patrolling the west coast of Africa to intercept any American vessels illegally engaged in the slave trade.

1843	Stephen Symonds Foster publishes *The Brotherhood of Thieves, or A True Picture of the American Church*, a searing indictment of American evangelical Christians for their complicity in the sin of slavery.
1844	The continuous efforts of Congressman John Quincy Adams, a former president of the United States, lead to the repeal of the Gag Rule.
	Joseph Smith, founder of the Church of Jesus Christ of Latter-day Saints (Mormons), supports the principle of compensated emancipation of slaves.
1845	Former slave Frederick Douglass publishes his influential *Narrative of the Life of Frederick Douglass, An American Slave, Written by Himself.*
	Abolitionist Lysander Spooner publishes the first part of his famous work, *The Unconstitutionality of Slavery*; the second part of the work appears in 1847.
1846	The American Missionary Association is organized to provide benevolent and educational assistance to African Americans and Native Americans.
	War breaks out between Mexico and the United States.
1847	Liberia, the West African colony of resettled African Americans, becomes independent.
	Former slave Frederick Douglass publishes the first issue of his abolitionist newspaper, *North Star*.
1848	Treaty of Guadalupe Hidalgo is signed, ending the Mexican-American War and transferring large tracts of territory from Mexico to the United States.
	The first women's rights convention held in the United States, the Seneca Falls Convention, meets in Seneca Falls, New York.
	The Free Soil Party is established in Buffalo, New York, by antislavery members of the Whig and Liberty parties.
	Congressman David Wilmot of Pennsylvania introduces into Congress a measure to ban slavery in all territories gained from Mexico.
1850	Former slave Harriet Tubman becomes a conductor on the Underground Railroad in Maryland.

With assistance from other abolitionists, illiterate former slave Sojourner Truth publishes her memoirs, *The Narrative of Sojourner Truth: A Northern Slave.*

In a speech delivered during the debate on the Compromise of 1850, New York senator William H. Seward speaks of a "higher law" beyond the Constitution, that is, God's law, that demands no compromise with slavery.

Congress passes the Compromise of 1850, a series of measures designed to compose differences between the North and South over the disposition of the new western territories won from Mexico; the Compromise includes passage of a new, more stringent Fugitive Slave Law, replacing the act of 1793.

1851   Former slave Sojourner Truth delivers her famous speech, "Ar'n't I a Woman?," at a women's convention in Ohio.

The Anti-Slavery Society of Canada is founded; Canada West (Ontario) becomes the terminus for the American Underground Railroad in the 1850s.

The so-called Jerry Rescue, involving the forcible rescue by Northern abolitionists of an escaped slave being returned to the South, occurs in Syracuse, New York.

1852   Harriet Beecher Stowe publishes her controversial novel, *Uncle Tom's Cabin.*

1854   George Fitzhugh publishes his first proslavery book, *Sociology for the South, or the Failure of Free Society.*

Congress passes the Kansas-Nebraska Act, which organized the two territories by applying the principle of popular sovereignty to determine if a state was to be free or slave; the measure effectively repealed the Missouri Compromise of 1820.

Escaped slave Anthony Burns is arrested in Boston under the provisions of the Fugitive Slave Act of 1850; despite demonstrations on his behalf, Burns is returned under guard to Virginia, although Boston abolitionists later purchase his freedom.

1855   Spurred by the arrest in Boston and return to captivity of escaped slave Anthony Burns, the Massachusetts legislature passes a state personal liberty law to thwart future efforts to return escaped slaves in Massachusetts to bondage.

Two years of violence, known as "Bleeding Kansas," erupts in Kansas Territory as pro- and antislavery forces fight one another for control of the territorial legislature and thus the right to determine the status of slavery in the territory.

1856   American pacifist Elihu Burritt publishes *A Plan of Brotherly Co-Partnership of the North and South for the Peaceful Extinction of Slavery*.

Proslavery Missourians destroy the free-soil town of Lawrence, Kansas, in an episode that becomes known as the "sack of Lawrence."

Abolitionist John Brown and his sons murder five proslavery settlers at Pottawatomie Creek in Kansas in retaliation for the sack of Lawrence.

1857   George Fitzhugh publishes his most famous proslavery volume, *Cannibals All! or Slaves without Masters*.

Hinton Rowan Helper publishes his controversial book, *The Impending Crisis of the South and How to Meet It*, which decries the economic effects of slavery on the South and vehemently attacks the region, the Democratic Party, and African Americans.

In the *Dred Scott* case, the U.S. Supreme Court declares that Congress has no constitutional right to prohibit slavery in the territories or the free states.

1859   Abolitionist John Brown, seeking to precipitate a slave uprising, unsuccessfully raids the federal arsenal at Harpers Ferry, Virginia.

1860   Harriet Jacob's *Incidents in the Life of a Slave Girl,* edited by Lydia Maria Child, is published.

1861   Civil War between eleven seceded states of the Confederate States of America and the federal government breaks out soon after the inauguration of Republican Party president Abraham Lincoln.

1862   During the American Civil War, the Union Army begins establishing "contraband camps" in the seceded states to house, feed, school, and employ runaway slaves and slaves whose homes were behind Union lines.

President Abraham Lincoln announces his Emancipation Proclamation, which will free slaves in areas under Confederate control, as of January 1, 1863.

1863	Fanny Kemble publishes her *Journal of a Residence on a Georgian Plantation* to persuade the British to stop supporting the Confederacy.
	President Abraham Lincoln's Emancipation Proclamation takes effect.
1865	General William T. Sherman issues Special Field Order No. 15, which sets aside certain lands in South Carolina, where the general's army was then operating, for exclusive settlement by slave refugees; the order in the twentieth century became the basis for calls for monetary reparations for slavery to African Americans.
	The federal Bureau of Refugees, Freedmen, and Abandoned Lands (the Freedmen's Bureau) is created to assist the former slaves with their transition to freedom.
	William Lloyd Garrison's newspaper, the *Liberator*, ceases publication.
	The Thirteenth Amendment, abolishing slavery in the United States, is ratified.
1866	Congress passes the Southern Homestead Act, setting aside public lands in Alabama, Arkansas, Florida, Louisiana, and Mississippi, for purchase by freed people for a $5 fee.
1867	The Paris Anti-Slavery Convention, organized in part by the British and Foreign Anti-Slavery Society, focuses on the abolition of the East African slave trade.
	Congress passes the Anti-Peonage Act to abolish Indian-Mestizo servitude in New Mexico and the Southwest.
1870	The Fifteenth Amendment is ratified.
	The American Anti-Slavery Society is disbanded.
1879	The "Negro Exodus," a three-year period which saw the first great African American migration following the end of slavery, begins; some 40,000 blacks migrate to Kansas from the Mississippi Valley.
1881	Former slave and abolitionist leader Frederick Douglass publishes a reminiscence of his career, entitled *Life and Times of Frederick Douglass*.

A

Abolitionist Women

In the antebellum United States, female abolitionists brought democracy to a higher level by engaging in social reform, including organizing, speaking, and writing. Many other abolitionist women worked on the Underground Railroad. Their work underscored the evils of slavery and the conditions of women. Many associate the abolitionists with white Quakers. While many were Quakers, abolitionist women were not of one mind or race. Free and emancipated black women took part in the movement, as well. White women of differing values and religions also participated. Some white abolitionists believed that blacks were inferior, but they did not support slavery. These abolitionists, despite the danger, took part in the most significant program of social reform that included women. Out of this movement, first-wave feminism was born. Angelina Grimké conflated the experiences of the enslaved with women who were oppressed and began a new movement. Black and white, all of these women were traumatized and humiliated, some by slavery, all by an oppressive patriarchal hierarchy.

Born Isabella in 1797, Sojourner Truth was the youngest of "ten or twelve" children. When sold at five years of age, she was traumatized. As a house slave, Isabella was bought by John and Sally Dumont. Isabella did housework and endured beatings and whippings. When she told her story as an older woman, Isabella said that John Dumont beat her, but it was Sally Dumont who sexually abused her.

In 1826, Isabella felt God telling her to escape from slavery. Guided always by her spirituality, she walked away from slavery, finding safety in the home of the Van Wageners, abolitionists. According to her autobiography, *Narrative of Sojourner Truth*, Isabella saw a vision of God that transformed her from victim to abolitionist and feminist. This change was symbolized in her name change, from Isabella Baumford to Sojourner Truth. Sanctified and baptized by the Holy Spirit, she became an itinerant preacher and spokesperson for the abolitionist movement. To understand Sojourner Truth, one must comprehend the depths of her spirituality.

During a meeting in which her friend Frederick Douglass was speaking, Sojourner called out from the back of the room, "But what about God?" Sojourner did not want to let Douglass drift away from the Lord, as she thought he was doing.

Unlike Sojourner Truth, Sarah Douglas was born a free black in Philadelphia. Her strength came not from her religion, but from her education. She started the Philadelphia Institute for Colored Youth, simultaneously working as a spokesperson for the abolitionist movement and contributor to an abolitionist newspaper, the *Liberator*. The *Liberator* had a "Ladies' Section," for which powerful abolitionist women wrote of the evils of slavery. Sarah Douglas was a forceful contributor.

Born in South Carolina to a prominent judge and slave holder, white Angelina Grimké witnessed the treatment of the slaves. So moved by their suffering, Angelina tried to imagine herself shackled in chains, as the slaves were. A pampered child, Angelina grew into a strong political force for freedom. Through her identification with the slaves, she realized the commonalities that white women shared with slaves: humiliation and oppression. As an adult, she allied herself to the radical abolitionists. She forged a connection between the abolitionists and the feminists. Angelina and her sister, Sarah, spoke against slavery in the South, where it was very dangerous to do so. Angelina wrote a dramatic article for the *Liberator* in which she asked God to give the women of South Carolina the strength to speak against slavery and to give men the courage to fight against it. South Carolina officials publicly burned her article and threatened to arrest Angelina if she returned to South Carolina. In her article she uses the words of the biblical martyr, Queen Esther, "If I perish, If I perish . . .," demonstrating her knowledge that she might be killed for using her wit to end slavery and her willingness to martyr herself for the abolitionist and feminist movements.

Ellen Harper lived in an underground railway station and spoke against slavery in many forums. She worked with feminists Susan B. Anthony and Elizabeth Cady Stanton until these woman opposed the Fifteenth Amendment. It was said that she sided with her race, not her gender.

In the North, Lucretia Mott organized against a plan to relocate blacks to Africa. Lucretia did not object to the concept of colonization, but she objected to a particular plan for colonization that did not respect the rights of the free blacks. Like other feminists, Mott fought for the Fifteenth Amendment. A Quaker, she spoke from her Inner Light, as Sojourner Truth did from her spiritual connection to God.

Among the bravest women in American history, Harriet Tubman was born into Southern slavery, the worst form of bondage. A childhood head injury left Tubman with seizures throughout her life. She received this blow to the head when she stood between an overseer and a fleeing slave. While recovering on the hard floor of her parents' cabin, Harriet had religious insights that made slavery incongruent with

Christianity. So motivated, she contemplated her escape. After recuperating, Harriet began her walk to freedom. When she arrived in Philadelphia, Tubman knew she was free but also alone. She returned nineteen times to slave states, freeing at least 300 slaves.

A common strand that runs through the stories of the women abolitionists is their profound belief in God. Many other women participated in this movement, but only a few of the brave women who joined the abolitionist cause are described here. Much time has passed since they spoke for freedom. Legal slavery in the United States ended. Women gained the right to vote. Despite the heroism of abolitionist women in the decades prior to the Civil War, the United States remained bereft of liberty for all. While abolitionist women tried to make democracy work to free the slaves, their brilliant rhetoric, their writings, and their spirituality did not end slavery. Instead, it took a civil war to end slavery—a war that was not energized by the feminine voice, but by the male patriarchy that dominated both the North and the South.

Mary Darcy

See also: Women's Antislavery Societies.

Further Readings

Baker, Jean H. *Votes for Women: The Struggle for Suffrage Revisited.* New York: Oxford Press, 2002.

Conrad, Earl. *Harriet Tubman. Soldier and Abolitionist.* New York: International Publishers, 1942.

Lerner, Gerda. *The Grimké Sisters from South Carolina: Pioneers for Women's Rights.* New York: Schocken, 1971.

Palmer, Beverly Wilson, ed. *Selected Letters of Lucretia Mott.* Urbana: University of Illinois Press, 2002.

Quarles, Benjamin. *Black Abolitionists.* New York: Oxford University Press, 1969.

Adams, John Quincy

John Quincy Adams was a diplomat, secretary of state, president, and congressman, as well as a prominent critic of slavery and territorial expansion as a member of the House of Representatives from 1831 to 1848.

Adams was troubled by the debates over slavery during the crisis of 1820 over the admission of Missouri as a slave state. But he did not embrace antislavery as a legislative cause until his election to Congress in 1830. He was never an abolitionist; he opposed the abolitionists' signal measure, the abolition of slavery in the

District of Columbia, as politically unwise. He was a staunch critic of the expansion of slavery into new territory. He also fought for the right to read antislavery petitions on the floor of the House and opposed the gag rule, the standing rule of the House from 1836 to 1844 that prevented such petitions from being read. In 1840 and 1841, Adams served as counsel for the thirty-nine African captives from the Spanish vessel, *Amistad,* and delivered the final arguments in their defense before the Supreme Court in February and March 1841.

Like many in the antislavery movement, Adams believed that a Slave Power conspiracy existed. He and other Northerners asserted that Southern politicians in Congress, the presidency, and judiciary had secretly combined to protect and extend the dominion of slavery and all related Southern interests while undermining and contracting the North's most cherished ideals—free labor, personal liberty, and political independence. The acquisition of Texas as a slave state was believed key to this conspiracy. Adams was influenced by the pamphlets of Benjamin Lundy. Lundy sent Adams a copy of his pamphlet, *The Origin and True Causes of the Texas Revolution Commenced in the Year 1835*, and Adams began using Lundy's arguments on the House floor. In 1838, Adams delivered a lengthy speech denouncing efforts to annex Texas. He cheered when the Senate rejected an annexation treaty in 1844, and considered the annexation by joint resolution in 1845 as the death of the union. Adams was one of the few Whigs to oppose the Mexican War, and he voted for the Wilmot Proviso, which proposed to bar slavery from any territory acquired from Mexico. To the end, Adams condemned the war as a war for slavery. Adams placed his last vote in the House of Representatives on February 21, 1848, two days before his death. He voted against a resolution thanking various generals for their service in the 1847 campaign in Mexico. Few statesmen of the 1830s and 1840s devoted as much of their energy to stopping the spread of slavery than John Quincy Adams.

Robert W. Smith

See also: Whig Party and Antislavery.

Further Readings

Bemis, Samuel Flagg. *John Quincy Adams and the Union*. New York: Alfred A. Knopf, 1956.

Miller, William Lee. *Arguing about Slavery: The Great Battle in the United States Congress*. New York: Alfred A. Knopf, 1995.

Nagel, Paul C. *John Quincy Adams: A Public Life, A Private Life*. New York: Alfred A. Knopf, 1997.

Richards, Leonard L. *The Life and Times of Congressman John Quincy Adams*. New York: Oxford University Press, 1986.

Africa Squadron

The Africa Squadron was a half-hearted attempt by the U.S. Navy to address British demands to assist in the suppression of the transatlantic slave trade after its abolition in the early nineteenth century. The beginning of the nineteenth century saw a renewed interest in the suppression of the transatlantic slave trade. In 1808—the year after the trade was made illegal in both Great Britain and the United States—Great Britain sent naval vessels to the west coast of Africa in an effort to intercept slavers. By 1833, slavery was abolished in the British Empire, and most western European powers had been cajoled, bribed, or bullied by Great Britain into agreeing to the equipment clause and the mutual right of search. The right of search allowed British officers on slave patrol vessels to halt and search other vessels suspected of being slavers. The equipment clause allowed these officers to seize the intercepted vessels if there was sufficient evidence that the craft was fitted out for the carrying of slaves. Indications that a vessel was destined to carry slaves included the presence of large cooking pots, shackles and manacles, and additional planks of wood that could quickly be constructed into a makeshift slave deck.

Although Great Britain had the permission of nearly every other relevant power to search suspicious vessels, the United States consistently refused to allow any person, other than American naval officers, to interrupt the journey of any ship flying the Stars and Stripes. This intransigent attitude can be traced to the impressment of American sailors before and during the War of 1812 and the determination by the American people that they would never again allow vessels belonging to their citizens to be subject to any type of unauthorized search by British naval officers. As understandable as this position was, it effectively allowed the illegal traffic to flourish, as slavers from countries such as Portugal and Brazil simply switched to the American flag when they suspected that British cruisers might be in the area.

In an effort to quash the illegal use of the U.S. flag and to improve Anglo-American relations, the government of the United States agreed to Section VIII of the Webster-Ashburton Treaty of 1842. This provision established that a regular American naval squadron, consisting of a minimum of eighty guns, would patrol the west coast of Africa to intercept any vessels suspected of being slavers and flying the American flag. Theoretically, the presence of American cruisers—designated the Africa Squadron—would solve the problem of British officers boarding suspicious American craft. In reality, the effectiveness of the squadron was negligible when compared to the results achieved by their British counterpart. Although American officers and men generally performed their duties diligently under extremely trying conditions, their force was never great enough to effectively guard the 3,000 miles of coastline used by slavers. The squadron rarely had more than a few ships on patrol at any given time, and the types of vessels sent to the area were usually too large to patrol the rivers and inlets favored by slavers for embarkation. In addition, the American supply base at Porto Praia was approximately 2,000 miles north from the main slaving areas. This meant that by the time any U.S. cruisers reached the principal slaving grounds, they were almost immediately forced to turn back if they were not to run out of supplies before the end of the voyage.

The orders sent to the first commander of the squadron, Captain Mathew Calbraith Perry, by Secretary of the Navy A.P. Upshur, also compromised the initial aims of the treaty. Upshur instructed Perry that his first responsibility was to protect the rights of American citizens engaged in lawful commerce and that this directive should take precedence over all other considerations. Upshur, in one brief, yet concise, set of orders, had changed the primary purpose of the Africa Squadron from suppressing the slave trade to the protection of U.S. nationals engaged in lawful commercial operations. For Upshur and many other Americans, it seemed more prudent to protect American citizens and commerce from British interference than to devote all energies and resources to what was, essentially, a moral issue that had so far bitterly divided the country. This division extended to the American judicial system, and members of the Africa Squadron were repeatedly disheartened by the lack of convictions brought against slavers.

Knowing that American cruisers were rarely to be encountered in slaving waters, traffickers simply flew the Stars and Stripes all but to guarantee safe passage for their hapless human cargo. Frequent complaints registered by the British condemned the American efforts as half-hearted and completely insufficient. Indeed, Royal Navy officers argued that since the American squadron had been formed, the trade had actually increased due to the protection afforded by the Stars and Stripes to those not legally entitled to fly the flag. The British government refused to officially relinquish the right of impressments, and so the American government continued to deny the Royal Navy the right of search, the one allowance necessary to effectively police the trade.

This situation continued until 1861, when all but one vessel were recalled to home waters to assist in the naval blockades of the Civil War. In January 1862, the remaining ship left the west coast of Africa. Fearful that Great Britain might enter the war in support of the South, and realizing the total impracticality of sending a squadron to police the west coast of Africa during a time of war, Secretary of State Seward, on March 23, 1862, agreed to sign a mutual right of search treaty. With the much-needed authority for the British to search all suspect vessels, the Atlantic slave trade was all but over within a three-year period. In comparison to the British West Africa Squadron, the American efforts proved disappointing. Although firm figures are difficult to arrive at, it is estimated that during the period that the

Africa Squadron was in existence, it captured approximately twenty-four slavers, although few were condemned. The Royal Navy captured 566 slave ships and well over 90 percent were condemned. For over half of its period of service, the Africa Squadron did not even fulfill its eighty-gun requirement.

Claire Phelan

See also: Atlantic Slave Trade and British Abolition.

Further Readings

Booth, Alan R. "The United States African Squadron, 1843–1861." In Jeffrey Butler, ed. *Boston University Papers in African History*, vol. 1. Boston: Boston University Press, 1964.

Lane, Calvin. "The African Squadron: The U.S. Navy and the Slave Trade, 1820–1862." *Log of Mystic Seaport* 50, 4 (1999): 86–98.

Lloyd, C. *The Navy and the Slave Trade: The Suppression of the African Slave Trade in the Nineteenth Century*. London: Frank Cass & Co. Ltd., 1968.

Ward, W.E.F. *The Royal Navy and the Slavers*. London: George Allen & Unwin Ltd., 1948.

African American Communities

African Americans in the antebellum United States lived in major cities throughout the country, usually in biracial neighborhoods. They also established independent free black communities. In 1850, the ten largest African American communities (including free and enslaved people) were New Orleans (23,916), Baltimore (22,774), Charleston (12,969), Washington, D.C. (9,525), New York (7,448), Louisville (6,893), Philadelphia (6,471), St. Louis (3,683), Cincinnati (3,217), and Brooklyn (1,783). Several factors assisted antislavery work in urban African American communities: black churches, schools, businesses, and benevolent institutions provided a supportive climate; lines between free and enslaved people were often blurred, and this assisted people to escape from slavery; these cities were all major ports, and ships and sailors provided important avenues both of communication and escape from slavery; and links with white allies brought resources into antislavery work. African American newspapers (including *Freedom's Journal*, New York, 1827–1829; the *Colored American*, New York, 1837–1841; the *North Star* and *Frederick Douglass' Paper*, Rochester, 1847–1859) played a major role in promoting antislavery agitation, as did national and state black conventions meeting in Philadelphia, New York City, and elsewhere, beginning in Philadelphia in 1830. Vigilance Committees, often biracial in composition, supported safe houses for the Underground Railroad (many of them kept by African Americans such as

Theodore Wright in New York, William Still in Philadelphia, Lewis Hayden in Boston, Stephen Myers in Albany, and Jermain Loguen in Syracuse). Freedom seekers often settled in Northern cities, especially those such as Cincinnati (located directly across the Ohio River from the slave state of Kentucky), 72 percent of whose free black population in 1850 had been born in a slave state, and Buffalo (on the border with Canada), 57 percent of whose free black population in 1850 were Southern-born.

African Americans also created independent communities. Many maroon communities emerged throughout the colonial and early national period without official sanction; the earliest official settlement was Ft. Mose, formed under Spanish control near St. Augustine in 1738. After 1820, African Americans (sometimes with the help of European American allies, including slaveholders turned abolitionists) established dozens of identifiable independent communities in rural areas of the free states, many of them on the midwestern frontier. Among the best known in the East were Timbuctoo, established in the Adirondacks of northern New York as part of a land grant by the abolitionist Gerrit Smith; Seneca Village, established by several hundred African Americans in what is now Central Park in New York City; and Sandy Ground on Staten Island, formed by farmers from New Jersey and oystermen from Maryland's Eastern Shore. Many other free black communities were formed in New York State, New Jersey, Pennsylvania, Maryland, and elsewhere. In the Midwest, the Beech and Roberts settlements in Indiana were established in the 1830s; Rocky Fork was an important stop on the Underground Railroad in Illinois; New Philadelphia, established by Frank McWhorter in Illinois, became the only documented township to be incorporated by African Americans before the Civil War.

These communities were generally small agricultural or fishing villages, formed not only for economic independence, but also for political purposes: to create a geographic base for cultural independence and political action and to provide a safe haven for freedom seekers and an alternative to emigration to Liberia, Canada, or elsewhere. Some of them, however, became substantial settlements. The largest was Carthagena, which in 1860 had a population of 600. The second largest, and the only one to have an urban, rather than a rural economic base, was Weeksville, established in the 1830s four miles east of downtown Brooklyn. Weeksville's African American population reached 521 by 1855.

Judith Wellman

Further Readings

Bordewich, Fergus M. *Bound for Canaan: The Underground Railroad and the War for the Soul of America*. New York: Amistad, 2005.

Curry, Leonard P. *The Free Black in Urban America, 1800–1850: The Shadow of the Dream*. Chicago: University of Chicago Press, 1981.

Harris, Leslie. *In the Shadow of Slavery: African-Americans in New York City, 1626–1863*. Chicago: University of Chicago Press, 2003.

Horton, James Oliver. *Free People of Color: Inside the African-American Community*. Washington and London: Smithsonian Institution Press, 1993.

Price, Clement Alexander. "Home and Hearth, The Black Town and Settlement Movement of Southern New Jersey." In Wendel A. White, ed. *Small Towns, Black Lives: African-American Communities in Southern New Jersey*. Oceanville, NJ: Noyes Museum of Art, 2003, pp. 168–175.

Rosenzweig, Roy, and Elizabeth Blackmar. *The Park and the People: A History of Central Park*. Ithaca, NY; London: Cornell University Press, 1992.

Vincent, Stephen A. *Southern Seed, Northern Soil: African-American Farm Communities in the Midwest, 1765–1900*. Bloomington: Indiana University Press. 2002.

Walker, Juliet E. K. *Free Frank: A Black Pioneer on the Antebellum Frontier*. Lexington: University Press of Kentucky, 1983.

Wright, Giles. *Afro-Americans in New Jersey: A Short History*. Trenton: New Jersey Historical Commission, 1988.

Allen, Richard

While Richard Allen remains best known as the founder of the African Methodist Episcopal Church (dedicated June 1794) in Philadelphia, he was also one of the leading black abolitionists of the early republic. Allen was born a slave, probably in Pennsylvania, but was soon sold to a small estate in Delaware. After converting to Methodism in 1777, Allen encouraged itinerant preachers to sermonize his master. A nominally antislavery lecture convinced Allen's second master, Stokeley Sturgis, to sign a freedom agreement with the young slave in 1780, which Allen paid off early in 1783. Allen became an itinerant Methodist preacher over the next several years, maintaining his belief that Christianity was an abolitionist religion. Allen's first major essay, "A Narrative of the Proceedings of the Black People during the Late Awful Calamity in Philadelphia, in the Year 1793" (published January 1794, the first copyrighted pamphlet by African Americans), was coauthored with Absalom Jones and featured a short, but sharp, attack on slavery. Subtitled "To Those Who Keep Slaves and Approve the Practice," the mini-essay condemned slaveholders as un-Christian and challenged masters to not only emancipate bondspeople, but treat them as equals. "If you love your children, if you love your country, if you love the God of Love," Allen declared, "clear your hands from slaves, burden not your children or country with them."

From the 1790s through the 1830s, Allen's "Mother Bethel" church became a key site of black abolitionist protest. Not only did Allen aid fugitive slaves, but he also welcomed antislavery advocates in protest meetings and conventions. In 1817, he hosted a massive anticolonization meeting, which produced a stirring pamphlet declaring free blacks' allegiance to enslaved Americans. In 1830, Allen welcomed the inaugural convention of free black activists to Mother Bethel, a meeting called to bolster black protest movements nationally and consider Canadian emigration as a viable alternative to continued American oppression. Allen was also an advocate of the Free Produce Movement, which supported the purchase of nonslave derived goods, allowing proponents to hold meetings in Mother Bethel.

Allen's career as an abolitionist was rich and varied. Although he was not allowed to join first-generation mainstream abolitionist organizations (e.g., the Pennsylvania Abolition Society), he did work with white abolitionists to aid kidnapped free blacks, secure indentures for recently liberated slaves, and inculcate principles of moral and religious uplift in free blacks. Frustrated by slavery's growth and entrenched racism in Northern locales, Allen also flirted with black-led emigration plans to Africa, Haiti, and Canada between the 1810s and 1830s. In 1799, he signed one of the earliest African American congressional petitions, a memorial seeking an end to the domestic slave trade, as well as consideration of gradual abolitionism. Though a firm opponent of violent abolitionist means, Allen also welcomed to his church black South Carolinians accused of supporting the Denmark Vesey's Conspiracy in 1822. Allen's spiritual autobiography, published posthumously in 1832, was also one of the earliest antebellum slave narratives, reminding Americans that enslaved people longed for freedom. In short, Allen was a "giant" of black protest, as the Anglo-African magazine would write in 1859.

Richard Newman

Further Readings

George, Carol. Segregated Sabbaths: *Richard Allen and the Rise of Independent Black Churches, 1760–1840*. New York: Oxford University Press, 1975.

Newman, Richard S. *Black Founder: Richard Allen and the Early American Republic*. New York: New York University Press, 2007.

Wesley, Charles H. *Richard Allen: Apostle of Freedom*. Washington, DC: Associated Publishers, 1935.

American and Foreign Anti-Slavery Society (AFASS)

Since the mid-1830s, contention had been growing in American abolitionist ranks over the stridently perfectionist positions advanced by the supporters of Boston editor William Lloyd Garrison, especially their harsh criticism of both religious denominations and governmental institutions as bulwarks of slavery. The Garrisonians often loudly denounced Northern churches for indirectly sanctioning slavery by continuing any form of fellowship with Southern slaveholders. Many Garrisonians endorsed extreme pacifistic or "non-resistant" principles and condemned most government activities as coercive. Further controversy arose when most Garrisonians also became advocates for a larger public role for females in the abolitionist movement.

These Garrisonian activities caused considerable consternation among more religiously orthodox and socially conservative abolitionists, who feared that the antislavery movement would be irreparably damaged by association with even less popular movements. Infighting among Massachusetts abolitionists caused a secession of Garrisonian opponents from the state antislavery organization and the formation of the Massachusetts Abolition Society in early 1839. After a Garrisonian majority at the annual meeting of the national abolitionist body, the American Anti-Slavery Society (AASS) selected a woman as an officer in May 1840, several hundred dissenters quit in protest and founded the American and Foreign Anti-Slavery Society (AFASS). Afterward, abolitionists often referred to the AASS and the AFASS as the "Old Organization" and the "New Organization," respectively.

The AFASS headquartered itself in New York City, where wealthy Congregationalist merchant Lewis Tappan immediately emerged as its guiding light. Throughout its history, evangelical clergymen, including a significant number of African American ministers, dominated the group's all-male leadership. These men kept the group's abolitionist activities focused on lobbying religious institutions, although most also endorsed the new antislavery Liberty Party. Despite limited financial resources, the AFASS attempted to sustain the abolitionists' traditional moral suasion tactics. It sponsored a number of periodicals and sent out itinerant lecturers. The organization also developed supportive ties with British abolitionists who shared their religiously shaped perspective toward reform. Most of the energies and resources of these religiously oriented abolitionists, however, were diverted into denominational antislavery campaigns, including the founding of "comeouter" sects such as the Wesleyan Methodist Connection, and interdenominational ventures such as the American Missionary Association.

Aside from these religious "affiliates," the AFASS failed to develop a system of auxiliary organizations. By the early 1850s, it had suspended most of its publishing activities and existed mainly as a New York City executive committee that held an anniversary meeting and issued an annual report chronicling antislavery activities in religious and political circles. In 1855, the AFASS merged its operations with the remnant of the Liberty Party led by Gerrit Smith and reorganized itself as the American Abolition Society. This new group focused so heavily on an unsuccessful effort to create a radical political abolitionist alternative to the Republican Party that some of its members launched the short-lived Church Anti-Slavery Society in 1859 to preserve the original religious abolitionist activism of the AFASS.

John R. McKivigan

See also: Come-Outerism.

Further Readings

Harrold, Stanley. *American Abolitionists*. New York: Longman, 2000.
McKivigan, John R. *The War against Proslavery Religion: Abolitionism and the Northern Churches, 1830–1865*. Ithaca, NY: Cornell University Press, 1984.

American Anti-Slavery Society (AASS)

Founded in Philadelphia on December 4, 1833, the American Anti-Slavery Society (AASS) actively promoted "immediatism"—the immediate emancipation of black slaves in the United States. The AASS "Declaration of Sentiments," written at its founding convention, stated that the organization called for the immediate emancipation of blacks, ending racial prejudice and securing equal rights for blacks in America. The AASS condemned colonization plans, such as those promoted by the American Colonization Society, which hoped to transport free blacks in America to West Africa, maintaining that such efforts were meant primarily to remove free blacks rather than assist them.

William Lloyd Garrison was a leading figure of the AASS. He wrote the "Declaration of Sentiments" and established "moral suasion" as the method by which the AASS would achieve its goals. With twenty-one Quakers and a strong evangelical presence led by two prominent businessmen, Arthur and Lewis Tappan, the moral argument against slavery became the centerpiece of the AASS. To spread their campaign, while the national executive office established itself in New York City, local chapters were created throughout most of the North. By 1838, there were as many as 1,350 affiliates and 250,000 members. The minister Theodore Dwight Weld has been considered one of the most influential members. He organized a series of famous student debates on abolitionism when he was a teacher in Cincinnati at the Lane Theological Seminary, edited the AASS weekly, the *Emancipator*, from 1836 to 1840, and pseudonymously published *American Slavery as It Is* in 1839.

Other additional efforts were made by the AASS to shape public opinion. Speakers, including ex-slaves like Frederick Douglass, were sent out to preach against slavery. In 1835, an intensive postal campaign sent abolitionist pamphlets throughout the country. To make slavery an issue of national political debate, the AASS also organized a petition campaign to Congress. Southern members of the House of Representatives, in response, successfully passed the Gag Rule in 1836, barring petitions relating to slavery from being read. In 1844, after congressman John Quincy Adams, the former president of the United States, maintained continuously that the Gag Rule violated the constitutional right to petition Congress, the ban was repealed.

With its strong egalitarian message, the AASS was a biracial and mixed-gendered organization. Several women played a prominent role in the AASS. Sarah and Angelina Grimké, sisters who left their slaveholding family in South Carolina, caused controversy within the AASS in the 1830s when they violated notions of the "female sphere." In doing so, they spoke publicly against slavery to male audiences and published criticism of the clergy. Controversy over the role of women culminated in 1840 at the annual meeting when Abby Kelley Foster was elected to the business committee. In response, fearing that equal inclusion of women would alienate the churches, Arthur and Lewis Tappan led a group away from the AASS to form the new American and Foreign Anti-Slavery Society.

Though subsequently becoming a minority and more radical fringe within the abolitionist movement, the AASS propaganda remained influential, continuing to make slavery an issue of public debate. In 1870, when the Fifteenth Amendment granted blacks the right to vote, the AASS disbanded.

Daniel P. Kotzin

See also: Garrisonians; Immediate Emancipation.

Further Reading

Stewart, James Brewer. *Holy Warriors: The Abolitionists and American Slavery.* New York: Hill and Wang, 1996.

American Colonization Society

The American Colonization Society was founded in 1816 to send African Americans, both slave and free, to Africa. It was supported by a broad array of groups, including prominent politicians, clergymen, and reformers who were attracted to the cause by quite different and even contradictory motives. Colonization achieved its greatest success during the decade following the creation of the colony of Liberia on the west coast of Africa in 1820, and retained considerable popularity among Northern whites throughout the antebellum era. But by the 1830s, numerous problems seriously diminished the organization's effectiveness.

The rapid growth of the free black population and mounting opposition to slavery following the American Revolution prompted numerous whites to call for the colonization of African Americans. Some Northern blacks also promoted emigration to Africa as a means of escaping white prejudice and ending the slave trade.

One of numerous benevolent organizations established after the War of 1812, the American Colonization Society promised various benefits for its diverse constituencies. For many antislavery groups and evangelical activists in the 1810s and 1820s—especially in the North and the Upper South—colonization represented a conscientious alternative to acquiescing to the existence of slavery, a relatively painless means of dealing with racism, and a vehicle for Christianizing and "civilizing" Africa. The Society attracted the support of nearly all the major religious groups, and clergymen and lay leaders played important roles in the movement.

Many Northern colonizationists also hoped that the repatriation of emancipated slaves would arouse slaveholders' benevolent impulses and eventually move them to end slavery, or at least ameliorate its worst abuses. Moreover, some of these colonizationists argued that only in Africa could African Americans escape the damaging effects of white prejudice and rise to positions of respect and influence.

Yet most white colonizationists believed that the removal of degraded blacks would preclude racial amalgamation and protect the classical republican virtues of order, morality, and harmony. Racial prejudice, they insisted, was the product of immutable popular attitudes, and African Americans were incapable of achieving equality with whites. In addition, many Southern colonizationists—including prominent slaveholders such as James Monroe and Henry Clay—considered free blacks a "troublesome presence" that gave slaves hope for emancipation; some owners claimed colonization would therefore serve to strengthen slavery. Finally, a few Northern blacks, such as John Russwurm, advocated colonization because they hoped for a better life in Africa than was possible in a racist America.

The organization thrived in the 1820s. By the early 1830s, over 200 local auxiliaries were active, and numerous state legislatures passed resolutions commending its program. The Society's board of directors, centered in Washington, D.C., received vital federal assistance for the creation of the colony of Liberia in 1820. Moreover, a voluntary system of support raised substantial revenue, Robert R. Gurley served capably as the Society's national secretary, and the organization's magazine, the *African Repository*, disseminated the colonization message. By 1830, the Society had sent well over 1,000 African Americans, most of them emancipated slaves, to Liberia.

Yet, beginning in the 1830s, the Society experienced serious problems. Escalating partisan political conflict, as well as sectional divisions over whether the organization should be an instrument for ending or perpetuating slavery, precluded federal subsidies. In addition, numerous slaveholders, resentful of the antislavery pronouncements of Northern colonizationists, concluded that colonization represented a threat to slavery, and thus left the Society.

At the same time, William Lloyd Garrison and other antislavery Northerners, convinced that colonization was an unrealistic and deceptive scheme that served to deepen racial prejudice and perpetuate slavery, defected from the colonization ranks and launched the abolitionist crusade. The immediatists' attacks placed colonizationists on the defensive and drained vital energy and money from the Society.

Most Northern blacks had long resented the colonizationists' racist stereotypes of African Americans and demanded freedom and equal rights in the United States. During the 1830s, they constructed alliances with white abolitionists and created their own organizations to combat colonization and racism. Consequently, between 1820 and 1833, only 169 of 2,886 emigrants to Liberia were Northern blacks. In fact, even during the 1820s and early 1830s, when the Society achieved its greatest success, in any given year the increase in the slave population far exceeded the number of emigrants sent to Liberia.

These groups' opposition effectively doomed the colonization cause to failure. The Society's mounting debt, produced by declining revenues and rising costs for transporting emigrants and maintaining the colony, as well as defections by a number of Northern antislavery colonizationists who sought to occupy a middle ground between colonization and abolitionism, compounded these problems. In addition, colonizationists in Maryland, New York, and Pennsylvania, who were critical of the national officers' mismanagement, turned to independent action. The national society responded to the state organizations' challenge by granting them considerable autonomy. But during the 1840s, Gurley was forced out as secretary, and the organization splintered.

Ironically, the colonization idea remained popular among Northern whites even as the Society struggled to survive. By the late 1840s, Liberia, which for many years had been a financial burden and poorly managed, became independent of the Society. Although revenues and the number of emigrants rose in the 1850s, the organization's vitality continued to wane. Emancipation during the Civil War virtually ended the Society's existence.

Hugh Davis

See also: Garrisonians; Liberia.

Further Readings

Edgerton, Douglas R. "Its Origin Is Not a Little Curious: A New Look at the American Colonization Society." *Journal of the Early Republic* 5 (1985): 463–480.

Staudenraus, Philip J. *The African Colonization Movement, 1816–1865*. New York: Columbia University Press, 1961.

Streifford, David M. "The American Colonization Society: An Application of Republican Ideology to Early Antebellum Reform." *Journal of Southern History* 45 (1979): 201–220.

www.denison.edu/waite/liberia/history/acs.htm.

American Convention of Abolition Societies

The American Convention of Abolition Societies met sporadically between 1794 and 1836, most often in Philadelphia, the home of the Pennsylvania Abolition Society. As the name implied, the American Convention gathered early abolition societies from around the young nation to discuss and coordinate (where possible) abolitionist tactics and strategies. The Convention's first meeting in Philadelphia attracted twenty-five delegates from nine different local abolition groups, including antislavery organizations from Pennsylvania, New York, Connecticut, Maryland, and even Virginia. Over the next several decades, groups from Delaware, Kentucky, and Tennessee attended Convention meetings. The American Convention—short for "the American convention of delegates from the abolition societies established in different parts of the United States"—assembled delegates a remarkable number of times: almost annually from 1795 onward (1795–1798, 1800–1801, and 1803–1805); then off and on in 1809, 1812, and 1815; annually again between 1825 and 1829; and once again for a final convocation in 1836. As this timeline suggests, early abolitionism was far from an inchoate collection of antislavery theorists, content merely to criticize slavery from afar. Rather, through the leadership of groups like the Pennsylvania Abolition Society, the New York Manumission Society, and the American Convention, the early abolition movement was well organized and savvy in its strategies during the early Republic.

Indeed, the American Convention's greatest success came in the 1790s, when it helped push Congress to pass the very first anti-slave trade law—a 1794 statute banning Americans from trading captured Africans to foreign traders. The law also prevented foreign ships from outfitting slaving vessels in American ports. Armed with the new law, abolitionists in Pennsylvania and New York successfully prosecuted several American slave traders who flouted the statute. In addition, members of the American Convention shared information on such developing problems as the domestic slave trade and the related issue of the kidnapping of free blacks. In Pennsylvania, for example, abolitionists used information gleaned from their own research and discussions with members of the American Convention to petition the state legislature for stronger penalties against kidnappers. In other states such as Connecticut and New York, local societies aided aggrieved slaves, free blacks, and the kidnapped with significant legal support.

Nevertheless, the American Convention was radically different from the second-wave abolitionists of the post-1830 era. To begin with, the overwhelming majority of delegates to the American Convention favored gradual abolition plans debated and promulgated exclusively at the state level. Second, the American Convention, like all early abolition societies, did not admit African American members. Finally, the American Convention did not prevent colonizationists or even slaveholders from becoming members. In fact, because early abolition societies in the Southern and Southwestern states often included slaveholders, the American Convention's Northern members refused to make manumission of one's slave a requirement for attendance.

The ascension of immediatist antislavery groups in the 1830s marginalized the American Convention. Nevertheless, its long history prior to that time illuminates important aspects of abolitionism's founding era.

Richard Newman

See also: Gradual Emancipation; Pennsylvania Abolition Society (PAS).

Further Readings

Adams, Alice Dana. *The Neglected Period of Anti-Slavery in America (1808–1831)*. Boston: Ginn and Company, 1908.

Locke, Mary Stoughton. *Anti-Slavery in America, from the Introduction of African Slaves to the Prohibition of the Slave Trade*. Boston: Ginn and Company, 1901.

Newman, Richard. *The Transformation of American Abolitionism: Fighting Slavery in the Early Republic*. Chapel Hill: University of North Carolina Press, 2002.

American Missionary Association (AMA)

Organized in 1846 when several antislavery and Christian mission groups combined, the American Missionary Association (AMA) provided benevolent and educational assistance to African Americans and Native Americans through a network of foreign and home missions.

Founding groups of the AMA included the Mendi Committee, which consisted of former members of the *Amistad* Committee. Following the *Amistad* trial, the group reorganized to aid the rebellious Africans who overtook the *Amistad* slave ship. The group helped these Africans or Mendians resettle in their homeland. The Union Missionary Society, organized by blacks to take Christianity into Africa, was another key addition to the AMA union of groups. Two smaller groups that also joined the AMA were the Western Evangelical Missionary Association and the Committee for West India Missions.

While the AMA was nondenominational, it aligned most strongly with the Congregational Church. Leaders of the AMA included Lewis Tappan, Simeon S. Jocelyn, Theodore S. Wright, Samuel Cornish, and Samuel Ringgold Ward. The goal of the group was to spread the Christian Gospel to all races. It did not allow membership by or support from slave holders. The group supported both foreign and home missions prior to the Civil War.

In October 1848, John G. Fee in Madison County, Kentucky, became the first Southern AMA minister. His fruitful work led to additional AMA work in the South. Notable Southern missionaries included Wilbur Fisk, Kentucky; Daniel Worth, North Carolina; as well as David Breed and George Bassett in Washington, D.C. When the AMA took a more aggressive position toward abolition in 1859, repercussions followed in the South. A number of AMA missionaries, including John Fee, were driven by force or threats from their Southern posts.

During this early period, the AMA supported foreign missions in Africa, Canada West (Ontario), Thailand, Egypt, the West Indies, and other places. The support of the Mendi Mission at Sierra Leone was of special interest to the group. Fugitive slaves in Canada were also of concern. The AMA also served Chinese immigrants in California.

During and after the Civil War, the AMA redirected its attention to aiding and educating African Americans, particularly newly freed persons. African Americans liberated by the war were generally destitute and homeless. Many lived in vast tent cities or camp towns, where living conditions were often unhealthy and overcrowded.

The AMA sent hundreds of teachers into the South and established numerous schools and churches during Reconstruction. The AMA opened numerous elementary schools in the South to all, regardless of race. The movement of hundreds of teachers into the South by the AMA and other groups gave rise to the stereotype of the Yankee schoolmarm.

In a time when few schools or colleges were open to blacks, the AMA established academies for teachers, as well as general colleges. Over time, some AMA primary schools developed into schools of higher learning. Unlike many short-lived Reconstruction projects, the AMA maintained educational efforts for African Americans in the South over a long period. The group possessed a clear and enduring vision of education as a vital tool to improve the lives and opportunities of American blacks.

Colleges with AMA roots include Atlanta University, Georgia; Berea College, Kentucky; Dillard University, Louisiana; Fisk University, Tennessee; Howard University, District of Columbia; LeMoyne Institute, Pennsylvania; and Talladega College, Alabama. These colleges formed the core of what is now known as historically black colleges and universities. The AMA is now a mission of the United Church of Christ and continues to support several of these colleges.

Jennifer Harrison

Further Readings

DeBoer, Clara Merritt. "Blacks and the American Missionary Association." In Barbara Brown Zikmund, ed. *Hidden Histories in the United Church of Christ.* Cleveland: United Church Press, 1984.

Green, Fletcher M. "Northern Missionary Activities in the South, 1846–1861." *The Journal of Southern History* 21, 2 (May 1955): 147–172.

Miele, Frank J. J. "The Amistad Research Center." *Cultural Resource Management* 21, 4 (1998): 48–49.

Quarles, Benjamin. *Black Abolitionists*. New York: Oxford University Press, 1969.

Amistad

The *Amistad* was a Spanish vessel carrying captured Africans from Havana, Cuba, to Puerto Principe, another port in the Spanish colony, in June 1839. The Africans had been taken off the coast of Africa by a Spanish slaver earlier in the year, in violation of an Anglo-Spanish treaty outlawing the transatlantic slave trade. On July 1, 1839, the thirty-nine captives, led by Cinqué, mutinied and seized the vessel, forcing the remaining crew to set course for Africa. The Spanish sailors, however, sailed secretly for the United States, and the *Amistad* arrived off the eastern end of Long Island on August 26. The crew of the USS *Washington* discovered the ship, hauled it to New London, Connecticut, and commenced a claim for salvage in federal court.

Abolitionists sought to use this claim, or prize case, as a test for the legality of slavery. Arthur Tappan, Joshua Leavitt, Simon Jocelyn, and other prominent abolitionists formed the *Amistad* Committee. They hired New Haven attorney Roger S. Baldwin, known as a lawyer for the downtrodden, as counsel for the captives. The case came before the Circuit Court, presided over by Supreme Court justice Smith Thompson and District Court judge Andrew T. Judson. Baldwin and his co-counsel argued that the captives were illegally taken into slavery and should go free. District Attorney William Holabird argued the position held by the administration of Democratic president Martin Van Buren that the Africans were Spanish property and should be returned under the terms of Pinckney's Treaty of 1795. Thompson ruled that the court had no jurisdiction over a piracy case aboard a Spanish vessel and sent the admiralty portion of the case back to the district court. In the meantime, the Spanish minister to the United States pressed the Van Buren administration to give up the captives.

In January 1840, Judson ruled that the captives were not slaves. The Spanish crewmembers that survived claimed the captives had been born in Cuba. Resourceful examination, however, revealed that the Africans did not speak Spanish; further inquiry determined that in fact they had been captured in the Sierra Leone region of West Africa. Therefore, seized illegally, they were not Spanish property. Holabird and the Spanish claimants appealed the case to the Circuit Court, which re-affirmed the decision in April. The case was then appealed to the Supreme Court.

For months, the *Amistad* Committee had tried to recruit John Quincy Adams as counsel for the captives. Finally, the aging and hesitant Adams relented and joined the legal team in late 1840, agreeing to argue his first legal case in thirty years. Adams delivered a nine-hour argument on February 24 and March 1, 1841. Justice Joseph Story delivered the opinion of the court on March 9. He ruled that the African-born captives had never legally been slaves and were free. As kidnap victims, they had a right to revolt against their captors. The cabin boy, who had been born a slave, was ordered to be returned to Cuba. Abolitionists had hoped for a broader condemnation of the legality of slavery, but Story's opinion was more narrowly based. The surviving captives set sail for Africa in November 1841. The abolitionists had hoped that the natural law of freedom would triumph over the statute law that upheld slavery, but Story's decision revealed that the courts could not be used to abolish slavery. Lewis Tappan foreshadowed the next phase of the abolition movement by helping the *Amistad*'s cabin boy escape to Canada before he could be returned to Cuba.

Robert W. Smith

See also: Democratic Party and Antislavery; Whig Party and Antislavery, Tappan, Lewis.

Further Readings

Bemis, Samuel Flagg. *John Quincy Adams and the Union.* New York: Alfred A. Knopf, 1956.
Jones, Howard. *Mutiny on the* Amistad. New York: Oxford University Press, 1987.

Antislavery Evangelical Protestantism

Antislavery evangelical Protestantism emerged in Great Britain and the United States in the last quarter of the eighteenth century within an environment of changing theological doctrines. While evangelicalism alone did not cause antislavery, there is little doubt that it contributed significantly to its rise and to a variety of other social reform efforts. The demand for immediate emancipation after 1830 sustained an especially strong link with evangelicalism. Many leading abolition-ists employed biblical language, and evangelical Protestants led the drive to found antislavery organizations. Yet, pronounced divisions within American Protestant-ism after 1840 revealed that not all evangelicals advocated immediate emancipa-tion. Nevertheless, antislavery evangelicals on both sides of the Atlantic shaped the movement in significant ways. Not only did they draw attention to slavery's immoral nature, but they agitated politically for an end to the international slave trade and for slavery's abolition. In the United States, their involvement in both radical and moderate antislavery efforts subsequently coincided with the collapse of the Second Party System and the increasingly divisive sectionalism that ulti-mately resulted in the Civil War.

Origins

Antislavery sentiment among evangelical Protestants can be traced to the influence of the Society of Friends, popularly known as Quakers, in both England and the American colonies, from the early eighteenth century. While an older generation of British Quakers, including George Keith and Benjamin Lay, had protested the buying and selling of slaves, it was not until the 1757 London Yearly Meeting that Quakers as a religious body began to consider the matter seriously. Pennsylvania Quakers like John Woolman and Anthony Benezet, expressing concern over the inherent sinfulness of slavery and its effect on the purity of Friends, encouraged their British counterparts to discipline Quakers who engaged in the slave trade. In 1761, London Yearly Meeting agreed to disown slave dealers. By 1774, the Phila-delphia Yearly Meeting adopted measures to ensure the eventual manumission of Quaker-owned slaves. Quaker insistence on the immorality of the slave trade and slaveholding drew attention from evangelical Protestants. Benezet, in particular, corresponded with British evangelicals such as John Wesley, the founder of Meth-odism, and Granville Sharp, an outspoken proponent of abolishing the foreign slave trade. In 1787, Sharp joined British Quakers and evangelicals to form the Abolition Committee, dedicated to ending the slave trade.

Evangelical theology was critical to the early British antislavery movement. Methodists and evangelical Anglicans stressed individual salvation and redemp-tion from sin over liturgical obedience. Emphasizing each believer's personal re-sponsibility to reform society and the nation, British evangelicals focused their energies on abolishing the slave trade. Like Quakers, they equated buying and selling slaves with moral corruption. In a 1791 letter to William Wilberforce, a member of Parliament, John Wesley called the slave trade, "that execrable villainy, which is the scandal of religion, of England, and of human nature." Wilberforce, who converted to the evangelical faith in 1785, spent twenty-two years struggling to secure passage by Parliament of a bill abolishing slavery. In 1807, he finally succeeded, a testament to the increasing weight evangelicals carried in the anti-slavery cause.

British antislavery evangelicals extended their influence beyond England's shores. Wilberforce, for example, maintained contact with Americans and congratulated President James Monroe on Congress's 1807 passage of a bill ending the U.S. participation in the international slave trade. After the British defeated Napoleon in 1814, evangelicals sought to make abolition of the European slave trade fundamental to a peace agreement and gathered nearly a million signatures on 800 antislavery petitions that they presented to Parliament. Although it is doubtful that these petitions swayed European leaders, the political pressure applied by evangelicals certainly encouraged British peace negotiators to represent their countrymen's position to the international community. In 1815, most continental powers agreed to abolish the slave trade either immediately or within a few years.

In America, early antislavery evangelicals responded powerfully to the Edwardsean theology that emerged from the Great Awakening. Even though influenced by both Quakerism and British evangelicalism, these reformers relied heavily on Jonathan Edwards's notion of disinterested benevolence, or good will toward one's fellow man that was not motivated by self-interest. Interpreting Edwards's abstract concept as a call to practical action, several of his disciples, including Samuel Hopkins, Joseph Bellamy, Jonathan Edwards Jr., and Lemuel Haynes, began preaching boldly against the evils of slavery during the Revolutionary period. In 1776, Samuel Hopkins informed the Continental Congress that slavery was a "very great and public sin." Once they linked slavery with sin, New Divinity preachers like Hopkins, a staunch Calvinist, demanded immediate repentance and complete emancipation. Among those employing Hopkins's interpretation of Edwards were British antislavery evangelicals William Wilberforce and Granville Sharp.

The American Revolution sharply impacted American antislavery evangelicalism. Imbued with the egalitarian language of the Declaration of Independence "that all men are created equal and endowed by their Creator with certain inalienable rights," New Divinity evangelicals tied abolition inextricably to the success of the young Republic. According to these reformers, the virtue necessary to be good republican citizens stemmed from disinterested benevolence and could not be sustained in a land of slaveholders. One New Divinity preacher, Nathaniel Niles, asked in 1774, "Would we enjoy liberty? Then we must grant it to others." These early evangelical calls for abolition, however, were overshadowed by the political exigency to preserve a newly created union, many of whose founders were slaveholders.

Two factors spurred the growth of antislavery evangelicalism in the first decades of the nineteenth century: the rapid social change accompanying the frontier's westward advance after the American Revolution and a transformation in Christian theology during the 1820s and 1830s. In the decades following the Revolution, New Englanders steeped in the Yankee heritage of Christian benevolence flooded western New England and upstate New York. When the market revolution and the Erie Canal transformed the region after the War of 1812, many individuals unfamiliar with Yankee Protestantism flocked to newly created boomtowns such as Utica and Rochester, New York. On a frontier where few churches existed, Protestants feared the rise of moral corruption and disruption in the social order. In this unsettled, anxious region, Protestant evangelists like Lyman Beecher and Charles Grandison Finney discovered a fertile field for missionary work. Preaching a liberalized Calvinism, they initiated a wave of enthusiastic spiritual revivals that inspired conversion and social reform.

The religious campaigns conducted by Finney between 1824 and 1834 throughout New York State supplied ample impetus for the antislavery movement. Departing from the Calvinist doctrine that sinners were completely passive during conversion, Beecher and Finney preached that the individual will, with the help of the Holy Spirit, was free to choose God's universal offer of grace. Declaring individuals responsible for their own repentance, the new doctrine indicated that revivals and believers could persuade others to repent as well and eventually transform all of society. Employing Edwardsean theology, Finney declared that "all sin consists in selfishness; and all holiness or virtue, in disinterested benevolence." Thus charged with the duty to pursue God's good selflessly in the world, converts initiated a variety of social reforms such as temperance and home missions, but embraced no reform with such impassioned dedication as they did abolitionism. Even though Quakers had been instrumental in the formation of early abolition societies like the Pennsylvania Abolition Society, evangelical Protestants in the 1830s invested in the movement with an unprecedented zeal.

The concept of perfectionism motivated many antislavery evangelical Protestants. Finney preached that individuals, by exercising their regenerated moral agency, could achieve perfect holiness or sanctification. Perfectionists believed that they could transform society one individual at a time and that eradicating sin would ultimately usher in Christ's millennial kingdom. Revivals and reform societies were deemed essential to hastening the millennium's arrival.

Rise of Immediatism

By the 1820s, antislavery evangelicals in both Great Britain and the United States considered the entire institution of slavery a national sin. Not content merely with an end to the slave trade, abolitionists organized more deliberately for complete abolition. In England, the early efforts by Quakers and their evangelical allies had created a climate conducive to immediate abolitionism. Employing often exclusively religious language, they proclaimed colonial slavery "a System full of Wickedness, hateful to God, and a Curse and Disgrace to Britain." Motivated by evangelical beliefs and by slave unrest in the West Indies, abolitionist activities multiplied after 1830. Activists spoke to overflowing crowds between 1830 and 1832, lecturing sometimes for hours to thousands of people. Notably, evangelical dissenters offered their churches for these assemblies.

Similarly, American agitation for immediate emancipation became more pronounced after 1830. Through the late 1820s, most opponents of slavery believed gradual emancipation—a policy of steadily releasing the enslaved over many years into society as free—was the most temperate and feasible plan. It was originally advocated by the American Convention of Abolition Societies and enacted in various Northern states in the late eighteenth century. However, after Finney's revivals through upstate and western New York from 1826 to 1831, antislavery activists in the North began to adopt a more radical position, rejecting gradualism and plans for black removal as far too compromised with slavery. Perfectionist and millennial in outlook, they espoused immediate and total emancipation as the only path to national regeneration. The relationship between evangelicalism and antislavery solidified in the ensuing decades.

Early Tactics

Evangelicals skillfully mobilized public opinion. In England, veterans from the battle over the slave trade joined with a new, younger generation of reformers to form the Anti-Slavery Society in 1823. It provided an organizational base from which to stir the public and government against slavery. During its first year, the Society printed over 200,000 tracts; by 1830, it published more than double that number. Key to their massive campaign were the thousands of antislavery petitions submitted to Parliament. Between 1826 and 1832, reformers gathered more than 3,500 petitions, many of which originated with church congregations. In addition, Wesleyan Methodists and other nonconformists worked together to encourage voters to elect members of Parliament who supported immediate emancipation. Public orations to large gatherings were also commonly employed. These tactics, combined with numerous other social, economic, and cultural factors, led to Parliament's 1833 passage of the Emancipation Act, abolishing slavery in the British Empire.

Significant and difficult as was gaining emancipation in Great Britain, it was a far more daunting assignment in the United States. In 1830, Southerners held two million slaves, planters commanded enormous political power, and the federal government was powerless to end slavery in the states. American evangelicals determined to deploy moral suasion as their principal tactic. Consistent with their perfectionist vision, moral suasionists such as Lewis Tappan, Elizur Wright Jr., and

William Lloyd Garrison believed that slaveholders could be brought to repentance and abolition by a constant declaiming upon moral truth and the barbaric character of slavery. Wright declared that only "direct repentance, confession, and reparation of injury" would bring about slavery's end. In 1833, Tappan, Wright, and other evangelicals, including Joshua Leavitt and James G. Birney, founded the American Anti-Slavery Society (AASS) as a national organization to bring abolitionists together under one association and, like their British counterparts, to mobilize public opinion. They sought to convert the entire nation to immediatism. With the Society's support, reformers petitioned state legislatures and flooded the postal system with antislavery pamphlets to induce Southern masters to emancipate their slaves. By 1838, evangelically inspired abolitionists had formed over 200 antislavery auxiliaries and submitted petitions to Congress with more than 400,000 signatures.

Employing religious language, antislavery activists compared conversion to immediatism with conversion to Christ. For these evangelicals, abolitionism was a sacred duty or calling. Theodore Dwight Weld, a Finney convert and AASS agent, proclaimed that "as long as I am a moral agent I am fully prepared to *act out* my belief in that thus saith the Lord—'*Faith without WORKS is dead.*'" Fueled by righteous faith, antislavery Protestants understood themselves as missionaries. In 1836, for example, the AASS permitted Weld to recruit sixty-nine other men to join him in his crusade. Like the "seventy" that Christ sent out to spread the Gospel message, these abolitionists preached the good news of immediatism.

Throughout the 1830s, especially after the Emancipation Act of 1833, British evangelicals sought to encourage American abolitionists. Theodore Dwight Weld, for example, embraced abolitionism after corresponding with the British Presbyterian, Charles Stuart. Baptists and Methodists, major American denominations, faced increasing pressure from across the Atlantic to oppose slavery more forcefully. British Methodists in 1837 castigated the Georgia Conference for refusing to declare slavery morally evil. The Board of Baptist Ministers In and Near London exhorted American Baptist clergy "to act in the spirit and with the firmness of Christian principle" to achieve abolition. Many American evangelicals welcomed this transatlantic support. Arthur Tappan claimed that it "greatly aided us in effecting that reformation of public opinion here which it is our object to effect." Although the 1840s brought new challenges to American activists, the British and Foreign Anti-Slavery Society continued to sustain and encourage them.

Division

Because American reformers, unlike British abolitionists, grappled with slavery within their nation's borders, they never approached unanimity on antislavery methods. Antislavery evangelical Protestantism encompassed a variety of positions from conservative to radical. For example, in 1834, a controversy over antislavery methods developed at Lane Seminary in Cincinnati, Ohio. The school's president, evangelical preacher Lyman Beecher, encouraged a harmonious working relationship between abolitionists and colonizationists—supporters of the American Colonization Society, which proposed removing free blacks from the country as the best method to prompt manumissions and ease interracial tensions. Student leader, Theodore Dwight Weld, however, strongly opposed the colonization plan. He considered the plan thoroughly sinful as it respected slaveholders and sanctioned racial prejudice. Instead, he advocated immediate emancipation and racial equality and a thorough rejection of colonizationism. While at Lane, he converted students to immediatism and engineered reform projects, including education programs for Cincinnati's African American community. When the seminary's evangelical trustees expelled Weld's group of students as too radical, the Tappan brothers, wealthy contributors to the school, founded Oberlin College as an alternative for abolitionist students and installed Charles Grandison Finney as professor of theology. Weld and his cohort relocated there. Oberlin became the first college in the country to accept both men and women, black and white.

By 1840, factional discord ruptured the AASS. Many Garrisonians renounced political action, withdrew from regular denomination fellowship, and favored full female inclusion in the governance and promotion of antislavery. The Tappans, Elizur Wright Jr., and Henry B. Stanton opposed these radical views and feared a conservative backlash against the antislavery movement if they were endorsed. The pressure to allow women an active voice within the Society finally forced the rancorous debate into the open, leading to the organization's fissure. The Garrisonians gained control of the AASS, while the Tappans and other similarly minded Protestants formed the new American and Foreign Anti-Slavery Society.

It was ironic that evangelicals should split over women's participation in the antislavery movement. Women who had been converted during the revivals of the 1820s and 1830s represented the majority of church members in the antebellum North and organized many antislavery auxiliaries. In addition, they signed legislative petitions and actively collected petition signatures. Angelina and Sarah Grimké, former slaveholders from South Carolina, became famous for speaking publicly for the AASS from 1836 to 1838. As evangelicals, the sisters employed Scriptural arguments against both slavery and women's oppression. After their retirement in 1838, other less well-known women continued to support abolitionism through churches and female antislavery societies. Nevertheless, gender conventions to which the vast majority of evangelical antislavery activists adhered mandated that men, not women, perform the public organizational and promotional activities of the societies.

During the 1840s and 1850s, the tension within abolitionism further disrupted established churches. Disgusted with the proslavery stand that many major denominations and clergymen had assumed, Methodist, Presbyterian, and Baptist abolitionists left their congregations, either by creating their own denominational antislavery wing or by forming nonsectarian churches. Evangelical abolitionists like Orange Scott and La Roy Sunderland, for instance, rejected fellowship with Methodist slaveholders to form the Wesleyan Methodist Church in 1843. Not all these "come-outers" maintained a relationship with a church body. Some, like Garrison and James G. Birney, championed radical anti-institutional and anti-ecclesiastical positions. They renounced churches altogether and espoused a more secular humanitarianism. Such heterodoxy appalled orthodox evangelicals like the Tappans, Stanton, and Wright, who favored church-centered activism. Yet, as the 1850s approached, even Wright abandoned orthodox Protestantism.

African American Evangelicalism

The relationship between African American abolitionists and antislavery evangelical Protestantism is complex. Although most free black reformers such as Samuel E. Cornish, Samuel Ringgold Ward, and Alexander Crummell were Protestant clergymen, their evangelicalism differed from white evangelicalism. Exposed to racial prejudice and social, economic, and legal discrimination, many free African Americans refused to embrace the perfectionist, millennial vision of white reformers. Often rejecting moral suasion, black evangelicals employed prophetic language, emphasizing God's judgment rather than slaveholders' repentance. Radicals like David Walker, Frederick Douglass, and Henry Highland Garnet all indicted white Christian hypocrisy for sustaining American slavery.

White evangelicals often limited African American involvement in the antislavery movement. When the AASS formed in 1833, just three of its original sixty-three delegates were African American. In 1842, Lewis Tappan gained control over the Union Missionary Society, an antislavery mission program founded by former slave and Congregational minister J.W.C. Pennington. He then replaced the organization's black leaders with white men. Tappan exemplified how strong racial prejudice remained in the North, even among those white evangelicals who actively supported radical abolition and denounced racism.

Along with antislavery activism, black evangelicals also concentrated their reform efforts on religious education and self-improvement programs. Many black reformers recognized their relative powerlessness within white assemblies and focused their energies on building and strengthening their disadvantaged communities. In 1830, black clergymen, along with white allies, founded the National Negro Convention Movement. Distinctly evangelical, it concentrated more on salvation and morality within the free African American community than immediate emancipation. Independent black churches like the African Methodist Episcopal (AME) and African Methodist Episcopal Zion (AMEZ) quietly, but diligently, supported antislavery efforts. Such evangelicals as the Reverend Jermain Loguen of New York aided many fugitive slaves on the Underground Railroad, and AME and AMEZ churches served as stops along the way. Where white reformers engaged in organizing and speaking, many more unheralded African Americans extended the antislavery movement to runaway slaves by providing them with clothing, food, and supplies.

Political Action

Finding moral suasion too limited, some evangelicals began to shift their attention to using politics to end slavery. In fact, the insistence by leaders within the AASS that members vote for antislavery candidates had helped catalyze its division in 1840. Dedicated to Christian anti-institutionalism, the Garrisonians adamantly refused any connection with a government they perceived as evil and ungodly. Non-Garrisonians, however, argued that moral suasion must be reinforced with more practical measures. Imbued with revival enthusiasm, men like Elizur Wright Jr., Gerrit Smith, Beriah Green, and Joshua Leavitt believed it was their religious duty to enter politics. In 1840, they founded the Liberty Party. Nominating former slaveholder and evangelical convert, James G. Birney, as its first presidential candidate, the party platform demanded abolition in the District of Columbia, termination of the domestic slave trade, and protection of the right to petition Congress.

A diverse group of evangelical Protestants, the Liberty Party leadership underscored the voter's Christian duty to support antislavery candidates. The party's conventions during the 1840s often resembled revival camp meetings, with prayers and sermons urging conversion to immediatism. Practicing "Bible politics," party members emphasized divine law and morality in government. Critics often pointed to these overtly religious politicians as self-righteous zealots and politically divisive. Tarred with the same brush as the Garrisonians, the Liberty contingent failed to garner broad-based support. Some evangelicals charged that, by engaging in political activism, Liberty men damaged the antislavery cause.

While many evangelicals did not share the Liberty Party's devotion to immediate universal emancipation, they strenuously opposed slavery's spread into new Western territories. In 1845, the United States' annexation of Texas prompted a strong reaction from both conservative and radical antislavery evangelicals. Recognizing the need for greater agreement among themselves, they joined, in 1848, with non-evangelical reformers to found the Free Soil Party. Committed to preventing slavery in the territories, the party gained support from evangelical Protestants. The Reverend Joshua Leavitt, former editor of the Tappans' antislavery newspaper, the

Emancipator, for example, supported Free Soil. Adopting the religious rhetoric and crusading style of the former Liberty Party, Free Soilers drew evangelical and non-evangelical slavery opponents away from the larger Democratic and Whig parties.

Confronted with the Compromise of 1850, evangelical Protestants again increased their political agitation. William Seward, a New York senator, proclaimed in his maiden speech to the Senate on March 11, 1850, that "there is a higher law than the Constitution, which regulates our authority over the domain." Free Soilers and antislavery evangelicals embraced "higher law" doctrine, convinced that Christians had a duty to disobey legislation if it contradicted divine law. This became especially important with the passage of the Fugitive Slave Law as part of the Compromise of 1850. The Fugitive Slave Law made Northerners complicit in the maintenance of the evil of slavery and ungodliness, an untenable position for antislavery evangelicals, conservative and radical.

The Kansas-Nebraska Act of 1854 cemented the bond among antislavery evangelicals. The repeal of the Missouri Compromise accompanying the Kansas-Nebraska bill assured slavery opponents that Kansas was being handed over to the devil. As antagonism between North and South escalated, evangelicals from all parties joined with other non-evangelical opponents of slavery to form the Republican Party in 1856. While evangelicals were not solely responsible for the party's existence, certainly their sense of Christian duty provided the party with much-needed energy and support. In 1860, some religious abolitionists read religious meaning into Abraham Lincoln's statement, "Let us have faith that right makes might, in that faith let us dare to the end to do our duty as we understand it." For former Free Soilers and Liberty men, this was a call to Christian action.

Conclusion

Antislavery evangelical Protestantism contributed to the movement toward Civil War. Both radical abolitionists and conservative antislavery reformers lent an urgency to the crusade against slavery by casting it in a moral light and keeping it continually so before the public. In a predominantly Protestant nation, evangelicalism deeply influenced the growing division between North and South. At the same time, reformers wielded little real power to effect change. While British evangelicals had continued their supportive relationship with American abolitionists throughout the decades preceding the Civil War, Americans faced social, political, economic, and cultural obstacles difficult to overcome. Given the scope of antislavery activity throughout the Atlantic world for over a century, however, the evangelical Protestant impact on the movement was profound.

Dianne Wheaton Cappiello

See also: Come-Outerism; Congregationalism and Antislavery; First Great Awakening and Antislavery; Quakers and Antislavery; Unitarianism and Antislavery.

Further Readings

Barnes, Gilbert Hobbs. *The Antislavery Impulse, 1830–1844.* 1933. Reprint, with an introduction by William G. McLoughlin. New York: Harcourt, Brace & World, Inc., 1964.

Bolt, Christine and Seymour Drescher, eds. *Anti-Slavery, Religion, and Reform: Essays in Memory of Roger Anstey.* Kent, England: Wm. Dawson & Sons Ltd., 1980.

Carwardine, Richard J. *Evangelicals and Politics in Antebellum America.* New Haven, CT: Yale University Press, 1993.

Cross, Whitney R. *The Burned-Over District: The Social and Intellectual History of Enthusiastic Religion in Western New York, 1800–1850.* Ithaca, NY: Cornell University Press, 1950.

Davis, David Brion. *The Problem of Slavery in the Age of Revolution, 1770–1823.* Ithaca, NY: Cornell University Press, 1975.

George, Carol V. R. "Widening the Circle: The Black Church and the Abolitionist Crusade, 1830–1860." In Lewis Perry and Michael Fellman, eds., *Antislavery Reconsidered: New Perspectives on the Abolitionists.* Baton Rouge: Louisiana State University Press, 1979, pp. 75–95.

Harwood, Thomas F. "British Evangelical Abolitionism and American Churches in the 1830's." *Journal of Southern History* 28 (August 1962): 287–306.

Loveland, Anne C. "Evangelicalism and 'Immediate Emancipation' in American Antislavery Thought." *Journal of Southern History* 32 (1966): 172–188.

Scott, Donald M. "Abolition as a Sacred Vocation." In Lewis Perry and Michael Fellman, eds., *Antislavery Reconsidered: New Perspectives on the Abolitionists.* Baton Rouge: Louisiana State University Press, 1979, pp. 51–74.

Stewart, James Brewer. *Holy Warriors: The Abolitionists and American Slavery.* Rev. ed. New York: Hill and Wang, 1997.

Walters, Ronald G. *The Antislavery Appeal: American Abolitionism after 1830.* New York: W.W. Norton & Co., 1984; Baltimore: Johns Hopkins University Press, 1978.

Wyatt-Brown, Bertram. *Lewis Tappan and the Evangelical War against Slavery.* Cleveland: Case Western Reserve University Press, 1969.

Antislavery Journalism in the United States and Great Britain

In their efforts to win support for an end to slavery, abolitionists used a variety of media both to maintain and expand their movement and to carry their messages to the general community. These media included the speaker's platform, pamphlets, books, dramas, magazines, and newspapers. The abolitionist press in the United

States became a focal point for the cause, but also resulted in countermeasures, particularly in the South, that included violence and death for one abolitionist editor, Elijah P. Lovejoy. In the United States, two abolitionist leaders in particular became identified with the newspapers they edited, William Lloyd Garrison of the *Liberator* and Frederick Douglass of the *North Star*. Douglass also edited a magazine, *Douglass' Monthly*, which circulated in England. The abolition press helped on both sides of the Atlantic to provide cohesion for efforts to end slavery.

Not long after the American Revolution, the push for an end to slavery gained momentum in England. Although the movement initially had a religious foundation, it gained support from changes in political and economic theory and the French Revolution. The antislavery movement in Great Britain relied less initially on the swaying of public opinion through the press than through initiatives in the courts and in Parliament.

The abolition movement in England generally had two phases: first, to end slavery in the country and its colonies and, second, to support the movement to end slavery in the United States. Zachary Macaulay founded what was probably the first abolition newspaper, the *Anti-Slavery Reporter*, in 1825. The newspaper eventually became the organ of the British and Foreign Anti-Slavery Society. It continued publishing, in some form, until 1994.

The abolitionist movement began in England in the 1700s, ostensibly as a religious movement of evangelicals and Quakers that opposed slavery and England's role in the slave trade. The abolitionists used books, pamphlets, lectures, and petitions to advance their cause. The movement achieved the most success in the courts. Granville Sharp, a civil servant, frequently challenged in the courts the right of West Indians to remove their slaves from England. The case of James Somerset in 1772 involved the right of a West Indian owner to forcibly remove a slave from England. The lord chief justice ruled that the no such right existed. Although it only limited the removal of slaves, it led to the end of slavery in England.

Sharp and Thomas Clarkson were cofounders of the Society for the Abandonment of the Slave Trade in 1787. The group formed from the London Quaker Abolition Committee, although Sharp and Clarkson both were members of the Church of England. William Wilberforce, who had served in Parliament since 1780, took up the twenty-year drive to end the slave trade in 1787. In an attempt to win public opinion, the English abolitionists decided to battle the slave trade rather than slavery itself. To sway public opinion, the movement used books and pamphlets and worked to win support in the general press. Parliament approved the Foreign Slave Trade bill in 1806, and the English slave trade ended on May 1, 1807.

British abolitionists thereafter turned their attention to slavery in the rest of the world, particularly the United States. Great Britain became a source of support of the U.S. abolition movement, including financial backing for antislavery newspapers in the United States and for contributors to these newspapers. Divisions in the U.S. abolition movement, however, also eventually resulted in divisions in the British movement. At issue were the views of Garrison. Among the British groups that supported Garrison was the Anglo-America Anti-Slavery Association. It sponsored the *Anti-Slavery Advocate*, a newspaper that published from 1852 to 1863. The *Anti-Slavery Reporter* and the *Anti-Slavery Advocate* were the two primary antislavery newspapers in Great Britain, but the Anti-Slavery Society's Agency Committee that sponsored antislavery lectures in Great Britain, beginning in the 1830s, sponsored its own antislavery publication, the *Tourist*.

The abolitionist press in the United States included not only the publications of antislavery organizations, but also coverage and editorial support in mainstream newspapers and in the black press. The U.S. abolitionist press served international, national, and regional audiences. Along with national publications such as the *Liberator*, the *National Anti-Slavery Standard*, published between 1840 and 1870, the *National Era*, and international publications such as *Frederick Douglass' Paper*, a number of regional abolitionist papers also were available, such as the *Instigator*, published in Providence, Rhode Island, and the *Liberalist*, published in New Orleans. Garrison's Pennsylvania organizations published the *Pennsylvania Freeman* through the 1850s. The Ohio Anti-Slavery Society, later the Western Anti-Slavery Society, published the *Anti-Slavery Bugle*. Mainstream newspapers also took a role in covering abolitionists and their crusade. The *New York Tribune*, under the leadership of publisher Horace Greeley, became the leading mainstream paper against slavery. Joseph Medill became an advocate for abolition with the *Chicago Tribune*.

The black press, beginning with *Freedom's Journal* in 1827, provided advocacy of abolition, a forum for abolitionists, and coverage of antislavery organizations. For the antebellum black newspapers, however, abolition was only one area they covered. They also reported on the social, economic, and educational advance of free blacks and former slaves in the North. *Freedom's Journal*, the *Colored American*, the *Ram's Horn*, the *Alienated American*, and late in the 1850s, the *Anglo-African* all addressed abolition as well as other issues of racial justice and improvement of immediate concern to the free blacks of the North. The pioneers of the black press, including *Freedom Journal's* John Russwurm and Samuel Cornish, also faced divisions over support for the colonization movement. The *Ram's Horn*, which included John Brown and Frederick Douglass among its contributors, took perhaps the strongest stance against abolition, publishing an editorial that directly addressed the slaves in the South.

Of those U.S. newspapers that focused almost exclusively on abolition, the earliest was Benjamin Lundy's the *Genius of Universal Emancipation*, the principal abolitionist organ in the 1820s. The newspaper initially was a one-man operation, and Lundy moved it from Ohio to Tennessee to Maryland in an attempt to build support. The paper closed early in 1829 because of lack of support from slavery states, but Lundy was able to reopen the publication later in 1829 with two associates, Elizabeth Chandler and William Lloyd Garrison. Garrison, who would become the central personality in the U.S. abolition movement, faced libel charges in Baltimore as a result of writing in the *Genius of Universal Emancipation* that a local slave trader had illegally transported some slaves. A jury convicted Garrison, who was jailed for forty-nine days before the New York City philanthropist, Arthur Tappan, paid his fine and secured his release.

Garrison's experiences in Baltimore, however, were only previews of his more than thirty-year role in the abolitionist press. Garrison's newspaper, the *Liberator*, began publication on January 1, 1831, in Boston, Massachusetts. Despite limited financial support and circulation throughout its operation, the newspaper presented its editor's views for immediate freeing of slaves, no payments to slaveholders, and no support for colonization of slaves and former slaves in Africa.

Garrison helped found the American Anti-Slavery Society (AASS) in 1833, but the *Liberator* continued to offer his personal views and was not the official publication of the society. The *National Anti-Slavery Standard* served that role. The society was a union of Philadelphia Quakers, Garrison's supporters in New England, and reformers from New York.

Despite the *Liberator's* limited circulation, Garrison used the newspaper-exchange system to get the paper into the offices of 100 newspaper editors, whose criticism of himself and abolition, Garrison gladly printed. As with other abolition publications, circulation of the *Liberator* in the South resulted in destruction of its copies and violence against its distributors. The U.S. postmaster general condoned efforts to bar circulation of the *Liberator* in the South.

The South was particularly wary of distribution of abolitionist publications after the Nat Turner slave revolt in South Carolina in 1831. The AASS launched a pamphlet campaign in 1835. Before 1836, it produced more than one million copies of antislavery items. Southern mobs also tried to bar distribution of these publications.

Garrison's critics contended that he and the *Liberator* were urging slaves to take violent actions against their owners. Southern states offered bounties for Garrison, who, nonetheless, opposed violence and Turner's rebellion.

Violent threats against the abolitionist press came not only from the South. In the 1830s, Elijah P. Lovejoy of Illinois published an abolitionist weekly. Mobs destroyed his press four times, and during the fourth attack in 1837, they killed him while he was trying to defend his press and his ideas. Lovejoy, a clergyman as well as an editor, began publishing a Presbyterian newspaper, the *St. Louis Observer*, in Missouri, a slave state, in 1834. Lovejoy advocated gradual elimination of slavery. Fearing for the safety of his family, Lovejoy relocated to Illinois, a free state, where he began publishing the *Alton Observer* and tried to form a state antislavery society. A mob also burned Pennsylvania Hall in Philadelphia in 1837. The hall had

An antiabolition mob attacks the warehouse of the *Alton Observer*, an antislavery newspaper, in Alton, Illinois, on November 7, 1837. Editor Elijah P. Lovejoy was shot dead defending his press. (Library of Congress)

housed the local antislavery office and was the site of the Anti-Slavery Convention of American Women, where blacks and whites freely mixed.

Lovejoy's death and other violence against abolitionists helped transform the movement from one only against slavery into a larger battle for civil liberties. Following closely after them were calls for direct action, including more political involvement, to win freedom for slaves. Previously, abolitionists had hoped that the soundness of their arguments alone would convince other rational citizens of the rightness of their cause. Now, some abolitionists like Gerrit Smith and Henry Highland Garnet turned to politics to fight slavery, and the abolitionist press helped to present their arguments.

Abolitionists, however, became divided. At the center of the divide was Garrison, whose *Liberator's* pages were open to a variety of reformers and causes, including women's rights. Maria Stewart, a black woman, began writing for the *Liberator* in 1831, and the unusual inclusion of a woman's voice in a newspaper brought opposition from both white and black males. The male-dominated black community so opposed her role at the newspaper that she opted to relocate to New York and seek reforms through education.

The issue of the appropriate role of women in the abolition movement generally divided the movement. Churches tried to limit women speaking about abolition in their communities, even if the events were not at their churches. Opponents tried to bar their voting rights in the AASS.

Garrison also condemned the government and Constitution as defenders of slavery and abjured political action as endorsing them. He questioned whether the Constitution could ever emancipate the slaves and protect them. During one protest in 1854, Garrison actually burned a copy of the Constitution.

In 1840, brothers Arthur and Lewis Tappan founded the American and Foreign Anti-Slavery Society (AFASS) to counter Garrison's recent seizure of control of the AASS. Garrison's espousal of reform causes other than abolition, especially that of women's rights, particularly worried them. The AFASS continued until 1855. Garrison's society was in place until the Civil War, but its role in the movement grew less prominent as antislavery became more part of the political mainstream with the rise of the Republicans by the mid-1850s.

Garrison's central role in the abolition movement was also somewhat eclipsed by the rise of Frederick Douglass, a fugitive slave, as a featured speaker of the abolition movement. An admirer of Garrison and of the *Liberator*, Douglass started the *North Star* despite some opposition from Garrison. Douglass received funding for a newspaper in 1847, and the first issue of the *North Star* appeared December 3, 1847. In December 1850, the newspaper became the *Frederick Douglass' Paper*.

Douglass's newspaper eventually exceeded the circulation of the *Liberator* and became an international newspaper with circulation in England and the West Indies. Douglass had traveled to England to lecture and raise money for the abolition movement in the United States. English abolitionists were patrons not only of Douglass's newspaper but also other abolition newspapers in the United States. Black abolitionists who traveled to England briefly or to live also found ready markets for their writings in the abolitionist press in the United States. *Frederick Douglass' Paper* remained in operation until 1861.

Both Garrison and Douglass saw the abolition movement change in the 1850s, when a number of factors brought the antislavery more to the forefront. The spread of slavery into the Western territories, the passage of the Fugitive Slave Law in 1850, and the publication of Harriet Beecher Stowe's *Uncle Tom's Cabin* in 1852 helped move the antislavery fight from the abolitionist movement to a wider population. *Uncle Tom's Cabin* first appeared in serial form in 1851 in the *National Era*, a newspaper with varied content that included opposition to slavery.

The election of Abraham Lincoln in 1860 brought secession of the Southern states and the Civil War. The Emancipation Proclamation in 1863 led to the freeing of slaves in the old Confederacy, and the ratification of the Thirteenth Amendment in 1865 resulted in the abolition of slavery throughout the rest of the United States. Garrison's *Liberator* ceased publishing on December 29, 1865.

The antislavery press played a pivotal role in galvanizing the abolition movement and providing a model to future reform movements for how to use the press both for internal organizational communication and for disseminating the message of reform to a broader public. In Great Britain and in the United States, public opinion became essential to the influencing and changing of public policy. Although the abolitionists used a variety of media to influence public opinion, the press dominated their efforts at moral suasion. As with the abolition movement itself, whose success made less important the roles of the antislavery societies, the success of the abolitionist press led to a larger role for the general, mainstream press in furthering the goal of ending slavery.

William J. Leonhirth

See also: British Slavery, Abolition of; Douglass, Frederick (1818–1895); Garrison, William Lloyd; Lovejoy, Elijah (1802–1837).

Further Readings

Anstey, Roger. *The Atlantic Slave Trade and British Abolition 1766–1810.* Atlantic Highlands, NJ: Humanities Press, 1975.

Blackett, R.J.M. "'To Reach the People with Abolition Doctrines': The Antislavery Press and the American Civil War." *Atlanta History* 42, 1 (1998): 35–44.

Dillon, Merton L. *Abolitionists: The Growth of a Dissenting Minority.* DeKalb: Northern Illinois University Press, 1974.

Hutton, Frankie. *The Early Black Press, 1827–1860.* Westport, CT: Greenwood Press, 1993.

Mayer, Henry. *All on Fire: William Lloyd Garrison and the Abolition of Slavery.* New York: St. Martin's Griffin, 1998.

Quarles, Benjamin. *Frederick Douglass.* Englewood Cliffs, NJ: Prentice-Hall, 1968.

Ripley, C. Peter, ed. *The British Isles, 1830–1865.* Vol. 1 of *The Black Abolitionist Papers.* 5 vols. Chapel Hill: University of North Carolina Press, 1985.

Streitmatter, Roger. *Mightier Than the Sword: How the News Media Have Shaped American History.* Boulder, CO: Westview Press, 1997.

Tripp, Bernell. *Origins of the Black Press: New York, 1827–1847.* Northport, AL: Vision Press, 1992.

Anti-Slavery Society

The movement against slavery in England was launched in the second half of the eighteenth century. In 1772, the Lord Chief Justice, William Murray, the first Earl of Mansfield, handed down the landmark *Somerset* Decision that once a slave set his foot on English territory he was considered free. This action had occurred with the help of a number of reformers who had become as concerned about the slavery question as they had about the condition of the poor or the reform of prisons.

In 1787, twelve of these men, including Granville Sharp and Thomas Clarkson, formed a society for the abolition of the slave trade. Anglicans and Quakers were represented on the committee with support from other religious groups. In the same year, Prime Minister William Pitt the Younger had a famous conversation with another reformer, William Wilberforce (under an oak tree it was said), in which Pitt asked Wilberforce to take over the lead of the antislavery forces in the House of Commons. Wilberforce, who was a convert to evangelical Christianity and already known as a reformer, agreed, joining the society sometime later.

This organization became one of the first single-issue groups to emerge in English history, setting the stage for such associations as the Anti-Corn Law League and the Women's Social and Political Union. It lobbied members of Parliament, and under the leadership of Wilberforce waged a constant battle to achieve its ends. He introduced a measure every year and was buttressed, after the Act of Union of 1801, by the addition of sympathetic Irish members to his ranks. In addition, the Society carried on electoral campaigns, distributed literature, sponsored rallies, supplied speakers, and petitioned the House of Commons. In addition, it publicized information about slave conditions and the atrocities that had taken place. Numerous obstacles were placed in the path of reform, but finally in 1807, under a sympathetic ministry, the slave trade was abolished.

The next step was, of course, to press for the complete abolition of slavery. Such a need was made clear from the practice of slaver captains to order slaves to be thrown overboard to lessen the fine paid for engaging in the slave trade. Thus, in 1823, the Anti-Slavery Society was founded to seek emancipation for the slaves. Wilberforce had become less involved in public life and had reservations about too hasty an abolition, but he did become a member of the Society.

In 1833, Parliament enacted the abolition of slavery. Because of age and illness, Wilberforce was not active and the leadership was taken by Thomas Clarkson and Thomas Buxton. It should be noted that women's antislavery societies also contributed to the cause. In dealing with emancipation, the most important question had become the need to compensate owners financially and provide a transition in which the slaves continued to work for masters for a period of time. Despite the misgivings of the more radical abolitionists, Buxton, seeing no alternative, made concessions on both points. It should also be noted that Wilberforce lived to see the bill passed, but died a few days later.

Problems continued, however, including how discussions concerning sugar tariffs would affect the condition of the newly freed slaves in the West Indies. Another question was where the Society should focus its attention now. Some wanted to pay attention to Africa, while others preferred to concentrate on India, and others were concerned to monitor the situation of the newly freed slaves in the West Indies.

Looking back, however, the achievement of the Society was substantial, especially considering that the emancipation of slaves in the United States took over twenty more years to be carried out. Moreover, the Society has been in the forefront of the fight against slavery to the present day.

Marc L. Schwarz

See also: Atlantic Slave Trade and British; British Slavery, Abolition of.

Further Readings

Fryer, Peter. *Staying Power: The History of Black People in Britain*. London: Pluto Press, 1984.

Oldfield, John. *Popular Politics and British Anti-Slavery*. London: Frank Cass, 1998.

Walvin, James. *England, Slaves and Freedom 1776–1838*. Oxford: University Press of Mississippi, 1987.

Antislavery Songs

The movement to end slavery in the United States produced what may be the country's first "protest" songs. As the antislavery sentiment of the late eighteenth and early nineteenth centuries merged with evangelical Christianity to form abolitionism, the new movement adopted every means at its disposal, including song, to disseminate its message. As a result, hundreds of antislavery songs were written, printed, and performed as part of the effort to eliminate slavery in the United States. In their words and music, these songs reflect both the main arguments of abolitionism and antebellum ideas about music and musicians in American society.

Drawing upon a long religious tradition of using words set to music for the moral edification of singer and listener, abolitionists produced songs from the beginning of the movement, commonly printing them in their newspapers. Nearly every issue of William Lloyd Garrison's *Liberator*, published weekly from 1831 to 1865, features one or more songs in its columns, and reports of meetings frequently indicate singing as an integral part of the activities. As early as 1836, Isaac Knapp of Boston published the first abolitionist songbook, *Songs of the Free, and Hymns of Christian Freedom*, compiled by Maria Weston Chapman, and at least a dozen songbooks would follow in the 1840s and 1850s, some running to hundreds of pages.

The songs contained all the main arguments and motivations of antislavery and abolitionism. Among the earliest songs, for example, are those supporting the movement to colonize former slaves in Liberia. These were rapidly replaced, however, by an outpouring of songs emphasizing three major dimensions of slavery's immorality: it was a sin in a professedly Christian nation; it betrayed the United States' upholding of liberty; and it destroyed families through the traffic in human beings. While a few songs on Liberia appear after 1830, they change from supporting black colonization there to opposing it, reflecting both abolitionists' rejection of this colonization and the increasing presence of free African Americans in the movement. Among the latter, especially important was Joshua Simpson of Ohio, the most prolific songwriter of the movement. Simpson wrote such lyrics as "Old Liberia Is Not the Place for Me" (1852), "Freedom's Call" (1852), and "Away to Canada" (1852) and claimed, in one songster, "This is the only book of Original Poetry and Songs, that was ever published by a Colored Author in the United States" (*The Emancipation Car*, 1854, flyleaf).

Although Simpson is responsible for writing more songs than any other author, the production and public performance of the songs was dominated by white Americans, both male and female. Women, important voices and organizers for abolitionism, also often wrote poetry and songs. The names of Lydia Maria Child and Lydia H. Sigourney are found on song lyrics, along with those identified only as "Mrs. Dr. Bailey," "Mrs. W.D.G.," or "Miss Ball."

The apparent purposes of the songs parallel not only the lyrics but also the occasions for which they were written and on which they were sung. Most commonly, regular meetings of antislavery societies from the local to national levels provided the main venue for singing. These meetings functioned much like church services, and music had an important place in them. Songs opened and closed the proceedings, often intervened throughout them, and reinforced the members' convictions that slavery violated Christian and American principles. Songs were also written for special occasions such as July 4 and August 1, when emancipation in the British West Indies was celebrated. On Independence Day, the contrast between national principles and actual practice was the theme of both meeting and song: in "Hymn" (1838), which includes the stanza, "Yet, though for all the boon was sought/Those rights for which they [patriots] bravely fought/Slavery their pure, their brightening fame/Has clouded with its hateful name." Festivities on August 1 emphasized the model Britain provided: a "Song for the First of August" (1845), indicating that it was "written for and sung at an antislavery picnic at Danvers," includes the lines, "Now let us turn to our own land/That claims to be so free."

Songs were performed by soloists, choirs, and the entire assembly. Occasionally children's choirs were featured, including those of African American children. Professional and semi-professional musicians were involved in the movement, and the most famous was the Hutchinson Family, a quartet of three brothers and a sister. The Hutchinsons modeled themselves on a successful European troupe, the Rainer Family, and toured the country (and later the battlefields), singing concerts in which they included abolitionist and other political songs. Their great exposure brought the songs to audiences not yet converted to abolitionism. The family's most famous song, "Get off the Track!" was written by Jesse Hutchinson

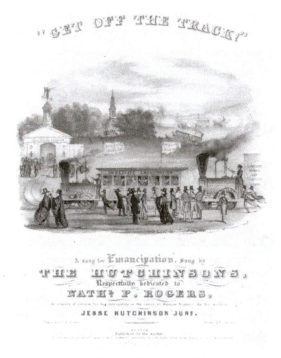

"Get off the track!" An illustrated sheet music cover for an abolitionist song composed by Jesse Hutchinson Jr. (Library of Congress)

in 1844. Set to the minstrel tune of "Old Dan Tucker," it was sung frequently, reproduced widely with varying lyrics, and may have been the most popular of all antislavery songs.

Adapting original lyrics to known tunes was a much more common practice than writing new tunes; thus "songwriters" were primarily authors of lyrics. In this respect, abolitionists were part of a long Western tradition of using popular melodies from the church, the home, or the tavern to serve varying causes. By the 1830s, debates were underway in the United States about what tunes were appropriate for various purposes and audiences (e.g., many objections were raised to hearing "Auld Lang Syne" in church or school). The tunes used most often for antislavery songs are typically eclectic in their sources: "America"; "Scots Wha Hae"; "Auld Lang Syne"; "Missionary Hymn"; and "Old Hundred." The use of minstrel tunes for antislavery songs apparently stirred a minor controversy, with Joshua Simpson defending the practice. In his *Original Anti-Slavery Songs* (1852), he wrote (p. 3), "My object in my selection of tunes, is to kill the degrading influence of those comic Negro Songs, . . . and change the flow of those sweet melodies into more appropriate and useful channels." That this was possible by then had been demonstrated by Francis Scott Key, who had written patriotic words to a drinking song and called it "The Star-Spangled Banner."

Vicki L. Eaklor

See also: Literature and Abolition.

Further Readings

Clark, George W. *The Liberty Minstrel.* 7 eds. New York, 1844–1848.

Eaklor, Vicki L. *American Antislavery Songs: A Collection and Analysis.* Westport, CT: Greenwood Press, 1988.

Hatfield, Edwin F., comp. *Freedom's Lyre: or, Psalms, Hymns, and Sacred Songs, for the Slave and His Friends.* New York, 1840; Miami, 1969.
Lincoln, Jairus, comp. *Anti-Slavery Melodies: for the Friends of Freedom.* Hingham, 1843.
Simpson, J[oshua] McC[arter]. *The Emancipation Car.* Zanesville, 1854; 1874.

Atlantic Slave Trade and British Abolition

The Atlantic slave trade was the forced migration of West African slave-captives from their homelands into slavery in the Americas by European and European American colonizers to labor as plantation, industrial, and domestic slaves. To date, this trade constituted the largest intercontinental migration of peoples in human history, perhaps as many as twenty million people forcibly relocated from the mid-fifteenth century through the latter nineteenth. Millions of Africans were shackled and tightly packed in the bellies of slave ships, in which they endured deplorable conditions as they crossed the Atlantic in what is called "the Middle Passage," a journey sometimes requiring up to three months, depending upon the weather and destination.

Several factors contributed to the development of the trade and to its longevity. One of the first documented events occurred in 1441 when Portuguese sailors kidnapped African slaves off the coast of Mauritania in northwest Africa. Three years later, Portuguese sailors took over 200 African captives back to the slave market in Lisbon, Portugal. By 1450, the Portuguese transported thousands of black slaves to Europe annually.

During this period, the Portuguese used African slave labor in their sugar factories on Atlantic islands off the coast of West Africa and later established plantations for growing cane sugar in their Brazilian colonies in South America. Their knowledge of operating large-scale plantations with enslaved labor expanded in the early seventeenth century when Dutch colonizers in Brazil introduced new technology. This knowledge would next be applied by the Dutch, English, and French in the West Indies, where sugar cultivation would explode in the second half of the seventeenth century. Described by historian Philip Curtin as a "plantation complex," an "economic and political order centering on slave plantations" in the Americas, they were owned and controlled by European and European American colonizers. These plantations supplied the developing Western civilization with key and valuable staples such as sugar, tobacco, cotton, and indigo.

With the addition of English, French, Danish, and Dutch colonizers, the Atlantic slave trade had grown enormously by 1700 and would continue to do so throughout the following century. Designed to enrich the colonizing nation, slavers from

Europe and North America organized and financed slaving voyages, hired captains and crews to man the ships to and from the west coast of Africa, and were responsible for successfully marketing the slaves. On slaving voyages, ships carried trading goods such as rum, European and Indian textiles, tobacco, weapons, and beads to barter for Africans with local brokers, chartered companies, and West Africans who kidnapped slaves far inland. Under these economic and social conditions, Africans became reduced to commodities.

Enslavement commonly resulted from capture during wars, but other factors were important as well. For example, during the eighteenth-century rise of the Asante kingdom, wars erupted against neighboring states and resulted in the capture of many Akan peoples who were then sold into slavery. Political instability could render a nation vulnerable to slavery. The fall of the Oyo kingdom in the nineteenth century forced many Yorubans to flee as refugees, and many of them were captured and sold. Africans were also victimized by organized slave-raiding, whose principal object was captives, not territory or political control. Some slaves were also secured through judicial punishments. In some West African cultural groups, adultery was a crime, and the accused, ostracized from society, could end up at a West African coastal slave market. Environmental factors could also increase the amount of the vulnerable. In times of famine or drought, West Africans fled to other lands and were preyed upon by kidnappers. Some nations like the Benin in the sixteenth century resisted involvement in the Atlantic slave trade. But by the seventeenth century, Benin would succumb, as would the vast majority of the nations and ethnic groups along the West African coast from the Niger River delta to the Senegambian region. The force of profits and military pressures by the seventeenth and eighteenth centuries made involvement almost inevitable.

Yet, on the other hand, other forces, especially by the eighteenth century, began to undermine this nefarious traffic and to disseminate an ideology morally and politically opposed to the trade and to slavery itself. West Africans themselves had long resisted enslavement at the time of capture and as they were being transported to the coast. There were also numerous incidences of organized rebellions on slave ships. The fact of this resistance had always made the traffic a potentially perilous venture for the sailors and captains involved in it.

But a combination of legal, social, and political activism in the Atlantic world after 1750 would be critical in eroding the scale of and sanction for the Atlantic slave trade. In 1772, British abolitionist Granville Sharp challenged the institution of slavery in English courts to argue against the kidnapping of slaves or former slaves in England. Sharp was influenced by Anthony Benezet's powerful, *A Short Account of That Part of Africa, Inhabited by the Negroes* (1762), which vividly illustrated the devastating effects of the slave trade upon West African peoples and their societies. Sharp corresponded with Benezet and reprinted *A Short Account of That Part of Africa* for distribution in England.

Based on his reading of Benezet's work, his legal studies, as well as his investigations of slave trading in England, Sharp came to oppose the trading and ownership of slaves. He published, in 1769, *A Representation of the Injustice and Dangerous Tendency of Tolerating Slavery*. In this publication, Sharp challenged a master's property rights in a slave. He argued these so-called property rights were actually antithetical to the natural rights of all human beings, and he advocated the use of a writ of habeas corpus to contest the recapture and reselling of a slave.

In 1771, Sharp encountered James Somerset, a runaway slave who resided in England as a personal servant to his master. Somerset had escaped, yet was recaptured by his master, who resold Somerset for slavery in Jamaica. Sharp interceded by using a writ of habeas corpus to prevent the export of Somerset. In Somerset's defense, his barristers denied the legality of slavery on English soil, even though the institution was allowed in the British colonies. Lord Chief Justice Mansfield's ruling on Somerset's status took the rights issue further by asserting that no law existed enabling a master's rights over a slave in England: "The state of slavery is of such a nature, that it is incapable of being introduced on any reasons, moral or political, but only by positive law." Since no such "positive law" existed, James Somerset was on "free soil" and was no longer a slave. Winning Somerset's freedom in 1772 would begin to stimulate the cause for abolition in England.

In 1787, Sharp joined forces with others opposed to the Atlantic slave trade, including numerous Quakers, Thomas Clarkson, William Wilberforce, James Ramsey, and others to form the Society for the Abolition of the Slave Trade. These men would prove integral to orchestrating the political machinery leading to Great Britain's abolition of its participation in the Atlantic slave trade in 1808, a momentous event given the dominant position Britain had occupied throughout the eighteenth century in the traffic. By the late 1780s, Clarkson had undertaken investigations of the conditions of slave ships departing slaving ports in England. In 1788, he produced a schematic drawing of *The Brookes*, a British slave ship, which illustrated the inhumane conditions under which Africans were shipped. This dominant image became a public testament to the horrendous conditions under which Africans suffered and was used with enormous effect to mobilize the British public against the trade. With the assistance of Quakers and dissenting congregations, Clarkson and the Society forged local oppositional committees that spearheaded a massive petition writing campaign to Parliament, resulting in over 400,000 signatories by 1792. Quakers and allies on a much smaller scale were also conducting similar petition campaigns in the United States at the same time. By 1792, inspired by the recent example of Denmark, which had enacted a measure to end their involvement with the slave trade gradually over the next ten years, the leader of the abolition cause in Parliament, William Wilberforce, had finally written a measure for the ending of Britain's own involvement and put it before the body. After much emotional debate, abolition passed the House of Commons, but was eventually blocked by the House of Lords, where the interests of West Indian planters brought great influence to bear. While further efforts to pass the legislation were pursued through 1795, dedication to it waned as the mounting crisis with France preoccupied the nation and diminished interest in promulgating any extensive reform measures.

Enthusiasm for abolition revived in the early years of the new century. While the Treaty of Amiens of 1802 appeared to leave Britain weakened and France resurgent in its West Indian colonies, Napoleon's reinstatement of colonial slavery and massive assault on Saint Domingue failed miserably, and France largely abandoned the islands for a renewed focus on continental conquests. In 1805, Britain's dramatic naval victory over the combined French and Spanish fleets at Trafalgar left it supreme in the Atlantic and in the seas beyond. If abolition were to be adopted now, Britain was capable of preventing any other nation from filling the void it would create if it suddenly withdrew from the trade. Abolitionists like Clarkson and Wilberforce, who ultimately sought an end to slavery itself, argued that once planters realized they could no longer rely on imported Africans to replenish their labor supply, they would improve the material and social conditions of the enslaved to increase their longevity and their notoriously low capacity for natural increase. Moreover, public weariness over the long war with France was eroding national morale at a time when a Britain isolated from the continent required a vigorous patriotism. Forging a great humanitarian crusade based on ending the inhumanities of the slave trade would hopefully reinvigorate the nation's flagging spirits by endowing the struggle with a great philanthropic and Christian mission. However, slavery itself in the British West Indies would remain untouched. When a bill for abolition was presented to Parliament again in 1807, it passed readily and was reinforced by a similar action in the U.S. Congress. On January 1, 1808, both nations ceased their involvement in the Atlantic slave trade.

Britain now almost immediately set about disabling the broader Atlantic slave trade. It began posting boats off the West African coast by key ports and passages used by slavers. In treaties concluded with Spain and Brazil prior to 1815, firm provisions against their participating in the slave trade were entered. Of course, Spanish Cuba and Brazil would violate these terms routinely, well into the second half of the nineteenth century. At the Congress of Vienna in 1815, which concluded the war with France, adjusted agreements with Spain and Brazil were struck which allowed them a few years to replenish their labor force with imported Africans and the French five years to do so, much to the dismay of abolitionists in England. Over the many following years, Britain would place commissioners in Cuba and elsewhere to attempt to enforce compliance with the treaties. By 1833, it had established a much larger fleet of vessels, called the Africa Squadron, to counteract the wide-scale slave trading that continued from West Africa into the 1850s. To this force, the United States added a few lackluster ships. Finally, British pressures and the decline of slavery in Cuba and Brazil after 1870 combined to bring the Atlantic slave trade to an end. Yet, as Britain and other European powers colonized Africa and Asia in the late nineteenth century, they justified their infringement in part on the basis of ending the slave trade in these various regions. Britain was as often as imperfectly successful in these locales as they were in the Atlantic as their professed humanitarian ideals were tempered by their colonialist need to reckon with regional customs and secure the cooperation of local potentates.

Gloria-Yvonne

See also: British Slavery, Abolition of.

Further Readings

Anstey, Roger. *The Atlantic Slave Trade and British Abolition*. New York: Macmillan, 1975.

Bailey, Anne C. *African Voices of the Atlantic Slave Trade: Beyond the Silence and the Shame*. Boston: Beacon Press, 2005.

Blackburn, Robin, *The Overthrow of Colonial Slavery, 1775–1848*. London: Verso, 1988.

Davis, David Brion. *The Problem of Slavery in the Age of Revolution, 1770–1823*. 2nd ed. Oxford: Oxford University Press, 1999.

Klein, Herbert S. *The Atlantic Slave Trade*. New Approaches to the America Series. Cambridge: Cambridge University Press, 1999.

Northrup, David, ed. *The Atlantic Slave Trade*. Problems in World History Series. 2nd ed. Boston: Houghton Mifflin, 2005.

Oldfield, J. R. *Popular Politics and British Anti-Slavery: The Mobilisation of Public Opinion Against the Slave Trade, 1787–1807*. London: Frank Cass, 1995.

Thomas, Hugh. *The Slave Trade: The Story of the Atlantic Slave Trade, 1440–1870*. New York: Simon and Schuster, 1999.

B

Bailey, Gamaliel

Gamaliel Bailey was a well-known journalist and newspaper editor during the first half of the nineteenth century. He was most famous for editing the *National Era* and became involved in the antislavery crusade in the 1830s. Bailey accomplished what no other antebellum individual achieved—he successfully established an antislavery press in the South.

To understand Bailey and other political economists, one has to make a crucial distinction between an advocate of antislavery and an abolitionist. An abolitionist was by definition antislavery, but the inverse commonly was not true for the antislavery advocate. For example, abolitionists called for the immediate, unconditional, and uncompensated emancipation of all slaves who would receive complete constitutional equality. They were morally driven; they viewed slavery as an abomination to all religious and right-thinking people, as a sin against God, and, in fact, as the most egregious sin of American society. Proponents of this position included William Lloyd Garrison, Gerrit Smith, and John Brown.

Advocates of antislavery, on the other hand, did not usually favor immediate abolition, but rather some scheme of gradual, compensated emancipation—gradual sometimes defined as into the 1900s. It was almost always coupled with some plan for African colonization. They also opposed the extension of slavery into the western territories. They were willing to constitutionally guarantee federal protection of that institution in the slave states, something a radical abolitionist would never do. They would form the core of the Free Soil Party of the late 1840s and eventually of the Republicans, who were motivated largely to protect the white laboring classes and maintain open land for them in the western territories. Many antislavery advocates detested black people and radical abolitionists, a number of whom were African Americans. They proudly proclaimed themselves supporters of a party for white men. For these late antebellum proponents of antislavery, free soil meant soil free of the blacks, whom they attacked as physically, mentally, and temperamentally inferior to whites and incapable of mixing with whites as equals. Their numbers included Frank Blair, B. Gratz Brown, and Gamaliel Bailey.

Born in Mount Holley, New Jersey, in 1807, Gamaliel Bailey early demonstrated his ability as a writer. He began by writing articles and editing various religious newspapers and by 1835 became involved in the antislavery crusade. He was one of the era's most interesting characters. Hardly an abolitionist, he at times nevertheless associated with them. However, he rarely endorsed their positions in his paper, the *National Era,* which he founded in Washington, D.C., in 1847. The reason was clear: Washington was a proslavery Southern city, a hostile environment in which to begin publication of an antislavery paper. Yet both antislavery advocates and abolitionists contributed some $63,000 to launch the paper, much of it from Arthur and Lewis Tappan.

Bailey was a conservative on the slavery issue. This orientation helped him to keep the *Era* afloat economically for he offended far fewer people. The *National Era* became a success, reaching a wider audience than any other antislavery or abolitionist newspaper. When the paper began, it had some 4,000 subscribers. By 1850 it had 25,000. Bailey hoped that the paper would spur a broad antislavery consensus that might even include Southerners. As a political organizer, he helped to found the Ohio Liberty Party, lobbied for early Free Soilers and later for Republicans in the nation's capital. While eventually his paper found little support in the South, it did have an extensive following in the Northwest, an area where the Republican Party quickly grew.

Bailey also stimulated a broader following by including writings on more than just antislavery topics. He hired top literary writers—who were also antislavery— including Lydia Maria Child and the eminent poet and literary editor, John Greenleaf Whittier. He had fiction and poetry, business and financial news; the *National Era* was not simply a "one idea" press.

Bailey vigorously attacked the Slave Power while simultaneously reaching out to the white working classes of the North and South. Slaveholders upheld an inefficient and oppressive system of labor that interfered with the advance of the nation's white working classes. And, by the 1850s, the slaveholders had so come to dominate the federal government that it served their interests alone. Bailey was an Anglo-Saxon supremacist; he believed the Anglo-Saxons were the "great civilizers" of the world. If anything, Bailey argued that American slaves, by being in contact with ethnic Saxons, were thereby at least being educated and uplifted under slavery. American slaves were better off than their African brothers, who still lived in barbarism. Therefore, until some scheme of gradual, compensated emancipation coupled with colonization could be settled upon by the North and South, blacks should remain in the South and continue under white tutelage. Bailey specifically called for black colonization to Haiti and endorsed Abraham

Lincoln's plan for an experimental settlement of black Americans on Île à Vache. Meanwhile, Bailey called for expanded European immigration to replace the colonized blacks.

James D. Bilotta

See also: Liberty Party.

Further Readings

Bilotta, James D. *Race and the Rise of the Republican Party, 1848–1865.* 3rd ed. Philadelphia: Xlibris, 2005.

Harrold, Stanley. *Gamaliel Bailey and Antislavery Union.* Kent, OH: Kent State University Press, 1986.

Benezet, Anthony

Anthony Benezet was born in St. Quentin, Picardy, France, on January 31, 1713. His father and mother were both Huguenots. Under the regime of Henry IV, the persecuted Protestant Huguenots experienced a period of semireligious freedom, which lasted from the promulgation of the Edict of Nantes in 1598, until its revocation in 1685. His family fled from France to Holland in 1715, then to England, and finally to Philadelphia in 1731. In 1735, he was naturalized as a British citizen, and on May 13, 1736, he married Joyce Marriot who was from a Quaker family.

In Philadelphia, Benezet became a schoolteacher and took charge of the William Penn School in 1742. After working for some years educating Quaker girls, he began to teach young black children, primarily in his home, in 1750. A few years later, he founded the *African School for Blacks* or the *Free African School.* His students would include Absalom Jones, the first minister of African descent in the Protestant Episcopal Church, and James Forten, the sail maker and entrepreneur.

Benezet fought actively to end slavery, but, unlike most whites, he also proclaimed the complete equality of enslaved Africans to whites. Building upon Quaker principles, Benezet wrote *A Short Account of the People Called Quakers* (1780), in which he advocated the equality of all before God and the particular full inclusion of blacks in civil society, nonviolence, and the avoidance of greed and sloth by Quakers.

His most important works, however, reckoned with Africa and the Atlantic slave trade. *A Short Account of That Part of Africa Inhabited by the Negroes, and the Manner by Which the Slave-Trade Is Carried On* was published in 1762 and *Some Historical Account of Guinea* in 1771. His study of Africa had a profound effect on the African-born abolitionists Ottabah Cugoano and Olaudah Equiano who were both kidnapped as children from Africa. Thomas Clarkson, the British abolitionist, also relied heavily on using Benezet's *Some Historical Account of Guinea* in preparing his own work on the Atlantic slave trade, *An Essay on the Slavery and Commerce of the Human Species, Particularly the African* (1786). In *Some Historical Account of Guinea,* Benezet had analyzed early travelers' accounts of Africa including those of Michel Adanson, Jacques Barbot, Williams Smith, and Willem Bosman to refute the proslavery descriptions of a benighted and barbaric Africa. He argued that, prior to the slave trade, Africans lived in relative freedom, with an abundance of the necessities of life. He argued that the trade morally corrupted Europeans and some Africans, who became their accomplices in the buying and selling of their fellow Africans.

Benezet had been deeply influenced by Montesquieu's argument in *The Spirit of Laws* that slavery had a destructive effect on both the state and "free men." He was equally persuaded by the Scottish moral philosopher George Wallace, who wrote in his *System of the Principles of the Law of Scotland* (1760) that men in their liberty are not *"in comercia*, they are not either saleable or purchasable," and his colleague, Frances Hutcheson, who asserted in *A System of Moral Philosophy* that "no endowments natural or acquired, can give a perfect right to assume power over others, without their consent."

Together with John Woolman, Benezet wrote *Epistles of Caution and Advice, Concerning the Buying and Keeping of Slaves,* in 1754. That same year, he edited Woolman's *Some Considerations on the Keeping of Negroes.* He also worked closely with Dr. Benjamin Rush, who later wrote anonymous tracts condemning slavery. He corresponded with Benjamin Franklin, who credited the antislavery petition and pamphlets of Benezet with the decision of the Virginia House of Burgesses to petition the king for an end to the slave trade in 1772. Benezet wrote many hundreds of letters, corresponding with religious leaders such as George Whitefield, John Wesley, and Moses Brown and secular leaders such as Benjamin Franklin and Benjamin Rush about his views on slavery and the slave trade. Upon receiving one of his pamphlets, Patrick Henry wrote on January 18, 1773, "I take this Opportunity to acknowledge ye receipt of Anthony Benezet's book against the slave trade. I thank ye for it. Would anyone believe that I am a Master of Slaves of my own purchase? I am drawn along by ye general Inconvenience of living without them; I will not, I cannot justify it." John Wesley's *Thoughts upon Slavery* (1774) was based almost entirely on Benezet's *Some Historical Account of Guinea.*

The correspondence between Benezet and the pioneer British abolitionist Granville Sharp proved one of the first links to the transnational fight against slavery and the slave trade. Copies of Benezet's pamphlets were delivered to Lord Chief Justice Mansfield and his fellow jurists in 1771 when Benezet and Sharp collaborated on the famous *Somerset* Decision. Justice Mansfield decided that James Somerset, a black who had been brought to England, could not be forcibly removed from the country by his master and was declared free. On May 14, 1772, Benezet wrote Sharp that "six hundred Copies had been delivered" of his pamphlet *A Caution and a Warning to Great Britain and Her Colonies* (1767) "to so many Members of both Houses of Parliament." Sharpe and Benezet developed new methods of collecting thousands of signatures on antislavery petitions and delivering them to their respective assemblies. His descriptions of Africa proved to be so central that William Wilberforce quoted Benezet at length in the great 1792 parliamentary debates about the abolition of the slave trade. Benezet also influenced the founders of the *Société des Amis des Noirs* in Paris.

Immediately after the American Revolution, Benezet was very involved in assisting Philadelphia's black community. When kidnapped blacks were transported through Philadelphia on their way south, Benezet intervened to obtain their freedom. He became the first president of the Society for the Relief of Free Negroes Unlawfully Held in Bondage on April 14, 1775. In 1784, a few months before Benezet's death, this organization was reformed as the Pennsylvania Abolition Society. After he died on May 13, 1784, over 400 local blacks marched in his funeral procession.

Maurice Jackson

See also: Quakers and Antislavery.

Further Readings

Armistead, Wilson. *Anthony Benezet.* London: A. W. Bennett, 1859.

Brookes, George S. *Friend Anthony Benezet.* London: Oxford University Press, 1937.

Bruns, Roger. "Anthony Benezet's Assertion of Negro Equality." *Journal of Negro History* 56, 3 (1971): 230–238.

Jackson, Maurice. "Anthony Benezet: America's Finest Eighteenth Century Antislavery Advocate." In Nancy L. Rhoden and Ian K. Steele, eds. *The Human Tradition in the American Revolution.* Wilmington, DE: Scholarly Resources, Inc., 2000, pp. 1–17.

Jackson, Maurice. "The Social and Intellectual Origins of Anthony Benezet's Antislavery Radicalism." *Pennsylvania History* 6 (1999): 86–112.

Straub, Jean S. "Anthony Benezet: Teacher and Abolitionist of the Eighteenth Century." *Quaker History* 57, 1 (Spring 1968): 3–16.

Vaux, Roberts. *Memoirs of the Life of Anthony Benezet.* New York: Burt Franklin, 1969. Reprint of 1817 ed.

Woodson, Carter G. "Anthony Benezet." *Journal of Negro History* 2 (1917): 37–50.

Birney, James Gillespie (1792–1857)

James Gillespie Birney was an abolitionist and Liberty Party candidate for the U.S. presidential elections of 1840 and 1844. Birney was born in Danville, Kentucky, on February 4, 1792, into a wealthy, slave-owning family. Despite being born into the culture of the Southern planter class, James Birney was exposed at an early age to opinions supporting antislavery. His father, James Birney, spoke out against the institution of human servitude to his young son, as well as did the aunt who helped to raise him. The younger Birney attended Transylvania University, then the College of New Jersey (later Princeton), and later studied law in Philadelphia, Pennsylvania. While in Philadelphia, Birney became further exposed to antislavery debates and became friends with a free black leader, James Forten, and an antislavery Quaker, Abraham L. Pennock.

After his training in the law, Birney returned to his native state, married Agatha McDowell, and served briefly in the Kentucky legislature in 1816.

Similar to others of his class, he migrated from his native state to the Deep South onto land being opened up for white families after the containment of Native American tribes. By 1817, Birney and his family had relocated to the Alabama Territory, and several years later, he was serving in the Alabama legislature. His early exposure to antislavery debates led to his introduction of legislation to allow for compensated emancipation. In addition, he helped create the University of Alabama in 1820.

Around this time, Birney was converted to the Presbyterian faith during a wave of evangelical revivals in the Southern communities. His conversion produced a stronger concern for humanitarian causes. His early exposure to antislavery debates and treatment of Native American populations in Alabama led to greater involvement into efforts to improve the conditions of both groups. In addition, his political views influenced by his religious conversion began to pull him away from the Democratic Party due in part to his opposition to policies and supporters of Andrew Jackson.

Birney became involved in the American Colonization Society, and later served as that organization's agent from 1832 to 1833. He moved his family back to Kentucky and began to devote more time in the antislavery movement. Birney rejected the colonization movement as ineffective and racist and freed his own slaves in 1834. He then became involved in the work of the American Anti-Slavery Society. Birney attempted to start an antislavery newspaper in Kentucky, but was forced by threats and mob violence to move his publication, the *Philanthropist*, to Cincinnati, Ohio, in 1836.

The following year, Birney moved to New York City and became secretary of the American Anti-Slavery Society. In an 1840 schism of that body, he became head of the anti-Garrison faction that advocated the need for a third party to find a political solution to end slavery. Birney became the presidential candidate of that new Liberty Party for the 1840 and 1844 U.S. presidential elections. In the 1844 election, Birney's candidacy materially affected the vote count for Whig Party candidate, Henry Clay, in the state of New York.

A severe fall from a horse in 1845 left Birney partially paralyzed and forced him to retire from politics. He moved to Michigan and engaged in land development there while vainly attempting to recover his health. In the 1850s, Birney offended some long-time antislavery associates by advocating compensated emancipation. In his final years, Birney and his second wife, Elizabeth Fitzhugh, moved to Raritan Bay Union in New Jersey and lived there until his death on November 18, 1857. Two of his sons, David Bell Birney and William Birney, later served as generals in the Union Army during the American Civil War.

William H. Brown

See also: Whig Party and Antislavery.

Further Readings

Birney, William. *James G. Birney and His Times: The Genesis of the Republican Party with Some Account of Abolition Movement in the South before 1828*. New York: Appleton, 1890.

Dumond, Dwight, ed. *Letters of James Gillespie Birney, 1831–1857*. 2 vols. New York: Appleton-Century, c.1938.

Fladeland, Betty. *James Gillespie Birney: Slaveholder to Abolitionist*. Ithaca, NY: Cornell University Press, 1955.

Bleeding Kansas

"Bleeding Kansas" was the name attached to the violence that gripped Kansas from 1855 to 1857. During those years, settlers from the North and South poured into Kansas Territory, hoping to gain control of the territorial legislature and thus the territory itself. The provisions of the Kansas-Nebraska Act of 1854, which applied the principle of popular sovereignty to the two territories, allowed the territorial legislature to determine the fate of the territory with regards to the issue of slavery. Instead, Kansas turned bloody over the issue of slavery as political institutions and practices broke down. The territory in fact mirrored what was occurring in the nation's capital with the two-party system. In many ways, the violence in Kansas presaged the civil war that was to grip the United States from 1861 to 1865.

The root of Kansas's troubles lay in the Kansas-Nebraska Act of 1854. Many Americans felt the lure of Manifest Destiny and headed west, especially to the

Pacific coast. Better transportation was sorely needed to link the new state of California with the eastern half of the nation. The most effective remedy would be a transcontinental railroad linking east and west. What route this railroad would take proved to be the stumbling block. Southerners wanted a line from New Orleans to southern California. Some Northerners sought routes that ran from Chicago out to San Francisco. Senator Stephen Douglas of Illinois was among this latter group. Douglas wanted to see Chicago prosper as the eastern hub of a transcontinental railroad. His interests were not only for the welfare of Illinois, but also for himself. Douglas owned real estate in Chicago and stood to make money if a transcontinental railroad was headquartered in that city. In order to build this railroad, though, the unorganized territory west of Iowa and Missouri had to be organized. Railroad promoters were not alone in this desire. Residents of Iowa and Missouri also wanted the land to be organized into territories so that further westward growth, which would be beneficial to their own economic futures, would be able to occur.

To gain approval for what became the Kansas-Nebraska bill, Douglas needed Southern support. There would be little interest among Southerners for a railroad that did not benefit their section; therefore, Douglas knew he needed something to attract the attention of Southerners. That something was the promise to secure the repeal of the Missouri Compromise restriction from 1820, which stated that there would be no slavery north of 36° 30', with the exception of Missouri. To replace the federal restriction in the 1820 compromise, the Kansas-Nebraska bill proposed the rule of popular sovereignty, which allowed the settlers themselves in each territory to determine whether or not slavery would exist there. This nebulous concept was the brainchild of Lewis Cass, the unsuccessful Democratic candidate for president in 1848. Cass was never definitive as to when settlers could decide the fate of slavery. He told Northerners that the settlers could decide during the territorial phase, while he told Southerners that the decision could be made only when the territory applied for statehood. This ambiguity with regard to the timing of the decision remained in 1854. Nevertheless, Douglas succeeded in attracting Southern support, and after a prolonged legislative battle, Congress passed the bill and President Franklin Pierce signed it on May 30, 1854.

After the passage of the act, migrants from Missouri began to enter Kansas Territory. As Nicole Etcheson argues, many Missourians viewed a slaveholding Kansas as vital to the future economic well-being of Missouri. Other Southerners, many of them non-slaveholders, also entered Kansas. Later in 1854, small farm families from Illinois and Indiana began to move to Kansas. Emigration from the New England states also began, aided by the efforts of the New England Emigrant Aid Company (NEEAC), which helped settlers obtain cheaper travel to Kansas because the NEEAC purchased steamship tickets in bulk quantities.

Early settlement went smoothly, but trouble began when it came time to elect a territorial delegate to Congress and a territorial legislature. In each case, the first in the autumn of 1854 and the latter in March 1855, Missouri "border ruffians" crossed into Kansas, intimidated election judges and voters with the threat of violence, and then voted in large numbers for the proslavery ticket. Missourians argued that they were residents while they were on Kansas soil, and thus had a right to vote. Through their efforts, proslavery forces voted a proslavery delegate to Congress, elected a proslavery territorial legislature, passed laws condemning abolitionism and restricting the right of free speech, and had Governor A. H. Reeder removed from office.

Free Soil settlers protested the unfair elections by withdrawing from the territorial legislature and creating their own territorial legislature. They knew that such a move would be viewed as treason, but they likened themselves to the American colonists, who when confronted with British oppression decided to revolt rather than be political slaves. In a series of meetings in Lawrence, Big Springs, and Topeka, the free state settlers drafted a constitution and formed a legislature. They elected Reeder as their delegate to Congress. Their actions angered the proslavery faction and led to calls to bring the free state faction to heel.

During the administration of Governor Wilson Shannon, open warfare between the two sides began. In the Wakarusa War, a proslavery force laid siege to Lawrence, but eventually withdrew. It was during this early phase of the conflict that several killings occurred that angered both sides. Tensions rose when a federal marshal and a force of about 500 Missourians destroyed much of the Free-Soil town of Lawrence in an episode known as the "sack of Lawrence" in May 1856. In retaliation for this attack, John Brown and several of his sons murdered five male settlers living in the proslavery town of Pottawatomie Creek. Brown's actions stunned both sides. Brown fled from justice but the killing continued. It would not be until the administration of Governor Robert Walker that the fighting subsided. Walker effectively used the U.S. Army to keep an unsteady peace between both sides. Peace would not come to Kansas until guerilla fighting ended at the close of the Civil War.

James C. Foley

See also: Compromise of 1850; Democratic Party and Antislavery.

Further Readings

Etcheson, Nicole. *Bleeding Kansas: Contested Liberty in the Civil War Era*. Lawrence: University Press of Kansas, 2004.

Fehrenbacher, Don E. *The Slaveholding Republic: An Account of the United States Government's Relations to Slavery*. Completed and edited by Ward M. McAfee. New York: Oxford University Press, 2001.

Potter, David M. *The Impending Crisis, 1848–1861*. Completed and edited by Don E. Fehrenbacher. New York: Harper & Row, 1976.

Rawley, James A. *Race and Politics: "Bleeding Kansas" and the Coming of the Civil War*. New York: J. B. Lippincott Company, 1969.

British Slavery, Abolition of

British abolitionists had hoped that the abolition of the slave trade, which they secured in 1807, would force West Indian planters to treat their slaves better. In its turn, this would encourage the slave population to increase naturally. There would follow, in some unspecified way, the natural decay of slavery itself. First of all, however, it was agreed that a system was needed to monitor the results of abolition, because no one really knew what the end of the slave trade would bring.

Josiah Wedgwood, an English abolitionist, created the most famous antislavery image of the eighteenth century. Wedgwood produced this medallion for the English Society for Effecting the Abolition of the Slave Trade, which was also formed in 1787. The Society distributed thousands of these medallions, which were reproduced in antislavery publications and even worn as bracelets and hairpins. The image quickly became well known as a symbol for the abolitionist movement in both England and the United States. (Library of Congress)

Before the Napoleonic wars, the Atlantic slave trade had been a relatively unquestioned feature of European maritime trade and prosperity. As the wars with France finally drew to a close in 1814–1815, Europe tried to put itself back together after a generation of warfare. The British, the senior partner among the victors, had renounced their slave trade and were anxious to prevent European diplomats, gathering at the various postwar Congresses, from allowing the defeated French to revive their own slave trade. Thomas Clarkson, the leading abolitionist in the drive to abolition in 1807, lobbied European statesmen at the peace negotiations for an international abolition of the slave trade. He was strengthened by public backing. Faced by the prospects of a renewal of French slave trading, the British abolition movement was revived in 1814–1815; something like one-and-a-half million people (from a population of twelve million) signed the new abolition petitions circulated in Great Britain. Talleyrand, the chief French negotiator at the Congress of Vienna, thought that British abolition had become "a passion carried to fanaticism, and one which the Ministry is no longer at liberty to check." However, the subsequent efforts of British and American abolitionists had to be set against the fact that a further million-and-a-half Africans were carried into the Americas and enslaved between 1807 and 1866.

News from the West Indies in the years after abolition was not encouraging for abolitionists. Slave unrest simmered away, and planters showed no signs of moderating their severity toward slaves. Nonconformist missionaries (mainly Baptists and Methodists) were converting ever more slaves, despite the planters' strenuous efforts to obstruct their work. And as Christianity became a dominant force in the slave quarters, slaves seemed to be ever more resistant to their bondage. Between 1815 and 1832, three major slave uprisings, each one more violent than the last, each one repressed with a violence that appalled British onlookers, seemed to confirm that West Indian slavery was a system that could be kept in place only by violence on a ghastly scale. Through all this, the West India lobby and its friends in London put up a rearguard action. To ever more Britons, they seemed to be defending the indefensible.

What also worried British abolitionists was the growing realization that cutting off the supply of imported Africans would not, in itself, bring slavery in the Americas to an end. This was particularly clear when abolitionists looked at the United States. Although North America had been in the vanguard of abolition in the era of the Revolution and had ended its own slave trade in 1808, there was little sign that slavery within the nation was in decline. Indeed, the rapid expansion of cotton cultivation in the South had brought a positive revival of North American slavery, with great material benefits for the United States in general. Cutting off supplies of Africans had clearly not brought slavery to an end in America.

But the British preoccupation was with the Caribbean. There was a growing body of information available in Britain about the slaves. First of all, large numbers of people in Britain (sailors, traders, settlers, and military) had detailed knowledge of the islands. In addition, the missionaries working in the islands sent regular reports back to Britain about slave life. Their words were edited and circulated by their sponsoring churches. The government also began its own information-gathering about slave society, beginning in recently acquired Trinidad in 1812. This "registration" of the slave population was a census and was the only accurate means of assessing the impact of the abolition of the slave trade. There followed a bitter parliamentary struggle about extending registration to all West Indian slaves, with planters and their backers inevitably resisting the idea of any form of interference between them and their slaves. Eventually, however, in 1819 an act was passed authorizing the registration of all slaves from 1820 onward. Though the data accumulated slowly, after 1820 indisputable demographic evidence came to hand about the exact consequences of ending the slave trade.

This raw demographic data provided abolitionists with material to promote slave emancipation. But in the process, a marked change came over the campaign for black freedom. Like the initial evidence about the slave trade in the 1780s and 1790s, the slave registration returns shifted the arguments about slavery from the impressionistic and hearsay, to the specific and the indisputable. Whatever flaws existed about that data, they were unimportant set against the powerful evidence now made available to the abolitionist camp.

Not surprisingly, planters were bitterly opposed to slave registration. They hated the abolitionist movement and resisted all attempts to make them answerable for their management of plantations and slaves. Perhaps above all, planters continued to be troubled about slave unrest. After all, Haiti had become an independent black nation as recently as 1804, and the specter of the Haitian Revolution continued to trouble planters throughout the Americas. Planters accused abolitionists and their friends of encouraging slave unrest and of elevating slave expectations. Then, in 1816, Bussa's rebellion erupted in Barbados.

Violent resistance was part of the story of African slavery in the Americas, although less strikingly so in North America. In the British Caribbean and Brazil, slave revolts had been common, and planters and colonial authorities lived in fear of them, never fully trusting the slaves who greatly outnumbered them. Despite that, Barbados seemed an unlikely place for a slave revolt. Its slave population was overwhelmingly local-born, and imported Africans no longer played a major economic or social role, as they did in so many of the other islands. Local planters, however, made a rod for their own back. They denounced slave registration, and their indiscreet table talk helped to persuade slaves that planters were denying them the freedom already granted by London. Bussa's rebellion of 1816, like most before it, was crushed—120 slaves killed, 144 executed, 132 deported. Barbadian planters had no doubt that simmering slave unrest had been fanned by the debate about emancipation.

Planters everywhere were beset by worries. Above all, they feared the slaves, with their simple but persistent demand for freedom; second, they feared British abolitionists' demanding positive action and change in the slaves' condition; third, they feared the missionaries who seduced armies of slaves to their church or chapel. Last, and not least, planters faced a British government that seemed ever eager to criticize planters on behalf of the slaves.

Slaves everywhere had traditionally resisted their bondage—in Africa, on the slave ships, and on the plantations—though their resistance was not always violent or threatening. Foot dragging, feigning ignorance, misunderstanding orders, escaping all formed the background to slavery in the Americas. But violence was always close to the surface.

Violence was visible in the raw, vicious realities of slave life. And it was a growing awareness of this endemic violence that helped to swing British opinion against slavery. The abolitionist campaign made effective use of slave sufferings to create a public mood that was resolutely opposed first to the slave trade, and later to slavery itself. The inhuman realities of slavery had become obvious to the British reading public even before the abolitionist campaign was launched in 1787. Slave cases in English courts, notably the *Somerset* Decision of 1772, the words of a small number of black writers and activists living in London in the 1770s and 1780s, and some powerful visual images helped expose the realities of Atlantic slavery. Black writers, for all their differences, returned, in their own distinctive way, to common themes: to the inhumanity of slavery, to the ungodly acts of Christian Britons, and to what independent black people (i.e., the authors) might achieve when free. These were essentially the same issues promoted by the abolitionist movement in order to establish the simple point that blacks were indeed men and women, brothers and sisters.

The full horror of what was being revealed about the slave trade sometimes overwhelmed even the staunchest of abolitionists, never more graphically than in the Zong massacre of 1781. Yet no one was brought to account for the mass murder of over 130 slaves. For all its unique horror, the Zong case was in keeping with the fate of slave rebels on other ships and plantations. Slave outbursts and violence were greeted by draconian white brutality, doled out by sailors, soldiers, planters, and colonial officials. From first to last, violence was the essential lubricant of the slave system, and slaves inevitably responded violently, though it merely provoked further white brutality against them and a tightening of the local slave laws. The permanent fear of slave violence hardened the heart of the whites against slaves in general. Planters believed that slaves were not to be trusted and that it was madness to tamper with the slave system. They also felt that the Haitian revolution proved them right.

Between 1787 and 1838, the details of slave life in the Caribbean were, then, basic to the ebb and flow of British abolitionist debate. With the coming of peace in 1815, there was a greatly heightened concern about slaves and slavery, partly because of slave revolts, beginning with Bussa's rebellion in 1816. For their part, the planters felt that slavery was being undermined from a number of different directions. Slaves' own resistance gnawed away at slavery, while missionaries, often unconsciously, were also digging away at slavery's foundations. In addition, the debates about the slave trade made headlines wherever European diplomats gathered after the war. Taken together, this all gave slavery an unprecedented political importance. Moreover, the slaves themselves were acutely aware of the debate in Britain.

Whites in the islands discussed, argued, and gossiped about the way slavery was being handled in London. Slaves heard the news (often garbled) from London via their masters' careless table talk. Speculation about the emancipation debate quickly passed from the Great House to the slave cabins. The enslaved Atlantic had traditionally been linked by information networks, with hard news and gossip filtering from one corner of that system to another by way not only of sailors and slaves, but also by merchants and planters. The upshot, after 1815, was that slaves knew they had friends in Britain. They also knew that the planters and their friends did not approve of what was unfolding in Britain.

At the same time, the work of missionaries was also unsettling slavery. Missionary work was guided by strict rules from their home churches in Britain. Preachers were ordered not to upset the delicate social balance in the slave colonies, but their very presence among the slaves was deeply unsettling. So, too, was their Christian message, however much it might be couched in theological terms. The established Anglican Church had never really worked with the slaves, but those failings were made good, from the 1780s, by a string of nonconformist missionaries who targeted the slave communities. Baptists and Methodists, following where German Moravians had begun in the midcentury, set sail for the islands, but with advice such as the following ringing in their ears: "Remember that the object is not to teach the principles and the laws of an earthly kingdom . . . but the principles and laws of the Kingdom of Christ."

Such a distinction looked easier in Britain than it did in the Caribbean, where there was an inevitable slide from the theological to the secular. What the missionaries said to the slaves about the equality of all before God seemed to the slaves to indict their worldly condition. Even more importantly, Christianity quickly passed into the hands of local black preachers, free and enslaved. Chapels, the Bible, hymns, and homegrown enslaved preachers all served to shape a potent weapon against slavery. Black enslaved congregations, black preachers, Old Testament fire and brimstone, communal singing—all of these Christian phenomena added up to a spiritual rod for the planters' back. Though British critics generally agreed that Christianity was the first step toward "civilizing" the slaves, many Anglicans, including prominent evangelicals, felt uneasy about the work of the missionaries on the islands. While Christianity was seen as a means of winning over enslaved peoples to a civilized form of society, it was hard to see how that could take place without causing unpredictable social consequences. The conversion of slaves was, then, a vital part of the aspirations of all abolitionists. In his "Sketch of a Negro

Code" (1792), Edmund Burke specified that "a competent minister of some Christian church or congregation shall be provided for the full instruction of the Negroes." Christianity would help to provide slaves with those personal and social skills needed to survive as free people. What few realized was that this Christian drive into the slave quarters would also help lay the foundation for ending slavery once and for all.

One unintentional result was to increase the number of British supporters for black freedom. The very groups actively converting the slaves, especially the Baptists and Methodists, were, at the same time, expanding rapidly in Britain. Inevitably British nonconformists felt a bond of sympathy for their enslaved co-religionists. There were, for example, more than a quarter of a million British Methodists by the 1820s, and perhaps 100,000 British Baptists twenty years later. By then, there were almost 15,000 dissenting places of worship across Britain. Nonconformity had clearly become a major force in Britain. This was to have a major impact on the campaign against slavery. Moreover, British nonconformity was increasing most rapidly in new, industrializing areas of rapid population growth. And it was the people of this "new Britain" who were the very people to lend their numbers and voices to demands for an end to slavery. Nonconformity could rally large numbers of British people, and its preachers spoke with great eloquence in the British campaign for slave emancipation in the 1820s and 1830s. At the same time, nonconformist Christianity transformed slave life itself.

The Atlantic slave trade had enabled planters, before 1807, to replenish their labor force by purchasing newly imported Africans. In time, some islands, notably Barbados, like North America, had been able to dispense with the Atlantic slave trade and rely on its own local-born slaves. But Britain's new colonies, acquired in the recent wars—Trinidad for example, or frontier societies, most notably Demerara/Guiana—continued to need new Africans. But after 1807, planters in those regions had to plan for a world without imported Africans and in the process had to rethink their slave management systems. As they did so, they were scrutinized with great suspicion by abolitionists, government officials, and other outsiders. The planters were renowned for their true hostility to abolition, and they continued to resist any outside interference with the slave colonies. They were permanently reluctant partners in any scheme emanating from London and made no secret of the fact that they would drag their feet in any change demanded of them by London.

The immediate consequence of the end of the slave trade in 1807 was a short-term fall in the slave population. Faced with a declining labor force, planters increased their demands on their labor force. They began to rearrange their workforce, switching slaves around, demanding more of all of them, and generally interfering with established, familiar work customs. Planters also began to relocate slaves from one property to another, rationalizing their overall labor force in ways that often caused great distress to the slaves. Women and children now undertook tasks once reserved for men. Skilled or elite slaves might now be expected to do rougher, more physically demanding work. People long accustomed to better working conditions now found themselves brutalized in the fields. Such changes made economic sense to planters, but it angered and confused the slaves. These changes are easily illustrated. There were now more women, and more "colored" slaves, working in the sugar fields. Stated crudely, fairer-skinned children might no longer expect the preferential treatment normally accorded to the offspring of black and white. On top of all this, it was clear enough that slaves were not becoming more docile. The optimistic expectations of the abolitionists were being dashed at the very time the fears of the planters were confirmed. At the same time, plantations were awash with rumors that full freedom, offered by the king, and/or Parliament, was being held back by the planters—all this at a time when the slaves' lives in the sugar economy on the older islands had become more demanding and more uncertain. The simple truth was that the abolition of the slave trade in 1807 had been a leap in the dark, and no one knew exactly what would happen when the transatlantic flow of Africans stopped. Planters hoped that as the old generation of Africans died out by natural aging, a new population of slaves born in the Caribbean and never having known freedom directly in Africa would become more manageable and compliant. Yet, the contrary seemed to be happening. Planters assumed that slave truculence was made worse by outside interference, by a critical British government and its colonial officers and by the swarm of missionaries wooing slaves to the chapels and prayer meetings. What happened after 1807 confirmed the planters' greatest fears. Bussa's rebellion (1816) in Barbados had been bad enough. But worse was to follow.

The newly developed slave lands in Demerara attracted a new breed of aggressive investors and planters including the father of William Gladstone. Slaves there were managed under a draconian system that appalled abolitionists. Missionaries arriving in that unforgiving climate were shocked by what they found. The most brutal treatment of slaves was often to be seen in the early days of settlement and expansion, in those societies that were, in effect, frontier communities. The crudeness of slavery in Demerara could be explained by its early state of development. It was perhaps more like seventeenth-century Barbados and Jamaica. But times and sensibilities had changed. What had gone unnoticed two centuries earlier was unacceptable now to an ever more inquisitive British gaze. Reports of the planters' wrongdoings sped back to British congregations by way of missionaries' correspondence.

The slaves in Demerara lived mainly on the coastal regions and along the rivers and had long been famed for their resistance and truculence. When the missionary, John Smith, arrived in Demerara in 1817, slaves flocked to his new congregations. Six years later in 1823, a major slave revolt erupted. It was suppressed by the military and planters. The subsequent summary and legal punishments were excessive even by local standards. The killing of three white people led to the killing of 250 slaves. Smith, too, was tried, in a hearing made all the more dramatic by Smith's own decline into consumption. He died in jail in February 1824 shortly before his Royal pardon had been received. There followed an outcry in Britain, though the outrage should have concentrated on the deaths of so many slaves, slaughtered for an indefensible system. Yet Smith's death served a purpose, once more focusing British attention on slavery. The flagging British abolition cause was promptly revived in 1823. It was abundantly clear to ever more people that West Indian slavery stood condemned by the actions of its principal proponents and benefactors.

Although the most important impact of the Demerara revolt was in Britain, the revolt naturally sent shock waves through the other slave colonies. Smith's death was used to goad a hesitant British government to move toward abolition. More and more people in Britain simply wanted to wash their hands of the entire slave system. It seemed obvious that planters would never bring justice, to say nothing of freedom, to the slaves. In a mood of profound national disgust, it was widely felt that slavery should be brought to an end. The practical problem remained: how to clinch black freedom.

As the data accumulated from the slave registration returns in the 1820s, the decline of the slave population became increasingly evident. That decline would continue until a new generation of slaves entered their child-bearing years. Everywhere, enslaved labor regimes were more brutal than ever, at the same time that Christian missionaries were winning over more and more slaves. Serious friction between planters and missionaries was ubiquitous. Viewed from Britain, the planters' open hostility to missionaries and to Christian slaves helped confirm the need to bring down slavery. In the very years when the British removed religious disabilities, most notably against Roman Catholics, it was ironic to see newly converted slaves harassed and obstructed in their worship in the West Indies. To make matters worse, excessive violence remained the hallmark of slave management and even of colonial administration. By the mid-1820s, the slave colonies seemed like survivors from a lost epoch. Any remaining optimism that the slave colonies could be expected to reform themselves was dispelled by the death of the Reverend Smith and the legions of slaves slaughtered at the same time. In 1823, it was time, once again, to rally the abolitionist troops.

The revived abolitionist campaign really began with the idea that slavery could be undermined by an economic attack, by undermining the sugar duties. The British Caribbean needed the protection of sugar duties to compete with sugar grown in other parts of the world. The abolitionists' new idea was simple: expose slave-grown sugar to free competition and it would simply collapse from its own inefficiencies. Some of the earliest abolitionist arguments (e.g., in the 1770s and 1780s) had embraced an economic critique of slavery, though rarely as a pivotal objection. Half a century later, however, other cheaper sugars were readily available on the world market. And, as the 1820s advanced, the economic critique gained in strength and persuasion. Promoted initially as a relatively minor objection by Quakers with East Indian interests in the early 1820s, by the late 1820s, it was widely accepted that a free trade and open competition for sugar would undermine West Indian slavery. The case was promoted most forcefully by James Cropper, a Quaker with East India interests, but he and other abolitionists were again convinced that their arguments needed public support. For that, they needed a reprise of the old abolitionist tactics.

With this in mind, the Society for the Amelioration and Gradual Abolition of Slavery was founded late in January 1823. Within a year, Thomas Clarkson, the durable survivor from the 1780s and 1790s, had spurred the formation of 250 societies across Britain. Over the next decade, these local societies—large numbers of them female—provided the impetus for the campaign to end slavery. A central London committee orchestrated the national campaign, with the country divided into organizational districts, and all were encouraged to rally support and organize petitions for black freedom. It was, instantly, a significant, national pressure group, made all the more influential by the energy and activities of female abolitionists, many working through their own associations.

By the 1820s, however, abolition had changed. The ideological core of the campaign was quite different from its forebears. The economics of antislavery had now shifted to the center of the arguments, though integrated with the older moral and religious objections. Slavery thus found itself under attack from a powerful combination of economic, religious, and moral objections. Large numbers of British people were attracted to the idea that slavery was both wrong and uneconomic. The West India lobby, on the other hand, now faced an impossible task: struggling to promote both the morality and the economic utility of slavery. Yet on both counts, they were repeatedly outflanked by events and by abolitionist arguments. How could they justify the recent treatment of slaves in Demerara, or the persecution of black Christians? And why should British consumers keep the slave system in place by paying more for their sugar? By the mid-1820s, the West Indians were clearly on the defensive and faced massive, well-organized, articulate ranks of British people who were now wedded to demands for black freedom sooner rather than later. Abolition had in effect captured both the economic and moral high ground.

Under this pressure, early in 1823 the Commons resolved to press for gradual slave emancipation. Once more the indefatigable Clarkson found support from ordinary citizens throughout the country, from all political quarters and, critically, from most churches. Despite a rearguard opposition in the House of Lords, black freedom no longer divided the British, but had, instead, become an issue that united the British people as no other. Abolitionists were confident that they could mobilize an outraged public opinion, which, in its turn, would make emancipation inevitable—Parliament would be unable to resist demands for black freedom.

After 1823, the campaign for black freedom reprised the familiar tactics: mass petitions, innumerable publications, and lectures, many of them of remarkable length, to packed audiences. Overspill audiences, people locked out, hundreds defying bad weather to get to a lecture hall and more bore testimony to the staggering popularity of the abolitionist campaign. Through all this, female abolitionists and their own, discrete organizations were vital; female abolitionists were at the heart of the campaign, as organizers, as lecturers, and as audiences. Female abolition was important in itself, but also as part of the much broader and more deep-seated shift toward female political activism. A profusion of abolitionist publications fluttered down on an increasingly literate people. Between 1823 and 1831, the Anti-Slavery Society issued more than three millions tracts, about half a million in 1831 alone. All of this was in addition to publications from local abolition groups and abolitionist material in the local and London newspapers.

Despite all this public pressure, abolition in Parliament languished. The figurehead, William Wilberforce, was old and weary, handing over the parliamentary leadership to Thomas Fowell Buxton. But by 1830, little headway had been made in Parliament. Of course, slave emancipation was only one of a number of reforming issues confronting Parliament. Dominating everything was the reform of Parliament. Nonetheless, younger abolitionists began to tire of their leaders' apparently endless patience in asking for black freedom, and in 1832 the Agency Committee was founded by George Stephen and Emmanuel and James Cropper (both Quakers) to press for immediate emancipation. Once again, unpredictable events took a hand, both at home and in the islands. Domestic British life was thrown into a national panic caused by the terrible cholera epidemic of 1832, which killed 32,000 people. Here was a disaster, some thought, provoked by divine punishment for national sins; and, what sin could have been greater than slavery? And, as if to confirm this judgment of the Almighty's wrath, Jamaican slaves revolted in 1831–1832.

The Jamaican revolt was quite unlike those in Barbados in 1816 or Demerara in 1823. It was a massive upheaval involving 60,000 slaves; it caused the death of 14 whites, and saw the killing of 540 slaves. Led by the inspirational preacher Sam Sharpe, the revolt raced through western Jamaica, with estates torched and Baptist slaves at the forefront. There was something different about this revolt. It was, above all, a revolt of Christians. Sharpe, though still a slave, personified the power of black Christianity, and he and other rebels spoke a language of radical, egalitarian Christianity.

News of the Jamaican revolt and of its violent repression caused another outcry in Britain. Missionaries returning from Jamaica on the eve of the debate for parliamentary reform roused British audiences with the latest news from Jamaica. They added an emotive element to the wider debate both for black freedom and for the Reform Bill. The coincidence of timing greatly helped abolition. When a parliamentary election was called in August 1832, using the new reformed franchise, abolitionists seized their chance. They forced parliamentary candidates to declare their views on slave emancipation. Something like 200 MPs declared themselves for black freedom. The reform of Parliament in 1832 thus paved the way for the ending of slavery.

Earl Grey's new government had little option but to end colonial slavery, though the Lords again remained doggedly supportive of the planters. After 1832, however, the parliamentary arguments were about when slaves would be freed and under what terms. Finally, the Abolition of Slavery Bill of August 1833 inaugurated black freedom the following year in August 1834. Even then, what was proposed had severe limitations founded primarily on the need to satisfy the planters' demands for a guaranteed source of labor. All slaves less than six years old were freed immediately; the rest became "apprentices" for up to six years, working most of their time without pay for their former owners. Bermuda and Antigua opted for immediate emancipation.

No less surprising, in retrospect at least, Parliament also allocated a staggering £20 million to be distributed on a per capita basis, not to the slaves, but to the slave owners. In effect, Parliament was buying the slaves' freedom by paying planters the current market value for their human property. Lord Harewood, for example, already fabulously wealthy from his family's sugar trading and West Indian plantations, received more than £26,000 for the 1,277 slaves still in his possession. Abolitionists asked the obvious question: why not compensate the slaves instead?

The interim apprenticeship scheme, monitored by a new breed of commissioners entitled Stipendiary Magistrates sent to the islands, was clearly a concession to the planters. But from the first, the scheme's failings (and abuses) were obvious, enabling abolitionists to continue their demands for full, immediate freedom. They kept up the pressure on Parliament using the old tactics. The abolition debate also reflected a major divide in British life. Abolitionists spoke for the "new" Britain, for urban, industrial, and dissenting British life; slavery tended to have its natural support in small-town, rural Britain and in the House of Lords. By then, however, there was little the slave lobby could do to save slavery. On August 1, 1838, apprenticeship was brought to an early end, and full emancipation was granted. Two centuries after their first ancestors had shuffled from the slave ships into the British colonies, something like three quarters of a million slaves were henceforth free people.

Planters understandably feared that ex-slaves had long memories and would remember the long litany of personal and collective grievances. They feared an understandable revenge. However, the ex-slaves celebrated their newly won freedom in the most peaceable of fashions: large numbers simply went to church.

Across the Caribbean and among abolitionists, black and white, in the United States as well, August 1, 1838, was celebrated peacefully. Freed people gathered in parades and public meetings, but above all, in crowded churches. Here was a staggering turn of events. For almost three centuries, African slavery had defined relations between black and white throughout the Americas, and it was a system rooted in violence. In Africa, in the mid-Atlantic, and on the American plantations, slavery had been characterized by violence. Although it is true that slavery in Haiti had been destroyed by the volcanic slave revolt of the 1790s and, although slavery in the United States was to end in the bloodshed of the Civil War, the British system of slavery ended peacefully. British slavery, and the British slave trade, had been infamous for their brutality, yet both ended without bloodshed by Acts of Parliament.

James Walvin

See also: Atlantic Slave Trade and British Abolition.

Further Readings

Blackburn, Robin. *The Overthrow of Colonial Slavery, 1776–1848*. London: Verso Books, 1988.

Costa, Emilia Viotti da. *Crowns of Glory, Tears of Blood: The Demerara Slave Rebellion of 1823*. Oxford: Oxford University Press, 1994.

Craton, Michael. *Testing the Chains: Resistance to Slavery in the British West Indies*. Ithaca, NY: Cornell University Press, 1982.

Davis, David Brion. *The Problem of Slavery in the Age of Revolution, 1770–1823*. 2nd ed. Oxford: Oxford University Press, 1999.

Drescher, Seymour. *Capitalism and Antislavery: British Mobilisation in Comparative Perspective*. Oxford: Oxford University Press, 1986.

Temperley, Howard. *British Antislavery, 1833–1870*. London: Macmillan, 1972.

Burned-Over District

The Burned-Over District occupied a region of upstate New York beyond the Catskill and Adirondack Mountains. Settled by New Englanders in the late 1800s, its early society reflected a culture of religious exuberance. The agrarian villages and small cities these migrants dominated shared a traditional Puritan concern for piety, morality, and communalism. Social trends and religious movements cultivated in the area contributed significantly to the history of religion and reform in the United States in the nineteenth century.

Identified with the intense religious enthusiasm that regularly blazed there, the Burned-Over District served as the epicenter for the early nineteenth-century revivals of the Second Great Awakening. The countryside and small cities of the region where the new emotional preaching styles typically flourished witnessed mass conversions and social change. Across the North, Protestant churches competed to host Presbyterian preacher Charles Grandison Finney, the era's most dynamic and persuasive revivalist. His controversial homiletic techniques, entitled the "New Measures," were designed both to inflame and to enlarge congregations. They ignited especially intense revival fires in the Western Reserve (1825) and Rochester (1831).

After the completion of the Erie Canal in 1825, formerly frontier environs in upstate New York developed swiftly into dynamic towns and farming regions, driven by a growing market economy. Families hoping to establish a secure social footing in an evolving middle class responded favorably to the revival culture. Women focused on elevating the moral and religious awareness of their husbands and children, while men associated with the revivals embraced religiously infused habits and values thought both to serve God and to advance a moral capitalism.

The Second Great Awakening also brought theological innovations emphasizing humankind's ability to achieve personal and social change. New moral imperatives spurred men and women alike to join the numerous benevolent and voluntary associations that sprang up across the district. New England missionary organizations offered spiritual aid to the early migrants, and soon the Yorker Yankees also supported the many Bible, tract, temperance, antislavery, and home mission associations that made the region a national nucleus for social reform.

At the heart of many reformers' efforts to perfect themselves and society was a widespread religious emphasis on perfectionism and millennialism. Along with other "ultraist" experimental views, these beliefs may have found more intense articulation in the Burned-Over District than elsewhere in the nation. As a result, a number of utopian groups resided in the area, including Fourier socialists and John Humphrey Noyes's controversial Oneida Community. Mesmerism, Swedenborgianism, phrenology, and other spiritual fashions also flourished.

This cultural milieu provided ready followers of the visionary native son and Mormon founder, Joseph Smith. Myths and religious issues long familiar to the region informed his writings. Smith was never well known there, however, and relocated to Ohio with one hundred devotees in 1831. On the other hand, Adventism, which originated elsewhere, provoked a sensation in the district. Founder William Miller and 50,000 adherents across the country augured and fervently anticipated Christ's return about 1843. Religious and social experimentation, popular nationwide in the nineteenth century, achieved their highest and most influential expression in the Burned-Over District.

Cathy Rodabaugh

See also: First Great Awakening and Antislavery.

Further Readings

Barkun, Michael. *Crucible of the Millennium: The Burned-Over District of New York in the 1840s*. Syracuse, NY: Syracuse University Press, 1986.

Cross, Whitney. *The Burned-Over District; The Social and Intellectual History of Enthusiastic Religion in Western New York, 1800–1850*. New York: Harper Torchbooks, 1965.

Johnson, Paul E. *A Shopkeeper's Millennium: Society and Revivals in Rochester, New York, 1815–1837*. New York: Hill and Wang, 1978.

Ryan, Mary P. *Cradle of the Middle Class: The Family in Oneida County, New York, 1790–1865*. Cambridge: Cambridge University Press, 1981.

Burns, Anthony

The *Anthony Burns* case involved an escaped slave who sought refuge in Boston, but was returned to his master under the Fugitive Slave Law of 1850. The case galvanized the antislavery movement in Boston.

Burns was a Virginia slave owned by Colonel Charles Suttle. He escaped in January 1854, arriving in Boston in February. On May 24, Judge Edward Loring issued a warrant for Burns's arrest as a fugitive slave. The warrant was served the next morning. Suttle's agent, William Brent, identified Burns as a runaway. Two prominent Boston attorneys, Richard Henry Dana Jr., and Charles Mayo Ellis, volunteered to serve as Burns's counsel.

The arrest coincided with two events that catapulted it to prominence. The first was anniversary week, the week when the reform societies of Massachusetts, including antislavery societies, convened their annual meetings. The second was the passage of the Kansas-Nebraska Act, which created and opened Kansas and Nebraska territories for settlement and possibly for slavery because the act revoked the Missouri Compromise line of 1820, which had prohibited slavery North of Missouri's southern boundary. Both events highlighted the slave question. Boston's abolitionists, led by Theodore Parker and Wendell Phillips, hastily summoned a meeting at Faneuil Hall on May 26, to plan a response to Burns's arrest. Thomas Wentworth Higginson assembled another group at the courthouse to attempt to free Burns from prison. About nine o'clock that night, a messenger informed the Faneuil Hall meeting that a riot had erupted at the courthouse, and Phillips, Parker, and the others rushed to join the effort there to free Burns. The attempt failed, and one deputy was killed.

The result of the trial, which began on May 29, was almost a foregone conclusion. Burns had already admitted that he was Suttle's slave. Ellis and Dana attempted various strategies, including challenging the constitutionality of the

Fugitive Slave Law and claiming that Brent and Suttle had misidentified Burns. A group of abolitionists attempted to buy Burns, but District Attorney Benjamin Hallett quashed the effort. On June 2, Judge Loring ruled that Burns was Suttle's slave, and Burns was taken under armed guard to a ship that would take him back to Virginia.

Boston philanthropists later purchased Burns. He trained as a minister at Oberlin College in Oberlin, Ohio, and later settled in St. Catherine's, Ontario, where he died in 1862. Parker, Phillips, and Higginson were indicted for their roles in the courthouse riot, but the charges were eventually dropped. The case propelled the Know-Nothing Party, both anti-Irish and antislavery, into power in the state and, in 1855, the Massachusetts legislature passed a personal liberty law designed to thwart future efforts to recover fugitive slaves.

Robert W. Smith

See also: Fugitive Slave Law (1850).

Further Readings

Commager, Henry Steele. *Theodore Parker: Yankee Crusader.* Boston: Beacon Press, 1947.
Korngold, Ralph. *Two Friends of Man.* Boston: Little, Brown and Company, 1950.
Thomas, John L. *The Liberator: William Lloyd Garrison.* Boston: Little, Brown and Company, 1963.
Von Frank, Anthony J. *The Trials of Anthony Burns: Freedom and Slavery in Emerson's Boston.* Cambridge, MA: Harvard University Press, 1998.

Burritt, Elihu

The author of *A Plan of Brotherly Co-Partnership of the North and South for the Peaceful Extinction of Slavery* (1856), American pacifist Elihu Burritt was an advocate of compensated emancipation. With tensions rising between the North and the South over the issue of slavery and its extension into the western territories, Burritt hoped that the United States might avert civil war by following the example of Britain in whose colonies slavery had been abolished peacefully in 1834, with former slaveholders receiving £20 million as compensation for the loss of their slaves. Burritt proposed that the federal government should sell all public lands in the western territories and use the funds generated to compensate Southern slaveholders for the emancipation of their slaves.

Burritt spent much of 1856 and 1857 lecturing throughout the Northern states and two Upper Southern states, promoting this plan for compensated emancipation. His campaign culminated in August 1857 in a national Compensated Emancipation

Convention held in Cleveland. While the convention was attended and supported by prominent abolitionist Gerritt Smith and resulted in the formation of the National Compensated Emancipation Society, not much came of Burritt's efforts. The Compensated Emancipation Society never truly became a society; it failed to attract anything but lukewarm support from a handful of individuals. Within a year it was essentially defunct.

Prior to this campaign for compensated emancipation, Burritt's contributions to abolitionism had been indirect and sporadic. He had risen to prominence in the late 1830s as the "learned blacksmith." Son of a cobbler and a workingman himself, Burritt had earned public acclaim for his extraordinary linguistic accomplishments; he was reputed to know fifty languages. In 1844, he launched a newspaper, the *Christian Citizen,* that was sympathetic to, but not formally associated with, the antislavery Liberty Party, and in that same year he stood as a Liberty Party candidate for the Massachusetts state senate. Like all state Liberty Party candidates that year, he lost. Between 1845 and 1855, Burritt devoted most of his energies to pacifism. He was the editor of the American Peace Society's *Advocate of Peace and Universal Brotherhood* in 1846; in that same year, he traveled to Great Britain, beginning a sojourn abroad that was to last the better part of a decade. In Britain, Burritt launched a reform organization called the League of Universal Brotherhood. The League was a transnational voluntary society of individuals who had pledged not to lend aid to any war effort of their nation. While the ending of slavery was not the principal goal of the League, the League's pledge did include "the abolition of all institutions and customs which do not recognize and respect the image of God and a human brother in every man of whatever clime, colour, or condition of humanity" as one of the League's central aims.

Robert K. Nelson

See also: Gradual Emancipation; Liberty Party.

Further Readings

Curti, Merle. *The Learned Blacksmith: The Letters and Journals of Elihu Burritt.* New York: Wilson-Erickson, 1937.
Tolis, Peter. *Elihu Burritt: Crusader for Brotherhood.* Hamden, CT: Archon Books, 1968.

C

Canada, Antislavery in

Antislavery in Canada divides into two distinct phases—the first beginning in the late eighteenth century while slavery itself was in full flower, and the second in the 1830s after slavery had disappeared from Canada and England, and British colonial slavery had been outlawed by Parliament. Antislavery sentiment in Canada first appeared when the Quaker Loyalist community of Beaver Harbour (New Brunswick) was established in 1783; slaveholders were not permitted to settle there. Nova Scotia and New Brunswick provided sanctuary for American refugee slaves in 1783 and again in 1814–1815. The presence of a significant number of freed blacks from and after 1783 set the stage for the antislavery movement to begin in Nova Scotia. By the time many of them left for Sierra Leone in January 1792, it was already underway.

The antislavery movement proper began in 1788 with the publication in Halifax in pamphlet form of the Reverend James MacGregor's *Letter to a Clergyman Urging Him to Set Free a Black Girl He Held in Slavery*. MacGregor (1759–1830), a Presbyterian dissenting minister, was almost alone among clergymen of his time in being a radical abolitionist. A product of Scotland, where slavery was illegal, and of the Scottish Enlightenment, MacGregor argued against slavery on both scriptural and philosophical grounds. He also practiced what he preached, redeeming slaves from their owners so that he might set them at liberty. He is reputed to have declared that he would rather burn at the stake than keep communion with a slaveholder.

Soon progressive lawyers and judges took up the cause and slavery was gradually but effectively extinguished, one slave at a time, over a period of thirty years. Courts held owners attempting to repossess fugitive slaves to an unrealistically high standard of proof of title. If an owner went to court to try to repossess an escaped slave, the onus would be on the owner to prove title. If he could not do so to the court's satisfaction, then the slave would go free, and most did. In practical terms, slavehold tenure became untenable; courts almost never returned slaves to their owners. Slavery was fatally undermined by the judicial emancipation of individual slaves. The central point, property in human beings, was never adjudicated. It could not be; slaves were chattels, and personal property was a common law right.

In the British North American colonies generally, antislavery took the form not of abolitionism but of emancipationism. In Nova Scotia, New Brunswick, and Lower Canada (Quebec), the few attempts to legislate on slavery—for or against—did not succeed. In Canada as in England, legislatures and courts were more concerned about violating private property than about violating human rights. Yet the years between statutory abolition of the transatlantic slave trade in 1807 and of colonial slavery in 1833 saw the complete and final extinction of the peculiar institution in British North America. No colonial legislature abolished slavery in its territory any more than Parliament abolished it in England. In 1825, however, after slavery had disappeared, Prince Edward Island repealed an act of 1781 declaring that slave baptism did not emancipate. Only Upper Canada (Ontario), in 1793, enacted a bill aiming at the gradual abolition of slavery, chiefly through the non-importation of slaves from the United States. It freed no slaves, and had little if any impact on the decline and disappearance of slavery.

By 1833, when the Colonial Slavery Abolition Act was passed, slavery had disappeared from all of British North America except for the West Indies; it was against plantation slavery that the act was exclusively aimed. Antislavery sentiment had to be redirected once slavery in both Canada and England had died a natural death through attrition, and been abolished in the West Indies. The center of attention moved to the Southern United States, where slavery continued to flourish. Churches, especially the Methodist and the Presbyterian, became outspoken in their denunciations of slavery and entered the controversy with their communions in the United States where deep rifts divided North and South over slavery. Canadian blacks became abolitionists themselves; they celebrated as Emancipation Day (first Wednesday in August) the anniversary of the final coming into force in 1838 of the Colonial Slavery Abolition Act, and they set up their own abolition societies and wrote antislavery tracts.

The second phase of antislavery activism in Canada reached its climax in the aftermath of the passage of the Fugitive Slave Law by the U.S. Congress in 1850. The Antislavery Society of Canada was founded in 1851 and Canada West (Ontario) became the ultimate northern terminus of the Underground Railroad. In Nova Scotia, Emancipation Day continued to be celebrated even after the end of the American Civil War. The fact that slavery disappeared from Canada, as from New England, relatively early and without a prolonged, bitter or violent struggle over its abolition, has tended to substitute a triumphalist antislavery narrative for the history of slavery in Canada.

Barry Cahill

See also: Atlantic Slave Trade and British Abolition; British Slavery, Abolition of.

Further Readings

Bell, D. G. "Slavery and the Judges of Loyalist New Brunswick." *University of New Brunswick Law Journal* 31 (1982): 9–42.

Cahill, Barry. "Slavery and the Judges of Loyalist Nova Scotia." *University of New Brunswick Law Journal* 43 (1994): 73–135.

Stouffer, Allen P. *The Light of Nature and the Law of God: Antislavery in Ontario, 1833–1877.* Montreal; Kingston: McGill-Queen's University Press, 1992.

Chase, Salmon P.

Salmon P. Chase was a senator, governor, cabinet secretary, and chief justice of the Supreme Court. Chase was born January 13, 1808, in Cornish, New Hampshire. He attended school in Keene, New Hampshire, and Windsor, Vermont. After his father died when Chase was nine years old, he lived with his uncle, the Protestant Episcopal Bishop of Ohio, Philander Chase. He continued to attend school and started college while living with his uncle. When his uncle went to England to raise money for a seminary, he returned to New Hampshire to attend Dartmouth College, where he graduated Phi Beta Kappa in 1826. Chase taught school and studied law in Washington, D.C., with Attorney General William Wirt before being admitted to the bar in 1829. He returned to Cincinnati in 1830 and established a law practice. While starting his practice, he compiled a three-volume compendium with commentary of the laws of Ohio, which became the standard work on the topic in Ohio's courts.

Initially more interested in other reform issues than slavery, Chase defended James G. Birney on charges of harboring a fugitive and became strongly committed to the antislavery cause. He saw slavery as a serious sin and often defended runaway slaves when their return to slavery was sought by former masters or slave catchers. His antislavery activities drew him into politics with first the Liberty Party, then the Free Soil Party, and finally the Republican Party.

In 1840, he was elected to the Cincinnati City Council and joined the Liberty Party the following year. He quickly emerged as a leader in the antislavery movement in Ohio and as a strong advocate for direct political action against slavery.

Salmon P. Chase was the founder of the national banking system and, as chief justice of the U.S. Supreme Court, managed to ensure that President Andrew Johnson received a fair impeachment trial. (Library of Congress)

Chase was elected to the U.S. Senate as a Free Soil candidate in 1848 and served from 1849 to 1855. He was a leader among antislavery forces in the Senate. He opposed both the Compromise of 1850 and the Kansas-Nebraska Bill because of their concessions to slavery. His pamphlet, "Appeal to Independent Democrats," attacking the Kansas-Nebraska Bill, received widespread attention nationally.

Support in Ohio for his position on these issues led to his election as governor as a Free Soil Democrat in 1855. In his campaign, Chase stressed the dangers of compromise with the South and strongly opposed the expansion of slavery. As governor, Chase was an economic conservative, but a reformer on social issues. He promoted education, the establishment of a geological survey, a railroad commission, a bureau of statistics, and women's rights. He was also supportive of radical antislavery measures, and during his term Ohio passed personal liberty laws and other strong antislavery legislation. He was reelected in 1857 as a member of the new Republican Party, but was less successful due to a scandal involving the state's treasurer. He remained personally popular and respected, however, and in 1860 he was elected to the U.S. Senate a second time.

Chase was a candidate for the Republican presidential nomination in 1860, losing to Lincoln in the convention. He was a member of the 1861 peace convention that tried to compromise the differences between the North and South and prevent the Civil War.

He resigned his Senate seat just two days after taking it to serve as secretary of the treasury in the Lincoln administration. He served as until July 1864 despite many differences with Abraham Lincoln over the conduct of the Civil War and policy toward the South. Chase wanted the elimination of slavery made an explicit war goal early in the conflict and supported General David Hunter when he recruited African Americans into the Union Army in the summer of 1862. Lincoln and most of the cabinet were more moderate and slower to move on issues related to race and slavery than Chase, who supported voting rights and full equality for African Americans. Chase had become identified with the anti-Lincoln faction within the Republican Party and was openly interested in the Republican nomination for president in 1864 when Lincoln accepted his resignation, offered during one of their arguments.

Despite their differences Lincoln appointed Chase chief justice of the Supreme Court, succeeding Roger Brooke Taney, author of the *Dred Scott* decision. As chief justice he presided over the impeachment trial of President Andrew Johnson and a number of Civil War and Reconstruction-related cases. He insisted that the Senate conduct itself as a judicial rather than a legislative body during the impeachment trial, alienating some of his former allies in the Senate. Chase served as chief justice from December 1864 until his death on May 7, 1873, in New York City, never completely giving up his presidential ambitions.

William H. Mulligan Jr.

See also: Democratic Party and Antislavery; Radical Republicans; Whig Party and Antislavery.

Further Readings

Blue, Frederick J. *Salmon P. Chase: A Life in Politics.* Kent, Ohio: Kent State University Press, 1987.

Middleton, Stephen. *Ohio and the Antislavery Activities of Attorney Salmon Portland Chase, 1830–1849.* New York: Garland Publishers, 1990.

Niven, John et al., eds. *The Salmon P. Chase Papers*, 5 vols. to date. Kent, Ohio: Kent State University Press, 1993.

Niven, John. *Salmon P. Chase: A Biography.* New York: Oxford University Press, 1995.

Child, Lydia Maria

Lydia Maria Child became an influential figure in the abolition movement through her great literary skills. In addition to her crusades on behalf of African Americans, she argued for the rights of Native Americans and women. Born Lydia Francis on February 11, 1802, in Medford, Massachusetts, to Convers Francis, Sr., and Susannah Rand, her social conscience was influenced by her father, a baker, who allegedly helped a fugitive slave escape in 1805. Child attended a dame school and Miss Swan's Academy, but her beloved older brother Convers Jr., was the only figure in her young life to take a serious interest in her academic abilities. The pair read voraciously and discussed philosophical matters, and Convers Jr., encouraged his sister to hone her writing skills. When he left home to attend Harvard, Child was devastated that she could not follow him to the all-male academy.

Susannah died of tuberculosis in 1814, and the following year Convers, Sr., pulled the thirteen-year-old Lydia out of school to live with her older sister, Mary, on the Maine frontier. At the time, Maine was still part of Massachusetts, but the social hierarchy on the frontier was fluid. During her years there, Child encountered the dispossessed Penobscot and Abenaki tribes, and she developed a deep sympathy for their plight. In 1824 she wrote *Hobomok*, her first novel. The book articulated her fierce belief in the humanity and goodness of the American Indians.

Her next book, the historic novel *The Rebels, or Boston before the Revolution*, attracted the attention of David Lee Child, editor of Boston's *Massachusetts Journal*. He courted her and proposed in October 1827. During the mid-1820s through mid-1830s, Lydia Child enjoyed a brilliant literary career, writing short stories and editing a children's magazine, the *Juvenile Miscellany*, which she founded in 1826. David and Lydia wed in October 1828, but the marriage was not a happy one. Her husband's persistent indebtedness impoverished them, and in 1829 she wrote *The Frugal Housewife* out of economic necessity. The book sold 6,000 copies in its first year and established her as an eminent American author.

Her popularity ended abruptly in 1833 with her publication of *An Appeal in Favor of That Class of Americans Called Africans*, in which she argued for radical abolition. Child had met William Lloyd Garrison when he worked as a printer for her husband, and she had quickly converted to his controversial doctrine of immediate emancipation. The general public responded to the *Appeal* with outrage. *The Juvenile Miscellany* lost so many subscriptions that it folded, and Lydia's popular *The Mother's Book* went out of print. Her message, however, did reach many Americans, including Charles Sumner, who credited her with his conversion to abolition. Child published *Oasis* (1834) and *Anti-Slavery Catechism* (1836) to address readers' concerns about immediate emancipation. She worked with local abolition groups and served on the business committee of the New England Anti-Slavery Convention.

Lydia's personal life remained unhappy. In the 1840s, David moved her to a farm in Massachusetts to grow sugar beets as part of an abolitionist effort to prove that the North could free itself from its dependence upon slave-grown crops. Child became so depressed that she stopped writing. Her husband's venture threw them deeper into debt, so she took work editing the Garrisonians' *National Anti-Slavery Standard*. She hoped to use her position to heal the growing rift between the Garrisonian and evangelical abolitionists, but the schism deepened and she resigned in disgust. Child reprinted her *Standard* column in two volumes of *Letters from New York* in 1843 and 1845.

The beating of her close friend Massachusetts senator Charles Sumner spurred her back into action. She wrote "The Kansas Emigrants," which encouraged abolitionists to unite behind those settlers in Kansas who sought to have the territory admitted as a free state. She also organized relief shipments to the emigrants. After John Brown's failed uprising at Harpers Ferry in 1859, Child petitioned Virginia's Governor Wise for permission to nurse Brown in prison. She published their letters in *Correspondence between Lydia Maria Child and Governor Wise and Mrs. Mason, of Virginia* in 1860, urging Northerners to risk Civil War. Child also raised money for the families of the Harpers Ferry victims and helped Garrison organize a mourning mass for Brown.

In 1860, Child edited Harriet Jacob's *Incidents in the Life of a Slave Girl*. During the Civil War, Child continued to agitate for immediate abolition, and she grew frustrated with Lincoln's slow, uncertain movement toward emancipation. She organized supplies for abolitionist-led regiments and contrabands. After the war, Child published *The Freedman's Book* and fought for black suffrage, land redistribution, women's rights, and the rights of American Indians. During her latter years, Child explored non-Western religions for means to advance gender and racial equality. Her husband died in 1874, and Lydia died October 20, 1880.

Susan Fletcher

See also: Literature and Abolition.

Further Readings

Abzug, Robert. *Cosmos Crumbling: American Reform and Religious Imagination*. Oxford: Oxford University Press, 1994.

Karcher, Carolyn. *The First Woman of the Republic: A Cultural Biography of Lydia Maria Child*. Reprint. Durham, NC; London: Duke University Press, 1998.

Karcher, Carolyn, ed. *A Lydia Maria Child Reader*. Durham, NC: Duke University Press, 1997.

Mills, Bruce. *Cultural Reformations: Lydia Maria Child and the Literature of Reform*. Athens and London: University of Georgia Press, 1994.

Clay, Cassius

Cassius Marcellus Clay was born at Clermont, his father's plantation, near Richmond, Kentucky, on October 19, 1810. His father, General Green Clay, was a veteran of the Revolutionary War and a cousin of Henry Clay.

Clay was educated at Madison Seminary, St. Joseph's College in Bardstown, Transylvania University in Lexington, and Yale University. While at Yale, in 1832 he heard William Lloyd Garrison speak and became an outspoken opponent of

Kentucky antislavery proponent Cassius Clay stirred up controversy in his native state by campaigning for emancipation and publishing an antislavery newspaper, the *True American*. (Library of Congress)

slavery for the rest of his life. Unlike Garrison, however, Clay was a supporter of the gradual emancipation of slaves through legal and political means. That same year he returned to Kentucky, completed a law degree at Transylvania, and married Mary Jane Warfield. He settled at White Hall, an estate near Richmond, Kentucky.

Clay inherited seventeen slaves in 1828, but freed them in 1844. While a supporter of the gradual, legal elimination of slavery, Clay was a powerful and forceful speaker and had a volatile personality. He elicited strong, often violent, reactions from his audiences. He served briefly in the Kentucky legislature from 1835 to 1837 and again in 1840, but his antislavery views effectively ended his political career in Kentucky. He fought a number of duels and was an expert knife fighter, writing a book on the subject. In 1843, he was shot during a debate and fought back with a large Bowie knife he carried for self-defense. Clay's large knife had blocked the bullet. He started a newspaper in Lexington, the *True American*, the only antislavery newspaper in the South. In August 1845, while Clay was ill with typhoid fever, his second cousin, James Brown Clay, a son of Henry Clay, and a number of others obtained an injunction from a proslavery judge and dismantled the paper's printing press and shipped it out of state. Clay reestablished the paper in Cincinnati, but defiantly kept Lexington as its dateline. He later won $2,500 in damages from Clay in court.

In 1846, Clay volunteered for service in the Mexican War and when the unit he commanded was captured, he managed to save them from execution by quick thinking. He returned to Kentucky a hero and had a somewhat easier time with audiences during his antislavery speeches, with one major exception. At the conclusion of an 1849 speech in Foxtown, Kentucky, Clay was clubbed as he finished his speech. His attacker was given a gun by someone in the crowd, but it misfired while

Clay lay on the ground. Clay had managed to stab his attacker several times with his knife and the attacker died several days later from his wounds. Clay survived but took many months to recuperate. Clay was charged with mayhem as a result of the affair, but was successfully defended by Henry Clay.

During the 1850s, Clay traveled extensively in the Northern states lecturing against slavery. In 1851, he was an unsuccessful candidate for governor of Kentucky, running on an antislavery platform. Among those he met during this decade was the Reverend John G. Fee, an antislavery minister from Kentucky. Clay gave Fee ten acres of land and some cash to establish a school for those opposed to slavery. The school became Berea College, a pioneer in racially integrated education. One of the places Clay spoke during his travels through the North was Springfield, Illinois, in 1854. Among those who heard him speak that day was Abraham Lincoln. Clay was involved in the formation of the Republican Party in 1854 and supported Lincoln during the 1860 presidential campaign.

Clay was to be appointed minister to Russia when Lincoln took office, but before taking that assignment he volunteered for service in the Union Army and was put in command of a unit pressed into the defense of Washington, D.C. Clay's Battalion, as the group was known, remained on duty until federal troops arrived to replace them. He served as minister to Russia in 1861 and 1862, returning to Washington during 1862 as a result of political maneuvering in the administration. He resumed his commission in the army and continued to give forceful antislavery speeches. Lincoln consulted him on how the Emancipation Proclamation would be received in Kentucky before issuing it. Clay referred to his role in the Emancipation Proclamation as "the culminating act of my life's aspirations." In 1863, Clay returned to Russia as U.S. minister and served there until 1869. He worked to keep the major European powers neutral during the Civil War with great success and later was involved in the American purchase of Alaska from Russia in 1867.

Clay returned to Kentucky in 1869 and quickly became alienated from the Republican Party due to the policies it pursued during Reconstruction. Clay's gradual emancipation approach to slavery had little common ground with the views of the Radical Republicans who controlled federal policy. He joined the Democratic Party, but sought no public office. His personal life included a divorce from his wife after forty-five years of marriage, a brief marriage, at age eighty-three, to the fifteen-year-old daughter of a neighbor, and acquittal on grounds of justified homicide when he was tried for the shooting death of an African American former employee. His daughter, Laura, became a crusader for women's rights based in part on the treatment her mother received as a result of the divorce and the legal position of women in Kentucky. Clay died on July 22, 1903, at White Hall.

William H. Mulligan Jr.

See also: Gradual Emancipation.

Further Readings

Brennan, Fletcher. *The Life of Cassius Marcellus Clay. Memoir, Writings and Speeches, Showing His Connection to the Overthrow of American Slavery, The Salvation of the Union, and Restoration of the Autonomy of the States.* 2 vols. Cincinnati: J.F. Brennan, 1886.

McQueen, Kevin. *Cassius M. Clay: "Freedom's Champion"; The Life Story of the Famed Kentucky Emancipationist.* Paducah, KY: Turner Publishing, 2001.

Smiley, David L. *The Lion of White Hall: The Life of Cassius M. Clay.* Madison: University of Wisconsin Press, 1962.

Clay, Henry

Henry Clay was born in Hanover County, Virginia, on April 12, 1777. His father, John Clay, was a minister who died while he was young. He was admitted to the Virginia bar in 1797 and moved to Lexington, Kentucky, that same year and began practicing law. He married Lucretia Hart, a member of a prominent local family. His political career began with his election to the Kentucky legislature in 1803.

The unifying principle of Clay's political career was his belief in the importance of the Union to all sections of the country and his strong economic nationalism. As a young man, he was a leading War Hawk who, with others, including John C. Calhoun, drove a reluctant president to war with Great Britain primarily over the security of the trans-Appalachian settlements. His vision of an interconnected and complementary national economy, known as the American System, tried to balance the economic needs of the various sections of the country in ways that helped each section prosper without any one section being left behind. It also sought a truly national economy rather than a series of sectional economies.

Clay's enduring reputation is as "the great compromiser," the one man who could craft legislation that kept slave and free states together in the Union and avoided a decisive showdown over slavery. He was the major architect of compromises in 1820 and, thirty years later, in 1850. A strong supporter of the Union who also owned slaves, Clay could bridge the ever widening gap between the North and South as no other politician of his era.

Slavery was both a central factor in Clay's political career and an issue he wrestled with on a personal level. Implementing his American System and otherwise advancing his economic vision for the nation's future was complicated by the increasing division and animosity between the nation's sections and political parties over slavery. Clay had come to maturity during the period when the merits and long-term future of slavery were still open to debate even in slave states.

Throughout his career his views on slavery were generally those of an earlier generation, one that was passing from the scene as his career was reaching the national stage.

His personal view of slavery was negative. He saw it as an evil institution—but he owned slaves, at times as many as sixty, and did so until his death. He had emancipated the majority of his slaves before he died, however. Clay did not see Africans as fully equal to whites and did not believe the two races could live together peacefully. In both of these views, he was very much a man of the time he lived in. He was an early supporter of the African colonization movement and presided at the meeting where the American Colonization Society was organized in 1816. In Congress, Clay opposed both the annexation of Texas and the Mexican War in the 1840s because of the additional territory this would open to slavery and the resulting increase in the political power of slave states. In the 1844 presidential election, his last realistic chance to be elected, his opposition to the annexation of Texas probably cost him the election. Clay never resolved the issue of slavery for himself and it remained an obstacle to his goals both in developing the integrated national economic policy he saw as essential for the nation's full development and in achieving the presidency.

He died in Washington on June 29, 1852. He lay in state in the Capitol Rotunda, a rare honor, and was buried in Lexington, Kentucky.

William H. Mulligan Jr.

See also: Compromise of 1850; Texas, Annexation of (1845); Whig Party and Antislavery.

Further Readings

Baxter, Maurice G. *Henry Clay and the American System.* Lexington: University Press of Kentucky, 1995.

Eaton, Clement. *Henry Clay and the Art of American Politics.* Boston: Little Brown, 1957.

Hopkins, James F. et al., eds. *The Papers of Henry Clay.* 11 volumes. Lexington: University of Kentucky Press, 1959–1992.

Remini, Robert V. *Henry Clay: Statesman for the Union.* New York: W.W. Norton, 1999.

Come-Outerism

Come-outerism describes the actions taken by antebellum church members to protest their denominations' antislavery policies. During the 1840s and 1850s, some Northern abolitionists separated from their congregations over their churches' willingness to accept slaveholders into membership. These "come-outers" adhered to the biblical command, "Come out of her, my people, that ye be not partakers of her sins, and that ye receive not of her plagues" (Rev. 18:4). Often influenced by the perfectionist strain of evangelical Protestantism, come-outers rejected communion with slaveholders as sinful and terminated any affiliation with churches unwilling to do the same.

Antislavery come-outerism was not a single unified movement. Some come-outers subscribed to radical abolitionist William Lloyd Garrison's position that no church, clergyman, or institution should stand between the believer and God. According to Garrisonians, individuals should be governed by God alone and, consequently, must separate themselves from any other institution that interfered with their ultimate obedience to God. For example, abolitionists Angelina Grimké and Theodore Dwight Weld refused clerical officiation at their 1838 wedding. For radical come-outers, clergymen epitomized the sinful church. Critics charged that this radical anti-ecclesiastical stand bordered on anarchy. In fact, some Garrisonians renounced association with any form of government.

Non-Garrisonians, on the other hand, represented more moderate come-outerism. At odds with their denominations' conservative slavery position, these abolitionists formed their own sects. In the 1830s and 1840s, some radical reformers such as William Goodell and Gerrit Smith attempted to form nonsectarian free churches whose sole test for membership was abolitionist and/or other moral convictions. Many come-outer sects, including the American Baptist Free Mission Society, the Free Presbyterian Church, and the Franckean Evangelical Lutheran Synod, originated as abolitionist wings of major denominations. Perhaps the most successful was the Wesleyan Methodist Church, founded in 1843 as an antislavery offshoot of the Methodist Episcopal Church. By 1845, members numbered close to 15,000. As Southern church members seceded from major denominations, however, many sectarians returned to the fold, and antislavery churches declined in significance and number.

Although not strictly come-outer churches, independent black congregations served the abolitionist cause as well. African Methodist Episcopal (AME) and African Methodist Episcopal Zion (AMEZ) clergymen such as Daniel Payne and Jermain W. Loguen engaged in important antislavery activities, supporting the Underground Railroad and opposing the Fugitive Slave Law.

Non-Garrisonian come-outerism was important for two reasons. First, it offered institutional support to abolitionists. Second, it allowed denominational church members a means to adhere to theological doctrines without compromising their consciences. Explaining the dilemma faced by come-outers, abolitionist and come-outer James G. Birney stated in 1846, "How to reconcile an intelligent love of freedom and a desire to remain in a proslavery church, under the preaching of a proslavery minister, I do not know." Come-outerism appeared to offer a balanced solution.

Dianne Wheaton Cappiello

See also: Antislavery Evangelical Protestantism; Garrisonians.

Further Readings

McKivigan, John R. *The War against Proslavery Religion: Abolitionism and the Northern Churches, 1830–1865.* Ithaca, NY: Cornell University Press, 1984.

Perry, Lewis. *Radical Abolitionism: Anarchy and the Government of God in Antislavery Thought.* Ithaca, NY: Cornell University Press, 1973.

Walters, Ronald G. *The Antislavery Appeal: American Abolitionism after 1830.* New York: W.W. Norton & Co., 1978.

Commonwealth v. Aves (1836)

An 1836 Massachusetts Supreme Court case, *Commonwealth v. Aves*, was the most important court victory for the antislavery movement of the 1830s and became a major precedent for Northern opponents of slavery. There are a number of ironies connected to those involved in the case. The author of this strongly antislavery opinion, Chief Justice Lemuel Shaw of Massachusetts, was not an abolitionist and probably opposed any agitation on slavery. In 1860, while most of his neighbors voted for Abraham Lincoln, Shaw cast a ballot for the Constitutional Union ticket. Similarly, the winning attorney, Rufus Choate, was a conservative opponent of abolitionists and other radicals. Later in his life, Choate would represent slave owners in fugitive slave cases. The losing attorney, who represented the interests of the slave owner, Benjamin Robbins Curtis, would later become an antislavery hero for his dissent in *Dred Scott v. Sandford* (U.S., 1857). However, despite his position in *Dred Scott*, he, too, remained a conservative opponent of the abolitionists and antislavery throughout his life.

The case involved Med, a six-year-old slave girl owned by Samuel Slater of New Orleans. In 1836, Slater's wife, Mary Aves Slater, went to Boston to visit her father, Thomas Aves. She brought Med with her, probably for companionship and to help her as a servant. Shortly after their arrival in Boston, members of the Boston Female Anti-Slavery Society began to investigate Med's status. They visited the Aves household in the guise of a "Sunday School Committee" to determine if Med was indeed being kept as a slave. Once they determined she was held as a slave, the antislavery women, led by Maria Weston Chapman, began to build a legal case to win her freedom. Although none of them were formally trained in the law, these women conducted an investigation and outlined a legal strategy. They then hired Rufus Choate, an elite Boston lawyer, to represent their interests in a *habeas corpus* proceeding. Joining Choate were two committed abolitionist attorneys, Ellis Gray Loring and Samuel Sewell. Like Choate, both were elite lawyers with ties to the highest levels of Boston society. But, unlike Choate, they would commit themselves to a lifetime of opposition to slavery. While styled as a prosecution—*Commonwealth v. Aves*—the case was really more like a private suit to release Med from the custody of Aves.

The writ of habeas corpus was directed to Thomas Aves, the father of Mary Aves Slater, because Med was in his house. It was brought in the name of Levin Harris, a male abolitionist, which was consistent with the notion at the time that women should not be in the public eye or public forum. The writ was served on Aves while his daughter was out of town, perhaps to spare her the embarrassment of being brought into court. The case was soon brought before Chief Justice Lemuel Shaw of the Massachusetts Supreme Judicial Court.

The legal issue was fairly straightforward. Slavery was illegal in Massachusetts. No one could be held as a slave under Massachusetts law. Curtis, representing Aves, argued that interstate comity—the respect one state gives the laws of another—required that Massachusetts give a temporary and qualified recognition to the laws of Louisiana and allow Slater to keep Med for a short time before returning her to Louisiana. Curtis argued that to do otherwise would undermine the Union.

In a lengthy opinion, Shaw examined and discussed numerous British and American cases on slavery and the slave trade. He also considered French cases and the general notion of international law. He also looked at how slavery ended in Massachusetts. He expressed surprise that the issue had never been decided before in Massachusetts. But, after examining various precedents, including the British case of *Somerset v. Stewart* (1772), Shaw concluded that Med became free the moment her owner voluntarily brought her into the state. Slavery could not exist in Massachusetts, except as regulated by the U.S. Constitution. The only person who could be treated as a slave in the state was a fugitive slave because the U.S. Constitution specifically provided for the return of fugitive slaves. Shaw speculated that a master might be able to cross a free state with a slave under some dire circumstances, or perhaps to return a fugitive slave to the South. But Med did not fall into this category. In offering this analysis of slave cases, Shaw noted that a number of Southern states, including Louisiana where Mary Slater and Med were from, accepted the principle that a slave became free if voluntarily taken by a master to a free state. He cited cases from both Louisiana and Kentucky showing that even the slave states understood that a slave voluntarily taken to a free jurisdiction would become free. He noted that in the British case *The Slave Grace* (1827), the High Court of Admiralty had ruled that a black who willingly went back to a slave jurisdiction after being brought to England could be re-enslaved. Shaw simply noted that this was not the case in the United States.

Commonwealth v. Aves proved to be a powerful antislavery precedent. In the next few years, most of the Northern states would accept the logic of Shaw's ruling: that slaves brought to free states would become free. Connecticut adopted this principle in *Jackson v. Bulloch* in 1837, while New York (1841) and Pennsylvania (1847) passed legislation declaring that all slaves brought into the state were immediately free. Ohio courts came to adopt this principle in 1841, and the Ohio Supreme Court confirmed this idea when it finally heard a case on the subject in 1856. By the eve of the Civil War, every Northern state except Indiana, Illinois, and New Jersey offered immediate freedom to any slave brought within its jurisdiction. By the eve of the Civil War, most Southern states no longer accepted the principles of *Aves* and *Somerset*. Thus, in Mississippi and Missouri courts rejected long-standing precedents and ruled that slaves did not become free if brought to free states. The Supreme Court affirmed their right to do this in *Strader v. Graham* (1851) and *Dred Scott v. Sandford* (1857). Indeed, if the Missouri Supreme Court had not reversed nearly thirty years of precedent in *Dred Scott*, the case would never have reached the Supreme Court because Scott, who won his freedom in a jury trial based on residence in a free territory and a free state, would have remained free.

While *Commonwealth v. Aves* was a victory for antislavery, it nevertheless raised some moral dilemmas. Mary Slater's husband owned Med's mother, who remained in Louisiana. Med was heartbroken when she found out that she would not be able to return to her mother and siblings in New Orleans. Instead, she was forced to remain in Massachusetts. The abolitionist women who brought the case took custody of Med. She was renamed Maria Somerset, after Maria Weston Chapman and the famous Somerset case. Eventually, she ended up in an orphanage, where some abolitionists tried to look out for her welfare.

Paul Finkelman

See also: Freedom Suits in North America.

Further Reading

Finkelman, Paul. *An Imperfect Union: Slavery, Federalism, and Comity.* Chapel Hill: University of North Carolina Press, 1981, reprint 2001.

Compromise of 1850

The Compromise of 1850, according to the hopes of its advocates, was to be a sectional compact between North and South that maintained the peace between the sections, much as the Missouri Compromise had since 1820. These hopes proved illusory. The Compromise of 1850 was, in the words of David Potter, more akin to an armistice than a lasting peace. Unlike the Missouri Compromise, which lasted for thirty-four years, the Compromise of 1850 began to break down shortly after its passage, due mostly to the aggravations caused by the Fugitive Slave Law of 1850, one of the elements of the Compromise of 1850.

A sectional compromise became necessary as a result of the Mexican War of 1846–1848. The United States had won a large section of northern Mexico as a result of the war. According to the terms of the Treaty of Guadalupe Hidalgo, the United States received present-day California, Arizona, New Mexico, and parts of Utah and Colorado from Mexico. The problem posed by slavery had become apparent during the war. David Wilmot, a freshman Democratic congressman from Pennsylvania, added an amendment to a military spending bill in 1846, which stipulated that slavery would not be allowed in any of the territories that the United States might win from Mexico. The Wilmot Proviso failed to win passage in the Senate, but its introduction sparked a political firestorm that had not been seen since the Missouri debates of 1819–1821. Southerners contended that this territory, won with the help of Southern money and the blood of soldiers from the South, should be open to slaveholders as well as non-slaveholders. A number of Northerners argued that Mexican law forbade slavery in the territory, but also that the territories should be reserved for free white labor, a key part of an ideology that quickly became known as Free Soil. Both sides championed liberty and freedom, but they defined these terms in different ways. Southerners argued that liberty and freedom meant the right to take slave property into the territories, unmolested by local abolitionist legislation. Upward mobility came from being able to purchase land and slaves and become a planter. Free Soilers argued that slavery hampered the ability of non-slaveholding white men to move upward in society because slaveholders purchased the best land, leaving lesser quality land to other white men. Thus planters had a monopoly of land, labor, economic gain, and cultural refinement. Moreover, the proximity of free labor to slave degraded the former. These two ideologies proved to be mutually exclusive when it came to the issue of the western territories.

The major source of contention between the two sides was California, which rapidly gained population as a result of the discovery of gold. Residents of California wished to enter the United States as a free state. At the time, however, there was an equal number of free and slave states. With the addition of California, the North would not only dominate the House of Representatives, but would also gain a majority in the Senate. Southerners had long feared becoming a minority section within the Union, because as a political minority it would be more difficult to protect slavery from antislavery legislation. These concerns led to fierce debate in Congress, which delayed California's entry into the Union. California was not the only concern. The Missouri Compromise line did not extend to the West Coast. What to do with the recently gained territories also became an issue of major concern.

Henry Clay, who had gained a reputation as the "great compromiser" for his work in 1820 and 1833, tried to solve the problems gripping North and South. As he had done in the Missouri Crisis, Clay formed a committee, the Committee of Thirteen, to study this problem and come up with compromise solutions. Clay and the committee attempted to solve all of the problems with an omnibus bill containing the following provisions: California would be admitted as a free state; New Mexico and Utah would be granted popular sovereignty to decide the slavery issue for themselves; the slave trade would be ended in the District of Columbia; the boundary dispute between Texas and New Mexico would be resolved, with New Mexico gaining land while Texas received monetary compensation for its losses; and there would be a new federal fugitive slave law to replace the original 1793 Fugitive Slave Act. The problem Clay faced was that the different provisions attracted too many enemies, and thus Congress rejected the omnibus bill. With the defeat of his bill, Clay left Congress in early August and returned later in the summer.

Prospects for sectional compromise appeared bleak during the period from May to early August 1850. President Zachary Taylor, a slave-holding Whig from Louisiana, staunchly supported California's admission to the Union as a free state. His death on July 9 would remove one major impediment from efforts to achieve a compromise, but other obstacles remained. Southern "fire-eaters" demanded immediate secession by the South in order to protect its rights, especially those associated with slavery. Radical abolitionists, such as William Lloyd Garrison, also supported disunionism, believing the Union would be better off without the stain of slavery.

Into this maelstrom stepped Senator Stephen Douglas, a Democrat from Illinois. He hoped to succeed where Clay had failed. His strategy was to shepherd through both houses of Congress the pieces of Clay's failed omnibus bill one at a time. Using this method allowed Douglas to build constituencies of support sufficiently strong to overcome the vociferous opposition that had doomed Clay's bill. The strategy worked. Throughout August and into the first week of September, with strong Democratic support and the absence of many Whig Senators on key votes, the separate pieces of legislation gained passage in both houses.

The Compromise of 1850 proved a palliative, rather than a lasting cure for sectional issues. Antislavery forces were pleased to see the slave trade, if not slavery, ended in the nation's capital. They were also pleased to see California admitted as a free state and Utah and New Mexico awarded popular sovereignty, believing as they did that the two latter territories would enter the Union as free states. The Fugitive Slave Law of 1850, however, had greater immediate impact on the North and antislavery advocates. This law forced Northerners to confront slavery face-to-face, because under the provisions of the act they had to help recapture fugitive slaves. Northerners thus became agents of the federal government, working on behalf of Southern slaveholders to help the latter recover their runaway property. The harsh features of the law angered many Northern whites, who feared their civil liberties were being eroded by this fugitive slave law. For free blacks and fugitive slaves, life after 1850 was filled with the dread possibility of recapture and enslavement. Nothing did more to aid the antislavery movement, and lead to Civil War, than this feature of the Compromise of 1850.

James C. Foley

See also: Clay, Henry; Democratic Party and Antislavery; Texas, Annexation of (1845); Whig Party and Antislavery.

Further Readings

Fehrenbacher, Don E. *The Slaveholding Republic: An Account of the United States Government's Relations to Slavery.* Completed and edited by Ward M. McAfee. New York: Oxford University Press, 2001.

Hamilton, Holman. *Prologue to Conflict: The Crisis and Compromise of 1850.* Lexington: University of Kentucky Press, 1964.

Potter, David M. *The Impending Crisis, 1848–1861.* Completed and edited by Don E. Fehrenbacher. New York: Harper & Row, 1976.

Confiscation Acts (1861, 1862)

The First and Second Confiscation Acts, passed during the American Civil War, contained the first provisions for freeing slaves in the rebellious states. The First Confiscation Act, signed by President Abraham Lincoln on August 6, 1861, authorized the president to seize any property used in "aiding, abetting, or promoting insurrection" if its owner permitted the use. The act also stated that anyone who used "the service or labor of any other person, under the laws of any State" to aid the rebellion, would lose any legal claim to that person's labor. While not explicitly authorizing emancipation, the provision was designed to liberate slaves. The First Confiscation Act directed seizures to be accomplished through *in rem* proceedings, a legal device for holding property, not its owner, guilty. This device entitled U.S. officials to condemn property without the owner's presence or other legal protections. Few actions were taken under the statute, however. President Lincoln worried that the act would antagonize the South and border states and did little to enforce it. Moreover, difficulties in proving that property had been used to aid rebellion prevented seizures of land and goods even when owned by known Confederates.

The Second Confiscation Act, signed into law on July 17, 1862, was intended to broaden the scope of the 1861 Act. The Second Confiscation Act authorized the taking of all property belonging to secessionists. Under the act, the president was authorized to seize the property of six classes of rebels and to condemn all land and goods of others who continued to aid the resistance sixty days after being warned publicly to desist. The statute instructed the president to use seized property to support the Union Army. Like the First Confiscation Act, the Second Act treated slaves separately from property. The statute stated that the slaves of those helping the rebellion would be "forever free of their servitude" if they reached the Union Army. Military officials also were prohibited from deciding the validity of claims to slaves.

The act offered few guarantees or specifics as to the status or future of those freed under the emancipation provision. Section 11 of the act authorized the president to employ African Americans "for the suppression of the rebellion," and the following section allowed him to make provisions for the voluntary colonization of those freed. Radical Republicans in Congress had wanted to distribute land seized under the act to African Americans. President Lincoln, however, forced the Radicals to abandon their plans, refusing to sign the act unless it limited the forfeiture of land to the natural life of the offender.

While the Second Confiscation Act expanded provisions of the 1861 law and added new and clearer language, enforcement of the Second Act also was problematic. Like the First Act, the Second Confiscation Act contained *in rem* procedures for forfeiture. The act, however, provided that confiscation proceedings for land should take place in the federal court with local jurisdiction. As courts could not operate in areas where fighting continued, it was nearly impossible to condemn real property.

The emancipation provisions also were difficult to implement. In liberating only the slaves of those aiding the rebellion, the act forced federal authorities to locate owners and find them guilty before their slaves could be legally freed. Moreover, as the military could not adjudicate claims to freedom, federal courts, which were not in session in much of the South, needed to hold that owners were rebels. Moreover, even if judges were sitting throughout the states in rebellion, emancipation would have required thousands of trials.

Military officials never enforced the provisions of the Second Confiscation Act related to emancipation, and less than $130,000 of property was seized under the act. Less than three months after signing the act, President Lincoln announced his preliminary emancipation proclamation on September 22, 1862.

Edward Daniels

See also: Lincoln, Abraham.

Further Readings

Donald, David Herbert. *Lincoln.* New York: Simon & Schuster, 1995.

Gerteis, Louis. *From Contraband to Freedman: Federal Policy toward Southern Blacks, 1861–1865.* Westport, CT: Greenwood, 1973.

Randall, James G. "Some Legal Aspects of the Confiscation Acts of the Civil War." *The American Historical Review* 18 (1912): 79–96.

Siddali, Silvana R. *From Property to Person: Slavery and the Confiscation Acts, 1861–1862.* Baton Rouge: Louisiana State University Press, 2005.

Syrett, John. *The Civil War Confiscation Acts: Failing to Reconstruct the South.* New York: Fordham University Press, 2005.

Congregationalism and Antislavery

Although many antislavery leaders sprang from Congregationalist religious backgrounds, the decentralized and lay-centered nature of Congregationalism prevented the denomination from ever taking a united stand against the "peculiar institution." Confined largely to New England and the states of the Old Northwest, few Congregationalists held slaves, and most clergy and laity in the antebellum era certainly disapproved of the practice. Nonetheless, Congregationalist churches seldom took strong antislavery stands, and most church leaders sought to distance themselves from organized abolitionism.

During the colonial era, Congregational clergymen constituted part of the elite "standing order" that governed New England society, and, as such, they generally shared a genteel lifestyle that often included domestic servants. A few ministers discountenanced slavery, such as Boston's Samuel Sewall (1652–1730), who, in 1700, published "The Selling of Joseph," the first antislavery tract written in America. But it was far more common for Congregationalist ministers to tolerate slaveholding, and some owned slaves themselves.

The influential theologian Jonathan Edwards (1703–1758), pastor of the Church in Northampton, Massachusetts, and a leading apologist for the Great Awakening, owned several slaves in his lifetime. His views were typical of Congregationalist clergymen of his generation. Like the great contemporary revivalist George Whitefield, who also owned several slaves, Edwards came to regard the African slave trade as an evil, in part because he believed it impeded evangelical missionary work. But he never identified slaveholding per se as sin, and never questioned the legitimacy of owning American-born slaves so long as masters treated them humanely and gave them Christian instruction.

Some of Edwards's "New Divinity" students and intellectual heirs developed a radical antislavery theological stance during the Revolutionary era. This may have had more to do with local circumstances and personal experience coupled with the heightened awareness of the tension between slavery and liberty fueled by the revolutionary struggle than anything intrinsic to Edwardsean logic. For example, Samuel Hopkins (1721–1803), perhaps the most influential of Edwards's many pupils, served the church in Great Barrington, Massachusetts, for a quarter of a century without advocating antislavery and for a time owned a slave. Then in 1769, Hopkins moved to Newport, Rhode Island, where he saw firsthand the brutality of the slave trade. He soon emerged as a passionate foe of both the slave trade and slaveholding. In 1776, Hopkins wrote a fiery antislavery address to the Continental Congress, denouncing slavery as sin.

Hopkins argued that the mark of a true Christian is first and foremost "disinterested benevolence" toward all beings, a readiness to set aside sinful self-interest for the sake of others. Christian slaveholders could not pursue their own liberty and rights while refusing it to others. In 1784, Hopkins led his Newport congregation in barring all slaveholders from communion. His position was embraced by many other New Divinity clergy of the Revolutionary era, including Levi Hart (1738–1808) and Jonathan Edwards Jr. (1745–1801), who in 1790 played a key role in founding the Connecticut Society for the Promotion of Freedom. Virtually all of the founding members of this early antislavery organization were Edwardsean Congregationalist clergy or lay leaders such as Noah Webster.

Despite the strong antislavery currents in late eighteenth-century Congregationalist circles, it did not develop into a consistent opposition to slavery during the antebellum years. Over time evangelical Congregationalist ministers became increasingly conservative, turning their attention to the conversion of individual souls rather than social action to end injustice. Generally they were far more likely to support gradualism and the work of the American Colonization Society than immediate abolition. Nonetheless, during the early nineteenth century, individual Congregationalist ministers and sometimes local ministerial associations did take strong stands against slavery, and a handful became committed abolitionist reformers. Among those ministers who took openly abolitionist stands were Owen Lovejoy, pastor of the Congregational Church in Princeton, Illinois; Henry Ward Beecher, the nationally famous pastor of Plymouth Church in Brooklyn, New York; and John Payne Cleveland of Providence, Rhode Island.

The Congregationalist churches lacked any national ecclesiastical structure, and thus chose to conduct their mission work primarily through interdenominational evangelical organizations like the American Home Missionary Society (AHMS) and the American Board of Commissioners for Foreign Missions (ABCFM). These associations drew financial support and recruits from Southern Presbyterian churches, and feared the divisiveness of organized abolition. Andover Seminary, the single largest theological school in antebellum America and the alma mater of many Congregationalist ministers across the United States, likewise drew students and financial support from every region of the republic. Although the Congregationalist faculty of Andover all supported the cause of colonization, they adamantly opposed the work of the American Anti-Slavery Society (AASS) and prohibited students from engaging in organized abolitionism on campus.

The reluctance of the Congregational churches to embrace abolitionism caused a crisis of conscience for many radicals who had been reared in the tradition. Some, like the Reverend Stephen Symonds Foster (1809–1881), a prominent lecturer for the AASS, followed William Lloyd Garrison in leaving the church and moving toward a more secular humanitarianism. In 1843, Foster penned one of the most effective tracts ever issued by the AASS, *The Brotherhood of Thieves, or A True Picture of the American Church*, a searing critique of the complicity of the nation's evangelical Christians in the sin of slavery. Other Congregationalist abolitionists, such as the lay reformer Lewis Tappan, never gave up their attachment to the church of their fathers or their hopes that it would eventually become an engine of social change. In the 1846, Tappan was instrumental in launching the American Missionary Association (AMA) as an antislavery rival to the AHMS and ABCFM. Accepting no funds from proslavery churches, the AMA was ostensibly nonsectarian but actually drew most of its support from antislavery Congregationalists. Although the new organization grew rapidly and soon funded numerous missions in both the United States and abroad, it never received the united backing of America's Congregationalist clergy.

James R. Rohrer

See also: Antislavery Evangelical Protestantism; New England Antislavery Society (NEASS).

Further Readings

Duncan, Troy, and Chris Dixon. "Denouncing the Brotherhood of Thieves: Stephen Symonds Foster's Critique of the Anti-Abolitionist Clergy." *Civil War History* 47 (2001): 97–117.

Kaplan, Sidney, ed. "'The Selling of Joseph': Samuel Sewall and the Iniquity of Slavery." In *American Studies in Black and White*. Amherst: University of Massachusetts Press, 1991, pp. 3–18.

Lovejoy, David. "Samuel Hopkins: Religion, Slavery, and the Revolution." *New England Quarterly* 40 (1967): 227–243.

McKivigan, John R. *The War against Proslavery Religion: Abolitionism and the Northern Churches*. Ithaca, NY: Cornell University Press, 1984.

Minkema, Kenneth P. "Jonathan Edwards on Slavery and the Slave Trade." *William and Mary Quarterly* 54 (1997): 823–834.

Minkema, Kenneth P. "Jonathan Edwards's Defense of Slavery." *The Massachusetts Historical Review* 4. NA (2002) http://www.historycooperative.org/journals/mhr/4/minkema.html.

Saillant, John. "Slavery and Divine Providence in New England Calvinism: The New Divinity and a Black Protest, 1775–1805." *New England Quarterly* 68 (1995): 584–608.

Thompson, J. Earl. "Abolitionism and Theological Education at Andover." *New England Quarterly* 47 (1974): 238–261.

Congressional Debate on Ending U.S. Atlantic Slave Trade

The U.S. Constitution allowed Congress to abolish the nation's involvement with the Atlantic slave trade as early as 1808, but did not guarantee that Congress would do so. In the end, Congress outlawed the practice by an overwhelming vote. Yet the crafting of the measure was riddled with sharp and revealing disputes between the North and South. What was said in these debates illustrated the danger of broaching subjects related to slavery and foreshadowed elements of later, more famous, controversies.

The disputes ranged throughout the second session of the Ninth Congress, from December 1806 to March 1807. A clear pattern emerged. While there was broad consensus behind abolishing the African slave trade, certain provisions of the bill provoked heated disagreements. The three most controversial issues were: what to do with blacks brought illegally to America; the penalty for violating the law; and whether the federal government could regulate the *domestic* seaborne slave trade. Although the divisions were sectional, Southerners carried all but the last point by gaining cooperation from Northerners.

How to deal with illegally imported people was the first question debated at length and showed the depth of sectional differences. A select committee reported a bill stipulating that persons of color imported after 1807 would be forfeited by the smuggler. James Sloan of New Jersey moved that the government liberate anyone thus forfeited. Southerners objected based on their fear of letting free blacks loose in the South. As he would at other times, Peter Early of Georgia elucidated the extreme form of the Southern position. He declared that a large number of freed black people in the South would inevitably lead to race war.

Many Northerners countered that should the federal government sell the contraband blacks as slaves, the taint of the slave trade would attach to the government. Others objected to the whole idea of the government confiscating human beings, for "the idea of forfeiture" relied on the "false principle" "that a property may be had in human beings." Early and his fellow Southerners perceived in such objections an attack on slavery itself. The principle behind these Northern objections, Early and others declared, "might in its effects strike at all the property held in slaves; . . . consequently it became their duty to resist it."

This question strained the spirit of compromise, but did not break it, at least for some Northerners. Timothy Pitkin of Connecticut, for one, declared that he would not consent to a provision confiscating human beings, "unless *absolute necessity* should require it." Passing a bill abolishing the Atlantic slave trade was clearly an "*absolute necessity*" in the North, and thus the bill ended with a compromise favorable to the South. The law decreed that the government would confiscate captured slave ships, but would deliver their human cargo to state authorities to be dealt with as they saw fit. The government would thus avoid directly countenancing property in man, but Southern officials would surely sell them into slavery. Meanwhile, Southerners received assurance that an intrusive federal government would not turn loose thousands of Africans or West Indians to slaughter or be slaughtered. Despite the strong sectional rhetoric, the South gained a victory with crucial Northern acquiescence.

Another heated exchange centered on the appropriate punishments for violations of the law. John Smilie of Pennsylvania began it by declaring captains of slave vessels guilty of "one of the highest crimes man could commit." Participation in the slave trade, he reasoned, should be a felony punishable by death. Other Northerners echoed this argument, forcing Southern representatives to defend not only slavers but all Southerners who had bought or sold human beings. They tried to defend the slave trade from complete moral stigma, although not as a positive good. They could not quite bring themselves to say that the trade was *moral*, only that it was not *immoral*.

The morality of the slave trade, and of slavery by implication, was the heart of the matter. Yet once again some Yankees backed the victorious Southern position. The act ultimately decreed a fine up to $10,000 and two to four years' imprisonment. It was not until 1820 that Congress affixed the death penalty to smuggling foreign slaves into the United States.

None other than Peter Early sparked the final debate over a provision of the bill when he proposed an amendment exempting from prohibition the seaborne slave trade between states. From this point forward, John Randolph took Early's place in the Southern vanguard, seeking to prevent Congress from setting any dangerous precedents. He objected that meddling with the internal traffic might someday "be made the pretext of universal emancipation." He also threatened to lead the secession of the South. "If the law went into force as it was," he warned, "he, for one, would say, if the Constitution is thus to be violated let us secede, and go home." Despite Randolph's threats, Congress voted along sectional lines to outlaw the coastwise internal trade, if only in vessels under forty tons. The North had won a qualified victory, a rarity in these proceedings.

There were signs of consensus on this bill throughout its legislative history. A straight-up vote in the House on whether to abolish the foreign slave trade produced a margin of 113–5 in favor. Jefferson signed the ban into law March 3, 1807, one day after Congress passed it. But these signs of unanimity obscured the deep fissures the debate over the specifics had revealed. The arguments in relation to this bill demonstrated the divisive potential of discussing slavery, for they featured forays into comments on slavery itself. It proved nearly impossible to discuss the slave trade without discussing the peculiar institution itself. As the players engaged this issue, many of the arguments prominent in later, more famous, controversies received attention and elucidation. The slave trade debates, then, have a place in the story of America's unfolding sectional drama.

Matthew Mason

See also: Atlantic Slave Trade and British Abolition.

Further Readings

Annals of the Congress of the United States, Ninth Congress, Second Session. Washington: Gales and Seaton, 1852.

Donnan, Elizabeth. *Documents Illustrative of the Slave Trade to America.* Carnegie Institution of Washington, 1932; reprint, New York: Octagon Books, 1965.

Du Bois, W.E.B. *The Suppression of the African Slave-Trade to the United States of America, 1638–1870.* 1898; reprint, New York: Russell and Russell, 1965.

Kaminski, John P. *A Necessary Evil? Slavery and the Debate over the Constitution.* Madison, WI: Madison House, 1995.

Locke, Mary Staughton. *Anti-Slavery in America from the Introduction of African Slaves to the Prohibition of the Slave-Trade.* Boston: Ginn and Company, 1901; reprint, Johnson Reprint Corporation, 1968.

Mason, Matthew E. "Slavery Overshadowed: Congress Debates Prohibiting the Atlantic Slave Trade to the United States, 1806–1807." *Journal of the Early Republic* 20 (Spring 2000): 59–81.

Robinson, Donald L. *Slavery in the Structure of American Politics, 1765–1820.* New York: Harcourt Brace Jovanovich, 1971.

Contrabands

During the U.S. Civil War, enslaved people who came into contact with Union forces were popularly known as "contrabands." This unusual moniker had its origin during the earliest days of the war, when three enslaved men sought protection at Union-occupied Fortress Monroe, in coastal Virginia. The Union commander, General Benjamin Butler, faced a quandary. The federal government's policy of

Contrabands arriving at the Union camp in Virginia during the Civil War. Escaped slaves who fled north to Union lines during the Civil War were first termed "contraband" by Major General Benjamin Butler, who refused to obey the laws of states that had seceded from the Union and therefore would not send the slaves back. (Library of Congress)

upholding the property rights of slaveholders obliged Butler to relinquish the men to their owner. Yet Butler knew that if the men were released, they would be forced to labor for the Confederacy, whereas if they stayed at Fortress Monroe, they could perform valuable work for the Union. Butler therefore declared the fugitives to be legally confiscated property, or "contraband of war," a move that provided a legal veneer for holding the men. The term quickly entered the popular lexicon, often shortened simply to "contraband."

The term contraband captured the fugitive slaves' ambiguous status during the first year and a half of the war. Indeed, as Union forces pushed into heavily populated plantation regions of the Confederacy early in 1862, the Union government had no organized policy toward the thousands of slaves with whom they came into contact. Contrabands became indispensable to the Union war effort. Throughout the Confederacy, they pressed toward Union lines, searching for freedom, and hoping to aid the Union. The earliest escapees were able-bodied men, whom the Union employed in a variety of ways, including building fortifications, caring for draft animals, staffing ships, and attending Union officers. Women also found employment as laundresses and food purveyors. Fugitives offered the Union not only their labor, but also invaluable information about unfamiliar terrain, Confederate positions, and Southern civilian morale.

Responding to political and military pressures in the fall of 1862, the Union government began establishing contraband camps, most of which were located within the seceded states. The camps were designed as hubs for government and philanthropic efforts to house, feed, school, and employ both displaced fugitives and slaves whose homes had come behind Union lines due to the advance of Union forces. The organization of contraband camps was also meant to reassure white Northerners that the Emancipation Proclamation (announced in September 1862) would not result in a massive northward migration of freed people.

Residents of contraband camps often suffered from exposure, disease, malnutrition, and abusive treatment by soldiers. Yet the camps were also places where people escaping bondage could reconstitute families, organize communities, earn a livelihood, debate politics, and begin to build their lives in freedom. Many had their first experiences with wage labor in and around the camps. The Union government employed contrabands not only in military labor, but also on abandoned and leased plantations. Indeed, at least 474,000 former slaves and free blacks participated in some form of government-sponsored free labor in the Union-occupied South. In regions where many former bondsmen joined the Union Army, contraband camps became homes for the women, children, and elderly members of soldiers' families. As the Emancipation Proclamation, the Union victory, and finally the Thirteenth Amendment made their status more secure, the contrabands of the Civil War became the freedmen of the postwar period.

Kate Masur

See also: Lincoln, Abraham.

Further Readings

Berlin, Ira, et al. *Slaves No More: Three Essays on Emancipation and the Civil War.* New York and Cambridge: Cambridge University Press, 1992.

Berlin, Ira, et al. *The Wartime Genesis of Free Labor: The Upper South. Freedom: A Documentary History of Emancipation, 1861–1867.* ser. 1, vol. 2. New York and Cambridge: Cambridge University Press, 1993.

Gerteis, Louis. *From Contraband to Freedman: Federal Policy toward Southern Blacks, 1861–1865.* Westport, CT: Greenwood Press, 1973.

Crandall, Prudence

White American abolitionist educator Prudence Crandall was born into a Quaker family in Hopkinton, Rhode Island, on September 3, 1803. She grew up in eastern Connecticut, in the town of Canterbury, and returned to Rhode Island to attend the

New England Yearly Meeting Boarding School from 1826 through 1830. Upon completing her studies, Crandall started teaching in Connecticut in 1830—exactly where is not clear—and converted to the Baptists. In late 1831, the village leaders in Canterbury endorsed her as principal for a female boarding school in the town. In September 1832, a local black woman, Sarah Harris, whose father, William Harris, served as local agent for the *Liberator*, asked Crandall if she could attend the school. When Crandall agreed, white villagers objected to having their daughters in the school, despite the fact that Sarah Harris had attended common schools with these same girls. When white parents withdrew their daughters, Crandall drew up a bold new plan. She sought the aid of Boston's William Lloyd Garrison, the editor of the radical antislavery newspaper, the *Liberator*, which had been supplied to her by her household assistant, Mariah Davis, a black woman from Boston who was affianced to Sarah Harris's brother, Charles.

With the active encouragement of Garrison and a racially integrated list of sponsors, Crandall reopened her school in April 1833, welcoming a class of black women and girls, most from the urban centers of the North. During the year and a half her school was open, twenty-one students are known to have attended, including Julia Williams, future wife of Henry Highland Garnet, Sarah Harris (who, with her husband, George Fayerweather, aided abolitionists in Rhode Island), and her sister Mary Harris, who would teach freedmen in Louisiana after the Civil War.

Crandall aimed to prepare black women to be teachers; her curriculum was among the most intellectually challenging for women prior to that offered them by Oberlin College in Ohio.

Abolitionists, led by Samuel Joseph May, a Unitarian minister in nearby Brooklyn, Connecticut, gave substantial support. Arthur Tappan assisted financially, and Garrison made the case famous through his press coverage. William Harris, Frederick Olney, and David Ruggles championed the school in the local African American community. What assured the school's fame, however, was the opposition it met. Even prior to its opening, the town leaders, directed by Andrew Judson, tried to block the school. A law was passed by the state legislature making it illegal to instruct blacks who were from out-of-state. This "Black law" was used to arrest Crandall. She intentionally endured a night in prison in June 1833 to draw attention to the case. Three separate trials were held. The first ended in a mistrial, while the second, adjudicated by the noted colonizationist David Daggett, led to her conviction. Her lawyers, who based their argument on a bold reading of the Constitution that assumed black citizenship, appealed. Although the state Court of Errors ultimately overturned the conviction, it did so on a technicality and refused to rule on the substantive issues at hand.

Vigilante violence and rude insults were daily fare at Crandall's Academy. Local people, including doctors, clergymen, and merchants, often refused to help the school. White youths threatened the students when they dared to stroll Canterbury's streets. The school building weathered incidents from egging to the fouling of the well water.

In August 1834, despite the misgivings of her friends, Crandall married Calvin Philleo (1787–1874), a Baptist minister and widower with three children to raise. Having a husband did not protect Crandall or her students from the anger of her frustrated enemies. Their legal avenues against Crandall exhausted, bitter townspeople viciously attacked her school on the night of September 9, rendering it uninhabitable. The next day, the school was closed.

Crandall's husband moved their family to Boonville, New York, where Prudence was unable to help when her brother, Reuben, was put on trial in Washington, D.C., for simply having copies of the *Liberator* in his luggage; he died in 1838 from the effects of his imprisonment. While Crandall enjoyed raising her stepchildren, her husband was a petty tyrant who sniped at her and tried to limit her reading material. In the 1840s, she made a few attempts to assert her independence from him, settling on land her father had purchased near Troy Grove in north central Illinois. By 1847, she permanently relocated to Illinois, and did some informal teaching of local farmers' children. During the Civil War she helped distribute abolitionist pamphlets written by her stepdaughter's husband, Charles Whipple.

When her husband died in 1874 after a protracted illness, Crandall and her older brother, Hezekiah, moved to Kansas in 1877. Here they homesteaded in Elk Falls, and Crandall became locally famous as an advocate of women's rights, temperance, and, most prominently, spiritualism. She was the center of an active spiritualist network in southeastern Kansas, to the extent that no local Protestant minister would deliver her funeral oration. The Connecticut legislature, prodded by novelist Samuel Clemens and descendants of her Canterbury persecutors, granted Crandall a pension in 1886, to compensate for her sufferings fifty years prior. She died on January 28, 1890.

Crandall's Academy recruited many to the abolitionist cause, and demonstrated a high degree of cooperation among abolitionist forces—black and white, New England and New York, male and female. The contrast between Crandall's benevolence and the prejudice of her opponents dramatically unmasked the agenda of the colonizationists, vindicating the criticisms that free blacks and white abolitionists had made concerning the goals and tactics of colonization. The arguments of her lawyers for black citizenship have been considered progressive, and similar ones were deployed in the landmark *Brown v. Topeka Board of Education* decision in 1953. The crucial roles of free blacks and of women in establishing and maintaining Crandall's school deserve greater attention. Her school in Canterbury is now open as a museum.

Jennifer Rycenga

See also: Garrisonians.

Further Readings

Abdy, E. S. *Journal of a Residence and Tour in the United States of North America, April, from 1833, to October, 1834.* 3 vols. London: John Murray.

Davis, Rodney O. 1835. "Prudence Crandall, Spiritualism, and Populist Era Reform in Kansas." *Kansas History* 3, 4 (Winter 1980): 239–254.

Foner, Philip S. and Josephine F. Pacheco. *Three Who Dared: Prudence Crandall, Margaret Douglass, Myrtilla Miner—Champions of Antebellum Black Education.* Westport, CT: Greenwood Press, 1984.

Friedman, Lawrence J. "Racism and Sexism in Antebellum America: The Prudence Crandall Episode Reconsidered." *Societas* 4, 3 (Summer 1974): 211–227.

Garrison, Wendell Phillips. "Connecticut in the Middle Ages." *Century* 30 (September 1885): 780–786.

Martineau, Harriet. *The Martyr Age of the United States of America.* Boston: Weeks, Jordan and Co., 1839.

May, Samuel J. *Some Recollections of our Antislavery Conflict.* Boston: Fields, Osgood, and Company. Reprinted New York: Arno Press, 1968.

Mayer, Henry. *All on Fire: William Lloyd Garrison and the Abolition of Slavery.* New York: St. Martin's Press, 1998.

Strane, Susan. *A Whole-Souled Woman: Prudence Crandall and the Education of Black Women.* New York: W.W. Norton and Company, 1990.

Welch, Marvis Olive. *Prudence Crandall: A Biography.* Manchester, CT: Jason Publishers, 1983.

Creole Affair (1841)

The *Creole* was an American intercoastal trading vessel owned by Johnson and Eperson of Richmond, Virginia, and captained by Robert Ensor. On the evening of October 25, 1841, the ship set sail from Richmond bound for New Orleans carrying a cargo of tobacco and slaves. There were at least 135 slaves on board and ten crew members. On the evening of November 7, first mate Zephaniah Gifford was informed by a slave that some of the other slaves had gone down aft with the female slaves who were being kept separately. At about 9:00 P.M., William Merritt was sent to investigate. When Merritt had the hatch removed from the hold for inspection, a slave named Madison Washington seized the opportunity to climb the ladder and make for the deck, calling on other slaves to help him. In the ensuing struggle, Captain Ensor was severely wounded and sailor John Hewell was killed. By about 1:00 A.M., Washington and nineteen other male slaves were in full control of the ship. Washington and the slaves initially wanted to sail for Liberia, but Merritt convinced them that, owing to insufficient provisions, the Bahamas were a more practical choice. Although Merritt was put in charge of the vessel, second mate Lucious Stevens was pressed into service as the navigator. On November 9, the ship arrived in Nassau. Before the vessel entered the harbor, Washington had all weapons collected and thrown overboard.

In harbor, first mate Gifford requested that the ship be guarded so that none of the slaves responsible for the murder of Hewell might go ashore. With the help of American counsel John Bacon, Gifford requested an interview with Governor Francis Cockburn, who sent a detachment of soldiers to take control of the vessel. This gave Cockburn a chance to determine the question of jurisdiction in the matter. The final official British position was that any slaves implicated in the murder would be detained, possibly to be remanded into custody of the American government. Any other slaves deemed blameless in the matter would be freed.

The final provision of the British decision did not please Bacon who, along with mates Gifford, Stevens, and a Captain Woodbine of the American ship *Louisa,* decided to retake the *Creole*. The attempt failed and British authorities decided at that point to cease taking depositions from those on board. Cockburn then directed Attorney General George Anderson to proceed to the ship with policemen, remove the troops and prisoners, and allow the remaining slaves to come ashore. Bacon reported back to Secretary of State Daniel Webster that he had been prevented from taking custody of the slaves remaining on the vessel by the British authorities and a mob on shore. On November 14, Bacon issued an official protest, citing the position he maintained in future dispatches. He contended that the slaves, as property, were legal cargo being transported under the American flag. The British government had no right to interfere with the officers of the vessel in the performance of their duties and cause the subsequent loss of property. He requested that the fugitives being held in custody be returned to American authorities and sent to New Orleans for trial. Cockburn, awaiting instructions from London, declined Bacon's request.

The *Creole* was subsequently released and arrived in New Orleans on December 2, unleashing a diplomatic firestorm. The question for Southern slave owners was whether or not British authorities could confiscate the property of Americans without their consent. Webster sent a dispatch to American minister to London Edward Everett demanding the return of the slaves and invoking the "comity of nations." In the U.S. Congress some Southern politicians threatened a retaliatory strike against the Bahamas. President John Tyler increased tensions by releasing the letters of Counsel Bacon, and the crew depositions that supported Bacon, to Congress. There was a very real possibility that the *Creole* incident would poison Anglo-American diplomacy. Tyler's lingering concerns over safe passage in the Bahama Channel and extradition insinuated their way into the negotiations for the Webster-Ashburton Treaty, delaying a resolution of the border between Maine and Canada.

Legal questions regarding the *Creole* incident required eleven years to resolve. In the case of at least seven insurance claims related to the *Creole*, courts only found the insurance companies liable in two cases. Judge Henry Adams Bullard of the Louisiana Supreme Court ruled that the slaves had not been lost through the negligence of British authorities. In fact, the vessel had been guarded at Counsel Bacon's request, and no complaint had been made until an attempt was made to retake the vessel. In short, the insurrection of the slaves broke up the voyage, not British authorities. Four other cases finding the insurance companies not liable cited almost identical findings. In 1853, the Anglo-American Claims Commission awarded the United States $110,330 for the loss of slave property.

As far as the slaves on board the *Creole* went, many were sent to Jamaica within a month of the ship's arrival in Nassau. As for those detained by the British government, two died in prison, and the rest were released. In the opinion of British legal experts, slaves seeking their freedom were not pirates and could not be held. And what of Webster's invocation of comity? Great Britain had outlawed slavery in 1832, and therefore slavery was not legally recognized in that nation. Recognition of comity in cases of extradition requires that a cooperating nation not find the law it is enforcing in the name of another nation to be offensive. Not having slavery, the British were under no obligation to honor American requests for extradition of the mutineers.

Stephen P. Budney

See also: *Amistad.*

Further Readings

Jervey, Edward D., and Huber, C. Harold. "The Creole Affair." *Journal of Negro History* 65 (Summer 1980): 196–211.

Jones, Wilbur Devereux. "The Influence of Slavery on the Webster-Ashburton Negotiations." *Journal of Southern History* 22 (1956): 48–58.

D

Declaration of Independence (1776)

Leading the rebellion of thirteen North American colonies against English rule, the Second Continental Congress formed a committee in June 1776 to compose a formal declaration of independence. Thomas Jefferson took the lead, leaving the other committee members—John Adams, Benjamin Franklin, Roger Sherman, and Robert Livingstone—the task of suggesting modifications. In early July, the Congress debated and altered the committee's draft, promulgating the Declaration on July 4. Beginning in early August, representatives from all the rebellious colonies signed the document. Jefferson later published the document the committee presented to Congress. The Declaration intersected the history of abolitionism in several ways.

Jefferson's draft contained a paragraph criticizing King George III for promoting the trade in slaves. Congress deleted this critique, which read as follows:

> he has waged cruel war against human nature itself, violating it's [*sic*] most sacred rights of life & liberty in the persons of a distant people who never offended him, captivating & carrying them into slavery in another hemisphere, or to incur miserable death in their transportation hither. This piratical warfare, the opprobrium of *infidel* powers, is the warfare of the *CHRISTIAN* king of Great Britain. Determined to keep open a market where MEN should be bought & sold he has prostituted his negative for suppressing every legislative attempt to prohibit or to restrain this execrable commerce: and that this assemblage of horrors might want no fact of distinguished die, he is now exciting those very people to rise in arms among us, and to purchase that liberty of which *he* has deprived them, by murdering the people upon whom *he* also obtruded them; thus paying off former crimes against the *liberties* of one people, with crimes which he urges them to commit against the *lives* of another.

105

Patriots in the Southern colonies did fear that slaves were responding to an offer made in 1775 to gain liberty by joining the English forces. Yet it was unrealistic to blame George III for the slave trade, for the trade predated his ascension to the throne and many colonists were traders and purchasers of slaves. Nonetheless Jefferson's words do suggest discomfort with the trade. Indeed the documents of the Continental Congresses do contain many cautions and reservations about slavery. Jefferson later recalled that the Congress excised his critique of the slave trade in order not to offend the delegates from slave trading and slaveholding areas. It is just as likely that many delegates disapproved of slavery but were unwilling to make a public pronouncement on it in the Declaration.

The Declaration was printed and disseminated. Many Americans first heard it in public readings. It is clear that some phrases inspired African Americans of the 1770s: "We hold these Truths to be self-evident, that all Men are created equal, that they are endowed by their Creator with certain unalienable Rights, that among these are Life, Liberty, and the Pursuit of Happiness." Particularly in the mid-Atlantic and the New England colonies, black men responded to this claim of equality, serving as patriots in the militia or the Continental Army and believing that the new nation to rise out of the War of Independence would be committed to an equality of rights. Legislation, constitutional statements, and judicial decisions did begin to end slavery in the North during the Revolutionary era, but a true equality of rights was not achieved.

The English philosopher John Locke has often been cited as an inspiration for the Declaration. Indeed, Locke's thoughts on rights and government were representative of an English tradition that was well known in the colonies. Locke himself, however, penned documents for colonial South Carolina that authorized slavery there. Yet one of Locke's concerns—property—was relevant to opposition to slavery and blacks' efforts to free themselves. For Locke, property was not only an object but also a skill or an ability such as literacy or craft. In the late eighteenth and early nineteenth centuries, more and more African Americans, even if enslaved, were acquiring property in the form of such marketable skills. Freedom was attractive at least partly because black men and women expected to be able to support themselves, their families, and their social institutions by exercising their skills in the marketplace. Today we usually think of property as physical, but if we want to understand that Americans, black as well as white, of the Revolutionary era were intent on the protection of their education, abilities, and skills, we should refer to Locke.

Finally, the Declaration, in the very phrases that inspired African Americans of the 1770s, became a focus of antebellum debate on slavery. In 1848, John C. Calhoun, a defender of slavery, argued that Jefferson's famous phrases were erroneous and irrelevant to the act of separating from England. In 1858, Abraham

Lincoln and Stephen A. Douglas, campaigning for nomination in the Illinois senatorial race, debated the meaning of the Declaration. Lincoln asserted that Jefferson had properly identified self-evident truths, that people remain convinced and moved by those phrases of the Declaration, and that they applied to blacks as well as whites. Although he believed that blacks might be inferior to whites in some ways, Lincoln insisted that both races—he also included the Indian—were equal in rights. Douglas would support Lincoln and the Union cause after hostilities commenced in early 1861 (he died later that year), but in 1858 he still believed in state sovereignty and compromise between North and South. He responded to Lincoln by satirizing him as a friend to blacks and by denying that the equality noted in the Declaration applied to blacks. Douglas, not Lincoln, won the Senate election, but the debates enhanced Lincoln's national reputation and helped set the stage for his victory in the 1860 presidential contest.

John Saillant

See also: U.S. Constitution and Antislavery.

Further Readings

Brion Davis, David. *The Problem of Slavery in the Age of Revolution, 1770–1823*. Ithaca, NY: Cornell University Press, 1975.

Jayne, Allen. *Jefferson's Declaration of Independence: Origins, Philosophy, and Theology*. Lexington: University Press of Kentucky, 1998.

Quarles, Benjamin. *The Negro in the American Revolution*. Chapel Hill: The University of North Carolina Press, 1961.

Delany, Martin Robison (1812–1885)

Martin Robison Delany was a prominent African American leader during the nineteenth century as an abolitionist, author, black nationalist, and a major in the Civil War.

Martin Delany was born in Charlestown, Virginia (now West Virginia), to a slave father and a free black mother. Since his mother had free status, Delany was legally free as well. Although denied the right to attend a school, Delany relentlessly pursued his education. In 1822, his family moved to Chambersburg, Pennsylvania, to escape the consequence of this illegal activity. In 1831, Delany departed to Pittsburgh to further his education and met John Vashon, a wealthy businessman who became his ideological mentor. Delany decided that he wanted to become a doctor to prove that blacks were capable of engaging in this profession, one traditionally denied to them.

In 1843, Delany practiced medicine. However, Delany was a man of indefatigable energy with varied interests. From 1843 to 1847, he founded and published the *Pittsburgh Mystery*. In 1847, Frederick Douglass invited Delany to work with him on the new antislavery weekly newspaper, the *North Star*. From 1847 to 1849, Delany served as coeditor and lecturer for the *North Star*. In 1850 and 1851, Delany attended Harvard Medical School.

In 1856, Delany moved his family to Chatham, Canada, where John Brown, the radical abolitionist, unsuccessfully sought Delany's support for an armed campaigned against slavery. Delany instead pursued plans for African American emigration. Delany had become disillusioned that black people could attain freedom and equality with their white counterparts in North America. Despite his new interest in emigration, Delany opposed the American Colonization Society's program because he believed that it was designed by the slave owners to rid America of free blacks. In 1859, Delany traveled to Liberia and Abeokuta (modern-day Nigeria), where he negotiated a treaty with the Alake to permit settlement for African Americans. Delany also conceived an economic scheme to undermine the South's economy, which was heavily dependent on cotton production by slaves, by growing cotton with free African labor.

With the onset of the Civil War, Delany saw the opportunities for blacks and became a recruiting officer in Massachusetts for blacks to join the Union Army. In 1865, Delany was promoted to a major and sent to South Carolina as a field commander, making him the first African American to attain such a high position. After the Civil War, Delany worked for Freedmen's Bureau in South Carolina to help former slaves reintegrate into the New South and held political office during Reconstruction.

Although Delany supported the Republican Party, in 1876 Delany endorsed the South Carolina Democratic gubernatorial candidate, Wade Hampton, III, who was a wealthy former slave owner. With the Democratic Party's victory, segregation would become the norm in the South. With no political office and facing old age, Delany slowly retreated from the political scene, devoting most of his time to writing.

Lumumba H. Shabaka

See also: Free Produce Movement; Radical Republicans.

Further Readings

Adeleke, Tunde. *Without Regard to Race: The Other Martin Robison Delany*. Jackson: University Press of Mississippi, 2003.

Delany, Martin R. *Martin R. Delany: A Documentary Reader*. Edited by Robert S. Levine. Chapel Hill: University of North Carolina Press, 2003.

Ullman, Victor. *Martin R. Delany: The Beginnings of Black Nationalism*. Boston: Beacon Press, 1971.

Democratic Party and Antislavery

Though the Democratic Party contributed important members and ideas to the anti-slavery movement, the party's antebellum policies were consistently proslavery. Those policies would encourage the birth of the antislavery Republican Party in 1854 and contribute to the coming of the Civil War. By the 1850s, most Southern Democrats interpreted the Constitution as a proslavery document that enabled slavery's expansion into federal territories. Institutionally, the party's core strength among Southern voters and its requirement of a two-thirds majority to select candidates in party caucuses blunted the power of the party's majority Northern wing. As a result, antislavery ideas and candidates failed to gain prominence in the party.

Still, individual Democrats did make important antislavery contributions. Ohio's Salmon P. Chase argued that the Constitution failed to recognize slavery in federal jurisdictions, giving Congress the power to prohibit slavery in the nation's territories. In August 1848, Pennsylvania congressman David Wilmot employed Chase's doctrine in the so-called Wilmot Proviso, which sought to prohibit slavery in territories gained in the Mexican War. However, Chase and Wilmot found little support among fellow Democrats.

Instead, their party embraced proslavery principles from its Southern wing. Employing John C. Calhoun's constitutional doctrine that the national territories were the joint property of the states, most Democrats argued that Congress could not exclude slavery from federal territories. As a consequence, the party spearheaded slavery's expansion in the 1850s. The Democratic administration of Franklin Pierce briefly sought the annexation of Spain's lucrative slave colony of Cuba in 1854 and also recognized the proslavery government of Southern filibusters who briefly took over Nicaragua in 1855. At home, Democratic senator Stephen Douglas's Kansas-Nebraska Bill repealed the slavery prohibition clause of the Missouri Compromise that had governed the Kansas and Nebraska territories. In its place, Douglas inserted the doctrine of popular sovereignty, which allowed settlers of those territories to determine whether or not to recognize slavery.

In protest, Chase and a small group of antislavery Democrats and Whigs published the "Appeal of Independent Democrats," criticizing Douglas's bill "as a gross violation of a sacred pledge," designed to make free territory into a "dreary region of despotism, inhabited by masters and slaves" (Potter 1976, 163). However, a majority of Northern Democrats and nearly all Southern members of the party combined to pass the bill in May 1854. Unsupported by Democrats and dissatisfied with the ineffective Whig Party, frustrated antislavery Northerners gradually began to switch their allegiance to the antislavery Republican Party, formed that same year. The expansion of slavery became the preeminent point of conflict between Republicans and Democrats by 1856.

Republicans charged Democrats with being an integral component of a Slave Power conspiracy to expand slavery's reach and political power at the expense of civil liberties and free labor. Republicans decried Democrats' supposedly violent proslavery principles. As evidence, they pointed to internecine warfare between antislavery and proslavery settlers in Kansas in 1856 and the caning that year of antislavery Senator Charles Sumner of Massachusetts by a proslavery Democratic congressman. In the *Dred Scott* case of 1857, Supreme Court chief justice Roger B. Taney sought to end this conflict and deal a death blow to antislavery and the Republican Party. In arguing that slavery could not be constitutionally prohibited from territories or even free states, the Democratic chief justice essentially declared antislavery unconstitutional.

Emboldened proslavery Democrats sought to build on that decision by pledging their party to protect slavery in all territories. Douglas and his supporters blocked that effort at the party's 1860 presidential convention. That impasse broke up the convention. Southern delegates consequently nominated John C. Breckinridge for president later that summer. Northern Democrats countered with Douglas. Former Whigs organized a compromise-oriented Constitutional Union ticket behind John Bell, while Republicans nominated Abraham Lincoln. The election essentially was a two-man race in each section: Douglas against Lincoln in the North and Breckinridge against Bell in the South. Northerners, hoping to check Southern power, chose Republican antislavery over the uncertainty of Douglas's principle of popular sovereignty. Lincoln carried every Northern state but New Jersey, winning the presidency with only 39 percent of the national popular vote.

Matthew Isham

See also: Mexican War and Antislavery; Radical Republicans; Slave Power Argument; Whig Party and Antislavery.

Further Readings

Earle, Jonathan. *Jacksonian Antislavery and the Politics of Free Soil, 1824–1854*. Chapel Hill: University of North Carolina Press, 2004.

Potter, David. *The Impending Crisis, 1848–1861*. Edited by Don E. Fehrenbacher. New York: Harper Torchbooks, 1976.

Richards, Leonard. *The Slave Power: The Free North and Southern Domination, 1780–1860*. Baton Rouge: Louisiana State University Press, 2000.

Silbey, Joel. "There Are Other Questions Beside That of Slavery Merely: The Democratic Party and Antislavery Politics." In Alan M. Kraut, ed. *Crusaders and Compromisers: Essays on the Relationship of the Antislavery Struggle to the Antebellum Party System*. Westport, CT: Greenwood Press, 1983.

Douglass, Frederick (1818–1895)

Frederick Douglass—abolitionist, journalist, and civil rights activist—was born Frederick Augustus Washington Bailey on the Eastern Shore of Maryland in February 1818. His mother, Harriet Bailey, was a slave and his father an unknown white man, but possibly his owner, Aaron Anthony. For the first six years of his life he lived with his grandmother, Betsy Bailey, in comparative comfort. In 1824, he was sent to Holme Hill Farm, on the plantation of Edward Lloyd, to live with his master, where he witnessed some of the horrors of slavery. In 1826, he moved to Baltimore to live with Hugh and Sophia Auld and serve as the companion to their young son, Tommy. Baltimore was the beginning of the end of his bondage. During his seven years there he learned to read, underwent a religious conversion, joined the Bethel A.M.E. church, and found hope in the word *abolition*.

In 1833, Thomas Auld, brother of Hugh and Frederick's new master, had Frederick returned to the Lloyd estate on Maryland's Eastern Shore. Auld considered him insolent, and in 1834 hired him out to Edward Covey, known in the area as a "slave breaker." After numerous beatings, Frederick stood up to Covey and instead beat him; thereafter, he was no longer whipped. "I was a changed being after that fight," he wrote. "I was *nothing* before. I WAS A MAN NOW." In 1836, Frederick and some other slaves plotted an escape that failed, and

Frederick Douglass was a foremost African American abolitionist and autobiographer, champion of civil rights and women's rights, orator, and circuit lecturer for the Massachusetts Anti-Slavery Society. Douglass's major works include three autobiographies, *Narrative of the Life of Frederick Douglass* (1845), *My Bondage and Freedom* (1855), and *Life and Times of Frederick Douglass* (1881, 1892). (National Archives)

he was sent back to Baltimore to live with Hugh and Sophia Auld. While he learned the caulking trade and joined a debating club, Frederick met his future wife, Anna Murray, a free black woman who worked as a domestic.

On September 3, 1838, masquerading as a sailor and carrying the free papers of a black seaman he had met in Baltimore, Frederick escaped north by train and boat. Later that month he married Anna Murray. They settled in New Bedford, Massachusetts, where Frederick found work, and on the recommendation of a black friend, he changed his last name to Douglass—taken from Sir Walter Scott's hero in *The Lady of the Lake*—to hide his identity as a fugitive. He and Anna started a family in New Bedford, and within a decade they had five children.

In New Bedford Douglass was drawn into the abolitionist movement. He read William Lloyd Garrison's newspaper, the *Liberator*, attended meetings, and, after speaking at an August 1841 convention of the Massachusetts Anti-Slavery Society on Nantucket, was hired as a lecturer. His oratorical skills brought him growing recognition, and in 1845 he published *The Narrative of the Life of Frederick Douglass, An American Slave, Written by Himself*. The book was an enormous success and made him famous. But fearing that the disclosure of his identity would endanger his freedom, he left for England, Ireland, and Scotland for an eighteen-month speaking tour. While there, British admirers raised money for him to purchase his freedom and start his own newspaper. He returned to the United States in 1847, moved to Rochester, New York, a center of radical reform, and started the *North Star*, a four-page weekly that promoted numerous reforms, especially immediate abolition, temperance, and women's rights.

Douglass's move to Rochester partly reflected his growing disenchantment with Garrison, the racial inequalities within the American Anti-Slavery Society, and the society's doctrine of nonresistance. By 1849, he endorsed slave violence, and after the passage of the draconian Fugitive Slave Law of 1850, he embraced abolitionist violence to combat the growing belligerence of the South's Slave Power. He formally broke with Garrison and the society in 1851 (Garrison was its president from 1843 to 1865), joined the National Liberty Party, and changed the name of his newspaper to *Frederick Douglass' Paper* to reflect his commitment to political action. In 1852 he published *The Heroic Slave*, his only work of fiction and the first African American novella. It explored the virtues of violence and featured an interracial friendship between the "heroic slave" and an abolitionist modeled on Gerrit Smith, the white friend to whom he dedicated *My Bondage and My Freedom*. *My Bondage*, which sold well when it was published in 1855, was one of the first African American autobiographies detailing at length not only the individual's experience with slavery but with freedom in the North as well. It also highlighted Douglass's emerging revolutionary ethos. Throughout the 1850s, Douglass was a close friend of John Brown, and he helped plan Brown's raid on the federal arsenal at Harpers Ferry. When the raid failed, Douglass fled to Canada to avoid arrest, then left for a speaking tour in England. For the rest of his life, Douglass considered Brown a hero, referring to him as "THE man of this nineteenth century."

With the onset of the Civil War, Douglass's prominence continued to grow. During the war he was invited to the White House three times by President Abraham Lincoln. From the beginning of the conflict he pressed the administration to make emancipation a war aim and to arm black troops, which he felt would hasten an end to slavery and racism. In 1863, he stopped publishing his newspaper after sixteen years as its editor, ending the tenure of the then longest-running black newspaper in America. By the end of the war, he was a committed Republican and would remain so for the rest of his life.

During Reconstruction, Douglass advocated black male suffrage and sought to prevent Confederate elites from returning to power. He met with President Andrew Johnson in 1866, urging him without success to endorse these measures. In 1870, he resumed his editorial career by purchasing the *New Era*, a Washington, D.C., weekly; he became editor-in-chief and changed its name to the *New National Era*. After his Rochester home burned down in 1872, he moved to Washington to be near his paper. But two years later, growing losses forced him to stop publishing it, and he became president of the insolvent Freedmen's Bank. His newspaper and bank failures cost him not only money but respect among other black leaders, who felt that he had become more moderate on questions of race. In many respects he had; he failed to criticize the Republican Party's abandonment of Reconstruction in 1876 when it removed federal troops from the South. That same year he was appointed marshal of the District of Columbia by president-elect Rutherford B. Hayes. His appointment masked the concessions Republicans had made to white supremacists to get Hayes elected.

Even after the failure of Reconstruction, Douglass continued to view the Republican Party as the most viable means for black empowerment. In 1881, President James A. Garfield appointed him the recorder of deeds for the District of Columbia. With his Republican appointments, he gave fewer lectures, no longer needing to rely on speaking fees for financial security. In 1882, he hired as a secretary Helen Pitts, a white woman who was twenty years his junior. That same year his wife, Anna Murray, who had never learned to read, died. He married Helen Pitts in 1884 and was attacked by whites and blacks alike, including members of his own family. His final Republican appointment came in 1889 when he was appointed U.S. minister to Haiti. He served in that position for two tumultuous years.

Douglass published *Life and Times of Frederick Douglass* in 1881, which was over twice as long as *My Bondage and My Freedom*. The book was largely a reminiscence and reviewed his career from the perspective of a senior Republican statesman. Instead of advocating radical social change, he sought to remind readers that the story of slavery—and his life—should not be forgotten. But his attempt to create a usable past failed, for the book sold few copies, and an updated edition in 1892 did no better. *Life and Times* reads as history, and Douglass's vision of progress was now linear, secular, and progressive. Gone was his hope for a sharp break with the past and for a new age. Although he viewed the war in apocalyptic terms, in the wake of Reconstruction it seemed as though the millennium had come but the new age was nowhere in sight. As a result, a heaven on earth increasingly seemed to him a sentimental delusion. He gradually abandoned his faith that God could enter into and affect the affairs of the world.

Despite his growing moderation and skepticism about the possibilities of substantive reform, Douglass remained a race leader until his death in 1895. He denounced the growing disenfranchisement of black men, Jim Crow laws, and the upsurge of lynchings. He was the most influential African American of the nineteenth century and never abandoned his activism or his outspoken hatred of oppression. "I was sent into the world to make an abolition speech," Douglass said during the Civil War. He continued to agitate for racial equality until his death.

John Stauffer

See also: Garrisonians; Radical Republicans.

Further Readings

Blight, David. *Frederick Douglass' Civil War: Keeping Faith in Jubilee*. Baton Rouge: Louisiana State University Press, 1989.

Martin, Waldo. *The Mind of Frederick Douglass*. Chapel Hill: University of North Carolina Press, 1984.

McFeely, William. *Frederick Douglass*. New York: W. W. Norton & Co., 1991.

Stauffer, John. *The Black Hearts of Men: Radical Abolitionists and the Transformation of Race*. Cambridge, MA: Harvard University Press, 2002.

E

Equiano, Olaudah

Olaudah Equiano was an emancipated African, abolitionist, writer, and explorer who became famous for his 1789 autobiography, *The Interesting Narrative of the Life of Olaudah Equiano, or Gustavus Vassa, the African.* Equiano gained fame in the Atlantic World for his ardent opposition to the transatlantic slave trade and to slavery. Equiano wrote *The Narrative* to illuminate for European audiences the experiences of an enslaved African. He hoped that raising awareness about the inhumane slave trade would lead to its demise. Equiano's objectives were achieved when English-speaking antislavery groups and abolitionists adopted his detailed autobiography to demonstrate vividly the evils of the transatlantic slave trade and the plantation slavery of the Americas. However, there was much controversy over Equiano's narrative. Several men sought to discredit the narrative, accusing Equiano of lying about his African birth. This dispute continues in related current scholarship.

Equiano wrote an elegant and profitable narrative despite never having had a formal education. According to Equiano, he was born in Essaka, present-day Nigeria, in 1745. At the age of eleven, he was kidnapped and sold into the British slave trade. Slave traders initially brought Equiano to Barbados, but he was later sold in Virginia and was given the name Gustavus Vassa. In 1766, he acquired freedom on the island of Montserrat. After emancipation, Equiano hired himself out as a seaman and worked for a brief time on a plantation scheme on the Mosquito Coast, present-day Nicaragua. Over the course of his life, Equiano traveled to North America, the circum-Caribbean, Europe, and the Arctic.

Although Equiano did not live to see the British slave trade abolished in 1807, both he and his autobiography were key forces in swaying the British public against the slave trade. Equiano published nine successful editions of *The*

Narrative. Each edition expanded readership including new subscriptions from very influential politicians, aristocrats, religious authorities, and others in Great Britain and America. Many readers were deeply moved by Equiano's ordeals as a slave and regretted British complicity in it. Equiano revealed the details of his capture and enslavement in Africa as a child, the horrors of the Middle Passage, and his work as an enslaved sailor. While Equiano was not condemned to plantation slave labor, he witnessed the ghastly living conditions forced on the enslaved onboard ship, on plantation estates, and in urban settings in the Americas. Equiano's devotion to Christianity—he was baptized in 1759—made his narrative even more credible to a broad British audience. Equiano expressed his desire to return to West Africa in *The Narrative*, and he frequently referred to many of the enslaved as his countrymen. In 1779, Equiano requested permission from the Bishop of London to accompany Governor Macnamara's mission to West Africa. Equiano's role in the mission was to Christianize West Africans, but he was denied the opportunity. In 1786, Equiano joined Henry Smeathmen's multiracial mission to settle London's black poor at Sierra Leone. The Committee for the Relief of the Black Poor approved the mission. However, in 1787 he was dismissed from the mission. Equiano believed that West Africans had viable economic and commercial alternatives to continued participation in the slave trade as a source of wealth. Rejection did not stop Equiano from accomplishing his personal religious and political goals. He continued his protest against the slave trade and slavery into the 1790s. He assisted various settlement missions to Sierra Leone from England, and he completed his autobiography.

Equiano long promoted the benefits of interracial relationships and, in 1792, he married an English woman, Susanna Cullen. They had two daughters, Ann Mary and Joanna Vassa. Joanna outlived her family and inherited Equiano's considerable estate in 1816.

Nadine Hunt

See also: Slave Narratives.

Further Readings

Braidwood, Stephen J. *Black Poor and White Philanthropists: London's Blacks and the Foundation of the Sierra Leone Settlement, 1786–1791*. Liverpool: Liverpool University Press, 1994.

Carretta, Vincent. "Olaudah Equiano or Gustavus Vassa? New Light on an Eighteenth Century Question of Identity." *Slavery and Abolition* 20, 3 (1999): 96–105.

Equiano, Olaudah. *The Interesting Narrative and Other Writings*. New York: Penguin Books, [1789] 1995.

Jones, G. I. "Olaudah Equiano of the Niger Ibo." In Phillip D. Curtin, ed. *Africa Remembered: Narratives by West Africans from the Era of the Slave Trade*. Madison: University of Wisconsin Press, 1967, pp. 60–98.

Lovejoy, Paul E. "Autobiography and Memory: Gustavus Vassa, Alias Olauduh Equiano, the Afrocan." *Slavery and Abolition* 27, 3 (2006): 31–47.

Walvin, James, *An African's Life: The Life and Times of Olaudah Equiano, 1745–1797*. London: Continuum, 1998.

F

Federalists and Antislavery

The relationship between the Federalist Party and opposition to slavery was complicated and ambiguous. Many leading Federalists worked for slavery's abolition, and the antebellum generation of abolitionists drew inspiration and nourishment from Federalism. But other Federalists could hardly be called abolitionists, and they and their traditions also nurtured antiabolitionism in the antebellum era.

In the late eighteenth and early nineteenth centuries, Northern Federalists joined, and at times led, efforts to abolish slavery. Their efforts and success varied from state to state. Among the most effective were New York's Federalists, who formed the vanguard in securing a gradual abolition law in 1799 and in defending African Americans' rights thereafter. Connecticut Federalism boasted the likes of Theodore Dwight, brother of Yale president Timothy Dwight. Theodore advocated the immediate abolition of slavery in the late eighteenth century and was a leading Federalist editor in the early nineteenth century.

But Massachusetts was the heart of Federalism, and most Massachusetts Federalists espoused a more political form of antislavery. There was a wing of the party, mostly comprised of preachers and some editors, that offered a moral critique of Southern slavery. But Federalist politicians in Massachusetts reviled slavery largely because it inflated the political power of their partisan rivals. If the Federalists' power base was New England, the Republicans' base was in the South. Out of national power after 1801, New England Federalists railed against "Virginia influence" in the federal government. That influence, they argued, was augmented by the Constitution's clause granting representation in Congress and the Electoral College for three-fifths of each slave inhabitant of the state in which they lived. Accordingly, as Republican policies heightened Federalist partisan and sectional grievances, their opposition to "slave representation" became more pronounced. It reached its zenith during the War of 1812, as the people joined the politicians in calling for the abolition of slave representation.

The Federalists thus kept slavery on the table in national politics. But the effectiveness of New England Federalists' sectionalist appeals in politics prefigured the Free Soil and Republican parties more than the antebellum abolitionists. Yet Federalism echoed in the program and rhetoric of those abolitionists. Both New England Federalists and abolitionists decried the Constitution's empowerment of slaveholders. They both urged Yankees to stand firm against slaveholders in defense of Northern rights. And the abolitionists carried on the religious Federalists' characterization of slavery as a national sin.

This was so partly because Federalism shaped many individual abolitionists. A teenage William Lloyd Garrison, for instance, served as an apprentice to Ephraim W. Allen, a leading Federalist printer in Newburyport, Massachusetts. In Allen's employ, Garrison immersed himself in Federalist political writings, which gave him a religious and sectional vision of the South and slavery, a deep ambivalence at best about the Constitution and Union, and some strident language in which to express such a worldview. In 1814, for instance, Allen's newspaper printed an article arguing that if New England's sufferings under the Republicans had "been foreshown to the men of New-England" when they helped draft and ratify the Constitution, "they would as soon have made *a covenant with death*, as a covenant of union with the states which have thus wantonly and cruelly oppressed them."

Other antebellum abolitionists also had deep roots in New England Federalism. The very names of two important abolitionists proclaimed these connections. The "P." in Elijah P. Lovejoy stood for "Parish," his name being a memorial to Elijah Parish, a Federalist preacher and sectional firebrand whose sermons scourged the South for the sin of slavery. Theodore Dwight Weld, like Lovejoy the son of a Congregationalist minister, was named after Theodore Dwight.

Multiple links of this sort are suggestive. But it was not until they came into contact with other influences that most of these people became abolitionists. Lovejoy, for instance, entered into an array of reform causes in the late 1820s and early 1830s. But he did not move toward abolitionism until he underwent evangelical conversion. When Garrison left Allen's employ in 1826, he pursued all manner of Christian reform activities. It was a chance meeting with Quaker abolitionist Benjamin Lundy in 1828 to which Garrison attributed his "conversion to abolitionism." The opposition of free people of color to the American Colonization Society pushed him beyond the colonizationist bias Allen helped instill in him. The immediatist Garrison had transcended his Federalist heritage in many respects, a process made possible by other influences.

Garrison's experience was not unique; Federalism made more colonizationists than abolitionists. This was true especially of the Congregationalist ministry, who continued to see the American Colonization Society as fully in keeping with their emphasis on godly reform and benevolence, promising gradual abolition without upheaval. Thus, even as abolitionists appropriated the ministers' moral urgency and religious rhetoric, they found themselves at odds with their more moderate position.

Abolitionists also contended with outright opposition from some of the remnants and descendants of Federalism, for this tradition produced at least as many antiabolitionists as abolitionists. For instance, in 1835, leading Massachusetts Federalist Harrison Gray Otis denounced the abolitionists as revolutionaries. Garrison, who had once idolized Otis, accused him of apostasy from the Federalist cause, but Otis represented Federalist conservatism and was far from alone. Sidney Edwards Morse, author of an important pamphlet during the War of 1812 attacking the expansion of Southern territory and power, emerged in antebellum years as a powerful opponent of the Garrisonians. Caleb Cushing, an acquaintance of Garrison's from Newburyport, prided himself on his moderate stance on questions related to slavery. As attorney general of the United States in the 1850s, he enforced the Fugitive Slave Law and defended the *Dred Scott* decision. He carried forward the Federalists' emphasis on order.

The Federalists' influence on antislavery, then, was more than many have realized but was also complex. Their tendency to emphasize the political aspects of slavery had wide appeal during their time but did not entitle most of them to be called abolitionists. Neither was the New England Federalists' influence on the next generation of antislavery simple or easily discerned. Yet the Federalist echoes were there nonetheless.

Matthew Mason

See also: Congregationalism and Antislavery; Garrisonians; Lovejoy, Elijah (1802–1837).

Further Readings

Abzug, Robert H. *Passionate Liberator: Theodore Dwight Weld and the Dilemma of Reform*. New York: Oxford University Press, 1980.

Arkin, Mark M. "The Federalist Trope: Power and Passion in Abolitionist Rhetoric." *Journal of American History* 88 (June 2001): 75–98.

Banner, James M. *To the Hartford Convention: The Federalists and the Origins of Party Politics in Massachusetts, 1789–1815*. New York: Alfred A. Knopf, 1970.

Dillon, Merton Lynn. *Elijah P. Lovejoy: Abolitionist Editor*. Urbana: University of Illinois Press, 1961.

Finkelman, Paul. "The Problem of Slavery in the Age of Federalism." In Doron Ben-Atar and Barbara B. Oberg, eds. *Federalists Reconsidered*. Charlottesville and London: University Press of Virginia, 1998, pp. 135–156.

Kerber, Linda K. *Federalists in Dissent: Imagery and Ideology in Jeffersonian America*. Ithaca, NY; London: Cornell University Press, 1970.

Mason, Matthew. "'Nothing Is Better Calculated to Excite Divisions': Federalist Agitation against Slave Representation during the War of 1812." *New England Quarterly* 75 (December 2002): 531–561.

Pease, Jane and William Pease. *Bound with Them in Chains: A Biographical History of the Antislavery Movement*. Westport, CT: Greenwood Press, 1972.

Richards, Leonard L. *Gentlemen of Property and Standing: Anti-Abolition Mobs in Jacksonian America*. New York: Oxford University Press, 1970.

Stewart, James Brewer. *Holy Warriors: The Abolitionists and American Slavery*. 1976; Rev. ed., New York: Hill and Wang, 1996.

Stewart, James Brewer. *William Lloyd Garrison and the Challenge of Emancipation*. Arlington Heights, IL: Harlan Davidson, 1992.

Wills, Gary. *"Negro President": Jefferson and the Slave Power*. Boston and New York: Houghton Mifflin Company, 2003.

Field Order No. 15

Abolitionists referred often to the debt that slaveholders owed their bondsmen and women for centuries of uncompensated labor. As the Civil War drew to a close, Union General William T. Sherman issued Field Order No. 15—an order cited repeatedly by reparationists as the origin of the U.S. government's promise of "forty acres and a mule." Proponents of reparations have argued that the government reneged on Sherman's wartime pledge to compensate the ex-slaves with land and farm animals. Reparationists continue to cite "forty acres and a mule" as justification for their appeals for a broad range of compensation—from cash payments to tax credits—for the descendants of America's four million black slaves.

On January 16, 1865, three months before Appomattox, Sherman issued his famous Special Field Order No. 15. This order set aside "the islands from Charleston south, the abandoned rice fields along the rivers for thirty miles back from the sea, and the country bordering the St. John's River, Florida," for the exclusive settlement of slave refugees. Sherman instructed General Rufus Saxton to grant each head of a black family not more than forty acres of land and to "furnish . . . subject to the approval of the President of the United States, a possessory title."

By June 1865, Saxton reported that approximately 40,000 blacks had settled on about 400,000 acres of land on what became known as the Sherman Reservation. Sherman authorized Saxton to loan the black families farm animals—decrepit creatures too broken down for military service. These presumably were the "mules" intended to work the proverbial "forty acres." In the summer and fall of 1865, however, President Andrew Johnson essentially reversed the government's policy of granting "forty acres and a mule" to the freedpeople. He pardoned former

Confederates and ordered the restoration of all property except that sold under a court decree. Few of the freedpeople who had claimed farms in the Sherman Reservation were allowed to retain their land.

Later events—creation of the Bureau of Refugees, Freedmen, and Abandoned Lands (the Freedmen's Bureau) in March 1865 and the passage of the Southern Homestead Act in June 1866—further complicated the role of the federal government in distributing land and farm animals to the freedpeople. The government authorized the Freedmen's Bureau to lease, not grant outright, "not more than forty acres" of abandoned or confiscated lands to freedmen with the option to "purchase the land and receive such title thereto as the United States can convey." The Homestead Act set aside public land in Alabama, Arkansas, Florida, Louisiana, and Mississippi, for purchase by the freedpeople for a $5 fee. The available land, however, was generally of inferior quality and the freedmen lacked sufficient capital to purchase implements and to farm the land properly. When, in 1876, Congress repealed the Homestead Act, blacks cultivated only several thousand acres, mostly in Florida.

For his part, Sherman denied any role in misleading the freedpeople in his Field Order No. 15. In his memoirs Sherman recalled that "the military authorities at that day . . . had a perfect right to grant the possession of any vacant land to which they could extend military protection, but we did not undertake to give a fee-simple title; and all that was designed by these special field orders was to make temporary provisions for the freedmen and their families during the rest of the war, or until Congress should take action in the premises." Sherman added that Secretary of War Edwin M. Stanton approved his field order before he announced it.

Though some Radical Republicans, including Thaddeus Stevens and George W. Julian, supported confiscation of Southern plantations with hopes of reforming the South's social and economic system, most nineteenth-century Americans held private property too sacred to endorse wide scale land redistribution. In the end, Congress failed to pass legislation certifying Sherman's field order—a military order designed to meet the exigencies of war, not peace. Today reparationists point to Sherman's Field Order No. 15 and "forty acres and a mule" as symbols of the government's broken promises and the ex-slaves' shattered dreams.

John David Smith

See also: Freedmen's Bureau.

Further Readings

Bentley, George R. *A History of the Freedmen's Bureau*. Philadelphia: University of Pennsylvania Press, 1955.

Oubre, Claude F. *Forty Acres and a Mule: The Freedmen's Bureau and Black Land Ownership*. Baton Rouge: Louisiana State University Press, 1978.

Sherman, William T. *Memoirs of General William T. Sherman. By Himself. In Two Volumes.* New York: D. Appleton and Company, 1875.

Westley, Robert. "Many Billions Gone: Is It Time to Reconsider the Case for Black Reparations?" *Boston College Law Review* 40 (1998): 429–476.

Finney, Charles Grandison (1792–1875)

Charles Grandison Finney was a Protestant evangelist whose dynamic preaching style and liberal theology galvanized the antislavery movement in the antebellum North. Born in Litchfield County, Connecticut, Finney moved to western New York as a child where he remained and eventually trained in law. Converted to evangelical Protestantism in 1821, he turned his energies toward the ministry. In 1826, Finney began a series of emotional religious revivals across upstate New York that earned the region the nickname, the "burned-over district." Because abolitionist efforts increased dramatically following these spiritual campaigns, Finney is often credited with inspiring the entire movement. His influence, however, was indirect. Rather than participating directly in abolitionist activities, he provided antislavery activists with a theological foundation for their views.

Finney's importance to the antislavery movement lay in his theology and his remarkable ability to convert individuals to evangelical faith. Repudiating the orthodox Calvinist doctrine that claimed human beings were passive recipients of God's saving grace, Finney emphasized the individual's own ability to obtain salvation. Finney employed various persuasive tactics to gain thousands of converts. These "new measures" included holding protracted meetings, demanding conversion immediately, allowing women to pray publicly, and inviting nonbelievers to sit on the "anxious bench" where they could contemplate their sins.

Finney's belief that individuals could achieve sanctification, or holiness and perfection, in this life sparked an enthusiastic response that bore fruit for the antislavery movement. Believing they could perfect society and, thereby, bring about Christ's millennial reign, Finney's followers embraced numerous benevolent and reform efforts including temperance, anti-Sabbatarianism, anti-Masonry, and abolitionism. According to Finney, slavery was a national sin that contravened God's moral law. After Finney's 1830–1831 Rochester revival, many antislavery evangelicals embraced immediate emancipation.

While Finney himself was no friend to ideas of racial equality, he supported his associates who were active in the abolition movement. At the same time that he required separate seating for African Americans at his New York City church, Chatham Street Chapel, he refused slaveholders communion. In 1833, he allowed his friends, New York City businessmen and ardent reformers, Arthur and Lewis

Tappan, to use Chatham Street Chapel for a meeting of the New York Anti-Slavery Society. The chapel subsequently became home to abolitionist activities and the target of antiabolitionist violence. Finney, however, feared that radicalism would disrupt his primary mission of converting souls.

In 1835, Finney continued his indirect influence on abolitionism by accepting a professorship in theology at reform-minded Oberlin College in Ohio. At Oberlin, Finney offered a voice of moderation to the antislavery movement, admonishing seminary students that they best served the cause by leading sinners, including slaveholders, to Christ. His views brought him into conflict with his most famous convert, radical abolitionist, Theodore Dwight Weld, who envisioned seminary as a training ground for antislavery reformers. During his thirty-year tenure at Oberlin, first as professor and later as president, Finney never wavered in his belief that spiritual revival offered the best hope for abolition.

Dianne Wheaton Cappiello

See also: Antislavery Evangelical Protestantism.

Further Readings

Hambrick-Stowe, Charles E. *Charles G. Finney and the Spirit of American Evangelicalism.* Grand Rapids, MI: William B. Eerdmans, 1996.

Hardman, Keith J. *Charles Grandison Finney, 1792–1875: Revivalist and Reformer.* Syracuse, NY: Syracuse University Press, 1987.

McLoughlin, William G. *Revivals, Awakenings, and Reform: An Essay on Religion and Social Change in America, 1607–1977.* Chicago: University of Chicago Press, 1978.

First Great Awakening and Antislavery

In the middle third of the eighteenth century, waves of revivals spread through the British North American colonies. Ministers as disparate as the theologically sophisticated Jonathan Edwards and the fervently histrionic George Whitefield—the first a New England Congregationalist, the second a Church of England missionary—led prayer meetings in which people felt their religion deeply and sometimes experienced saving grace on the spot. These revivals, particularly such excesses as believers crying out and fainting away, were criticized by less enthusiastic ministers of the time. They chided that the outpourings of the spirit were too quick and shallow to indicate true faith, and they reasserted traditional means such as prayer, reading the Bible, and attending services as better preparation for receiving grace. Some modern historians have expressed skepticism in another form, asking whether there were enough revivals and conversions to constitute a "Great Awakening." The majority view, however, is that the revivals were significant in American history. These revivals intersected with the history of abolitionism at several points.

One intersection was institutional, relating to the role of blacks in Christian denominations. Much of African American religious history from the middle of the eighteenth to the beginning of the nineteenth century was rooted in the First Great Awakening. Revivalists—Edwards and Whitefield were exemplary—preached to whites, blacks, and Native Americans. Both ministers noted conversions among their black auditors. Yet although some blacks, both slave and free, joined Congregational or Anglican churches, the First Great Awakening involved the growth and spread of denominations that would soon attract many African American members. The Baptists and Methodists became the most important evangelicals, and Methodists were among the most active exhorters to slaves both in North America and in the West Indies. It was often as evangelical lay exhorters or prayer leaders that black men and a few black women gained leadership roles in these denominations in the eighteenth century. Historians have often asserted that churches emphasizing immediate conversion more than preparation through traditional means readily gained more black members. The black church population and the evangelical denominations increased together in the late eighteenth and early nineteenth centuries.

The Silver Bluff Church, Aiken County, South Carolina, for instance, was the first African American Baptist Church. After having gathered the members in 1774 or 1775, David George, with some congregants, fled to Savannah for the protection of a British camp in the War of Independence; then in 1782 he departed for Nova Scotia, where he formed another black Baptist church. Most of the black Nova Scotians (usually called black loyalists) had freed themselves from slavery by seeking British protection during the war. About 1,200 of them furthered their quest for freedom by migrating to Freetown, Sierra Leone, in the early 1790s. George was among the emigrants, and he formed another black Baptist church in Africa. He traveled from Sierra Leone to England, where his recollections of slaveholders' cruel treatment were recorded and published. Moreover, independent black denominations such as the African Methodist Episcopal Church and the African Methodist Episcopal Zion Church grew out of the denominations that had grown strong in the First Great Awakening. Leading spokesmen for black rights such as Richard Allen and Absalom Jones were ministers in these churches.

The second intersection was theological. The theology of the First Great Awakening was Calvinism. Revivalism made Calvinism more accessible to ordinary people, and experiences of the outpouring of the spirit added a more loving face to the stern God of predestinarian religion. Most of the early black authors who criticized slaveholding—Jupiter Hammon, James Albert Ukasaw Gronniosaw, Lemuel Haynes, Phillis Wheatley, John Marrant, Quobna Ottobah Cugoano, and Olaudah Equiano—were Calvinists. The theological views of several early African American spokesman, such as Prince Hall and Richard Allen, cannot be determined today with available evidence, but in Hall, for instance, we see enough interest in Calvinist theologians like Jonathan Edwards to motivate a thirty-five-page commentary in the black man's hand.

With this Calvinist inspiration, black abolitionists transposed to black people at large the story of the suffering sinner who at last received saving grace in a revival meeting. God had predetermined the sufferings of blacks in the slave trade and slavery just as he had mandated the trials of the Jews in captivity and he had demanded the crucifixion of Jesus as expiation for sin. The sufferings were trials of God's faithful and they were intended to reveal his glory in judging and his mercy in forgiving. God would gather his faithful unto him—in Calvinist-inspired black religion this meant not only grace and salvation, but also civic freedom with all its benefits. The black arch-Calvinist Lemuel Haynes, who argued for both predestination and civic freedom, exhibited this faith. For some black Christians like John Marrant, in the wake of the First Great Awakening it meant establishing themselves in Africa. For instance, the black Methodists called Huntingdonians because of the encourage and support given them by the Calvinist Lady Huntingdon of England were members of a sect that had left both the Church of England and the Wesleyan Methodists over the freedom of the will. Huntingdonians were strict predestinarians. Marrant attended one of George Whitefield's revivals during the missionary's 1769–1770 tour. Crying out and falling to the ground, Marrant converted. He was soon in service in the British Navy, and then traveled to England, where he exhorted in London and received holy orders in a Huntingdonian chapel. He became a popular preacher among black and white Bostonians, claiming that blacks were among God's chosen people, predestined to be tried in the slave trade and slavery as well as to reestablish a holy society in Africa. Marrant himself died just before the 1,200 black Nova Scotians migrated to Sierra Leone, but indications of the power of his ideas included the exodus of his entire congregation to Freetown and the strong role of the black Huntingdonians in Africa in demanding black rights in the faces of the imperial officials and English investors in the colony. Thus the First Great Awakening affected the institutions and the beliefs of black Christians in North America, the West Indies, Sierra Leone, and England.

John Saillant

See also: Congregationalism and Antislavery.

Further Readings

Brooks, Joanna, and John Saillant, eds. *"Face Zion Forward": First Writers of the Black Atlantic, 1785–1798.* Boston: Northeastern University Press, 2002.

Frey, Sylvia R., and Betty Wood, *Come Shouting to Zion: African-American Protestantism in the American South and British Caribbean to 1830.* Chapel Hill: The University of North Carolina Press, 1998.

McLoughlin, William G. *Revivals, Awakenings, and Reform: An Essay on Religion and Social Change in America, 1607–1977.* Chicago: The University of Chicago Press, 1978.

Fitzhugh, George

One of the first sociologists in the United States was also one of the most famous proslavery advocates in the antebellum period. George Fitzhugh of Virginia argued that slavery was a positive good, that it was superior to Northern free labor, and that Southern slaves were better off than Northern workers. In fact, Fitzhugh believed that slavery was such a superior social system that many white workers ought to be enslaved as well. His bold defense of slavery made Fitzhugh a pariah in the North and spurred abolitionists to action responding to his writings.

Born in Prince William County, Virginia, in 1806, Fitzhugh grew up in a society that seemed to be in decline. Generations of planting tobacco on the same land had led to soil exhaustion, and many Virginians were choosing to move to newly opened areas to the West. Impressed by the writings of the agrarian philosopher John Taylor, who had argued that the soil could be replenished through scientific agriculture, Fitzhugh held to the belief that Southern agriculture and Southern slavery produced a society in which ignorance, crime, and poverty were unknown. This ideal served as the foundation for his defense of slavery, and he contrasted it with the baleful conditions in modern industrial society.

A lawyer by profession, Fitzhugh struggled financially in his rural practice. He married well and lived largely off of his wife's inheritance, a small plantation on the Rappahannock River. Although he continued to practice law, he was not successful, in large part because he disliked the law and hated the routine of a regular practice. Fitzhugh also despised most of his clients and refused to listen to them. He found the politics of slavery much more to his liking, especially after the abolitionists began to attack the South's peculiar institution. Throughout the 1840s, Fitzhugh read the works of abolitionists like William Lloyd Garrison and formed friendships with such defenders of slavery as George Frederick Holmes and James D. B. DeBow. He also read the works of Thomas Carlyle, the Scottish historian who criticized not only abolitionism but also modern society as a whole. Carlyle believed that the modern world had erred in making labor a commodity and idealized premodern society. With the ideals of Taylor and Carlyle in his mind, Fitzhugh set out to defend the South and slavery.

Fitzhugh published proslavery pamphlets in the early 1850s and followed these with his first book, *Sociology for the South, or the Failure of Free Society*, in 1854. In this work, he attacked the American view that all men were created equal, arguing that human society was organic and that inequality was natural. Northern industrial society brought individualism and notions of equality and liberty that were dangerous and, if left unchecked, would destroy God's natural order. Unrestrained selfishness was at the heart of modern society and unchecked it would bring chaos and anarchy. These arguments were taken even further in Fitzhugh's most famous book, *Cannibals*

All! or Slaves without Masters, published in 1857. There, he attacked the ideal of progress and the American ethic of individualism. Fitzhugh argued that Northern workers were worse off than slaves, being exploited by the capitalists who took their profits and left the poor to fend for themselves. Northerners believed that they were free, but were actually slaves. They were wage slaves, slaves without masters. True freedom came not from free labor, but from a paternalism like that found in the South. According to Fitzhugh, under Southern slavery, the masters cared for their workers, treated them well, fed them well, and saw to their needs. Southern slaves, he asserted, "are the happiest, and in some sense, the freest people in the world."

Although few Southerners agreed with Fitzhugh's most radical ideas, Northern abolitionists argued that he was representative of the South. For many in the North, Fitzhugh was the symbol of Southern proslavery views and that he was a typical Southerner. Indeed, Southerners did applaud his books, but few of them were ready to support all that he argued. While they agreed with his arguments on behalf of slavery and believed that their slaves were happy and well cared for, few of them were ready to argue that the North was so bad, and still fewer supported the idea that any whites should be enslaved. In the end, Fitzhugh served to heighten the sectional tensions of the 1850s. His radicalism allowed abolitionists to paint all Southern defenders of slavery as extremists. His arguments against modernity fit well with Northern fears of the Slave Power conspiracy and made it more difficult to find common ground to avert civil war.

Probably the most famous apologist for slavery, he is best remembered for his attacks on capitalism, and some of his criticisms of industrial society later would be renewed by socialists. When the Civil War began, it destroyed Southern slavery and dashed Fitzhugh's idealistic dreams of paternalism. But he quickly found new friends, taking a job as a judge in the Freedmen's Bureau, and eventually coming to embrace industrial capitalism. By the time of his death in 1881, he believed that modern capitalism brought monopoly, a system that truly expressed the inequality that he believed was natural to humanity.

A. James Fuller

See also: Slave Power Argument.

Further Readings

Fitzhugh, George. *Cannibals All! or Slaves without Masters*. 1857. Reprint: Cambridge, MA: Harvard University Press, 1960.

Genovese, Eugene. *The World the Slaveholders Made: Two Essays in Interpretation*. Hanover, NH: Wesleyan University Press, 1969.

Wish, Harvey. *George Fitzhugh: Propagandist of the Old South*. 1943. Reprint: Gloucester, MA: Peter Smith, 1969.

Foster, Abby Kelley (1811–1887)

Abby Kelley was born in 1811 in Massachusetts and was raised in the Quaker faith. As a Quaker, she developed her sense of "independent thinking" and a strong moral commitment to human rights. While teaching, she was inspired by William Lloyd Garrison and became committed to the abolitionist movement. In 1838, she gave her first public speech at an antislavery convention in Philadelphia. During a period in history when white women were often relegated to political silence, she became known as one of the more radical and fearless orators and a major fundraiser who helped to propel the abolitionist movement's causes forward.

During the 1840s while living in the Western Reserve, she established the Western Anti-Slavery Society. In her ongoing work, she also helped to establish *The Anti-Slavery Bugle*. That same year she married fellow Quaker and abolitionist Stephen Foster, and they moved to their sprawling lovely home known as Liberty Farm in Massachusetts. The Foster homestead became a major regional link in the Underground Railroad as they assisted numerous slaves escaping to the North and Canada.

Abby Kelley and her husband added one child to their union, a daughter, while continuing their work as key activists and speakers on the antislavery circuit. In addition, Abby Kelley spoke passionately for equal rights for women. She was an important organizer of the women's suffrage movement and brought many of the movement's then little known women to the forefront, including Lucy Stone and Susan B. Anthony. Labeled by some opponents as "Jezebel," and often verbally attacked and physically threatened, she was never silenced nor intimidated and continued working for human equality until late in life when illness finally slowed her activism. Abby Kelley Foster died in 1887.

Iris Hunter

See also: Quakers and Antislavery.

Further Reading

Sterling. Dorothy. *Ahead of Her Time: Abby Kelley and the Politics of Antislavery.* New York: W. W. Norton & Co., 1991.

Free Produce Movement

The free produce movement boycotted any products made by slave labor and lasted from the 1790s until the 1860s. Free produce proponents believed that consumers who purchased slave produce ensured the economic viability of slavery.

Free produce activists maintained that purchasers of slave goods were as culpable as slaveholders for the survival and growth of the institution.

The movement began among individual members of the Society of Friends (or Quakers) in the late eighteenth century. As pacifists and believers in the spiritual equality of all humankind, Quakers were among the first religious sects to oppose slavery, and by the 1770s and early 1780s, they had eliminated slaveholding among their members. In the decades that followed, a growing number of Quakers—inspired by radical Friends such as John Woolman and Anthony Benezet—argued that merely opposing slave ownership was not enough. For these Quakers, the consumption of slave labor products was akin to the use of "prize goods," or products obtained through acts of war, which pacifist Quakers had long refused to trade or use. The transatlantic reach of the Quaker community ensured that these ideas found an audience in both the United States and Great Britain. In 1787, British Friends, in alliance with leading abolitionists, established the London Abolition Committee to end British involvement in the international slave trade. Six years later, the committee endorsed the tactic of abstention from slave-produced sugar and rum. Abolitionist Thomas Clarkson optimistically estimated that 300,000 Britons had joined this early free produce campaign.

But it was in the United States that the free produce movement found its widest support. In the 1810s and 1820s, Quaker minister Elias Hicks urged his coreligionists to boycott all slave produce, and in 1826 Quaker abolitionists established the first formal free produce organization in Wilmington, Delaware. In Baltimore that same year, Quaker Benjamin Lundy opened a store that sold goods produced exclusively by free labor. In 1827, Philadelphia Quakers and like-minded antislavery activists established the Free Produce Society of Pennsylvania, and in 1838, free produce supporters from a variety of Northern states met in Philadelphia as the American Free Produce Association. The leaders of these organizations hoped to establish alternative production and distribution networks that were untainted by slavery, and they soon set to work identifying and promoting sources of free labor produced staples (or appropriate alternatives) in the South and throughout the world. Activists also established free produce retail outlets and mail order services in Pennsylvania, New York, New England, Ohio, and Indiana. The most ambitious free produce effort took place in the early 1850s when Philadelphia Quaker George W. Taylor established a textile mill so as to increase the quality and supply of free labor cotton goods. Free produce organizations promoted their cause through a variety of broadsides, pamphlets, and journals, the most important of which was the *Non-Slaveholder*, published in Philadelphia between 1846 and 1854.

In addition to the Quakers who supported free produce because it offered a nonviolent and legal way to undermine slavery, some African American abolitionists embraced the concept. In 1830, African Americans in Philadelphia established their own organization, the Colored Free Produce Society of Pennsylvania, with a corresponding female organization created the following year. A number of African Americans also launched free produce stores, including Lydia White, who opened her Philadelphia establishment in 1830 and stayed in business for sixteen years, and William Whipper who began his Philadelphia grocery store in 1834. Other black abolitionists, such as the New York–based Presbyterian minister Henry Highland Garnet, promoted the cultivation of free labor products to end Northern and British dependence on slave-produced goods. In 1858, Garnet established the African Civilization Society in cooperation with British abolitionists to promote the voluntary migration of black Americans to the Niger Valley where they would teach native Africans Christianity and grow cotton to sell to British and American manufacturers. Though denounced by many black abolitionists as another colonization scheme designed to remove African Americans from the United States, Garnet argued that finding alternative free labor cotton sources would strike a decisive blow against slavery.

Female antislavery activists also played a central role in the free produce movement from its outset. In a culture that viewed women as the primary source of moral virtue, and, more practically, as the principal consumers of domestic goods, the success of any free produce campaign depended upon female participation. Accordingly, many free produce publications (and female abolitionists such as Abby Kelley Foster and Lucretia Mott) urged women to eschew slave products.

Despite such endorsements, the free produce movement failed to garner continuing support. Indeed, by the late 1840s, abolitionist William Lloyd Garrison openly ridiculed the scheme, arguing that it was at best an impractical distraction from more important abolitionist work and, at worst, it salved the consciences of selfish Northerners at the expense of slaves who failed to benefit. The lack of broader abolitionist support hastened the collapse of the American Free Produce Association in 1847, though an exclusively Quaker organization survived to 1856. Nevertheless, a market consisting primarily of Quakers and small numbers of African Americans was too limited to enable supporters to forge a sustainable free produce supply, production, and distribution network. Lacking economies of scale, free produce merchants could offer only higher cost, lower quality goods that had little appeal to a broader buying public. Garrison was certainly correct. The free produce movement was impractical, not because the idea lacked merit (as prior and subsequent consumer boycott campaigns have revealed), but because slavery had so deeply penetrated all aspects of the transatlantic economy.

A. Glenn Crothers

See also: Quakers and Antislavery.

Further Readings

Garrison, Wendell P. "Free Produce among the Quakers." *Atlantic Monthly* 22 (October 1868): 485–494.

Glickman, Lawrence B. "'Buy for the Sake of the Slave': Abolitionism and the Origins of American Consumer Activism." *American Quarterly* 56 (December 2004): 889–912.

Midley, Clare. *Women against Slavery: The British Campaigns, 1780–1870.* London: Routledge, 1992.

Nuremberger, Ruth Ketring. *The Free Produce Movement: A Quaker Protest against Slavery.* Durham, NC: Duke University Press, 1942.

Schor, Joel. *Henry Highland Garnet: A Voice of Black Radicalism in the Nineteenth Century.* Westport, CT: Greenwood Press, 1977.

Freedmen's Aid Societies

Freedmen's Aid Societies were founded during the U.S. Civil War throughout the Northeast and Midwest to assist the hundreds of thousands of former slaves who had fled into the North or lived in territory occupied by the Union Army. Many of the leaders and members of these Societies had been abolitionists before the war, although not all. Nearly half of the membership had not been active in antislavery at all before the war.

The main objective of the Societies was the education of the freedmen. At the war's end, there were nearly four million freedmen. Few had any education, only 5 percent were literate, and the Freedmen's Aid Societies felt that the best service they could provide was to prepare these former slaves to become productive citizens. As Union soldiers moved into Confederate territory, they were soon followed by Society members, mostly women, who established schools for freedmen. The Societies had sent more than nine hundred teachers into the former Confederate states, and others operated schools for those freedmen who had escaped into the North. After the war, the Freedmen's Bureau constructed school buildings while the Aid Societies provided the teachers. Local whites often threatened or socially ostracized these teachers. The vision of the Aid Societies went beyond basic education. An important legacy of the Societies can be found in many of the South's traditional black colleges, such as Atlanta University, which was founded in 1865.

Although best known for their work in providing education for former slaves at the end of the war, the Societies were very active during that conflict, supplying basic material aid to African American refugees such as food, shelter, and medical care. They helped ex-slaves find work and negotiate fair wages. The Union Army was unable and in many cases unwilling to care for these refugees, officially referred to as "contraband" by the army and newspapers. The Freedmen's Aid Societies offered the only institutional help available to former slaves.

The war all but cut off the supply of cotton to the textile manufacturers of the North. As the Union Army occupied the cotton-growing regions of the South, the demand for cotton could not be met. Many freed slaves were put back to work on plantations, some even on the ones they had fled. These plantations were managed by the army or their former owners. The freedmen worked for wages that most never received. Many Freedmen's Aid Societies sent members to act as labor superintendents in a futile effort to ensure fair treatment.

The Freedmen's Aid Societies successfully lobbied the Union government on behalf of former slaves. It was through their efforts that the Freedmen's Inquiry Commission was created in 1863, the chief accomplishment of which was the Freedmen's Bureau. The Societies also influenced the choice of officers to manage occupied Southern territory.

The services offered by the Freedmen's Aid Societies were replaced by the Freedmen's Bureau and state agencies of the Reconstruction governments in the decade following the war. Even though their influence as a whole was diminished, some individual members continued to work with the freedmen for the rest of their lives.

Wesley Moody

See also: Freedmen's Bureau; Reconstruction Acts in the United States (1867–1868).

Further Readings

Faulkner, Carol. *Women's Radical Reconstruction: The Freedmen's Aid Movement.* Philadelphia: University of Pennsylvania Press, 2003.

McPherson, James. *The Struggle for Equality, Abolitionists and the Negro in the Civil War and Reconstruction.* Princeton, NJ: Princeton University Press, 1964.

Freedmen's Bureau

By the spring of 1865, the Union Amy controlled much of the former Confederacy, a military triumph, but an administrative burden. In addition to the vast acreage in Union hands, much of it abandoned, the former slaves needed help in adjusting to their new circumstances, finding either land or work, and, more immediately, with sustenance and shelter. In order to deal with these issues, Congress passed legislation creating the Bureau of Refugees, Freedmen, and Abandoned Lands, quickly shortened to the Freedmen's Bureau. President Abraham Lincoln signed the law on March 3, 1865.

On May 12, 1865, Major General Oliver Otis Howard became the commissioner of the Bureau. A native of Maine and a graduate of both Bowdoin College and the U.S. Military Academy, Howard's antislavery leanings began at an early age when he spent considerable time with Edward Johnson, an African American who worked for

Engraving titled "The Freedmen's Bureau" depicts a representative of the agency standing between armed blacks and whites. The Freedmen's Bureau was a national organization set up by the U.S. Congress in 1865 to help refugees and freed slaves in the South recover from the ravages of the Civil War. (Library of Congress)

Howard's father. Howard's combination of religious conviction and antislavery feelings made him, in the eyes of most, the ideal candidate to head the Freedmen's Bureau. Initially the Bureau had no budget or funding other than rent received from the abandoned lands under their control, so Howard staffed the Bureau with military officers.

Howard and his men viewed the Bureau as largely a stopgap measure necessary only until the free labor system could take hold in the former slave states. Howard viewed the written contract between laborers and the owners of capital as the way to ensure a smooth transition to free labor, and he directed the Bureau's agents immediately to begin arranging these contracts between freedmen and planters. In addition to coordinating these contracts and enforcing their terms, the Freedmen's Bureau provided clothing and food to those in need, whether they were white or black. The Bureau also helped establish schools for the newly freed people, set up hospitals, and helped former soldiers obtain their bounties.

As President Andrew Johnson grew more accustomed to the office of the presidency, he began to make policy changes that dramatically affected the Freedmen's Bureau and its charges. Initially, lands that had been abandoned during the war were seized by the government and placed under the Freedmen's Bureau. The Bureau had begun dividing the abandoned lands up among the former slaves, but Johnson instead ordered that the abandoned lands be restored to their former owners. How-ard opposed the measure and unsuccessfully attempted to retain the abandoned lands for the freedpeople.

The Bureau, with only 900 men on staff at its peak, was far too small to ad-equately cover the vast area of the former Confederacy. Additionally, while How-ard and his men were dedicated to helping the freedmen, their low opinions of the capabilities of the former slaves limited their ability to be truly effective advocates. An overriding fear that the former slaves would become too dependent on govern-ment help led the Bureau to offer far less support than they could have.

The agency was short lived. As early as 1868, the Bureau began to phase out the services it offered and ceased to provide any programs by 1872. While the Bureau had provided some needed assistance to the freedpeople after the Civil War, it was largely a disappointment to the former slaves who felt the Bureau held them back as much as it helped them up.

Jared Peatman

See also: Freedmen's Aid Societies; Reconstruction Acts in the United States (1867–1868).

Further Readings

Foner, Eric. *Reconstruction: America's Unfinished Revolution, 1863–1877.* New York: Harper & Row, Publishers, 1988.

McFeely, William S. *Yankee Stepfather: General O.O. Howard and the Freedmen.* New Haven, CT: Yale University Press, 1968.

Freedom Suits in North America

Freedom suits, or cases in which a slave sues his or her master for freedom, have been an important, yet not always successful route to freedom for slaves in North America. Most freedom suits did not challenge slavery as an institution, but instead just sought freedom for an individual slave who was illegally enslaved. Under the English common law tradition that most states followed, slaves usually contested their enslavement by a plea of trespass, arguing that they had been injured by their owner. The owners would then respond by contending that they could not injure a slave as the enslaved was the owner's property. The court would then have to decide if injury took place and subsequently whether the person was a slave or not. The success, frequency, and style of freedom suit depended upon local law and the social, economic, and cultural environment.

Freedom suits sat at the nexus of two primary American ideals: the owner's right to unfettered control of his or her property and the slave's right to liberty. The general ideal of liberty as found in the Declaration of Independence sometimes led to freedom for slaves. A few states such as Louisiana and Missouri restricted slaves' access to the courts, except in the case of freedom suits. Other states, like Massachusetts and New Hampshire, ended slavery as a result of freedom suits. The protection of slave owners' property pressed other states, however, to curb slaves' rights to the court altogether.

Due to the federal system in the United States and the influence of the common law tradition, most slave law operated under local conditions. The landmark case, *Somerset v. Stewart* (1772; see *Somerset* Decision), decided that slave law depended on local legal sanction. As a result, state law dictated whether slavery existed or not and defined the body of laws around the institution. Thus, slaves in different states and colonies had very different legal rights. Slaves' access to rights generally mirrors the social and economic environment of the locality. Places more reliant upon slave labor tended to insist upon oppressive laws that sometimes made freedom suits a near impossibility. In contrast, localities with less reliance on slave labor could liberalize their law to endow slaves with some civil rights and provide for some access to the courts.

In Massachusetts, for example, freedom suits were very successful because the state recognized broad legal rights for slaves. Slaves could sue, be witnesses, own property, and enter into contracts. Slaves took advantage of this situation and sued for their freedom in the relatively friendly era of the American Revolution. While many of these cases brought freedom to individuals, two cases, *Walker v. Jennison* (1781–1783) and *Brom and Bett v. Ashley* (1782), actually ended slavery in the state. Both cases argued that the 1780 Massachusetts State Constitution did not support slavery because in its preamble it declared all men "free and equal" and because no positive law enabled slavery. When Walker won his final case in 1783 at the Massachusetts Supreme Judicial Court, slavery was legally dead in the state.

In contrast, South Carolina law provided very little space for slaves to become free and had only three freedom suits, all occurring between 1770 and 1800. South Carolina law gave less recognition to slaves' legal rights than any other state, and consequently slaves rarely brought suits.

Many Virginia slaves used freedom suits as a route to freedom, but the opening was limited to the Revolutionary era. Virginia lawmakers debated ending slavery in their state during the Revolutionary era and opened up the courts to slaves who could prove free lineage. In order to bring a successful case, slaves had to prove that they had a maternal ancestor who had been free. Hundreds of slaves came to the courts with evidence of free ancestry and became free. By the nineteenth century, however, Virginia began curbing the rights of slaves to the courts and virtually stopped the flow of freedom suits.

Louisiana provided yet another type of environment for freedom suits as a former colony under Spain and France. Under Spanish rule, the law was fundamentally unlike that in most English colonies because it recognized that slavery was not "the natural condition of man" and that slaves should have an avenue to freedom as long as the owners were compensated for their property loss. Colonial Louisiana slaves had a right to gain their freedom and sue for it if they paid for it. Once under the United States, Louisiana law became as oppressive toward slaves as the other Deep South states except for one important distinction: the *Civil Code of the State of Louisiana*, a holdover from French rule, explicitly allowed slaves to enter into a contract for freedom and to sue for their freedom. This law allowed the slaves to evade the necessity under common law of beginning an action of trespass as a way to become free. Instead, slaves might sue on the grounds that their right to be free had been taken away. Hundreds of slaves took advantage of this opening in the law and became free. In the 1830s and 1840s, Louisiana's close relationship to the "free" nation of France provided a common opening for freedom, as many slaves sued on the basis of having traveled in France.

Another variation in freedom suits came from Missouri whose relevant laws changed from when it was a territory under congressional oversight. An 1807 territorial statute granted slaves the specific right to sue for their freedom. The statute was reinstated when Missouri became a state. Just as slaves in Massachusetts had learned, however, the legal environment had to be right for freedom suits to succeed. Missouri had its own "golden age" of freedom suits between 1824 and 1844, after the Supreme Court set the favorable precedent "once free, always free" in *Winny v. Whitesides* (1824). This doctrine translated into freedom for slaves who traveled into a free state. After a visit to a free state, Missouri courts would no longer recognize the owner's right to the person. This precedent held fast until *Dred Scott v. Sandford* was brought before the U.S. Supreme Court in 1857.

During the antebellum era, abolitionists throughout the United States used freedom suits as a way to test the boundaries of freedom. In particular, abolitionists tried to advocate for the freedom of men and women whose owners traveled North with them. They pressed free states to grant freedom to slaves who legally entered free territory for extended periods of time. These cases began at the same time as the militant abolitionist movement took hold in the 1830s. The plaintiffs and their abolitionist advocates tested the conflicting laws in different regions of the United States. The Massachusetts Supreme Judicial Court made the first bold statement in *Commonwealth v. Aves* (1836) where Justice Lemuel Shaw argued that slavery, like bigamy, was so repugnant that his state did not have to recognize the laws of another state where it did exist. Connecticut, Pennsylvania, and New York soon followed with court decisions and statutes that did not allow owners to maintain their right to slave property when traveling in their states. Southern states with more open legal systems, such as Kentucky, Missouri, and Louisiana, also witnessed successful freedom suits for slaves traveling to free states. One of these cases was heard before the Supreme Court: *Dred Scott v. Sandford.*

Just as *Aves* advanced slave law well beyond the freedom of one young female plaintiff, Dred Scott's famous case meant much more than a denial of freedom for Scott and his family. Dred Scott filed his freedom suit in 1846 because he had spent extended periods of time in the free territories of Wisconsin and Illinois. The case wound its way through the appeal system with Scott losing more cases than winning. Abolitionists took over his case once it reached the federal level, culminating in a battle in the U.S. Supreme Court. In a 7–2 decision, the Court denied Scott his freedom. The decision written by Chief Justice Roger B. Taney effectively demolished personal liberty laws for slaves throughout the United States. The decision declared that no black person could be a citizen of the United States. The Court also stated that it was unconstitutional to restrict slavery in particular territories. The decision was one of many events in the late 1850s that helped polarize the United States, pressing the nation toward Civil War.

Emily V. Blanck

See also: *Commonwealth v. Aves* (1836); *Somerset* Decision (1772).

Further Readings

Blanck, Emily. "Seventeen Eighty-Three: The Turning Point in the Law of Slavery and Freedom in Massachusetts." *New England Quarterly* 75, 1 (2002): 24–51.

Fehrenbacher, Don E. *The Dred Scott Case: Its Significance in American Law and Politics.* New York: Oxford University Press, 1978.

Hanger, Kimberly S. *Bounded Lives, Bounded Places: Free Black Society in Colonial New Orleans, 1769–1803.* Durham, NC: Duke University Press, 1997.

Higginbotham, A. Leon Jr. *In the Matter of Color, Race and the American Legal Process: The Colonial Period.* New York: Oxford University Press, 1978.

Nicholls, Michael L. "'The Squint of Freedom': African-American Freedom Suits in Post-Revolutionary Virginia." *Slavery and Abolition* 20, 2 (1999): 47–62.

Schafer, Judith. *Becoming Free, Remaining Free: Manumission and Enslavement in New Orleans, 1846–1862.* Baton Rouge: Louisiana State University Press, 2003.

Freemasonry and Antislavery

Freemasonry is a fraternal organization that took hold in the American colonies before the American Revolution, and later reflected the bitter divide in the young nation over the slavery issue in the nineteenth century. Freemasonry itself had its foundation in the stonemason guilds in Europe during the Middle Ages. The organization linked itself to the building of King Solomon's Temple that was found in the Bible's First Book of Kings. Its members follow the principle of fatherhood of God, brotherhood of man, and moral life principles. Prospective members have to be initiated through a series of degrees based on principles and stories found in the Old Testament of the Bible. The fraternity emphasizes itself not as a religion, but as an organization promoting brotherhood. It is not uncommon to find lodges in municipalities, businesses, and military units.

By the nineteenth century, masons and their lodges were scattered throughout the fabric of American society. Each state had its own Grand Lodge as a governing body. American territorial growth into western lands led to the extension of the Masonic brotherhood into the new states of the Union. The Masonic use of secret handshakes and passwords provided a method where information could be secretly passed along without attracting attention. This secrecy fostered the suspicion that freemasonry threatened democratic principles. By the 1820s, a political reform movement was directed against the Masonic movement and its members' prominence in many political institutions. The Anti-Masonic Party was created in New York as a response to a supposed killing of a Masonic critic. This political party briefly became a factor in elections in the northeastern United States, and served as a launching pad for such politicians as Thaddeus Stevens.

Despite claims that their fraternity did not discriminate members based on their racial background, nearly all U.S. Grand Lodge affiliated lodges were white-only. However, African Americans had started their own lodge in Boston, Massachusetts, in 1784. This lodge, African Lodge Number 459, consisted of African American Masons who had previously been members of an Irish military lodge while Boston was occupied by the British Army. These African Americans were led by Prince Hall, who was later master of this lodge. Hall used his lodge to push for a free school for African American children within the city. In addition, he and other lodge members provided a network of contacts to provide aid and support to the local African American community and runaway slaves from the Southern United States. African American or Prince Hall lodges never extended to the Southern states due to the fear of slave revolts. After 1866, however, Prince Hall lodges began to appear in Southern cities and society.

William H. Brown

See also: Hall, Prince.

Further Readings

Coil, Henry W. *Freemasonry through Six Centuries.* 2 vols. Richmond, VA: Macoy Publishing Co., 1967.

Tabbert, Mark A. *American Freemasons: Three Centuries of Building Communities*. Lexington, MA: National Heritage Museum; New York: New York University Press, 2005.

Wesley, Charles H. "The Prince Hall Story, the Origin of Prince Hall Masonry." *Prince Hall Masonic Directory*. Washington, DC: Conference of Grand Masters, Prince Hall Mason, 1981.

Fugitive Slave Law (1850)

The return of fugitive slaves from the South was one of the most important causes of tension between the North and the South in the antebellum era. Article Four, Section Two, Clause Three of the U.S. Constitution stated that fugitives from justice or service were to be turned over to the state or person asking for their return. This process worked only when there was comity between the states, a willingness to honor each other's laws and return fugitives to the offended state. To help ensure comity Congress passed a fugitive slave law in 1793. Under the terms of the 1793 law, a Southern slaveholder who wished to recapture a fugitive slave had to go north himself or send one of his agents to track down the fugitive and arrest him or her. Then the slaveholder or his agent had to go before a judge in federal circuit court to obtain a certificate so that he could return the slave to the original state from which the fugitive had fled.

"Effects of the Fugitive Slave Law." An impassioned condemnation of the Fugitive Slave Act, the print shows a group of black men—possibly freedmen—ambushed by a posse of armed whites in a cornfield. (Library of Congress).

This process was laborious and expensive and contributed to the rising number of fugitive slaves in the antebellum North. Further complicating matters was the rise of the abolition movement and the Underground Railroad, which provided assistance to Southern slaves as they fled northward. In the 1840s, Northern state legislatures also began to enact personal liberty laws to protect free blacks who lived in their states. Who was a free black and who was a fugitive slave became a difficult question to prove, especially if a free black lost his or her freedom papers. As a result of these developments, comity between Northern and Southern states began to collapse.

Southern slaveholders desired a tougher fugitive slave law that would help them reclaim their runaway slaves. Senator James Mason of Virginia introduced legislation for a new fugitive slave law on January 4, 1850. It quickly became caught up in the tangle of legislation that would form the Compromise of 1850. It was not until September 18, 1850, that President Millard Fillmore signed the bill. The Fugitive Slave Law of 1850 was one of the provisions of the Compromise of 1850, and it proved to be the most controversial element of that sectional compromise.

What made the new law so controversial was that it put the federal government on the side of the slaveholder in helping him to recapture his runaway slave property. If a slaveholder believed that one of his slaves had run away, he would report the disappearance, along with a description of the runaway, to a court in his home state. Other courts, federal or state, along with commissioners appointed by the federal courts, or federal marshals, had to accept this statement as the slaveholder's testimony. The slaveholder, or his agent, could either obtain a warrant for the fugitive's arrest or track down the fugitive himself in a free state, arrest the runaway slave, and present him or her to a federal judge or commissioner. If the slaveholder could prove this runaway was his slave, he received a certificate from the judge or commissioner and took his property home with him. The slave could neither testify on his or her own behalf, nor did the alleged runaway enjoy the right of habeas corpus. If a person in the free states tried to assist or hide a runaway slave, or prevent the runaway's recapture, and that person knew the runaway to be a fugitive slave, then that Northerner could be arrested, tried, and if found guilty, fined $1,000, and sentenced to six months in jail. If a marshal asked for assistance in the effort to recapture a fugitive slave, and a person refused his request, then that person could be charged with obstruction and suffer the penalties of fine and/or imprisonment. Commissioners were the only federal employees who benefited materially from this process. They received $10 if the alleged runaway was found guilty and returned to slavery, but only $5 if the alleged runaway was found not guilty. The claimant paid the commissioner's fee. Clearly, there was a financial reward for finding alleged runaways guilty and returning them to slavery.

The harsh provisions of this act shocked the sensibilities of many Northerners. For the first time, Northerners were made complicit in the recapture of fugitive slaves. To assist runaway slaves in their flight to freedom put white and free black Northerners at risk for being prosecuted by federal courts. Civil liberties, such as freedom of speech, habeas corpus, and the liberty of conscience, all appeared to be under attack by the new law. These liberties applied not only to runaway slaves but also Northern whites. Northern free blacks faced the threat of being kidnapped if they resembled an alleged runaway slave or if they lacked their freedom papers. Many runaway slaves began to flee to Canada to put them beyond the reach of the new law.

When the Fugitive Slave Law of 1850 went into effect, Northerners were brought face-to-face with slavery. Slaveholders and their agents began to head north, searching for fugitive slaves. Runaway slaves began to be captured and sent back to the South. One of the most spectacular, and controversial, cases involved Anthony Burns, a fugitive slave from Virginia who had escaped to Boston. He was arrested and placed in prison awaiting his hearing. Black and white Bostonians attempted to free him from jail, but they failed. One marshal died in the raid. The mood in Boston was ugly. Tens of thousands of city residents lined the streets to protest Burns's rendition to Virginia. It took hundreds of well-armed soldiers and marines to accomplish this mission. Episodes such as the rendition of Anthony Burns in 1854, when combined with the passage of the Kansas-Nebraska Act of that year, led growing numbers of Northerners to believe that a Slave Power Conspiracy existed and was turning the national government to the benefit of Southern slaveholders. As a result, more Northerners became sympathetic to the cause of antislavery. The publication of Harriet Beecher Stowe's *Uncle Tom's Cabin* in 1851, which offered the Northern public a view of Southern slavery in the form of a sentimental novel, also helped turn Northern opinion against the law. Northerners were deeply affected by such scenes as Eliza fleeing across the Ohio River from slave-catchers and their hounds. The final straw, though, was the Supreme Court's decision in *Dred Scott v. Sanford* (1857), which stated that Congress could not regulate slavery in the federal territories, and which also declared unconstitutional both popular sovereignty and the Missouri Compromise of 1820. Northern state legislatures began to pass personal liberty laws to protect fugitive slaves in defiance of both the 1850 law and the *Dred Scott* decision. As a result, sectional tensions increased between North and South, tensions that finally boiled over in 1860–1861 into secession and civil war.

James C. Foley

See also: Compromise of 1850; Freedom Suits in North America; Slave Power Argument.

Further Readings

Campbell, Stanley W. *The Slave Catchers: Enforcement of the Fugitive Slave Law, 1850–1860.* Chapel Hill: University of North Carolina Press, 1968.

Fehrenbacher, Don E. *The Slaveholding Republic: An Account of the United States Government's Relations to Slavery.* Completed and edited by Ward M. McAfee. New York: Oxford University Press, 2001.

Finkelman, Paul. *An Imperfect Union: Slavery, Federalism, and Comity.* Chapel Hill: University of North Carolina Press, 1981.

Potter, David M. *The Impending Crisis, 1848–1861.* Completed and edited by Don E. Fehrenbacher. New York: Harper & Row, 1976.

Von Frank, Albert J. *The Trials of Anthony Burns: Freedom and Slavery in Emerson's Boston.* Cambridge, MA: Harvard University Press, 1998.

G

Gabriel's Conspiracy (1800)

The enslaved revolutionary known only as Gabriel was born in 1776 near Richmond, Virginia, at Brookfield, the Henrico County plantation of Thomas Prosser. By Virginia standards, Brookfield was a large plantation, with a population of approximately fifty laborers. The identity of Gabriel's parents is lost to history, but he had two older brothers, Martin and Solomon. Most likely, Gabriel's father was a blacksmith, the occupation chosen for Gabriel and Solomon. Status as a craft artisan provided the young blacksmith with considerable standing in the slave community, as did his ability to read and write. By the mid-1790s, as he approached the age of twenty, Gabriel stood "six feet two or three inches high." A long and "bony face, well made," was marred by the loss of two front teeth and "two or three scars on his head." In later years, a legend arose which held that Gabriel wore his hair long in naive imitation of Samson, in hopes that his locks would give him extraordinary strength. Contemporary descriptions say only that his hair was cut short and was as dark as his complexion. According to journalist James T. Callender, blacks and whites alike regarded him as "a fellow of courage and intellect above his rank in life."

In the fall of 1798, Gabriel's old master died, and ownership of Brookfield passed to twenty-two-year-old Thomas Henry Prosser, who maximized his profits by hiring out his surplus slaves. Despite all of the work to be done at Brookfield, Gabriel spent a considerable part of each month smithing in Richmond for white artisans. Although still a slave under Virginia law, Gabriel enjoyed a rough form of freedom. Indeed, his ties to the plantation became so tenuous that several historians have identified him as a free man. Emboldened by this quasi-liberty, in September 1799 Gabriel moved toward overt rebellion. Caught in the act of stealing a pig by a white neighbor, Gabriel wrestled the man to the ground and bit off the better "part of his left Ear." Under Virginia law, slaves were not tried as whites. They were prosecuted under a colonial statute of 1692 that created special segregated tribunals

145

composed of five justices of the peace. Gabriel was formally charged with attacking a white man, a capital crime. Although found guilty, Gabriel escaped the gallows by pleading "benefit of clergy," which allowed him to avoid hanging in exchange for being branded on the thumb with a small cross as he was able to recite a verse from the Bible.

Gabriel's branding and incarceration served as a brutal reminder that despite his literacy and privileged status, he remained a slave. By the early spring of 1800, his fury began to turn into a carefully considered plan to bring about his freedom, as well as the end of slavery in Virginia. Slaves and free blacks from Henrico County would gather at Brookfield on the evening of August 30 to march on Richmond. If Governor James Monroe and the town leaders agreed to Gabriel's demands for black liberty and an equitable distribution of the property, the slave general intended to "hoist a white flag" and drink a toast "with the merchants of the city."

The conspiracy matured in the context of Atlantic and political affairs of the late 1790s. Since 1793, large numbers of refugees from the slave rebellion in French Saint Domingue had arrived in Virginia, many of them bringing their bondservants with them. Monroe worried that the "scenes which are acted in Saint Doming[ue], must produce an effect on all the people of colour" in the Chesapeake. But if the uprising in the Caribbean helped to inspire mainland rebels, it was the divisive election of 1800 that provided Gabriel with his opportunity. Rumors about Richmond held that if Jefferson was victorious, the Federalists would not relinquish power, and one Federalist newspaper predicted an "ultimate appeal to arms by the two great parties." Most likely, Gabriel not only hoped to exploit this fissure among white elites, but also to throw his lot in with whichever side would benefit the slaves the most in the coming civil conflict.

The planned uprising collapsed just before sunset on the appointed day, when a severe thunderstorm hit the Richmond area. The chaos of the storm convinced two Henrico slaves that the revolt could not succeed. They informed their owner of the conspiracy, and he hurried word to Monroe. After hiding along the James River for nearly two weeks, Gabriel risked boarding the schooner *Mary*. Captain Richardson Taylor, a recent convert to Methodism, spirited Gabriel downriver to Norfolk. There Gabriel was betrayed by an enslaved crewman, who had heard of Monroe's $300 reward for Gabriel's capture. Returned to Richmond under heavy guard, Gabriel was quickly tried and found guilty of "conspiracy and insurrection." On October 10, 1800, the young revolutionary died on the town gallows near Fifteenth and Broad Streets. He was twenty-four. In all, twenty-six slaves, including Gabriel and his two brothers, were hanged for their part in the conspiracy. Eight more rebels were transported to Spanish New Orleans; at least thirty-two others were found not guilty. Reliable sources placed the number of slaves who knew of the plot to be between 5 and 600.

In the aftermath, as was the case with most slave conspiracies, white authorities, as one newspaper put it, moved to "re-enact all those rigorous laws" that had been allowed to lapse after the Revolution. In late 1802, Monroe established the Public Guard of Richmond, a nighttime police force designed to protect the public buildings and militia arsenals. The state assembly passed a law ending the right of masters to hire out their surplus slaves, and in 1806 the legislature amended the state's Manumission Act of 1782 by requiring liberated bondpeople to leave Virginia or face re-enslavement.

Douglas R. Egerton

See also: Manumission; Turner, Nat; Vesey's Conspiracy (1822).

Further Readings

Egerton, Douglas R. *Gabriel's Rebellion: The Virginia Slave Conspiracies of 1800 and 1802.* Chapel Hill: University of North Carolina Press, 1993.
Schwarz, Philip J. *Twice Condemned: Slaves and the Criminal Laws of Virginia, 1705–1865.* Baton Rouge: Louisiana State University Press, 1988.
Sidbury, James. *Ploughshares into Swords: Race, Rebellion, and Identity in Gabriel's Virginia, 1730–1810.* New York: Cambridge University Press, 1997.

Garnet, Henry Highland (1815–1882)

Throughout the antebellum era Henry Highland Garnet was among the most radical of black abolitionists. Born in 1815, Garnet escaped slavery as a boy when his family fled Maryland. Two childhood events helped shape his growing defiance toward whites. When Garnet was fourteen, slave catchers seized his sister, prompting him to buy a knife to defend his family. Five years later, he discharged a shotgun in self-defense against a white mob. In his mid-twenties, Garnet accepted a Presbyterian pastorate in Troy, New York, which served as a platform for his antislavery work. He assumed a leading role in the black convention movement and spearheaded organizing in the 1840s and 1850s for African Americans to regain the suffrage in New York.

In 1840, Garnet helped establish the American and Foreign Anti-Slavery Society when he became dissatisfied with William Lloyd Garrison's unwillingness to use politics in fighting slavery. Garnet became nationally prominent in 1843 when he delivered a controversial speech before the National Convention of Colored Citizens in Buffalo, New York. In his address, he called on Southern slaves to stage work stoppages and insurrections against their masters. Slaves had nothing to lose and everything to gain, he argued. Not only was resistance a moral duty, but God required that they refuse to submit further to their oppressors. To fail to oppose them, Garnet emphasized, was to offend and anger God. Resistance was the only path for them to secure their liberty. Frederick Douglass immediately condemned Garnet's speech as too inflammatory, which sparked a personal rivalry between them that would span two decades.

In the early 1850s, Garnet lectured in Great Britain, lobbying for an economic boycott of slave-manufactured goods. After a three-year missionary stint in Jamaica, he returned to America and settled in New York City where he became minister of Shiloh Presbyterian Church. Garnet had also by then become an advocate of overseas emigration. The Fugitive Slave Law of 1850 had made free blacks more receptive to relocating outside the United States. In 1858, Garnet and Martin Delany cofounded the African Civilization Society, which promoted the voluntary colonization of African Americans in Africa. Through the society, Garnet sought to destroy slavery and the slave trade, end prejudice through black economic advance, disseminate Christianity in Africa, encourage the cultivation of free labor cotton in Africa in order to undermine the Southern economy, and build an independent black state as a bulwark of black nationalism. With the advent of the Civil War, Garnet shifted his priorities, supporting the Union and the Republicans and lobbying for the use of black troops, and after 1862, recruiting them. In 1864, he moved to Washington, D.C., to pastor the prestigious Fifteenth Street Presbyterian Church. His stature led to an invitation to speak before the U.S. House of Representatives.

On February 14, 1865, Garnet became the first African American to address Congress. In his discourse, over which he reviewed the many long decades of black struggles against slavery and injustice, he called for the enfranchisement and equal treatment of black Americans as the Civil War was ending. Garnet receded from the spotlight after the war, returning to a New York church at which he had served as pastor earlier. In 1881, President Garfield appointed Garnet as minister resident to Liberia. Although advanced in years and declining in health, Garnet accepted the diplomatic post, intent on strengthening the economic ties between the two countries. He arrived in Liberia at year's end, but died less than seven weeks later on February 13, 1882. After sixty-six years, Garnet died in Africa, the place he had yearned for since his youth.

Shawn Mosher

See also: Garrisonians.

Further Readings

Ofari, Earl. *"Let Your Motto Be Resistance": The Life and Thought of Henry Highland Garnet.* Boston: Beacon Press, 1972.

Pasternak, Martin B. *Rise Now and Fly to Arms: The Life of Henry Highland Garnet*. New York: Garland Publishing, 1995.

Schor, Joel. *Henry Highland Garnet*. Westport, CT: Greenwood Press, 1977.

Garrison, William Lloyd

Through his indefatigable activities as an editor and reformer, William Lloyd Garrison became one of the most outspoken and radical abolitionists of the antebellum United States.

Born in 1805 as the fourth child to a merchant seaman, Abijah Garrison, and a housekeeper, Frances Lloyd, William spent his early years in an impoverished and unstable but religiously pious household in Newburyport, Massachusetts. Abijah's drinking led him to abandon his family in 1808, at the height of the economic dislocation caused by the 1807 Embargo Act. William's mother, a devout Baptist familiarly called "Fanny," moved the family several times while searching for work and suitable apprenticeships for her sons. In 1818, she left William in the care of the editor of the Newburyport *Herald*, Ephraim Allen, who instructed Garrison in the techniques of the print trade that he would use in his antislavery crusade.

When his apprenticeship ended in 1826, William became editor of the *Free Press*, also in Newburyport, and subsequently traveled to edit a series of newspapers in Massachusetts and Vermont. As an editor, Garrison was adept at spotting literary talent, publishing the first works of the Quaker poet John Greenleaf Whittier. As a

As a propagandist, William Lloyd Garrison polarized the nation on the issue of slavery more than any other single abolitionist. (National Archives)

businessman, Garrison was a failure; each of the papers he edited during this period folded soon after his arrival, for Garrison cared less about holding an audience of readers than in preaching to them through his press. Garrison looked on electoral politics with disdain at a time of vast, though white and male, voter participation, telling readers that politics was an activity corrupting to observant Christians. Readers soon refused to pay for such editorials, and Garrison's early journalism career was populated by failures.

His fortunes were reversed, however, by two events, both in 1828. Garrison joined a newspaper in Boston called the *National Philanthropist* that advocated a broad set of anti-gambling, religious, and pacifist reforms. He also was invited to Baltimore by the Quaker abolitionist Benjamin Lundy to coedit a weekly paper called the *Genius of Universal Emancipation*. This introduction to radical abolitionism—calling for immediate rather than gradual emancipation—landed Garrison in Baltimore's city jail in 1830. He was convicted for libeling a prominent Boston merchant, Francis Todd; Garrison said that Todd was engaged in the interstate slave trade and called him a "murderer." Convicted and unable—or unwilling—to pay a fine, Garrison was held in Baltimore's city jail for forty-nine days. From there, he labored to write a pamphlet and send out regular dispatches condemning slavery, calling for immediate abolition, and drawing attention to his plight; his quasi-martyrdom propelled him to prominence among abolitionists throughout the Northeast, and his imprisonment ended when the New York merchant brothers Arthur and Lewis Tappan paid his fine.

Garrison spent the following months delivering lectures throughout the region, a minor celebrity honing his religious message. Slavery, he believed, was so offensive to God that it required vehement, but peaceful, opposition on the part of all Christians, who had to seek *immediate* liberation for the enslaved and penitence from their oppressors. This view put Garrison at odds with the prevailing goals of the abolitionist movement: *gradual* emancipation and relocation. The American Colonization Society, which sought to resettle free blacks in Africa, would merely create a country more suitable for slavery, Garrison believed, by banishing free blacks and making slavery a normative condition.

To carry his message, Garrison founded a newspaper called the *Liberator* in 1830 and printed his first edition on January 1, 1831. His opening editorial proclaimed, "I am in earnest—I will not equivocate—I will not excuse—I will not retreat a single inch and *I will be heard.*" The paper's motto was, "Our country is the world. . . . Our countrymen are mankind." Financially supported by free blacks and religious whites in Northern cities, the *Liberator* eventually swelled to 30,000 subscriptions and made Garrison the leader of a movement then in the early stages of defining itself. Garrison gained respect in abolitionist circles and became a target for Southern slaveholders who peppered him with death threats.

Nevertheless Garrison's influence grew. In 1832, he cofounded the New England Anti-Slavery Society; it called for immediate abolition and an end to social and legal distinctions among races. That same year, he penned a pamphlet that attacked the American Colonization Society, *Thoughts on African Colonization*, and took an increasingly harsh and confrontational tone in his newspaper that garnered him further attention as he led a multi-front attack on slavery.

In 1833, Garrison sailed to Great Britain, meeting there with veteran abolitionists Thomas Buxton, Daniel O'Connell, George Thompson, and William Wilberforce. Garrison had come to view the antislavery cause as a global one, and sought both moral and financial support from British for his mission at home.

In December 1833, Garrison and fifty others founded the American Anti-Slavery Society in Philadelphia, making common cause among Quaker abolitionists John Greenleaf Whittier and Lucretia Mott, religious evangelicals Joshua Leavitt, William Jay, and Samuel Sewall, and free blacks such as Robert Purvis. The organization's *Declaration of Sentiments*, authored by Garrison himself, made clear that it aspired to be something wholly new to the American political landscape: a racially and gender-integrated network of pacifist activists who sought the establishment of smaller grassroots societies, newspapers, and campaigns to aid them in wiping slavery away. Instead of working by the ballot or through legislatures, they appealed to individuals' consciences through the religious revivalism of the period and what they called "moral suasion."

Proslavery partisans did not sit idly by as Garrison and his allies made their attacks. Garrison was harassed by a mob in Boston in 1835, while copies of his newspaper were confiscated and sometimes burned in Southern post offices. Within the abolitionist movement, Garrison's disdain for politics provoked a fissure within the American Anti-Slavery Society; his views on clerical authority, the Scriptures, and women's rights put him in opposition to many of his most prominent fellow abolitionists who feared that such positions would cost them public support.

The division that began in the mid-1830s between Garrisonians favoring a holistic moral shift in American society and anti-Garrisonians focused solely on slavery provoked, in 1840, the formation of the splinter American and Foreign Anti-Slavery Society. Secession, experienced within Garrison's pared-down American Anti-Slavery Society, led him to advocate for Northern secession; the *Liberator's* masthead urged, "No Union with Slaveholders." Throughout the 1840s and 1850s, Garrison represented the wing of abolitionism that would sacrifice the union to escape what they saw as slavery's broad taint. When he burned a copy of the Constitution in 1854, Garrison only cemented this position, making himself gradually more marginal in the political struggles of the decade.

Yet Garrison did shift positions, embracing Abraham Lincoln's affirmation of the Union in 1860 and defending the 1863 Emancipation Proclamation, in spite of its narrow limitations. This put Garrison on the more conservative side of many of his antebellum allies, including Wendell Phillips. While Phillips sought political equality for blacks, Garrison insisted that political rights were privileges that could be conditioned on educational and behavioral standards and tests. With emancipation in 1865, Garrison saw his work as done; he closed the *Liberator* and left the American Anti-Slavery Society after failing to disband it. Apart from a few pamphlets and articles, Garrison was largely silent in the 1860s and 1870s and died in New York City, leaving a still debated legacy over his historical importance and influence in the *causus belli* of the Civil War.

Brian Murphy

See also: American Anti-Slavery Society (AASS); New England Antislavery Society (NEASS); U.S. Constitution and Antislavery.

Further Readings

Mayer, Henry. *All on Fire: William Lloyd Garrison and the Abolition of Slavery.* New York: St. Martin's Griffin, 2000.

Ruchames, Louis, and Walter Merrill, eds. *The Letters of William Lloyd Garrison, 1805–1879.* 6 vols. Cambridge, MA: Belknap Press, 1963–1981.

Stewart, James Brewer. *William Lloyd Garrison and the Challenge of Emancipation.* Wheeling, IL: Harlan Davidson, 1992.

Garrisonians

Named after the antislavery activist William Lloyd Garrison, Garrisonians were members of a radical and relatively small segment of the abolitionist movement that emerged in the early 1830s. Its adherents rejected compromise with slave owners and called for an immediate end to slavery. Based mainly in Boston, they included prominent abolitionists such as Maria Weston Chapman, Henry C. Wright, Wendell Phillips, Samuel J. May, Parker Pillsbury, and most notably the group's leader William Lloyd Garrison. Garrisonian abolitionists were predominantly pious non-denominational Christians or practitioners of less-organized and nonhierarchical forms of Christianity, including the Quakers and the Unitarians. While Garrisonian attitudes toward the role of women in the antislavery movement evolved, they generally were the most inclusive of abolitionists. This impulse stemmed from the many Quakers in the group who favored gender egalitarianism as well as the influence of Garrison's many female supporters. As a result, Garrisonian women played a central part within this wing of American abolitionism.

Most Garrisonians refused to participate directly in politics because they viewed the American political system as a process that was rooted in human bondage and bound to compromise with the evil institution: some went so far as to argue that the U.S. Constitution itself was an inherently proslavery document. Therefore, voting or other political activities rendered individuals personally complicit in the sin of slavery. By the early 1840s, Garrison himself believed that the Northern states should secede from the South if its elite insisted on upholding a slave system. However, Garrisonians argued against violence as a means to achieve their goals because they considered such behavior un-Christian.

Instead, they argued that an end to slavery could best be accomplished through the moral suasion of women and men. In January 1831, Garrison began publishing a weekly newspaper entitled the *Liberator*, which was the central mouthpiece through which Garrisonian abolitionists spread their message until December 1865, when the newspaper concluded its uninterrupted run. While Garrison was the principal contributor to the production of the newspaper, Chapman and May, among many others, frequently played important supporting roles in its production and distribution. Consequently, the *Liberator* was effective in uniting Garrisonians by giving them a project to work on together.

As a result of their radical, uncompromising, and vocal views on both slavery and how best to end it, Garrisonians often found themselves at odds with their fellow abolitionists. These conflicts became particularly intense during the early 1840s, when Garrisonians gained control of the American Anti-Slavery Society (AASS) after a bitter convention of the Society in New York City in July 1840 at which a female supporter of the Garrisonian faction, Abby Kelley Foster, was elected to the executive. In response to this transgression of gender roles, in addition to a number of other disputes plaguing the organization, the dissidents broke away from the AASS and formed the American and Foreign Anti-Slavery Society (AFASS). However, the inclusiveness frequently demonstrated by Garrisonians, particularly toward women, had limitations. While Garrison and his supporters encouraged black antislavery activists, especially ex-slaves, to speak at their rallies, they were not comfortable with African American abolitionists such as Frederick Douglass, editing their own newspapers. Partially as a result of the condescending attitude that Garrisonians showed toward black abolitionists, Douglass distanced himself from the group during the 1840s and 1850s. Yet many of the prominent black abolitionists in the Boston area including John T. Hilton, Lewis Hayden, William Wells Brown, and Charles Lenox Remond were ardent Garrisonians.

Opposed to participation in politics, Garrison and his supporters largely were unsupportive of the 1840 and 1844 antislavery Liberty Party presidential campaigns of James G. Birney. Despite frequent disputes among Garrisonians, they largely remained united in their support of Garrison's crusade to end slavery, often describing him in religious terms. However, with the rise of the Republican Party in the 1850s, the nonpolitical abolitionism advocated by Garrisonians became less relevant to the debate over slavery in America. As a result, Garrison and his supporters were often less antagonistic toward the Republican Party than they had been toward the Liberty Party. In addition, Garrisonian opposition to the use of violence became less extreme in the 1840s and 1850s, showing sympathy for militant antislavery activism in Bleeding Kansas and John Brown's uprising.

Garrisonians represented a far more important part of the abolitionist movement than their modest base of support would suggest. William Lloyd Garrison and his supporters wielded considerable influence in the debate over slavery in the United States. Furthermore, the prominent positions female abolitionists were able to take within Garrison's inner circle allowed women to challenge prescribed antebellum gender roles.

David M. Greenspoon

See also: Radical Republicans; Whig Party and Antislavery.

Further Readings

Friedman, Lawrence J. *Gregarious Saints: Self and Community in American Abolitionism: 1830–1870.* Cambridge: Cambridge University Press, 1982.

Mayer, Henry. *All on Fire: William Lloyd Garrison and the Abolition of Slavery.* New York: St. Martin's Press, 1998.

Stewart, James Brewer. *Holy Warriors: The Abolitionists and American Slavery.* Rev. ed. New York: Hill and Wang, 1996.

German Coast (Louisiana) Insurrection of 1811

On January 20, 1811, Governor William Claiborne wrote to Thomas Jefferson regarding a slave rebellion that had just taken place north of New Orleans, in the German Coast county of Lower Louisiana, "We have lately experienced much alarm in consequence of an Insurrection among the Slaves in this vicinity. It at first assumed a menacing aspect; but was very soon quelled by the prompt and decisive movements of the armed force of the United States, and the Body of the Militia." Stressing the swiftness of the repression, Governor William Claiborne minimized the actual scope of the slave rebellion and described the rebels as mere desperate brigands. Across the United States though, the rebellion became known as "the miniature representation of the horrors of Santo Domingo," and alarming accounts of the rebellion were printed in American newspapers North and South.

The Territory of Orleans, which was soon to be admitted as an American state, had experienced its largest slave rebellion to date. Again and again, this momentous event has been labeled as one of the largest slave revolts in U.S. history. Yet, information regarding the rebellion itself remains scattered and at best superficial.

Four days before William Claiborne's reassuring letter was penned, Jean, a teenage slave, had narrowly escaped capital punishment. He had, "with force and arms, [made] or [caused] to be made an insurrection in the Territory of Orleans." The St. Charles parish authorities had sentenced him to attend the execution of his fellow slave, Gery, convicted the day before, and to receive a punishment of thirty lashes in the public jail. Jean was among the yet-undetermined number of slaves—between 150 and 500—who had risen up in arms in the two densely populated sugar parishes of St. Charles and St. John the Baptist, about thirty miles upriver from New Orleans.

The parish of St. John the Baptist, where the revolt started, had a slave population of 1,500. Plantations were moderately large in size—an average of twelve slaves per plantation—and were relatively larger on the left bank of the Mississippi River. The largest plantation, which had a slave population of about ninety slaves, was that of Manuel Andry. It was there that the revolt erupted. Just south of St. John the Baptist, the St. Charles parish had a slave population of 2,300, which made it the parish with the largest concentration of slaves in the Territory of Orleans. There were, on average, twenty slaves per plantation. On the left bank of the parish, however, most slaves lived on much larger plantations, which averaged more than fifty slaves. Throughout the parish, there were four slaves for each white inhabitant, a factor largely contributing to the sense of hysteria provoked by the slave rebellion. The two parishes had recently received large groups of new African slaves and the slave labor force of the sugar plantations had markedly increased. The Pointe Coupée Rebellion of 1795 had taken place a long way away from the capital, but now the danger seemed to lay at the threshold of the city and faubourgs where in excess of 13,000 slaves lived.

Louisiana planters had long been used to the problem of slave resistance, but revolt on this scale was unheard of, and it was all the more disquieting as Louisiana had become increasingly dependent upon the labor of its slave population. To make matters worse, it was often deplored that police forces were unable to effectively control the activities and whereabouts of slaves. In the late eighteenth century, James Pitot, a Frenchman who had recently arrived in Louisiana, observed that "the patrols are insignificant; the garrison is inconsequential; the militia not in uniform . . . Negroes, less subject to authority and more able to move around without supervision on the main roads and in town, are in a position to learn the ways of corruption . . . and *the anxious owner lives in a state of war with his slaves.*" In 1811, many planters would have still agreed with this characterization. William

Claiborne was apparently convinced of the existence of such a state of war; no sooner had the slave rebellion been crushed, then he called for the complete overhaul of the militia.

The insurrection was led by a mulatto slave driver named Charles Deslondes, who was born in Saint Domingue. As in Saint Domingue, the insurrection started with the sound of drums which issued from the plantation of Manuel Andry on the evening of January 8, 1811. Manuel Andry was wounded and his son was killed; the slaves took the ammunition they could find and then marched to other plantations in the two parishes of the German Coast. Whites fled to New Orleans, where the City Guard was ordered to patrol the streets and check for any signs of possible insurrection. The slave rebels were joined by bands of runaway slaves but their progression was brutally checked two days later by regular soldiers, volunteer corps, and militiamen. All in all, sixty-six slaves were killed during the repression, twenty-two were imprisoned, and nineteen were reported missing. Of all the slaves arrested, twenty-two were executed, including Charles Deslondes. The brutality of the repression called to mind the similarly brutal suppression of the Pointe Coupée rebellion a few years earlier.

The German Coast insurrection laid bare the tensions interwoven in the slave and African American community. Unlike the Pointe Coupée conspiracy, free people of color were not involved in the plot and did not support the forced abolition of slavery. On the contrary, they were praised for their participation in suppressing the revolt. In addition, the authorities felt confident enough to assert also that "great fidelity has been evinced by the Slaves towards their master in the most trying circumstances." Such self-confidence was, of course, grossly overrated, but some slaves did indeed fight the rebels to defend their masters' plantations. Bazile, for instance, a mulatto belonging to the estate of the deceased Meuillon, was praised for fighting the rebels who had set fire to his master's house.

The structure and causes of the German Coast insurrection are maybe best understood when compared with the Pointe Coupée Rebellion of 1795. Both rebellions took place in times when the Louisiana slave demography was being dramatically altered. The 1780s saw the arrival of shipload after shipload of African slaves from two of the Caribbean's most active slave ports: Kingston and Roseau. The 1800s was a period marked, in particular, by the brisk reexport trade in slaves from Cuba and Charleston and by the arrival of refugee slaves from Saint Domingue and Cuba. Plantation demography was destabilized each time, and rebellious strains came to the fore. The Pointe Coupée slave conspiracy was blamed in part on the arrival of too many slaves from the Caribbean, which led planters and authorities to call for a total suspension of the slave trade. William Claiborne similarly appraised the German Coast insurrection and called for checks on the influx of slaves from other American states. But the similarities end there. Planters did not agree with Governor Claiborne and did not petition for the imposition of new checks on the slave trade; they needed as many slaves as possible to develop their new, prosperous cotton and sugar plantations. Planters would continue importing large numbers of slaves, no matter what.

To do that safely and avert further insurrections, they needed, however, to re-form existing modes of slave control. The reorganization of the militia and the several plans for the creation of a gendarmerie for the city, suburbs, and other districts of New Orleans who would be in charge of arresting runaway slaves and controlling slaves in general were two clear steps in that direction. The failure of the German Coast insurrection did not mean the end of slave resistance, but it signaled to planters that a slave society needed adequate and reliable forces capable of controlling the slaves and deterring rebellion. It served to unite planters at the same time as it tested the rebellious resolve of the slave population.

Jean-Pierre Le Glaunec

See also: Gabriel's Conspiracy (1800); Turner, Nat; Vesey's Conspiracy (1822).

Further Readings

Aptheker, Herbert. *American Negro Slave Revolts.* 5th ed. New York: Columbia University Press, 1987.

Ingersoll, Thomas. *Mammon and Manon in Early New Orleans. The First Slave Society in the Deep South, 1718–1819.* Knoxville: University of Tennessee Press, 1999.

Pitot, James. *Observations on the Colony of Louisiana from 1796 to 1802.* Baton Rouge; London: Louisiana State University Press, 1979.

Rodriguez, Junius Peter. "Ripe for Revolt: Louisiana and the Tradition of Slave Insurrection, 1803–1865." Ph.D. Dissertation: Tulane University, 1992.

Rowland, Dunbar, ed. *Official Letter Books of William C. C. Claiborne, 1801–1816.* Jackson, 1917.

Thrasher, Albert, *"On to New Orleans." Louisiana's Heroic 1811 Slave Revolt,* New Orleans: Cypress Press, 1995.

Germantown Antislavery Petition (1688)

Written at a Quaker meeting in Germantown, Pennsylvania, on April 18, 1688, the petition is believed to be the first public protest against slavery in British North America. The four Quaker men who signed the petition—Francis Daniel Pastorius, Gerret Hendericks, Derick op de Graef, and Abraham op de Graef—were recent immigrants from Germany who had settled in Pennsylvania to escape religious persecution.

Founded in 1681 by Quaker leader William Penn, Pennsylvania granted freedom of conscience to Protestant Christians of any denomination, earning it the byname of the "holy experiment." The Germantown petition denounced the incongruities between the spiritual and social aspirations of the Quaker founders and the inhuman institution of slavery practiced by many Quakers. Recognizing the profound moral, social, and political ramifications of this issue, the monthly and quarterly Quaker meetings shifted the petition to the Yearly Meeting, the highest policy-making authority, which ultimately dismissed it. Although the petition had no immediate effect on the Quakers' stance toward slavery, the protest is notable for presaging their strong antislavery commitment.

George Fox, founder of the Society of Friends (Quakers), had admonished slaveholders in America to free slaves after a number of years and to ensure proper religious instruction. Removed from their own experience of oppression in England, however, many American Quakers kept slaves for life. Except for Pastorius, the signers of the Germantown protest were Mennonites who had only recently converted to Quakerism. In sixteenth- and early seventeenth-century Europe, Anabaptist groups such as the Mennonites had suffered severe persecution, including torture and public executions. While no longer fearing for their lives in the late seventeenth century, radical Protestants such as the Mennonites were still barred from a free exercise of their religion and a full participation in civic life. In America, however, slavery dashed these immigrants' utopian hopes for a society free from the moral and social vices of Europe.

While most of the early Germantown settlers had little formal education, Pastorius had a legal degree and years of classical training. He was the only German Quaker able to compose a formal petition in English. Pastorius was grounded in the Pietistic renewal of Lutheranism in Germany and joined the Society of Friends after his arrival in Pennsylvania. Both Pietism and Quakerism sought to reform orthodox Protestantism through an emphasis on the workings of the spirit within each individual and the primacy of personal conscience over religious and secular authority. They are evident in the petition—a handwritten, two-page document—which appealed to Christian principles in general and Quaker ethics in particular. Throughout, the protest admonished readers to apply the "Golden Rule," the biblical injunction to "do unto others as you would have them do unto you," to the problem of slavery. Instead of asking white Christians to imagine slavery theoretically, the document recalled the dread most Europeans felt about the common occurrence of enslavement by Turkish pirates. The petition also applied this mirroring technique to the possibility of slave insurrections: since Europeans would defend their precious liberty by any means possible, why should enslaved Africans not be allowed to do the same?

The protest furthermore listed a series of abominations originating in the slave trade, particularly that the separation of husbands and wives resulted in adultery.

Following the Quaker doctrine against trading in stolen goods, Pastorius repeatedly described slavery as the robbing of humans. The petition worked most effectively in pointing out the inconsistency between the founding principles of Pennsylvania and the practice of slavery: "In Europe there are many oppressed for Conscience sacke; and here there are those oppressed wch are of black Colour." In another line of reasoning, the document asked Quakers to consider their own reputation, especially among their critics. The petitioners lamented that slavery might prevent other religious dissenters from coming to Pennsylvania. Finally, the petition insisted that slavery is an issue that precludes moral ambiguity, asking the community to "consider well this thing, if it is good or bad?" In reducing the problem to a simple moral choice, the petition did not allow for equivocation or economic justification. Yet the Quakers' response to this test of their collective conscience admitted no such moral clarity. According to the minutes, the members of the Yearly Meeting at Burlington judged the issue too complex to be dealt with, "It having so General a Relation to many other Parts, and therefore at present they forebear It."

Patrick M. Erben

See also: Antislavery Evangelical Protestantism.

Further Readings

Binder-Johnson, Hildegard. "The Germantown Protest of 1688 against Negro Slavery." *Pennsylvania Magazine of History and Biography* 65 (1941): 145–156.

Learned, Marion Dexter. *The Life of Francis Daniel Pastorius*. Philadelphia: Campbell, 1908.

Soderlund, Jean R. *Quakers and Slavery: A Divided Spirit*. Princeton, NJ: Princeton University Press, 1985.

Gradual Emancipation

Between 1780 and 1888, slavery ended in more than two dozen societies in the Western Hemisphere. A growing number of government officials and interest groups who were influenced by Enlightenment ideas that emphasized a rationalist vision of the world, a developing sense of cultural relativism, new currents in religious thought that deemed slavery a sin against humanity, and economic theory that considered slavery an anachronism which could not compete with free labor, concluded that slavery was no longer a legitimate institution.

Yet, in the North of the United States, Canada, the British, French, and Danish West Indies, the Spanish American republics, Brazil, Cuba, and Puerto Rico, emancipation enacted gradually—or, gradual emancipation was the dominant pattern. Many factors contributed to the slow pace of emancipation including resistance by slaveholders, an attachment to property rights, the fear of social disorder, widespread confidence in the efficacy of piecemeal reform, a concern by metropolitan elites in the colonial empires that abolition would disrupt imperial relations, the enormous wealth generated by slave labor, and a pervasive racism directed toward Africans in the Americas. Thus, with few exceptions, gradual emancipation was promulgated only after years of debate and important concessions to slaveholders' demands.

Gradual emancipation made inroads earliest in the Northern states of the United States. During the Revolutionary era, religious groups such as the Quakers and evangelical Protestants concluded that slavery was contrary to God's will. They and others who considered America as the last refuge of freedom came to view the system as the antithesis of the Revolution's fundamental aims. In addition, African Americans increasingly demanded freedom.

With antislavery activism and support for the Revolution fully intertwined, slavery gradually moved toward extinction in the North. In comparison with the U.S. South, relatively few Northerners depended upon slaves for their social standing, political power, or economic well-being, and there were too few slaves to threaten white supremacy once emancipation occurred. Moreover, an extensive system of free labor not only made slavery less necessary, but also led many white wage laborers to oppose cheaper slave labor.

In 1780, Pennsylvania enacted the first emancipation law in the Western Hemisphere, which proved to be the most restrictive passed in the North between 1780 and 1784. Intended to avoid a disruptive end of slavery and economic loss for slaveholders, the law did not free a single slave. All slaves born before the law went into effect were to continue to be held in lifetime bondage, and all children born of a slave after 1780 would not be freed until they reached age twenty-eight. In fact, the last slave in Pennsylvania was not freed until 1847.

Despite its severe limitations, the Pennsylvania law encouraged the antislavery forces in other Northern states during the Revolution. The Massachusetts Constitution of 1780 did not mention slavery, but its declaration that all men were born free and enjoyed equal rights became the basis for a freedom suit that judicially abolished the institution. However, that decision, the *Jennison* case, in fact produced gradual emancipation, for slavery after Jennison had no legal foundation in the state and any individual who challenged his or her enslavement would win. By the early 1790s, slavery had all but disappeared in Massachusetts.

The pattern of emancipation was similar in New Hampshire, where the 1783 constitution's statement that all men were born equal and independent and enjoyed natural rights was sufficiently unclear with regard to slavery that nearly a decade later 150 slaves still resided in the state, although by then more than 600 had been freed. Vermont was the exception to the pattern of gradual emancipation in the North. Its 1777 constitution, which embodied the principle of "higher law" justice, explicitly abolished slavery.

Unlike in Massachusetts, Vermont, and New Hampshire, the Rhode Island legislature passed a gradual emancipation law in 1783 but, at the same time, continued the slave trade. The law protected slaveholders' interests by making all children of slaves born after 1783 apprentices; girls could not be freed until age eighteen and boys at age twenty-one. Until that time, masters could rid themselves of the expense of sustaining these children by freeing their mothers and having their communities support the children.

In Connecticut, Revolutionary ideology also prompted legislative action against slavery. After rejecting three emancipation bills between 1777 and 1780, the legislature passed a law in 1784 that provided for black and mulatto children born after that year to be freed at age twenty-eight. Although a 1794 bill that would have ended slavery the following year was defeated, in 1797 the legislature reduced the age of manumission to twenty-one years of age. However, the state did not enact total abolition until 1848.

Among the Northern states, New York and New Jersey, which had the region's largest slave populations, were the last to enact gradual emancipation laws. During the 1780s, the influence of Revolutionary ideals moved the New York legislature to allow slaveholders to manumit their slaves without posting bond and to establish a uniform system of justice for blacks and whites. The creation of the New York Manumission Society reflected growing antislavery sentiment in the state, but slaveholders represented a large minority of its members and officers. Indeed, it consciously refrained from directly attacking slavery in New York and preferred to reform the institution and achieve emancipation with a minimum of disruption. Thus, an effort to abolish slavery in 1785 failed.

The gradual emancipation act of 1799 provided significant safeguards for slaveholders. All slave children were required to serve the masters of their mothers until males were twenty-eight and females were twenty-five, and masters could abandon these children a year after their birth. In addition, the fact that masters were paid by the state for every child over one year of age whom they kept amounted to compensated emancipation. Consequently, most slaves remained in bondage for many years; only in 1817 could African Americans born before 1799 have any realistic hope of soon being freed. Slavery in fact was not abolished in New York until July 4, 1827.

Emancipation occurred even more gradually in New Jersey. Antislavery groups labored for nearly twenty years before an emancipation act was finally passed in

1804. This law was extremely gradual in its effect, and explicitly protected slave-holders' property rights. Indeed, no slaves were freed at the time, and masters retained the right to the services of young slaves. Much as in New York, owners could assign children to overseers of the poor, and these children could then be reassigned to their masters, who were paid a monthly allowance by the state. Male slaves were to be freed at age twenty-five and females at twenty-one, but if females bore children, masters owned them until they reached a working age.

With a weak antislavery movement, interest in total abolition did not revive until the 1830s, and the state did not formally abolish slavery until the following decade. Even then, the remaining slaves were still subject to a form of servitude. Indeed, a small number of slaves were not freed until the ratification of the Thirteenth Amendment in 1865.

All in all, the Northern states generally moved slowly and cautiously toward emancipation, even where there were often relatively few slaves. This was also the case in Lower Canada, where fewer than fifty slaves resided, and in Upper Canada, where there were fewer than 100 slaves. Indeed, emancipation laws passed there provided freedom only for those born in or after 1793 and only after they reached their age of majority at twenty-five. A security against former slaves becoming a public charge was also required to be posted.

From 1780 through 1830, antislavery Americans generally employed gradualist rhetoric and tactics and achieved limited success in their efforts to end slavery throughout the nation. At the Philadelphia Convention in 1787, the Founding Fathers chose national unity over liberty because they wanted to avoid secession by the Lower South delegates, were convinced that the Revolution's goals were inextricably linked to the sanctity of private property, and were hopeful that slavery would gradually die out. Likewise, during the late eighteenth and early nineteenth centuries, the organized antislavery movement—most notably represented by the Pennsylvania Abolition Society—was decidedly gradualist in tone and philosophy. The Pennsylvania organization was led by elites who sought gradual emancipation through lawsuits, legislative action, and petitioning on behalf of African Americans. From the 1790s through the 1820s, the American Convention of Abolition Societies, which was largely dominated by the New York and Pennsylvania groups, served as a clearinghouse for gradual emancipation efforts and sought to pressure government leaders to ameliorate the slave trade and to end slavery in the District of Columbia.

Another form of gradualism was espoused by many Northern antislavery colonizationists during the 1820s and 1830s. These colonizationists hoped that by persuading masters to free their slaves and send them to Liberia, slavery could eventually be eradicated. Most slaveholders, however, resented the antislavery pronouncements of these colonizationists, and by the 1830s Southern whites, as well as Northern free blacks, had turned against the movement.

By the 1840s, a growing number of antislavery Northerners had embraced yet another form of gradualism. Those who supported the Wilmot Proviso, which sought to prohibit slavery in the vast area that would be purchased from Mexico at the end of the Mexican War, hoped that this bill would effectively contain slavery in the South and thereby, they believed, moving it toward extinction. Large numbers of Free Soilers and, by the mid-1850s, Republicans embraced this gradualist approach, which they believed would ultimately convince non-slaveholding Southerners to abolish slavery in their states. In the final analysis, slavery in the United States was not destroyed until the Union armies defeated the Confederacy, thus enabling the Emancipation Proclamation to take effect throughout the South in 1865.

British abolitionists in the 1790s who sought to end the importation of slaves into the British West Indies, much like those Americans who later attempted to halt the spread of slavery into the western territories, disavowed any intention of interfering with slavery where it had long existed and mistakenly assumed their actions would soon lead to the eradication of slavery. In fact, the road to emancipation in the British West Indies was both long and difficult.

Vigorous opposition to emancipation by West Indian planters, as well as the British government's reluctance to risk disruption of the existing system of imperial rule by forcing emancipation on the colonies, combined to slow the move toward eradicating slavery. Following major slave rebellions in Jamaica and other islands, the British government abolished slavery in 1834. However, the planters had resisted so strenuously that Parliament agreed to compensate them generously and to establish a six-year apprenticeship for the former slaves, which perpetuated various methods of exploitation. Nevertheless, bitter apprenticeship strikes and other forms of unrest ultimately brought the system to a premature end in 1838.

British emancipation influenced the policies of the French and the Danish in the Caribbean. Much as in the British West Indies, ferocious planter opposition to emancipation forced these governments to provide compensation for slaveholders when slavery finally ended in 1848. Sustained agitation by the French and Danish ex-slaves, however, prevented the creation of an apprenticeship system prior to freedom. Likewise, when the Dutch, following years of debate, freed the remaining slaves in Surinam and their Caribbean islands in 1863, no effort was made to limit the former slaves' freedom.

Although the number of slaves in the Spanish American republics was approximately the same as in the Northern United States and the process of gradual emancipation lasted nearly as long in Venezuela and Peru as it did in New Jersey, the wars of liberation in Latin America had a greater impact on slavery than did the American Revolution. Much as in the U.S. North, slaveholder resistance, concern for property rights, racial prejudice, and delays in translating the rhetoric of liberation into effective antislavery action slowed the movement toward abolition in Latin America. Even where there were relatively few slaves, such as in Chile, attempts at gradual emancipation encountered stiff opposition; this delayed the eradication of slavery in that country for more than a decade.

Moreover, while so-called free womb laws freed the children of slaves in the Spanish American republics, long-term apprenticeships under their old masters were often imposed on the *libertos*, or *manumisos*. Because no slave born prior to the decrees of the 1820s was actually freed, slavery continued, albeit with declining numbers, well into the 1840s and 1850s in most of the republics. The experience of Venezuela, Columbia, and Ecuador, which formed a unified confederation following independence, was quite typical. In 1821, the confederation freed all slaves born after that year and established local juntas to purchase the freedom of slaves born prior to 1821. But the dissolution of the confederation weakened the abolitionist movement, and slaveholders were able to postpone emancipation until the 1850s, when they received compensation.

The Peruvian experience was quite similar. The liberating army decreed gradual emancipation in the free birth act of 1828, but apprenticeship laws forced the *libertos* to work for their masters during the next twenty years. When slavery was finally abolished in 1854, compensation was provided for the owners. Other republics followed much the same pattern. For example, in 1831 Bolivia declared all slaves born since independence in 1825 to be free, but slavery did not in fact end until 1851. Likewise, Uruguay enacted a free womb law in 1825 but slavery lasted until 1842; and, while Argentina's free birth law of 1813 was the first enacted in Spanish America, total abolition was not accomplished until forty years later. The few slaves held in Central America were freed, with compensation provided for masters, in 1824, but in Mexico all slaves were not freed until nearly a decade after independence was achieved in the early 1820s.

In the lucrative Spanish colony of Cuba, the large slave population was not freed until the 1880s. Not only was the Spanish government generally controlled by groups that were either indifferent or hostile to abolition, but even Cuban liberals tended to favor only a very gradual emancipation. Not until the first Spanish republic was created in 1868 did the government seriously consider emancipation. Nevertheless, the outbreak of the Cuban rebellion in the same year prevented any action. Finally, in 1870 Moret's Law freed all slaves born after its enactment as well as those over sixty-five years of age, and apprenticed, with no wages, all *patrocinados* under age twenty-two. In fact, Moret's Law was merely a step toward gradual emancipation, for it did not alter the essential nature of slavery and was difficult to implement in the midst of the Cuban rebellion. The law was not fully applied until 1880. Much as in the British and French West Indies earlier in the century, the former slaves in Cuba strenuously opposed apprenticeship and demanded immediate abolition. In 1886, this agitation led the Spanish government to end the apprenticeship system two years before it was slated to expire and to free the remaining slaves.

Because slavery had never taken deep root in Puerto Rico and no insurrection against Spanish rule had occurred there, Moret's Law went into effect sooner than in Cuba. Thus, emancipation, with compensation for slaveholders, was effected by a series of enabling decrees in 1872 and 1873.

In Brazil, slavery was so deeply rooted that antislavery sentiment developed much later than elsewhere in Latin America. Finally, the American Civil War and mounting international pressure led Brazilians to adopt a law of free birth in 1871, with a provision for apprenticeship until age twenty-one. A state-supported emancipation fund was established to purchase freedom for slaves born before 1872. But not until 1880, did a popular antislavery movement, which included many free blacks and mulattoes, effectively challenge slavery. Although slave owners responded by passing a harsh fugitive slave law in 1885, antislavery pressure continued to mount. A mass exodus of slaves from the plantations into safe havens in the cities ultimately prompted the government in 1888 to decree the immediate and total abolition of slavery. At last, slavery had been eradicated throughout the Western Hemisphere.

With relatively few exceptions, the process of emancipation in Western Hemisphere societies extended over many years. Those who advocated emancipation not only encountered stiff resistance from the slaveholders, but they often shared with many others in their societies a concern for property rights, an abiding fear of disruption and conflict, and a deep-seated racial prejudice. Even when gradual emancipation laws were enacted, their implementation was often uneven and prolonged. Apprenticeship systems frequently followed emancipation, thus denying the former slaves real freedom. Ultimately, those who were placed in apprenticeship, along with free blacks, mulattoes, and others still held in bondage, joined with antislavery whites to force an end to both the slavery and apprenticeship systems.

Hugh Davis

See also: Immediate Emancipation.

Further Readings

Corwin, Arthur F. *Spain and the Abolition of Slavery in Cuba, 1817–1886*. Austin: University of Texas Press, 1967.

Craton, Michael. *Empire, Enslavement, and Freedom in the Caribbean*. Princeton, NJ: Markus Weiner, 1997.

Davis, David Brion. *The Problem of Slavery in the Age of Revolution, 1770–1823*. Ithaca, NY: Cornell University Press, 1975.

Klein, Herbert S. *African Slavery in Latin America and the Caribbean*. New York: Oxford University Press, 1986.

McManus, Edgar J. *Black Bondage in the North*. Syracuse, NY: Syracuse University Press, 1973.

Newman, Richard S. *The Transformation of Abolitionism: Fighting Slavery in the Early Republic*. Chapel Hill: University of North Carolina Press, 2002.

Zilversmit, Arthur. *The First Emancipation: The Abolition of Slavery in the North*. Chicago: University of Chicago Press, 1967. www.antislavery.org/breakingthesilence

Grimké, Angelina

Angelina Emily Grimké was born in Charleston, South Carolina, of French Huguenot descent in 1805. She was a member of a prominent slaveholding South Carolina family, and her father was a justice of the South Carolina Supreme Court.

Angelina Grimké was a prominent Southern antislavery activist. She and her sister, Sarah, were the first abolitionists to advocate civil and political rights for women through their lectures and writings. (Library of Congress)

At his death, her father owned fifty slaves and two plantations. So, Grimké knew firsthand about slave life in Charleston.

Yet, from these inauspicious beginnings Angelina Grimké became a leading abolitionist and proponent of women's rights. She and her older sister, Sarah Grimké, are believed to have been the first women to publicly speak against slavery. Angelina's appetite for reform influenced all aspects of her life; she left the Episcopal Church for the Presbyterian Church and eventually the Society of Friends (Quakers).

In November 1829, Angelina left Charleston and followed her sister to Philadelphia. There they united with the Orthodox Branch (the more conservative wing) of the Society of Friends. Although Orthodox

Quakers did not own slaves and opposed slavery, they also opposed Quaker participation in public life and in the antislavery movement.

In Philadelphia, Grimké struggled with the Orthodox position as she sought to further her education and to find her life's work. By 1835, she was reading abolitionist newspapers and, despite the opposition of her Quaker friends, attending abolitionist meetings. On August 30, 1835, she wrote William Lloyd Garrison a letter that changed her life forever. In that era, women did not write to men they did not know. Yet Grimké wrote commending Garrison's plea for a fair hearing for the abolitionist perspective. Abolitionist lectures frequently led to riots, making it difficult to reach audiences. Garrison published her "soul-thrilling epistle" about slavery in the *Liberator.*

In Philadelphia, the Grimké sisters also championed the rights of the free African Americans who made up 10 percent of the population, but were treated as second-class citizens even in Quaker meetings. They participated in the Free Produce Movement effort to boycott slave-produced goods and developed ties with Lucretia Mott, Abba Alcott (mother of Louisa May Alcott), and with such leading African American women such as Charlotte, Sarah, and Marguerite Forten and Harriet Purvis.

During the summer of 1836, Grimké wrote an "Appeal to the Christian Women of the South." The American Anti-Slavery Society printed the moving "Appeal" and it became a mainstay of the abolitionist movement. The mayor of Charleston, South Carolina, however, told her mother that he could not guarantee Grimké's safety if she returned to Charleston. As a result, Grimké never saw her mother or Charleston again.

In the fall of 1836, the Grimké sisters crossed another divide when they traveled to New York City to speak against slavery. They were breaking barriers for women while they sought to permanently rid the country of slavery. In December, they began their speaking tour. They worked without pay for the American Anti-Slavery Society. Theodore Weld, another member, edited the Society's publication, the *Emancipator.* A respected lecturer and writer, Weld attracted the attention of the Grimkés.

Angelina Grimké and her sister were heckled, threatened, and criticized for their views and for enunciating them in public. In the nineteenth century, most people did not consider public speaking women's work. As a result, life in the public sphere and within the abolitionist movement was difficult for the Grimkés. Opposition to their public roles strengthened the sisters' feminist leanings as they advocated rights for African Americans and women.

In 1837, Angelina and Sarah Grimké moved to Boston and began a speaking tour in Massachusetts. Opponents attacked their speaking as "unnatural" for women. Some contended that they equally advocated women's rights and abolition.

Rather, Angelina Grimké emphasized women's moral responsibilities, while her sister Sarah was more forthright in her call for women's rights. During 1837, Weld attended the sisters' lectures, visited with them, and corresponded with them. In February 1838, he wrote Angelina and stated his love for her, after which they became engaged.

Grimké was the first woman in the United States to address a state legislature. On February 21 and 23, 1838, she addressed a committee of the Massachusetts state legislature opposing slavery in the District of Columbia. Grimké eloquently described herself as a "repentant slaveholder" who was "exiled from the land of my birth by the sound of the lash, and the piteous cry of the slave." A series of lectures at the Odeon followed these groundbreaking addresses. Before and during the lecture series, Angelina Grimké and Theodore Weld planned their wedding.

On May 14, 1838, abolitionists dedicated Pennsylvania Hall in Philadelphia. That evening, between thirty and forty interracial guests attended the wedding of Grimké and Weld. No minister officiated as the Quaker Grimké and the Presbyterian Weld exchanged vows they had written. William Lloyd Garrison was one of the guests.

Two days later, Angelina Grimké Weld spoke in the newly dedicated Pennsylvania Hall. Protestors shouted insults. As Grimké spoke of the horrors of slavery and her firsthand experience, the mob outside threw bricks and rocks through the windows. Though she never faltered, this address was another turning point for Grimké. Arsonists burned the building the next day, and Grimké did not again speak in public for twenty-five years.

The Welds and Sarah Grimké lived in Fort Lee, New Jersey. The sisters aided Weld's research for the monumental study, *American Slavery as It Is: Testimony of a Thousand Witnesses*, published in 1839. When their mother died that year, the Grimké sisters freed the four slaves she had owned. The Welds had three children, Charles Stuart Faucheraud Weld, Theodore Grimké Weld, and Sarah Grimké Weld.

In 1840, the Welds purchased a farm in Belleville, New Jersey. By 1848, they had found a new calling as they began operating Belleville School. In 1853, a number of families joined together to form the Raritan Bay Union, a cooperative community. They invited the Welds and Sarah to join the union and open a school, Eagleswood. The Welds accepted and, after a year, Sarah joined them. Although the union failed, the school succeeded. Eagleswood was an innovative, coeducational school with an advanced curriculum. Students were encouraged to ask questions and to learn by experience.

With the outbreak of the Civil War, the Welds resumed speaking. Their older son became a conscientious objector and refused to fight, and the younger son developed an incurable disease and had to be institutionalized. On her twenty-fifth wedding anniversary, Angelina Grimké Weld addressed the National Convention of the Woman's League. Grimké also submitted a resolution urging federal soldiers in this "Second Revolution" to secure freedom for all. The League collected 400,000 signatures asking the U.S. Congress to immediately free the slaves. In 1863, that petition helped bring about the Thirteenth Amendment to the U.S. Constitution.

In 1863, the Welds and Sarah Grimké returned to Massachusetts, taught at a school in Lexington, and worked to support the rights of the freedmen. In 1868, they learned of a brilliant African American student at Lincoln College named Archibald Grimké. The Welds wrote him and learned that he was the son of Angelina's brother Henry and a slave named Nancy Weston. An abolitionist teacher in Charleston had arranged for Archibald and his brother, Frank, to attend Lincoln College. Angelina and Sarah embraced these unknown nephews and contributed to their education and to their other family members who remained in Charleston. Archibald Grimké became a prominent lawyer and leader in the National Association for the Advancement of Colored People (NAACP). He named his only daughter, Angelina Weld Grimké.

In 1870, the sisters again made history as they and other women organized and voted in a town election. Although their ballots were not counted, this was the first time women in Massachusetts went to the polls. Sarah Grimké died on December 23, 1873, and Angelina on October 26, 1879. Theodore Weld lived until 1895. The woman who dared much for causes so close to her heart lies in an unmarked grave. Yet, her legacy lives as Americans continue the fight for racial justice and women's rights.

Alexia Helsley

See also: Grimké, Charlotte Forten.

Further Readings

Todras, Ellen H. *Angelina Grimké: Voice of Abolition*. North Haven, CT: Linnet Books, 1999.

Wilbanks, Charles, ed. *Walking by Faith: The Diary of Angelina Grimké, 1828–1835*. Columbia: University of South Carolina Press, 2003.

Grimké, Charlotte Forten

Charlotte Forten was born in 1837 and was the granddaughter of James Forten, Sr., an affluent member of Philadelphia's black upper class. James and other Forten family members were key organizers of the antislavery movement: their home served as the meeting place where the American Anti-Slavery Society was founded in 1833. Charlotte thus matured in a household deeply imbued with the understanding that slavery was immoral and that she would be expected to find her niche in the movement to abolish it and foster racial egalitarianism in America. As a gifted adolescent, she wrote antislavery poetry, which was published in such antislavery newspapers as the *Liberator* and the *Anglo African.* Charlotte chose to attend college so she might teach and help to eradicate the ills wrought by slavery upon African Americans. She graduated from college in 1856, and by 1863 she had become one of the first African American teachers in the pioneering experiment to educate former slaves at the captured town of Port Royal, South Carolina. She, along with other "Gideonites"—dedicated teachers who were also ardent evangelicals and abolitionists—labored through 1865 to educate newly freed slaves for independence and eventual land ownership, a hope that would be bitterly quashed by mid-summer 1865. After almost two years of diligent work, Charlotte was forced to resign due to illness.

Although unable to continue with the "Port Royal Experiment," Charlotte did continue her mission of activism while also working for the U.S. Treasury Department. In 1878, she married the Reverend Francis Grimké, the African American nephew of the renowned abolitionist sisters Angelina and Sarah Grimké. Together, Charlotte and her husband continued in the tradition of their heritage denouncing racism and oppression and promoting equality. Charlotte Forten Grimké died in 1914.

Iris Hunter

See also: Grimké, Angelina.

Further Readings

Forten, Charlotte. "Life on the Sea Islands." *Atlantic Monthly* 23 (May and June 1864): 587–596, 666–676.

Stevenson, Brenda, ed. *The Journals of Charlotte Forten Grimké.* New York: Oxford University Press, 1988.

Winch, Julie. *A Gentleman of Color: The Life of James Forten.* New York: Oxford University Press, 2002.

H

Haitian Revolution

The insurgency of the African slaves on the French West Indian colony of St. Domingue (present-day Haiti) was one of the major events of the eighteenth and nineteenth centuries. The Haitian Revolution marked a critical juncture in attitudes and policies toward slavery and race in the Atlantic world. The black revolution signaled the emergence of Afro-America on the scene of international politics. It was the first anticolonial racial war, and it was also the first instance of immediate mass emancipation in a slave society. It was the first—and only—slave revolt to culminate in a modern independent state, and it resulted in the second republic to win its independence in the Americas. It established a precedent for U.S. military intervention in the Caribbean, and it legitimated the proslavery orientation of American foreign policy.

The Haitian Revolution precipitated the collapse of French power in the Western Hemisphere and helped solidify the domination of U.S. slaveholders over the Old Southwest by creating the opportunity for the Louisiana Purchase (1803). The Haitian insurgents defeated the Spanish (1793–1795), British (1793–1798), and French (1802–1803) armies sent against them, and the insurgents destroyed the power of the plantation owners in the island itself (1793). From the perspective of the slaveholders, who backed the European expeditions against the rebels, the black revolution was not about freedom and equality; instead blacks sought revenge, and their relentless destruction would result in economic ruin and the annihilation of the white property owners. Despite the prodigious efforts of slaveholders in the British, French, and Spanish islands, and the metropolitan governments of Europe, the Haitians did achieve their freedom and independence, which was declared by Jean Jacques Dessalines on January 1, 1804. But the movement for independence did not appear until late in the Haitian Revolution; it was not until the French emperor, Napoleon Bonaparte, ordered the restoration of slavery in the French islands in 1802 that the blacks and free coloreds formed an alliance against the

French whites and drove them from the colony and declared independence, events critical to the later emancipation of slaves in the Americas.

From 1776 to 1823, abolitionists and slaveholders fought their first great struggles over the slave trade and slavery in the Atlantic world. These epic struggles were main themes of the American and French Revolutions, the Napoleonic wars, and the Latin American wars of independence. A principal consequence of these struggles was the emancipation of hundreds of thousands of slaves and to narrow the geographical expanse of the near universal institution of slavery in the Americas while enlarging the "free soil" regions of the Atlantic world. The Haitian Revolution was integral to these broader struggles, and many of the most important leaders of the Haitian Revolution—André Rigaud, Henri Christophe, Jean-Baptiste Chavannes—would serve first as soldiers against the British during the American Revolution.

From an ideological point of view, the Haitian slave revolution spoke to both the defenders and opponents of slavery, providing both sides with ideological armor that helped them combat or support calls for emancipation in the United States and the Americas. After 1791, the antislavery movement found itself confronted with charges that it promoted anarchy by calling publicly for freedom for the blacks and encouraged slave violence. Antislavery advocates found that the unwelcome spread of violence in the Americas dampened the ardor of Americans for emancipation of the slaves; politically, antislavery kept a safe distance from the black rebels, objected to black violence, and some even expressed the hope that the blacks would be defeated. The Haitian slave revolution deeply influenced international politics. Thus, as a war measure against England, the French National Convention emancipated the slaves of their empire throughout the Americas on February 4, 1794, as they sought African allies in their wars against the enemy and recruited slaves as soldiers or allies. In 1805–1807, the British, currently at war with France, adopted their own wartime antislavery measure by abolishing the slave trade to the colonies of their enemies and to their own colonies. Responding to the collapse of French power in St. Domingue and the elimination of French competition in the slave trade in 1803, the British initiated what became a crusade against the international slave trade, a dominant theme of British foreign policy in the nineteenth century.

Following Haiti's declaration of independence on January 1, 1804, the new republic was ostracized by the Atlantic powers. Despite the isolation of Haiti, the great leaders of their revolution, such as Toussaint L'Ouverture, Henri Christophe, Jean-Jacques Dessalines, and others, sought to maintain sugar production. But the black cultivators were not interested in changing one set of white masters for new sets of black or colored masters. Subsequent to independence, the African and African Creole populations drifted into the island's mountainous interior where they cultivated their own garden plots, much as the maroon Africans had done during the centuries of white rule. Haiti achieved a thorough-going peasant society that celebrated individual freedom, independence, land ownership, and faith. For the first time, Haitians achieved a self-sustaining population, a population that grew by natural increase rather than by importations from Africa.

Tim Matthewson

See also: German Coast (Louisiana) Insurrection of 1811; Turner, Nat; Vesey's Conspiracy (1822).

Further Readings

Davis, David B. *The Problem of Slavery in the Age of Revolution, 1776–1820*. Ithaca, NY: Cornell University Press, 1975.

Geggus, David P. *Haitian Revolutionary Studies*. Bloomington: Indiana University Press, 2002.

Geggus, David P., ed. *Impact of the Haitian Revolution in the Atlantic World*. Columbia: University of South Carolina Press, 2001.

James, C.L.R. *The Black Jacobins: Toussaint L'Ouverture and the San Domingo Revolution*. 1938. 2nd ed. New York: Vintage, 1963.

Lawless, Robert. *Haiti's Bad Press*. Rochester, VT: Schenkman Books, 1992.

Matthewson, Tim. *A Proslavery Foreign Policy: Haitian-American Relations during the Early Republic*. Westport, CT: Greenwood Publishing Group, Inc., 2003.

Plummer, Brenda G. "Le Vogue Nègre." In Brenda G. Plummer, ed. *Haiti and the United States*. Athens, Georgia: University of Georgia Press, 1992, pp. 121–138.

Trouillot, Michel-Rolph. *Silencing the Past: Power and the Production of History*. Boston: Beacon Press, 1995.

Hall, Prince

Born in or about 1735, Prince Hall was likely a slave in the household of William Hall in Boston, Massachusetts, until he was manumitted by Hall in 1770. Prince Hall worked as a leather dresser and merchant and was the principal in the founding of African Lodge #459, the world's first duly chartered Masonic Lodge comprised exclusively of persons of African descent. Prince Hall and the lodge were also distinguished by their pronounced opposition to slavery. While Freemasonry's core tenets of universal fellowship and benevolence could be arrayed against slavery, no lodge of white Masons adopted any similar antislavery position.

Prince Hall deployed the democratic ideology of the American Revolution to attack slavery and racial injustice. In January 1777, Hall, Lancaster Hill, Peter Bess, and other black men in Boston sent a petition to the Massachusetts legislature, requesting the abolition of slavery. In 1787, Hall and numerous other black residents again petitioned the Commonwealth either to provide public education for black children or else to cease taxing blacks. In 1788, Hall and twenty-two other African American Masons signed and sent a petition to the state legislature imploring it to intervene on the behalf of three free African American men who had been kidnapped and transported out of Boston to be sold as slaves in the West Indies. One of the kidnaps was a member of African Lodge. On March 26, 1788, the Massachusetts legislature acted; it made kidnapping of Africans in Massachusetts unlawful and provided grounds for compensation to the affected families. This petition was key to the state's ensuing abolition of the slave trade in the same year.

The seed of black Freemasonry in North America was planted in 1775 in Boston when Hall and thirteen local black men were initiated into an Irish Regimental military lodge. This action granted permission to Hall and the others to meet and bury their dead as Masons among themselves, but they did not constitute a lodge and were thus unable to admit any new members to their assembly. By 1787, however, Prince Hall had secured a charter from the Grand Lodge of England, which designated them African Lodge #459. Over the ensuing years, black masonry grew slowly but steadily in the Northeast. By 1814, African Lodge #459 had chartered one lodge in Providence, Rhode Island, and four in Philadelphia. In 1808, the first African Grand Lodge was formed in Boston and, in 1815, the African Grand Lodge of Pennsylvania was constituted. Some applications by free black men had been submitted to white lodges in these states and others and were rejected, sometimes on the grounds that a man must be "freeborn" to become a Mason, a policy that the Grand Lodge of England would explicitly reject in 1838. While prevailing racial attitudes certainly informed the reluctance of white American Masons to embrace black men as equal Masonic brothers, no evidence exists that Prince Hall or any other masters of black lodges ever approached white grand lodges seeking admission of their black lodge into the larger, dominant white Masonic structure. Prince Hall and his followers were well satisfied with the legitimacy of their lodges and their knowledge of the Craft's rituals and procedures and confidently established a Masonry for black men.

Two "Charges" which Prince Hall presented to African Lodge #459 in 1792 and 1797 vividly evinced his antislavery and that of black Freemasonry as a whole. In 1792, Hall argued that the core duties of a Mason were to love God and to practice "love and benevolence to all the whole family of mankind, as God's make and creation." Thus, "he that despises a black man for the sake of his colour, reproacheth his Maker." In 1797, he upheld the African influences upon the rise of Masonry and Christianity. He condemned the disgraceful and violent discrimination blacks confronted daily in Boston while forbidding his brothers from displaying any "slavish fear of man." Finally, he praised his "African brethren" in St. Domingue for rebelling against their enslavement and overthrowing their brutal masters. "Thus doth Ethiopia begin to stretch forth her hand, from a sink of slavery to freedom and equality," he exclaimed. For Hall and his black brothers, slavery was utterly incompatible with the ideals and practices of Freemasonry. In the decades before the Civil War, many local lodges and leading black Masons, including John Telemachus Hilton, David Walker, Benjamin Hughes, Thomas Paul, Lewis Hayden, and Martin Delany, would spearhead the fight against slavery and racial injustice. In honor of their founder, who died in December 1807, most black Masons would in 1847 denominate themselves Prince Hall Masons.

Peter P. Hinks

See also: Freemasonry and Antislavery.

Further Readings

Brooks, Joanna. *American Lazarus: Religion and the Rise of African-American and Native American Literatures*. New York: Oxford University Press, 2003.

Kaplan, Sidney, and Emma Nogrady Kaplan. *The Black Presence in the Era of the American Revolution*. Rev. ed. Amherst: University of Massachusetts Press, 1989.

Upton, William H. *Negro Masonry, Being a Critical Examination of Objections to the Legitimacy of the Masonry Existing among the Negroes of America*. Cambridge, MA: M.W. Prince Hall Grand Lodge, 1902.

Wesley, Charles H. *Prince Hall: Life and Legacy*. Washington, DC: The United Supreme Council, Prince Hall Affiliation, 1977.

Helper, Hinton

Hinton Helper was born in Mocksville, Rowan County, North Carolina, an area where slavery had neither the presence nor influence that it did in the eastern regions of the state. He attended the Mocksville Academy and displayed an early aptitude for writing. This aptitude would serve him well as the U.S. Civil War approached for he would become an important Republican oracle and help found and lead the party in Baltimore.

Helper detested slavery not because he viewed it as an immoral or sinful institution, but—like Gamaliel Bailey—because he believed it threatened to degrade free white labor. Hence he spent little time in the South and usually moved between Baltimore and New York City. He loved to travel and wrote about his experiences in California in 1850 in his first book, *The Land of Gold,* published in 1852. He loathed what he saw there. Helper, an arch Anglo-Saxon supremacist, was deeply offended by the polyglot population he found there. He attacked Native Americans, Mexicans (in fact, all Latins), Catholics, and Asians, but especially the black man, of whom some 8,000 were in the gold mining industry. Helper feared that racial mixing or miscegenation as it was then called would produce a mongrel population, which in turn would ruin the prospects for American economic development. He did not wish to see the rest of the western territories become another California or American South. He articulated some of late-antebellum America's most virulent racism.

Gripped with this fear of America's "mongrelization," Helper wrote his second and most famous book, *The Impending Crisis of the South and How to Meet It*, first published in 1857. The work vehemently attacked the South, the Democratic Party, and the black man. He used the 1850 Federal Census to concoct a series of distorted statistics to claim that the South was an economic drag on the nation and that this "fact" was due wholly to its reliance on Negro slavery. Helper skewed statistics by, for example, comparing a Northern state where some product or crop was produced very successfully with a Southern state where it was not an important product. He would thus use this evidence to deduce the unprofitability of slavery. He ended his work by calling for an annual federal tax of $60 on each slave, the money to fund black colonization outside of the United States.

Helper's book enjoyed rapid and enormous political influence with leading members of the Republican Party, such as John Sherman, Salmon P. Chase, and Abraham Lincoln, and it quickly became the bible of the new party. Numerous publishers refused to produce it because of its incendiary nature, but once available, it became an instant success. During the campaign of 1860, Horace Greeley's *New York Tribune* alone printed some 140,000 copies, a prodigious amount for that time period. The book caused such a furor in Congress during the 1859 speaker of the house contest—when sixty-eight Republican congressmen endorsed it—that the nation's attention became even more focused on Helper's book. It played an instrumental role in rallying the North against the South on the eve of the Civil War.

In 1860, Lincoln appointed Helper consul to Argentina, where, ironically, he met and wed a Catholic Argentinian. During Reconstruction, he continued to write, turning out two of the most vicious attacks on the black man ever written, *Nojoque, a Question for a Continent*, and *The Negroes in Negroland*, in which he called for the extermination of the black race. Helper was obsessed with race and ethnicity and is a paradigm of the nineteenth-century American strain of racist ethnocentrism. His earlier fame gone and living alone, he committed suicide in Washington, D.C., in 1901.

James D. Bilotta

See also: Radical Republicans.

Further Readings

Bailey, Hugh C. *Hinton Rowan Helper: Abolitionist-Racist*. Montgomery: University of Alabama Press, 1965.

Bilotta, James D. *Race and the Rise of the Republican Party, 1848–1865*. Philadelphia: Peter Lang Publishers, 2005.

Higher Law and Antislavery

In its simplest formulation, "higher law" refers to a moralistic argument advanced by Northern abolitionists opposed to the 1850 Fugitive Slave Law, one of the key pieces of legislation contained in the Compromise of 1850. Intended to appease Southern slaveholders after the admission of California as a free state, abolitionists were outraged that the 1850 Fugitive Slave Law required citizens of the Northern free states to assist in the apprehension of runaway slaves. This privileging of slaveholders' property rights over Northerners' religious and moral convictions convinced many abolitionists that the federal government no longer protected basic civil liberties, and that continued obedience to the Constitution made them complicitous in perpetuating the institution of slavery. Presupposing that slavery was morally incompatible with divine law, higher law advocates argued that the religious imperative to respect God's ultimate authority and to obey His commandments released individuals from any ethical duty to obey immoral civil laws.

The relatively similar rhetoric of abolitionists' higher law arguments masks a broad range of underlying philosophical and theological foundations, as well as vastly different understandings of the moral authority and legitimacy of the federal government and its Constitution. Antebellum-era higher law arguments were often premised on moral intuitionism, a subjectively valid means of ascertaining divine law developed simultaneously, but separately, within evangelical Protestant theology, Quaker pietism, and Romantic philosophy. The eighteenth century, however, produced a number of rationalist (as opposed to intuitionist) higher law arguments grounded in the natural philosophy of the Enlightenment. In 1772, the English abolitionist Granville Sharp asserted, "No legislation on Earth . . . can alter the Nature of Things, or make that to be lawful, which is contrary to the law of God." For Sharp, evidence of the existence of divine law was best ascertained through the objective, empirical study of nature.

This rationalist understanding of higher law found later expression in the key political documents of the American Revolution, the Declaration of Independence and the U.S. Constitution. The "laws of nature and of nature's God," in Jefferson's memorable phrase, provided the philosophical foundation for the Declaration's assertions of "self-evident" truths and "inalienable" human rights. Premised on a belief in the existence of a rational Creator and on an authoritative, yet rationally ascertainable Providence or divine will, natural law functioned as higher law within the framework of eighteenth-century Enlightenment philosophy.

The civil liberties articulated in the Bill of Rights and ratified in the first eight Amendments (the freedoms of conscience, speech, press, and assembly; the right to bear arms, to due process, etc.) led many Americans to view the U.S. Constitution as a complex symbol of the identity between the nation's civil laws and divine or natural higher law. For this reason, few Americans other than the most radical abolitionists ever entirely repudiated the moral authority of the Constitution when advancing higher law arguments. William Henry Seward, an abolitionist Whig senator from upstate New York and author of the best-known statement of higher law doctrine, asserted in his March 11, 1850, Senate speech that "[A] higher law than the Constitution regulates our authority" over the western territories. Nowhere in the speech, however, delivered during debate over the expansion of slavery into the newly acquired Mexican territories, did Seward disavow or call for the disavowal of the Constitution. A committed Free Soiler and a devout evangelical Protestant, Seward's appeal to higher law should be understood as a call to return the nation to its moral foundations, as expressed originally in the Declaration of Independence and in the Constitution, rather than as a repudiation of the moral authority of these documents. For Seward, as for many moderate abolitionists, the crises of the 1850s were attributable not to manifest flaws in the Constitution but to the disingenuous and politically dangerous attempts by John C. Calhoun and other Southern ideologues to reconstruct the Constitution as a militantly proslavery document.

Seward's continued faith in the Constitution, as well as his abolitionist appeal to higher law, was consistent with, and likely influenced by, the perfectionist higher law doctrine formulated in the late 1830s by Charles Grandison Finney, the leading evangelical Protestant preacher of the period. Perfectionism demanded of evangelical Christians that they rid themselves of sin and morally reform American society in accordance with God's laws. For Finney, as for many Northern evangelicals, slavery symbolized the widespread moral corruption of American society and provided the clearest example of civil laws deemed incompatible with divine law. After passage in 1839 of an Ohio fugitive slave law, Finney presented a series of higher law resolutions to the Ohio Anti-Slavery Slavery. "We regard it, as a settled principle of both common and Constitutional law," Finney affirmed, "that no human legislation can annul, or set aside, the law or authority of God." "Whatever is contrary to the law of God," Finney added, "is not law." Alternately, however, Finney insisted that Americans were obligated to obey those civil laws, including the articles of the U.S. Constitution, which remained in accord with divine law.

Finney's enormous popularity, as well as his later prominence as president of Oberlin College, a hotbed of abolitionist activism, undoubtedly contributed to the popularization of higher law doctrine. Nevertheless, Finney's political moderation, which grew out of his belief that revivalism and moral reformation, not civil disobedience, were the primary agents of social change, led many abolitionists to embrace William Lloyd Garrison's far more radical formulation of higher law doctrine, which condemned the federal government and the Constitution as morally corrupt institutions. As early as 1832, just one year after he began publication of the *Liberator*, Garrison denounced the Constitution as "the most bloody and heaven-daring arrangement ever made for the continuance and protection of a system of the most atrocious villainy ever exhibited on earth." In 1843, Garrison more succinctly described the Constitution as "a covenant with death and an agreement with hell," and on July 4, 1854, he burned a copy of the Constitution in public protest. Bound up with the radical abolitionist doctrine of immediatism, Garrison articulated an uncompromising higher law argument that demanded an absolute repudiation of the sinfulness of slavery and of the moral complicity of the nation's political institutions.

Influenced by Quaker pietism, Garrison counterbalanced his radical abolitionist doctrine with an equally firm commitment to pacifism and to nonviolent forms of social protest. The political passions of the 1850s, however, produced another group of radical abolitionists committed to a higher law doctrine that sanctioned violence as a legitimate means of combating slavery. The best known of these militant higher law advocates was the radical Unitarian minister Theodore Parker. Passage of the 1850 Fugitive Slave Act led Parker to author a classic statement of higher law doctrine. Premising his argument on Romantic philosophy, specifically German post-Kantian idealism, Parker asserted, "So far as the statutes of man are just—conformable to the moral Nature of man, and the constitution of the Universe, they are entitled to obedience by citizens of the country where they are made and known. But so far as they are unjust they have no claims to be obeyed; it is a sin to obey them." Parker's understanding of the implications of his higher law doctrine led him to openly support John Brown's failed raid on the federal armory at Harpers Ferry, Virginia, which Brown and his followers hoped would instigate a violent slave insurrection throughout the South. Until his premature death in 1859, violence remained a recurring theme in Parker's abolitionist writings.

Despite their rhetorical similarities, Seward, Finney, Garrison, and Parker articulated antebellum-era higher law arguments that contained vastly different interpretations of the moral authority of the federal government and the U.S. Constitution, and that advocated very dissimilar means for practically applying higher law doctrine to abolitionist protest. In each case, the specific content of each author's respective higher law doctrine was intimately related to the theological or philosophical system through which he viewed the world, and with that author's broader political commitments.

Neil Brody Miller

See also: Antislavery Evangelical Protestantism; Immediate Emancipation; Unitarianism and Antislavery.

Further Readings

Davis, David Brion. "The Emergence of Immediatism in British and American Antislavery Thought." *Mississippi Valley Historical Review* 42 (September 1962): 209–230.

Fellman, Michael. "Theodore Parker and the Abolitionist Role of the 1850s." *Journal of American History* 61, 3 (December, 1974): 666–684.

Parker, Russell D. "The Revivalism of Charles G. Finney: Higher Law and Revivalism." *Ohio History: The Scholarly Journal of the Ohio Historical Society* 82, 3–4 (1973): 142–153.

Pease, Jane H. "The Road to the Higher Law." *New York History: Quarterly Journal of the New York State Historical Association* 40, 2 (1959): 117–136.

Szasz, Ferenc M. "Antebellum Appeals to the 'Higher Law,' 1830–1860." *Essex County Historical Collections* 110, 1 (1974): 33–48.

Wilson, Major L. "The Repressible Conflict: Seward's Concept of Progress and the Free-Soil Movement." *Journal of Southern History* 37, 4 (November 1971): 533–556.

Hiring-Out and Challenges to Slavery

The hiring-out of slaves has long been, and continues to be, a subject of considerable debate among historians. Some scholars contend that hiring-out challenged slavery because hired-out slaves engaged in "semi-free" activities or because the practice was a manifestation of slavery's incompatibility with certain environments. Other historians assert that hiring-out did not challenge slavery at all, or that it did so only in particular circumstances and in regard to specific types of hired-out slaves.

Particular facets of hiring-out enabled some hired-out slaves to enjoy a degree of autonomy greater than that experienced by slaves without these privileges. Some employers of hired-out slaves paid board money with which the slaves procured their own meals and lodging, and so avoided housing the slaves on their premises. Also, some employers gave hired-out slaves overwork payments, that is, cash for the performance of labor beyond the contracted amount, as an incentive toward greater levels of production. Typically, hired-out slaves used this cash for discretionary expenses such as consumption and personal entertainment, or for savings. Such hired-out slaves commonly had more mobility than other slaves; they traveled between their residence and their employment each day, socialized at night, and, in the case of slave draymen, for example, had jobs which required them to move over a broad geographical area. Despite some whites' opposition to cash disbursements to hired-out slaves, the payments continued, as white employers were not inclined to alter a practice that both facilitated their use and management of slave labor, and sustained the profitability of their operations. Self-hired-out slaves had even more individual discretion than most other hired-out slaves. Self-hired-out slaves were not hired out by their owner to an employer of the owner's choosing, but rather made their own working arrangements and received cash payments directly from employers. In return, self-hired-out slaves remitted to their owner a stipulated sum of money from what they earned. In some instances, self-hired-out slaves challenged slavery by earning enough money to accumulate property, purchase the freedom of loved ones, and purchase their own freedom. Most self-hired-out slaves were painters, carpenters, bricklayers, blacksmiths, or other types of skilled workers.

Although it was contrary to law and elicited complaints from skilled whites who competed for work with such slaves, self-hiring-out remained pervasive because white owners of self-hired-out slaves derived numerous benefits from the practice. Also, fines imposed upon whites who allowed their slaves to hire out their own time were rather lenient. Receipt of cash in the form of bonus money and overwork payments, mobility, discretion in arrangement of living and working situations, and purchase of freedom lead some historians to liken the lives of hired-out slaves to those of free persons, and to assert that hired-out slaves' experiences were located somewhere between slavery and freedom. These historians, particularly Clement Eaton, Lynda Morgan, and Richard Wade, among others, conclude, therefore, that hiring-out challenged slavery's long-term institutional viability. Significantly, however, these historians focus on cities, and on hired-out, skilled men and boys, by 1860 estimated to number in the thousands in Virginia's major urban centers of Richmond, Lynchburg, and Petersburg. Consideration of hired-out slave women and children in rural areas, rather than only skilled men and boys in cities, has led other historians to diverge from the premise that hiring-out challenged slavery. Only skilled male slaves, these scholars contend, had even the hope of challenging slavery by gaining privileges like cash or mobility. Rather, these historians assert, most hired-out slaves endured exploitation, separations, low standards of living, and virtually no opportunities for manumission or self-purchase. Hiring-out, moreover, gave larger numbers of whites access to slave labor, and provided slavery with the flexibility it required to survive in diversifying economies. This was especially the case in rural, mixed-farming regions such as Fauquier and Loudoun Counties in Virginia, where several hundred slaves were hired out in 1860 alone. For these historians, hiring-out did not challenge slavery.

Most recent scholarly investigations of hiring-out continue to be characterized by attention to variables of setting (i.e., urban, rural, agricultural, industrial, or household), and whether men, women, the young, or elderly were the hired-out. Yet historians remain divided on whether hiring-out challenged slavery or sustained it. A recent investigation of urban slavery acknowledges hired-out slaves' opportunities for autonomous activities, but asserts that slavery, facilitated by hiring-out, sustained the city's economic development. Conversely, another historian writes that hired-out slaves evaded their owners' supervision and control, which facilitated hired-out slaves' acts of rebellion. Similarly, while another inquiry acknowledges the role of hiring-out in the westward expansion of slavery and in placing slaves in the hands of non-slaveowners, it emphasizes hired-out slaves' challenge to slavery by bringing owners and hirers into conflict with each other, fracturing the white racial solidarity upon which slavery rested. Several decades of conflicting conclusions, along with research currently underway, suggests that hiring-out challenged slavery in certain settings and with respect to certain hired-out slaves, but reinforced the institution in other settings. Studies of skilled males in cities have concluded that hiring-out rendered slaves "virtually free," "quasi-free," or "semi-free." On the other hand, consideration of all hired-out slaves and their varied locales, rather than only urban, skilled males, has often revealed that hiring-out did not always challenge slavery or bring benefits to slaves, but rather strengthened slavery and worsened the hired-out slaves' conditions. Present research on hiring-out stresses all white class, ethnic, occupational, and other groups involved in hiring-out, and concludes that while hiring-out may have afforded skilled males in cities opportunities to challenge slavery's limitations, it fortified slavery in other settings, in part by transcending potential fault lines in white society. Ultimately, the precise focus of hiring-out research has determined, and will continue to determine, the extent to which hiring-out challenged slavery.

John J. Zaborney

See also: Manumission.

Further Readings

Martin, Jonathan D. *Divided Mastery: Slave Hiring in the American South*. Cambridge, MA: Harvard University Press, 2004.

Schnittman, Suzanne. "Black Workers in Antebellum Richmond." In Gary M. Fink and Merl E. Reed, eds. *Race, Class, and Community in Southern Labor History*. Tuscaloosa; London: University of Alabama Press, 1994.

Schweninger, Loren. "The Underside of Slavery: The Internal Economy, Self-Hire, and Quasi-Freedom in Virginia, 1780–1865." *Slavery and Abolition* 12 (September 1991): 1–22.

Zaborney, John J. "Slaves for Rent: Slave Hiring in Virginia." Ph.D. dissertation, University of Maine-Orono, 1997.

Immediate Emancipation

The demand for an immediate end to racial slavery was manifested widely beginning in the early decades of the nineteenth century. The movement that was established upon that basic precept was transatlantic in scope (Great Britain and the
United States especially), and comprised agitators of all stripes—men and women,
white and black. Indeed, because of the Catholic nature of the activism on behalf
of immediate emancipation of slaves, the history of that doctrine is best told as a
story of the key figures who helped develop and spread it.

When Massachusetts native William Lloyd Garrison emerged from Baltimore
Jail on June 5, 1830, the twenty-four-year-old journeyman newspaper editor—most
recently as coeditor, with the Quaker abolitionist Benjamin Lundy, of the Baltimore-
based antislavery press, the *Genius of Universal Emancipation*—was ever more
determined to combat American social iniquities: human enslavement and antiblack prejudices in particular. To be sure, Garrison was already an outspoken
journalist before he served a nearly two-month prison term, as evidenced by his
scathing comments in the *Genius* concerning the involvement of ship owner and
fellow Bay stater Francis Todd in the domestic slave trade that initiated the criminal
charges (libel) responsible for Garrison's imprisonment. His incarceration, however, was not cause for his conversion to what he called the "immediate and complete emancipation of slaves," to which he was committed prior to his employment
with the *Genius* in September 1829. Rather, Garrison's confinement cemented his
adherence to that cause and increased the intensity and urgency of his abolitionist
appeal. Nor is this a scholar's interpretation, for he indicated as much while behind prison bars. "A few white victims," proclaimed this self-styled martyr, "must
be sacrificed to open the eyes of the nation, and to show the tyranny of our laws.
I am willing to be persecuted, imprisoned and bound for advocating African rights,
and I should deserve to be a slave myself, if I shrunk from that duty or danger."
Garrison's liberation would mark the opening salvo of an unrelenting and radical

campaign on behalf of African Americans (enslaved and free), as well as against slaveholders and racially prejudiced whites, best exemplified in his vehement and vituperative abolitionist weekly, the *Liberator*, inaugurated from its Boston publishing headquarters on January 1, 1831.

Although Garrison did not originate the doctrine of immediate emancipation, his espousal represented a fundamental shift from earlier exponents. "A belief in the slave's right to immediate freedom," according to historian David Brion Davis, "was at least implicit in much of the antislavery writing of the eighteenth century." Unlike his humanitarian predecessors (secular and sacred), Garrison's intellectual worldview was not defined or limited by the belief that societal change must occur slowly and indirectly, or the concomitant fear that sudden change would disrupt the social order and deter historical progress. That Garrison and his small cadre of abolitionist allies thought differently from the outset of their organized movement (first through the regional New England Anti-Slavery Society (NEASS), founded in 1832, then, the national American Anti-Slavery Society (AASS), established in 1833) is indicated by the cumbersome phrase that they championed. Although immediatism eventually became the clarion call for antebellum American abolitionists, the principles epitomized by that watchword signified a clear and decisive break with past and contemporaneous antislavery alternatives. The activists who agitated for the immediate, uncompensated emancipation of slaves without expatriation rejected as a halfway measure the tenet of gradualism embodied in such late eighteenth-century organizations as the Pennsylvania Abolition Society and the New York Manumission Society; utterly renounced as deceptively philanthropic if not sinister the program of voluntary emancipation of slaves by slaveholders and their subsequent colonization in West Africa offered by the American Colonization Society as a safe and gradual solution to the nation's growing black population—slave as well as free; and repudiated the idea of monetary compensation for slaveholders (which the parliamentary Emancipation Act of 1833 extended to British West Indian slave owners in return for the loss of their bondsmen, and the U.S. Constitution mandated in the Fifth Amendment), for to do otherwise was tantamount to a recognition of the rightfulness of property in humans.

Despite the significant role that Garrison played in the transformation of American abolitionism from a gradualist to an immediatist phase, he alone was not responsible for that change. That is, just as Garrison reshaped antislavery reform in the country, he himself was influenced by slavery's foes at home and abroad. Indeed, several years before Garrison adopted an unyielding antislavery stance, the Leicester, England, Quaker abolitionist, Elizabeth Heyrick, unleashed an immediatist broadside that would reverberate across the Atlantic. In 1824, Heyrick anonymously authored the pamphlet, *Immediate, Not Gradual Emancipation*, exposing for readers what she considered the misguided and derelict approach to the issue of British colonial slavery within Parliament and among leading antislavery advocates. In no uncertain terms, Heyrick condemned gradualism as "the grand marplot of human virtue and happiness;—the very masterpiece of satanic policy." Calling the struggle against slavery a "holy war," and dismissing planters' claims to slave property as unnatural and irreligious, there was but one just and humane remedy for this pamphleteer—immediate emancipation. Such a course, argued Heyrick, would not only restore to slaves what was rightfully theirs (liberty), but would also remove that which slaveholders most feared: slave insurrections. To achieve this, she called upon not just the politically influential, but all Britons; she recommended not a popular petition drive, but a massive consumer boycott of slave-grown produce (West Indian sugar in particular).

Conscience revolt against slavery and the belief that all individuals were implicated in slavery's perpetuation underlay Heyrick's forceful polemic and animated the transatlantic movement for immediate emancipation. Among the most truculent expressions of the inhumanity of slavery and the absolute sinfulness of slaveholding, however, appeared several years before Heyrick's work helped redefine British antislavery efforts. Published in 1816, *The Book and Slavery Irreconcilable* asserted many of the religious and moral arguments that American abolitionists deployed, beginning in the 1830s, to justify and propagandize a nationwide immediatist campaign. The English Presbyterian minister residing in western Virginia who authored that tract, George Bourne, also defended his antislavery positions in a style most characteristic of William Lloyd Garrison's fiery writing. Aiming his rhetorical barbs at supposed Christian slaveholders, Bourne variably denounced them as thieves or man-stealers, and unequivocally as sinners; concerning slaveholding clergymen and church officials, Bourne adjudged them not simply as hypocrites, but as subverters of Holy Scripture. Yet, regardless of worldly status, "no slaveholder," he declaimed, "is innocent . . . he is an unjust, cruel, criminal Kidnapper, who is guilty of the most atrocious transgression against God and Man." The same applied to ministers who abetted slave ownership among the laity—indirectly by their refusal to censure it, and directly by their enlistment of the Bible to sanction it. Indeed, for Bourne, human enslavement "is so entirely corrupt that it admits of no cure, but by a total and immediate, abolition. For a gradual emancipation is a virtual recognition of the right, and establishes the rectitude of the practice." "If it be just for one moment," he concluded, "it is hallowed for ever; and if it be inequitable, not a day should it be tolerated." That such uncompromising language greatly influenced Garrison is undeniable; the editor himself stated in the March 17, 1832, issue of the *Liberator*, "Next to the Bible, we are indebted to this work for our views of the system of slavery."

Heyrick's and Bourne's respective publications provided American abolitionists with inspiration and the argumentative tools to defend the immediatist cause.

Although their work was pivotal in the history of antislavery thought and in the emergence of a more aggressive phase of abolitionism, those pamphlets alone did not establish the raison d'être for the immediatist turn in antislavery reform. Rather, the crucial component mobilizing American abolitionists was rooted in broader sociocultural developments, particularly the outburst of evangelical Christian activity during the first four decades of the nineteenth century. This period of religious ferment, often called the "Second Great Awakening," resulted not simply in increased levels of church attendance, but most dramatically in the redirection of the spiritual lives of hundreds of thousands of Americans. Religious rebirth, however, had worldly repercussions, for the evangelical faith as dispensed by such preachers as upstate New Yorker Charles G. Finney, and New Englander Lyman Beecher, was directed inward (at one's soul) and outward (at the individual body as well as the body politic).

Because of theological revisions, and in some instances outright rejection, of the tenets of Orthodox Calvinism, the Second Great Awakening's emphasis on moral agency and accountability enabled individuals to achieve salvation, rather than receive it as a gift from God. The corollary to this was the demand that individuals immediately recognize and repent for their own sins. Once cleansed, the converted abandoned lives of selfishness, leading instead selfless existences dedicated to social usefulness and benevolence. Although rebirth occurred at religious revivals, evangelical Christianity received secular expression through voluntary associations—(e.g., temperance, peace, and Bible and tract societies) dedicated to moral and social uplift. Involvement in benevolent pursuits allowed the regenerated to wage personal warfare against sin among like-minded individuals collectively striving for the perfection of self and society and, according to a millennial desire, to usher in the Kingdom of God on Earth. To be sure, not all of the reborn entered the ranks of humanitarianism; and of the active minority who participated in interdenominational reform organizations, but a small segment gave witness to immediate emancipation.

Since immediatist abolitionists were originally so few, conversion to immediate emancipation (itself a religious experience replicating evangelical rebirth) marked one as a visible saint. Yet, because many abolitionists derived their belief systems from evangelicalism, and based their reformist approaches and vocabularies on that model, the surrogate religion that immediatism became was similarly open to any who repented and renounced the sin of slavery. Recognition of slavery's sinfulness, however, was hardly limited to slaveholders, for all Americans, according to these abolitionists, were guilty by association. That is, since the U.S. Constitution, as immediatists contended, recognized and protected slavery, the South's "peculiar institution" was anything but that—it was indisputably a national institution and a national sin. It was such "change[s] of disposition," to borrow the historian Anne C. Loveland's apt phrase, that distanced antebellum abolitionists from their antislavery predecessors and, as it became apparent, their fellow countrymen. At the forefront of that shift was William Lloyd Garrison, immediatism's messianic minister.

In the period from Garrison's prison release in the summer of 1830 until the *Liberator* was launched on New Year's Day, 1831, the unemployed editor lectured to reform-minded audiences throughout the North. Garrison hoped that his speaking tour would raise the necessary funds to support a new publication dedicated to his special brand of immediatism and simultaneously lay the necessary groundwork for the creation of a national abolitionist organization. To be sure, Garrison was not greeted with outright hostility, nor did he experience its antithesis. The inroads that were made, however, as well as the opposition that blocked abolitionism's progress, ultimately convinced the young activist that his immediatist quest must recommence not in the nation's capital—as he initially anticipated—but in Boston, Massachusetts.

Because Garrison espied among New Englanders "contempt more bitter, opposition more active, detraction more relentless, prejudice more stubborn, and apathy more frozen, than among slave owners themselves," he resolved himself "to lift up the standard of emancipation in the eyes of the nation, *within sight of Bunker Hill and in the birth place of liberty.*" Garrison further stressed in the first issue of the *Liberator* that the free states presented a most difficult challenge; it was there that a "greater revolution in public sentiment" was most needed. Yet, despite this rather grim portrayal, New England also possessed remarkable promise. After one lecture in Boston, Garrison continued his discussion with a few of the attendees late into the evening. "That night," Unitarian minister Samuel J. May recalled years later, "my soul was baptized in his spirit, and ever since I have been a disciple and fellow-laborer of William Lloyd Garrison."

For Garrison, immediatism was less a plan of action than a doctrine of common humanity and a revelation of inherent black equality (insights that prompted May to declare Garrison "a prophet"). Thus, such questions confronted by historians as whether immediatism meant gradual emancipation immediately begun or immediate emancipation gradually achieved are misdirected. Indeed, from Garrison's viewpoint, time was of the essence; a timeline, however, was less essential. The demand for the immediate abolition of slavery was an urgent one because redeemed proponents contested for the souls of slaveholders and slaves on the one hand, and for the fate of the nation and its inhabitants more generally on the other. Most importantly—and pressingly—immediatists, ever aware of their countrymen's hypocrisy of proudly proclaiming their freedom and boasting of their libertarian heritage while millions remained enslaved, feared for that moment when slaves revolted for what naturally belonged to them and against those who had oppressed them for so long.

Although Elizabeth Heyrick and George Bourne also warned readers of the ever-present danger of violent insurrection should slaves remain in bondage, the potential of widespread slave uprisings appeared increasingly imminent after a free black used-clothing dealer from Boston, David Walker, issued his *Appeal to the Colored Citizens of the World, but in Particular, and Very Expressly, to Those of the United States of America* in the fall of 1829. Although previously anonymous, if not nonexistent, to white Americans, Walker's fervid protest (against slavery, antiblack biases, the country's sham equalitarianism) quickly made his presence known to the majority population, for with the forcefulness of a thunderclap, the author's prediction and encouragement of racial warfare horrified slaveholders and non-slaveholders alike. "I tell you Americans!" proclaimed Walker, "that unless you speedily alter your course, *you* and your *Country are gone!!!!*" Garrison, who reviewed the work in the *Genius* and returned to its contents several times in the *Liberator*, took heed of such a prophecy and shared Walker's notion of divine retribution for slavery's continuance. Yet, unlike (and partially because of) Walker's warlike solution, Garrison passionately and stridently struggled for the immediatist answer: the pacifistic means to avoid an apocalyptic end.

That Garrison never established a firm date (or any date for that matter) for the abolition of slavery was based on his refusal to recognize slavery's legitimacy and his faith in immediatism's regenerative capabilities. Although an emancipation schedule largely represented a compromise with sin, such a scheme, in his opinion, was more simply deemed unnecessary. For the evangelically inspired Garrison, immediatism was powerful and persuasive because it could and, as it was originally believed, would purify slaveholding consciences and cleanse racist souls. The emancipation of slaves and of white Americans, as well as national absolution, would immediately occur once the sin of slavery and the attendant evil of antiblack prejudices were recognized and duly repented. Perhaps this was an impractical and naïve approach to some in hindsight, but Garrison and many other abolitionists thought differently when they organized nationally in 1833. Their expectations were practical, and the evangelical Christian example only buttressed them. Yet, what immediatists considered logical was unthinkable, impossible, and fanatical to the vast majority of their contemporaries.

Raymond James Krohn

See also: First Great Awakening and Antislavery; Garrisonians; Gradual Emancipation.

Further Readings

Abzug, Robert H. *Cosmos Crumbling: American Reform and the Religious Imagination.* New York: Oxford University Press, 1994.

Abzug, Robert H. "The Influence of Garrisonian Abolitionists' Fears of Slave Violence on the Antislavery Argument." *The Journal of Negro History* 55, 1 (January 1970): 26–28.

Christie, John W., and Dwight L. Dumond. *George Bourne and the Book of Slavery Irreconcilable*. Wilmington: The Historical Society of Delaware, 1969.

Davis, David Brion. "The Emergence of Immediatism in British and American Antislavery Thought." *The Mississippi Valley Historical Review* 49, 2 (September 1962): 209–230.

Jacobs, Donald M., ed. *Courage and Conscience: Black and White Abolitionists in Boston*. Bloomington: Indiana University Press, 1993.

Loveland, Anne C. "Evangelicalism and 'Immediate Emancipation' in American Antislavery Thought." *The Journal of Southern History* 32, 2 (May 1966): 172–188.

Midgley, Clare. *Women against Slavery: The British Campaigns, 1780–1870*. London: Routledge, 1992.

Newman, Richard S. *The Transformation of American Abolitionism: Fighting Slavery in the Early Republic*. Chapel Hill: University of North Carolina Press, 2002.

Internal Slave Trade and Antislavery

Following congressional action to make the importation of slaves to the United States illegal in 1808, the movement of slaves within American borders became an increasingly controversial topic in politics and popular culture in the period leading up to the Civil War. The close of the slave trade coincided with the development of short-staple cotton agriculture in the Lower South and Southwest. This brought about a movement of slaves from the Upper South to such new states as Alabama and Mississippi, creating an important source of revenue for slaveholders and slave traders. It also brought about a massive movement of slaves that has been described as nothing short of a "Second Middle Passage" for slave families and communities. Estimates indicate that between the ratification of the Constitution and the Civil War, approximately one million slaves moved from the Upper to the Lower South, approximately two thirds of whom were sold through a network of traders and slave markets which made up America's domestic slave trade. The trade in slaves made up roughly 15 percent of the South's economy in the antebellum period, a figure that does not account for the many slaves smuggled into the country long after the 1808 importation ban was established.

Slaveholders claimed that the trade was an odious, if necessary, part of life in the Old South. Even proslavery polemicists characterized the slave traders as one of the most detestable groups in Southern society. But to antislavery activists, the domestic slave trade represented the most egregious aspect of the peculiar institution. With the publication of tracts such as Theodore Dwight Weld's *American Slavery as It Is* (1839) and Harriet Jacob's autobiography, *Incidents in the Life of a Slave Girl* (1861), the antislavery movement focused its growing energies on the slave trade as representing all that was immoral and irreligious about American slave-holding. The constant threat of sale also provided a potent and pervasive theme in more sentimental antislavery literature. For example, Harriet Beecher Stowe's popular *Uncle Tom's Cabin* (1852) depicted the sale of slaves as an inherently immoral act that broke up black families, exposed slaves to the harshness of life in the Lower South, and disconnected children from their parents. Stowe's effort to reveal how slavery destroyed familial life struck a chord with Northern readers at a time when Americans viewed the family as the bedrock of stability and a foundation of communal life. These works incurred the wrath of slaveholders, who fought to suppress the distribution of antislavery tracts in their states, and pushed for the congressional suppression of antislavery petitions, which came to be known as the "Gag Rule" (1836). Abolitionist pressure and slaveholder reactions created a politically charged environment that spurred a growing sense among Northerners in the 1850s that Southerners would stop at nothing to use the federal government to protect their property. As antislavery rhetoric won a wider audience within the Northern electorate, the internal slave trade became a central symbol of the slave-holder's unrestrained power.

Erik Mathisen

See also: Literature and Abolition.

Further Readings

Bancroft, Frederic. *Slave Trading in the Old South*. 1931. Columbia: University of South Carolina Press, 1996.

Berlin, Ira. *Generations of Captivity: A History of African-American Slaves*. Cambridge, MA: Belknap Press of Harvard University Press, 2003.

Johnson, Walter. *Soul by Soul: Life Inside the Antebellum Slave Market*. Cambridge, MA: Harvard University Press, 1999.

Tadman, Michael. *Speculators and Slaves: Masters, Traders, and Slaves in the Old South*. Madison: University of Wisconsin Press, 1989.

J

Jefferson, Thomas and Antislavery

Thomas Jefferson (1743–1826) is at the center of the most insurmountable paradox in American history. Prior to serving as the nation's first secretary of state, second vice president, and third president, Jefferson was the primary author of the Declaration of Independence, in which he insisted, "All men are created equal." Nevertheless, before he died on July 4, 1826, Jefferson owned hundreds of slaves, many of whom were sold to settle his notoriously unruly debts, but only eight of them (all members of the Hemings family) were ever freed (three during his lifetime and five at his death). Sally Hemings was Jefferson's slave, as well as half sister-in-law and, as a 1998 DNA analysis proved, mother to at least one of his children.

Born the son of a rich Virginia planter and educated with many of the nation's future leaders at William and Mary College, Jefferson inherited several hundred acres and a keen understanding of the value of slaves. He acquired even more land, the now-famous Monticello, through marriage to Martha Wayles Skelton, who died in 1782 shortly before turning thirty-four. Martha Jefferson gave birth to six children, only two of whom reached adulthood. Jefferson never knew life without slaves.

Yet Jefferson's view of slavery has long been contested. In the infamous *Dred Scott v. Sandford* majority opinion of 1857, Supreme Court chief justice Roger Taney confidently observed: "[The Declaration] would seem to embrace the whole human family. . . . But . . . the enslaved African race were not intended to be included . . . the conduct of the distinguished men who framed the Declaration of Independence would have been utterly and flagrantly inconsistent with the principles they asserted. . . . They perfectly understood the meaning of the language they used and how it would be understood by others; and they knew that it would not in any part of the civilized world be supposed to embrace the negro race" (60 U.S. 393 [1856]). Before becoming president, Abraham Lincoln, in his 1858 U.S. Senate campaign debate with Stephen Douglas, responded to Taney and the *Dred Scott* decision: "While Mr. Jefferson was the owner of slaves, as undoubtedly he was, in speaking upon this very subject, he used the strong language that 'he trembled for his country when he remembered that God was just'" (Fifth Debate, October 7, 1858). Did Jefferson never intend that "all men" included blacks, as Taney suggested, or was he a reluctant and remorseful slave owner, as Lincoln suggested?

Among historians, Jefferson's supporters insist that he often wrote or spoke against slavery and even tried, in Congress in 1784, to eliminate the slave trade. Jefferson detractors claim that his antislavery assertions were pitifully few and only appeared in private letters. While some biographers portray Jefferson as a frustrated but tireless proto-abolitionist, still others proclaim he did almost nothing to end slavery. As it turns out, determining Jefferson's stance on slavery is anything but simple.

Jefferson recognized the detestable character of slavery, and he seems to have been at least theoretically bothered by it. His most significant repudiation of the institution can be found in *Notes on the State of Virginia*, written and rewritten by Jefferson in the 1780s. In Query XVIII of that collection, Jefferson observed, "There must doubtless be an unhappy influence on the manners of our people produced by the existence of slavery among us." Of Jefferson's concerns regarding slavery, none are more quoted than this line from an 1820 letter to a friend: "We have the wolf by the ear, and we can neither hold him, nor safely let him go. Justice is on one scale, and self-preservation is on the other."

Although Jefferson often advocated freedom for slaves, there is little indication he made much effort toward emancipation. Furthermore, any effort he did make was predicated upon the complete removal of freedmen from the United States. More remarkable than anything he wrote in *Notes on the State of Virginia* rejecting slavery are his reflections relating to the inferiority of blacks. The pages of *Notes* are filled with pseudoscientific descriptions and observations of blacks like the following:

- "the preference of the Oranootan for the black women over those of his own specie"
- "they secrete less by the kidnies . . . which gives them a very strong and disagreeable odour"
- "seem to require less sleep [and] . . . will be induced by the slightest amusements"
- "brave, and more adventuresome. But . . . from a want of forethought"
- "they are more ardent after their female"
- "their griefs are transient"
- "An animal whose body is at rest, and who does not reflect, must be disposed to sleep . . . in memory they are equal to the whites; in reason much inferior"

Some historians insist that Jefferson was a product of his age; his racism, like his spelling, was indicative of the times. Opposition to slavery, they say, was socially and legally impossible for a wealthy Virginian. Still other historians disagree, insisting that some among Jefferson's contemporaries did far more to contain or even end slavery.

In 1782, the Virginia legislature passed a law allowing manumitted slaves to remain in the state. That law stood for twenty-three years, during which time George Washington freed all his slaves in his will. Unlike Jefferson, Washington also refused to break up slave families through sale, "as you would do cattle at a market." Another fellow Virginian and member of the state council, Robert Carter III, not only freed over 500 slaves, he also provided them with land to farm. Edward Coles, a neighbor of Jefferson, wrote the ex-president in 1814, seeking endorsement for a plan he had to free all his slaves. Jefferson dissuaded Coles, contending slaves were as "incapable as children of taking care of themselves" and that emancipated slaves were "pests in society by their idleness." Ignoring Jefferson's advice, Coles moved to Illinois where he became the state's second governor and the man most responsible for keeping Illinois a free state prior to the Civil War. As for Jefferson, he remained a slaveholder all his life, and his antislavery seems to have been little more than rhetoric.

R. Owen Williams

See also: Declaration of Independence (1776).

Further Readings

Ellis, Joseph J. *American Sphinx*. New York: Vintage, 1996.
Finkelman, Paul. *Slavery and the Founders*. Armonk, NY: M.E. Sharpe, Inc., 2001.
Miller, John Chester. *Wolf by the Ears*. Charlottesville: University of Virginia Press, 1991.
Peterson, Merrill, ed. *Thomas Jefferson: Writings*. New York: The Library of America, 1984. See especially, *Notes on Virginia, Queries XIV, XVIII*.

Jerry Rescue (1851)

One of the most important episodes in the history of antebellum antislavery, the Jerry Rescue involved the forcible rescue by Northern abolitionists of a captured fugitive who was being returned to slavery in the South. The incident occurred on October 1, 1851, in Syracuse, New York, which had become by that time a hotbed of abolitionism and reform activity. The rescue constituted deliberate and open defiance of the Fugitive Slave Law that had been passed by the U.S. Congress as part of the Compromise of 1850. Signaling an increasing radicalism and aggressiveness in the abolitionist movement, the Jerry Rescue marked the beginning of a shift away from the moral persuasion and legal reform tactics of the 1840s, advocated most notably by the Garrisonians, toward more open acts of resistance and civil disobedience that would characterize abolitionist agitation in the years leading up to the Civil War.

William Henry, known as "Jerry," was an escaped slave from Missouri who had lived in Syracuse for about two years, working in a carpentry studio as a cooper. On October 1, federal marshal Henry Allen and his deputies arrested Jerry under the false charge of petty theft. Jerry offered no resistance while the deputies handcuffed him and transported him to the office of U.S. commissioner Joseph L. Sabine. Only at the commissioner's office was Jerry informed that he had been arrested under the authority of the Fugitive Slave Law. His arrest marked the first time a fugitive slave had been captured in Syracuse under that law and accordingly drew much immediate attention.

At the time, many visitors were in Syracuse attending both a county agricultural fair and a local convention of the Liberty Party, the political arm of the abolitionist movement. When news of Jerry's arrest reached that convention, the abolitionists were outraged and the meeting was immediately adjourned. Its delegates included prominent philanthropist and abolitionist Gerrit Smith, Unitarian minister Samuel J. May, and Reverend Jermain W. Loguen, a fugitive slave and leader of the Underground Railroad network. Church bells were tolled to alert the members of the local Vigilance Committee to the arrest of a fugitive slave. A crowd of abolitionists, residents, and curious spectators flocked to the commissioner's office.

Jerry's hearing was delayed while court officials attempted to find a large room to accommodate all the people who had crowded into the office. Not allowed to testify on his own behalf and fearing a guilty verdict, Jerry attempted to escape with the help of some sympathetic members of the crowd. Recaptured by police officers and volunteer agents, he was taken to the police office and placed in a back room under heavy guard with his legs shackled. As the crowd grew to what historians have estimated to be nearly 2,000 people, the local authorities began to fear a riot. Marshal Allen wanted to call out the militia to prevent disorder, but it never arrived.

Early that evening, the local Vigilance Committee met secretly to plan the rescue. By 8:30 P.M., a group of approximately fifty-two abolitionists marched down the street toward the police office carrying a long wooden beam that they then used as a battering ram to destroy the windows and doors of the office. As the abolitionists forced their way into the building, Marshal Allen and the other authorities fled. The crowd carried Jerry into the street, transporting him to a horse and buggy that had been waiting for him. Jerry was taken to a safe house in the city where he waited for four days before he left for Oswego, New York, on the shores of Lake Ontario. He then sailed for Kingston, Canada West (Ontario), where he died of tuberculosis in 1853.

Although abolitionists regarded the rescue of Jerry as the action of virtuous citizens defying an unjust law, most Northerners who desired reconciliation and compromise with the South held the opposite opinion. Indeed, newspapers outside of central New York frequently denounced the rescue as mob rule. Fearing prosecution, many participants in the rescue, including Loguen, fled to Canada West. Thirteen men were eventually arrested. After a number of postponements, the trials of the rescuers began in January 1853. However, only one person, Enoch Reed, was found guilty. He appealed, but died before the appeal was heard. Another rescuer was acquitted, and the remaining cases were postponed, adjourned, and then the charges were dropped against all the other rescuers. In a bold countermove, the abolitionists charged Marshal Allen with kidnapping a citizen of Syracuse. Although a grand jury indicted and tried him in June 1852, Allen was acquitted of the kidnapping charges because the court determined that he was merely enforcing federal law.

In Syracuse, abolitionists held public commemorations of the Jerry rescue every October 1 until the Civil War. They hoped to promote the same spirit of resistance to slavery and the legal system that supported it as the rescuers demonstrated in 1851. The Jerry rescue came to be so celebrated because successful rescues of fugitive slaves were rare in the 1850s; the vast majority of slaves who were captured by federal agents were returned into slavery.

Michelle Orihel

See also: Fugitive Slave Law (1850).

Further Readings

Roach, Monique Patenaude. "The Rescue of William "Jerry" Henry: Antislavery and Racism in the Burned-Over District." *New York History* 82, 2 (Spring, 2001): 135–154.

Sokolow, Jayme A. "The Jerry McHenry Rescue and the Growth of Northern Antislavery Sentiment during the 1850s." *Journal of American Studies* 16, 3 (December, 1982): 427–445.

K

King, Boston

Boston King freed himself twice, became a leader of a black Loyalist community of freed slaves in America and then in Africa, and wrote and had published one of the most revealing and poignant memoirs of an individual's struggles in slavery and in freedom. Over the course of his eventful life, King was born into slavery in South Carolina, escaped to British lines during the American Revolution, was evacuated from New York to Nova Scotia in 1783, joined the migration from Nova Scotia to Sierra Leone in 1792, and spent two years in England training to be a Methodist missionary before returning to Sierra Leone.

As with so many slaves who freed themselves, in King's first twenty-five years, he combined luck, ingenuity, and persistence to escape slavery and to stay free. King was born on the South Carolina plantation of the Waring family; his father was a Christian, a native African, and a leader of the local black community, and his mother was most likely born in America and may have been at least partly American Indian. A favorite of his horse-racing owner, King traveled extensively in the colonies as a stable attendant before being apprenticed to a Charles Town (now Charleston) carpenter. The American Revolution offered the young, resourceful man a chance to escape the abusive carpenter; in 1780, King fled and joined the British Army in Charles Town. After a series of adventures, including being accidentally left behind by his regiment, being recaptured and reenslaved by American forces, and a daring night-time escape during low tide from New Jersey to Staten Island, King was in British-occupied New York City when peace was declared in 1783. He joined the 2,700 others listed in the Book of Negroes whom the British, at their own expense, evacuated to Nova Scotia and promised land and supplies for farming. Like many of the free blacks in Nova Scotia who suffered poverty and hardship, King struggled to make ends meet, though eventually was able to parlay his carpentry skills into a modest living.

But it was King's inspiration by Methodism that led to his remarkable Atlantic world career. King's most memorable childhood experience involved a religious revelation during a dream, and he continued to study the Bible as best he could during the American Revolution. However, he did not consider himself fully converted to Christianity until his first few years in Nova Scotia. After that, he began preaching and managed to gain a pulpit. When John Clarkson came to Nova Scotia in 1792 to recruit settlers for the new British-sponsored colony in West Africa, Sierra Leone, King convinced Clarkson to include him as a missionary despite the fact that King's modest living excluded him from the Sierra Leone Company's requirements that only very poor people be taken. Though his wife became sick on the journey to Africa and died soon after their arrival, King survived and began his work as a teacher and missionary, with limited success. In 1794, he accepted an invitation to go to England at the Sierra Leone Company's expense to study; he spent the next two years at a Methodist school in Bristol, during which time he wrote his memoirs, published serially in the *Methodist Magazine*. King then returned to missionary work in Nova Scotia, where he died in 1802.

Along with his amazing success at establishing himself as an educated free man and community leader, King's main legacy lay in his autobiography. King's 9,000-word account in some ways typified the abolitionist-sponsored, conversion narratives of former slaves; his description of his slavery and freedom is paralleled by the story of his call to Methodism and his growing sense of brotherhood with white Methodists. While compared to the writing in his own letters, the narrative's language clearly bears the mark of an editorial hand; yet it conveyed his distinctive sense both of religious inspiration and of passion for freedom which was never surpassed by any other slave narrative. Although not as widely acknowledged at the time of its publication as was that of Olaudah Equiano, the memoir offers an eloquent account of one man's spiritual journey and efforts to gain and keep freedom through the turmoil of the American Revolution, the black Loyalist colony in Nova Scotia, and the free black colony in Sierra Leone.

Andrew M. Schocket

See also: British Slavery, Abolition of.

Further Readings

Black Loyalists: Our History, Our People [Online, June 2005]. Canada's Digital Collections, http://collections.ic.gc.ca/blackloyalists/index.htm.

King, Boston. "Memoirs of the Life of Boston King, a Black Preacher. Written by Himself, during His Residence at Kingswood School." In Vincent Carretta, ed. *Unchained Voices: An Anthology of Black Authors in the English-Speaking World of the Eighteenth Century*. Lexington: University of Kentucky Press, 1996, pp. 351–368.

Walker, James W. St. G. *The Black Loyalists: The Search for a Promised Land in Nova Scotia and Sierra Leone, 1783–1870*. Reprint. Toronto: University of Toronto Press, 1993.

L

Lane Seminary Debates (1834)

Theodore Weld, a student at Lane Seminary, Cincinnati, organized a series of debates regarding slavery in February 1834. Son of a Presbyterian minister, Weld and twenty-four other students had recently transferred to the new school from Oneida Institute, New York. Most of these students were men of some accomplishment and maturity. The debates addressed two main questions: first, whether or not slavery should be immediately abolished; and second, whether Christians should support colonization of American blacks in Africa.

For the times, these were two highly controversial issues. Even those who held antislavery views did not agree upon methods with which to end slavery. The debates, held over two weeks, were moving and far-reaching. They systematically challenged the audience, mostly other students, to thoughtfully examine these issues. The nation tuned-in to the debates through antislavery newspapers. In their remarks, Weld and the former Oneida students revealed the strong influence of revivalist Charles G. Finney and his ideas of moral perfectionism.

Finney had taught students how to generate a conversion experience or change in beliefs. The first step was sharing solid facts that appealed to reason. The second was creating an emotional connection. In these debates, that connection was building empathy for enslaved persons. Student speakers related firsthand experiences observing injustices endured by slaves. Henry Thompson of Kentucky, Andrew Benton of Missouri, and Colemen Hodges of Virginia spoke of cruelty to slaves that each had witnessed, including separation of families, torture, and murder. Finney had taught that once reason and emotional connection were brought to bear, time and individual reflection could create a sincere change in a person's beliefs.

The issue of colonization, or the plan to deport free blacks to Africa, was also debated. At this time many believed whites and blacks could not live together peacefully in freedom. Some feared numerous free blacks would deprive white Americans of what was often seen as limited resources including jobs, food, and land. In addition, a widely held view of racial inferiority led many people to believe free blacks would remain dependent upon whites. This supposed inferiority was long used to justify racial, hereditary slavery. This pervasive false belief caused racial prejudice in the 1830s and continued to do so for more than a century to come.

Examples of racial equality were often used by antislavery debaters to help dispel this myth. James Bradley, a former slave, spoke of being taken by force from Africa. Yet he rose to manage his master's Kentucky plantation, while saving to purchase his freedom. He was an articulate and forceful example of how a black person, despite adversity, was more than equal to persons of other races.

The debates succeeded in converting nearly all Lane students to support both immediate emancipation and oppose colonization. Following the debates, Lane students formed an antislavery society. They also raised money to support a library and aid Cincinnati blacks. Students also conducted night school and Sunday school for free blacks living in Cincinnati. Some Lane students even resided in free black homes.

The debates, as well as the mission work among black residents, angered authorities at Lane Seminary. The next fall trustees took disciplinary action against the students who organized the debates and then performed mission work among free blacks. As a result, Theodore Weld and William T. Allan and a group of at least seventy-three other Lane students withdrew from the school in the fall of 1834. They became known as the Lane Rebels. Soon the student group issued their own account of events at Lane and "The Statement of Reasons" for withdrawal. It was signed by fifty-one students.

Some Lane Rebels continued to study in nearby Cumminsville and work with Cincinnati's black community. In the fall of 1835, part of the group moved to Oberlin College in northern Ohio. That new school had agreed to accept black students, thanks to pressure from this group. But most significantly, a number of Lane Rebels, including Weld and Allan, went on to devote themselves to the antislavery cause. Lane Rebels eventually fanned out across the North as ministers, speakers, and reformers. Many years of their hard work helped bring about a change in how the public viewed slavery and African Americans.

Jennifer Harrison

See also: American Colonization Society.

Further Readings

Hagedorn, Ann. *Beyond the River: The Untold Story of the Heroes of the Underground Railroad*. New York: Simon & Schuster, 2002.

Horton, James Oliver, and Lois E. Horton. *In Hope of Liberty: Culture, Community, and Protest among Northern Free Blacks, 1700–1860*. New York: Oxford University Press, 1997.

Lesick, Lawrence Thomas. *The Lane Rebels: Evangelicalism and Antislavery in Antebellum America*. Studies in Evangelicalism, No. 2. Metuchen, NJ: Scarecrow Press, 1980.

Liberia

Liberia was founded in 1822 along the West African coast by the American Colonization Society (ACS) as a site to settle emancipated slaves from the United States, making it the first American colony. It became an independent country in 1847. Between its founding and the outbreak of the U.S. Civil War, approximately 12,000 Americans migrated to Liberia.

The idea of colonizing freed blacks in Africa was not new when the ACS was organized in December 1816. The concept was discussed by Americans dating back before 1800, and the British founded what would become Sierra Leone for that purpose in 1787. The ACS was supported by many prominent white Americans, such as Henry Clay and Bushrod Washington, and in 1819 Congress allocated $100,000 for the encouragement of relocating former slaves. The capital city, Monrovia, would even be named for President James Monroe. Chapters of the ACS would open in several states in addition to the creation of other independent state and city colonization societies.

An abortive effort was made to found the colony in 1820. In 1821, with the assistance of a U.S. Navy vessel, land was purchased from the West African natives.

A Vey town (i.e., Vai) near Monrovia. (Library of Congress)

Another effort to establish a colony was made in 1822, and this time succeeded in laying the foundation for Liberia. Other state colonization societies such as in Maryland also founded colonies in the same regions and would eventually be incorporated into a larger Liberia.

Liberia was a colony from 1822 to 1847. Among those who resided in the colony were freed slaves from the United States who gained their freedom on condition of leaving, and free blacks who were looking for a better life away from the openly racist white America. The former slaves from the United States would become Americo-Liberians. Former slaves from the Caribbean would become the Congo People. Both Americos and Congo peoples would eventually become separate ethnic groups in modern Liberia. The population was augmented by recaptureds, blacks liberated from illegal slave ships working along the West African coast, as a well as a large indigenous population. With attitudes somewhat similar to whites who migrated to the United States, many of the new settlers saw themselves as coming to civilize the native population. The new society they created was based on the American culture, including the Southern plantation culture they knew in the United States. The expense of maintaining Liberia for the ACS was great, and there were potential threats from colonial powers. In 1846, the colony voted to become an independent state and a year later it did so. Joseph Jenkins Roberts was elected its first president. While an American creation, independent Liberia was not recognized by the United States until after the start of the Civil War because of persistent Southern opposition.

The supporters of Liberia had varied reasons for endorsing it. For those who did not believe freed slaves could be integrated into American society, it was a way to rid the nation of their presence and to return blacks to their supposedly "natural" home in Africa. Some whites even believed the presence of Liberia would hasten the end of slavery by affording a site where hesitant slaveholders might require their slaves to go as a condition of manumission. Slave owners would also benefit by getting rid of those free blacks whose presence "corrupted" slaves and who might even encourage the murder of slave masters or whites in general.

The society's efforts were opposed vigorously in the 1820s by black anticolonizationists, and they gained some significant white support in the early 1830s as they won more whites over to oppose the ACS, Liberia, and slavery. Abolitionists, white and black, understood the colony as an effort to strengthen slavery by eliminating the free black presence. Blacks themselves were not enthusiastic about abandoning their native land for an Africa that was no more their homeland than it was that of white Americans.

The country of Liberia was ruled by "Americo-Liberians" from 1847 to 1979. The role of indigenous tribes in the rule of Liberia was sharply curtailed throughout much of the nation's history. In 1862, they were declared subjects with limited political rights, but there was only a very gradual acceptance of their role in society. In a 1979 coup the rule of Americo-Liberians was ended and replaced by a period of turmoil lasting over two decades. In modern Liberia, Americo-Liberians have become just one of many ethnic groups in the country, constituting approximately 2.5 percent of the population, with Congo people comprising another 2.5 percent.

Donald E. Heidenreich

See also: American Colonization Society.

Further Readings

Beyan, Amos Jones. *African American Settlements in West Africa: John Brown Russwurm and the American Civilizing Efforts*. New York: Palgrave, 2005.

Burin, Eric. *Slavery and the Peculiar Solution: A History of the American Colonization Society*. Gainesville: University Press of Florida, 2005.

Clegg, Claude Andrew. *The Price of Liberty: African Americans and the Making of Liberia*. Chapel Hill: University of North Carolina Press, 2004.

Reef, Catherine. *This Our Dark Country: The American Settlers of Liberia*. New York: Clarion Books, 2002.

Liberty Party

The Liberty Party developed from a split in the antislavery movement over the question of participation in the political process and acceptance of the Constitution as a valid form of government for the United States. Supporters of political involvement wanted a new, third party committed to the elimination of slavery. Those who favored forming such a third party included Gerrit Smith and Myron Holley of New York, Edwin Stanton of Ohio, and Joshua Leavitt of Massachusetts, editor of the *Emancipator*.

In 1839, a series of meetings beginning at the national convention of the American Antislavery Society led to the formation of the Liberty Party and its nomination of James G. Birney of Michigan for president and Thomas Earle of Ohio as his running mate. The Liberty Party's effort in the 1840 election was minimal, and the party received little more than 7,000 votes nationally.

The Liberty Party platform in 1840 focused on a single issue, slavery, and took no position on other important issues of the day such as the tariff and internal improvements. The party enjoyed some success at the state and local levels during the early 1840s in the Northern states, drawing support largely from members of the Whig Party. In 1844, Birney was again nominated for president and was seen as enough of a threat to be attacked by the Whig Party press with a forged letter calling into question his opposition to slavery. The Liberty Party attracted some 62,300 votes in the election, which was very close between the two main party candidates, James K. Polk and Henry Clay. In New York State, Birney's vote exceeded the margin between Polk and Clay; carrying New York would have made Clay president. The Liberty Party was strengthened by these results and saw itself as now holding the balance between the two principal parties.

This success and political issues of the post-election period, especially the Mexican War, led many in the party to seek alliances with other reform groups and reform or antislavery members of the Whig and Democratic parties. This "broad platform" approach had been discussed prior to 1844, but gained strength afterward and had prevailed by the 1848 election. Coalitions between the Liberty Party and other reform groups, or antislavery elements of other parties, led to a number of electoral successes for Liberty Party members in a number of Northern states.

In 1848, the Liberty Party nominated John P. Hale of New Hampshire for president. When Martin Van Buren bolted from the Democratic Party over the issue of slavery, Hale and his running mate, Leicester King, withdrew in favor of the new Free Soil Party candidate. Van Buren, however, was not acceptable to the entire "broad platform" faction because of his record on other reform issues and his earlier, much softer, stand on slavery. A rump convention formed the National Liberty Party and nominated Gerrit Smith for president. A coalition of several reform groups also nominated Smith, but with a different running mate.

The Liberty Party did not survive this division. Some of its more politically successful and ambitious members returned to the Democratic or Whig parties. Those with stronger antislavery views joined the Free Soil Party. The Liberty Party was replaced by the Free Soil Party, if anything a more committed antislavery party, but with a much broader base. Both the Liberty Party and the Free Soil Party made little, if any, effort to attract Southern voters for support, as did the later Republican Party. The Liberty Party had succeeded in its principal goal—bringing the debate over slavery into electoral politics.

William H. Mulligan Jr.

See also: Democratic Party and Antislavery.

Further Readings

Holt, Michael F. *The Rise and Fall of the Whig Party*. New York: Oxford University Press, 1999.

Sewell, Richard H. *Ballots for Freedom: Antislavery Politics in the United States, 1837–1860*. New York: Oxford University Press, 1976.

Volpe, Vernon L. *Forlorn Hope of Freedom: The Liberty Party in the Old Northwest, 1838–1848*. Kent, OH: Kent State University Press, 1990.

Lincoln, Abraham

On February 12, 1809, Abraham Lincoln was born in Kentucky to Thomas and Nancy Lincoln. In 1816, the family moved to Indiana, "partly on account of slavery; but chiefly on account of the difficulty in land titles in Ky," according to Lincoln. Lincoln's year of formal schooling was in Indiana, but most of his time was spent working on the farm or as a hired hand. In 1830, the Lincoln family moved to Illinois, and shortly thereafter Lincoln struck out on his own. When the Black Hawk War broke out in 1832, Lincoln joined a volunteer company and was elected captain, gaining his first experience as an elected leader.

After the war, Lincoln ran unsuccessfully for the state legislature. He ran again in 1834 and won. While in the legislature, Lincoln began studying law and had gained his license by 1836. Lincoln was reelected three times, and was soon the leader of the Illinois Whigs. In 1837, reacting to the murder of abolitionist Elijah Lovejoy, the legislature passed a resolution condemning abolitionist societies, declaring the right of property in slaves to be sacred, and asserting that the federal government could not abolish slavery in the capital. Lincoln was one of six legislators who voted against the resolution, and in March he helped to write a protest declaring, "The institution of slavery is founded on both injustice and bad policy." However, Lincoln also asserted, "The Congress of the United States has no power, under the constitution, to interfere with the institution of slavery in the different States."

In 1846, Lincoln was elected to the U.S. House of Representatives. During a break in the session in 1847, Lincoln represented a slaveholder in a lawsuit, arguing that the man should not be deprived of his slaves. In 1849, Lincoln authored a referendum calling for the gradual, compensated abolition of slavery in the District of Columbia, but could not get support for the measure. Lincoln did not run for reelection, and for the next ten years practiced law.

As slavery became an increasingly important issue, the new antislavery Republican Party began to siphon members, including Lincoln, away from the Whigs. In 1858, Lincoln campaigned against Stephen Douglas for a senatorial appointment. In a series of debates, Douglas, who favored not interfering with slavery where it already existed and allowing popular sovereignty to decide on it in the territories, argued that Lincoln sought equality between the races. Lincoln stated his preference that no new slave states be admitted to the Union, and that slavery be abolished in the District of Columbia, but also asserted, "I am not, nor ever have been in favor of bringing about in any way the social and political equality of the white and black races . . . I am not nor ever have been in favor of making voters or jurors of negroes, nor of qualifying them to hold office, nor to intermarry with white people." Lincoln did not receive the appointment, but the debates brought him national attention.

In February 1860, Lincoln spoke at the Cooper Institute in New York, arguing that slavery should not be allowed to spread to new areas, but neither should it be abolished where it already existed. While the position was unacceptable to extremists on both sides, the majority of Northerners agreed with Lincoln's moderate stance, earning him even more national prominence. Lincoln was not the favorite to receive the Republican nomination in 1860, but he was acceptable to most factions of the party, and when the frontrunners ran into opposition, it was Lincoln who was nominated. In November, Lincoln was elected to the presidency even though he received less than half the popular vote and did not appear on the ballot in most Southern states.

By the time Lincoln assumed the presidency, seven states had already left the Union, and soon afterward four more followed them. Lincoln knew he had to keep the border states—Delaware, Maryland, Kentucky, and Missouri—in the Union, something he could not do if he moved against slavery, so he held off, even rescinding early freedom proclamations issued for runaways by military commanders John Frémont and David Hunter. However, by July 1862 and after the successful implementation of the First and Second Confiscation Acts, Lincoln saw that he could move against slavery as a military measure, thereby forestalling much criticism, and drafted an Emancipation Proclamation freeing the slaves in areas that were in rebellion. After showing the draft to his cabinet, they encouraged him to keep the document secret until the Union forces had won a major battlefield victory so as to avoid appearing desperate. Lincoln took their advice, kept the proclamation to himself, and waited for a victory. On August 14, 1862, Lincoln met with a group of African Americans and advocated colonization, the voluntary deportation of former slaves, saying that the racism and distrust on both sides would never allow the races to live together. In the months prior to this meeting, Lincoln had actually appointed some individuals to inquire into the possibility of creating a site for African American colonization in the black republic of Haiti. Nowhere, however, in the draft of the Emancipation Proclamation did he mention colonization.

Eight days later, Lincoln wrote, "My paramount object in this struggle *is* to save the Union, and is *not* either to save or to destroy slavery. If I could save the Union without freeing *any* slave I would do it, and if I could save it by freeing *all* the slaves I would do it; and if I could do it by freeing some and leaving others alone I would also do that." In September, after the Union victory at Antietam, Lincoln announced the preliminary Emancipation Proclamation. Foreign intervention, which had recently seemed a possibility, became a dead letter because no nation wanted to be seen as interfering in a war for freedom. While Lincoln may have wavered on slavery before signing the Emancipation Proclamation, afterward there was no doubting how he felt. In 1864, Lincoln wrote, "I am naturally anti-slavery. If slavery is not wrong, nothing is wrong. I can not remember when I did not so think and feel."

In 1864, Lincoln worked hard for his reelection and a constitutional amendment abolishing slavery. In November, Lincoln was reelected easily and in January the Thirteenth Amendment was passed. Lincoln's second inaugural address, delivered just over a month before he was assassinated by Southern sympathizer John Wilkes Booth, showed just how far he had come: "Fondly do we hope, fervently do we pray, that this mighty scourge of war shall soon pass away, yet if God wills it continue till all the wealth piled by two hundred years of bondage shall have been wasted, and each drop of blood drawn by the lash shall have been paid for by one drawn by the sword, the judgments of the Lord are true and righteous altogether." In his 1876 "Oration in Memory of Abraham Lincoln," Frederick Douglass proclaimed "in his heart of hearts he loathed and hated slavery."

Jared Peatman

See also: Democratic Party and Antislavery; Radical Republicans; Whig Party and Antislavery.

Further Readings

Basler, Roy P., ed., and Marion Dolores Pratt and Lloyd A. Dunlap, asst. eds. *The Collected Works of Abraham Lincoln*, 9 vols. New Brunswick, NJ: Rutgers University Press, 1952–1955.

Oates, Stephen B. *With Malice toward None: The Life of Abraham Lincoln*. New York: Harper and Row, 1977.

Literature and Abolition

The institution of slavery in the United States galvanized the literary community as writers sought to present the cruelties meted out against human beings to preserve a social system that defied the founding principles of the revolution and the basic tenets of Christian beliefs. From the introduction of the slave trade at the Jamestown colony in 1619 to the Emancipation Proclamation of 1863, freed and enslaved African American and white writers, many of whom were active in religious organizations, revolutionary movements, and women's rights groups, along with individuals compelled by indignation against social injustice, sought to press upon the emerging nation's conscience the inherent wrong of forcing men, women, and children into bondage and maintaining a caste system that terrorized the powerless to enrich the privileged white landowners, particularly of the Southern states.

The term "abolition" in this context refers to the abolishing of slavery throughout the United States, especially as it concerned the trafficking of Africans from their native lands to be sold as property, the oppression of those descendants of enslaved Africans within a primarily agrarian system of labor, and the denial of these people from achieving self-determination through laws and prohibitions, both by individual states and the federal government. The survey of literature concerned with abolition includes sermons, speeches, political tracts and essays, autobiographical narratives, poetry, and fiction.

In the seventeenth century, although few voices spoke out against "the peculiar institution," one remarkable group, the Quaker community, began to organize on behalf of freedom of worship for black slaves. In their yearly meetings from the 1680s on, the Quakers called for the abolition of slavery, which they referred to as the "traffick in menbody." They pointed out that such a practice undermined the "democratic egalitarianism" of Christianity. The early eighteenth century witnessed an awakening of the American conscience against slavery with Puritan Samuel Sewell's antislavery pamphlet "The Selling of Joseph, A Memorial" (1700). The pamphlet was published during the heated controversy about the holding of slaves, which the Puritan-enacted *Body of Liberties* had established in New England in 1641. By 1700, the slave trade was an institution. A burgeoning population of slaves brought the need for a reconsideration of such a practice as it contradicted egalitarian Christian beliefs that all people were children of God and therefore heirs to God's kingdom, principles that the Quakers had voiced earlier. Puritan leader of the Massachusetts Bay Colony, Cotton Mather lamented the practice of slavery in 1702 in his famous work *Magnalia Christi Americana*. In 1706, he published an *antislavery* sermon, "The Negro Christianized," which spoke of the need to view African Americans as part of the body of Christ, to treat them as brothers and sisters in the faith, and to encourage literacy to make the Bible available to them.

In the period from the mid-eighteenth century to the beginning of the nineteenth, voices spoke out against slavery and urged abolition. John Woolman of Massachusetts (1720–1782) published an essay dealing with the issue in "Some Considerations on the Keeping of Negroes" (1754). Meanwhile, African writers very early on recounted their experiences with slavery from firsthand experience. Among those slaves was Lucy Terry (born in West Africa in 1730), considered the first African American writer, whose poetry was passed down in the oral tradition. Only one of her poems, "Bars Fight," has survived, published in 1855, over thirty years after her death. Although the poem itself does not deal with abolition, Terry is acknowledged to be one of the first women to fight for equality, unsuccessfully arguing the case for the admittance of one of her sons to Williams College.

In New England, African American men of the cloth represented another voice for equality and abolition. John Marrant, a black preacher, led a congregation of black loyalists in Nova Scotia, impressing on his brethren the idea of a Zion, a promised land, which, according to his view, would be the return of blacks to Africa and the establishment of an all-black community in Sierra Leone. He died before realizing his vision, but paved the way for others, such as David George, who saw the resettlement of African American slaves as a solution to the problem of slavery. Marrant's autobiography of his life as a preacher, published in 1790, was one of the first to reach a wider audience. In Boston, two other notable black writers, Prince Hall and Boston King, spoke out against slavery in the years leading up to the Revolutionary War. Hall's petition to abolish slavery in Massachusetts in 1777 affected the eventual end to slavery in the Commonwealth in 1783. Connecticut's Lemuel Haynes, writer and preacher of the New Light Ministry, contributed to abolition in his essay "Liberty Further Extended: Or Free Thoughts on the Illegality of Slave-Keeping," which was first published in 1783 in the *William and Mary Quarterly*. Although these black Atlantic writers called for abolition, Prince Hall and Boston King considered a return to Africa a more viable way to release their brothers and sisters from bondage and fulfill their dream of a new Zion. Later, whites would take up the idea of colonization, returning blacks to Africa, as an alternative to abolition, most notably Thomas Jefferson himself.

The Founding Fathers addressed the issue in the late eighteenth century as they grappled with the inherent contradiction of slavery within a new democracy. Benjamin Franklin published an editorial, "On the Slave Trade" (1790), where he urged readers to abolish the institution. Thomas Jefferson, in his *Notes on the State of Virginia*, "Queries XIV and XVII" (1785), strongly condemned the institution of slavery, but argued that emancipation should be accompanied by the removal of blacks to a separate colony, where they could be "free and independent people." As leaders of the new republic searched for a compromise, slave narratives began to circulate, bringing the conditions by which people were stolen from their homes, forced to endure the Middle Passage to the United States, humiliated through the slave trade, and denied the most basic of human rights as outlined in the Declaration of Independence. Olaudah Equiano, kidnapped from what is now Nigeria, published *The Interesting Narrative* in 1789, an autobiography of his life as a slave and later a freeman. Ignatius Sancho was the author of a publication, *Letters of the Late Ignatius Sancho, an African* (1782), which included correspondences with British writer Laurence Sterne. Sancho's letters described the inhumane conditions of blacks forced into slavery and helped raise awareness of their plight.

In the early nineteenth century, three developments gave momentum to both sides of abolition: the Fugitive Slave Act of 1793, which handed slave owners legal recourse to reclaim runaway slaves captured in the North; the Missouri Compromise of 1820–1821, allowing Missouri to enter the Union as a slave state; and Nat Turner's Rebellion in 1831. Turner, a black preacher in Virginia, exhorted his parishioners to rise up against their white oppressors. Their fury led to a massacre of both adults and children before the rebellion was forcibly put down. Turner,

Captured in the interior of West Africa as a young boy and sold to Europeans as a slave, Olaudah Equiano endured many years of enslavement before eventually purchasing his own freedom. He published an autobiographical account, *The Interesting Life of Olaudah Equiano or Gustavus Vassa, the African*, in 1789 and became an important figure in the eighteenth-century British abolition movement. Frontispiece and title page from *The Interesting Narrative of the Life of Olaudah Equiano*. (Library of Congress)

arrested, tried, and convicted, was sentenced to death, but before his execution in 1831, his confession was recorded by Thomas R. Gray, whose publication of these last words, *The Confessions of Nat Turner, the Leader of the Late Insurrection in South Hampton, Va.*, was circulated to a reading public curious about the man and the events. The description of his life and times created an uneasy stir among both Northerners and Southerners. In fact, shortly after these events, several states passed laws forbidding slaves to learn to read, citing the fact that Turner had been able to read to study the Bible and preach in the black churches. Additionally, it became increasingly difficult for black preachers to operate freely in the South. In short, the Nat Turner Rebellion created a generalized suspicion and hostility toward blacks. The Missouri Compromise demonstrated that legislators were unwilling to champion the cause of abolition. The Fugitive Slave Act of 1793 was superseded by the Fugitive Slave Law of 1850, which was more injurious to blacks. This legislation stripped runaway slaves of any legal guarantees that their liberty would be protected in the North. By midcentury, the promise of emancipation had become remote.

Given the political climate of these decades, abolitionists began to speak out forcefully, only to be met with scorn and violence. Many of these social reformers, ministers themselves, wrote essays and political tracts condemning the situation in the South. Meanwhile, the slave narrative gained a wider readership. Frederick Douglass, a runaway slave, orator, and leader of the growing antislavery movement in the Boston area, published his *Narrative of the Life of Frederick Douglass, an American Slave* in 1845. The author of the preface was the famous abolitionist William Lloyd Garrison. In this account of the cruelties he endured, Douglass brought the conditions of this institution to the conscience of the white readership of the North. Later, he published the essay, "What to the Slave Is the Fourth of July?" returning to the inherent contradiction of a nation built on democratic principles and denying at the same time, liberty to millions of black Americans. Henry Highland Garnet, another black writer of the mid-nineteenth century, addressed the gradual incorporation of African Americans in the society. He gave a speech, later published as *An Address to the Slaves of the United States of America, Buffalo, N.Y., 1843*, at a Negro National Convention. Another slave narrative, but unique in that it spoke for the black woman, was published in 1861. Although it was several years later than Douglass, Harriet Jacobs's account of being a slave and a woman impressed upon the nation's conscience that the issue of disenfranchisement was two-fold. In *Incidents in the Life of a Slave Girl*, Jacobs assumes a fictional protagonist to deal not only with the conditions of the blacks, but specifically of black women: sexual harassment, concubinage, and the selling of children. Her narrator pleads, "Pity me and pardon me, O virtuous reader. You never knew what it is to be a slave; to be entirely unprotected by law or custom; to have the laws reduce you to the conditions of chattel, entirely subject to the will of another." The confluence of these two movements was to give voice to Sojourner Truth, the sisters Angelina and Sarah Grimké, and Harriet Beecher Stowe at midcentury.

Radical abolitionists brought the controversy to the public forum. Most notable was William Lloyd Garrison, whose antislavery tracts raged against the idea of "gradual abolition," and called for a militant "immediate" abolition of slavery. The abolitionist movement found a charismatic leader in Garrison, whose weekly newspaper, the *Liberator* (1831–1865), gave voice to many categories of social reformers in the North. Among those who worked with Garrison was John Greenleaf Whittier, whose *Justice and Expediency* was an antislavery tract. In the 1830s and 1840s, abolitionists were often met with mob violence. However, such writers as Garrison, Whittier, and Frederick Douglass persevered, passionately arguing the rightness of their cause. Whittier's poem "Massachusetts to Virginia" is based on an account of fugitive slave George Lattimer, who pleaded for his freedom in Boston against the attempt of his former owner to return him to the South. Eventually, Lattimer was given his free papers. The poem illustrates the hypocrisy of the Fugitive Slave laws.

William Garrison was unswerving in his crusade against slavery. Inspired by another editor, Benjamin Lundy, whose newspaper the *Genius of Universal Emancipation* (1828) was the only publication exclusively devoted to the cause, Garrison, however, disagreed with Lundy's position of gradual, not immediate, emancipation and colonization in Africa. In 1831, he and Isaac Knapp began publishing issues of the *Liberator,* pressing upon Americans the crime perpetrated on millions of black Americans. Garrison maintained that only immediate emancipation would redeem the nation. Included in his vision of universal emancipation were women. Among the early abolitionists, Garrison was preeminent, tirelessly promoting other writers, such as Frederick Douglass, whose narrative saw print through Garrison's efforts.

Garrison's influence on women writers was profound. Lydia Maria Child, a young, white novelist of the genteel tradition, turned her efforts toward abolition after meeting with Garrison. Her first abolitionist pamphlet, *An Appeal in Favor of That Class of Americans Called Africans* (1831) was directed to middle-class women. The Grimké Sisters, Angelina and Sarah, were also profoundly moved by Garrison and joined the abolitionist movement in the 1830s. Alarmed by the angry mobs in Boston who attacked women abolitionists, both sisters began lecturing throughout New England. Sarah Grimké, in her *Appeal to the Christian Women of the South* (1836), argues the urgency of the cause by appealing to their Christian principles. The abolition movement clearly found allies in the women's movement.

One woman instrumental in turning the tide of public opinion in favor of abolition was Harriet Beecher Stowe, daughter of an illustrious churchman, Lyman Beecher, and wife of a learned theologian. A New Englander, she became aware of the Underground Railroad while living in Cincinnati, Ohio, and felt compelled to address the cause and wrote the novel that dramatized the cruelties of slavery. *Uncle Tom's Cabin,* published serially and then as a volume in 1852, captured

UNCLE TOM'S CABIN;

OR,

LIFE AMONG THE LOWLY.

BY

HARRIET BEECHER STOWE.

VOL. I.

BOSTON:
JOHN P. JEWETT & COMPANY.
CLEVELAND, OHIO:
JEWETT, PROCTOR & WORTHINGTON.
1852.

Title page of *Uncle Tom's Cabin,* by Harriet Beecher Stowe. Originally serialized in the weekly publication the *National Era* beginning in June 1851, the entire work was later published as a book in 1852. The controversial book stoked sectional tensions in the United States. (Library of Congress)

the hearts and minds of readers across the nation and became perhaps the nation's first best seller, selling 300,000 copies in the first year. Although from our contemporary perspective her characters seem stereotyped, the story led readers of her day to understand how the system of slavery tore at the fabric of the family. Even the term "Uncle Tom" later became a label for those African Americans who accommodated themselves to the white racist system, rather than rebel against it. By the end of the decade, the divisions deepened to the point that any compromise to Southern slavery had become remote. Stowe wrote other sketches, stories, and essays, one concerning Sojourner Truth (1797–1883), a black evangelist, abolitionist, and women's rights activist. Her piece "Sojourner Truth, the Libyan Sibyl" (1863) is a lively exchange, an authentic record of the colloquial speech of her time. Although others recorded her speeches, Olive Gilbert transcribed Sojourner Truth's powerful *Narrative* (1850), one of several slave narratives that fueled the abolitionist movement.

Other black women emerged to speak out against such injustices. Frances Ellen Watkins Harper, writing at midcentury, is regarded as the first black woman to publish a short story in the United States, "The Two Offers," which describes the problems created within the black family—drunkenness and child abuse—resulting from the slave system. Her poetry directly concentrates on the issues of slavery and the need for moral reform. "The Slave Mother" dramatizes the mother's anguish when she is forced to give up her child. Her speeches, published in 1857, urge an end to slavery and the equal treatment of women.

One important literary figure, William Wells Brown, an escaped slave from Kentucky, became active in the antislavery movement and spoke as a delegate to the National Negro Convention, held in Buffalo in 1843. He published his own slave narrative in 1847. Brown's novel, *Clotel*, published in London in 1853, later in New York in 1861, is considered one of the earliest fictional renderings of life from a black antislavery perspective. As the novel crossed the Atlantic, it was heavily revised, published in installments in the *Weekly Anglo-African* and finally brought out in 1867 as the novel *Clotelle: or The Colored Heroine*. Other novels by black men of the late-antebellum period included Frank Webb's *The Garies and Their Friends* and Martin Delany's *Blake*.

As President Abraham Lincoln took office in 1861, the nation was so deeply divided on the issue of slavery that any compromise or accommodation had become untenable. The secession of South Carolina and the firing on Union troops at Fort Sumter in April of that year plunged the nation into a civil war that was to last for four wrenching years, during which time Lincoln's Emancipation Proclamation, delivered in 1863, formally ended slavery in the United States. The Proclamation demanded a release of all persons from bondage. As the war continued for one more year, the slaveholding states eventually surrendered their arms, their lands, and their way of life to the more powerful, rapidly industrializing North. In the years to come, African Americans would continue to struggle for equal rights and equal protection under the law, but the abolition of slavery, in principle, had been achieved. Writers, both black and white, had borne witness to the "peculiar institution" that deprived human beings of life and liberty; they had, by speaking out, contributed to the demise of an unjust system that undermined the democratic ideals upon which the nation has been founded.

Sonja Lovelace

See also: Child, Lydia Maria; Douglass, Frederick; Equiano, Olaudah; Garrison, William Lloyd; Jefferson, Thomas and Antislavery; Stowe, Harriet Beecher.

Further Readings

Brooks, Joanna, and John Saillant, eds. *Face Zion Forward: First Writers of the Black Atlantic, 1785–1798*. Boston: Northeastern University Press, 2002.

Gates, Henry Louis, ed. *The Slave Narratives*. New York: Signet, 1987.

Gates, Henry Louis, and Nelly Y. McKay, eds. *The Norton Anthology of African American Literature*. New York: Norton, 1996.

Gould, Phillip. *Barbaric Traffic: Commerce and Antislavery in the Eighteenth-Century Atlantic World*. Cambridge, MA: Harvard University Press, 2003.

Lauter, Paul, and Richard Yarborough, eds. *The Heath Anthology of American Literature*. vol. 1. 4th ed. New York: Houghton-Mifflin, 2001.

Merish, Lori. *Sentimentalism Materialism: Gender, Commodity Culture, and Nineteenth-Century American Literature*. Durham, NC: Duke University Press, 2000.

Lord Dunmore's Proclamation

On November 7, 1775, the Earl of Dunmore, the last royal governor of Virginia, issued a proclamation imposing a state of martial law on the rebellious colony that he had governed since 1771. In an unusual, indeed unprecedented, step he declared free those slaves "appertaining [belonging as a possession or right] to Rebels" who would abscond and fight for the king. It was a daring act by a desperate man, short on troops and trying unsuccessfully to govern the colony from on board a warship. Despite not being a professional soldier, Dunmore was looking to raise an army not only of slaves but also of Indians with which to quell the rebellion. Most Virginians, Tory and Patriot alike, were slaveholders, as was Dunmore himself. Many thought that suborning slaves to desert en masse was opening Pandora's Box. It might lead to a slave revolt—a prospect too dreadful to contemplate. Such an uprising would be difficult to contain; it would inevitably spread from the slaves of rebels to the slaves of Tories; together they would make common cause against the common oppressor, slaveholders. Normally, martial law would place slaves—all slaves—under greater restrictions; no slave would ever be declared free in return for military service.

Slaves were not loyal or disloyal subjects; they were not subjects at all. They owed allegiance only to their master, not to the king. The rationale of Lord Dunmore's proclamation was that the treason of the rebels had discharged their slaves from allegiance. Invoking martial law gave the governor the right to invade and expropriate private property, which the slaves were. He was not freeing slaves so much as confiscating them. Fugitive slaves (the property of rebels) thus became wards of the crown, and, at the pleasure of the crown, could "earn" their liberty by taking up arms in its defense. In the manner of convicts released into military service, the slaves were to be mercenaries paid in the coin of their own freedom. Though royal authority was scarcely enforceable anywhere in Virginia, many slaves, thinking compulsory military service not too high a price to pay for liberty, responded to Lord Dunmore's proclamation and rushed to the governor's assistance. Many were slaughtered at the battle of Great Bridge in December 1775; the survivors spent the next few months cruising off the coast of Virginia with the governor and his little fleet. Most died from disease.

The proclamation served little purpose other than to inflame further popular feeling against Lord Dunmore. The patriot convention responded by issuing an edict to the effect that fugitive slaves taken in arms would be summarily executed. An unintended result was that slaves loyal to their patriot owners were armed by them and fought against the British, as was their duty. Subsequent proclamations by British army commanders liberated slaves who fled rebel masters, but they were never allowed to fight. A punitive war measure rather than an antislavery measure, Lord Dunmore's proclamation was an experiment in brinkmanship too risky to repeat. Declaring slaves of rebels free so that they could help put down a rebellion by their masters was thought to be impolitic, a menace to the very fabric of the socio-legal order to which both parties to the conflict wholeheartedly subscribed. Some eighty-seven years later, during a much greater rebellion and civil war in which slavery was the central issue, Lord Dunmore's proclamation would find its echo in President Lincoln's Emancipation Proclamation.

Barry Cahill

See also: British Slavery, Abolition of.

Further Readings

Berkeley, Francis L. *Dunmore's Proclamation of Emancipation....* Charlottesville, VA: The Tracy W. McGregor Library, University of Virginia, 1941.

Caley, Percy B. "Dunmore, Colonial Governor of New York and Virginia, 1770–1782." Ph.D. dissertation, University of Pittsburgh, 1939.

Quarles, Benjamin. "Lord Dunmore as Liberator." *William & Mary Quarterly* 3rd ser. 15 (1958): 494–507.

Lovejoy, Elijah (1802–1837)

Elijah Parish Lovejoy was an educator, newspaper publisher and editor, religious leader, abolitionist, and political activist. Lovejoy was murdered by an angry mob of men on November 7, 1837 in Alton, Illinois. Many of the local residents opposed his antislavery beliefs printed in the local newspaper, the *Alton Observer*. After the shocking incident, the American Anti-Slavery Society, American abolitionists, free blacks, and enslaved Africans commemorated Lovejoy as a hero and martyr of the U.S. antislavery movement.

Lovejoy was born near Albion, Maine, to the Reverend Daniel and Elizabeth (Moody) Lovejoy on November 9, 1802. Lovejoy boasted Puritan roots and was raised in an evangelical household. The young Lovejoy first studied at home and later attended local academies in Monmouth and China, Maine. He graduated from the Baptist-supported Waterville College, now Colby College, in September 1826. Upon his graduation, Lovejoy became a schoolmaster at China Academy.

In 1827, Lovejoy moved to St. Louis, Missouri, where he established a private high school, the curriculum for which was grounded in classical education. Three years later, he entered a partnership with T.J. Miller and became the editor of the *St. Louis Times*. In 1833, he graduated from Princeton Theological Seminary, and was later licensed as a preacher. He returned to St. Louis to edit the *St. Louis Observer*, which espoused politics informed by Christianity and antislavery. In 1835, he married Celia Ann French.

The *Observer*, however, came to disturb local residents, primarily because of Lovejoy's abolitionism. In 1835, Lovejoy was denounced by residents for shipping the *Emancipator*, a New York newspaper published by the American Anti-Slavery Society, with a box of Bibles to a Jefferson City branch of the American Bible Society for St. Louis. In 1835, a mob destroyed his press and he witnessed the lynching of a man named Francis J. McIntosh. Lovejoy then decided to move to Alton, Illinois, with his wife, Celia, and their son, Edward Payson. In 1836, Lovejoy established the *Alton Observer* and resumed his antislavery publishing. Angry residents in Alton twice destroyed Lovejoy's press and during the latter attack, he was murdered when he sought to defend his office.

Nadine Hunt

See also: American Anti-Slavery Society (AASS).

Further Readings

Curtis, Michael Kent. "The 1837 Killing of Elijah Lovejoy by an Anti-Abolition Mob: Free Speech, Mobs, Republican Government, and the Privileges of American Citizens." *UCLA Law Review* 44 (1997): 1109–1184.

Dillon, Merton L. *Elijah P. Lovejoy: Abolitionist Editor.* Urbana: University of Illinois Press, 1961.

Educational Resources: Elijah Lovejoy [Online, August 2005] Center for State Policy and Leadership, http://pphsp.uis.edu/elijah_parish_lovejoy.htm.

Simon, Paul. *Freedom's Champion: Elijah Lovejoy.* Carbondale: Southern Illinois University Press, 1994.

Lundy, Benjamin

Benjamin Lundy, the most significant American antislavery advocate of the 1820s, edited the *Genius of Universal Emancipation.* Born to Joseph and Elizabeth Shotwell Lundy on January 4, 1789, in Sussex County, New Jersey, Lundy was a birthright Quaker. He witnessed the dehumanizing effects of slavery firsthand while learning the trade of saddlery in Wheeling, Virginia. He relocated to Ohio, where he married Esther Lewis and established his own shop in 1815. He soon began his activist career, helping to cofound the Union Humane Society in 1816 in Mount Pleasant, Ohio. Short-lived though this group proved, its tenets would remain consistent across Lundy's career: opposition to slavery through both moral and political means, use of all legal means to free slaves, and assisting free blacks.

After a frustrating sojourn in Missouri during the tumultuous statehood debates of 1819–1820, Lundy recognized the importance of an antislavery press. With the 1820 death of Elihu Embree, the Tennessee editor of the *Emancipator,* Lundy picked up his mantle with the *Genius of Universal Emancipation* in June 1821. The next year he moved his family and his paper from Ohio to Greeneville in eastern Tennessee, to foster antislavery sentiments in the South.

From the beginning, Lundy based his abolitionist analysis on the ideals of the Declaration of Independence, decrying the blatant hypocrisy that slavery entailed politically, ethically, religiously, and economically. Though he embraced the Quaker heritage of John Woolman and Anthony Benezet and counted on Friends' support, his paper was never partisan, maintaining an ecumenical, even eclectic tone. He supported efforts to prove that free labor was more profitable than slavery. Lundy was ambivalent toward colonization; he saw through its underlying racism, and ridiculed the impossibility of relocating all American blacks to Africa, but he also appreciated any movement that freed slaves and provoked reflection on the benefits of manumission. One result of this was a trip to Haiti in 1826 to investigate possibilities for American blacks resettling there. Not only was the trip a failure, but also Lundy's wife died while he was away; relatives raised their five children.

Based in Baltimore since 1824, the *Genius of Universal Emancipation (GUE)* became the national voice of antislavery. Through Lundy's paper, forces that shaped abolition and related movements first came to prominence. Lundy cautiously supported Frances Wright's Nashoba project, and more enthusiastically published Elizabeth Heyrick's bold *Immediate, Not Gradual Abolition*. His serious treatment of women as co-workers and intellectuals continued with his mentoring of the Quaker poet Elizabeth Margaret Chandler, who would become editor of the women's page of *GUE* in 1829. Lundy also befriended free blacks in Baltimore, including William Watkins, and published their writings occasionally.

In 1828, Lundy traveled north to raise funds, meeting with many Northern philanthropists, such as William Goodell and George Benson. But the most important meeting was with William Lloyd Garrison. Inspired by Lundy, and choosing to focus his energies on antislavery, the young Garrison became an associate editor of *GUE* in 1829. His more strident tone resulted in legal problems for himself and the paper. Once Garrison was out of prison, he and Lundy amicably ended their business relationship, leaving Garrison free to launch the *Liberator* in 1831. Despite ideological differences and public quarrels over the next decade, the importance of Lundy's influence in converting Garrison to antislavery and encouraging his editorial skills cannot be underestimated: it cements Lundy's role in bridging earlier antislavery movements to later abolitionists.

In the spring of 1832, Lundy traveled to Texas, investigating conditions in this part of Mexico for black American settlement. While negotiations with the Mexican government ultimately evaporated, he gained intimate knowledge of Southern white American plans to usurp this land and, he feared, turn it into several new slaveholding states. He wrote two widely circulated pamphlets in 1836, *The War in Texas* and *The Origin and True Causes of the Texas Revolution*. John Quincy Adams used Lundy's writings and testimonies to delay the annexation of Texas to the United States.

Texas propelled Lundy from a nearly forgotten relic to a central player in the growing antislavery movement of the late 1830s. However, he was suffering ill health and losing his hearing. While preparing for his move to Illinois to live with his children, Lundy's papers were destroyed in the mob arson of Pennsylvania Hall in 1837. Arriving in Illinois the next year, antislavery forces there saw Lundy and *GUE* filling the gap left by Elijah Lovejoy's martyrdom, and so the paper resumed for twelve issues. Lundy died August 22, 1839, in Lowell, Illinois, from fever brought on by overwork on his farm. Lundy was widely eulogized, but his contributions have still been underestimated, now and then. His newspaper fanned a flame of abolition that was nearly extinguished, and brought its fire to a new generation. His ecumenical approach was not only religious, but sectional, too. He consistently tried to reach the conscience of white Southerners, and to place slavery in international perspective. He was tireless (to his own detriment), almost always impoverished, open-minded to new ideas, and consistent in his principles. Relatively free of class snobbery, he evaluated ideas on their merits rather than on the respectability of their authors. He intuitively grasped the difficulties involved in ending slavery, and thus encouraged a pluralism of ideas to further that goal.

Jennifer Rycenga

See also: Quakers and Antislavery.

Further Readings

Armstrong, William C. *The Lundy Family and Their Descendants*. Belleville, Ontario, Canada: Mika Publishing Company, 1987.

Dillon, Merton L. *Benjamin Lundy and the Struggle for Negro Freedom*. Urbana: University of Illinois Press, 1966.

Earle, Thomas. *The Life, Travels and Opinions of Benjamin Lundy*. New York: Arno Press, 1969 [originally published 1847].

Landon, Fred. "Benjamin Lundy in Illinois." *Journal of the Illinois State Historical Society* 33 (March 1940): 53–67.

Lundy, Benjamin. *The Origin and True Causes of the Texas Revolution Commenced in the Year 1835*. Philadelphia, 1836.

Lundy, Benjamin. *The Poetical Works of Elizabeth Margaret Chandler, With a Memoir of Her Life and Character*. Mnemosyne Press, 1969.

Lundy, Benjamin. *The War in Texas*. Upper Saddle River, NJ: Literature House, 1970 [reprint of 1836 edition].

Miller, Randall M. "The Union Humane Society." *Quaker History* 61, 2 (1972): 91–106.

Sandlund, Vivien. "'A Devilish and Unnatural Usurpation': Baptist Evangelical Ministers and Antislavery in the Early Nineteenth Century: A Study of the Ideas and Activism of David Barrow." *American Baptist Quarterly* 13, 3 (1994): 262–277.

Manumission

Manumission involves the liberation of individual bondpersons in a society that continues to maintain slavery. It is distinct from emancipation, which connotes the freeing of all slaves within a society. Wherever slavery existed, manumission occurred. Manumission rates varied across time and space, a heterogeneity borne of disparate demographic, economic, geopolitical, and social conditions. Dissimilar manumission rates in the Americas produced free black and "free colored" populations that differed in size, composition, and outlook. Even so, the actual process of manumission was remarkably uniform. Everywhere, manumission was a protracted enterprise involving multiple parties. Critical negotiations between slaveholders, bondpersons, and others came before and after the bestowal of freedom. In short, manumission was a ubiquitous and complex practice, one whose frequency, character, and consequences changed as historical circumstances changed.

Manumission rates varied among societies. Slave liberations occurred more frequently in Brazil than in the United States, to give an oft-cited example. Yet even in the most manumission-adverse societies, some slaveholders emancipated bondpersons.

Manumission rates also varied within societies. Brazil provides an illustrative example. The differences could be regional: in the early nineteenth century, manumission rates were higher in Minas Gerais than in Sao Paulo. The distinctions could be temporal: in the sugar-producing regions of northeast Brazil, slave liberations were relatively uncommon in the dynamic mid-seventeenth century, but they increased thereafter as the economy sputtered. The dissimilitude could be demographic: in Brazil (as elsewhere), some slaveholders and bondpersons were more likely to engage in manumission than others.

Intersocietal and intrasocietal differences in manumission rates influenced the size of free black and free colored populations. In Spain's mainland colonies, free people of color outnumbered slaves by the early nineteenth century. In Brazil, the freedperson population approximated the slave population by the early 1800s and surpassed it by midcentury. In most areas colonized by northern Europeans, the free colored population was smaller than the white population and usually dwarfed by the slave population. All totaled, by 1800, there were close to two million free persons of color in the Americas, compared with approximately three million slaves.

Governmental authorities outlined the means by which slaveholders could legally free bondpersons. The most common methods of manumission were gratis, conditional, delayed, self-purchase, postmortem, and state-sponsored. When slaveholders emancipated bondpersons gratis, they did not explicitly demand compensation. In conditional manumissions, slaves obtained liberty, but additional requirements were made of them, such as attending to their ex-owner until his or her death. Delayed manumissions were instances wherein slaveholders withheld immediate liberty, but promised to grant freedom at a future date. In self-purchase arrangements, bondpersons bought their liberty, the price for which could be above, below, or at the market price for slaves. In post-mortem manumissions, slaveholders liberated bondpersons upon their demise, usually with a testamentary decree. State-sponsored manumissions took many forms, including bestowing liberty to slaves who revealed insurrection plots and to those who served in the military, with the latter policy sometimes resulting in mass liberations. Although these modes of manumission differed in many respects, they shared at least one characteristic: normally, they granted freedom to select slaves only—large-scale, state-sponsored manumissions notwithstanding. Put another way, slaveholders rarely emancipated bondpersons en masse.

Manumission was not just a legal act. It was also a social process, often a lengthy one, in which important events preceded and followed the official confirmation of liberty. At each stage of the process, bondpersons, slaveholders, and other parties sought to advance their own interests.

For slaves, the trek to freedom was often difficult. Not surprisingly, some bondpersons were better situated to make the journey than others. The law inhibited a number. Restrictions on emancipating superannuated slaves were common, for instance. Even more important were the economic, demographic, and social forces that molded manumission patterns. The result was a distinctive population of freedpersons: females, mixed-race persons, skilled workers, urbanites, and creoles were overrepresented among the manumittees' ranks, largely because their sex, color, occupation, residence, and level of acculturation gave them greater access to the avenues of freedom. While no single characteristic predetermined whether a slave would achieve liberty, bondpersons with the aforementioned traits generally had the most opportunities for freedom.

Female slaves were more likely to secure liberty than male slaves. Despite the fact that bondmen usually outnumbered bondwomen on slaving vessels and large plantations, 60 to 65 percent of manumittees in the Americas were females. This overrepresentation occurred for a number of reasons. In some cases, male slave-holders liberated their bonded sexual partners. In others, slaveholders emancipated bondwomen because they assumed the latter would be dependent on them, and there-fore would remain an accessible, exploitable labor force. A gendered division of labor also contributed to the preponderance of freedwomen. Traditionally "female" occupations such as housekeeper, cook, nurse, laundress, and vendor allowed some bondwomen to make money and meet sympathizers, and thereby increased their opportunities to obtain freedom. Sex-specific customs could have the same effect, as was the case in eighteenth-century Surinam, where some planters transferred preg-nant slaves to urban Paramaribo in order to better monitor their health, a procedure that introduced such women to persons and practices that bolstered their chances for freedom. Like slavery itself, manumission was a gendered experience.

It was also a familial endeavor. Freedom was usually not given gratis, so slaves who wanted to liberate themselves and their kin had to pool their resources and gradually buy their way out of bondage. The objective was to have one family mem-ber buy his or her freedom, and then that manumittee would accumulate funds and purchase other kin. Strategy was essential, and gender and sex influenced bond-persons' deliberations. Often the choice was between liberating a male, whose comparatively high wages could underwrite additional manumissions, or freeing a female, whose children after emancipation would be born free. To complicate matters, different slaveholders often owned different members of a slave family. In these situations, familial reconstitution necessitated enlarging the strategy for manumission. Expansive undertakings of this sort sometimes irked neighboring slaveholders. Protests were most common in places where manumissions occurred infrequently, such as the nineteenth-century U.S. South. Slaves' familial bonds thus rendered manumissions intricate affairs, ventures that required determination, sagacity, and deftness on the slaves' part.

Counterpoised against the slaves' objectives were their owners' ambitions. Individuals freed bondpersons for any number of reasons. Some manumitted their bonded concubines. Other emancipators, especially free black ones, liberated their own kin. Still others were moved by humanitarian, religious, or philosophical con-siderations. To dismiss manumitters' professions concerning morality, gratitude, and affection as mere rationalizations for pecuniary objectives is to overlook how non-economic forces influenced manumission practices and to ignore slaves' own efforts to attract the positive attention of their owners, and thereby increase their odds for liberation. Nevertheless, it is clear that many slaveholders initiated manu-missions for financial reasons.

Slaveholders freed bondpersons during good times and bad. Manumission rates usually increased when the economy declined. Rising manumission rates in

Pernambuco, Brazil, during the late seventeenth century and in the Chesapeake region during the late eighteenth century, for example, coincided with downturns in sugar and tobacco production, respectively. On occasion, food shortages prompted slaveholders to liberate bondpersons. This was the case in eighteenth-century Curacao, where spikes in manumission rates corresponded with periodic famines. In some instances, however, manumission rates rose during eras of economic growth. In early nineteenth-century Baltimore, manumission abetted commercial and industrial expansion. A similar story unfolded during the early to mid-1700s in the gold-mining region of Sabara, Minas Gerais, Brazil. Viable during both booms and busts, manumission was a protean practice.

From the slaveholders' perspective, manumission promised an exceptionally productive and flexible labor force. This was especially true in regard to self-purchase arrangements. Slaveholders assumed that bondpersons who were trying to buy their freedom would work harder and be less apt to run away. They also figured that self-purchase agreements would allow them to slowly liberate their older, less profitable slaves and use the manumittees' ransom money to purchase additional bondpersons. And all the while, slaveholders retained the legal rights to would-be manumittees' children. In some instances, children born to self-purchasing women were deemed slaves for life; in others, the offspring were entitled to freedom at a later date—when they reached adulthood, for example. Either way, slaveholders could take possession of the youngsters or leave them with their parents, depending upon the costs of child upkeep and their need for child labor. For many slaveholders, manumission meant profit maximization.

Some slaveholders were more likely to embrace manumission than others. Proportionally speaking, small, urban, and free black slaveholders liberated bondpersons more frequently than their large, rural, and white counterparts. In a like manner, females were overrepresented among the manumitters' ranks. Such women were not exhibiting antislavery sympathies. If anything, slaveholding women, having fewer vocational options and less material wealth than most slaveholding men, were particularly dependent on slave-generated revenue, and they wanted their bondpersons to labor diligently and faithfully. Thus, the profusion of female manumitters was attributable to legal strictures, gender conventions, familial concerns, and slave acumen, not tenderheartedness. Throughout the Americas, lawmakers impaired females' property rights. Generally speaking, only unmarried and widowed women exercised full control over their property. As a result, female slaveholders' options regarding slave management were comparatively circumscribed, and this may have made them more reliant on manumission than men. Similarly, gender norms, while varying from society to society, restricted female slaveholders' management choices, especially in regard to personally inflicting corporal punishment, and manumission may have emerged as a favored method of motivating bondpersons. Familial concerns may have also contributed to the overrepresentation of females among manumitters. Whereas male slaveholders might expect bondpersons to serve their widows and children, widows may have had more discretion in disposing of their property, a flexibility that could bode well for favored slaves. Finally, bondpersons understood female slaveholders' legal, social, and familial situation, and manipulated it to their advantage. In short, slave-owning women were as invested in bondage as their male counterparts, but differing circumstances led many to utilize manumission as a way to protect their profits.

Slaves and slaveholders were not the only ones involved in the domain of manumission. Other parties made their presence felt, including lawmakers. The legislators' influence fluctuated over time. Until the mid-1700s, manumission statutes tended to be unobtrusive. Thereafter, government officials made manumission a more cumbersome process, although Brazil was somewhat of an exception to this trend. In Martinique, Barbados, and Jamaica, the crackdown reflected growing white fears about free black economic competition and servile revolt. The same anxieties were evident in the nineteenth century in the United States and Cuba where the profitability of the cotton and sugar revolutions fuelled slaveholders' concerns that the supply of bondpersons would diminish due to restrictions on the Atlantic slave trade. By the early nineteenth century, legislators not only required emancipators to post bonds to insure that manumittees would not become public charges, they also prohibited various methods of liberation such as testamentary emancipations and banned the freeing of certain bondpersons, especially the elderly.

Public opinion also affected manumission patterns. When local attitudes countenanced slave flight, bondpersons had greater leverage in negotiating for manumission. In the post-Revolutionary Northern United States, for example, slavery collapsed more quickly than lawmakers had intended, partially because slaves used the burgeoning antislavery sentiment to exact promises of expeditious freedom from their owners. Comparable events transpired in northeastern Brazil 100 years later, when private manumissions outpaced the statutory timetable for gradual abolition. Conversely, when public opinion was not in the slaves' favor, bondpersons had more difficulty securing freedom. Simply put, outside parties always affected emancipatory ventures.

The ventures did not end once slaves obtained liberty. There was also the question of the freedpersons' place in the social order. Two important factors in determining manumittees' status was their relationship with their former owner and the character of the larger society. Some ex-slaves fared better than others, but none enjoyed socioeconomic and political equality.

Manumission conferred freedom, not independence. Many emancipators expected subordination and fealty from their former slaves. Consequently, freedpersons struggled to escape their ex-owners' control. For some, the terms of manumission obliged them to additional labor. For others, the law demanded that they show deference to their former owners and serve them dutifully. For still others, affective bonds with enslaved kin kept them within their ex-owner's sphere of power. Destitution likewise impaired manumittees' quest for autonomy. Self-purchase agreements could leave freedpersons penniless and past their most economically productive years, with the result being that they remained dependent on their old owners. Even individuals with valuable occupational skills found that white antipathy might stall their drive for independence. Similarly, rural manumittees who could not acquire land were frequently at their ex-owners' mercy. In sum, the mode of manumission, legal regulations, familial considerations, and economic matters affected freedpersons' chances for self-determination.

A multiplicity of variables also influenced freedpersons' status in the larger society. Racial attitudes, demographic trends, economic conditions, and legal codes were among the most important. This tumult of forces never produced a racially egalitarian culture in the Americas, but by the early nineteenth century three distinctive societal patterns had emerged. First, in most of the Spanish- and Portuguese-speaking areas, freedpersons' numerical strength (25 to 50 percent of the population) and economic power (especially in urban locales) provided opportunities for upward mobility, but white racism and civil disabilities limited their prospects, rendering free people of color a large and diverse caste unto themselves. Second, in many parts of the British and French Caribbean, as well as in Dutch Surinam, "free coloreds" served as a racial buffer between an overwhelming slave majority and a white minority that feared servile insurrections. The free people of color exploited their advantage, sometimes becoming large slaveholders and even citizens, yet they still labored under the stigma of their mixed-racial ancestry and former servile status. Last, in the antebellum United States, free blacks constituted only 6 to 8 percent of the Southern population, but they faced a level of enmity that was perhaps unparalleled in the history of slavery, a hostility that inspired laws that required the departure of new manumittees and a colonization movement that championed the removal of African Americans beyond the country's borders. Thus Southern free blacks probably understood better than anyone that manumission was a protracted, multiparty undertaking that resulted in liberty, not equality.

Eric Burin

See also: Freedom Suits in North America.

Further Readings

Brana-Shute, Rosemary, and Randy Sparks, eds. *Paths to Freedom: Manumission in the Atlantic World.* Columbia: University of South Carolina Press, 2009.

Burin, Eric. *Slavery and the Peculiar Solution: A History of the American Colonization Society.* Gainesville: University Press of Florida, 2005.

McGlynn, Frank, ed. *Perspectives on Manumission*, special issue of *Slavery and Abolition* 10, 3 (December 1989).

Nash, Gary B., and Jean R. Soderlund. *Freedom by Degrees: Emancipation in Pennsylvania and Its Aftermath*. New York: Oxford University Press, 1991.

Patterson, Orlando. *Slavery and Social Death: A Comparative Study*. Cambridge, MA: Harvard University Press, 1982.

Tannenbaum, Frank. *Slave and Citizen*. New York: Alfred A. Knopf, Inc., 1946.

Whitman, T. Stephen. *The Price of Freedom: Slavery and Manumission in Baltimore in Early National Maryland*. Lexington: University Press of Kentucky, 1997.

Memorialization of Antislavery and Abolition

Throughout the history of slavery, there have been individuals of various races and from various countries who have fought for its abolition. Several of these abolitionists have been honored with memorials, including statues and plaques, conventions, celebrations, and the naming of various buildings and public spaces.

One of the most famous American abolitionists was Sojourner Truth. Born Isabella Van Wagenen in New York in 1797, Truth was sold many times as a slave. Although she escaped from slavery and helped others to do the same, her freedom was not fully secured until after abolition in New York, in 1827. Truth eventually made Battle Creek, Michigan, her home for more than twenty years, and that city has erected a Monument Park in which Truth has a memorial dedicated to her fight for women's rights and to her efforts to guide escaped slaves through the Underground Railroad. There have also been numerous other monuments built in her honor. A portion of highway I-194 and M-66 in Michigan has been designated the Sojourner Truth Memorial Highway. Other noteworthy commemorations of Truth include her induction into the Michigan Women's Hall of Fame in Lansing in 1983 and, in 1986, a postage stamp issued by the U.S. government. In 2002, the bronze Sojourner Truth Memorial Statue was erected in Florence, Massachusetts; it stands atop an eight-foot pedestal surrounded by gardens and flowers.

The renowned abolitionist, William Lloyd Garrison, has also been memorialized, although not as extensively as Truth. In Boston, a statue of William Lloyd Garrison is prominently situated in the Commonwealth Mall with the inscription "My countrymen are all mankind." The statue sits in the middle of one of the busiest streets in Boston.

Harriet Elizabeth Beecher Stowe knew Garrison well. Stowe was born in Litchfield, Connecticut, and is best remembered for her book *Uncle Tom's Cabin* and other literary efforts attacking slavery. She also assisted fugitive slaves on the Underground Railroad. Today Stowe has a library and museum named after her in

Hartford, Connecticut, where her papers and memorabilia are housed along with many unique works and correspondence of other noteworthy abolitionists.

A memorial was erected in honor of the highly regarded orator and abolitionist Frederick Douglass in New Bedford, Massachusetts, where he lived in the late 1830s. The statue sits outside of the New Bedford City Hall and mentions that Douglass changed his name from Frederick Baily to Frederick Douglass to make it more difficult for Southern slave catchers to find him. Douglass and his dedication to freedom are memorialized in innumerable sites in the United States and beyond.

As antislavery and abolition did not only take place in the United States, the United States is not the only place where one finds them memorialized. The centennial of the abolition of slavery in Cuba was celebrated with the holding of several conferences in 1986. Also, in 1988, conferences were held to commemorate the abolition of slavery in Brazil, an event that involved numerous historical congresses and other ceremonies. The editor of the journal *American Historical Review* decided to dedicate the entire August 1988 issue to mark the anniversary. Also, a statue of Abraham Lincoln freeing the slaves stands nearby London's famed Westminster Abbey.

A memorial to the slaves at Mount Vernon, the former home of President George Washington, was dedicated on September 21, 1983. The memorial sits on the slaves' burial site, where it is believed over 300 enslaved people were interred. In 2001, in Lawnside, New Jersey, the Peter Mott House officially opened to the public. The house is a memorial for those who ran the Underground Railroad. The house stands as a museum to those who helped the slaves find their way to freedom. The house, constructed over 160 years ago, was inhabited by black businessmen and farmers whom helped escaped slaves to freedom.

On January 1, 1883, in Washington, D.C., a large and important celebration took place. It was the twentieth anniversary of the signing of the Emancipation Proclamation and a celebration of black abolitionist men. This was the first time an assemblage of influential African American leaders had gathered together. It was at this dinner and all across the country that African Americans first began to commemorate their struggles for freedom. January 1 became Emancipation Day and was celebrated within the African American communities in the North and South. This celebration and commemoration was the first of many in 1883, most of which memorialized black and white abolitionists and their fight for freedom and equality.

The Robert Gould Shaw Memorial to the Massachusetts Fifty-Fourth and Fifty-Fifth Colored Regiments is one of the most eminent commemorations of African Americans' struggle against slavery. It was dedicated in the Boston Common in May 1897 with a large, solemn parade that included veterans from the two regiments and over 3,500 cadets, seamen, militia, and mounted police. It remains the single most important memorial to the over 180,000 black men who fought against

Southern slavery from January 1863 to the Civil War's end. Many of the Fifty-Fourth's men died at the Battle of Fort Wagner in Charleston Harbor in July 1863, a battle that the *New York Tribune* proclaimed, "made Fort Wagner such a name to the colored race as Bunker Hill had been for ninety years to the white Yankees." This memorial was of enormous significance for it served to remind an American public of a fact that most had forgotten by the century's end—that the bloody and ultimate Union victory in April 1865 had been very dependent upon the tens of thousands of courageous black troops from the North and South who enthusiastically volunteered to smash the institution which had beleaguered them for so long.

The timing for the Shaw installation was propitious for the nation as a whole, as the South, in particular, was actually then engaged in a very contrary memorialization. Throughout the South, Confederate soldiers were being commemorated with statues and large monuments for their brave defense of their states and the Confederacy. As laws disenfranchising and segregating blacks were being passed throughout the South at century's end, and Northerners were encouraged to leave the white South alone to resolve its race "problem," a new and amicable reunion between the white North and South was promoted. Newly erected memorials both North and South celebrated only white veterans and their heroism, and all but denied the vast involvement of African Americans in the great struggle. The acme of this process of forgetting was the great encampment of white veterans in Gettysburg, Pennsylvania, in July 1913 to celebrate the fiftieth anniversary of the terrible battle. No black veterans were invited to this event, which highlighted the renewed bond of national fellowship between Southern and Northern white men.

In the early decades of the twentieth century, many historians who wrote about the Civil War and the crisis preceding it in the 1850s blamed the abolitionists and irresponsible antislavery forces in the North for causing the war. Through their ceaseless and distorted propaganda against slavery and supposed support for John Brown's raid on Harpers Ferry in 1859, they had needlessly inflamed an anxious South about the security of their control over their legal property—the slaves—and led them to choose secession as their only feasible recourse. By the mid-twentieth century, however, a vast revision of the history of slavery, antislavery, and the causes of the Civil War was undertaken, which highlighted the causative significance of Southern intransigence in the 1850s and the bold courage rather than corrupt fanaticism of the abolitionists. The bravery and dedication of civil rights workers in the South in the 1950s and 1960s helped stimulate a rethinking of the role and importance of the abolitionists in antebellum America. The civil rights movement and the reevaluation of the role of antislavery in antebellum America contributed to a new endeavor to commemorate the struggles of those who had fought against slavery before and during the Civil War. Along with a host of Web sites affording a positive history of abolitionism, the most prominent example of this drive to memorialize antislavery is the recent completion in Cincinnati of the National Underground Railroad Freedom Center.

Johnathan L. Carter

See also: Douglass, Frederick; Garrison, William Lloyd; Truth, Sojourner.

Further Readings

Blight, David W. *Race and Reunion: The Civil War in American Memory.* Cambridge, MA: Belknap Press. 2001.

Drescher, Seymour. *The Abolition of Slavery and the Aftermath of Emancipation.* Durham, NC: Duke University Press, 1988.

Foster, Gaines M. *Ghosts of the Confederacy: Defeat, the Lost Cause, and the Emergence of the New South.* New York: Oxford University Press, 1987.

Hedrick, Joan D. *Harriet Beecher Stowe: A Life.* New York: Oxford University Press, 1994.

Mexican War and Antislavery

The Mexican War (1846–1848), prosecuted by the Democratic administration of James K. Polk, inspired the emergence of a broad-based, politicized antislavery movement that eclipsed the abolitionism of the 1830s and intensified the bitter debate over whether to prohibit or recognize slavery in the federal territories.

Antislavery Northerners complained that the Mexican War was an unprovoked act of aggression whose territorial accessions would mainly benefit Southern (slaveholding) migrants. South Carolina senator John C. Calhoun had boldly asserted the annexation of Texas (the primary cause of war with Mexico) was necessary to provide slavery a western outlet for expansion. This alarmed many Northern free-white-labor advocates who hoped to see slavery restricted to the existing Southern states. The seemingly proslavery nature of the war inspired Henry David Thoreau to write his essay *Civil Disobedience*. Nevertheless, most Northerners of both parties accepted the war.

Still, many people tried to prevent slavery's expansion into territories gained in the war, though not all for the same reason. On August 8, 1846, David Wilmot, an obscure Democratic representative from Pennsylvania, authored an amendment to a war-time appropriations bill that stipulated "as an express and fundamental condition of the acquisition of any territory from the Republic of Mexico . . . neither slavery nor involuntary servitude shall ever exist in any part of said territory." Though Congress failed to adopt it, the Wilmot Proviso's principle of congressional prohibition of slavery's expansion would serve as the ideological foundation of the new antislavery Free Soil Party in 1848.

The proviso was not an abolitionist document. It made a broader appeal to Northerners' self-interest in defending freedom, especially free labor, rather than to their moral objections to slavery. Wilmot authored his proviso in part out of contempt for black labor and a desire to keep it out of the West. Notwithstanding such instances of racism, many antislavery proponents were quite progressive at the time. Although some Free Soilers, such as Salmon P. Chase, Charles Sumner, and Joshua Giddings, consistently promoted citizenship and voting rights for free black men, they were a distinct minority. Most antislavery supporters had never espoused immediate abolitionism, believing instead that to restrict the expansion of slavery was to set it on the path to peaceful extinction.

In the Compromise of 1850, the antislavery movement met with partial success in prohibiting slavery from the territories gained in the Mexican War. That compromise, an omnibus bill consisting of several elements, admitted California as a free state. Importantly, it also allowed for popular sovereignty—a doctrine by which territorial settlers would determine, among other matters, whether or not to recognize slavery—to govern the New Mexico Territory. Inspired directly by the conflicts over the Mexican War, popular sovereignty achieved only limited acceptance among the antislavery movement. When it was incorporated into the 1854 bill to organize the Kansas and Nebraska territories, antislavery leaders bitterly resisted since those territories had previously been pledged to freedom by the provisions of the Missouri Compromise. Yet, by 1856, popular sovereignty in Kansas meant internecine warfare between antislavery and proslavery settlers. The Mexican War further inflamed the dispute over slavery and the territories. Antislavery and proslavery forces would clash over "ownership" of the territories with increasing frequency throughout the 1850s, indeed, until secession and the U.S. Civil War itself.

Matthew Isham

See also: Immediate Emancipation; Texas, Annexation of (1845).

Further Readings

Hietala, Thomas. *Manifest Design: Anxious Aggrandizement in Late Jacksonian America.* Ithaca, NY: Cornell University Press, 1985.

McPherson, James M. *Battle Cry of Freedom: The Civil War Era.* New York: Oxford University Press, 1988.

Potter, David. *The Impending Crisis, 1848–1861.* Completed and edited by Don E. Fehrenbacher. New York: Harper Torchbooks, 1976.

Sewell, Richard. "Slavery, Race and the Free Soil Party, 1848–1854." In Alan M. Kraut, ed. *Crusaders and Compromisers: Essays on the Relationship of the Antislavery Struggle to the Antebellum Party System.* Westport, CT: Greenwood Press, 1983, pp. 101–124.

Missouri Compromise (1820)

In 1803, when President Thomas Jefferson authorized American negotiators to purchase Louisiana from Emperor Napoleon Bonaparte of France for $15 million, Jefferson believed that he had secured the independence of the yeoman farmer for centuries. Jefferson, however, lived to see his purchase become a fierce battleground between North and South over the issue of slavery. As Americans moved westward, so too did slavery. Matters came to a head in 1819, when Missouri Territory applied for statehood. Missouri had the requisite number of inhabitants to apply for statehood, but it also had roughly 3,000 slaves. Missouri thus threatened to become the first slaveholding state that lay completely west of the Mississippi River.

On February 13, 1819, Representative James Tallmadge, a Jeffersonian Republican from New York, offered an amendment to the Missouri statehood bill. This amendment contained two parts. The first part called for a ban on further importations of slaves into Missouri. The second part outlined a gradual emancipation plan similar to that of New York's, in which the children of adult slaves would receive their freedom at the age of twenty-five. Adult slaves would remain in bondage. Tallmadge's amendment created a political firestorm that lasted for two days in the House of Representatives, and two years in the nation.

The House of Representatives, in which the North enjoyed a numerical majority, voted to support the Tallmadge Amendment, but the Senate, which was evenly divided between free and slave states, rejected it. This voting alignment repeated itself throughout most of the Missouri Crisis of 1819–1821. Supporters of slavery in the Senate not only enjoyed the balance of free and slave states, but also the support of senators from states such as Illinois and Indiana, technically free states, but ones with a pronounced Southern influence.

As the House and Senate failed to agree, the bill could not proceed and had to wait until the next session of Congress before any action could occur. While Congress was between sessions, the Missouri issue caught fire in the Northern states. Large assemblies of citizens around the North met and wrote petitions that they sent to their members of Congress, asking them to support Missouri statehood without slavery. Residents of Missouri, likewise, held meetings to protest the actions of the House of Representatives. These meetings also produced petitions, urging Congress to grant Missouri statehood without restriction as to slavery.

The Sixteenth Congress began its first session in this highly charged atmosphere in November 1819. Missouri took up much of the agenda from November until early March 1820. Speeches poured forth from representatives and senators, as did essays in newspapers. Men argued about the place of slavery in the American republic, the effect of slavery on national character, the degrading influence of slavery on free labor, the three-fifths clause and its impact on national politics, whether Congress had the power to restrict slavery in a territory and a state, and whether Congress had the power to regulate the movement of slaves across state lines. Antislavery Northerners, such as Representatives Timothy Fuller of Massachusetts and Arthur Livermore of New Hampshire, had railed against slavery as an institution in the previous session, going so far as to call it a sin. Some Southerners, such as Senator William Smith of South Carolina, openly defended slavery in the session in late 1819 and launched a new intellectual trend in the South. Representative William Plumer Jr., of New Hampshire, reported that talk of secession regularly dropped from the lips of Southern members of Congress, should Missouri enter the Union without slavery.

A compromise was already in the works, designed to prevent the possibility of secession. Speaker of the House Henry Clay of Kentucky and Senator James Barbour of Virginia were in close contact with President James Monroe. Monroe favored Missouri becoming a slave state, but he also supported the idea of a compromise. Maine had been a province of Massachusetts for several decades, but its residents had grown both in numbers and in desire for independence. The Massachusetts legislature granted them the opportunity to apply for statehood in 1819. The Senate linked the statehood bills of Maine and Missouri. If Missouri failed to enter the Union, Maine would suffer the same fate. Despite howls of protest from antislavery Northerners, the Senate approved the bills for Maine without slavery and Missouri without restriction as to slavery. After much debate, the solidarity of the Northerners in the House of Representatives broke, and by a vote of 90–87, the House approved the bill for Missouri to form a state government without restriction as to slavery. As part of this package, the House and Senate approved legislation that created a geographic line at 36° 30', the southern boundary of Missouri. There was to be no slavery north of this line, with Missouri being the only exception to this rule.

The compromise was unpopular in much of the North, as well as in Virginia. Antislavery Northerners believed that this failed effort to halt the westward spread of slavery represented a capitulation to the South, a conclusion buttressed by Representative John Randolph of Virginia, who sneered that the men who voted with the South were doughfaces. Many Virginians felt much the same as many antislavery Northerners. These Virginians believed that the slaveholding South had given up too much territory in this compromise.

The compromise reached earlier in 1820 almost came undone that summer when the Missouri legislature wrote a state constitution that called for a ban on free black and mulatto immigration into the new state. This proposed clause angered many Northerners, as well as some Southerners. The clause raised the issue of black citizenship and whether the proposed ban violated the privileges and immunity clause of the U.S. Constitution. Under the terms of this clause, all citizens share federal rights in all of the states in the Union. There was much debate over the place of African Americans in the republic, but no consensus. Congress finally agreed to require Missouri's legislature never to pass any law that might infringe on the privilege and immunities of an American citizen. The Missouri legislature agreed, and Missouri entered the Union in August 1821. With this second compromise the American republic had navigated its way through the most threatening political crisis that had yet gripped the nation. The compromise would last until the Kansas-Nebraska Act of 1854 repealed it.

James C. Foley

See also: Compromise of 1850; Mexican War and Antislavery.

Further Readings

Foley, James C. "'Make the Iron Enter into Their Souls': Slavery and Race in the Missouri Crisis, 1819–1821." Ph.D. Dissertation, University of Mississippi, 2005.

Forbes, Robert Pierce. "Slavery and the Meaning of America, 1819–1837." Ph.D. Dissertation, Yale University, 1994.

Moore, Glover. *The Missouri Controversy, 1819–1821.* Lexington: University of Kentucky Press, 1953.

Mott, Lucretia Coffin

Lucretia Coffin Mott was a Quaker minister and advocate of abolition, women's rights, and peace. She was born on January 3, 1793, on the island of Nantucket, Massachusetts, the daughter of Thomas and Anna Folger Coffin. Like many on Nantucket, her father engaged in the East India trade; Mott later attributed the independence of Nantucket women to the frequent absence of men from the island. At home, school, and in meeting, Mott absorbed Quaker theology and antislavery sentiment. In 1804, her family moved to Boston and Mott soon left to attend Nine Partners, a Quaker Boarding School in Dutchess County, New York. She chafed against the authority of her instructors, but eventually became a teacher at the school and learned firsthand of sexual discrimination through her unequal salary. She also met fellow teacher James Mott, a Quaker from Westchester County, New York, whom she married in 1811.

After their marriage, the couple moved to Philadelphia, where Mott soon discovered her skill as a public speaker. James embarked on several unsuccessful careers before finally settling on a cotton commission business in 1822. Mott gave birth to the first of her six children in 1812, and her youngest daughter was born in 1828. She also taught in a Quaker school in 1817. But her son Thomas died in 1817, plunging Mott into a spiritual crisis from which she emerged renewed as a minister and follower of Elias Hicks, the radical Quaker preacher from Long Island, who railed against the Philadelphia Elders and their complicity with slavery. In 1827, the Motts and other Hicksites left the Philadelphia Yearly Meeting of Friends to form a parallel organization more sympathetic to Hicks's teachings. Lucretia Mott became one of the most famous and controversial Hicksite preachers, as she found the new denomination disappointingly conservative. In her sermons, she castigated the Society of Friends for not taking a strong enough stand against slavery, and for allowing superficial indications of spirituality to outweigh the individual's inner experience of God's teachings. She adopted as her motto "truth for authority, not authority for truth."

In the 1820s, the Motts first began to advocate the use of free produce, or goods made without slave labor, and James gave up his cotton commission business for wool in 1830. Both James and Lucretia Mott attended the founding meeting of the American Anti-Slavery Society in Philadelphia in 1833. James signed the Society's declaration, but Mott, as a woman, did not, although she was the only woman to speak at the meeting. Shortly thereafter, Mott and other white and black women formed the Philadelphia Female Anti-Slavery Society, which thrived for the next thirty-six years with Mott as its frequent president. She participated in the Anti-Slavery Convention of American Women, speaking at its first meeting in New York in 1837. When the Convention met in Philadelphia the following year, an angry antiabolition mob burned Pennsylvania Hall, the meeting site, to the ground, and then headed for the Motts' house before being diverted at the last moment by an abolitionist ally.

In 1840, Mott was one of several female American delegates to the World Anti-Slavery Convention in London, who were refused seats by British abolitionists upon their arrival. This rebuff, following so soon after the American Anti-Slavery Society split over the proper role of women in the movement, galvanized Mott and another American woman, Elizabeth Cady Stanton. Mott began speaking more frequently on women's rights, motivated also by further factionalism in the Society of Friends over slavery and women's authority. Mott's visit to her sister, Martha Coffin Wright, in Auburn, New York, prompted the organization of the first women's rights convention at nearby Seneca Falls in 1848.

Mott spent the next three decades traveling the country, attending meetings on a variety of reforms. Mott viewed the antislavery, women's rights, temperance, and peace movements as contributing to the spread of true democracy and Christianity. She spoke against the false authority men derived from organized religion, tradition, politics, and law, urging people to follow their personal understanding of God's will, not society's prescriptions. In 1853, Mott gave an antislavery speech in Maysville, Kentucky. While local slaveholders feared she would incite rebellion, her lecture was so well received that the audience demanded she speak again on women's rights. Mott tolerated no compromises with slavery, but she did seize every opportunity to talk individually with slaveholders. But when the Civil War loomed, Mott would have preferred that President Lincoln allow the South to leave the Union.

Committed to the peaceful and nonviolent doctrine of nonresistance, Mott deplored the Civil War, but she celebrated emancipation with other abolitionists. She never attributed this success to the military, however, but to the moral warfare waged by William Lloyd Garrison and other abolitionists. Like many abolitionists, Mott turned her attention to aiding former slaves, joining the Friends Association for the Aid and Elevation of the Freedmen. After the war, Mott devoted herself to women's rights, peace, and free religion, an antisectarian movement committed to a liberal understanding of Scripture. Her beloved husband James died in 1868, but Mott continued her struggle for human progress, attending an anniversary meeting of the Seneca Falls Convention in 1878. However, her increasingly failing health limited her ability to attend reform meetings, and she died at home on November 11, 1880.

Carol Faulkner

See also: Women's Antislavery Societies.

Further Readings

Bacon, Margaret Hope. *Valiant Friend: The Life of Lucretia Mott*. New York: Walker and Company, 1980.

Palmer, Beverly Wilson, Holly Byers Ochoa, and Carol Faulkner, eds. *The Selected Letters of Lucretia Coffin Mott*. Urbana: University of Illinois Press, 2002.

Myers, Stephen (1800–1870) and Myers, Harriet (1807–1865)

Stephen Myers came to be the most important leader of the Underground Railroad movement in Albany, New York, in the 1830s, 1840s, and 1850s. Together with his wife, Harriet, they were the focal point of assistance in helping freedom seekers, or fugitives from slavery, who had arrived in Albany on their way to Canada or settling in New York State. While there had been other significant figures of the Underground Railroad in Albany, they met untimely fates, or moved to other theaters of action. It is well documented that Stephen and Harriet Myers assisted thousands of individuals to settle in or move through Albany to points west, north, and east on the Underground Railroad. Initially, in the 1830s, Myers used his own resources. By the 1840s, Myers organized *The Northern Star Association*, utilizing its resources in support of freedom seekers and in support of the publication of the *Northern Star and Freeman's Advocate* newspaper. By the 1850s, Myers was the principal agent of the Underground Railroad in Albany, and was receiving financial assistance from a broad range of backers. Under his leadership the Albany branch of the Underground Railroad was regarded by some as the best-run part of the Underground Railroad in New York State.

Stephen was born a slave in 1800 in Rensselaer County in Hoosick Four Corners. While not much is known of his early years, it is known that at the age of twelve he was in the service of Albany's General Warren of Revolutionary War connections, and was freed at the age of eighteen. Over the next decade and a half he worked as a grocer and steamboat steward, starting his journalistic enterprises in the late 1830s and early 1840s. His first newspaper venture was short lived. It was called the *Elevator*. It concentrated on news and information targeting the free African people in Albany. Stephen and Harriet were married in 1827. Harriet worked with him on his newspaper ventures. He was a leading spokesperson for antislavery and the rights of free blacks in Albany in the late 1840s and 1850s. His newspaper, the *Northern Star and Freeman's Advocate*, was a vehicle for reform around education, temperance, black rights, and the need to abolish slavery. Toward the end of the 1840s, the newspaper may have taken on the name *Northern Star and Colored Farmer* when Myers was involved in organizing an economic project call the Florence Farming and Lumber Association. Later in his life he had other publishing ventures including the *Pioneer*, and *Telegraph and Temperance Journal*. Stephen Myers was an active speaker and shared the podium with other black orators of his day, such as Frederick Douglass and William H. Johnson. He spoke in Albany and Troy, as well as in Massachusetts and the New York City area.

Myers was not only involved in abolitionist activity, but he showed leadership in addressing a wide range of civil rights issues. Through his newspapers he was deeply involved in education and advocacy. He also provided leadership as the superintendent of one of the area's first schools for black children, The Free Colored School in Albany based at Israel African Methodist Church in 1843. He was active in organizing Suffrage Clubs to encourage black voting rights, petitioning the state legislature for reforms, and the early organization of free black labor. He was also involved in economic development through the Florence Farming and Lumber Association where he worked with philanthropist Gerrit Smith to provide farms and farming skills to black farmers.

Harriet Myers was born in 1807 as Harriet Johnson. While the source of her education is not known, she collaborated with her husband in the production of the various newspaper projects and was known for providing a "skilled" editorial hand in proofreading. She was also involved in various women's organizations popular among black women that raised funds through bazaars and sewing circles to support the work of the Underground Railroad.

Harriet Myers died in August 16, 1865. In the obituary, which appeared in the Philadelphia *Christian Recorder* of September 2, 1865, she was described as one of "nobleness" of heart, "unselfish hospitality," and "her house was ever a refuge for the oppressed and friendless." Stephen Myers was buried February 16, 1870, but no record has been thus far found identifying the specific date of his death.

Paul Stewart

See also: Underground Railroad.

Further Reading

Williams, Peter. "Letters from Negro Leaders to Gerrit Smith." *Journal of Negro History* 27, 4 (October 1942).

N

New England Antislavery Society (NEASS)

Founded in 1832 in Boston, the New England Antislavery Society (NEASS) was the first American abolitionist organization to embrace the doctrine of immediatism. The NEASS thereafter became the model for all "second-wave" abolitionist organizations, including the American Anti-Slavery Society, founded in Philadelphia in 1833. The NEASS also proved innovative by hiring traveling agents and publishing a short-lived organizational magazine, the *Abolitionist*. The group also offered a public platform to some of the most important antislavery activists of the nineteenth century, including Frederick Douglass. The NEASS was perhaps best identified with its founding figure, William Lloyd Garrison, publisher of the radical abolitionist newspaper, the *Liberator*. But the group also drew inspiration and support from Boston's black community, which offered intellectual and monetary capital to the burgeoning immediate abolition movement, both in New England and nationally. Garrison himself was influenced by black Bostonian David Walker who authored *An Appeal to the Colored Citizens of the World* (1829), a rousing rejection of prevailing abolitionist tactics of gradualism and colonization. In addition, African Americans provided nearly a quarter of the seventy-two signatures to the group's constitution at the first annual meeting of the NEASS. In this sense, the NEASS was the first biracial reform organization in America—a significant achievement when considered against the history of segregation in early abolitionist societies such as the Pennsylvania Abolition Society.

The NEASS's activism rested on attacking Southern slavery and routing racial prejudice in Northern states. Just as the group hoped to convince and coerce Southern masters to liberate enslaved people, so too did it aim to challenge racial injustice above the Mason-Dixon Line. As the group's constitution boldly put it, "The objects of the society shall be to endeavor, by all means sanctioned by law, humanity and religion, to effect the abolition of slavery, to improve the character and condition of the free people of color . . . and obtain for them equal civil and political rights and privileges with the whites." Group activists challenged Massachusetts's laws prohibiting racial intermarriage and aided in early school desegregation lawsuits. They also signed petitions against both slavery and the slave trade in the District of Columbia. Despite espousing ideals of racial equality, white activists within the NEASS could also practice a form of "romantic racialism," which depicted African Americans—both free and enslaved—as desperately in need of white leadership.

Outside of attacking Southern slaveholders (and antiabolitionist Northerners), the NEASS struggled against members of the American Colonization Society, who argued that abolitionism was folly and removal by transportation of freed blacks was the only safe solution to America's racial ills. NEASS members constantly debated the efficacy of colonizationist policies in town meetings throughout New England, and waged a similar war against colonizationist thinking in printed publications.

In February 1835, the NEASS was officially renamed the Massachusetts Anti-Slavery Society (MASS), and it functioned for several years as an auxiliary to the American Anti-Slavery Society. Although female activists in New England created a bevy of their own abolitionist organizations, the MASS supported women's activism, admitting female reformers and hiring female agents. While schisms within the broader antislavery movement—particularly over women's roles and political abolitionism—certainly impacted the MASS, the group functioned through the Civil War, holding a memorable thirtieth anniversary meeting in 1862.

Richard Newman

See also: Garrisonians; Immediate Emancipation.

Further Readings

Mayer, Henry. *All on Fire: William Lloyd Garrison and the Abolition of Slavery*. New York: St. Martin's Griffin, 2000.

Newman, Richard. *The Transformation of American Abolitionism: Fighting Slavery in the Early Republic*. Chapel Hill: University of North Carolina Press, 2002.

New York Committee of Vigilance

One of the most radical African American abolitionist societies of the 1830s, the New York Committee of Vigilance was organized on November 21, 1836, although its activities began informally the year before. The New York Committee of Vigilance especially sought to halt the practice of kidnapping of self-emancipated slaves and free blacks from the streets of the city. Slave catchers, using the 1793 Fugitive Slave Act as a pretense, would bring their captives before a city magistrate, who would then rule the person a fugitive slave. Quickly, the black person would be taken in chains to a waiting ship and spirited off to slavery in the Southern states. The New York Manumission Society's radical wing had contested such practices since the 1790s and local blacks had commonly demonstrated and even rioted against slave catchers, calling them man stealers.

Organizing the committee was an important step in uniting middle-class blacks, sympathetic whites, and the black working class against kidnapping. At the organizing meeting, David Ruggles was appointed secretary. A radical abolitionist, Ruggles already had experience accosting slave catchers and indicting sea captains taking part in the illegal slave trade. Other significant members included Thomas Van Rensellaer, a former slave and now a prominent black restaurateur and community leader; William Johnston, an English-born abolitionist; George R. Barkers, a New York City broker; and James W. Higgins, a local grocer. Ruggles found a number of enslaved people held illegally by their masters who were often on Northern tours. This integrated group, led by Ruggles, embarked on a number of sensational slave rescue cases, using a legal device known as a *writ de homine replegiando* that freed individuals imprisoned or held by a private party by giving security that the accused would appear in court. It is now replaced in American law by the writ of *habeas corpus*; Ruggles and the committee cooperated with the New York Manumission Society in the Dixon Case, which forced the judiciary to grant jury trials to fugitives. In 1838, Ruggles created the nation's first black magazine, the *Mirror of Liberty*, to chronicle the hundreds of instances in which the committee helped fugitive slaves. Ruggles's zeal eventually caused trouble when he printed a letter in the *Colored American* accusing a local black boardinghouse keeper of hiding fugitives for slave catchers. The boardinghouse keeper successfully sued Ruggles, the newspaper, and the committee for libel. An ensuing investigation uncovered financial irregularities, and Ruggles was forced to resign his post. In 1840, lobbied by the manumission society, the New York State legislature passed a bill requiring jury trials for blacks, although it was weakened several years later in the *Prigg v. Pennsylvania* case. The committee continued on into the 1840s but on a lower profile. It inspired the New York State Committee, innumerable local organizations, and was a key, early safe harbor on the Underground Railroad.

Graham Russell Gao Hodges

See also: Ruggles, David; Underground Railroad.

Further Reading

Ripley, Peter C., et al. *The Black Abolitionist Papers*. Chapel Hill: University of North Carolina Press, 1991, Vol. 3, pp. 168–180.

New York Manumission Society (NYMS)

Founded in 1785 in New York City, the New York Manumission Society (NYMS) was one of the most important abolitionist groups of the early national period. Counting elite statesmen such as John Jay and Alexander Hamilton as members, the group helped shepherd the gradual emancipation act through the state legislature in 1799. Less well-known group members—particularly adherents of the Religious Society of Friends, also known as Quakers—pestered ship captains engaged in the international slave trade through the port of New York, aided free black kidnapping victims, and even helped fugitive slaves. Together with the Pennsylvania Abolition Society and the American Convention of Abolition Societies, the NYMS put a tactical face on the early antislavery movement.

Originally called the New York Society for Promoting the Manumission of Slaves and Protecting Such of Them as Have Been or May be Liberated, the NYMS was formed during the country's first broad public debate over slavery's status in post-Revolutionary culture. Beginning with Pennsylvania in 1780, every Northern state passed a gradual abolition law during the next twenty-five years. Although New York's law, which took effect July 4, 1799, was the second to last Northern abolition act (New Jersey's statute passed in 1804), debate over abolitionism in the state dated back to 1777. The NYMS took shape in January 1785 to bolster the passage of such a law. Although the group attracted support from some celebrated New York politicians and merchants, Quakers and Anglicans dominated its day-to-day membership. The Society's constitution declared that slavery violated the religious and political underpinnings of American culture—equality and justice for all. By the time NYMS members helped push through the abolition act in 1799, New York contained roughly 21,000 enslaved people. The law stipulated that all slaves born after the passage of the act would be freed gradually, women at twenty-five and men at twenty-eight. The law was revised in 1817 so that all slaves would be liberated on July 4, 1827.

As Patrick Rael has written, the NYMS also "worked to tighten loopholes in other state laws: it sought to strengthen prohibitions on the import and export of slaves to the state, to prevent inhuman treatment of slaves, and to remove provisions of the slave code permitting courts to deport slaves deemed guilty of crimes." Perhaps the Society's most unheralded act was the creation of an African Free School in November 1787. By the 1820s, abolitionists watched over roughly 800 students in seven different schools. Eventually, protest in the first half of the 1830s by the black community compelled abolitionists to turn over running the schools to African American leaders. The city of New York incorporated the two principal African Free Schools into the public school system in 1834.

Like other gradual abolitionist groups of the early national era, the NYMS did not admit black members—it was a segregated group. Moreover, its members were accused of treating New York City's free black community paternalistically and even as inferiors. By the 1830s, when second-wave abolitionists appeared nationally declaring black activists "coadjutors" of a new movement to destroy slavery immediately, the NYMS was in decline. The group officially folded in 1849. Yet its several decades of abolitionist activism formed an integral part of the early antislavery movement, particularly the sectional erosion of slavery in Northern states via gradual abolition laws.

Richard Newman

See also: New York Committee of Vigilance.

Further Readings

Davis, David Brion. *The Problem of Slavery in the Age of Revolution*. Ithaca, NY: Cornell University Press, 1976.

Rael, Patrick. "The Long Death of Slavery." In Ira Berlin and Leslie Harris, eds. *Slavery in New York*. New York: New Press, 2005.

Northwest Ordinance (1787)

The Northwest Ordinance is perhaps the most significant piece of national legislation passed by the U.S. Congress during the period when the Articles of Confederation formed the basis for national government. Enacted on July 13, 1787, it was among the last measures passed by the Confederation Congress.

Designed to facilitate the orderly settlement of the territory west of the Appalachian Mountains and north of the Ohio River, the ordinance had several elements. Most generally, it established the principle that new territories, when sufficiently settled, would become states, fully equal to the original thirteen, and not remain permanently or even for very long in a subordinate position. Land in the territories would be sold directly to occupiers in small parcels, not in large parcels to speculators and others with political connections. Federal land would be surveyed prior to sale using a grid system and specific lots were set aside to support public education. These principles continued to govern the territorial expansion of the United States for the next century as the nation reached its current borders. Finally, slavery was prohibited from the entire territory, although provision was made for the return of fugitive slaves from the territory when claimed by their owners or their owners' agents. The exclusion of slavery from the territory was not controversial at the time, unlike later efforts to legislate on the status of slavery in the territories, and reflects both the spirit of equality that emerged from the Revolution and the general sense in the 1780s that slavery was an economically marginal institution and would soon disappear.

While the ordinance appeared to free those slaves already in the territory, territorial governor Arthur St. Clair did not move to free slaves already in the territory and acted to prevent slaves being freed by court order, ruling that pre-1787 slaves must remain in bondage.

When Indiana was established as a separate territory, it permitted the importation of African Americans as indentured servants who were bought and sold openly. When Illinois became a separate territory, it adopted the same practice. There were 746 indentured blacks in Illinois as late as 1830. Both territories continued this practice, as well as lax enforcement of antislavery provisions in their constitutions, after attaining statehood. Both indenture and slavery in the Northwest Territory and the states formed from it were largely limited to areas near the Ohio River.

William H. Mulligan Jr.

Further Readings

Hyman, Harold M. *American Singularity*. Athens: University of Georgia Press, 1986.

Onuf, Peter S. *Statehood and Union: A History of the Northwest Ordinance*. Bloomington: Indiana University Press, 1987.

Taylor, Robert M. *The Northwest Ordinance of 1787: A Bicentennial Handbook*. Indianapolis: Indiana Historical Society, 1987.

Williams, Frederick D. *The Northwest Ordinance: Essays on Its Formulation, Provisions, and Legacy*. East Lansing: Michigan State University Press, 1989.

P

Parker, John Percial

A former slave from Virginia, John Percial Parker is believed to have aided 900 or more slaves during his fifteen-year career as an Underground Railroad conductor. At age eight, he was sold by his master, probably also his father. Purchased by a Mobile, Alabama, doctor, he drove the doctor to see his patients, and became friends with the doctor's two sons, who secretly taught him to read and write.

After being separated from his master's sons when they went north to complete their educations, Parker's master apprenticed him to a plasterer. An argument with his employer landed him in a slave hospital, from which he fled after a fight with the hospital's sadistic caretaker. He spent several months on the run, and was only accidentally reclaimed by his master.

Following this abortive escape, his master arranged employment for him in a foundry. Parker quickly became a skilled iron molder, but his tendency to quarrel with his employer and coworkers led to trouble. His master decided to sell him south as a field hand. Desperate to avoid this fate, Parker persuaded one of his master's patients to purchase him with the understanding that he would pay her back his purchase price plus interest, in exchange for his freedom.

By working hard, Parker was able to repay the widow in eighteen months. In 1845, he was given his freedom papers, traveled north to Cincinnati, and found employment as an iron molder. Though he states in his autobiography, *His Promised Land*, that his master never mistreated him, he nevertheless harbored a deep resentment for having been enslaved. Therefore, he was not averse to the idea of assisting in the escape of two Kentucky slave girls. This first experience of guiding fugitive slaves from Kentucky to the home of a Ripley, Ohio, abolitionist, was the start of his career as an Underground Railroad conductor.

Parker married in 1848, after which he moved from Cincinnati to Ripley, where he had already been working with the town's many abolitionists. For the next fifteen years, he was actively involved in conducting escaping slaves across the Ohio

River. Among his many antislavery colleagues were Ripley Presbyterian minister John Rankin, as well as Levi Coffin. Although he had a $1,000 price on his head, he made almost-nightly trips into Kentucky to bring groups of fleeing slaves to Ripley. He recounted many of his harrowing (and sometimes amusing as well) adventures in *His Promised Land.*

Although the traditional lore of the Underground Railroad has painted a picture of a movement organized and headed by Caucasian abolitionists, without whom runaway slaves would never have been able to make their bids for freedom, the truth is quite different. They were much more apt to trust fellow African Americans over white men, and their first contact after they had entered a Northern state was most often with a free black like Parker. Many cities had sizeable free black communities; their residents frequently concealed runaways, forwarding them further north to both black and white abolitionists when it was safe to do so.

These Northern blacks, despite being free, did not find life easy. They encountered bitter prejudice from whites, which limited jobs they might hold and where they might live. The Ohio Black Laws, originally enacted in 1804, for example, required that all free blacks entering the state not only possess free papers, but also register themselves with the clerk of courts in the county they resided in. Later Black Law legislation required that free blacks coming into the state post a $500 bond to ensure that they would not become a public charge. Other Northern states enacted similar laws. In addition to such obstacles, they ran the risk of being kidnapped and sold into slavery by white slave hunters.

John Parker was a respected member of the Ripley, Ohio, community. He established himself not only as a successful businessman, running his own foundry, but also as an inventor. One of the first African Americans to hold patents for his inventions, he manufactured and marketed his soil pulverizers and tobacco presses throughout the midwestern United States.

Susannah C. West

See also: Underground Railroad.

Further Readings

Gara, Larry. *The Liberty Line: The Legend of the Underground Railroad.* Lexington: University Press of Kentucky, 1961.

Griffler, Keith R. *Front Line of Freedom: African Americans and the Forging of the Underground Railroad in the Ohio Valley.* Lexington: University Press of Kentucky, 2004.

Hagedorn, Ann. *Beyond the River.* New York: Simon & Schuster, 2002.

Horton, James Oliver, and Lois E. Horton. *In Hope of Liberty.* New York: Oxford University Press, 1997.

Ripley, Ohio: Its History and Families. Ripley, OH: Ripley Historical Committee, 1965.

Sprague, Stuart Seely, ed. *His Promised Land: The Autobiography of John P. Parker, Former Slave and Conductor on the Underground Railroad*. New York: W.W. Norton & Company, 1996.

Paul, Nathaniel

Born in Exeter, New Hampshire, Nathaniel Paul was an outspoken African American clergyman and abolitionist during the 1820s and 1830s. He founded the First African Baptist Church in Albany, New York, in 1820, where he served as pastor for ten years. The son of a veteran of the American Revolution, Paul adhered uncompromisingly to the republic's founding principles of liberty and equality for all. He was one of the earliest agitators for complete and immediate emancipation, staunchly opposing the American Colonization Society's scheme for gradual emancipation. Throughout his career, he pursued various avenues to end slavery and racial discrimination.

Paul was instrumental in founding the nation's first African American newspaper. In 1827, spurred by racially disparaging comments from white journalists, Paul joined with other free black abolitionists including Presbyterian minister Samuel E. Cornish and Episcopal pastor Peter Williams Jr., to establish *Freedom's Journal* (1827–1829), in New York City. As an authorized agent for the paper in Albany, New York, Paul promoted its efforts to present a black voice in the nation's debate over slavery.

Paul is probably best known for his address at Albany's First African Baptist Church on July 5, 1827, celebrating New York's official termination of slavery, which took effect on July 4, 1827. In lauding the New York legislation as a triumph "over tyranny and oppression," Paul employed religious, sometimes prophetic, language to denounce slavery as "contrary to the laws" of God. He declared that "not only throughout the United States of America, but throughout every part of the habitable world, where slavery exists, it will be abolished."

Despite his opposition to African colonization, Paul and his brother, Benjamin, moved in 1830 to Wilberforce Colony, Canada, a free black community led by former slave and Rochester businessman, Austin Steward. After a year of acting as the colony's agent and minister, Paul departed to travel throughout the British Isles, raising funds to establish a manual labor college at Wilberforce. Although his expenses exceeded the $8,000 he raised, his many lectures before thousands of people attracted attention and support from leading British and American abolitionists such as George Thompson, Thomas Clarkson, and William Lloyd Garrison. Upon his return to the United States in 1836, he continued his public antislavery work with the Albany Anti-Slavery Society and as a supporter of Cornish's new newspaper, *Colored American*.

A strong proponent of education, Paul believed that black religious, social, and moral improvement would advance the antislavery cause and weaken racial prejudice. Consequently, he devoted considerable attention to African American self-improvement efforts, becoming the first president of Albany's Union Society for the Improvement of the Colored People in Morals, Education and Mechanic Arts. In addition, Paul continued in the ministry, leading Albany's Union Street Baptist Church until his death.

Dianne Wheaton Cappiello

Further Readings

Pease, William H., and Jane H. Pease. *Black Utopia: Negro Communal Experiments in America*. Madison: State Historical Society of Wisconsin, 1963.

Quarles, Benjamin. *Black Abolitionists*. New York: Oxford University Press, 1969.

Swift, David E. *Black Prophets of Justice: Activist Clergy before the Civil War*. Baton Rouge: Louisiana State University Press, 1989.

Pennsylvania Abolition Society (PAS)

Founded in 1775, "the Pennsylvania Society for Promoting the Abolition of Slavery and for the Relief of Free Negroes Unlawfully Held in Bondage," also known as the Pennsylvania Abolition Society (PAS), was the world's leading antislavery organization during the early republic. Indeed, only the rise of Garrisonian reformers in the 1830s dethroned the PAS as the abolitionist vanguard in the United States. The PAS remains in existence today, supporting African American educational endeavors and the memory of the abolitionist struggle, among other things.

After its initial organization, the PAS lapsed during the Revolutionary War, but was revived in 1784. Reorganized in 1787, the PAS formed a constitution, created a committee system assigning specific abolitionist tasks to members (from educational activities in the free black community to raising funds among philanthropists), and organized a legal aid system for endangered blacks that became a model for other abolitionists. The group was officially incorporated by the state in 1789. According to its constitution, the PAS would "use such means as are in their power to extend the blessings of freedom to every part of the human race." The PAS's committee of correspondence communicated with abolitionists and reformers in

England, France, the Caribbean, and almost every state in the American union. Indeed, under the PAS's leadership, Philadelphia became a worldwide capital of the first-wave abolitionism.

The PAS's first incarnation comprised a small group of men who wanted to expand Quakers' attacks on slavery. The Society of Religious Friends, commonly known as Quakers, had a long history of antislavery activism, particularly in Pennsylvania, where figures from Ralph Sandiford to Anthony Benezet had published consciousness-raising essays against bondage. The PAS grew from these roots, attracting support from other religious denominations as well as statesmen and governing elites. During the late eighteenth and early nineteenth centuries, nearly 2,000 members would officially join the PAS, and many more reformers would express sympathy with its motives. While men of standing joined the group—including America's leading statesman, Benjamin Franklin, who served as president of the group from 1787 to 1790; its leading doctor, Benjamin Rush; and its leading jurist, William Rawle—so too did tailors, middling merchants, and candle makers.

The PAS advocated gradual abolitionism, both in Pennsylvania and in other states. PAS members, including Thomas Paine, helped pass the Quaker State's gradual abolition statute in March 1780. The first of its kind in the Western world, the law outlined slavery's gradual demise in Pennsylvania: all slaves born after the law's passage would be free at twenty-eight. This statute, combined with PAS lawyers' advocacy of black rights in state and federal courts, compelled even fugitive slaves to run away to "free" Pennsylvania.

Tactically, the PAS favored action in legal and political venues rather than mass organizing of American citizens. The PAS was the first abolitionist group to issue antislavery petitions to federal institutions. In 1787, the group asked PAS member Benjamin Franklin to present an antislavery memorial to the Constitutional Convention then meeting in Philadelphia (Franklin pocketed the petition for fear of its divisive consequences). In February 1790, the PAS petitioned the first federal Congress for an end to overseas slave trade and consideration of gradual abolitionism. "We have observed with great satisfaction," the petition told Congress, "that many important and salutary powers are vested in you for 'promoting the welfare' and 'securing the blessings of liberty' to the people of the United States." Such power should be aimed at slavery. The memorial infuriated Deep South slaveholders and was not acted upon by Congress. Subsequent PAS memorials were less radical in tone. Nevertheless, both on its own and as the leader of the American Convention of Abolition Societies, a biennial meeting of local and state abolitionist groups from 1794 to 1836, the PAS presented many other petitions to state and federal governments on subjects ranging from ending the domestic slave trade to abolishing slavery in the federally controlled District of Columbia.

The PAS had a complex relationship with Pennsylvania's free black community. On the one hand, the group rendered important aid to African Americans by finding apprenticeships for former slaves, opening schools for free blacks, and even offering business loans to black leaders such as Richard Allen and Absalom Jones. On the other hand, the PAS remained a segregated organization until the 1830s. The group would not ask black leaders to become fellow activists, as did Garrisonians, because they believed that abolitionism should be left to legal and political elites. African Americans could be helped by white abolitionists but they could not be considered coadjutors of the movement.

As slavery expanded both geographically and numerically during the nineteenth century, the PAS faced its toughest challenges. Indeed, slavery's growth in the South and Southwest offset the passage of gradual abolition laws in every Northern state. In addition, the creation and expansion of the American Colonization Society (or ACS, formed December 1816) allowed Northern and Southern citizens to unite behind a quasi-antislavery movement, one that pictured free blacks—and not bondage—as America's major problem. While the majority of blacks opposed the ACS, the PAS did not publicly rebuke colonizationism until the late 1820s. Although some PAS members believed that colonization would fail, others, such as well-known reformer Roberts Vaux, considered the ACS a worthy reform group.

By the 1820s and 1830s, as blacks in Philadelphia, New York, Boston, and other locales engaged in more radical forms of abolitionism (from mass pamphleteering to confrontational fugitive slave defenses), and a new generation of white reformers began embracing the doctrine of immediate abolitionism, the PAS was further marginalized. Labeled "modern" abolitionists, these new reformers included white evangelicals, black elites, and for the first time in mainstream antislavery organizations, women. Modern abolitionists formed the American Anti-Slavery Society (ironically in the PAS's home of Philadelphia), supported Garrison's *Liberator*, and spawned a whole new wave of local and state abolitionist societies. By the mid-1830s, the era of PAS dominance was over. "Has abolition gone defunct in Pennsylvania," some old-time activists wondered?

Still, the PAS remained active over the next several decades, with some members joining the modern abolitionist crusade (the first immediatist antislavery society appeared in Philadelphia in 1834, attracting some key PAS supporters). Other PAS members worked with fugitive slaves, became further involved in black education efforts, and remained dedicated to a more moderate brand abolitionism. The group has never folded.

Though it receives little credit in contemporary histories of antislavery, the PAS was an important part of American abolitionism. During the post-Revolutionary era in particular, when many statesmen supported antislavery ideals but feared abolitionist action, the PAS attacked slavery in a highly efficient and formally organized manner. The group helped launch gradual abolitionism in Northern states and establish (with black runaways and kidnapping survivors) the concept of "free" Northern culture well before the Free Soil and Republican Parties would do so. And the group was among the first to put slavery on the federal radar via petitions against the overseas slave trade. Even Garrison would salute the PAS as among the most "thorough-going" antislavery reformers prior to the 1830s. In sum, the group formed a critical part of first-wave abolitionism.

Richard Newman

See also: Democratic Party and Antislavery; Gradual Emancipation; Immediate Emancipation; Radical Republicans; Whig Party and Antislavery.

Further Readings

Nash, Gary, and Jean Soderlund. *Freedom by Degrees: Emancipation and Its Aftermath in Pennsylvania*. New York: Oxford University Press, 1991.

Newman, Richard S. *The Transformation of American Abolitionism: Fighting Slavery in the Early Republic*. Chapel Hill: University of North Carolina Press, 2002.

Phillips, Wendell

One of the most effective and influential abolitionist orators of the nineteenth century, Wendell Phillips was born on November 9, 1811, as the eighth child of John Phillips, a wealthy lawyer, politician, and philanthropist, and Sarah Walley. His family occupied the highest caste in Boston, tracing their North American roots back to early seventeenth-century Salem, Massachusetts.

First educated at the Boston Latin School, Phillips later attended Harvard and graduated in 1831. Although he harbored an interest in studying history, he was recognized as a skilled debater and carried that talent with him to Harvard Law School. A Boston attorney and member of the Suffolk County bar, Phillips quickly grew bored with the legal profession.

In Ann Terry Greene, Phillips found both a wife and a vocation. Ann was the daughter and heir to one of Boston's wealthiest families, and a political radical. She was an avowed abolitionist, a supporter of antislavery newspaper editor William Lloyd Garrison, and a member of the Boston Female Anti-Slavery Society. Phillips followed her both down the aisle and into the ranks of Boston's abolitionists, dedicating himself to the cause at a March 1837 meeting of the Massachusetts Anti-Slavery Society. He was married on October 12, 1837, and only weeks later found the voice that would define his career.

Phillips revealed his oratorical powers at a critical moment in the antislavery movement. In Alton, Illinois, on November 7, 1837, a proslavery mob murdered abolitionist newspaper editor Elijah P. Lovejoy and destroyed his printing press. Barricaded in the warehouse where he had hidden a new press—three others had been thrown into the nearby Mississippi River—Lovejoy was killed when he tried to prevent the mob from setting fire to the building. Word of the event electrified anti- and proslavery activists, and a month later, on December 7, Phillips attended a heated meeting at Faneuil Hall in Boston to discuss the case. What he heard enraged him. James T. Austin, the Massachusetts attorney general, denounced Lovejoy and compared the murderous mob to the Revolutionary War patriots who threw off British rule in 1776. For Phillips, this was too much; at the urging of friends, he rose with a spontaneous address celebrating Lovejoy's intrepid resistance. The gathered crowd was stunned by Phillips's clarity and eloquence, and thus, at the age of twenty-six, Phillips thrust himself to the forefront of the antislavery movement.

Following that debut, Phillips became a confidant of Garrison. The two saw abolitionism as a larger cause that embraced women's rights, rejected religious denominations, and was set apart from politics itself. Like Garrison, Phillips believed that the partisan electoral system was tainted by slavery; to be successful, abolitionism would have to be radical and revolutionary. He was even more hostile to proslavery forces than Garrison, dissenting from the latter's pacifism. For Phillips, a war against slavery would be a just war.

In 1840, Phillips and his wife were traveling in Europe where they attended the World's Anti-Slavery Convention in London as representatives of the American Anti-Slavery Society. Hoping to win support from British abolitionists for their movement, they were disappointed by their inability to convince the international gathering to allow women to vote at the event. The couple's failure in Britain demonstrated that a transatlantic abolitionist movement would be less radical and more conventional than what Garrison and his cohort sought. Mainstream abolitionism continued to work through elections and politics to achieve its ends; Garrison, Phillips, and their associates continued to pursue a broader and more ideological reform agenda.

Throughout the 1840s and 1850s, Phillips continued to be at Garrison's side, professing before audiences the sentiments Garrison conveyed in print. Among his other writings, he penned two pamphlets on the defects of American politics: *The Constitution—A Proslavery Document* (1842), and *Can an Abolitionist Vote or Hold Office under the United States Constitution?* (1843). Both pamphlets laid out the Garrison-Phillips argument that abolitionists who continued to be involved in American politics were coconspirators in a corrupt system. The U.S. Constitution, as he saw it, was inherently proslavery.

Despite his power as a public speaker, Phillips also engaged in social reforms and civil disobedience in the cause of racial equality and abolition. He was a member of the executive committee of the American Anti-Slavery Society and the Boston Vigilance Committee; in the latter capacity, he helped protect fugitive slaves from capture in Boston after the passage of the 1850 Fugitive Slave Law. He also worked to overturn segregation in the city's public schools. Phillips wanted such activities to heighten, rather than assuage, the growing tensions between free and slave states. Agitation, he believed, could eventually split the Union; years before any slave states contemplated secession, Phillips advocated that Northern states peel away from the United States, leaving only the slaveholding states behind.

Phillips made this case throughout the 1850s, touring as a lecturer who delighted audiences with discourses on all kinds of topics, from natural science to the arts and architecture. But most came to hear him discuss slavery, blending his quick wit and accessible style with his uncompromising platform. He traveled throughout the northeastern and midwestern United States, never using a script, lending rhetorical support to the increasingly confrontational tactics of antislavery activists like the Free Soilers in Kansas, John Brown's followers at Harpers Ferry, and those who spirited away fugitives.

When war came, however, Phillips reversed his course. While supportive of the idea of Northern states seceding to escape slavery, he was now unwilling to permit Southern states to leave the Union to protect their peculiar institution. Demanding war and the return of the slave states, Phillips became one of the most radical of Republicans during the Lincoln administration. He wanted the war to be about slavery, a radical revolutionary conflict that would result in emancipation and aggressive land redistribution in the South.

Parting ways with Garrison after the war, Phillips did not view emancipation as the endpoint of the abolitionist struggle. Reconstruction represented a new beginning, and in 1865 Phillips succeeded Garrison as president of the American Anti-Slavery Society. He served in that position until 1870, when the Fifteenth Amendment was passed.

In that year, Phillips ran for governor of Massachusetts as the candidate of both the Labor Reform and Prohibitionist Parties, garnering 20,000 votes. Phillips continued his activism on behalf of freed African Americans and began to speak out on issues of labor relations. In 1871, he supported former Civil War general Benjamin Butler's candidacy for governor of Massachusetts. In public, he called for eight-hour workdays and cooperative workplaces. Phillips made his last public speech on December 26, 1883, and died on February 2, 1884.

Brian Murphy

See also: Bleeding Kansas; Radical Republicans; Underground Railroad.

Further Readings

Bartlett, Irving. *Wendell Phillips: Brahmin Radical*. Westport, CT: Greenwood Press, 1973. Originally published in 1961.

Stewart, James Brewer. *Wendell Phillips: Liberty's Hero*. Reprint ed. Baton Rouge: Louisiana State University Press, 1998.

Port Royal (South Carolina)

One of the oldest place names on the eastern coast of North America, Port Royal is an important site in the history of New World slavery. In 1562, Jean Ribaut, while seeking a haven for French Huguenots in the New World, sailed into a broad harbor on the coast of South Carolina and named it Port Royal. Since then, the name has applied to the region, to the harbor, to an island, a river, and a town.

As a region, Port Royal includes the Sea Islands of South Carolina. The Sea Islands were one of the great incubators of the Gullah culture that combines elements of several African cultures with those of Europe. Thousands of African slaves from Senegambia, Angola, and other parts of Africa came to the Sea Islands to grow indigo, cultivate rice, and produce the famed Sea Island cotton. Living isolated lives away from commercial centers, the Sea Island slaves developed their own language, arts, and culture.

The harbor and river of Port Royal were the training grounds for African American pilots and sailors. African Americans not only produced the staples that made white Beaufortonians rich, but they also took the crops to markets in Charleston and Savannah. In the first decades of European settlement in the region, these waterways were escape routes for hundreds of slaves who fled to St. Augustine. So many slaves fled South Carolina that the Spanish officials allowed them to settle and govern their own town—Garcia Real de Santa Teresa de Mosa north of St. Augustine. The settlement was the site of a major defeat for Carolina troops during General James Oglethorpe's siege of Saint Augustine in 1740.

The Sea Islands were also home to the "Port Royal Experiment"—an effort to transform the lives of the former slaves through education and religion. After the surrender of Forts Beauregard and Walker, federal troops occupied the Sea Islands in 1862. One of their immediate challenges was to care for the slaves who lived in the area, as well as the thousands of others who fled to the Union lines for freedom. A public-private response involved abolitionist teachers and preachers from Pennsylvania, Massachusetts, and other Northern states who came South and opened schools for the freedmen. Later, the Freedmen's Bureau provided housing and food, negotiated labor contracts, and tried to reconnect broken families. A few fortunate freedmen acquired land and many became successful farmers, craftsmen, and small businessmen.

One of the first schools founded during the Port Royal Experiment was the Penn School on St. Helena Island. This school trained and educated African Americans in the Port Royal area for decades. Today, it continues its mission as the Penn Community Center.

The Sea Islands, with their large African American majorities, were politically significant during Reconstruction. Robert Smalls of Beaufort served as a U.S. congressman and was a member of both the South Carolina Constitutional Conventions of 1868 and 1895. He remained a political power in the region until his death. The Carolina low country was the last bastion of black power in the state.

The island of Port Royal was the site of Old Fort Plantation. From there on New Year's Day 1863, the Reverend William Brisbane read the Emancipation Proclamation to thousands of freedmen with great ceremony. Also, the Reverend Mansfield French presented regimental colors to the First Regiment of South Carolina Volunteers, a troop of freedmen who had enlisted in the Union Army. The First Regiment of South Carolina Volunteers, later known as the 33rd U.S. Colored, was the first African American regiment commissioned during the Civil War. Federal forces raised both the First and Second South Carolina Regiments in the Port Royal area. Therefore, the Port Royal region and name have deep, multifaceted significance for the history of slavery and African Americans.

Alexia Helsley

See also: African American Communities.

Further Readings

Helsley, Alexia Jones. *Beaufort, South Carolina: A History*. Charleston: The History Press, 2005.

Rose, Willie Lee. *Rehearsal for Reconstruction: The Port Royal Experiment*. New York: Oxford University Press, 1964.

Rowland, Lawrence S., et al. *History of Beaufort County, South Carolina*. Vol. 1, *1514–1861*. Columbia: University of South Carolina Press, 1996.

Postal Campaign (1835)

In May 1835, at the second annual meeting of the American Anti-Slavery Society (AASS), AASS Publications Committee Chair Lewis Tappan announced an aggressive campaign to deliver each week issues of the society's four publications to social and political leaders throughout the United States. Tappan called upon abolitionists throughout the country, including especially women and children, to donate generously toward the cost of publishing and mailing AASS materials through the federal mails to *"inquiring, candid, reading* men" who had not yet embraced the message of immediate emancipation. Although the Society targeted religious leaders, educators, businessmen, and politicians throughout the nation, the campaign was designed especially to reach leaders in the Southern states who might throw their influence behind abolition.

Tappan and editor Elizur Wright Jr., who orchestrated much of the great postal campaign, counted upon a certain degree of violent opposition to help put their cause at the forefront of national attention. As Wright stated in the first issue of the serial *Human Rights*, published in July 1835, "If you wish to draw off the people from a mad or wicked custom . . . you must make an excitement, do something that everybody will notice." During the following year, the AASS mailed more than one million pieces of antislavery literature to post offices throughout the nation, triggering a public outcry against abolitionism that far exceeded their expectations. The postal campaign was premised upon the mistaken assumption that antislavery sentiment ran wide and deep within the Christian public, including Southern churches, and that a determined appeal to Christian conscience would persuade many leaders to ally themselves with the cause of the slave. Instead AASS leaders found themselves vilified in both Northern and Southern states as advocates of disunion and racial war. Although free blacks were not on the AASS mailing list, it was widely rumored that they were the chief target of abolitionist organizing efforts, leading to a spate of new state laws to police free negroes and demands for more vigorous enforcement of existing race laws.

The postal campaign triggered a dramatic rise in antiabolitionist violence during the summer of 1835. Almost every major city in the nation saw antiabolitionist rallies and torchlight parades. News of mobs and antiabolitionist speeches filled the newspapers each day. In both North and South, pastors took to their pulpits to denounce abolitionists as irresponsible incendiaries who deserved to be censured by the public and prosecuted by the government for crimes against humanity. In many towns, committees formed to inspect the mails and destroy offensive abolitionist literature, an action that Postmaster General Amos Kendall virtually endorsed. On July 29, 1835, a mob broke into the Charleston, South Carolina, post office and carried off recently arrived mailbags filled with AASS literature. Identifying themselves with the patriots of the Boston Tea Party in 1773, the following night the thieves held a rally on the Charleston parade grounds attended by over 2,000 citizens, who watched approvingly as the abolitionist mail was burned beneath a large mock gallows where antislavery leaders hung in effigy. A grand jury in Virginia indicted and demanded the extradition of all officers of the AASS, while many Southern vigilance committees offered large bounties to anyone who would deliver prominent AASS officers to them dead or alive.

The postal campaign was a defining moment in the history of antislavery. The campaign helped to drive a wedge between more conservative churchmen and those who wished to see the evangelical churches align themselves with the cause of emancipation. The concerted opposition to the campaign across the nation and the virtually universal condemnation expressed by Southern citizens underscored the futility of antislavery tactics based upon moral suasion and helped to provide impetus to political approaches to the problem. Just as importantly, the violence sparked by the postal campaign succeeded in making the abolitionist cause a topic of daily conversation. According to Elizur Wright Jr., the violence directed at the AASS did more to advance the cause of antislavery than the arguments of 1,000 agents could have accomplished. Between May 1835 and May 1836, more than 15,000 people subscribed to AASS publications and the number of AASS auxiliaries grew from 200 to 527 chapters. Abolitionism could never again be dismissed as a fringe movement.

James R. Rohrer

See also: American Anti-Slavery Society (AASS).

Further Readings

Richards, Leonard D. *"Gentlemen of Property and Standing." Anti-Abolition Mobs in Jacksonian America*. New York: Oxford University Press, 1970.

Snay, Mitchell. *Gospel of Disunion: Religion and Separatism in the Antebellum South*. New York: Cambridge University Press, 1993.

Wyatt-Brown, Bertram. *Lewis Tappan and the Evangelical War against Slavery*. New York: Atheneum, 1971.

Wyly-Jones, Susan. "The 1835 Anti-Abolition Meetings in the South: A New Look at the Controversy over the Abolition Postal Campaign." *Civil War History* 47 (2001): 289–309.

Q

Quakers and Antislavery

The Christian denomination of the Society of Friends, better known as the Quakers, has a long history of involvement with antislavery causes. While the Quakers have been hailed as leaders in the antislavery struggle, they sometimes suffered internal dissension over the issue. The Friends, started in England in the 1640s as a radically egalitarian reaction to the left of the Puritans, always maintained a strong tenet of human spiritual equality. As the denomination developed, Quakers possessed the intellectual and communal forms for critiquing slavery, as well as its attendant ills of racism, formalism, and inherited institutional power. This did not ensure, however, that Quaker antislavery testimony would be consistently applied, nor skillfully articulated at all points in their history. While the common impression that the Quakers were in the forefront of antislavery activism should be tempered, they were nevertheless in the antislavery vanguard among predominantly white groups.

As Quakers settled in the growing colonies of North America and the Caribbean, the founder of the Society, George Fox (1624–1691), began to express qualms about slavery. His concerns, though, were not directed against the institution of slavery, but focused on the proper obedience and religious instruction of slaves, and upon the conduct of masters. On a 1671 visit to Barbados, Fox took more care to dispel rumors that the Quakers were inciting slave revolts than he did to condemn the institution of slavery. Fox's travel companion, William Edmundson (1627–1712), however was shocked by the slavery he saw in North America in the 1670s. In his widely circulated journal, he speculated that Christianity and slavery were incompatible.

More forthright in their criticisms were a brave group of Dutch Quaker immigrants to Pennsylvania. In 1688, they addressed a strongly worded denunciation of slavery to their monthly meeting, pointing out the incompatibility of slaveholding with the Golden Rule: "There is a saying that we shall do to all men like as we

OBSERVATIONS

On the Inflaving, importing and purchafing of

Negroes;

With fome Advice thereon, extracted from the Epiftle of the Yearly-Meeting of the People called Quakers, held at *London* in the Year 1758.

When ye fpread forth your Hands, I will hide mine Eyes from you, yea when ye make many Prayers I will not bear; your Hands are full of Blood. Wafh ye, make you clean, put away the Evil of your Doings from before mine Eyes Ifai. 1, 15.

Is not this the Faft that I have chofen, to loofe the Bands of Wickednefs, to undo the heavy Burden, to let the Oppreffed go free, and that ye break every Toke, Chap. 58, 7.

Second Edition.

GERMANTOWN: Printed by Christopher Sower. 1760.

Title page of Anthony Benezet's "Observations on the inslaving, importing and purchasing of Negroes . . ." presented at the yearly meeting of Quakers in London, 1760. (Library of Congress)

will be done ourselves; making no difference of what generation, descent or colour they are. . . . Is there any that would be done or handled at this manner? viz. To be sold or made a slave for all the time of his life?" This remonstrance disappeared from history until republished by abolitionists in 1844. A similar denunciation of slavery from the schismatic followers of George Keith in 1693 was likewise fleeting in its impact.

Through the early eighteenth century, increasingly prosperous Quakers involved themselves in all aspects of slavery and the slave trade, economic success undercutting any strict application of their ideals of equality. These ideals did not, however, disappear. A few lone voices were raised against slavery in the 1720s and 1730s, most notably Ralph Sandiford (1693–1733) and Benjamin Lay (1682–1759), each of whom published antislavery arguments. However, the outstanding individual leaders of the movement to purge slaveholding from American Friends were Anthony Benezet (1713–1784) and John Woolman (1720–1772). Benezet's pamphlets on slavery had wide currency in both America and Europe, among Quakers and outside of the Society; his writings are credited with awakening the conscience of English abolitionist Thomas Clarkson. Furthermore, Benezet, who opened a school for free blacks in Philadelphia in the 1760s, became one of the first antislavery advocates to denounce as well the ideology of racial inferiority which undergirded slavery: "I have found amongst the negroes as great a variety of talents as amongst a like number of whites; and I am bold to assert, that the notion . . . that the blacks are inferior in their capacities, is a vulgar prejudice."

John Woolman's method included the written word, but succeeded more through a quiet but persistent personal witness. He would visit slaveholding Quakers, speaking against the practice, then insist on giving wages to slaves who had assisted him during his stay. He attended meetings in many districts, raising the inconsistencies of slavery and Christianity, without condemning slaveholders as individuals. By the late 1740s, slaveholding was decreasing among Quakers, and in 1754 the Philadelphia Quarterly Meeting declared slaveholding a sin, a resolution with which the Yearly Meeting concurred in 1758. Other Quaker meetings followed them; by 1780 slaveholding among Quakers was virtually unknown, as it had been determined an offense requiring disowning by other Friends. John Woolman's gentle, unrelenting style achieved ongoing resonance through his *Journal*, which became standard devotional reading for generations of Friends.

As Jean Soderlund demonstrates, Woolman's personal quest could not have succeeded without a change in the economic status of Quaker leadership. In the 1730s, many of those who deliberated and published the proceedings of Yearly Meetings were, themselves, slave owners. By the late 1750s, leadership had passed to more reform-minded, middle-class Friends, who had no personal stake in upholding slavery.

Even as Quaker political power dissipated during the American Revolution, Friends seized on the congruency between republican language and antislavery. In April 1775, Anthony Benezet called the initial meeting of the Society for the Relief of Free Negroes Unlawfully held in Bondage. Thomas Paine was among the attendees of this first interreligious abolition group, but the majority were Quakers. Moses Brown (1738–1836), a wealthy merchant destined to play a key financial role in the industrialization of New England, manumitted his slaves and joined the Friends on the eve of the Revolution. Brown used his social prominence to fund numerous antislavery organizations over the next half-century. In the decades following the Revolution, a large-scale internal migration of Quakers occurred because of slavery; large numbers of Quakers in Southern states relocated to Ohio and Indiana, removing themselves from slave culture and governments that eyed their ideological differences with suspicion. Others moved to Canada, where they would later assist escaped blacks.

Arguably the most important international action of American Quakers during the Revolutionary era came when the Philadelphia Yearly Meeting urged their London counterparts to action. This resulted in English Friends submitting the first formal petition to Parliament opposing the slave trade in 1783, which would deeply influence the men who would become the leaders of the English movement to abolish the Atlantic slave trade including William Wilberforce, Thomas Clarkson, and Thomas Buxton, none of whom were Quakers. Quaker meetings would also form a crucial grassroots backbone for the antislavery cause.

With the slave trade officially banned in 1808, white American and English antislavery entered a more quiescent, gradualist phase. The most notable Quakers in this period were the American editor Benjamin Lundy (1789–1839) and the English woman writer Elizabeth Heyrick (1769–1831). Lundy edited an antislavery newspaper, the *Genius of Universal Emancipation*, which kept the flame of abolition alive in the 1820s by entertaining all approaches to mitigating and ending slavery. One such approach came in the stirring tones of immediatism, first enunciated by Elizabeth Heyrick. Her call for an immediate end to the sin of slaveholding jarred her more conservative Quaker brethren in England when her pamphlet, *Immediate, Not Gradual Abolition*, was published in 1824. However, her logic impressed women's antislavery groups in England, and, when republished in Lundy's paper in 1826, initiated a radicalization of white abolitionists in the United States.

Immediatism was the rampart of the English Quaker abolitionist Joseph Sturge (1793–1859), who led the struggle to end slavery in all English territory in 1835. Realizing that Parliament's recent passage of gradual, compensated emancipation in the British colonies could be compromised by racism, apprenticeship requirements, and the persistence of proslavery sentiments, Sturge undertook visits to the Caribbean and the United States to eradicate slavery in the British West Indies once and for all. He also helped organize the 1840 World's Anti-Slavery Convention in London, which extended antislavery internationally.

With the advent of more radical abolitionist organizations in the United States after 1830, Quakers were divided among themselves on questions of tactics. There had been schismatic movements among the Friends in the early nineteenth century which resulted in an official distancing of those called Orthodox Quakers from abolitionist causes, despite a high level of individual Quaker participation in the movement. Quakers who played key roles in the abolitionist struggle included poets John Greenleaf Whittier (1807–1892) and Elizabeth Margaret Chandler (1807–1836), and especially Philadelphians Lucretia Coffin Mott (1793–1880) and her spouse James Mott (1788–1868).

Lucretia Mott's antislavery activism highlights the contradictions present among Quakers. Because women had always participated equally in the Society, functioning as traveling ministers as well as speaking at meetings, Quaker women nurtured many organized women's antislavery groups. But as Quakers became more religiously conventional, they adopted some of the prejudices of their time, and objected to women's public political presence. Mott was also criticized for bringing black women to Quaker meetings; despite Benezet's early witness, Quakers had long discouraged African Americans from joining. Even though Mott was a member of the more socially radical Hicksite group, her actions left her threatened with disownment. The famous 1840 London conference refused to seat her as a full delegate; this led to her meeting Elizabeth Cady Stanton and planning what would eventually become the Seneca Falls Convention.

Many other abolitionists had been born Quakers, or sojourned with them, but had to leave the Society to continue their antislavery activism. Isaac Hopper (1771–1852), Arnold Buffum (1782–1859), Angelina Grimké (1805–1879), Sarah Grimké (1792–1873), Abby Kelley Foster (1811–1887), Prudence Crandall (1803–1890), Laura Haviland (1808–1898), Susan B. Anthony (1820–1906), and even Elias Hicks (1748–1830) himself all found themselves at odds with Quaker meetings. Ironically, many of them are now claimed as Quaker heroes.

Similar tensions marked Quaker involvement in the Underground Railroad. Many Quakers assisted runaway slaves, but those who made it a priority were often chastised. Along the border states of Indiana and Ohio, heated disputes led to ruptures. Levi Coffin (1798–1877) and his wife Catherine White Coffin (d. 1909) were among those who were dismissed for meeting with non-Quaker abolitionists and for their willingness to break the law against harboring runaways. They and other radicals started the Indiana Yearly Meeting of Anti-Slavery Friends in 1843, which rejoined the main branch once most Quakers evolved to a similarly militant stance by 1857. Another noted Quaker "conductor" on the Underground Railroad was Lucretia Mott's associate, the Hicksite Thomas Garrett (1789–1871). Positioned strategically in Delaware, he assisted over 2,000 runaways, and provided financial and logistical support to Harriet Tubman (ca. 1820–1913).

The American Civil War posed the ultimate test for the pacifist Quakers, dramatically pitting their ideal of equality against their nonviolence. Some, such as Garrett and Mott, had already reconciled themselves to the likely need for violence to overthrow the Slave Power. A few Iowa Quakers allied with John Brown (1800–1859) as he planned for his raid at the Harpers Ferry arsenal. Once the war began, Confederate states imprisoned Friends on suspicion of being against both slavery and the war. In the North, individual Quakers agonized over support for the war, and young men faced the even more grueling decision about whether to fight. Records show that as many as a quarter of eligible Quaker men did enlist; very few disownments were made despite this blatant disregard of a foundational tenet of the denomination.

Quakers remained active as missionaries during the late nineteenth century expansion of British imperialism in Africa. In Zanzibar and Kenya, slaves were held under a variety of indigenous Muslim and Swahili social systems. Quakers vociferously maintained the need for immediate abolition. Henry S. Newman, the honorary secretary of the Friends Foreign Mission Association, established the "industrial mission" of Banani on the island of Pemba in 1897. Former slaves were welcomed, providing Newman with the means to agitate for abolition throughout the region. However, the Quakers of the time did not question the presumptions of imperialism, the paternalism of racism, or the exploitations of British capitalism; Friends had become part of the establishment, even if still occasionally a gadfly. While slavery was abolished in most colonial territory of East Africa by 1909, labor relations between the former slaves and the plantation owners was virtually unchanged. Quakers continued their antislavery agitation following World War I, joining in petitions to the League of Nations to monitor imperialist labor practices verging on slavery.

Contemporary Quakers are rightfully proud of their legacy of involvement in antislavery, but have not rested on their laurels. The American Friends Service Committee continues the struggle by working against debt-bondage, sexual slavery, and slavery in civil wars.

From the time they renounced slaveholding among themselves, Quakers became an integral part of antislavery struggles internationally. Because of their strong intragroup communication, they provided activists with organizational models and access to existing networks. The prominent public role of women in Quaker polity paved the way for the emergence of feminism from within the awakened political consciousness of female abolitionists. Yet Quakers have also suffered from their own internal problems including an incomplete dismantling of racial prejudice and debilitation from internal disputes, which have limited their cohesion at key moments in the struggle.

Jennifer Rycenga

See also: Immediatism; Mott, Lucretia Coffin.

Further Readings

Anstey, Roger. *The Atlantic Slave Trade and British Abolition, 1760–1810*. London: Macmillan, 1975.

Bacon, Margaret Hope. *Mothers of Feminism: The Story of Quaker Women in America*. San Francisco: Harper and Row, 1986.

Coffin, Levi. *Reminiscences of Levi Coffin*. New York: Arno Press, 1968 (Reprint of 3rd edition, 1898).

Cooper, Frederick. *From Slaves to Squatters: Plantation Labor and Agriculture in Zanzibar and Coastal Kenya, 1890–1925*. New Haven, CT: Yale University Press, 1980.

Davis, David Brion. *The Problem of Slavery in Western Culture*. Ithaca, NY: Cornell University Press, 1966.

Dorland, Arthur Garratt. *The Quakers in Canada, A History*. Toronto: Ryerson Press, 1968.

Drake, Thomas E. *Quakers and Slavery in America*. New Haven, CT: Yale University Press, 1950.

Frost, J. William. *The Quaker Origins of Antislavery*. Norwood, PA: Norwood Editions, 1980.

Hamm, Thomas D. "Indiana Quakers and Politics, 1810–1865." In Barbara A. Heavilin and Charles W. Heavilin, eds. *The Quaker Presence in America: "Let Us then Try What Love Will Do." Quaker Studies* Volume 5. Lewiston, NY: Edwin Mellen, 2003, pp. 219–242.

Hamm, Thomas D. *The Quakers in America.* New York: Columbia University Press, 2003.

Hewitt, Nancy A. "Feminist Friends: Agrarian Quakers and the Emergence of Woman's Rights in America." *Feminist Studies* 12, 1 (Spring 1986): 27–49.

Hornick, Nancy Slocum. "Anthony Benezet and the Africans' School: Toward a Theory of Full Equality." *Pennsylvania Magazine of History and Biography* 99, 4 (1975): 399–421.

Jennings, Judith Gaile. "The Campaign for the Abolition of the British Slave Trade: The Quaker Contribution, 1757–1807." Ph.D. dissertation, University of Kentucky, 1975.

Nelson, Jacquelyn S. *Indiana Quakers Confront the Civil War.* Indianapolis: Indiana Historical Society, 1991.

Newman, Henry S. *Banani: The Transition from Slavery to Freedom in Zanzibar and Pemba.* London: Headley Brothers, 1898 (Reprint edition. New York: Negro Universities Press, 1969).

Nwulia, Moses D. E. *Britain and Slavery in East Africa.* Washington, DC: Three Continents Press, 1975.

Soderlund, Jean. *Quakers and Slavery: A Divided Spirit.* Princeton, NJ: Princeton University Press, 1985.

Walvin, James. *England, Slaves, and Freedom, 1776–1838.* Jackson: University of Mississippi, 1986.

Quok Walker Decision (1783)

In 1783, in *Commonwealth of Massachusetts v. Jennison*, the Supreme Court of Massachusetts under Chief Justice William Cushing pronounced Quok Walker—and all other slaves in Massachusetts—free. Through that single action, the court transformed Massachusetts from the first colony to legalize slavery into the first state to deny any of its citizens the right to hold human property.

This historic decision did not emerge, however, until Massachusetts courts oversaw two years of legal battles. In 1781, Quok Walker sued Nathaniel Jennison of Barre for assault and battery. While Quok considered himself a free man, Jennison thought Walker was his runaway slave. When Jennison found him working for John and Seth Caldwell, and Walker refused to accompany Jennison back to his home, Jennison and two other men beat him. After this brutal beating, Jennison imprisoned Walker in a barn.

Within a month, Quok Walker sued Jennison on a plea of trespass. The Worcester County Inferior Court of Common Pleas ordered Jennison to appear for the case *Walker v. Jennison* (1781). People illegally enslaved usually used a charge of trespass to sue for freedom. Trespass, the unlawful injury of another's person or property, determined status because a master could legally injure a slave, but not a free person. Therefore, if the jury found the defendant had injured the plaintiff, they had decided that he or she was free. From Jennison's perspective, injury was not possible, for he could not injure his own property. As his property, Jennison had a right to beat or restrain Walker as he willed. Walker and his lawyers responded that Walker was a free man and had therefore suffered injury. Before Jennison owned him, Walker had made an agreement with James Caldwell, Walker's original owner, to free him at the age of twenty-five. Jennison acquired Walker through marriage with one of Caldwell's daughters. After the daughter died and Walker came of age, Jennison refused to uphold Caldwell's agreement. The jury found Walker's argument most convincing and decided that Jennison had injured Walker, and, thus, Walker was free.

The initial case blossomed into three other cases between Walker, Jennison, and the Caldwell family. In each of these cases, the attorney, Levi Lincoln, offered an impassioned plea for the abolition of slavery in Massachusetts; yet none of these cases declared anyone free, but Walker himself. The scope of the case would change, however, when the Commonwealth of Massachusetts arrested Jennsion for imprisoning and beating Walker in the final and most important case, *Commonwealth of Massachusetts v. Jennison* (1783).

The remarkable aspect of this case was Chief Justice Cushing's charge to the jury. Cushing pushed aside the traditional adherence to points of law and looked to the state constitution of 1780 to instruct the jury. He thought that the concept of natural rights bound the framers to "declare *that all men are born free and equal*" and stated furthermore that *"every subject is entitled to liberty."* In his legal instruction he deemed slavery "as effectively abolished as it can be." He, therefore, ordered the jury not "to consider whether the promises of freedom to Quaco . . . amounted to manumission or not." After issuing his oral charge, Cushing wrote out his instructions in his legal notebook. Almost in amazement of what had happened, he ended the entry with a statement in his notebook that explained the significance clearly: "The preceding Case was the one in which by the foregoing Charge, Slavery in Massachusetts was forever abolished."

Despite this seemingly unequivocal assertion, slavery did not instantaneously end in Massachusetts. The immediate legacy of these cases was very murky. Most importantly, the abolition of slavery by judicial decree did not result in a mass emancipation but made it impossible for masters to maintain their ownership when brought to court. For this reason, some scholars have questioned whether the case indeed ended slavery. As legal scholar A. Leon Higginbotham expressed it, however, the court had indeed "signaled that it would no longer protect the legality of slavery." But the burden lay upon the enslaved men and women who had to assert their freedom to their master. The first substantial evidence that slaves actually became free was the 1790 Census when Massachusetts reported no enslaved inhabitants.

Emily V. Blanck

See also: Freedom Suits in North America.

Further Readings

Blanck, Emily. "Seventeen Eighty-Three: The Turning Point in the Law of Slavery and Freedom in Massachusetts." *New England Quarterly* 75, 1 (2002): 24–51.

Cushing, William. Massachusetts Historical Society, William Cushing Papers, Notes on Law Cases, 1783, 98.

Higginbotham, A. Leon. In the Matter of Color: Race and the American Legal Process, The Colonial Period (1978).

O'Brien, William. "Did the Jennison Case Outlaw Slavery in Massachusetts?" *William and Mary Quarterly* 17, 2 (1960): 219–241.

Zilversmit, Arthur. "Quok Walker, Mumbet, and the Abolition of Slavery in Massachusetts." *William and Mary Quarterly* 25, 4 (1968): 614–624.

R

Radical Republicans

The Radical Republicans earned their label by advocating policies of radical social change during the Civil War era. Radicals interpreted the U.S. Constitution's guarantee of republican government in the several states as a mandate for vastly expanded national power during the Civil War and Reconstruction. Inspired by this view, Radical Republicans invoked federal power not only to destroy slavery, which they viewed as antithetical to republican freedoms, but also the political and economic systems that had supported it. Especially through Reconstruction, Radicals envisioned remodeling the entire South into a region of small producers and free laborers, characterized by political equality for all men, regardless of race. Though not wholly successful in implementing their goals, they did inaugurate dramatic social and political change in the South, and throughout the United States.

Pointing to slavery as the fundamental cause of the Civil War, Radicals prodded President Abraham Lincoln early in the conflict to wage war for emancipation. Lincoln's shrewd reluctance to propose emancipation prematurely—so as to preserve the loyalty of slaveholding Unionists in the border states—greatly frustrated Radicals. For the most part though, they supported Lincoln's policies and greeted his preliminary Emancipation Proclamation in September 1862 with great enthusiasm. Through their leadership of the Joint Committee of the Conduct of the War, Radicals also sought to aid the president in prosecuting the war, assistance that likely complicated his management of the war as much as it helped.

Radicals also differed with Lincoln on the subject of Reconstruction. The president sought the quick restoration to the Union of seceded states in which 10 percent of the adult, male population pledged their allegiance to the Constitution. Radicals, though, thought the destruction of the South's old political regimes was more important than hasty restoration to the Union. In July 1864, Senator Benjamin F. Wade of Ohio and Congressman Henry Winter Davis of Maryland sponsored a Reconstruction bill that required oaths of allegiance from over half of a state's adult males and disenfranchised Confederate leaders. Lincoln pocket-vetoed the bill, but Radicals did not abandon demands for harsher Reconstruction measures.

Thaddeus Stevens of Pennsylvania, a leader in the House of Representatives, advocated redistributing plantation property to freedmen in small freeholds, and other Radicals proposed legislation to guarantee black male suffrage. However, few Americans supported land redistribution, and several Southern states passed Black Codes in 1865 and 1866 that severely circumscribed black freedoms and voting rights. President Andrew Johnson (who succeeded to the presidency on Lincoln's assassination) vetoed the Freedmen's Bureau and civil rights bills in 1867, which had been designed to protect the freedoms and rights of freedmen. In response, Charles Sumner led other Radicals in holding up congressional passage of the Fourteenth Amendment in 1867 until it incorporated protection of citizenship rights and suffrage regardless of color. Radicals also combined with moderates to assume control of Reconstruction in 1867 and orchestrate the impeachment of Johnson the following year.

Inspired in large part by George Julian, Stevens, and other Radicals, Congress's Reconstruction Acts of 1867 divided the South into five military districts, directed the military to register voters for new state constitutional conventions, and enfranchised adult, black males to vote in those elections. These measures enfranchised over 700,000 African American voters, outnumbering the region's white voters, and led to the first biracial state governments in the nation's history. Those governments funded public education and other social programs designed to enhance economic and social opportunities for small producers, both white and black.

However, this radical change proved short-lived. Waning Northern support for the ongoing, costly Reconstruction process caused many moderates to abandon Radical Reconstruction by 1868. The combination of Southerners' dissatisfaction with new state taxes and a wave of racist violence aimed at Republican voters soon toppled Republican governments in the South. Democrats' return to power in most Southern states by 1872 effectively ended Radical Reconstruction. Though Radical Republicans' policies proved short-lived in the South, they had paved the way for greater political and social equality for Northern blacks and greatly expanded the powers of federal and state governments to effect social change.

Matthew Isham

See also: Democratic Party and Antislavery; Whig Party and Antislavery.

Further Readings

Foner, Eric. *Reconstruction: America's Unfinished Revolution, 1863–1877*. New York: Harper & Row, 1988.

Hyman, Harold. *The Radical Republicans and Reconstruction, 1861–1870*. Indianapolis, Indiana: Bobbs-Merrill, 1967.

Perman, Michael. *The Road to Redemption: Southern Politics, 1868–1879*. Chapel Hill: University of North Carolina Press, 1984.

Trefousse, Hans. *The Radical Republicans: Lincoln's Vanguard for Racial Justice*. New York: Knopf, 1969.

Reconstruction Acts in the United States (1867–1868)

Between March 1867 and March 1868, the U.S. Congress passed four Reconstruction Acts to facilitate the reentry of the former Confederate states into the Union. The First Reconstruction Act divided the South into five military districts under the command of army generals. The act also subjugated the citizens of those districts to the authority of military courts. The first district was comprised of Virginia; the second of the Carolinas; the third of Georgia, Alabama, and Florida; the fourth of Arkansas and Mississippi; and the fifth of Texas and Louisiana. Tennessee was not part of any district as it had already ratified the Fourteenth Amendment and was considered reconstructed. In addition to establishing military districts, the First Reconstruction Act barred former high-ranking Confederates from holding public office, demanded that states enact new constitutions guaranteeing universal male suffrage regardless of race, and required states to ratify the Fourteenth Amendment. President Andrew Johnson vetoed the bill, but was overridden by Congress. The presidential veto and ensuing congressional override was a pattern that would be upheld for all of the Reconstruction Acts. In response to the passage of the First Reconstruction Act, President Johnson removed Secretary of War Edwin Stanton from office in an attempt to curb the power of the Radical Republicans. However, Stanton was sustained in office by the Tenure of Office Act, and Johnson was impeached and nearly removed for his actions.

Faced with a choice of granting suffrage to former slaves or living under continued military occupation, many Southerners decided they would rather deal with the army than enfranchised African Americans. Recognizing this, Congress waited less than a month before passing the Second Reconstruction Act and giving the military district commanders directions on holding state constitutional conventions. The act proscribed the loyalty oath that was required of former Confederates, established the system for choosing delegates to write the new state constitutions, and laid out the methods and procedures for elections. The federal government was going to make sure the Southern states wrote new constitutions and ratified the Fourteenth Amendment whether they wanted to or not. President Johnson, unhappy with compelling citizens to write a new constitution against their will, interpreted the bill as narrowly as possible.

In July 1867, Congress passed the Third Reconstruction Act, allowing district commanders to remove state officials from office. The act also declared that former U.S. government officials who then served in the Confederate government were not entitled to register to vote, and established who could serve on the voter registration boards and how they would work. In March 1868, the Fourth Reconstruction Act allowed the new state constitutions to be approved by a simple majority vote. By the summer of 1870, all of the former Confederate states had been readmitted to the Union, bringing an end to the necessity of the Reconstruction Acts.

Jared Peatman

See also: Lincoln, Abraham.

Further Reading

Foner, Eric. *Reconstruction: America's Unfinished Revolution, 1863–1877.* New York: Harper & Row, Publishers, 1988.

Republicanism and Antislavery

In their struggle to convince Americans of the necessity of immediate, uncompensated emancipation of slaves without expatriation, and to persuade them of the sinfulness of human enslavement, antebellum abolitionists directly and indirectly invoked the legacy, language, and values of republicanism (as well as those of liberalism and evangelical Christianity). Indeed, to justify their cause, to embolden adherents and inspire converts, and to realize the nation's libertarian pretensions, immediatists often enlisted the past—particularly the memory of the American Revolution—to achieve a more perfect future (and union for that matter). The republican ideological heritage that partly informed abolitionist perceptions of slavery and helped shape abolitionist arguments against slaveholding was distinctive and sophisticated, extending across great amounts of space and time— from classical antiquity, Renaissance Italy, seventeenth- and eighteenth-century England, and Revolutionary America—and embracing such theorists and writers as Niccolo Machiavelli, James Harrington, Algernon Sidney, Thomas Gordon, John Trenchard, and Thomas Jefferson, to name only a few.

Although abolitionists espoused that lineage, they never systematically adhered to a unitary framework of republican thought, nor, for the most part, did their intellectual ancestors. That is, American republicanism, hardly a static concept, has been shaped and reshaped, applied and reapplied, depending on the individual and the context. Indeed, the manner in which abolitionists utilized republican ideas often differed markedly from the usages of their contemporaries—Whig and Democratic politicians, urban laborers, slaveholders, and so on. Yet, despite republicanism's protean nature, certain central tenets nonetheless define that term and distinguish that worldview.

At the epicenter of republicanism was liberty, specifically how best to secure and preserve it. Liberty could mean different things to different people; for Americans, however, liberty referred to traditional rights, such as the ones guaranteed by the state and federal constitutions. To ensure liberty's enjoyment and existence, citizens must restrain their private desires and interests for the sake of the common good and be ever vigilant against plots that might endanger the body politic and jeopardize established freedoms. Should such conspiracies remain undetected, unchecked, or ultimately succeed, tyranny and oppression would assuredly follow (late eighteenth-century colonial American rebels deployed similar rhetoric in defense of independence from England). Because of such ever-present threats, civic-minded republicans were the perpetual sentinels against arbitrary arrangements and encroachments of power. Such responsibilities, at least in the antebellum United States, ceased to be the exclusive domain of property holders—those individuals originally deemed appropriately independent, sufficiently capable of disinterested decision making, and necessarily invested in a republic's proper maintenance. Yet, the democratization of America in the early nineteenth century, particularly the expansion of the suffrage to include all white adult males regardless of land ownership, incorporated greater numbers among the ranks of the productive, responsible, and virtuous citizenry. At about the same time, abolitionists completely undercut newly created racial and gender strictures for republican guardianship that matured during the Jacksonian era—for white male activists embraced not only black men as among those worthy of vigilant citizenship, but also black and white women as crucial participants. (It does not follow, however, that white-male antislavery agitators were without racial prejudices and gender biases.)

According to one historical argument that has asserted the strongest link between republicanism and abolitionism, immediatists believed that slavery "embodied the frightening force of arbitrary power [and] acted as an expansive and conspiratorial menace that smashed all barriers to authority, infected the moral character of a people, created widespread misery, and destroyed the fragile principles of human liberty" (McInerney, 8–9). To be sure, republican-sensitive abolitionists judged human enslavement utterly reprehensible, if only because masters were virtually all powerful and slaves nearly powerless. Such an extreme was a blatant contradiction of basic republican hallmarks, balance and order on the one hand, and self-control and self-determination on the other. And if power corrupted, republican-inspired abolitionists specifically feared the direful consequences that might arise from the absolute power that slave masters wielded.

Yet, when numerous antislavery delegates, primarily from across the North, gathered in Philadelphia in 1833 to establish what became the American Anti-Slavery Society, the national movement that they inaugurated did not originate in counter subversion. That is, at the outset of their campaign, antebellum abolitionists espied anything but a scheming planter oligarchy that, because of its determination to safeguard the "peculiar institution," threatened to subvert the liberty of everyone else. The suppression of traditional civil rights (e.g., the abolitionist postal and petition campaigns of the middle 1830s, the decades-long debates over the status of slavery west of the Mississippi River, and the perceived attempt to seemingly nationalize the institution of slavery (the 1850 Fugitive Slave Law and the proslavery decision in the 1857 Supreme Court case, *Dred Scott v. Sanford*) all unequivocally stirred in abolitionists' republican misgivings. By the time the slave states of the Deep South greeted the election of Republican candidate Abraham Lincoln to the presidency in 1860 with secession from the Union, abolitionists had proven themselves the inveterate foes of what was called the Slave Power and the most outspoken agitators against the conspiracy thought to be waged by a cabal of aggressive and rapacious slaveholders to extend and protect slavery wherever slaveholders might travel or reside.

Indeed, soon after the founding of immediate abolitionism's national organization, antislavery activists confronted violence and endured hostility—in the press, in the streets, and in legislative halls, and against their property, against their persons, and against their basic rights—for nearly three decades before the eruption of sectional military conflagration. Because of the accumulated negative reactions that immediate emancipation intentionally and unintentionally provoked (largely stemming from abolitionist-instigated controversies surrounding the repeated incursions of the slavery issue into the national public and political discourse), abolitionists-cum-republicans were convinced that some malevolent, designing force impeded the emancipation of slaves, wrought havoc on the sanctity of liberty, and prevented the nation's return to founding principles as enshrined in the opening paragraph of the Declaration of Independence, thereby assisting in the republic's desolation and approaching demise. The Civil War, however, allowed for the potential of an appropriately restored republican course, one that extended personal freedoms to and protected the individual liberties of all the country's inhabitants. Such a hope enabled normally nonviolent and anti-war abolitionists to tentatively support the Union cause. Such a hope, moreover, ensured that abolitionists would remain ever vigilant on behalf of the enslaved, as they continually agitated for stronger antislavery measures from the Republican-controlled Congress and Executive.

Raymond James Krohn

See also: Democratic Party and Antislavery; Slave Power Argument; Whig Party and Antislavery.

Further Readings

McInerney, Daniel J. *The Fortunate Heirs of Freedom: Abolition and Republican Thought.* Lincoln: University of Nebraska Press, 1994.
Rodgers, Daniel T. "Republicanism: The Career of a Concept." *The Journal of American History* 79, 1 (June 1992): 11–38.

Ruggles, David

David Ruggles was a prominent African American abolitionist, publisher, and bookseller. He was born in Norwich, Connecticut, on March 15, 1810, the first of eight children of David and Nancy Ruggles, a free black couple. David, Sr., was a blacksmith; his wife Nancy was a locally famous cook and caterer. Ruggles spent his early years in the family home in an old tenement located on a tiny triangular plot just off the main road in Bean Hill, a prosperous rural neighborhood of Norwich. Though his parents were members of the Methodist Church, David was educated at a charity school operated by the First Congregational Church. In his teens, he worked as a mariner on coastal vessels. At seventeen, he left home, moved to New York City and opened a grocery store on Courtland Street. Initially he sold alcohol, but soon announced his conversion to temperance in an advertisement in the *Freedom's Journal*, the newspaper of black New Yorkers.

Ruggles became active in the local antislavery and anticolonization movement. By the early 1830s, he employed self-emancipated slaves in his grocery. In 1833, he abandoned the store to concentrate on antislavery work as an agent for the *Emancipator*. He traveled around New England and the Mid-Atlantic states, making speeches, honing his ideas, and making valuable contacts. He attended the National Conventions of Colored Peoples in Philadelphia and New York City and was a founding member of the Phoenix Society of New York, the Garrison Literary and Benevolent Association, and the New York Temperance Society, groups that combined reform, education, and antislavery. He opened the nation's first African American bookstore and lending library at his home at 67 Lispenard Street in New York City and operated it until a mob destroyed it in late 1835. In 1834,

Ruggles published his first pamphlet, the anticolonization satire, *Extinguisher Extinguished . . . Or David M. Reese, M.D. Used Up*. In this pamphlet and an 1838 piece entitled *An Antidote for the Furious Combination*, he attacked Dr. David M. Reese, a prominent doctor and proponent of colonization policies. In 1835, Ruggles published the Abrogation of the Seventh Commandment, on his own press, another black first. This pamphlet appealed to the nascent feminist movement to shun Southern wives and daughters of slave masters. Ruggles began to write dozens of letters to the editors of abolitionist and other newspapers, extolling the value of education and antislavery journalism.

Ruggles began working with local abolitionists, Barney Corse and Isaac Hopper, to counteract the illicit slave trade, kidnappings of free blacks, and capture of self-emancipated slaves in New York City. Working with them or by himself, Ruggles took part in highly publicized arrests of sea captains smuggling slaves in New Bedford, Massachusetts, and New York City. He also routinely boarded vessels in New York harbor or entered private homes in search of blacks held unlawfully by masters and mistresses. In 1835, Ruggles formalized such activities by organizing the New York Vigilance Committee. Over the next few years, the committee enabled hundreds of blacks including Frederick Douglass to avoid arrest and help them to freedom and work in New England or Canada.

Ruggles worked equally with whites and blacks. Between 1838 and 1841 he chronicled his activities in the *Mirror of Liberty*, the nation's first black magazine. He also published an annual report of the vigilance society. In 1839, his fervor proved his undoing. A successful suit for libel brought against Ruggles and Samuel Eli Cornish, the editor of the *Colored American,* threatened to bankrupt the newspaper. Ruggles had made hasty claims that a local black boarding house keeper was hiding slaves. Ruggles and Cornish parted ways over the suit; accompanying audits of the vigilance society revealed unexplained deficits attributed to Ruggles's careless bookkeeping. Alienated, broken in health (he suffered from declining sight, stomach ailments, and other diseases), Ruggles fought his old colleague Cornish bitterly for two years before quitting New York.

After a fund-raising tour of New England where many black organizations feted him for his courage, Ruggles showed his old grit in 1841 by refusing to move to the segregated cars on a railroad between New Bedford and Boston, Massachusetts. Tossed off the train, Ruggles suffered more injuries. This injustice sparked numerous protests, including attempts by William Lloyd Garrison and the newly famous Douglass to integrate the trains. Ruggles meanwhile had settled at the Northampton (Massachusetts) Association of Education and Industry, a communitarian society formed by abolitionists. There he mended his body, though he eventually lost his sight. He continued his work on the Underground Railroad. Ruggles studied hydrotherapy and opened first a clinic and later a hospital where he treated and cured patients ranging from Sojourner Truth to the wife of a Southern slaveholder. By the late 1840s, Ruggles was a respected practitioner and was on the cusp of expanding his business when he died on December 16, 1849, of a severe bowel inflammation.

Graham Russell Gao Hodges

See also: Underground Railroad.

Further Readings

Hodges, Graham Russell Gao. *David Ruggles: A Radical Black Abolitionist and the Underground Railroad in New York City*. Chapel Hill: University of North Carolina, 2012.
Hodges, Graham Russell Gao. "David Ruggles: The Hazards of Anti-Slavery Journalism." *Media Studies* (Summer 2000): 11–18.

Rush, Benjamin

A famed physician, statesman, and reformer, Benjamin Rush was also one of the leading abolitionists of the early national period. A native of Pennsylvania, Rush was an active member of the Pennsylvania Society for Promoting the Abolition of Slavery (best known as the Pennsylvania Abolition Society), the world's leading abolitionist organization before the 1830s and based in Rush's longtime home of Philadelphia. Rush served as secretary of the group (1787–1789) and worked on various abolitionist committees during his life. He corresponded with leading abolitionists in America and England and served as a delegate to the American Convention of Abolition Societies several times during the 1790s. Like other members of the Pennsylvania Abolition Society, Rush advocated gradual emancipation and supported Pennsylvania's 1780 law guaranteeing enslaved blacks born after that date freedom at the age of twenty-eight.

Years before this, Rush had authored one of the first broad attacks on slavery and the slave trade in the American colonies, a 1773 essay entitled "An Address to the Inhabitants of the British Settlements in America, Upon Slave-Keeping." Rush was also a patron of free blacks in post-revolutionary Philadelphia, helping to raise money for the first autonomous free black churches. Although some of his racial pronouncements sound odd to modern ears—Rush once argued that African Americans suffered from a form of leprosy, which accounted for their darker pigmentation—he was also part of an antislavery vanguard in late eighteenth-century transatlantic culture, which not only envisioned slavery as a moral wrong, but abolitionism as a practical good. Ironically, but not unlike some members of first-generation abolition societies in both New York and Virginia, Rush owned at least one enslaved person during his life.

Richard Newman

See also: American Convention of Abolition Societies; Jefferson, Thomas and Antislavery.

Further Readings

Brodsky, Alfred. *Benjamin Rush: Patriot and Physician.* New York: Truman Talley Books, 2004.
Nash, Gary B. *Race and Revolution.* Madison, WI: Madison House, 1990.

S

Secession Crisis and Abolitionists

Between Abraham Lincoln's election on November 6, 1860, and the attack on Fort Sumter in mid-April 1861, seven Southern states left the Union, and four more would join them in the spring and early summer, making up the Confederate States of America. For many Southerners, particularly slaveholders, this moment was the culmination of a long, tortuous process of anxious negotiation. By balancing a desire for independence with an attention to the fragile regional unity that created the Confederacy, Southerners built a society on the understanding that slavery was right and just, and that the white man was intended by Scripture and nature to rule over the black.

Several moments in earlier decades of the nineteenth century suggested that secession might be an option that would allow Southerners to protect slavery. During one of the first options—South Carolina's 1832 Nullification Controversy with the federal government—the citizens of the state proved unwilling to declare independence. By the 1850s, what had earlier seemed a dim possibility became a growing reality. The efforts of Northern abolitionists by then were important to the development of a common perception among many Southerners that secession was the only option for protecting slavery, their key labor source. Important turning points were the eruption in Kansas of a bloody conflict between slaveholders and Free Soilers in the mid-1850s and John Brown's raid into Harpers Ferry, Virginia, in 1859. Events in Kansas showed Southerners the lengths to which abolitionists were willing to go to thwart the slaveholder's right to human property. Brown's raid in 1859 exposed the efforts of a few radical abolitionists to topple slaveholder power by storming a military battery and potentially spurring slaves into rebellion.

Though these incidents proved especially powerful in setting Southern opinion in favor of secession, it was Lincoln's election that proved the central catalyst. Secessionist "fire eaters" painted a picture of manipulation and abolitionist control of the central government that they elaborated into an 1860 campaign filled with images of racial mixing, intermarriage, and the overturn of white supremacy.

"Black Republican" became a watchword for a national political party firmly in the control of a radical group bent on the destruction of the South. Despite the Republicans' best efforts to show that a Lincoln administration would check the growth of slavery in western territories, and not the institution's eradication, most Southern slaveholders fervently believed that any attempt to abrogate their right to own slaves would propel the South into a subservient position to the industrializing North. However, as each Southern state deliberated on its future, deep and important divisions emerged which threatened a new Southern nation from the beginning. Secession in Mississippi and Alabama passed, respectively, on January 9 and 11, 1861, but not before exposing divisions between slaveholding southern counties and non-slaveholding northern counties in each state. Georgia seceded from the Union on January 19, 1861, but not before a protracted deliberation that revealed the fragility of slaveholder control over politics in the state; non-slaveholding counties which had long supported the Democratic Party shifted their support in the secession election against slaveholders who wished to join the Confederacy, creating anxiety among secession leaders that they were losing an assumed base of support. There were also constant concerns in the Deep South over the loyalties of the Upper South. Virginia, Arkansas, North Carolina, Tennessee, and Kentucky were all initially cool to secession, but the Confederate attack on Fort Sumter on April 14, 1861, and Lincoln's call for 75,000 troops the following day to put down the Southern "insurrection," brought all the reluctant states, save for Kentucky, into the Confederacy by the following June.

Erik Mathisen

See also: Bleeding Kansas; Radical Republicans.

Further Readings

Barney, William. *The Secessionist Impulse: Alabama and Mississippi in 1860*. Princeton, NJ: Princeton University Press, 1974.

Crofts, Daniel W. *Reluctant Confederates: Upper South Unionists in the Secession Crisis*. Chapel Hill: University of North Carolina Press, 1989.

Johnson, Michael. *Toward a Patriarchal Republic: The Secession of Georgia*. Baton Rouge: Louisiana State University Press, 1977.

Potter, David M. *The Impending Crisis, 1848–1861*. Completed by Don E. Fehrenbacher. New York: Harper & Row, 1976.

Secret Six

"The Secret Six" were the six Northern abolitionists who helped to finance John Brown's antislavery violence in Kansas and his raid on the federal arsenal at Harpers Ferry, Virginia, in October 1859. They comprised Thomas Wentworth Higginson,

Samuel Gridley Howe, Theodore Parker, Franklin Sanborn, Gerrit Smith, and George Luther Stearns. Their identities became public after the failed raid at Harpers Ferry, when federal troops discovered papers abandoned by several of Brown's cohorts in a farmhouse near Harpers Ferry. Two of the men, Howe and Stearns, appeared before a U.S. Senate committee, chaired by Senator James Mason of Virginia, that investigated the raid at Harpers Ferry. The committee failed to prove decisively that Howe and Stearns had advance knowledge of Brown's plans.

"The Secret Six" were fortunate the Mason Committee was unable to link them in any conclusive way to Brown's raid, because their support was incontrovertible. They had raised money for Brown from contacts within their social and ideological circles, given him money themselves, hosted him in their homes, introduced him to local notables such as Ralph Waldo Emerson and Henry David Thoreau, and shipped rifles to him in Kansas. Two of the six, Higginson and Smith, were fanatical in their support of Brown's violent attacks on slaveholders and their followers. Higginson would go on to lead a regiment of African American soldiers in the Union Army during the Civil War.

These men who became the "Secret Six" were pillars of their communities. They were the descendants of some of the most prominent families in the northeastern United States. Higginson, who had begun studies at Harvard at age thirteen, was a well-respected author, editor, and minister, who also supported disunion abolitionism in the 1850s. He believed that the Constitution was a proslavery document, and believed that slavery had corrupted American politics. The best thing that could happen would be a separation of North and South. Howe was a medical doctor whose wife, Julia Ward Howe, would gain fame for writing the "Battle Hymn of the Republic" during the Civil War. This song was based on "John Brown's Body," a song written to commemorate Brown's execution by Virginia authorities and which helped him achieve martyr status in many parts of the North. Howe's relatives had participated in major events in the American Revolution, such as the Boston Tea Party and the building of fortifications for the Battle of Bunker Hill. Howe had also supported republican revolutions in Greece, France, and Prussia in the late 1820s and early 1830s.

Sanborn instructed the sons of prominent families from both North and South at his school. Some of his students, in fact, prevented federal marshals from seizing Sanborn in a late night raid. They sought to bring him to Washington to testify before the Mason Committee. Not surprisingly, parents of Southern boys withdrew their sons from his school as sectional tensions escalated after Brown's raid and the revelation of Sanborn's involvement. Parker was a well-respected Unitarian minister whose failing health forced him to leave the United States before Brown's raid. Parker died in Florence, Italy, on May 10, 1860, roughly six months after the raid on the federal arsenal. Smith was a wealthy landowner who lived near Syracuse, New York. He had supported Frederick Douglass's newspaper, the *North Star*, and had set aside 120,000 acres of land in upstate New York, near Lake Placid, for black freedmen. Smith also was one of the founders of the Liberty Party in 1840, a party that promoted abolition and ran candidates on its antislavery ticket.

Members of the "Secret Six" became radicalized by two important events of the 1850s, the passage of the Fugitive Slave Law of 1850 and the Kansas-Nebraska Act of 1854. Gerrit Smith led an armed rescue of a fugitive slave, Jerry McHenry, from a Syracuse jail in the autumn of 1852. Thomas Wentworth Higginson led a raid that attempted, but failed, to free a fugitive slave, Anthony Burns, from prison in Boston in 1854. Higginson and Parker condemned the Fugitive Slave Law in sermons, while George Luther Stearns, who was a wealthy businessman, joined the antislavery effort because the same law was anathema to him.

The Kansas-Nebraska Act of 1854 led to the overturning of the Missouri Compromise of 1820, which had banned slavery north of 36° 30', with the exception of Missouri. The 1854 act allowed settlers to decide if slavery would exist in the two new territories. Wealthy men from Boston established the New England Emigrant Aid Company to help settlers move west and populate Kansas with enough free-state settlers to gain control of the territory and form a government opposed to slavery. When "border ruffians" from Missouri began raiding free-state settlements, Parker began buying guns and bullets for the migrants from New England.

Their hatred of slavery, the "Slave Power," and the perceived injustice of the Fugitive Slave Law, led the "Secret Six" to support John Brown. He was a man willing to wage war on slavery, as he proved in Kansas, most notoriously in the Pottawatomie Creek massacre in 1856, and he believed that he could launch a massive slave rebellion in the valley of northwestern Virginia. The idea of provoking civil war between North and South appealed to members of the "Secret Six," especially Smith and Higginson. Not all of the six believed this idea was prudent, a sentiment shared by Frederick Douglass. None of the six abolitionists faced prosecution for their actions, though they suffered ignominy from their conservative friends and associates for a time. Some of the six, such as Sanborn, continued to defend Brown from critics for as long as he lived. The episode of the "Secret Six" revealed the depth of passion aroused by slavery and the events of the 1850s.

James C. Foley

See also: Bleeding Kansas; Jerry Rescue (1851).

Further Readings

Renehan, Edward J. Jr. *The Secret Six: The True Tale of the Men Who Conspired with John Brown.* New York: Crown Publishers, Inc., 1995.

Reynolds, David S. *John Brown, Abolitionist: The Man Who Killed Slavery, Sparked the Civil War, and Seeded Civil Rights.* New York: Alfred A. Knopf, 2005.

Slave Narratives

Slave narratives were autobiographies written by ex-slaves. There were two major periods in which slave narratives were published, 1760–1807 and 1831–1865. During the initial period, slave narratives described the authors' lives as slaves. In the later period, authors provided more brutal descriptions of slavery, overtly agitating for the abolition of slavery.

In the early period, slave narratives were part of the larger genre of colonial autobiography and narrated the adventures of Africans who became enslaved. Authors portrayed slavery as the absence of physical freedom, with the dehumanizing elements of slavery rarely emphasized. Rather, the focus was on the protagonist who usually assimilated into Western culture and converted to Christianity, with freedom offered as a reward. Some of the most noteworthy examples of this genre are Venture Smith, *A Narrative of the Life and Adventures of Venture, a Native of Africa* (1798); Boston King, *Memoirs of the Life of Boston King, a Black Preacher* (1798); Quobna Ottobah Cugoano, *Thoughts and Sentiments on the Evil and Wicked Traffic of the Slavery . . .* (1787); and Olaudah Equiano, *The Interesting Narrative of the Life of Olaudah Equiano, or Gustavus Vassa, the African* (1789).

While a handful of slave narratives appeared in the early decades of the nineteenth century, the growth of the American abolitionist movement in the 1830s renewed interest in publishing slave narratives. White abolitionists understood that slave narratives could serve as a powerful propaganda tool for their cause. Often ex-slaves were aided by sympathetic abolitionist editors in writing their autobiographies. Many narratives also included testimonials about the author, generally written by white abolitionists or ministers, to authenticate the author's good character and the truth of his story. With slavery becoming increasingly controversial during the antebellum period, many Northern whites became interested in the lives of slaves. Reflecting the power of these firsthand accounts of slavery, several slave narratives went through multiple editions.

Antebellum slave narratives provided much more graphic descriptions of slavery than their eighteenth-century counterparts. The physical hardship and brutality of slavery were narrated in detail. The emotional, intellectual, and spiritual deprivations were also provided, revealing the human side of the slave experience. Many of the most popular slave narratives, such as Frederick Douglass's *Narrative of the Life of Frederick Douglass, an American Slave* and Harriet Jacobs's *Incidents in the Life of a Slave Girl*, emphasized the authors' pursuit of individual freedom and their perseverance through slavery, gross exploitation, and the dangerous flight to freedom. Slave narratives often adopted the sensational and sentimental literary styles of the nineteenth-century United States. To speak effectively to a highly religious audience, the religious contradictions of slavery were also exposed.

While slave narratives have been extremely useful to historians because of their firsthand accounts of slavery, they are not fully representative of the antebellum slave experience. Less than 15 percent of the antebellum slave narratives were written by women, and most of the slave narratives describe slavery in the Upper South, leaving few accounts of slavery in the Lower South. In their ability to escape from slavery and subsequently write perceptively about it, the authors of slave narratives were also exceptional and, not infrequently, privileged slaves with the occupational and geographical mobility to enhance success at flight.

Daniel P. Kotzin

See also: Douglass, Frederick (1818–1895); Equiano, Olaudah.

Further Readings

Davis, Charles T., and Henry Louis Gates Jr., eds. *The Slave's Narrative*. New York: Oxford University Press, 1985.

Foster, Francis Smith. *Witnessing Slavery: The Development of Antebellum Slave Narratives*. Madison: University of Wisconsin Press, 1979.

Slave Power Argument

The three-fifths clause in the U.S. Constitution called for three-fifths of the Southern slave population to count in the total population of the slave states, both for tax purposes and for representation in the U.S. House of Representatives, and therefore in the electoral college as well. Thus, the slave states increased their representation in Congress; in fact, they continuously had one-third more seats than if only their free populations had counted for representative purposes. In 1793, the slave states (not including those Northern states such as New Jersey and New York that enacted plans of gradual emancipation after 1793) had forty-seven seats as opposed to the thirty-three that their free population warranted. In 1812, they had seventy-six instead of fifty-nine, and in 1833, they had ninety-eight instead of seventy-three. This inflated representation for proslavery Southerners formed the basis of the Slave Power.

Due to their inflated congressional representation and incredible unity, the slave states needed only to sway a few Northern voters in order to enact their policies in the House of Representatives, while the balance of free and slave states meant only one Northern vote was necessary for the Slave Power to succeed in the Senate. This magnified representation also helped in presidential elections, as it was only necessary for a Southern candidate to carry a small portion of the Northern electoral votes to win the election. With the exception of the two single-term Adams presidencies, from 1797 to 1801 and from 1825 to 1829, the president hailed from a slave state for the entire first half of the nineteenth century. Therefore, between the election of George Washington and Abraham Lincoln, at least nineteen of the thirty-four appointees to the Supreme Court were slaveholders. Due to this power, a string of proslavery laws and court decisions were put into effect. For example, the Slave Power defeated the Tallmadge Amendment to the Missouri statehood bill in 1819, which proposed banning the further introduction of slavery into Missouri and gradual emancipation to manumit slaves born there. The Slave Power also crushed the Wilmot Proviso, which proposed banning slavery in all territory taken from Mexico. The same forces were behind the admission of Texas into the Union as a slave state, the Fugitive Slave Law, and the Kansas-Nebraska Act that repealed the Missouri Compromise. The Taney Court's 1857 *Dred Scott* decision—which ruled against the power of Congress to regulate slavery in the territories—was decided by a staunchly pro-South Court. These laws and decisions greatly alarmed antislavery Northerners. Concerned about this slave oligarchy extending slavery at the expense of the rights and liberty of Northern whites, antislavery fervor increased, culminating with the rise of the Republican Party in the North. The Whig Party disintegrated, and the Northern Democrats sustained irreparable damage. Increasing numbers of immigrants had substantially swung the representative balance of power back to the North, so with the elections of 1858 and 1860, the Republicans seized control of Congress and the White House, crushing the Slave Power.

John French

See also: Adams, John Quincy; Democratic Party and Antislavery; Radical Republicans; Texas, Annexation of (1845); Whig Party and Antislavery.

Further Readings

Gara, Larry. "Slavery and the Slave Power: A Crucial Distinction." In John R. McKivigan, ed. *History of the American Abolitionist Movement*. New York: Garland Publishing, Inc., 1999, pp. 203–217.

Richards, Leonard L. *The Slave Power: The Free North and Southern Domination, 1780–1860*. Baton Rouge: Louisiana State University Press, 2000.

Smith, Gerrit

Among the most renowned abolitionists and nineteenth-century philanthropists, Gerrit Smith devoted his life and most of his great wealth to the cause of equal rights for all men and women. Over a twenty-year period, from 1838 until the Civil War, the immediate abolition of every sin was his most passionate desire, and he went to great lengths to effect it. Smith, along with his close friend, John Brown, was virtually unique among white reformers in his efforts to overcome enormous

Philanthropist and reformer Gerrit Smith was involved in such nineteenth-century reform movements as temperance, dress reform, women's suffrage, and vegetarianism, but he made his greatest contribution as an abolitionist. (Library of Congress)

class and racial barriers and to establish close affinities with other blacks. But following John Brown's raid on Harpers Ferry in 1859, Smith suffered a crisis of faith that resulted in his support for more conservative reform measures during the Civil War and Reconstruction; he supported Lincoln and the Republican Party, emphasized the suppression of the Rebellion over emancipation, and after the war advocated clemency to former rebels.

Smith was born in Utica, New York, on March 6, 1797, into one of the wealthiest families in the country. In 1806, his parents, Peter and Elizabeth Livingston Smith, moved the family to Peterboro, a village they founded in Madison County, part of the "Burned-Over District" of western New York, where Gerrit lived for the rest of his life. As a young patriarch, Smith had visions of becoming a man of letters, an eminent lawyer, a respected minister, or a statesman. But immediately after graduating as valedictorian from Hamilton College in 1818, a series of incidents occurred which precipitated his turn to reform work including the death of his mother, the death of his new bride, and the retirement of his father, who requested that Gerrit manage his vast property concerns. In little more than a year after reaching "manhood," he found himself back in the family mansion house overlooking the village green of Peterboro, bound to his ledger books and land office, with his dreams shattered and the two most important people in his life dead.

In 1823, he married Ann Carroll Fitzhugh Smith, a cousin of George Fitzhugh and a fervent evangelical. She was instrumental in fueling her husband's religious zeal and spawning his vision of a broad sacralization of the world. He soon became an avid temperance reformer, and in 1827 he joined the American

Colonization Society, whose efforts to colonize blacks in Africa represented for him the most effective way to bring about gradual emancipation and an end to the degradation of free blacks. His complete break with colonization and whole-hearted embrace of immediate abolition occurred in 1837, and it corresponded to a fundamental shift in the source of his values; he became a self-described "outsider" and "fanatic," rejected existing social conventions and authority, and turned inward by affirming his spiritual instincts and passions of the "heart." His belief in the preservation of the social order and distinct hierarchies—values on which the principles of colonization were based—had crumbled. This profound shift was due in part to the Panic of 1837, which brought him to the brink of bankruptcy; to the deaths of two children, one in 1835 and the other in 1836; and to his newfound reliance on "sacred self-sovereignty."

One of the most important applications of Smith's religious vision was his re-interpretation of the Golden Rule as empathy. He continually sought to participate in the feelings and sufferings of his black brethren and to see himself as a black man. "To recognize in every man my brother—ay, another self" was his wish, and he often described his efforts "to make myself a colored man." His empathic awareness and black identification had tangible results: He was instrumental in turning Madison County into the most fervent abolition county in the country; his own village of Peterboro, which the black leader Henry Highland Garnet likened to "heaven," became an antebellum model of interracial harmony; and in 1846, he gave to each of some 3,000 poor blacks from New York roughly fifty acres of land in the Adirondacks (where John Brown eventually settled) as a way for them to attain the franchise, become self-sufficient, and remain isolated from the virulent racism in the cities. Black leaders throughout the North, from Garnet and Frederick Douglass to James McCune Smith and Samuel Ringgold Ward, became respected friends and allies; and the black abolitionist paper, the *Ram's Horn*, went so far as to say, "Gerrit Smith is a colored man!"

Smith's radical reform efforts from 1840 to the Civil War closely paralleled those of black leaders in New York, who overwhelmingly embraced political abolitionism and lost patience with peaceful means of abolishing slavery, especially following the Fugitive Slave Law of 1850. Smith helped found the Liberty Party in 1840, which interpreted the Constitution as an antislavery document, and in 1852 he was elected to the House of Representatives on an abolition ticket that advocated immediate abolition, universal suffrage for men and women, and land grants to the landless. He never completed his term in Congress, however. Immediately following the passage of the Kansas-Nebraska Act in 1854, Smith resigned out of disgust with Congress and the white laws perpetuating slavery, and became a revolutionary. The tension between his boundless reform visions and the present, sinful reality had reached a breaking point; he began to see himself as a prophet and accepted blood atonement as a necessary means for vanquishing the forces of evil. He donated over $16,000 in "emigrant aid" that sent fighting men and munitions to "save" Kansas from slavery; and he became a lead conspirator in John Brown's efforts to liberate slaves that culminated with the attack on the federal arsenal at Harpers Ferry in October 1859.

The Harpers Ferry raid profoundly affected Smith's world views and reform visions. He was the only conspirator who, in the aftermath of the raid, considered it wrong and experienced profound guilt over his participation in it. He believed himself culpable for all the lives lost in the incursion, and suffered a complete, but brief, emotional collapse. Following his recovery in early 1860, he distanced himself from blacks, and viewed his black identification and close friendship with blacks, as well as his acceptance of prophecy belief and blood atonement, as the dark sources of violence. In May 1860, he acknowledged that "much of the year 1859," his most active period of pursuing violent remedies for ending slavery, was "a black dream," and he described the link between his black identification and his descent to violence in a short story called "The Ruinous Visit to Monkeyville." He never again identified so closely with blacks, became considerably more moderate in his reform efforts, and for the rest of his life denied his complicity in the Harpers Ferry raid. Before the Civil War officially began, Smith became a casualty in his own civil war, and he lost faith in the power of empathy and sacred self-sovereignty.

Shortly after the election of 1860, Smith began to support Abraham Lincoln and the Republican administration. Although he was himself nominated for president on a radical abolition ticket, he did not take his candidacy seriously, and felt that Lincoln was "in his heart an abolitionist." As the Southern states seceded, he advocated the compromise measures of a lower tariff and compensated emancipation to lure the South back into the Union without bloodshed. But following the firing on Fort Sumter, he fervently embraced the war efforts of the administration to "put down the Rebellion," and believed that its suppression would be the means for ending slavery. The war had dissolved all party distinctions, he argued, and he viewed all Northerners as either Unionists or disloyal Rebels who must be crushed: "We are assembled . . . not as Republicans, nor Democrats, nor Abolitionists—but as Americans," he said in the first of many speeches to raise money and troops for the war effort; "we are all on the side of the Government," which "must be upheld at whatever expense to friend or foe." The Rebellion was "simply slavery in arms."

Smith's primary role in the war was to lend his support to the Lincoln administration by urging unified support to the Union cause. He published numerous speeches to this effect, and campaigned for Lincoln in 1864. He spent over $10,000 of his own money and raised thousands more for troops, equipment, and the relief of afflicted families, and he urged a stiff income tax on the wealthy to help fund the war. For the first time since becoming a radical abolitionist in 1838, he was no longer considered an "outsider" and "fanatic," but a respected, though eccentric, elder statesman.

Smith's attitude toward the use of black troops highlights the enormous shift that occurred in his attitude toward blacks following the Harpers Ferry raid. He urged black participation as early as August 1861, but primarily as a tactical measure: "The party that gets the blacks to fight for it gets the victory." Although he believed that arming blacks would facilitate the cause of equal rights, in 1863 he also compared blacks (and Indians) to devils and suggested that putting "down a base, brutal, abominable, causeless, accursed Rebellion" required the use of dark-skinned, base, and brutal savages: "Common-sense teaches us that we should get the negro to help us if we can; and the Indian also if we can; and the devil himself if we can. I would that we could succeed in getting our harness upon his back and in making him work for us. It would by the way, be doing a great favor to the old rascal to make him serve a good cause once in his life." While he never abandoned his quest for equal rights, he now considered blacks to be potentially dangerous and by nature less civilized than whites. His first utterance that betrayed a belief in the prevailing pseudo-scientific arguments for innate black inferiority occurred in late 1861, when he admitted, "were the laws of nature allowed free play, the dark-skinned races would find their homes within and the light-skinned races without the tropics." Simultaneously he renewed his faith in colonization—after having denounced it for twenty years as inherently racist—as the most effective way to solve the race problem, so long as the decision to colonize rested with blacks themselves.

As Smith moved into the mainstream role of elder statesman and "insider," his racial views became increasingly conservative, and his position during Reconstruction was one of moderation. Initially he refused to support the Thirteenth Amendment because of his long-held belief that the Constitution was already an antislavery document and because he felt it would detract from the war effort, but he eventually endorsed it. Similarly, he initially advocated literacy as a condition of voting for both blacks and whites before accepting universal black suffrage. Throughout Reconstruction he sought amnesty for rebels, and in 1867, he alienated himself from most Northern radicals by signing Jefferson Davis's bail bond—along with mainstream leaders Horace Greeley and Cornelius Vanderbilt.

Smith's declension from his perfectionist vision and close identification with blacks in the 1840s and 1850s did not go unnoticed by black leaders. His correspondence with them, which surpassed that of all other white reformers combined before the war, waned considerably following Harpers Ferry. Some former friends and allies harshly rebuked him; the black physician and intellectual, James McCune Smith, began criticizing Gerrit as early as August 1861: "I charge you . . . with being unequal to the exigency of the hour. After lives spent in signal devotion to the cause of the slave you fairly abandon that cause in the hour of its trial and triumph." But black leaders never forgot the great lengths Smith went to for the cause of equal rights in the twenty years before the war. In 1873, a year before Gerrit's death, Henry Highland Garnet summed up the feelings of many black reformers by saying: "Among the hosts of great defenders of man's fights who in years past fought so gallantly for equal rights for all men," Smith was "the most affectionately remembered and loved."

John Stauffer

See also: Bleeding Kansas; Radical Republicans.

Further Reading

Stauffer, John, *The Black Hearts of Men: Radical Abolitionists and the Transformation of Race.* Cambridge, MA: Harvard University Press, 2002.

Smith, James McCune

James McCune Smith, black abolitionist and physician, was born in New York City, the son of slaves. All that is known of his parents is that his mother was, in his words, "a self-emancipated bond-woman." His own liberty came on July 4, 1827, when the Emancipation Act of the state of New York officially freed its remaining slaves. Smith was fourteen at the time, a student at the African Free School no. 2, and he greeted the day as a "real full-souled, full-voiced shouting for joy" that brought him from "the gloom of midnight" into "the joyful light of day." He graduated with honors from the African Free School, but was denied admission from Columbia College and Geneva, New York medical schools on account of his race. With assistance from the black minister Peter Williams Jr., he entered the University of Glasgow, Scotland in 1832, at the age of nineteen, and earned the degrees of B.A. (1835), M.A. (1836), and M.D. (1837). He returned to America in 1837 as the first professionally trained black physician in the country.

Smith resettled in New York City, married Malvina Barnett, who bore him five children, and established himself as a successful physician. He set up practice in Manhattan as a surgeon and general practitioner for both blacks and whites, became the staff physician for the New York Colored Orphan Asylum, and opened a pharmacy on West Broadway, one of the first in the country owned by a black.

It was his activities as a radical abolitionist and reformer, however, that secured his reputation as one of the leading black intellectuals of the antebellum era. As soon as he returned to America, he became an active member of the American Anti-Slavery Society, which sought immediate abolition by morally persuading slaveholders to renounce the sin of slavery and emancipate their slaves. By the late

1840s, he had abandoned the policies of nonresistance and non-voting set forth by William Lloyd Garrison and his followers in the Society, for political abolitionism, which interpreted the Constitution as an antislavery document and advocated political, and ultimately violent, intervention to end slavery. In 1846, Smith championed the campaign for unrestricted black suffrage in New York state; that same year he became an associate and good friend of Gerrit Smith, a wealthy white abolitionist and philanthropist, and served as one of three black administrators for his friend's donation of roughly fifty acres to each of some 3,000 New York blacks on a vast tract of land in the Adirondacks. He became affiliated with the Liberty Party in the late 1840s, which was devoted to immediate and unconditional emancipation, unrestricted suffrage for all men and women, and land reform. In 1855, he helped found the New York City Abolition Society, which was organized, as he put it, "to Abolish Slavery by means of the Constitution; *or otherwise*," by which he meant violent intervention in the event that peaceful efforts failed (though there is no indication that he resorted to violence). When the Radical Abolition Party, the successor to the Liberty Party, nominated him for New York Secretary of State in 1857, he became the first black in the country to run for a political office.

In his writings Smith was a central force in helping to shape and give direction to the black abolition movement. He contributed frequently to the *Weekly Anglo-African* and the *Anglo African Magazine*, and wrote a semi-regular column for *Frederick Douglass' Paper* under the pseudonym "Communipaw," an Indian name that referred to a charmed and honored black settlement in Jersey City, New Jersey. He also wrote the introduction to Douglass's 1855 autobiography, *My Bondage My Freedom*, and he often expressed his wish that Douglass relocate his paper from Rochester to New York City. Douglass considered Smith the "foremost" black leader to have influenced his reform vision.

Smith's writings focused primarily on black education and self-help, citizenship, and the fight against racism; and these themes represented for him the most effective means through which to end slavery and effect full legal and civil rights. He was a life-long opponent of attempts among whites to colonize blacks in Liberia and elsewhere, and a harsh critic of black nationalists who, beginning in the 1850s, encouraged emigration to Haiti and West Africa rather than continuing to fight for citizenship and equal rights. Although he defended integration, he also encouraged blacks to establish their own presses, initiatives, and organizations. "It is emphatically our battle," he wrote in 1855. "Others may aid and assist if they will, but the moving power rests with us." His embrace of black self-reliance in the late 1840s paralleled his departure from Garrisonian doctrines and the American Anti-Slavery Society, which largely ignored black oppression in the North—even among abolitionists—by focusing on the evils of slavery in the South. Black education in particular, he concluded, led directly to self-reliance and moral uplift, and these values in turn provided the most powerful critique against racism. He called the schoolhouse the "great caste abolisher," and vowed to "fling whatever I have into the cause of colored children, that they may be better and more thoroughly taught than their parents are."

The racist belief in innate black inferiority was for Smith the single greatest and most insidious obstacle to equality. In 1846, he became despondent over the racial "hate deeper than I had imagined" among the vast majority of whites; fourteen years later he continued to lament that "our white countrymen do not know us"; "they are strangers to our characters, ignorant of our capacity, oblivious to our history." He hoped his own distinguished career and writings would serve as both a role model for uneducated blacks and as a powerful rebuttal against racist attacks. And as a black physician he was uniquely suited to combat the pseudo-scientific theories of innate black inferiority. In two important and brilliantly argued essays—"Civilization" (1844) and "On the Fourteenth Query of Thomas Jefferson's Notes on Virginia" (1859)—he incorporated his extensive knowledge of biology and anatomy to directly refute scientific arguments of innate black inferiority.

The driving force behind Smith's reform vision and sustained hope for equality was his supreme "confidence in God, that firm reliance in the saving power of the Redeemer's Love." Much like other radical abolitionists such as Douglass and Gerrit Smith, he viewed the abolition movement and the Civil War in millennialist terms; slavery and black oppression were the most egregious of a plethora of sins ranging from tobacco and alcohol to apathy and laziness that needed to be abolished in order to pave the way for a sacred society governed by "Bible Politics," as he envisioned God's eventual reign on earth. He strove to follow his Savior's example by embracing the doctrine of "equal love to all mankind" and at the same time remaining humble before Him; he likened himself to "a coral insect . . . loving to work beneath the tide in a superstructure, that some day when the labourer is long dead and forgotten, may rear itself above the waves and afford rest and habitation for the creatures of his Good, Good Father of All." Following his death in 1865 from heart failure, his writings and memories remained a powerful source of inspiration, "rest and habitation" to future generations of reformers.

John Stauffer

See also: Liberty Party.

Further Readings

Blight, David W. "In Search of Learning, Liberty, and Self Definition: James McCune Smith and the Ordeal of the Antebellum Black Intellectual." *Afro-Americans in New York Life and History* 9, 2 (July 1985): 7–25.

Dain, Bruce. *A Hideous Monster of the Mind: American Race Theory in the Early Republic*, 2002.

Rael, Patrick. *Black Identity and Black Protest in the Antebellum North,* 2002.

Stauffer, John. *The Black Hearts of Men: Radical Abolitionists and the Transformation of Race.* Cambridge, MA: Harvard University Press, 2002.

Somerset Decision (1772)

The *Somerset* case, decided in 1772 by Lord Mansfield (William Murray), helped launch the movements to abolish slavery in England and the United States, and became a significant part of the common law of slavery in the English-speaking world.

James Somerset was born in Africa, sold into the slave trade, and then taken to Virginia where Charles Stewart purchased him. Stewart took Somerset to England in 1769. In October 1771, Somerset escaped, and when Stewart recaptured him, he immediately imprisoned Somerset on a boat headed to Jamaica where he planned to sell him. Three abolitionists, Thomas Watkins, Elizabeth Cade, and John Marlow, came to Somerset's aid and submitted affidavits to the court for a writ of habeas corpus. Mansfield agreed to hear the plea and summoned Thomas Knowles, the owner of the ship, to bring himself and Somerset to court on December 9, 1771.

Knowles testified that Somerset belonged to Charles Stewart, that he had never been "manumitted, enfranchised, set free or discharged," and that Somerset had "departed and absented himself" from service without permission from Stewart. Mansfield believed the case had merit and arranged court dates in February and in April 1772 to hear arguments from both sides.

The two lead lawyers, Francis Hargrave and John Dunning, gave sophisticated arguments before the court. The primary question confronting the court was whether an owner could remove a slave from England. Although Hargrave had never argued before the bar, he presented a subtle and compelling case that slavery was contrary to English common law. Seeming to anticipate almost every counterargument, Hargrave admitted that *villenage,* or conditions pertaining to feudal serfs, and colonial slavery were legal, but forced the court to recognize the way that English common law had steadily progressed *in favorem libertatis* or in favor of liberty. He argued that if England accepted American racial slavery, it would be forcing the law to regress rather than progress. Furthermore, English law required consent in all service relationships, and Hargrave contended that "no man can by compact enslave himself." His arguments were published in the United States and England and were widely used by abolitionists.

John Dunning, a well-respected lawyer who had argued just a year before that no one could be detained as a slave in England, defended Knowles and Stewart's right to imprison and sell Somerset. He tried to argue from fact and law to unsettle the emotional strength of Somerset's case. He contended that the emancipation of Somerset would undermine the respect that the court should hold for the law of

Virginia where Somerset was purchased, and where slavery was legal. More effectively, he argued that the emancipation of Somerset could precipitate the emancipation of all enslaved blacks in England, a scenario that would divorce men from their property and place a great burden on England's poorhouses.

Mansfield did not feel compelled to write the decision in this case, but Somerset's unwillingness to settle out of court forced him to do so. Mansfield's greatest contribution finally to English law was not the *Somerset* Decision, but his promotion of commercial law, which helped England's emerging capitalism to flourish. His brief decision reflected the tenuous relationship between capitalism and slavery. He recognized that his decision could disrupt the property rights of thousands of slave owners, but concluded, *"fiat Justitia, ruat coelumtet"* (let justice be done whatever the consequences). Slavery, he argued, was different in each locality and "so odious, that nothing can be suffered to support it, but positive law." The case, as Mansfield made clear, did not end slavery in any of the British colonies, nor, as he showed in subsequent cases, did it end slavery in England; however, it did prevent owners from forcibly detaining slaves and deporting them for sale. This careful decision, historian David Brion Davis notes, preserved the service of the slaves to their masters, but at the same time established an important precedent that labor is voluntary, an important legal foundation for a capitalist society.

Whatever Mansfield's intention, the case had a much wider influence. It was the first step toward the emancipation of blacks in England. In America, some slaves and abolitionists incorrectly used the case to support the end of slavery. Other opponents of slavery more correctly used the case as support to end slavery in only parts of the United States, requiring positive law to maintain slavery and contending that slavery could be upheld in one locality but not another. This understanding of slave law, as requiring positive law, became the common law in the United States and is reflected in the Constitution's support of slavery without mentioning slavery by name. Slavery became a local (state) issue, not a national one and required positive law to be upheld in each locality. Somerset was almost immediately cited in court cases and petitions in Massachusetts. Likewise, throughout the antebellum era, judges and legal commentaries on slavery used the case as the foundation of opposition to slavery in America.

Emily V. Blanck

See also: British Slavery, Abolition of.

Further Readings

Davis, David Brion. *The Problem of Slavery in the Age of Revolution 1770–1823*. 2nd ed. Oxford: Oxford University Press, 1999.

Hall, Kermit L. *The Magic Mirror: Law in American History*. New York: Oxford University Press, 1989.

Hargrave, Francis. *An Argument in the Case of James Sommersett a Negro.* London: E. Russell, 1774.

Higginbotham, A. Leon. *In the Matter of Color: Race and the American Legal Process, The Colonial Period.* New York: Oxford University Press, 1978.

Somerset v Stewart, Lofft 1–18; 20 Howell's State Trials 1, 79–82; 98 Eng Rep 499–510 (King's Bench, 22 June 1772).

Spooner, Lysander

Lysander Spooner was an American legal theorist who became a prominent member of the radical abolitionist community in the 1840s when he wrote *The Unconstitutionality of Slavery*. His argument that the U.S. Constitution did not sanction slavery was made two decades before the ratification of the Thirteenth Amendment. Spooner's theory challenged the view, held by William Lloyd Garrison and Wendell Phillips, that the Constitution was a "covenant with death, and an agreement with hell" that permitted and protected slavery. In later life, Spooner wrote about anarchism, but his abolitionist writings were his most influential; both the Liberty Party and Frederick Douglass embraced his theory.

Whether the subject matter was deism, economics, jury trials, or slavery, Spooner always made legalistic arguments based on individuals' natural rights. In his most famous abolitionist work, *The Unconstitutionality of Slavery*, published in two parts in 1845 and 1847, Spooner said that written laws violating these natural rights were not legitimate and that people were not legally obliged to obey them. The only permissible exception was when a law specifically stated, in unequivocal language, that the government was permitted to infringe on these rights. The Constitution was not such a law; it did not mention "slavery" or "slaves."

This interpretation is based on an understanding of the original meaning of the language used by the Framers of the Constitution, and directly challenged the arguments made by Wendell Phillips. Phillips used historical documents (e.g., James Madison's notes from the Constitutional Convention in 1787) to show that the original *intent* of the Framers had been to build into the Constitution a series of compromises that protected slavery. Spooner rejected the legal relevance of these documents, because he believed that a law could only be legally binding as it was specifically written down.

Spooner was not the first to argue that slavery was unconstitutional, or to reach this conclusion using natural rights arguments. The intellectual ancestry of his theory is seen in the 1830s works of, for example, Alvan Stewart and William Goodell. His was, however, the most comprehensive and legalistic of these analyses of the relationship between slavery and the U.S. Constitution.

Although he never again reached an audience matching that of the 1840s, Spooner continued to write antislavery works. In 1850, in *A Defence for Fugitive*

Slaves, he challenged the legality of the fugitive slave acts of 1793 and 1850. Consistent with his lifelong distrust of government officials, he encouraged people to facilitate the escape of fugitive slaves. If this resulted in their arrest, Spooner believed that the best course of action was to challenge the constitutionality of the fugitive slave laws. He combined the natural rights theory of *The Unconstitutionality of Slavery* with the elements of judicial process that formed the core of his later work on jury trial. While his argument was radical, the civil disobedience that he advocated was a strategy widely adopted by opponents of the 1793 and 1850 laws.

Spooner enjoyed less support for the views expressed in *A Plan for the Abolition of Slavery (and) to the Non-Slaveholders of the South*, an 1858 pamphlet responding to the Supreme Court's *Dred Scott* decision (1857). His radicalism continued to increase, as he saw no hope for a political end to slavery. He now advocated, if necessary, violent rather than merely legal challenges to laws. Illustrating his argument by using examples from the American and French Revolutions, Spooner called upon whites and blacks alike to engage in a revolutionary uprising in the South to liberate slaves. This ignited a wellspring of criticism, and most abolitionists were unwilling to condone this plan at a time of increasingly volatile sectional divisions. Spooner initially sought to ensure widespread distribution of his pamphlet, but John Brown persuaded him to suppress the publication because Brown feared it would jeopardize his planned raid at Harpers Ferry in 1859. Their ideas were similar, but consistent with his other writings Spooner focused on the theory of a revolution, whereas Brown intended to put ideas into practice.

Overall, during his lifetime the influence of Spooner's work was limited; he never achieved the fame he expected his writings to bring. He lacked the social benefits of a college or law school education, having learned the law as an apprentice to several prominent Massachusetts lawyers (including Governor, and later Senator, John Davis). His status as a serious legal scholar was undermined by some of the radical positions that he adopted, and, as a result, history has generally regarded him as an abolitionist whose writings, while voluminous, were of limited legal or theoretical importance.

Helen J. Knowles

See also: Fugitive Slave Law (1850); Garrisonians; Liberty Party; U.S. Constitution and Antislavery.

Further Readings

Cover, Robert M. *Justice Accused: Antislavery and the Judicial Process*. New Haven, CT: Yale University Press, 1975.

Lysander Spooner Web site: www.lysanderspooner.org.

Spooner, Lysander. "The Unconstitutionality of Slavery." In Charles Shively, ed. *The Collected Works of Lysander Spooner*. Vol. 4: *Anti-Slavery Writings*. Weston, MA: M&S Press, 1971.

Wiecek, William M. *The Sources of Antislavery Constitutionalism in America, 1760–1848*. Ithaca, NY: Cornell University Press, 1977.

Stowe, Harriet Beecher

Harriet Beecher Stowe's contribution to the antislavery movement centers upon her novel, *Uncle Tom's Cabin*, which rapidly attracted worldwide attention, above all along a transatlantic axis running between the United States and the United Kingdom and Europe. *Uncle Tom* concentrates upon the stories of two families of slaves "owned" by a Southern planter family, the Shelbys, and on the fates of Uncle Tom on the one hand and George and Liza Harris on the other. The novel first appeared in serial form in the abolitionist newspaper, the *National Era*, during 1851–1852, and immediately afterward as a book published by John P. Jewett, entitled *Uncle Tom's Cabin; or, The Man That Was a Thing*.

Connecticut-born Harriet Beecher Stowe is famous as the author of the best-selling antislavery novel *Uncle Tom's Cabin* (1852), which aroused Northern feeling against slavery in the United States. (National Archives)

Stowe, from late adolescence onward, had developed growing antislavery sympathies, first in New England and, after 1832, in Ohio. But she had almost no direct experience with slavery in the American South save for one brief visit to Kentucky in 1834. Thus she largely relied upon anecdotes related by others, for example, the stories told to her by escaped slaves, including her own servant, Eliza Buck, when she was living in Cincinnati from 1832 to 1850. Stowe also drew upon antislavery publications, such as the pamphlet written by Theodore Dwight

Weld, Angelina Grimké Weld, and Sarah Grimké, *American Slavery as It Is: Testimony of a Thousand Witnesses* (1839). The pamphlet drew on a mélange of sources, including escaped slaves' stories, but chiefly on newspaper reports, particularly accounts in numerous Southern newspapers. Stowe also spoke to an escaped slave, Josiah Henson, and read his 1849 autobiography. In the subtitle of later editions of his book, Henson claimed to be "Mrs. Harriet Beecher Stowe's 'Uncle Tom.'" However, Stowe never accepted this claim, and, though there are similarities with Henson, Tom is substantially a fictional character—the creation of a white female writer seeking to stir up active resistance to the continuation of slavery in the United States, and especially to the 1850 Fugitive Slave Law.

Stowe succeeded in her aim. Abraham Lincoln, on meeting her in 1862, is said to have exclaimed, "So you're the little woman who wrote the book that started this great war?" The persistence of this apocryphal story provides an indication of the scale of *Uncle Tom's* success. The first printing of the book (5,000 copies) sold out in a few days, and it was to be constantly reprinted in the United States and the United Kingdom and across Europe (in translation). Over 300,000 issues were sold in the first year in the United States, a figure still dwarfed by British sales, which soared over 1.5 million. Voyaging abroad to receive an antislavery petition composed by the duchess of Sutherland, the earl of Shaftesbury, and the earl of Carlisle, and signed by half a million women inspired by *Uncle Tom's Cabin*, Stowe discovered how much of an international antislavery celebrity she had become. She subsequently traveled widely in Europe, particularly in Britain and Ireland, rallying support for American antislavery efforts.

Yet, *Uncle Tom's* reliance on anecdote, its force as an antislavery polemic, and its targeting of a white audience have given the book a controversial history. White Southerners were incensed, claiming the book distorted the workings of the institution of slavery. Faced with such criticism, Stowe rushed out *A Key to Uncle Tom's Cabin Presenting the Original Facts and Documents upon Which the Story Is Founded* in 1853. African Americans, for very different reasons, were also uneasy, particularly about the book's portraits of black slaves. For example, the portrayal of Topsy, the young slave girl, as a naïve, mischievous, capering, dishonest self-hater, came in for heavy criticism—Stowe's unthinking reliance on blackface minstrelsy's excesses were all too clear. But Uncle Tom himself attracted the heaviest criticism. As early as 1852, William C. Nell criticized Tom for his passive reliance on the efficacy of Christian forgiveness. By 1865, Frederick Douglass, despite his *Paper*'s initial enthusiasm, in a speech to the Annual Meeting of the Massachusetts Anti-Slavery Society, expressed concern about Tom's readiness "to take off his Coat whenever required, fold his hands, and be whipped by anybody who wanted to whip him." By 1926, William Stanley Braithwaite observed in the *Negro in American Literature* that "the moral gain and historical effect of Uncle Tom have been artistic loss and setback." In 1956, J.C. Furnas, in his *Goodbye to Uncle Tom*, described the "theological terror" that the book invoked as comparable to the "terror" upon which the Southern States' "lynch mob[s]" had relied. Consequently, Furnas ·claimed, "American Negroes have made . . . ["Uncle Tom"] a hissing and a by-word." Or, as James Baldwin put it in his *Partisan Review* essay of 1949, "Tom . . . has been robbed of his humanity and divested of his sex."

In contrast, outside the South, the white reception of the book was generally characterized by respect, if not admiration. Initial reviews from antislavery sympathizers on both sides of the Atlantic were eulogistic, although some advocates of "immediate" or "ultra" abolition found Stowe's message too conservative. Those unconvinced about abolition's desirability were even more wary, if compelled, to recognize the book's power. For example, on September 3, 1852, a London *Times* reviewer wrote that "with the instincts of her sex, the clever authoress takes the shortest road to her purpose, and strikes at the convictions of her readers by assailing their hearts." As this passage implies, Stowe's novel is carefully contrived, strategically aiming to appeal as widely as possible to its audiences, be they antislavery converts, the unconverted or—perhaps above all—agnostics. Part of the problem would seem to be Stowe's relative naiveté concerning abolitionist politics. Before the publication of *Uncle Tom's Cabin*, Stowe was only a sympathizer, not an active abolitionist; she only learned to negotiate with confidence the politics of abolition—the competing claims of Garrisonian advocates of immediate abolition on the one hand and gradualists on the other—after being thrust into the international limelight.

Yet Stowe's naiveté can be overstated. Acknowledging this provides a way of analyzing why *Uncle Tom's* narrative splits into two stories. As the fugitive slaves George and Eliza Harris escape North, Tom, however, progresses southward, deeper into servitude and suffering. As George and Eliza travel North, their story increasingly engages with the public politics of abolitionism and the solutions posited by those abolitionists, political abolitionists, who saw the remedy for slavery as primarily residing in political change. The passage of the Fugitive Slave Act marked a significant defeat for these political abolitionists, by dramatically *extending* slavery's impact. Stowe traces the act's consequences for Eliza and George during their northward journey. Bounty hunters strive to recapture the Harrises during their journey; Senator Bird and his wife debate the act's rectitude; George makes his "Declaration of Independence" in an armed stand-off; and the British colony of Canada is ironically identified as the runaways' blessed land of freedom. The repeated sense is that in the public domain of politics, insuperable institutional impediments block the achievement of perfect Christian charity. Indeed doubt is shed upon the idea that any public human institution can deliver the necessary reform.

In counterpoint with this political, Northward plotline, Tom's involuntary progress South effectively takes up the arguments of those abolitionists who saw a resolution to the issue of slavery residing not in the political arena, since even the U.S. Constitution itself countenanced slavery but in the persuasive efficacy of the moral arguments against both slavery—as when the saintly Little Eva disputes with the slave-owning St. Clare—and racism—as when St. Clare shows Ophelia how she dreads "touching" Topsy. This sort of moral persuasion is climactically advanced by Tom's Christ-like death and final words: "Ye poor miserable critter [Legree]! . . . I forgive ye, with all my soul!" (II: 275). The focus of the political plot-strand centering on Eliza and George is primarily external/public, demanding political action and resistance, while the moral suasionist strand of Tom's story is primarily internal/domestic. Tom practices perfectionism in his faith, residing in his belief that, even unto death, God's justice will prevail.

Focusing upon this narrative division and the implicit support it provides to moral suasionists provides a way of understanding how some feminist critics came to take *Uncle Tom* as highly significant in its advocacy of moral nurturing, archetypally depicted in the Quaker matriarch, Hannah's harmoniously organized Christian kitchen. More significantly, the novel's double plotline also, at least apparently, provides a way of rebutting those critics dismayed by Tom's passivity: George, unlike Tom, actively fights his persecutors. Though George is a light-skinned quadroon, so raising the issue of how skin color ranks high in many abolitionists' calculations of "worth" (as in Richard Hildreth's *The White Slave* [1836] and its use of a "white" hero to stir up antislavery anger), vigorous resistance is also offered in Stowe's novel by the dark-skinned Jim Selden. This surely contradicts Baldwin's 1949 suggestion that Tom is Stowe's "only black man." Yet it is clear why Baldwin errs; Selden appears only briefly, and elsewhere St. Clare ponders how, since "there is a pretty fair infusion of Anglo-Saxon blood among our slaves now . . . with all our haughty feelings burning in their veins," they "will not always be bought and sold" (II: 76). African Americans' unease with this novel's color politics cannot be dismissed.

Yet it is important to distinguish between the novel itself and variations that have constantly flourished in popular culture. The illustrations to the novel have often emphasized a sentimentalized Uncle Tom, or brought out the blackface traces in Stowe's characterizations. Much more damagingly, Southern racist popularizations, as in the staging of *Uncle Tom's Cabin as It Is* in Baltimore in 1852, or in *Aunt Phillis's Cabin; or Southern Life as It Is* by Mary Henderson Eastman in 1852, portrayed Southern slavery as a pastoral idyll overseen by paternalistic planters and "Uncle Tom" suffering racism in the North and gladly returning South to his cabin. Such deformations explain well just why "Uncle Tom" became so much of a "hissing and a byword," in J.C. Furnas's 1956 verdict. As a tentative counterbalance to this emphasis, reference needs to be made to Stowe's other antislavery novel from 1856, *Dred; a Tale of the Great Dismal Swamp*, which offers a messianic portrait of a runaway maroon. Concealed in the swamps, Dred resists white attempts at recapture, while denouncing slavery—if in an overly melodramatic and apocalyptic fashion. However, Stowe has always primarily entered public consciousness as Uncle Tom's creator, and, in her depiction of George and Eliza resolving to travel to Africa in line with American Colonization Society propaganda, as a colonizationist. One sign of the resulting problem of this legacy is how, in the late 1960s, Tom once again needed reinventing—this time, in the wake of the rise of black power—as a resistant hero quite unlike the original. Stowe's *Uncle Tom* remains deeply discomforting.

Richard J. Ellis

See also: Literature and Abolition.

Further Readings

Hedrick, Joan D. *Harriet Beecher Stowe: A Life*. New York: Oxford University Press, 1994.
Weinstein, Cindy. *The Cambridge Companion to Harriet Beecher Stowe*. Cambridge: Cambridge University Press, 2004.

T

Tappan, Arthur

Arthur Tappan, with his younger brother, Lewis Tappan, became one of the most famous abolitionists in the United States. The brothers helped establish the American Anti-Slavery Society in 1833 and led the fight against slavery throughout the antebellum period. Together, the brothers made millions in business and used their wealth to fund abolitionist and other social reform organizations. Less well remembered than his brother because of Lewis's role in the famous *Amistad* case, Tappan's influential leadership helped create and shape the direction of abolitionism.

Born in 1786 in Massachusetts, in his early life Tappan was directed by his mother, Sarah. More forceful than her husband, Benjamin, Sarah instructed her children in a strict, yet loving, way that emphasized a Calvinistic interpretation of the Christian religion. While Lewis often required his mother's reproof and punishment, Tappan was a submissive boy who rarely needed discipline. As Lewis put it in his biography of his brother, Tappan "had the good fortune to escape much chastisement at home, or in school." His submission was rooted, no doubt, in his introspective personality, but may also have stemmed from his mother's constant reminders of the uncertainty of life. She often told him how he had nearly died on several occasions. When combined with his reserved nature, his mother's interpretation that he was alive only by the miracle of God made Tappan an obedient boy. Her influence was so strong that Tappan apparently did not experience an emotional conversion to Christianity. It was as if he had always been saved, and there was no room for doubting this. While his brother briefly became a Unitarian, Lewis's return to orthodoxy was treated with the kind of celebration that often accompanied conversion in evangelical Christian circles. But Tappan inherited his mother's sense of religious mystery and alternating feelings of guilt and gratefulness for being alive.

Tappan entered into business as a teenager, working as a merchant apprentice in Boston. Later he went to Montreal to sell blankets for trade with the Indians.

The War of 1812 interrupted his business, and he lost money in the venture. Upon his return, he borrowed money from Lewis to start an importing business in New York City. He was successful, especially as a silk merchant, and his firm flourished. Located on Pearl Street, his store was a center of fashion, with the latest styles of hats and umbrellas and ladies' apparel. As his business and wealth expanded, Arthur became involved in social and religious reform. Like many other Calvinists in the early nineteenth century, he became an evangelical and joined with other Christians to improve society and save souls. He was one of the founders of the American Tract Society in 1825, gave liberally to the American Sunday School Union, and worked hard to promote education, help prostitutes get off the streets, stop the evils of alcohol, and pass Sabbatarian legislation. His reserved personality and aversion to the urban environment took its toll, however, and he invited his brother to join him in business in 1828. Not long after Lewis arrived, Tappan moved his family to the quieter atmosphere of New Haven, Connecticut.

Even as he struggled with his own guilt, Tappan became convinced of the nation's sin. Urged on by the great revivalist, Charles Grandison Finney, Tappan and his brother had become part of a circle of wealthy Christian philanthropists who funded various benevolence organizations, founded colleges, and promoted reform. This included Tappan's generous contributions to Oberlin College in Ohio, a school that became a hotbed of Christian perfectionism and abolitionist activity. Convinced of the abolitionist position in the mid-to-late 1820s, Tappan founded an antislavery newspaper, but was hesitant to embrace what he perceived to be the radicalism of outspoken abolitionists such as William Lloyd Garrison. This changed by the early 1830s when he helped organize the American Anti-Slavery Society, which came to lead to national movement for abolitionism.

His activism made Tappan very unpopular, and he became the target of mobs and was lampooned in songs and newspapers across the country. When the brothers experienced financial setbacks in the late 1830s after a fire destroyed their warehouses, followed by the Panic of 1837, the Tappans did not despair. They struggled on, honoring their debts and rebuilding their business empire. Tappan responded to all adversity with stoicism and a dogged determination to do his duty. Along with Lewis, he founded the Mercantile Agency, the country's first credit-rating service, to help stabilize the economy in the wake of the Panic of 1837.

Elected president of the American Anti-Slavery Society when it was founded, Tappan soon became known as a conservative influence in the organization. Although a devoted abolitionist, he also wanted to remain respectable and was suspicious of the methods of radicals like Garrison. His quiet personality made him an unlikely choice for top leadership and, although other abolitionists appreciated his financial donations, they doubted his abilities to bring about real change. In the movement, as in his own business, Tappan followed a strict, cautious line of financial responsibility. While this worked well in keeping the society solvent, it was unpopular with those who wanted to move more quickly and use dramatic methods. His cautious nature also led him to move briefly toward gradual emancipation, rather than the more radical immediatism called for by Garrison. This brought widespread criticism, and Garrison used it to ask Tappan to step aside. Instead, Tappan recanted his heresy, returned to supporting immediate emancipation, and donated a large sum of money to buy the forgiveness of the radicals.

Tappan made many mistakes and often seemed reluctant to support the radical abolitionists completely. From the perspective of later generations, he was not a saint and not a great hero. In part this was due to his personality and the fact that he left very few papers and made very few public speeches. His brother, Lewis, was by far the more popular candidate for abolitionist sainthood, as he remained active in the movement up to the Civil War, pushed for the most radical methods, and supported the *Amistad* slaves in their famous case. Eventually, Lewis himself tried to restore Tappan to his proper place in the history of abolition by publishing a biography of his brother, but even that was not enough. Some scholars believe that Lewis was too modest and attributed some of his own work to his older brother. Despite his flaws and his somewhat ambivalent record, Tappan was an important leader of the abolitionist movement and his contributions were more than just financial in nature. In the context of the 1830s, he was at the forefront of the fight against slavery and deserves to be remembered for his efforts.

A. James Fuller

See also: Garrisonians.

Further Readings

Tappan, Lewis. *The Life of Arthur Tappan*. 1870. Westport, CT: Negro Universities Press, 1970.

Wyatt-Brown, Bertram. *Lewis Tappan and the Evangelical War against Slavery*. 1969. Baton Rouge: Louisiana State University Press, 1997.

Tappan, Lewis

Lewis Tappan, Christian reformer, businessman, and philanthropist, epitomized evangelical abolitionism in nineteenth-century America. A signal leader in numerous benevolent associations, Tappan believed in antislavery as a righteous cause. No American abolitionist had a longer or more dedicated career.

Raised in Massachusetts by devout Congregational parents, Benjamin and Sarah Tappan, Lewis retained a lifelong dedication to piety and social conscience. After a short-lived youthful embrace of Unitarianism in Massachusetts, Tappan joined the New York silk merchandising firm of wealthy older brother Arthur Tappan in 1827, where he not only managed operations but also entered Arthur's world of orthodox evangelicalism. Together with other pious New York businessmen, they founded the *Evangelist* in 1827 and hired Joshua Leavitt to edit the new journal. The Tappans supported the Free Church movement to make seating and membership in a church not contingent upon payment of a fee. Combining this policy with their new dedication to popular enthusiastic preaching associated with the Second Great Awakening, they helped organize the Chatham Street Chapel as a part-time home for fiery revivalist Charles G. Finney.

The Tappan brothers' conversions to abolitionism came gradually, but by 1833 Arthur had helped launch the *Emancipator*, hiring Elizur Wright Jr., as secretary. Conversations with Theodore Dwight Weld turned Lewis to immediate emancipation, and in 1833 the Tappans, staying just ahead of an antiabolitionist mob, inaugurated the New York Anti-Slavery Society at the Chatham Street Chapel. That December the first national antislavery convention witnessed Lewis bridging the interests of the New York organization and the more liberal Boston-based Garrisonians. Both Tappan brothers held high positions in the American Anti-Slavery Society (AASS) that issued from that meeting, and helped author its declaration that slavery was both a crime and a sin. To promote Christian abolitionism's westward expansion, they supported Lyman Beecher and Lane Seminary in Cincinnati; later, Arthur put his substantial fortune behind founding the more radically antislavery Oberlin College in northeastern Ohio.

Lewis Tappan's talents as an editor, fund-raiser, and administrator were tremendously useful in the war against slavery. Belief that moral suasion could produce manumissions led him to mount a massive postal campaign in 1835 directed at Southern slaveholders. The South's furious reaction against this campaign earned the antislavery movement national attention and chastened Lewis's confidence that moral suasion alone would convert the South to abolition.

William Lloyd Garrison's growing radicalism only increased the Tappan brothers' discomfort with non-evangelical abolitionists, and contributed to a schism in the national organization in 1841 and the Garrisonians gaining control of the AASS. Lewis immediately led a handful of men centered in New York City to form the American and Foreign Anti-Slavery Society (AFASS) that, like its British model, stressed international cooperation among antislavery reformers. Their numbers were small: internecine bickering and the challenges of conducting business in a climate of notoriety had recently led Arthur to retrench from visible antislavery activity, while other former cohorts stayed with Garrison in the AASS, retired, or sought political solutions through participation in the newly formed Liberty Party.

In 1839, Lewis Tappan formed a committee to free jailed Africans who had recently mutinied and murdered some crew members on the Cuban slaving schooner *Amistad*. The case, which attracted national attention, provided a ready outlet for Tappan's talents as administrator, publicist, religious teacher, and legal advisor. A few years later, the crisis over Texas annexation inspired Tappan to travel to England, where he failed to convince British leaders to acquire Texas for the empire and concurrently block the spread of American slavery.

In England, Tappan witnessed the potential value of third-party political action. Upon his return, he began to support the Liberty Party, and founded their popular journal, the *National Era*, under the editorship of the dynamic Gamaliel Bailey. Politically, antislavery's propensity for pragmatism and compromise disquieted Tappan, however, and when its various factions combined with assorted disaffected partisans to form the Free Soil Party in 1848, Tappan, shocked and wounded, refused to join.

Political interest soon gave way to pursuits more suited to a pious evangelical whose primary objection to slavery had always been its spiritually destructive effects. Tappan refocused his efforts on Christian abolitionism. In 1842, his *Amistad* committee had merged with the black-founded Union Mission, an alliance that within a few years expanded into a reconstituted American Missionary Association (AMA), an officially nonsectarian organization that nonetheless drew heavily from Congregationalist support. Largely in pursuit of Tappan's dream of an interracial Christian fellowship, the AMA by 1860 had spent over $1 million on antislavery missions worldwide.

Tappan's visibility as an antislavery reformer waned, yet sectional violence in the 1850s led him to resurrect the AFASS as the American Abolition Society and renew his condemnation of bondage as criminal and unconstitutional. During this period, he also challenged evangelicals who continued to tolerate slavery, an effort that climaxed in a dramatic clash at the American Tract Society's convention in 1856. Although best remembered for his evangelical abolitionism, Tappan was also the founder in 1827 of the *Journal of Commerce* and in 1841 of the Mercantile Agency (later Dun and Bradstreet), the country's first credit reporting agency.

Cathy Rodabaugh

See also: Garrisonians; Tappan, Arthur.

Further Readings

McKivigan, John R. *The War against Proslavery Religion: Abolitionism and the Northern Churches, 1830–1865*. Ithaca, NY: Cornell University Press, 1984.

Wyatt-Brown, Bertram. *Lewis Tappan and the Evangelical War against Slavery*. Baton Rouge: Louisiana State University Press, 1969.

Texas, Annexation of (1845)

The annexation of Texas was the central issue in the expansion of slavery into new territories, and the various factions of the antislavery movement united in opposition to it.

In the 1820s, the Mexican government encouraged Americans to migrate to the very sparsely settled lands of Mexico's most northern province, Texas. Many came from the Southern states, and brought their slaves with them. But having abolished slavery in 1829, Mexico reversed its settlement policy in 1830 and prohibited both further American immigration and the importation of slaves. In 1835, Texas revolted against Mexican rule, winning its independence in 1836 and establishing the Republic of Texas. Immediately after and for the next nine years, Texas nevertheless actively sought annexation to the United States.

In 1835, the abolitionist Benjamin Lundy wrote two pamphlets denouncing the Texas revolution as an effort to restore slavery where it had been abolished and create the opportunity for the United States to annex it. Most opponents of annexation followed his lead. John Quincy Adams delivered lengthy speeches in 1836 and 1838 opposing the annexation of Texas, casting the measure as risking war for the benefit of slavery. Texas was a key component in what antislavery forces saw as a Slave Power conspiracy. On March 3, 1843, Adams and several other antislavery congressmen issued an address depicting the annexation of Texas as a measure to insure the permanent rule of the slave states over the free states.

The antislavery furor prevented Jackson and Van Buren from annexing Texas. In 1843, John Tyler actively revived the project. He sent Duff Green as his personal representative in Great Britain to speak to Texas officials there and to ascertain British intentions in Texas. Green concluded that British abolitionists wanted to use the promise of guaranteed loans to force Texas to abolish slavery, which would serve as a prelude to attacking the institution in the United States, in part by encircling the Southern states with colonies and nations where slavery had been outlawed. Tyler and his allies tried to portray the annexation of a slave state as a benefit to the North. In January 1844, Senator Robert J. Walker put forth the theory that a slave Texas would tend to draw slavery further south, and prevent the migration of escaped slaves to the North. Walker cited statistics from the 1840 census, which purported to show a high incidence of insanity among free blacks. The effort failed, and the Senate rejected an annexation treaty in June 1844. In the closing days of his administration, Tyler achieved the annexation of Texas through a joint resolution of Congress. Opponents of annexation considered the joint resolution as the triumph of the Slave Power over the U.S. Constitution. It certainly helped prompt the United States' war with Mexico.

Robert W. Smith

See also: Slave Power Argument.

Further Readings

Hietala, Thomas R. *Manifest Design: Anxious Aggrandizement in Late Jacksonian America.* Ithaca, NY: Cornell University Press, 1985.
Merk, Frederick. *Slavery and the Annexation of Texas.* New York: Alfred A. Knopf, 1972.
Pletcher, David. *The Diplomacy of Annexation: Texas, Oregon and the Mexican War.* Columbia: University of Missouri Press, 1973.

Thirteenth Amendment (1865)

The Thirteenth Amendment abolished slavery and involuntary servitude in the United States. Adopted by two-thirds of Congress in January 1865, and declared ratified by three-fourths of the states in December of that year, the measure declared in its first clause that "neither slavery nor involuntary servitude, except as a punishment for crime whereof the party shall have been duly convicted, shall exist within the United States, or any place subject to their jurisdiction." In its second clause, the amendment added that "Congress shall have power to enforce this article by appropriate legislation."

The amendment represented a monumental, if largely unanticipated, consequence of the Civil War. In the first year of the war, political leaders of the Union promised not to interfere with slavery where it already existed, a promise that Abraham Lincoln and others of the Republican Party had made in the 1860 election campaign. Lincoln even supported a constitutional amendment, sometimes called the "first Thirteenth Amendment," adopted by Congress in March 1861, which prohibited federal interference with slavery where it existed. The proposed amendment was signed by President Lincoln, on the day of his inauguration (March 4, 1861)—the only amendment ever signed by a president—and later that day was sent to all states for ratification. Three states actually ratified it and more might have had it not been for events unfolding in the South.

As the war continued beyond the first year, more Northern whites accepted, if not encouraged, the use of emancipation as a war measure against the Confederacy. Union commanders, who during the first year of the war had been instructed by the Lincoln administration to return escaped slaves to their owners, began to follow the lead of General Benjamin Butler, who from the beginning of the war had refused to return African Americans and instead declared them "contraband" of war. Congress endorsed the contraband policy by passing Confiscation Acts in 1861 and 1862, which declared that all rebel property, including slaves, would be seized by the Union. The initiative taken by runaway slaves, by military commanders, and by Congress ultimately led President Lincoln to issue the Emancipation Proclamation, which declared "forever free" all slaves in rebellious areas. However, the Proclamation exempted those slaves in Union-controlled regions of the South and border states. Lincoln signed the final Emancipation Proclamation on January 1, 1863.

After Lincoln signed the Proclamation, abolitionists used petition drives to press for a broader act of emancipation. In April 1864, the U.S. Senate adopted a resolution for an antislavery amendment, but the House of Representatives failed to carry it in June. Lincoln ensured that the amendment was on the national platform of the Republican Party that summer. Lincoln and the Republicans scored victories in the fall elections, and the president claimed the vote as a popular endorsement of the amendment. He urged the House of Representatives to take up the measure again. Using informal cajoling as well as offers of patronage, Lincoln applied pressure to lame-duck Democratic congressmen to win their votes. Rumors floated through Washington that Lincoln's agents were bribing congressmen on behalf of the amendment, but no evidence of bribery has ever been uncovered. Enough Democrats changed their vote or absented themselves so that on January 31, 1865, the House of Representatives carried the amendment. States across the North immediately began to ratify the amendment, though some such as New Jersey initially voted against ratification. After Lincoln's assassination and the end of the war, President Andrew Johnson made ratification a condition of Southern states' readmission to the Union. On December 18, 1865, Secretary of State William Henry Seward issued a proclamation that the amendment had been ratified by three fourths of the states.

Almost immediately, Congress began to debate the meaning of the amendment. While Democrats and conservative Republicans argued that it merely abolished chattel slavery and secured no rights to the freedpeople, moderate and Radical Republicans claimed that the measure guaranteed equal rights for African Americans. The argument for equality won the day: Republican congressmen used the amendment's enforcement clause to create the Civil Rights Act of 1866, the first clause of which guaranteed "full and equal benefit of all laws and proceedings" to African Americans. They also invoked the amendment to renew the Freedmen's

Bureau, which had been created in 1865. Congress carried both the act renewing the Freedmen's Bureau and the Civil Rights Act of 1866 over the veto of President Andrew Johnson, who had begun to court the support of conservatives. Ultimately, the Thirteenth Amendment was eclipsed by the Fourteenth Amendment, which was adopted in 1868 and added specificity to freedom by setting the terms of citizenship and explicitly prohibiting states from denying "due process" and equality before the law.

The long-term effects of the Thirteenth Amendment were limited. The measure became an important weapon against various forms of involuntary servitude, but its phrasing allowed peonage, or debt slavery, to persist into the twentieth century. The most common victims of this form of servitude were African Americans, the very people meant to benefit from the Thirteenth Amendment.

Although the Thirteenth Amendment is overshadowed by the Fourteenth, the measure retains great significance. Civil rights lawyers still use the amendment, sometimes with success. In the Supreme Court case of *Jones v. Mayer* of 1968, for example, the Court accepted the Thirteenth Amendment as the basis for overturning discriminatory housing practices. The amendment remains a perpetual monument to the cause of freedom in the United States. Slavery, a word not used in the original Constitution, had long been protected by it. With the Thirteenth Amendment, slavery was officially abolished.

Michael Vorenberg

See also: Democratic Party and Antislavery; Radical Republicans; U.S. Constitution and Antislavery.

Further Readings

Hyman, Harold M., and William M. Wiecek. *Equal Justice Under Law: Constitutional Development, 1835–1875*. New York: Harper and Row, 1982.

Tsesis, Alexander. *The Thirteenth Amendment and American Freedom*. New York: New York University Press, 2004.

Vorenberg, Michael. *Final Freedom: The Civil War, the Abolition of Slavery, and the Thirteenth Amendment*. Cambridge: Cambridge University Press, 2001.

Truth, Sojourner

Sojourner Truth was born Isabella Van Wagenen in about 1797 as a slave in Hurley, New York. During her life as a slave, she allegedly bore thirteen children, of which three were sold into slavery. She served five masters until slavery was abolished in the state of New York on July 4, 1827. After experiencing a religious epiphany, the ex-slave Isabella changed her name to Sojourner Truth and became a singing preacher traveling throughout New York and Connecticut.

In 1847, Sojourner Truth became associated with the Northampton Association of Education and Industry, which was founded in 1841 as a community dedicated to abolitionism, pacifism, equality, and the betterment of human life. It was there at Northampton that she became immersed in the abolitionist movement and began working with many of the movement's leaders including William Lloyd Garrison and Frederick Douglass.

Although illiterate, Sojourner Truth's memoirs were published in 1850 with the assistance of Oliver Gilbert (a fellow abolitionist) as *The Narrative of Sojourner Truth: A Northern Slave*. Her book, along with her speaking skills, propelled her to the front of both the abolitionist and women's rights movements and she spoke broadly in the lyceum circuit. Her most famous speech—"Ar'n't I a Woman?"—was made at a women's convention in Ohio in 1851.

In 1857, Sojourner Truth moved to Battle Creek, Michigan, and after the Emancipation Proclamation she relocated to Washington, D.C., where she worked to gain support for a land distribution program for former slaves. This effort failed when Congress refused to enact the bill. Afterward, she returned to her home in Battle Creek. All in all, she dedicated over forty years of her life to denouncing slavery, promoting women's equality, and later, after slavery ended, to promoting equality for blacks and providing assistance to ex-slaves in need. Surrounded by family and friends, this influential icon died in 1883.

Iris Hunter

See also: Douglass, Frederick.

Further Reading

Painter, Nell Irvin. *Sojourner Truth: A Life, A Symbol*. New York: W.W. Norton & Co., 1996.

Tubman, Harriet

Born into slavery as Araminta Ross, Harriet Tubman was a self-emancipated woman, conductor of the Underground Railroad, abolitionist, feminist, soldier, and philanthropist. As a multifaceted person, her family, friends, and acquaintances also knew her as Moses, Aunt Harriet, Minty, and General Tubman. Tubman fought to eradicate slavery in the United States by rescuing enslaved Africans and their families from a life of anguish.

Tubman was born near Bucktown in Dorchester County, Maryland, to Harriet (Rittia) Green and Benjamin Ross. As an enslaved child, Tubman was hired out to several families, working as a muskrat trapper, nursemaid, and domestic. In her adolescent years, she was assigned to manual labor. In 1844, Tubman married a free black, John Tubman. In 1849, she escaped the bonds of slavery, leaving her former slave life and moving to Philadelphia, where she initiated contacts and networks with local abolitionists. Tubman's marriage ended shortly after her escape.

In 1850, she returned to Maryland as a conductor of the Underground Railroad and made her first rescue. Initially, Tubman focused her efforts on relocating her siblings and their families to St. Catherine's, Upper Canada (present-day Ontario, Canada) via Underground Railroad networks in Maryland, Pennsylvania, and New York. However, her fight against slavery expanded to include non-family members from the Dorchester county area. She confidently rescued and directed approximately 120 enslaved Africans and their families to free states in the North and to Upper Canada.

Harriet was not formally educated and relied on her impeccable memory, her astute Christian beliefs, her prophetic abilities, and use of pictographs to complete successful Underground Railroad journeys. Her successful career as an Underground Railroad conductor was extraordinary, since she was one of the most famous and most wanted runaways in the United States. Several slaveholders and planters in the Maryland area offered large bounties for Tubman's arrest or her head.

As General Tubman, she participated in fund-raising efforts for John Brown's unsuccessful war against the U.S. government to end slavery. She recruited African American soldiers for Brown's war and for the Union Army during the Civil War. She served in the South Carolina branch of the Union Army, working as a laundress, cook, nurse, and spy. During Reconstruction, she directed her attention to women's suffrage movements and dedicated her life to the betterment of African Americans. In 1869, Tubman wedded Civil War veteran, Charles Nelson Davis. Davis and Tubman spent the rest of their lives committed to improving the lives of African Americans in Auburn, New York.

In 1897, Tubman was recognized by Britain's Queen Victoria and awarded the Silver medal for her fight against slavery. In 1990, President George H.W. Bush declared March 10 as Harriet Tubman Day, acknowledging her passion and dedication to ending slavery in the United States.

Nadine Hunt

See also: Underground Railroad.

Further Readings

Clinton, Catherine. *Harriet Tubman: The Road to Freedom*. New York: Little, Brown and Co., 2004.

Harriet Tubman Historical Society [Online, August 2005]. www.harriettubman.com.

Humez, Jean. *Harriet Tubman: The Life and the Life Stories*. Madison: University of Wisconsin Press, 2003.

Larson, Kate Clifford. *Bound for the Promised Land: Harriet Tubman, Portrait of an American Hero*. New York: Ballantine, 2004.

Underground Railroad Web links [Online, August 2005]. Harriet Tubman Resource Centre on the African Diaspora www.yorku.ca/nhp.

Turner, Nat

Nat Turner is best known for the 1831 slave revolt he led in plantation-dotted Southampton County, Virginia. A decade before his eponymous revolt, Turner had a vision that he would lead a slave rebellion. Despite having escaped from slavery in 1821, Turner's vision compelled him to return voluntarily to his former plantation, where he would bide his time until the moment for rebellion was nigh. In the late 1820s, Turner began preaching to slave congregations. His sermons focused on themes like freedom, liberation, and redemption. His powerful exhortations attracted many followers, some of whom would refer to Turner as "the Prophet." As a preacher, Turner had the liberty to travel to different plantations, which was ideal for reconnaissance and rallying support from local slaves.

Turner interpreted a solar eclipse in February 1831 as a sign to begin his rebellion. He planned to launch it on July 4; the date was chosen intentionally for its symbolic importance. However, Turner fell ill, so the revolt was postponed until August 22. (This was the anniversary of the 1791 slave uprising in Saint Domingue, which probably inspired Turner and his coconspirators.) The revolt began at the home of Joseph Travis (Turner's owner), where the rebels killed everyone in the household. Turner planned to move from plantation to plantation, killing all the whites. He made it clear that this strategy was only a means of intimidating whites and inspiring other slaves to join his cause. Once the rebellion had achieved critical mass, Turner expected the indiscriminate violence to abate.

Turner turned his insurgents toward an arsenal in Jerusalem, Virginia. However, as more supporters joined the rebellion, Turner had to contend with collapsing organization in his ranks. After three days, the rebels were dispersed by militiamen, who killed more than 100 slaves while suppressing the revolt. Turner survived as a fugitive until he was captured on October 30, 1831. He was tried, sentenced to death, and hanged on November 11, 1831. While awaiting execution, Turner recounted his hopes and plans to his attorney, Thomas Gray. Gray later published *Nat Turner's Confessions.*

Nat Turner's revolt was the most violent slave uprising in American history. The brief rebellion and its brutal repression left almost 200 people dead on the plantations of Southampton County, Virginia. Later, more than 100 slaves were executed for their involvement in the uprising. Eugene Genovese, the noted historian of American slavery, has suggested that Turner's revolt was a turning point in the movement toward the U.S. Civil War because it stiffened the resolve of both abolitionists and proslavery advocates. It seemed to vindicate the position of those abolitionists who believed that slaves would fight for their freedom if they were organized and armed from without. (This attitude would have significant implications for someone like John Brown.) As with previous slave revolts, Turner's rebellion encouraged many Southerners to demand harsher restrictions on slaves. After 1831, American abolitionists became more radical in their demands and plantation owners became more bellicose in their support for slavery. The myth of the happy slave died with Nat Turner.

Jennifer J. Pierce

See also: Gabriel's Conspiracy (1800); Haitian Revolution; Literature and Abolition; Vesey's Conspiracy (1822).

Further Readings

Genovese, Eugene. *From Rebellion to Revolution: Afro-American Slave Revolts in the Making of the Modern World.* Baton Rouge: Louisiana State University Press, 1979.
Greenberg, Kenneth S. *Nat Turner: A Slave Rebellion in History and Memory.* New York: Oxford University Press, 2003.

U

Uncle Tom's Cabin (1852)

In 1852, Harriet Beecher Stowe took the nation by storm with her antislavery novel, *Uncle Tom's Cabin*. A cultural phenomenon rather than a mere book, *Uncle Tom's Cabin* sold some 300,000 copies within a year of its release and went on to become, after the Bible, the second-best-selling book in the world during the nineteenth century. *Uncle Tom's Cabin* almost immediately gave rise to a number of dramatic productions and spawned a cottage industry in figurines, collectors' plates, and other decorative items that represented popular scenes and characters from Stowe's story. As late as the 1930s, some eighty years after the novel's publication, "Tom shows" toured the United States, making Uncle Tom, Eliza, Topsy, Little Eva, and Simon Legree some of the most recognized literary figures in the nation.

Originally serialized in the *National Era, Uncle Tom's Cabin* emerged out of Harriet Beecher Stowe's anger over the Fugitive Slave Law of 1850. Like many white Northerners at the time, Stowe was not an abolitionist. But as a former resident of Cincinnati, gateway to the free North for many slaves, she felt outraged at the cruelty the system inflicted, and was particularly appalled at its destruction of slave families. Prompted by her sister-in-law to "write something" on the subject, Stowe designed a novel that would tug at the heartstrings of men, women, and children who had previously felt little personal connection with, or individual responsibility for, Southern slavery. She also hoped to effect the conversion of slaveholders with her sentimental portrayal of the suffering that slaves endured regardless of the kindness or cruelty of any individual master. As Stowe suggested in *Uncle Tom's Cabin*, even when a slave was owned by an indulgent or compassionate slaveholder, the laws that supported slavery made the existence of all slaves precarious, and likely to be rendered unbearable at a moment's notice.

While Stowe's fictional portrayal of Southern slavery attracted an unprecedented following among white Americans, it also drew considerable criticism.

Uncle Tom and Eva from *Uncle Tom's Cabin*. Originally serialized in the weekly publication the *National Era* the entire work was later published as a book in 1852 by Harriet Beecher Stowe. (Library of Congress)

Many Northerners and Southerners alike viewed *Uncle Tom's Cabin* as an affront to slaveholders and a threat to the Union, prompting the publication of both angry reviews and over two dozen "anti-Tom" novels intended to discredit Stowe's representation of slavery. Some abolitionists, on the other hand, pointed out that *Uncle Tom's Cabin* reinforced negative stereotypes of African Americans. Stowe allowed the light-skinned slaves George and Eliza Harris to escape to Canada, even depicting the highly capable George shooting and wounding a white slave catcher along the way. Yet the much blacker, more simple-minded Uncle Tom died a martyr on a Louisiana plantation, rejecting violence to the very end as a legitimate means of gaining freedom. Scholars have long debated whether Tom's choices represent resistance to slavery and loyalty to the slave community or submissiveness to, and even a complicity in, white power. Finally, Stowe's conclusion, in which the entire Harris family relocated to Africa rather than becoming integrated into American society, troubled abolitionists who regarded colonization as a racist policy that worked against black equality.

Sarah N. Roth

See also: Literature and Abolition.

Further Reading

Sundquist, Eric, ed. *New Essays on Uncle Tom's Cabin*. New York: Cambridge University Press, 1986.

Underground Railroad

The essence of the Underground Railroad, to use the National Park Service's Network to Freedom's definition, was "the effort of enslaved African Americans to gain their freedom by escaping bondage." The origin of the term "Underground Railroad" is not known, but it appears to have come into use by the 1830s. As Frederick Douglass noted, "secrecy and concealment were necessary conditions to the successful operation of this railroad, and hence its prefix 'underground.'" Several different stories explain the origin of the term. One of the best-known relates to Tice Davids, a freedom seeker who swam the Ohio River from Kentucky to Ripley, Ohio, and disappeared so quickly that his master thought he must have "gone off on an underground road."

Freedom seekers (generally known as fugitives) traveled alone or in groups, with or without help. Usually they were young men, but many women and children also escaped, often as families. Fear of imminent sale was a common motivation. They walked, used horses, boats, ships, wagons, or railroads. Most often, they escaped from the Upper South (Maryland, Virginia, Kentucky, or Tennessee), but sometimes people escaped from port cities along the Mississippi River, the Gulf, or the Atlantic. Sometimes they escaped for only a few days to nearby woods or to maroon communities. Often, however, they left permanently. Many headed for

Engraving by John Osler depicting fugitive slaves' escape from the eastern shore of Maryland. Illustration from *The Underground Railroad* by William Still, 1872. (Library of Congress)

Canada. A few went to Mexico or the Caribbean, but many also settled in Northern free states. By the late 1830s, Vigilance Committees—the first of them started by David Ruggles and other black abolitionists in New York City in 1835—were quickly organized by black and white Underground Railroad supporters throughout the North, and they openly assisted freedom seekers.

Both African Americans and white Americans kept safe houses. In Wilmington, Delaware, Quaker Thomas Garrett, friend of Harriet Tubman, noted that he had helped 2,038 fugitives by 1856. In many Northern cities, African Americans kept the major safe houses, sustained by a wide biracial network. Robert Purvis and William Still, both African Americans, worked with whites J. Miller McKim and Lucretia Mott in Philadelphia. Oliver Johnson and Sydney Howard Gay assisted African Americans David Ruggles and Theodore Wright in New York City. Stephen Myers, the Reverend Jermain Loguen (known as "the king" or "the prince" of the Underground Railroad, probably for his central location, his importance, and his size), and John Jones, all African Americans, kept the main safe houses in Albany, Syracuse, and Elmira, New York. In Newport, Indiana, and later Cincinnati, Ohio, Quaker Levi Coffin kept a major safe house. In Detroit, William Lambert and George De-Baptiste, African Americans, worked with Seymour Finney, a white hotel operator.

While it is impossible to know how many people escaped on the Underground Railroad, 1,500 per year is a generally accepted estimate. Certainly, enough people escaped to make passage of a Fugitive Slave Law a top priority for white Southerners as part of the Compromise of 1850. The Fugitive Slave Act required federal marshals to assist slave-catchers to capture accused fugitives. Freedom seekers had no right to testify on their own behalf. Underground Railroad helpers could be jailed for six months and fined $1,000 for each person they helped. Commissioners received $10 for ruling on behalf of slave-catchers and $5 for ruling on behalf of the freedom seeker. Fearing recapture, many freedom seekers who had settled in the Northern United States fled to Canada. Others, including Shadrach Minkins in Boston and William "Jerry" Henry in Syracuse, successfully escaped federal agents. The federal government did capture Anthony Burns in Boston, however, and returned him to slavery under the terms of the Fugitive Slave Act.

William Still's extensive notes formed the basis for his 1872 book, *The Underground Railroad*. Memoirs of people such as Quaker Levi Coffin, Harriet Tubman, and John Parker, themselves freedom seekers, offer important primary source evidence. Historians in the late twentieth century generally ignored the history of the Underground Railroad, citing the unreliability of oral traditions and the lack of written primary evidence. A closer look at both oral traditions and written evidence, however, has led to a rejuvenation of interest in this field.

Judith Wellman

See also: Jerry Rescue (1851); Tubman, Harriet.

Further Readings

Bordewich, Fergus. *Bound for Canaan: The Underground Railroad and the War for the Soul of America.* New York: HarperCollins, Amistad Press, 2005.

Bradford, Sarah. *Scenes in the Life of Harriet Tubman.* Auburn, NY: W.H. Moses, 1869.

Hagedorn, Ann. *Beyond the River: The Untold Story of the Heroes of the Underground Railroad.* New York: Simon and Schuster, 2002.

Gara, Larry. *The Liberty Line: The Legend of the Underground Railroad.* Lexington: University of Kentucky, 1961.

Griffler, Keith P. *Front Line of Freedom: African Americans and the Forging of the Underground Railroad in the Ohio Valley.* Lexington: University Press of Kentucky, 2004.

Grover, Kathryn. *The Fugitive's Gibraltar: Escaping Slaves and Abolitionism in New Bedford, Massachusetts.* Amherst: University of Massachusetts Press, 2001.

Hudson, J. Blaine. *Fugitive Slaves and the Underground Railroad in the Kentucky Borderland.* Jefferson, NC: McFarland and Company, 2002.

Parker, John. *His Promised Land: The Autobiography of John P. Parker, Former Slave and Conductor on the Underground Railroad.* Edited by Stuart Seely Sprague. New York: W.W. Norton, 1996.

Sernett, Milton. *North Star Country: Upstate New York and the Crusade for African American Freedom.* Syracuse, NY: Syracuse University Press, 2002.

Siebert, Wilbur. *The Underground Railroad from Slavery to Freedom.* New York: Macmillan, 1898.

Still, William. *The Underground Railroad.* Philadelphia, 1872.

Unitarianism and Antislavery

It is difficult to summarize the relationship of Unitarians to the antislavery movement. Most Unitarians, it appears, were opposed in principle to slavery. Many Unitarians tacitly, if not actively, supported the moderate antislavery movement and its agenda of gradual emancipation, slaveholder compensation, and African colonization. With the emergence of William Lloyd Garrison and the abolitionist movement in the 1830s, however, leading members of the Unitarian clergy publicly chastised the Garrisonians for their advocacy of immediate emancipation and for their confrontational, socially disruptive tactics. Still other Unitarians emerged in the 1850s as spokespersons for the radical vanguard of the abolitionist movement. While it is difficult, therefore, to generalize about Unitarianism and antislavery, it is possible to identify the socioeconomic and cultural factors behind their initial conservatism, and to chart the relationship between their evolving radicalism and the major political events of the day.

The Reverend William Ellery Channing, (1780–1842), the leading Unitarian minister of his generation, lamented privately to a friend, that "no sect in this country has taken less interest in the slavery question" than the Unitarians. As a small sect of liberal Congregationalist ministers located initially in and around Boston, the Unitarians were closely associated with the city's wealthy mercantile families and elite cultural institutions. Many Boston merchants had long-established relationships with Southern slaveholders, first as owners of the merchant ships that trafficked in African slaves, and later as owners of and investors in New England's growing textile industry, which depended on a regular supply of Southern cotton. Economic self-interest, compounded by a social conservatism and cultural elitism shared by Boston's merchants and Unitarian clergy, sanctioned expression of only the most moderate antislavery sentiments. The Reverend Henry Ware Jr., a professor at Harvard Divinity School, was pressured in 1834 by Harvard administrators, Boston newspapers, and members of his own congregation, to renounce his affiliation with the Cambridge Anti-Slavery Society, a moderate antislavery association. Another member of Harvard's faculty, Carl Follen, a distinguished German scholar, was dismissed for publicly voicing antislavery views. By the early 1850s, one-third of Harvard's undergraduates were the sons of Southern planters, and with the outbreak of Civil War in 1861, Harvard could claim the dubious honor of counting seventeen Confederate generals among its alumni.

William Ellery Channing typifies the relationship of many Unitarian ministers to the antislavery movement. Channing was born and raised in Newport, Rhode Island, a town still referred to in the late eighteenth century as "the slave market of America." After graduating from Harvard in 1798, Channing spent two years in Virginia tutoring the children of a prominent Richmond slaveholder. Channing married into a wealthy Newport mercantile family whose fortune had been earned in part by selling rum to slavetraders, who occasionally settled their debts in slaves. In 1830, troubled by poor health, Channing vacationed on a slave plantation on the Caribbean island of St. Croix, where he once again witnessed firsthand the harsh realities of the plantation system.

Despite these experiences, or perhaps more accurately, due largely to these experiences, Channing refrained from commenting publicly on or participating in the antislavery movement until the last years of his life. Criticized by Maria Weston Chapman, a radical member of his congregation, and by the Reverend Samuel J. May, a young Unitarian minister converted to abolitionism, Channing admitted in 1834 that he had been "silent too long" on the subject of slavery. *Slavery*, Channing's first public statement in support of antislavery, was published in 1835. From that year onward until his death, Channing took an increasingly public stance against slavery. In 1837, Channing organized a memorial service for the murdered Illinois abolitionist, Elijah P. Lovejoy, over the protests of Andrews Norton, another leading Unitarian minister, and despite increasingly hostile condemnations by members of his Federal Street congregation and other prominent Bostonians. A cursory reading of *Slavery* and Channing's other published antislavery works reveals, however, that despite his heightened political activism, Channing's views never evolved beyond a moderate antislavery position. Even as he proclaimed his devotion to the antislavery cause, in nearly every work Channing reserved his harshest criticism for the abolitionists, whom he criticized repeatedly as irresponsible, if well intentioned, extremists.

Channing's evolving views on slavery are significant only in comparison to the intransigent and often intemperate condemnations of the antislavery movement voiced throughout the 1830s and 1840s by Andrews Norton, Ezra Stiles Gannet, and other leading Unitarians. Despite the social conservatism of Channing's generation, by the 1850s younger Unitarian ministers like Thomas Wentworth Higginson and Theodore Parker had repudiated their elders' views on antislavery and achieved prominence as leading spokespersons in the vanguard of the abolitionist movement. The radicalism of these younger Unitarians achieved its fullest expression in the abolitionist activism of the Reverend Theodore Parker.

Parker's radicalism had several sources. Parker was particularly proud of the fact that his grandfather led the local militia in the Battle of Lexington, and references to the American Revolution recur throughout his antislavery writings. Like many New Englanders, Parker was also outraged by passage of the Fugitive Slave Law and by the outcome of the case of Anthony Burns. The failed efforts to prevent Burns's reenslavement, compounded by news of the outrages committed in Kansas by proslavery forces, compelled Parker and many other Unitarians to accept violence as a legitimate tactic in the war against slavery. Parker took to carrying loaded pistols, and supported the movement to arm Kansas free-state settlers, including the militant abolitionist John Brown. Parker's support for Brown continued even after Brown's massacre of unarmed, proslavery settlers at Pottawatomie Creek. In 1859, Parker, along with Higginson, became a member of the Secret Six, a group of prominent, proviolence abolitionists who provided Brown with funds for his intended, and ultimately unsuccessful, slave insurrection at Harpers Ferry, Virginia. By the time Brown's ill-fated raid came undone in October 1859, Parker lay dying in Rome, Italy, where he had hoped to recuperate from tuberculosis. Nevertheless, upon learning of Brown's indictment and pending execution, Parker used "what poor remnant of power is left to me," to celebrate Brown as a martyr and a saint, and to assert that the slave "has a natural right to kill everyone who seeks to prevent his enjoyment of liberty."

Neil Brody Miller

See also: Bleeding Kansas.

Further Readings

Commager, Henry Steele, ed. *Theodore Parker: An Anthology*. Boston: Beacon Press, 1960.

Howe, Daniel Walker. *The Unitarian Conscience: Harvard Moral Philosophy, 1805–1861*. Middleton, CT: Wesleyan University Press, 1988.

Pease, Jane H. and William H. Pease. "Confrontation and Abolition in the 1850s." In John R. McKivigan, ed. *History of the American Abolitionist Movement: A Bibliography of Scholarly Articles*. New York: Garland Publishing, 1999, pp. 293–307.

Stange, Douglas C. "Abolitionism as Treason: The Unitarian Elite Defends Law, Order, and the Union." *Harvard Library Bulletin* 28 (1980): 152–170.

Stange, Douglas C. *Patterns of Antislavery among American Unitarians, 1831–1860*. Rutherford, NJ: Associated Universities Press, 1977.

United States, Antislavery in

Organized antislavery in the United States has a long history that can be roughly divided into four somewhat overlapping phases. The movement began during the American Revolution and for the most part ended with the adoption of the Thirteenth Amendment, which abolished slavery in the United States. However, some opponents of slavery and a few organizations continued to be active in the United States well after slavery was abolished in the nation. One of the earliest antislavery organizations, the Pennsylvania Society for the Abolition of Slavery, never disbanded and continues to work for better race relations.

Early Abolition Societies

During the American Revolution, opponents of slavery in most of the Northern states, and a few states of the Upper South, organized what were known at the time as abolition societies. The most important was the Pennsylvania Society for Promoting the Abolition of Slavery, the Relief of Free Negroes Unlawfully Held in Bondage, and for Improving the Condition of the African Race, more commonly known as the Pennsylvania Abolition Society, or the PAS. The PAS was first organized in 1775, but became moribund during the British occupation of Philadelphia. A revived society reemerged in 1784. However, members and future members of the Society helped work for the passage of the Pennsylvania Gradual Abolition Act of 1780, the first American legislative act to begin the process of dismantling slavery. Similar organizations in other states successfully worked for gradual abolition acts in Rhode Island (1784), Connecticut (1784), New York (1799), and New Jersey (1804). Societies in Delaware, Maryland, Virginia, and Kentucky were

Abolitionists, including William Lloyd Garrison and Frederick Douglass, met at Tremont Temple, in Boston on December 3, 1860. The rally commemorated the anniversary of John Brown's execution but ended with the abolitionists being expelled by other Bostonians. (Library of Congress)

unsuccessful in moving those states toward abolition, and by 1810, the Southern societies were moribund or simply no longer functioning. Many of the leaders of these societies were leaders of the new nation itself. Benjamin Franklin and Dr. Benjamin Rush, a signer of the Declaration of Independence along with Franklin, served as presidents of the Pennsylvania Society. The president of the New York Society was John Jay, the diplomat and future chief justice of the United States. Another key member was Alexander Hamilton, who coauthored the *Federalist Papers* with Jay and then served as secretary of the treasury. James Wood, who served as governor of Virginia from 1796 to 1799, was also the vice president of the Virginia Abolition Society. Other members of these societies included Thomas Paine; James Otis; James Pemberton, a Quaker merchant; Philadelphia mayor, Hilary Baker; Rufus King, a signer of the U.S. Constitution; Judge James Duane; and Daniel D. Tompkins, a future governor of New York.

The Northern abolition societies had four general goals. The first was to abolish slavery in their own states. In this they were remarkably successful. In addition to those Northern states which ended slavery through gradual abolition acts, Massachusetts, New Hampshire, and Vermont (the fourteenth state) abolished slavery through constitutional provisions. By 1804, all of the Northern states had either ended slavery outright or were in the process of gradually destroying it. The slave population in the North dropped precipitously, while the free black populations grew rapidly. For example, in Pennsylvania the slave population dropped from 6,855 in 1780 to 211 in 1820. In New York there were 21,324 slaves in 1790 and just over 10,000 in 1820. In 1827, the state freed all remaining slaves. New England had 3,870 slaves in 1790 and 145 by 1820.

Second, the societies agitated for an end to the African slave trade. In the first session of Congress, the Pennsylvania Society petitioned Congress to end the commerce. The Constitution prohibited an absolute ban on the trade at that time. Nevertheless, the Society petitioned Congress to end the trade, which led to an astounding attack on abolitionists by Southern members of Congress. Benjamin Franklin responded, in his last published essay before he died, with a brilliant satirical attack on the slave trade. In this essay, Franklin took on the voice of a North African Moslem, praising the virtue of enslaving Christians. Even though Congress could not yet ban the trade, the individual states could. Thus, the Northern states and a number of Southern states prohibited their citizens from participating in the trade. The abolition societies worked to make sure these laws were enforced.

Third, the societies fought to protect free blacks. The PAS, for example, agitated for legislation to protect free blacks from kidnapping and reenslavement. This led, in 1788, to an elaborate amendment strengthening the 1780 gradual abolition act. The PAS, as well as other societies, also used litigation to protect free blacks, help emancipate slaves, and make life miserable for slaveowners. At one point, President George Washington complained to political leaders in Pennsylvania that the PAS was harassing too many Southern masters. The PAS and its New York counterpart also initiated litigation to secure the liberty of blacks who had a legal claim to freedom. The threat of a lawsuit was probably the reason Thomas Jefferson reluctantly signed a paper agreeing to free his slave James Hemings, after he brought him to Philadelphia. Ironically, intervention by the PAS on behalf of a kidnapped free black ultimately led to the adoption of the 1793 fugitive slave law. However, despite that outcome, the abolition societies throughout the North used the legal talent of their members to secure the freedom of a number of blacks. In many ways, these societies were the first public interest organization to use litigation to achieve social reform. They can be seen as the precursors of the NAACP Legal Defense Fund or the American Civil Liberties Union.

Fourth, the societies worked to enhance the social conditions of blacks. They built schools for blacks, helped raise money for black education, black churches, orphanages, and other social institutions. In an age before public education and a social safety net, the abolition societies provided significant material aid to black communities.

The abolition societies continued to function into the early part of the nineteenth century. With immediate abolition in northern New England and the last gradual abolition act passed in New Jersey in 1804, the mission of the societies evolved to protecting free blacks from kidnapping and helping black communities provide education for their children. Except for the African slave trade, the societies were mostly focused on local issues. Their purpose was to end slavery in their own backyard and end the African slave trade. By 1808, they had accomplished both. By the 1820s, they had ceased having national conventions as they had done in the 1790s and generally disbanded or, like the PAS, faded into obscurity, continuing to help runaway slaves and black schools, but otherwise not participating in the emerging new attack on slavery in the 1830s.

American Colonization Society

In 1816, a diverse collection of humanitarians, opponents of slavery, slave owners fearful of free blacks, and various politicians, organized the American Society for Colonizing the Free People of Color, better known as the American Colonization Society (ACS). The early leaders of the ACS included Henry Clay, the speaker of the House of Representatives; Congressman Charles Fenton Mercer of Virginia; Maryland lawyer and author of the *Star Spangled Banner*, Francis Scott Key; and James Monroe, who would become the fifth president of the United States. The first president of the Society was Supreme Court justice Bushrod Washington, the nephew of President George Washington. The ACS transported free blacks and recently manumitted slaves to Africa, where they established colonies and settlements and eventually the country of Liberia. The goals of the Society were mixed. Many of the slaveholding Southern members saw the Society as a vehicle for removing free blacks from the United States. They believed free blacks were subversive to slavery. Other members, such as the Massachusetts politician Daniel Webster, believed the ACS would encourage masters to free their slaves by providing a safe place to send them. Thus, the ACS combined proslavery racism with antislavery humanitarianism. Over the years, some masters took advantage of the ACS to emancipate their slaves. This was particularly applied in states like Virginia and North Carolina, which had made manumission without also removal from the state extremely difficult. Some free blacks supported the ACS because they felt Africa offered them more opportunity than the United States.

Most free blacks, however, saw the ACS as a threat to their liberty. In Philadelphia, the Reverend Richard Allen led a huge protest against the ACS. The black revolutionary David Walker vigorously attacked colonization in his pamphlet,

An Appeal to the Colored Citizens of the World (1829). The free black opponents of the ACS understood that its slave-owning leaders and proslavery supporters, such as the Virginians John Tyler and Abel Upshur, were hardly friends of emancipation or free blacks. These Southerners wanted the ACS to remove free blacks, not slaves, from American shores. In the 1830s, the new antislavery movement attacked the ACS as a friend of slavery, not of blacks. In fact, it was a friend of slavery, but at the same time, the ACS facilitated the private manumission of a few thousand or so slaves.

The Emergence of Immediatism

Opponents of slavery objected to colonization because the colonizationists were not, ultimately, interested in ending slavery. At best, the ACS facilitated liberty for a few slaves through private manumission. But, the cost of this private manumission for the African Americans was high; to gain freedom they had to leave the land they knew, the United States, and relocate to another land where they had never been, Africa. They had to leave friends and relatives behind and venture to an unknown place. Most of all, however, colonization retarded any direct assault on slavery.

Blacks like David Walker and Richard Allen were the first to condemn colonization, but in the early 1830s, white opponents of slavery also attacked the ACS. The most important of these—indeed, the most important opponent of slavery for the next three decades—was William Lloyd Garrison, a native of Newburyport, Massachusetts, and a printer by trade. In 1831, Garrison began publishing the *Liberator*, which became the nation's leading antislavery paper. Garrison, along with other early white abolitionists including Arthur and Lewis Tappan, had been deeply influenced by the intensity of black opposition to colonization, their increasing attacks on slavery, and their dedication to faith and self-improvement. This influence was critical in moving the previously procolonization Garrison and the brothers Arthur and Lewis Tappan out of the fold and toward a demand for total and immediate abolition. Quoting the nation's founding document in the inaugural issue of the *Liberator*, Garrison asserted his support for "the 'self-evident truth' maintained in the American Declaration of Independence, 'that all men are created equal, and endowed by their Creator with certain inalienable rights—among which are life, liberty and the pursuit of happiness.'" Garrison proclaimed, "I shall strenuously contend for the immediate enfranchisement of our slave population." Setting the tone for the next three decades, Garrison declared the following in his newspaper:

> I am aware that many object to the severity of my language; but is there not cause for severity? I will be as harsh as truth, and as uncompromising

as justice. On this subject, I do not wish to think, or to speak, or write, with moderation. No! no! Tell a man whose house is on fire to give a moderate alarm; tell him to moderately rescue his wife from the hands of the ravisher; tell the mother to gradually extricate her babe from the fire into which it has fallen; but urge me not to use moderation in a cause like the present. I am in earnest—I will not equivocate—I will not excuse—I will not retreat a single inch—AND I WILL BE HEARD. The apathy of the people is enough to make every statue leap from its pedestal, and to hasten the resurrection of the dead.

A year later, in 1832, Garrison helped found the New England Anti-Slavery Society, which advocated immediate abolition. In December 1833, sixty-two opponents of slavery met in Philadelphia to form the American Anti-Slavery Society (AASS). The delegates included three blacks and four women, in an age when men and women rarely gathered in public meetings and blacks and whites rarely worked together. Most of the delegates were religiously motivated and saw their movement as part of a moral crusade to rid America of sin. Many came out of the temperance movement. The abolitionists demanded the "immediate, unconditional, uncompensated emancipation" of the nation's slaves. They rejected the gradualism of the earlier abolition societies and the absurd position of the ACS that free blacks had to be removed from the nation. Such a position was unfair to blacks and at the same time made ending slavery impossible, because the prerequisite for emancipation—moving the former slaves to Africa—was impossible. There were simply not enough ships or resources to move American slaves to Africa or anywhere else, assuming they wanted to go.

The new "immediate" abolitionists believed that they could accomplish their goals through moral suasion—that is, by persuading slave owners that they should free their slaves because it was their Christian duty to do so. Their tactics included flooding the mails with pamphlets and letters and trying to convince leading Southerners, especially churchmen and lay leaders, to take a stand against slavery. Later, the abolitionists would flood Congress with petitions against slavery. The AASS developed local and state organizations throughout the North. While women continued to work within the men's organizations, they also formed their own groups, such as the Boston Female Anti-Slavery Society. Members of this group found an attorney to petition for a writ of habeas corpus to test whether a visitor could bring a slave into Massachusetts. In *Commonwealth v. Aves* (1836), they succeeded in getting the Massachusetts Supreme Judicial Court to hold that slaves brought into the state immediately became free.

Abolitionists were trapped by their own language—immediate emancipation—because no one believed this was either possible or desirable. Almost all whites, even those opposed to slavery, believed that most of the two million or so slaves in the nation were not ready for immediate freedom. Furthermore, even opponents of slavery understood that the overwhelming majority of whites in the North as well as the South were not prepared to accept so many free blacks living among them. This led to the complicated explanation that the new abolitionists favored "immediate abolition, gradually achieved." They believed the ending of slavery must start immediately, and the Americans, especially slaveholders, had to commit to emancipation to save the very soul of the nation. This led to the tactics of moral suasion.

These early abolitionists met with little success. In the North they were mobbed and in the South they were ignored or banned. Between 1833 and 1835, citizens in Canterbury, Connecticut, repeatedly attacked a boarding school for black girls run by a Quaker abolitionist, Prudence Crandall. In 1835, a mob in Boston threatened to lynch William Lloyd Garrison, dragging him through the streets with a rope around his neck. In 1837, an abolitionist printer, the Reverend Elijah P. Lovejoy was killed as he tried to defend his business and printing press from a proslavery mob attempting to throw his press into the Mississippi River. Mobs in Utica, New York City, Philadelphia, and elsewhere broke up antislavery meetings and even burned buildings. Some abolitionist speakers were beaten up and chased out of towns in the North. Congress passed a "gag" rule to prevent the reading of abolitionist petitions, and relatively few Northerners joined antislavery organizations.

Abolitionists also struggled with each other over a variety of issues. Garrison and his allies were not content with focusing on antislavery. Garrison campaigned for women's rights, world peace, pacifism, and temperance. He attacked the organized churches and became increasingly disaffected with politics. By the end of the 1830s, he was moving to the position that abolitionists should reject political activity altogether. Declaring the Constitution to be a "covenant with death and an agreement in hell," he adopted as a slogan for his newspaper, "No Union with Slaveholders." This radical disunionism made him even less popular among most white Northerners. Most of the subscribers to his newspaper were blacks. However, despite his personal unpopularity, and the small number of whites or blacks who joined the AASS, Garrison's message began to take hold. Northerners who had never thought about slavery could no longer avoid the issue. In addition, Garrisonians used the courts in Massachusetts and elsewhere to challenge slavery where they could. Members of the Boston Female Anti-Slavery Society brought the issue of visiting slaves before the Massachusetts Supreme Judicial Court in *Commonwealth v. Aves* (1836). The conservative chief justice, Lemuel Shaw, sided with the abolitionists, holding that a slave became free the moment he or she entered the state, unless as a fugitive slave. Within a decade, most other Northern states had followed this rule. The AASS also provided legal help to fugitive slaves. The AASS continued to operate until the end of the Civil War. Small in numbers, the Society had powerful speakers, including Wendell Phillips who was perhaps the greatest orator of the age. Frederick Douglass began his career as a Garrisonian, and as an agent for the Massachusetts Anti-Slavery Society. Women speakers like Abby Kelley Foster were also important in spreading the gospel of strong antislavery ideas. The AASS served as a powerful force for changing opinion, even if it lacked members and convinced few to accept all of its goals. Northerners introduced to abolitionist ideas by AASS pamphlets, books, and its many speakers might not have become immediate abolitionists, but many became strongly antislavery, and those sentiments eventually affected politics, law, and social relations.

Political Antislavery

Garrison's increasing radicalism led to a split within the movement. In 1840, moderate abolitionists, led by James G. Birney and Lewis and Arthur Tappan, formed the American and Foreign Anti-Slavery Society. The AFASS rejected women's rights, pacifism, and other causes and focused only on slavery. The election of Abby Kelley to the AASS board precipitated the creation of the new organization, but this was not the only cause of the schism. Garrison and other leaders of the AASS had mounted an unrelenting campaign against the organized churches— "synagogues of Satan" and "cages of unclean birds" as one Garrisonian called them. But other abolitionists, evangelicals such as Arthur and Lewis Tappan, James G. Birney, and William Jay (the son of former Chief Justice John Jay), were more orthodox in their religious beliefs and support for existing churches. They were also not ready to mix antislavery with support for women's rights and other issues. Thus, in 1840 a number of key AASS members, led by the Tappans and Birney, formed the AFASS. The organization would continue to operate until the mid-1850s, when it faded from the scene. The split between the two antislavery societies left both of them weaker. But, by competing with each other, they probably increased the total number of antislavery books, pamphlets, and newspapers in circulation, and gave more people access to antislavery ideas.

Initially, the new organization ignored politics, but shortly after the schism, the Tappans and Birney helped form the Liberty Party, with Birney as its first presidential candidate in 1840. The Liberty Party was the first political party in the nation's history to openly oppose slavery. By this time, the antislavery movement was beginning to have an effect on electoral politics. Antislavery sentiment was particularly strong in northern New England, northern and central New York, much of Massachusetts, northern Ohio, and the new state of Michigan. Some Whig members of Congress, such as John Quincy Adams of Massachusetts, Seth Gates of New York, Joshua Giddings of Ohio, and William Slade of Vermont, were openly sympathetic to antislavery. So too were some important state politicians, like Governor William H. Seward of New York. But antislavery Whigs were a minority in their party. While a few Democrats also opposed slavery, for the most part the office holders and rank and file of the Democracy were deeply hostile to antislavery. The national Democratic Party was dominated by Southerners, and most Northern Democrats followed their lead on issues of slavery and race. The Liberty Party offered antislavery voters an opportunity to express their opposition to slavery and their disgust that neither of the two major parties was willing to take a stand against slavery. In 1840, the new party won only 7,000 votes nationally, and had no effect on the election.

In 1844, Birney again ran for president on the Liberty ticket. This time he won slightly over 62,000 votes. The party won no electoral votes, but may have taken enough votes from the Whig candidate, Henry Clay, to give the election to the Democrat, James K. Polk. In the popular vote, Polk beat Clay by just over 38,000 votes. In New York, Clay lost to Polk by fewer than 5,000 votes, while the Liberty Party won about three times that many votes. Clay believed the Liberty Party cost him New York, and the election. He was certain that he would have won most of the votes going to Birney had there been no Liberty Party, and thus but for the third party would have been elected president. But, this analysis, supported by some historians, assumes that the antislavery voters who supported Birney would have been willing, in the absence of an antislavery party, to vote for the slaveholding Clay. This is at least debatable. It is just as likely they would have stayed home and refused to vote for either slaveholding candidate.

In 1848, another antislavery party emerged, the Free Soil Party. In the wake of the war with Mexico, the Free Soilers insisted on preventing the spread of slavery into the West. Unlike the Liberty Party, the Free Soilers were not dedicated to ending slavery where it existed. The new party nominated Martin Van Buren, the former Democratic president, who had great popularity among Northern Democrats, particularly in his home state of New York. Despite the party's refusal to attack the existence of slavery, the Free Soilers' commitment to stopping the spread of slavery made their organization an important and powerful alternative to the Whigs and Democrats for those voters who opposed slavery. Before 1848, mainstream antislavery politicians had generally been Whigs. But in 1848, the Democrats faced the problem of a rank-and-file revolt against allowing slavery to exist in the newly acquired territories. This was perhaps a testament to the success of the abolitionists. While neither of the two major antislavery societies had gained very many members, together they had helped usher in a sea change in Northern opinion. Thus, many Northern Democrats now had to offer some antislavery sentiments to their constituents. The Free Soil Party appealed to these Democrats, as well as to the Liberty Party voters.

The Free Soil Party's candidate, former Democratic president, Martin Van Buren, gained over 290,000 votes. Van Buren clearly took votes away from the Democratic candidate, Lewis Cass, setting the stage for the Whig candidate to win the election. Meanwhile, other Free Soilers were elected to state legislatures and Congress. In Ohio, a small group of Free Soilers held the balance of power between the Democrats and Whigs. They leveraged this position to gain repeal of most of Ohio's black laws and to send an abolitionist, Democrat Salmon P. Chase, to the U.S. Senate. Joining him that term was the Whig abolitionist, William Henry Seward of New York. Scores of others in the House and Senate were now adamantly opposed to slavery in one form or another. Few came close to the Garrisonian position of immediate abolition. Almost all believed the federal government had no power to end slavery in the states. However, the antislavery men in the House and Senate were determined to prevent the spread of slavery into new territories and states, and were willing to fight to chip away at slavery where they could—such as in the District of Columbia, the federal territories—and by more effectively enforcing the ban on the African slave trade. They unsuccessfully opposed the stringent Fugitive Slave Law of 1850, but its repeal would be part of the political agenda of antislavery activists for the rest of the decade.

By the 1850s, antislavery was part of mainstream politics in the North. The AASS and the AFASS continued to agitate, send out speakers, publish attacks on slavery, aid fugitive slaves, and fight segregation and racism. William C. Nell, a black Garrisonian, spearheaded a drive to integrate Boston's schools. His work led to the first school desegregation case, *Roberts v. Boston* (1850), which was argued by Charles Sumner, the soon-to-be abolitionist U.S. senator, and Robert Morris, one of the first black attorneys in the nation. The plaintiffs lost before the Massachusetts Supreme Judicial Court, but Nell did not stop there. Despite the Garrisonian rejection of voting, Nell persistently petitioned the state legislature, ultimately succeeding with a law in 1855 that banned segregation in the state's public schools.

Informal and small antislavery groups helped fugitive slaves evade capture and aided them in seeking shelter in the United States or in Canada. They included some groups that were exclusively black and some that were integrated. In the 1830s, the black leader, David Ruggles, organized the New York Committee of Vigilance in New York City. The committee helped hide fugitive slaves and helped expose professional slave catchers. After the adoption of the 1850 Fugitive Slave Law, blacks, sometimes working with whites, organized more vigilance committees to help protect themselves from slave catchers. In 1851, at Christiana, Pennsylvania, scores of blacks and whites showed up when horns were blown because a master was trying to recover his fugitive slave. The abolitionists tried to talk the master out of seeking his slave, and when this failed, gunfire broke out. The master was killed, the slaves escaped, and the government indicted numerous bystanders for treason. Abolitionist lawyers, including the Whig congressman Thaddeus Stevens, defended those indicted, all of whom were acquitted.

The major antislavery organizations persistently denounced the fugitive slave laws and helped raise money for fugitives in Canada. Attorneys who were members of the AASS and AFASS often represented fugitive slaves or those charged with helping them escape. In New York City, for example, William Jay and his son John Jay Jr., were extremely active in supporting fugitive slaves, as were a number of Liberty Party men. American abolitionists corresponded with members of the Anti-Slavery Society of Canada and other Canadians who were dedicated to helping fugitive slaves. Americans like Frederick Douglass and Wendell Phillips lectured in Canada. John Brown, who operated outside of any organizational structures that were not his own, held a meeting in Ontario to plan his raid on Harpers Ferry.

Most of the antislavery societies were integrated—at least if there were blacks in the area. Many local societies were in the rural North, where few, if any, blacks lived. African Americans organized numerous societies and conventions, focusing on their social, political, and legal rights. Slavery, and especially the protection of fugitive slaves and stopping the kidnapping of free blacks, was always on their agenda. But, these organizations were far broader than the traditional antislavery societies. Overlapping interests led to cooperation between black and white groups on a variety of issues. Indeed, one of the great legacies of antislavery was the development of interracial cooperation. Equally important was the development of separate black groups that provided leadership training and organizational skills that helped develop Northern black communities and set the stage for black leadership in the post–Civil War South.

Mainstream Politics and the End of Slavery

In 1854, the Democratic majority in Congress passed the Kansas-Nebraska Act, opening almost all of the western territories to slavery. This led to the formation of the Republican Party. By 1856, most political abolitionists had become Republicans. The AFASS virtually disappeared, as did what was left of the Liberty Party. The Republicans were not a single-issue party. The party took positions on tariffs, land policy, Mormon polygamy, banking and currency, and foreign policy. But, the party's biggest issue was slavery. The Republican Party captured Northern state legislatures, elected governors, congressmen, and senators. In 1860, it would capture the presidency. The first Republican president, Abraham Lincoln, personally hated slavery. He correctly understood the Constitution to protect slavery where it already existed, but he was determined to prevent its spread to new places.

Lincoln's election was an ironic culmination of decades of abolitionist agitation. The Garrisonians sneered at Lincoln. Referring to one case where Lincoln represented a slave owner (and lost), Wendell Phillips called him "the slave hound of Illinois." Lincoln similarly despised the disunionism of Garrison and Phillips and the violence of their new hero, John Brown. In fact, however, Lincoln and his party owed much of their success to the organized antislavery movement of the previous three decades. Abolitionists like Phillips, Garrison, Douglass (who voted for Lincoln), Theodore Dwight Weld, Elizabeth Cady Stanton, Abby Kelley Foster, Harriet Beecher Stowe, and Gerrit Smith had convinced the vast majority of Northern whites that slavery was simply wrong, that it was sinful and unnatural, and that it violated the basic principles of American society. Lincoln and his party provided an effective political vehicle for implementing these sentiments.

During the Civil War, the Republican Party and the U.S. Army became the most effective instrument of antislavery philosophy and politics. Abolitionists like Chase and Seward entered Lincoln's cabinet. Other abolitionists were military officers, including the Reverend Thomas Wentworth Higginson. In the 1840s, he was a member of the Essex County Antislavery Society. He later ran for Congress as a Free Soiler. At the same time he worked with Garrison and supported women's rights. In 1854, Higginson had helped storm a Boston jail in an unsuccessful attempt to rescue the fugitive slave Anthony Burns. He was allied with Garrison intellectually, on some issues, but rejected nonresistance and pacifism. In 1854, Higginson also helped organize the Massachusetts Kansas Aid Committee, which worked with the Kansas Emigrant Aid Society. Higginson's "aid" to settlers in Kansas often took the form of rifles known as "Beecher's Bibles." In 1857, he organized a "disunion" convention in Worcester, Massachusetts. In 1858 and 1859, he was one of the "secret six" who backed John Brown in his abortive raid on Harpers Ferry. In 1862, he accepted a commission as a Colonel in the First South Carolina Volunteers, a regiment made up of former slaves who enlisted on the South Carolina Sea Islands. He spent the next two years fighting slavery as a soldier and a commander of black troops. In 1864, he left the army because of illness.

Meanwhile, other abolitionists moved to the South to set up schools for former slaves and in other ways to help them adjust to freedom. In 1862, for example, James Miller McKim organized the Philadelphia Port Royal Relief Committee, which later became known as the Pennsylvania Freedmen's Relief Association. Before the war, McKim had been the general agent for the Pennsylvania Anti-Slavery Society. McKim illustrates the flexibility of abolitionists. He was Garrisonian in his view that the Constitution was proslavery, but he worked closely with legislators in Pennsylvania and also supported John Brown. And, when the war began he worked with former slaves. He was also a member of the Union League of Philadelphia and helped recruit black regiments in the state. He remained involved in helping former slaves until 1869. He also fought for a ban on segregation in public transportation in Pennsylvania.

Unlike McKim, Garrison thought his work was done in 1865 when he dissolved the American Anti-Slavery Society, believing that the adoption of the Thirteenth Amendment had rendered his organization no longer necessary. In retrospect, we know that conclusion was a mistake. After slavery, blacks needed support, education, and activist allies. Some white abolitionists like McKim stayed longer. Wendell Phillips continued to be concerned about the plight of blacks, but also focused on labor reform after the war. Black abolitionists like Frederick Douglass continued their work until the end of their lives.

In the end, the antislavery movement set the moral tone for the nation. The leaders of the movement developed organizing skills and propaganda techniques. Despite intramural disputes and disagreements over tactics and theories, in retrospect the antislavery movement was surprisingly coherent. The schisms and internal disputes mask the diversity of opinions and the ability of abolitionists to accept a variety of tactics and goals. Garrison, Phillips, or McKim may not have voted, but they worked well with politicians in their own states and many of their followers did vote. The non-voting abolitionists helped create a huge constituency of fellow travelers who did vote, and who would ultimately only vote for opponents of slavery. At the social level, not all abolitionists were integrationists, or even racial egalitarians. But, the organizations almost universally opposed discrimination and emphatically supported black rights. Abolitionists fought for integrated education, antidiscrimination laws, and black suffrage. Abolitionist women in Massachusetts successfully petitioned the legislature to repeal the state's ban on interracial marriage, because they believed the state should have no laws that sanctioned racial discrimination. Even nonpolitical Garrisonians agitated for blacks to have the same right to vote as whites. Interracial cooperation within the movement was never perfect. But, nowhere else in the United States was there as much cooperation and interracial opportunity. Much of the postwar black leadership came out of the antislavery movement. Similarly, women in the movement gained valuable experience, which they applied to their fight for legal equality after the war. The top leaders of the women's movement— Elizabeth Cady Stanton, Lucretia Mott, and Susan B. Anthony—had all been active abolitionists before the war. A final legacy of organized antislavery was its persistence and staying power. For more than three decades abolitionists labored against the monstrous injustice of slavery. They provide a model of how to keep an eye on the prize through decades of struggle and discouragement.

Paul Finkelman

See also: Immediate Emancipation; Mexican War and Antislavery; Postal Campaign (1835); Whig Party and Antislavery.

Further Readings

Finkelman, Paul. *Slavery and the Founders: Race and Liberty in the Age of Jefferson.* Armonk, NY: M.E. Sharpe, 1996.

Foner, Eric. *Free Soil, Free Labor, Free Men: The Ideology of the Republican Party before the Civil War.* Reprint ed. New York: Oxford University Press, 1995.

Stewart, James Brewer. *Holy Warriors: The Abolitionists and American Slavery.* 2nd ed. New York: Hill and Wang, 1997.

Walters, Ronald. *The Antislavery Appeal: American Abolitionism after 1830.* New York: W.W. Norton and Company, 1985.

U.S. Constitution and Antislavery

The U.S. Constitution protected slavery in a variety of ways. Article I, Sec. 2. Par. 3, contained the three-fifths clause, which counted three-fifths of all slaves for purposes of representation in Congress. That provision vastly increased the power of the South in Congress. The three-fifths clause also gave the South extra power in electing the president because the allocation of presidential electors was based on the number of representatives in Congress. Thomas Jefferson, who owned nearly 200 slaves, would not have been elected president in 1800 without the extra electors produced by the three-fifths clause. Article I, Sec. 8, Par. 15, known as the domestic insurrections clause, empowered Congress to call "forth the Militia" to "suppress Insurrections," including slave rebellions. Southerners were delighted by this provision, as well as one in Article IV, Sec. 4, known as the domestic violence provision guaranteeing that the U.S. government would protect states from "domestic violence," including slave rebellions. Article I, Sec. 9, Par. 1, popularly known as the "slave trade clause," prohibited Congress from banning the African slave trade before 1808. Under this clause, more Southerners imported about 100,000 Africans into the United States in the early nineteenth century. The amendment provisions of Article V further protected the slave trade by specifically prohibiting any modification of that provision before 1808. Article I, Section 9 and Section 10 prohibited taxes on exports, which Southerners demanded as a way of prohibiting an indirect tax on slavery and slave produced products. Article IV, Sec. 2, Par. 3, the fugitive slave clause, prohibited the states from emancipating fugitive slaves and required that runaways be returned to their owners "on demand."

Besides specific clauses of the Constitution, the structure of the entire document ensured against emancipation by the new federal government. Because the Constitution created a government of limited powers, Congress lacked the power to interfere in the domestic institutions of the states. Thus, during the ratification debates, only the most fearful Southern Anti-Federalist opposed the Constitution on the grounds that it threatened slavery. But most Southerners agreed with the Federalists, who argued that the Constitution created a limited government that could not harm slavery. For example, General Charles Cotesworth Pinckney of South Carolina crowed to his state's house of representatives, "We have a security that the general government can never emancipate them, for no such authority is granted and it is admitted, on all hands, that the general government has no powers but what are expressly granted by the Constitution, and that all rights not expressed were reserved by the several states." Similarly, at the Virginia ratification convention, Edmund Randolph asserted, "Were it right here to mention what passed in [the Philadelphia] convention . . . I might tell you *that the Southern States, even South Carolina herself, conceived this property to be secure*" and that "there was not a member of the Virginia delegation who had *the smallest suspicion of the abolition of slavery.*"

The amendment process, set out in Article V, further secured slavery. Under Article V, an amendment required the ratification of three-fourths of the states. As long as the slave states voted against an amendment, it could not pass. In 1860, for example, there were thirty-three states, of which fifteen were slave states, thereby eliminating the possibility of twenty-five states (three-fourths of all the states) voting against Southern interests. Voting as a block, these states can still prevent any amendment to the Constitution, even in the modern fifty-state nation.

Because of these many proslavery provisions and compromises with slavery, and the impossibility of ending slavery through a constitutional process, William Lloyd Garrison, the great nineteenth-century abolitionist, called the Constitution a "covenant with death" and "an agreement with Hell." Garrison and his followers refused to participate in American electoral politics, arguing that if they did so, they would be supporting "the pro-slavery, war sanctioning Constitution of the United States." Instead, under the slogan "No Union with Slaveholders," the Garrisonians repeatedly argued for dissolution of the Union.

Part of Garrisonian opposition to the Union stemmed from their desire to avoid the corruption that came from participating in a government created by what they considered a proslavery Constitution. But their position was also at least theoretically pragmatic. The Garrisonians were convinced that the legal protection of slavery in the Constitution made political activity not only futile, but actually counterproductive. They believed that traditional political activity created popular support for the constitutional order, which in turn strengthened the stranglehold slavery had on America. In his pamphlet, *Can Abolitionists Vote or Take Office under the United States Constitution* (1845), Wendell Phillips pointed out that in the years since the adoption of the Constitution, Americans had witnessed "the slaves trebling in numbers—slaveholders monopolizing the offices and dictating the policy of the Government—prostituting the strength and influence of the Nation to the support of slavery here and elsewhere—trampling on the rights of the free States, and making the courts of the country their tools." Phillips argued that this experience proved "that it is impossible for free and slave States to unite on any terms, without all becoming partners in the guilt and responsible for the sin of slavery."

The Garrisonians ultimately argued that since the political system and the Constitution were stacked in favor of slavery, it was a pointless waste of their time and money to try to fight slavery through electoral politics. The Garrisonian critique of the Constitution logically led to the conclusion that the free states should secede from the union. Garrisonians thus rallied to the slogan "No Union with Slaveholders."

Other nineteenth-century antislavery leaders disagreed with the Garrisonians. Salmon P. Chase, the most successful antislavery politician of the period, fought throughout the antebellum period to convince his colleagues in Congress, the judiciary, and Northern voters that the Constitution was really antislavery. Chase argued that abolitionists should use the political process to prevent the expansion of slavery and the addition of new slave states. He believed repeal of the fugitive slave laws and other laws protecting slavery was a way in which the Constitution could be used to fight bondage. Frederick Douglass, who began his career as a Garrisonian, eventually came to accept the idea that the Constitution could be used to fight slavery. He went so far as to argue that the "three-fifths clause" leaned toward freedom. This analysis ignored the fact that the clause gave extra representation in Congress to the South for its slaves, but of course did not give the slaves any particular power. If the clause leaned toward freedom, it was only because it did not give the South full representation for its slaves.

Despite their creative perseverance, the efforts of Chase, Douglass, William H. Seward, and other political abolitionists failed. The U.S. Supreme Court almost always protected slavery in the cases it heard. Likewise, almost all American presidents and their cabinet officers protected slavery in foreign and domestic politics. Perhaps most frustrating to the political abolitionists was the fact that some of their most brilliant allies in the crusade against slavery, the Garrisonians, agreed with their enemies on the meaning of the Constitution. Thus, one Ohio Liberty Party man, who believed in using politics to fight slavery, expressed his frustration with the Garrisonians after reading Wendell Phillips's pamphlet on the Constitution: "Garrison, Phillips, and Quincy; Calhoun, Rhett, and McDuffie; all harmoniously laboring to prevent such a construction of the Constitution as would abolish slavery."

Once the Civil War began, however, the Lincoln administration was able to use the Constitution to attack slavery. Lincoln found the necessary authority to issue the Emancipation Proclamation in his powers as commander-in-chief. Furthermore, with eleven of the fifteen slave states no longer participating in the government, Congress was free to limit slavery as much as possible. Thus, Congress repealed the Fugitive Slave Laws, banned slavery in the territories, and then ended slavery in the District of Columbia. In 1865, Congress sent the Thirteenth Amendment— ending slavery—to the states. The slave states could come back to the Union only if they ratified this amendment. Thus, in four years of the Civil War, the proslavery Constitution was remade as an antislavery document. Over the next five years, antislavery Republicans would pass two more amendments that further changed the Constitution to give blacks equal political and constitutional rights.

Paul Finkelman

See also: Declaration of Independence (1776); Radical Republicans; Thirteenth Amendment (1865).

Further Readings

Finkelman, Paul. *Slavery and the Founders: Race and Liberty in the Age of Jefferson.* 2nd ed. Armonk, NY: M.E. Sharpe, 2001.

Foner, Eric. *Free Soil, Free Labor, Free Men.* New York: Oxford University Press, 1970.

Wiecek, William M. *The Sources of Antislavery Constitutionalism in America, 1760–1848.* Ithaca, NY: Cornell University Press, 1977.

U.S. South, Antislavery in

Long before the dramatic rise of the organized abolitionist movement in the early nineteenth century, slaves themselves commenced resistance and rebellion in the U.S. South, which had become the heartland of the nation's slave system. In numerous ways slaves signaled their discontent with servitude, by running away, by malingering, sabotage, and arson. Because during the seventeenth and eighteenth centuries parts of the South were still sparsely settled, especially sections of swamps, woods, and mountains, entire small groups hid out as maroons, evading capture for months or even years at a time. While there were no large-scale revolts like those led by Spartacus against Rome, there were sporadic uprisings, such as that of a small but determined group of slaves who killed several whites at Stono, South Carolina, in 1739, apparently aiming to escape to the colony of free blacks under the Spanish at St. Augustine in Florida.

In addition to actions such as these, the culture and daily life of slaves provided ways to resist as well. Folklore is replete with tales of slaves who outwitted their masters, who like the "trickster" Br'er Rabbit, found their way to safety in the "briar patch." Songs such as "Jimmie Crack Corn," composed by Daniel Emmett with the likely help of African Americans, made fun of the pomposity of the masters, and took covert satisfaction when they were "accidentally" killed by the Blue Tail Fly.

During the American Revolution, tens of thousands of slaves fled to the British side, having been promised freedom if they did so. All these aspects of early American slave life suggest the constant pressure of slaves themselves against the system.

Small religious groups such as the Quakers had long expressed their opposition to slavery, as did figures like the Deist Thomas Paine. The Presbyterian leader David Rice made an impassioned plea against slavery at the Constitutional Convention in Kentucky in 1792, but that state was admitted with its "peculiar institution" intact.

In the first two decades of the nineteenth century, the South provided many examples of small groups, mostly of religious leaders, who opposed slavery. In Jonesborough, Tennessee, the Quaker Elihu Embree published seven issues of the *Emancipator* in 1820. After his death that same year, Benjamin Lundy started the *Genius of Universal Emancipation* in Greeneville, but moved it to Baltimore in 1824. While it is sometimes claimed that these initiatives represented the beginnings of the abolitionist movement, they usually took a gradualist position, and even supported the "return to Africa" colonization societies. However, William Lloyd Garrison was clearly inspired by Lundy's example, and thus there are some valid connections between these isolated and beleaguered Southern antislavery writers and the militant groups that emerged in the 1830s.

The Nat Turner Revolt of 1831 led to a complex but open debate about slavery in the Virginia legislature, where opponents tended to come from the western mountain sections, while proponents were from the tidewater and piedmont sections where tobacco produced by slaves was carried out on a large scale. The antislavery forces were defeated, but at least there had been a frank discussion on the issue.

By the middle of the 1830s, Northern abolitionists launched a campaign to saturate the South with their literature, but this only led to violent opposition, including the dramatic burning of U.S. mail by a mob in Charleston in 1835. While the Deist "Founding Fathers" had tended to hope that slavery might eventually and gradually disappear, the 1830s saw a new rigidity on the part of the masters. Gradualism, after all, might be postponed indefinitely, while the immediatism of Garrison and his followers presented them with a more urgent challenge to the entire system. Even though at this time Garrison remained a pacifist or "nonresistant," any kind of opposition was met by determined force. As the number of slaves had grown to three million, now almost entirely confined to the South (with emancipation now in effect throughout the North), and their labor was essential to the profitability of the industrialized system of agriculture, the stakes were high indeed.

The tier of Deep South states from South Carolina to Texas was the heart of large-scale rice and cotton production, with tobacco predominating in Virginia and

North Carolina. The border states from Maryland to Missouri included mountain areas where poor whites already disliked the predominance of the lowland, tidewater, and river districts, and sometimes assisted escaping slaves. These states provided distinct enclaves of safety and support, both for slaves and for abolitionist sympathizers, from the mountains of what would be separated from Virginia to form the new state of West Virginia in 1863, to urban centers like Louisville and St. Louis, where one could hide out at least temporarily.

In spite of this heightened bitterness, Southern figures like Cassius M. Clay of Kentucky continued to argue against slavery, though his case emphasized the harmful effects of slavery not so much for its own sake, but because it threatened the well-being of free white labor. In 1845, a mob seized the press of Clay's newspaper the *True American* and shipped it north to Cincinnati. Though Clay courageously continued his struggle, he had little success; while there was a debate about slavery in the Constitution Convention of 1849 in Kentucky, all efforts to abolish it went down to defeat. While Clay remained in the state, many other Southern abolitionists found it necessary to move North in order to avoid assassination. However, their experiences told in books and speeches inflamed Northern opinion. Scores of slave narratives provided vivid details of oppression, brutality and suffering.

The operations of the Underground Railroad, as well as less organized individual escapes, meant that by the 1850s, 50,000 slaves per year were attempting to flee. Most of these were captured, but the sheer effort required to try to maintain the system in place was enormous.

By the mid-1850s, a significant component of the antislavery movement included the new immigrants from Germany and other European countries, largely consisting of radical veterans of the Revolutions of 1848. As far west as San Antonio, Adolph Douai published an antislavery German language newspaper until he, too, was forced to leave Texas in 1856. By 1860, things had become so violent in Texas that a peddler who was found with copies of Hinton Helper's *The Impending Crisis* in his wagon was suspended from a tree branch, the wagon soaked with oil, and the man burned to death by his own wares.

The sum of this history suggests that the gradualist and colonization tendencies of the emancipation struggle were doomed to be ineffective. Similarly, pacifist and other strategies that emphasized moral persuasion did not succeed. The dynamic convergence of blacks and whites in the Underground Railroad and the broader movement threatened the basis of the slavery system, but in the end it was force in the form of the Union Army that led to the end of slavery in the South.

Fred Whitehead

See also: Clay, Cassius.

Further Readings

Aptheker, Herbert. *American Negro Slave Revolts*. 5th ed. New York: International, 1983.

Degler, Carl N. *The Other South: Southern Dissenters in the Nineteenth Century*. New York: Harper & Row, 1974.

Dillon, Merton L. *Slavery Attacked: Southern Slaves and Their Allies 1619–1865*. Baton Rouge: Louisiana State University Press, 1990.

Franklin, John Hope, and Loren Schweninger. *Runaway Slaves: Rebels on the Plantation*. New York: Oxford University Press, 1999.

Harrold, Stanley. *The Abolitionists and the South, 1831–1861*. Lexington: University Press of Kentucky, 1995.

Osofsky, Gilbert, ed. *Puttin' on Ole Massa*. New York: Harper, 1969.

V

Vesey's Conspiracy (1822)

Perhaps the largest slave conspiracy in North American history, the Charleston, South Carolina, plot was organized by Denmark Vesey, a free black carpenter. Although brought into the city in 1783 as a slave of Captain Joseph Vesey, Telemaque, as he was then known, purchased his freedom in December 1799 with lottery winnings. For the next twenty-two years, Vesey earned his living as a crafts-man and, according to white authorities, was "distinguished for [his] great strength and activity," and the black community "always looked up to [him] with awe and respect." His last (and probably third) wife, Susan Vesey, was born a slave but became free prior to his death. But his first wife, Beck, remained a slave, as did Vesey's sons, Polydore, Robert, and Sandy, who was the only one of his children to be implicated in his 1822 conspiracy.

Around 1818, Vesey joined the city's new African Methodist Episcopal con-gregation. The African Church, as both whites and blacks called it, quickly be-came the center of Charleston's enslaved community. Sandy Vesey also joined, as did four of Vesey's closest friends: Peter Poyas, a literate and highly skilled ship carpenter; Monday Gell, an African-born Ibo, who labored as a harness maker; Rolla Bennett, the manservant of Governor Thomas Bennett; and "Gullah" Jack Pritchard, an East African priest purchased in Zinguebar in 1806. The temporary closure of the church by city authorities in June 1818, and the arrest of 140 congre-gants, one of them presumably Vesey himself, only reinforced the determination of black Carolinians to maintain a place of independent worship and established the initial motivation for his conspiracy. The "African Church was the people," Monday Gell insisted. He and Pritchard had considered insurrection in 1818, he swore, "and now they had begun again to try it."

At the age of fifty-one, Vesey resolved to orchestrate a rebellion followed by a mass exodus from Charleston to Haiti. President Jean-Pierre Boyer had recently encouraged black Americans to bring their skills and capital to his beleaguered

345

republic. Vesey did not intend to tarry in Charleston long enough for white military power to present an effective counterassault. "As soon as they could get the money from the Banks, and the goods from the stores," Rolla Bennett insisted, "they should hoist sail for Saint Doming[ue]" and live as free men. For all of his acculturation into European American society, Vesey, as a native of St. Thomas, remained a man of the black Atlantic.

Vesey planned the escape for nearly four years. His chief lieutenants included Poyas, Gell, Pritchard, and Rolla Bennett. Although there are no reliable figures for the number of recruits, Charleston alone was home to 12,652 slaves. Pritchard, probably with some exaggeration, boasted that he had 6,600 recruits on the plantations across the Cooper and Ashley Rivers. The plan called for Vesey's followers to rise at midnight on Sunday, July 14—Bastille Day—slay their masters, and sail for Haiti and freedom. As one Southern editor later conceded, "The plot seems to have been well devised, and its operation was extensive."

Those recruited into the plot during the winter of 1822 were directed to arm themselves from their masters' closets. Vesey was also aware that the Charleston Neck militia company stored their 300 muskets and bayonets in the back room of Benjamin Hammet's King Street store, and that Hammet's slave, Bacchus, had a key. But as few slaves had any experience with guns, Vesey encouraged his followers to arm themselves with swords or long daggers, which in any case would make for quieter work as the city bells tolled midnight. Vesey also employed several enslaved blacksmiths to forge "pike heads and bayonets with sockets, to be fixed at the end of long poles."

Considerably easier than stockpiling weapons was the recruitment of willing young men. With Vesey and Pritchard employed about the city as carpenters, it is hardly surprising that so many other craftsmen became involved in the plot. Most of all, Vesey and his lieutenants recruited out of the African Church. As a class leader, Vesey was not only respected by the church membership, but he knew each of them well; he knew whom to trust and whom to avoid. As former Charleston slave Archibald Grimké later wrote, Vesey's nightly classes provided him "with a singularly safe medium for conducting his underground agitation."

The plot unraveled in June 1822 when two slaves, including Rolla's friend, George Wilson, a fellow class leader in the African Church, revealed the plan to their owners. Mayor James Hamilton called up the city militia and convened a special court to try the captured insurgents. Vesey was captured at the home of Beck, his first wife, on June 21 and hanged on the morning of Tuesday, July 2, together with Rolla, Poyas, and three other rebels. According to Hamilton, the six men collectively "met their fate with the heroic fortitude of Martyrs." In all, thirty-five slaves were executed. Forty-two others, including Sandy Vesey, were sold outside the United States; some, if not all, became slaves in Spanish Cuba. Robert Vesey lived to rebuild the African Church in the fall of 1865.

In the aftermath of the conspiracy, Charleston authorities demolished the African Church and banished Morris Brown to Philadelphia. The state assembly subsequently passed laws prohibiting the reentry of free blacks into the state, and city officials enforced ordinances against teaching African Americans to read. The city council also voted to create a permanent force of 150 guardsmen to patrol the streets around the clock at an annual cost of $24,000. To deal with the problem of black mariners bringing information about events around the Atlantic into the state's ports, in December 1822 the legislature passed the Negro Seamen Act, which placed a quarantine on any vessel from another "state or foreign port, having on board any free negroes or persons of color." Although U.S. Circuit Court judge William Johnson struck the law down as unconstitutional, a defiant assembly renewed the act in late 1823. It would be no coincidence that many of those who nullified the federal law in 1832—including then-governor James Hamilton, who resigned his office in 1833 to command troops in defense of his state's right to resist national tariffs—were veterans of the tribunals that tried Vesey and his men a decade before.

Douglas R. Egerton

See also: Gabriel's Conspiracy (1800); Turner, Nat.

Further Readings

Egerton, Douglas R. *He Shall Go Out Free: The Lives of Denmark Vesey*. Madison, WI: Madison House, 1999.

Freehling, William W. *The Reintegration of American History: Slavery and the Civil War*. New York: Oxford University Press, 1994.

Lofton, John. *Insurrection in South Carolina: The Turbulent World of Denmark Vesey*. Yellow Springs: Antioch Press, 1964.

Paquette, Robert L. "Jacobins of the Lowcountry: The Vesey Plot on Trial." *William and Mary Quarterly*, 59 (January 2002): 185–192.

Violence and Nonviolence in American Abolitionism

A common assumption shared by historians as well as people generally is that the great majority of American abolitionists were doctrinaire pacifists. Accordingly, John Brown and other antislavery activists who either advocated or engaged in violent tactics were exceptional. Yet, while abolitionists acknowledged the desirability of relying on peaceful tactics, they were not inflexible in regard to violent means. They recognized that white Americans had won freedom from Great Britain through violent means, and they refused to rule out a similar option for African Americans. In January 1842, for example, white abolitionist leader

John Stuart Curry's illustration *The Tragic Prelude* depicts abolitionist John Brown during the Harpers Ferry raid. (National Archives)

Gerrit Smith noted that although "there are . . . some persons in our ranks who are opposed to the taking of human life in any circumstances . . . the great majority of abolitionists justify their forefathers' bloody resistance to oppression." They could, therefore, oppose slave revolt only on the basis of "expediency." In other words, most abolitionists were ambivalent concerning means. They endorsed violent or nonviolent tactics depending on their perception of conditions. Immediate abolitionism arose in the North at a time when black antislavery violence in the South made it expedient for antislavery societies to endorse nonviolence. But, as time passed, abolitionists found violence to be increasingly expedient.

Black Antislavery Violence

During the 1820s and early 1830s, violent black liberators in the South and violent black rhetoric in the North influenced the rise of immediate emancipation. In 1822, a free black carpenter named Denmark Vesey led a slave-revolt conspiracy in Charleston, South Carolina. The conspiracy collapsed when informants revealed it to their masters. Until recently historians believed the conspiracy, for which

Vesey and with thirty-five others were executed, had little impact beyond South Carolina. But historian Peter P. Hinks indicates that unrest within Charleston's black community, if not Vesey himself, directly influenced black abolitionist David. Walker. Walker, who had been born free in North Carolina and visited Charleston during the early 1820s, published his *Appeal to the Colored Citizens of the World* in Boston in 1829. The *Appeal* urged black men to assert their masculinity through violent resistance to their masters. It recalled the successful slave revolution in Haiti led by Toussaint L'Ouverture and predicted that God would raise up a black warrior to deliver African Americans from oppression.

By relying on black and white seamen, Walker, who died in 1830, was able to circulate his *Appeal* in the South. This, along with William Lloyd Garrison's initiation of his newspaper, the *Liberator*, in January 1831, led many white Southerners to assume that Northern abolitionists encouraged Nat Turner's August 1831 slave revolt in Southampton Country, Virginia. There is no proof that such a linkage existed. But when Turner and his band of more than sixty black men killed approximately fifty-seven white men, women, and children, they convinced white Southerners that a real threat of violent abolitionism existed.

White militia overwhelmed Turner's uprising. He and seventeen of his associates were hanged, and white vigilantes killed at least 100 other African Americans in Virginia and North Carolina. In the North, black and white abolitionists joined in a general revulsion against the bloodshed that Turner had unleashed. Although abolitionists compared Turner to George Washington, L'Ouverture, and other liberators, they emphasized that they did not endorse his violent methods. Instead, they warned that without immediate peaceful abolition, additional slaves would follow his violent example. In other words, they urged a peaceful solution to slavery backed with a violent threat.

Nonviolence

Memories of Turner's revolt and white Southern accusations of abolitionist complicity in it were fresh as immediatists organized in the Northeast during the early 1830s. Invariably they pledged themselves to nonviolent means. The New York Anti-Slavery Society at its initial meeting in October 1833 declared, "We have no force but the force of truth." Those assembled promised never to "countenance the oppressed in vindicating their rights by resorting to force." Two months later, the American Anti-Slavery Society's Declaration of Sentiments called on slaves "to reject the use of all carnal weapons for deliverance from bondage."

Sincere Christian morality, including Quaker and evangelical strains, influenced these pledges. Nonviolence remained a powerful component of immediatism until the Civil War, especially among Garrison and his associates. But circumstances as much as Christianity shaped early immediatist rejection of force. A tiny band of abolitionists, already suspect because of its radical views on slavery and race, and accused of involvement in Turner's revolt, dared not put itself beyond the law and outrage public opinion by appearing to justify race war.

Once established as policy, nonviolence among abolitionists developed during the 1830s under the influence of a feminized masculinity common among northeastern reformers. Many abolitionist men favored what they regarded as feminine persuasion over male aggressiveness. Conscious of slavery's brutality, a few of them renounced involvement in any system that rested on force. In 1838, Garrison and his friend Henry C. Wright formed the Nonresistance Society, which renounced involvement in any form of violence. Members refused to defend themselves. They also became anarchists because all human government is based ultimately on force. The great majority of abolitionists, including some leading Garrisonians, however, opposed nonresistance. They associated it with heretical religion and saw in its rejection of human government a threat to the Northern social order. Yet Lewis Tappan and other church-oriented abolitionists fervently embraced peaceful means. Tappan and a few other evangelicals approached nonresistance in their refusal to defend themselves or their property against antiabolitionists or to sue in court those who harmed them.

Led by the American Anti-Slavery Society (AASS), abolitionists during the 1830s initiated a variety of peaceful strategies (usually referred to as "moral suasion") that continued throughout the following decades. They rapidly formed local antislavery societies across the Northeast and Old Northwest, so that by 1838 the AASS claimed to have 1,350 affiliates and a total of 250,000 members. In 1835, the AASS executive committee, under the leadership of Lewis Tappan, organized an ambitious postal campaign designed to send huge amounts of antislavery literature to white Southerners. At about the same time, the AASS initiated a gigantic petitioning campaign calling on Congress to abolish slavery in the District of Columbia. Abolitionists designed the latter campaign to raise the slavery issue in Congress and to bring non-abolitionist Northerners into the antislavery movement. Abolitionist women led in circulating the petitions.

As historian Carlton Mabee establishes, abolitionists also engaged in a variety of nonviolent direct actions. They integrated churches, left churches that did not denounce slavery, and formed new abolitionist churches. They engaged in "ride-ins" in attempting to integrate Northern railroads and worked to integrate Northern schools. Some of them supported boycotts of slave produce sold in Northern markets. They worked peacefully to repeal Northern state laws that discriminated against African Americans. From the mid-1840s through the 1850s, antislavery missionaries, supported by the abolitionist American Missionary Association and other groups, risked their lives to distribute antislavery literature and provide Bibles to slaves in the Upper South. During the 1840s, many advocates of the abolitionist Liberty Party contended that political engagement was a peaceful form of antislavery action, although nonresistants pointed out that politics, like government, rested on force.

In most instances, these peaceful efforts produced disappointing results. Many white Southerners, fearing that abolitionist literature would reach slaves, responded with anger to the postal campaign. A mob in Charleston, South Carolina, burned antislavery publications that reached that city. President Andrew Jackson and several Southern state legislatures called on Northern states to suppress the abolitionist movement. Southern members of the House of Representatives, with considerable Northern help, passed the Gag Rule in 1836, banning the reading of antislavery petitions. Abolitionist speakers, editors, organizers, and missionaries faced mob violence during the 1830s and to a lesser extent during the 1840s and 1850s. It seemed that peaceful moral suasion was not enough to make progress against slavery.

Defensive Violence

From the 1830s into the 1840s, as angry antiblack, antiabolition mobs attacked abolitionists and black communities in the North and Border South, numerous abolitionists forcefully defended themselves and their property. During an antiblack, antiabolitionist riot in New York City in 1834, AASS president Arthur Tappan distributed guns to employees at his business. In 1836 in Cincinnati, abolitionist organizer James G. Birney and his sons used guns to defend their home against rioters. In Alton, Illinois, abolitionist newspaper editor Elijah P. Lovejoy died defending his printing press against a proslavery mob. In the Border South, where abolitionists were more isolated than in the North, organized defensive violence became increasingly common. Kentucky abolitionist Cassius M. Clay used a knife in 1849 to kill a proslavery antagonist. During the early 1850s, Clay raised armed bands to defend his nonviolent associate John G. Fee. Moral power, Clay contended, had to be supplemented with "cold steel and the flashing blade"—"the pistol and the Bowie knife."

Slave Rebels and a Revolutionary Heritage

Despite their commitment to nonviolence and embrace of feminine values, white Northern abolitionists admired slave rebels. Americans, they realized, regarded violent struggles for freedom to be heroic. Although black abolitionists shared their white colleagues' ambivalence toward violent means, a few during the 1830s openly praised Turner. In part this was because a masculine image of a violent Southern black liberator challenged pervasive stereotyping of black men as meek and submissive. By the late 1830s, as well, abolitionists had come to regard slavery as a war of extermination against African Americans. Many of them concluded that Christian morality allowed for black violence in self-defense. The American revolutionary heritage reinforced this point of view. As early as 1837, Garrison observed that the Declaration of Independence "authorized" slaves to "cut their masters' throats." Although outright calls for slave revolt were rare during the 1830s, black and white abolitionists praised such violent black liberators as L'Ouverture, Vesey, and Turner. In December 1841, Liberty Party abolitionists on Long Island, New York, declared that Madison Washington, who a month earlier had led a successful slave revolt aboard the brig *Creole*, "acted in accordance with the principles of the Declaration of Independence." Those attending the meeting hoped that Washington's example would "be imitated by all in similar circumstances."

The Underground Railroad versus the Fugitive Slave Laws

Garrison argued in 1844 that helping slaves to escape was a nonviolent activity, carried out "in the spirit of good will to the oppressed, and without injury to the oppressor." But assisted slave escapes often turned violent. Armed masters used force against escapees, and the escapees sometimes carried weapons to protect themselves. Black and white slave rescuers, ranging from Charles T. Torrey during the early 1840s to Harriet Tubman during the 1850s, carried guns and threatened to use them against masters, slave catchers, and law enforcement officials. Black Underground Railroad operative John P. Parker, who helped slaves escape from Kentucky to Ohio during the 1850s, recalled that there was "real warfare" between antislavery and proslavery forces in the Ohio River Valley. Like Tubman, Parker always carried weapons when he ventured into the South. Also like her, he sometimes threatened to shoot fugitives who endangered the rest of his charges.

The Fugitive Slave Law of 1850 pushed northward and widened violent conflict between practical abolitionism and angry masters. Increased numbers of black and white abolitionists aided escapees. Masters enlisted federal marshals to help them recapture their human property. African Americans had violently resisted the earlier Fugitive Slave Law of 1793 since its inception. After 1850, the violence became more biracial and more common as non-abolitionist Northerners joined abolitionists in defying the new law. Influenced by Harriet Beecher Stowe's dramatization of the plight of fugitive slaves in her novel, *Uncle Tom's Cabin*, large numbers of Northerners favored forceful resistance to the law. Although such resistance centered in New England, New York, Ohio, and Pennsylvania, white Southerners believed that militant abolitionists, who used violence against the property rights of masters, pervaded the North.

Although there were numerous instances in which abolitionists violently resisted the Fugitive Slave Law, five cases gained notoriety. In February 1851, a black mob, supported by black and white abolitionists, forcefully rescued fugitive slave Shadrack Minkins from a Boston courtroom. The following September, African Americans, led by underground railroad agent William Parker, killed a master who attempted to recover a fugitive slave at Parker's house in Christiana, Pennsylvania. That November, a biracial mob led by black abolitionist Jermain Wesley Loguen and white abolitionists Gerrit Smith and Samuel Joseph May stormed the Syracuse, New York, police station to rescue William Henry—known as "Jerry." In 1854, black and white abolitionists in Boston unsuccessfully attempted to rescue Anthony Burns from the city courthouse. One of Burns's guards died in the melee. Later, local authorities had to call in state and federal troops to protect those who escorted Burns to a southbound ship in Boston Harbor. Another biracial abolitionist mob composed of faculty and students from Oberlin College forcefully rescued fugitive John Brice from a Wellington, Ohio, tavern where he had been held.

In each of these cases, abolitionist rescuers enjoyed the support of local public opinion. In each case there were indictments and some rescuers went to jail pending trial. But there were few convictions and none at all in the especially violent Christiana and Burns cases. Just as popular opposition had contributed to abolitionist nonviolence during the 1830s, awareness of support encouraged abolitionist violence during the 1850s. Prior to the *Jerry* rescue, Smith predicted that the local fugitive slave law commissioner would very likely release the fugitive. "But," Smith advised, "the moral effect of such an acquittal will be as nothing [compared] to a bold and forcible rescue. A forcible rescue will demonstrate the strength of public opinion against the possible legality of slavery and this Fugitive Slave Law in particular."

Bleeding Kansas

Abolitionist participation in violent resistance to the Fugitive Slave Law increased white Southern fear of the movement. Democratic and Whig Party leaders responded by pledging to "crush out" agitation of the slavery issue. The Kansas-Nebraska Act, introduced into Congress in January 1854 and passed the following May, destroyed what chance there was of carrying out such a pledge. The act further divided the two sections of the country and accelerated violent tendencies among abolitionists.

Stephen A. Douglas, a Democratic senator from Illinois, had proposed to organize territorial governments in Kansas and Nebraska chiefly as a means of routing a transcontinental railroad through Kansas. To secure Southern support for his bill, he added a clause repealing the Missouri Compromise prohibition of slavery in the two territories and providing that the settlers of each territory vote to decide whether or not to admit slavery. This encouraged Southern leaders to try to make Kansas a slave territory and eventually a slave state. It also outraged most Northerners, who believed Douglas had sold out the interests of free labor, and set the stage for a violent struggle in Kansas Territory between free state and slave state settlers. Free state settlers, who constituted the overwhelming majority in Kansas, battled against "border ruffians" from Missouri, federal officials, and federal troops sent to Kansas by proslavery U.S. president Franklin Pierce. Proslavery aggression in Kansas convinced most abolitionists that force should be used not only on behalf of fugitive slaves but also to defend freedom in the territory.

Although few abolitionists went to Kansas, those who did either set out with violent intentions or gave up their commitment to peaceful means after they arrived. Charles B. Stearns, for example, was a nonresistant before he arrived in Kansas in 1855. Shortly thereafter he declared, "These pro-slavery Missourians are demons from the bottomless pit and may be shot with impunity." A year later, John Henry Kagi, a correspondent of several abolitionist newspapers, killed a proslavery man during a brawl. The most famous abolitionist who fought in Kansas was John Brown. At least since the late 1840s, Brown had advocated violent action on behalf of slaves and against slaveholders. In May 1856, in reprisal for a proslavery attack on the free state town of Lawrence, Brown and several of his sons brutally executed five proslavery settlers at Pottawatomie Creek. Although few, if any, abolitionists knew the details of his actions at Pottawatomie, many of them lionized him and contributed funds to pay for his ambitious plan to assault slavery in the South.

Events in Kansas Territory helped break down what nonviolent principles remained among the great mass of abolitionists. Gerrit Smith, Garrison's friend Wendell Phillips, and other immediatists contributed money to arm antislavery migrants to Kansas. Smith contended that "the shedding of blood [in Kansas] was unavoidable." Leading abolitionist women, such as Lydia Maria Child and Angelina Grimké Weld, professed continued preference for peaceful means while recognizing the legitimacy of antislavery violence in Kansas. Weld lamented, "We are compelled to choose between two evils, and all that we can do is take the *least*, and baptize liberty in blood, if it must be so." By the late 1850s, Garrison and Lewis Tappan, who persisted in their formal commitment to peaceful means, represented a distinct minority among immediate abolitionists.

Northern Abolitionists and Slave Revolt

Although abolitionists had long admired slave rebels, before 1850 they rarely called for revolt. Even black abolitionist Henry Highland Garnet in his famous Address to the Slaves of August 1843 qualified his demand for resistance with a warning that revolt was inexpedient. But by the late 1850s, amid resistance to the Fugitive Slave Law, guerrilla war in Kansas, and rumors of widespread slave unrest following the Republican Party's first presidential election campaign in 1856, immediatists began forthrightly to call for a slave uprising. That formally nonresistant white Garrisonians often joined black abolitionists in such appeals indicates that the long-term ambivalence among abolitionists concerning peaceful and violent means had decisively shifted in favor of the latter. Still claiming to be a nonresistant, Wright declared in 1857, "We owe it as our duty to ourselves and to humanity, to excite every slave to *rebellion* against his master."

Traditional notions of masculinity rebounded among abolitionists during the contentious 1850s. Under the racialist assumption that white men were more aggressive than black men, white abolitionists, such as Thomas Wentworth Higginson and Theodore Parker, contended that they had to instruct black men in martial valor. To a degree, black abolitionists shared this view. Frederick Douglass declared, "My people can never be elevated until they elevate themselves, by fighting for their freedom, and by the sword obtaining it."

Few prominent abolitionists, however, were willing, prior to the U.S. Civil War, to transform violent rhetoric into action. That was left to Underground Railroad operatives on what historian Keith P. Griffler calls "the front line of freedom" and the few abolitionists who went to Kansas. John Brown belonged to both groups. Emerging from a Garrisonian meeting in 1859, he scoffed, "Talk! talk! talk!— that will never set the slave free." Support from Gerrit Smith, Higginson, and Theodore Parker for Brown's plan to invade the South to launch a black guerrilla war against slavery reflected violent sentiment among abolitionists during the 1850s. But Brown had begun to formulate a plan to lead a slave rebellion during the 1840s. Thirty years of abolitionist admiration for slave rebels and twenty years of abolitionist contacts with slaves in the Border South established the context for his plan. Long-standing aggressive tendencies within the antislavery movement contributed as much as the heightened sectionalism of the 1850s to the raid on Harpers Ferry, Virginia, in October 1859.

Brown's raid failed to spark a slave uprising as members of his tiny interracial band were killed, captured, or forced to flee northward. But Brown, who was among those captured, used the month between his trial and his execution to employ a surprising eloquence against what remained of abolitionist pacifism. "I, John Brown, am now quite *certain* that the crimes of this *guilty land* will never be purged away but with *blood*," he declared on the day he died. Although a few Garrisonians, such as Parker Pillsbury, Marius Robinson, and Moncure Conway, continued to disavow violence, most now agreed that black men must follow Brown's example if African Americans were to gain freedom. Garrison declared, "Give me, as a non-resistant, Bunker Hill, and Lexington, and Concord, rather than the cowardice and servility of the southern plantation." On the day of Brown's execution, Garrison proclaimed, "Success to every slave insurrection in the South!" Frederick Douglass suggested that "posterity will owe everlasting thanks to John Brown [because] he has attacked slavery with the weapons precisely adapted to bring it to the death."

Many correctly predicted that Brown's raid would spark civil war between the North and South. When the war began in April 1861, abolitionists became fervent supporters of Union cause, urging from the start that black men be allowed to enlist in Union armies and that emancipation be a war aim. Older abolitionists, including Douglass, helped raise black troops. Younger abolitionists, including sons of Douglass and Garrison, enlisted in what became a successful war against legalized slavery. Several white abolitionists, including Higginson, became officers in segregated black regiments that distinguished themselves in battle. Years later, after the Civil War and Reconstruction had failed to secure equal rights for African Americans, elderly white abolitionists regretted that armed conflict had superseded their peaceful crusade. Violence, they implied, could not end racism. Yet their movement had been rooted in violence, had never been entirely nonviolent, and had achieved important objectives through violent means.

Stanley Harrold

See also: Bleeding Kansas; Democratic Party and Antislavery; Jerry Rescue (1851); Radical Republicans; Vesey's Conspiracy (1822); Whig Party and Antislavery.

Further Readings

Dillon, Merton L. *Slavery Attacked: Southern Slaves and Their Allies 1619–1865*. Baton Rouge: Louisiana State University Press, 1990.

Griffler, Keith P. *Front Line of Freedom: African Americans and the Forging of the Underground Railroad in the Ohio Valley*. Lexington: University Press of Kentucky, 2004.

Harrold, Stanley. *The Abolitionists and the South 1831–1861*. Lexington: University Press of Kentucky, 1995.

Harrold, Stanley. *The Rise of Aggressive Abolitionism: Addresses to the Slaves*. Lexington: University Press of Kentucky, 2004.

Hinks, Peter P. *To Awaken My Afflicted Brethren: David Walker and the Problem of Antebellum Slave Resistance*. University Park: Pennsylvania State University Press, 1997.

Mabee, Carlton. *Black Freedom: The Nonviolent Abolitionists from 1830 through the Civil War*. London: Macmillan, 1970.

McKivigan, John R., and Stanley Harrold, eds. *Antislavery Violence: Sectional, Cultural, and Racial Conflict in Antebellum America*. Knoxville: University of Tennessee Press, 1999.

Perry, Lewis. *Radical Abolitionism: Anarchy and the Government of God in Antislavery Thought*. Ithaca, NY: Cornell University Press, 1973.

Walker, David

David Walker was born in Wilmington, North Carolina, in the Lower Cape Fear District, in about 1796. His mother was a free black and he thus acquired her status. Slave labor and society was very evident in this region where rice was cultivated and naval stores were produced in the extensive pine barrens. Slaves here proved both very religious and restless. The early Methodist church in Wilmington was overwhelmingly black and probably was the foundation of Walker's lifelong dedication to the denomination. The pervasive swamps of the Lower Cape Fear were commonly refuges for runaways and small maroon encampments, and several incidences of slave rebellion issued from them between 1775 and the early nineteenth century. This black world of religiosity and restlessness likely helped shape David Walker.

Sometime in the 1810s, Walker journeyed to Charleston, South Carolina, which had a much larger free black population than Wilmington, as well as greater employment opportunity. By 1818, Charleston also had one of the earliest congregations of the recently launched African Methodist Episcopal (AME) church, established by Richard Allen in Philadelphia in 1817. Vehemently opposed by local white authorities, it was comprised of both free blacks and slaves and quickly became the center of black Charleston. It also was an important nexus for the plotting of a major slave conspiracy led by Denmark Vesey, a free black carpenter who was a member of the church, and a number of other free blacks and slaves in the town. The intensely religious and Methodist Walker likely attended this church and may have been exposed to the conspiring in one form or another. He certainly knew of the plot when it was uncovered in June 1822 and violently crushed by the local magistrates. More than thirty free blacks and slaves were executed, and a number of leaders of the church including its minister, Morris Brown, fled the town soon after the plot's exposure. Walker probably left at about the same time and may have roamed along the eastern seaboard of the country. It is very likely that he went to Philadelphia where the seat of the AME church was located and to where most of those blacks fleeing Charleston went. The name David Walker appears in Philadelphia municipal records for 1824. There is even some indication that he may have gone briefly to Haiti when a number of American blacks were emigrating there to accept President Jean-Pierre Boyer's offers of free land and other assistance to settlers.

By 1825, David Walker had settled in Boston, Massachusetts. He soon opened a used-clothing store, married, became an African Mason, bought a house, and joined the Reverend Samuel Snowden's black Methodist church. He was the local agent for the first black newspaper, *Freedom's Journal*, and he was a principal in the formation in 1828 of one of the nation's first explicitly black political organizations, the Massachusetts General Colored Association. In December 1828, he addressed the Association and passionately decried slavery, the colonization movement, and racial injustice.

Walker is best known for his publication in September 1829 of his *Appeal to the Colored Citizens of the World*. This booklet was one of the most vivid and incisive denunciations of American slavery, racism, and hypocrisy produced in the country in the nineteenth century. In it, Walker clearly empathized with the suffering, both physical and psychological, endured by the slaves in the South, a people whose world he knew well from his earlier years. But he also chided them for any tendency to succumb to demoralization induced by their brutal treatment and to surrender themselves to slavery and slavishness. He admonished them to refuse to submit to enslavement any further; to do so was to make themselves complicit in the sin of slavery. To whites, he counseled an immediate acknowledgment of their horrible sinning in imposing slavery and degradation upon blacks. They must seek God's forgiveness for their sins and publicly repent. Finally, they must reach out to blacks in Christian fellowship and seek a nonviolent path to reconciliation with blacks and the forging of a new free and interracial society in the United States. Walker believed such a reunion was possible, but was also fully aware of the daunting obstacles confronting it. If whites proved unrepentant and continued to enslave blacks, then they had no choice but to reject their enslavement and violently oppose the whites who had in effect rendered themselves devils. For blacks to do otherwise was the grossest of affronts to God. In the pamphlet, Walker struggled to harness the optimistic activism inherent to evangelical Christianity and revolutionary republicanism to inspire African Americans to a new sense of personal worth and to their capacity to challenge the increasingly systematized ideology and institutions of white supremacy.

By early 1830, Walker had launched a remarkably resourceful circulation of his *Appeal* in Georgia, South, and North Carolina, Virginia, and New Orleans. White authorities throughout the South were enraged and sought to check its influx into their states by monitoring local slaves and free blacks carefully, impeding the movement of Northern white and free black sailors in their ports, and guarding the mails and newspapers from importing any seditious materials. Still, the pamphlet found its way into black hands in the South, especially in North Carolina where an impressive network of runaway slaves, free blacks, and perhaps some white Quakers moved it along the state's eastern counties. Walker implored literate slaves and free blacks to read his work to their less educated brethren and apparently some did. The pamphlet failed, however, to spark the wide scale resistance for which Walker hoped. But his passionate words fired black activism in the North throughout the antebellum era and beyond. Maria Stewart, Frederick Douglass, and Henry Highland Garnet all looked to Walker as seminal in the movement over which they became so prominent. Even as late as 1940, W.E.B. Du Bois lauded the *Appeal* for its "tremendous indictment of slavery" and for being the first "program of organized opposition to the action and attitude of the dominant white group," as well as for its "ceaseless agitation and insistent demand for equality."

Peter Hinks

See also: Vesey's Conspiracy (1822).

Further Reading

Hinks, Peter. *To Awaken My Afflicted Brethren: David Walker and the Problem of Antebellum Slave Resistance.* University Park: Pennsylvania State University Press, 1997.

Washington, D.C., Compensated Emancipation in

On April 16, 1862, President Abraham Lincoln signed a bill to end slavery in Washington, D.C. The bill, entitled "An Act for the Release of Certain Persons Held to Service or Labor in the District of Columbia," marked the first time that the federal government authorized the emancipation of any slave and the only time that it compensated former owners as part of an emancipation plan.

While compensation was not included in later acts, emancipation in the nation's capital was an early sign of the end of slavery in the United States. The District of Columbia Emancipation Act was received with joy in Washington's African American community and is now remembered in the District's Emancipation Day celebration.

Throughout the antebellum era, ending the slave trade and slavery in Washington, D.C., was a popular cause for abolitionists. They focused on Washington because of the symbolic importance of slavery in the capital of a free republic and because of the ability of the federal government to end it there. Under Article I, Section 8 of the U.S. Constitution, Congress has exclusive power to pass laws for the nation's capital.

On December 16, 1861, Senator Henry Wilson of Massachusetts introduced the District of Columbia Emancipation Act in the Senate. The bill provided for immediate emancipation of all slaves in the District of Columbia as well as compensation for their masters and funds for the foreign colonization of slaves who chose to emigrate outside the United States. Wilson's three-point plan linking emancipation with payment to owners and colonization was similar to earlier proposals to end slavery. Supporters reasoned that connecting emancipation with payments to owners and funds to encourage former slaves to emigrate would make the abolition of slavery more palatable to the slaveholding states that had not seceded to join the Confederacy, such as Kentucky and Missouri.

The compensation provision of the District bill, however, divided antislavery members of Congress. Senator Samuel Pomeroy of Kansas criticized compensation for owners on the grounds that it wrongly recognized slaves as property. He argued that if Congress authorized any compensation, it should be paid to former slaves. Senator Charles Sumner of Massachusetts answered Senator Pomeroy, stating that payment to masters was acknowledgment of Congress's responsibility for slavery in Washington and would dull opposition to the bill. Despite this resistance to compensation, it remained in the District of Columbia Emancipation Act.

As passed by Congress and signed by the president, the act appropriated as much as $1 million to be paid to owners in the District of Columbia, provided that the total amount paid did not exceed an average of $300 per slave. Under the statute, owners could be compensated only if they were loyal to the Union. The act directed the president to appoint three commissioners to receive and investigate petitions and to assess the value of slaves freed by the statute. The act also appropriated $100,000 for voluntary colonization.

After signing the District of Columbia Emancipation Act, President Lincoln appointed commissioners to the three-member board in April 1862. The commissioners met throughout the following three months, receiving claims, determining ownership and loyalty to the Union, and setting compensation for former slaves. Compensation payments were ostensibly based on estimates of the former slaves' intrinsic value to their owners. To determine the intrinsic utility of each, the commissioners began by estimating salable price before the start of the war, relying on the assessments of Bernard Campbell, a slave dealer from Baltimore. As estimated price usually exceeded the average compensation allowed by law, the commissioners granted payments of $300 in most cases.

The loyalty provision prevented only secessionists from recovering compensation. The commissioners interpreted the restriction to apply only upon proof that the "claimants have borne arms against the Government of the United States in the present rebellion or in any way given aid or comfort to the enemy." They justified their interpretation of the statute by noting that its language was similar to the Constitution's treason provision in Article III, Section 3. Since the Constitution defined treason to apply only in specific circumstances with adequate proof, the commissioners accepted claims even of Confederate sympathizers.

The commissioners received 966 petitions, claiming 3,100 former slaves. Of those petitions, the commissioners granted 909 in their entirety and 21 in part, accounting for 2,989 former slaves. The remaining petitions were rejected because former owners had voted for secession or moved south to join the Confederate military or had failed to appear before the board.

On July 12, 1862, a supplemental bill to the District of Columbia Emancipation Act was signed into law. The Supplemental Act allowed slaves and former slaves whose former masters had not filed compensation petitions to assert their own claims to freedom under the April 16 or July 12 statutes. The act also specified that any slave who had lived or been employed in the District of Columbia with the consent of his or her owner after April 16, 1862, was legally free.

As with the District of Columbia Emancipation Act, the Supplemental Act charged the emancipation commissioners with receiving and investigating petitions. The statute provided that African Americans could not be excluded from testifying. The commissioners received 161 petitions under the Supplemental Act and granted 139.

Edward Daniels

See also: Lincoln, Abraham.

Further Readings

Fladeland, Betty L. "Compensated Emancipation: A Rejected Alternative." *The Journal of Southern History* 42 (1976): 169–186.

Green, Constance. *The Secret City: A History of Race Relations in the Nation's Capital.* Princeton, NJ: Princeton University Press, 1967.

Guelzo, Allen C. *Lincoln's Emancipation Proclamation: The End of Slavery in America.* New York: Simon & Schuster, 2004.

H. Exec. Doc. 42, 38th Cong., 1st Sess. (1864). (Letter from the Secretary of the Treasury, in answer to a resolution of the House of Representatives, of the 11th of January, transmitting the report and tabular statements of the commissioners appointed in relation to emancipated slaves in the District of Columbia.).

Kurtz, Michael J. "Emancipation in the Federal City." *Civil War History* 24 (1978): 250–267.

Milburn, Page. "The Emancipation of the Slaves in the District of Columbia." *Records of the Columbia Historical Society* 16 (1913): 96–119.

Weld, Theodore Dwight

Theodore Dwight Weld was an influential abolitionist in the United States during the 1830s and early 1840s. For much of his young life it appeared that Weld, son of a Congregationalist minister, was destined for a career in the ministry. He briefly attended Andover Seminary, but withdrew after experiencing vision impairment, which may have been a psychosomatic manifestation of his dissatisfaction with orthodox Calvinism. In 1826, Weld's religious fervor was renewed after he was converted to evangelicalism by the famed minister Charles Grandison Finney. Weld devoted himself to Finney, becoming one of his most trusted aides. His work as a revivalist soon led him into the temperance and manual labor reform movements. As an agent for the Manual Labor Society, he helped establish Lane Seminary in Cincinnati, Ohio, which he entered as a student in 1833 to prepare for the ministry.

Lane instead launched Weld into abolitionism. In 1834, Weld led a revolt among the students of Lane against the school's administration over the issue of slavery. In February of that year, Weld helped organize an eighteen-day debate at the seminary where he and his fellow students discussed the duties of Christians regarding slavery, specifically debating the comparative merits of the scheme proposed by colonizationists to end slavery gradually and the demands of radical abolitionists for its immediate abolition. The students emerged from the debate certain of the utter sinfulness of both slavery and racial prejudice, convinced that colonizationism did not offer adequate means to repent those sins, and eager to put their newfound immediatist convictions into practice. They founded an antislavery society at the seminary and, led by Weld, they began to reach out to the local African American community, setting up both secular and religious education programs in Cincinnati's "Little Africa" district. The activism of the Lane students drew harsh criticism from many in Cincinnati's white community, who called upon the trustees of Lane Seminary to restrain them. In October, the trustees bowed to this pressure, passing resolutions that banned student organizations not directly related to ministerial education and allowing the trustees to expel offending students. Led by Weld, the majority of the students promptly withdrew from the seminary rather than compromise their antislavery beliefs.

This dispute at Lane propelled many of its former students into abolitionist activism, none more so than Weld. Weld spent two years as a full-time agent of the American Antislavery Society (AASS) touring Ohio, New York, and other western areas agitating the antislavery cause and helping to establish local abolitionist societies. Despite persistent, sometimes violent, harassment from antislavery mobs, Weld was remarkably successful, helping to establish numerous local societies and converting many who came to hear him speak to abolitionism. In the mid-1830s, Weld's voice was compromised following years of nonstop speaking, and thereafter he assumed a less public role in abolitionism as correspondent, editor, and pamphleteer at the headquarters of the AASS in New York. In 1836, he recruited and trained dozens of abolitionist agents for the AASS including Angelina and Sarah Grimké. Daughters of an elite South Carolina slaveholding planter, the Grimké sisters had been converted to Quakerism and then to abolitionism. Coached by Weld, the sisters spent much of the following two years touring New England promoting abolitionism. In the midst of this tour, Weld began courting Angelina, and they were married in May 1838.

Collaborating with his wife, Angelina, and sister-in-law, Sarah, Weld produced *American Slavery as It Is: Testimony of a Thousand Witnesses* (1839). In this widely circulated pamphlet, Weld and the Grimkés amassed firsthand accounts of the horrors of slavery compiled from Southern newspapers and personal testimonies solicited from Southerners. The pamphlet documented in grisly detail the violence and cruelty endemic to the institution of slavery. *American Slavery as It Is* ranks as one the most influential works of American antislavery literature. Over 100,000 copies were sold in the first year, and Harriet Beecher Stowe later reported that it was an important source for *Uncle Tom's Cabin*.

From 1841 to 1843, Weld labored as a researcher and lobbyist for antislavery congressmen in Washington. In particular, he helped in the fight against the Gag Rule, which suppressed debate regarding antislavery petitions. This fight was ultimately successful and the Gag Rule was rescinded in 1844. Following his stint in Washington, Weld withdrew from an active role in abolitionism.

Robert K. Nelson

See also: American Anti-Slavery Society (AASS); Immediate Emancipation.

Further Readings

Abzug, Robert H. *Passionate Liberator: Theodore Dwight Weld & the Dilemma of Reform.* New York: Oxford University Press, 1980.

Barnes, Gilbert H., and Dwight L. Dumond, eds. *Letters of Theodore Dwight Weld, Angelina Grimké Weld, and Sarah Grimké, 1822–1844.* Gloucester, MA: Peter Smith, 1965.

Nelson, Robert K. "'The Forgetfulness of Sex': Devotion and Desire in the Courtship Letters of Angelina Grimké and Theodore Dwight Weld." *Journal of Social History* 37 (Spring 2004): 663–679.

West Indies Emancipation Day Celebration

On August 1, 1834, the emancipation bill of 1833 was promulgated in the British West Indies and placed the former slaves under the transitional system of apprenticeship, which was to last for six years before the enactment of full emancipation. Under apprenticeship, the former slaves were required to labor forty-five hours each week for their master; beyond that time, they could earn wages for themselves. Yet apprenticeship was abolished two years early on August 1, 1838. Both events of August 1 were welcomed by black and white American abolitionists as auspicious signs that success was inevitable in their own country as well, and throughout the remainder of the antebellum period, many commemorated the "First of August" as an antislavery holiday. Although it was also sporadically observed in Great Britain, it became most important as a platform for antislavery agitation in America.

At a time when the Fourth of July was developing into an annual occasion for patriotic effusions about freedom, the First of August was a subversive surrogate for the hypocritical rituals of Independence Day. By celebrating Great Britain's virtue, abolitionists spotlighted America's vice. Simultaneously, they highlighted the path to repentance: by publicizing the perceived peacefulness and profitability of West Indian emancipation, they used the First of August to argue that immediate abolition would be safe and expedient for the American South. In addition to its usefulness as a rhetorical platform, however, the First of August contributed to the movement culture of Northern abolitionists, both black and white, providing them with annual opportunities to congregate, celebrate, and rejuvenate their commitment to reform.

Observances of the First of August clustered around the geographical centers of immediatism, specifically Boston and New England, New York City and upstate New York, Philadelphia, and Ohio. Ceremonies were often held in meeting houses or rustic "groves," and audiences numbered from hundreds to thousands at the largest events. Especially in Massachusetts and New York, assemblies were frequently biracial and composed of both men and women, particularly in the mid- to late-1830s. In the next two decades, however, First of August celebrations were marked by the divisions that plagued the antislavery movement, both among white abolitionist factions and between black and white reform communities. Garrisonians in the Massachusetts Anti-Slavery Society and the American Anti-Slavery Society consistently observed the day with official "picnics" up to the Civil War, but African American leaders within Boston, New York, and Philadelphia increasingly organized separate celebrations, both to demonstrate the solidarity of black communities and to legitimize their own claims to community leadership.

First of August celebrations drew on many of the cultural traditions that shaped the Fourth of July, but they also manifested the same class tensions that were exhibited on Independence Day. Much like middle-class celebrations of the Fourth, which contrasted with the rowdy celebrations of the urban working class, ceremonies for the First usually emphasized orations and songs. Attending orations allowed abolitionists to display their respectability and temperance, even while espousing radical views; but if the First demonstrated abolitionist decorum, it was also a day for rest and recreation. The resulting tension between recreation, respectability, and radical reform helped produce a diversity of opinions about how the First of August should be observed, just as many contemporaries argued about the proper way to celebrate the Fourth of July.

Recent scholarship has focused on the First of August as a window onto community formation and political mobilization among Northern African Americans. Long before British emancipation in the 1830s, black Northerners had developed holiday alternatives to the Fourth of July, a day on which they were often targeted by racist discourse and dangerous rioters. Many celebrated July 5 (New York state emancipation), instead of the Fourth, or preferred other holidays, like the anniversary of Crispus Attucks's death in March or of the slave trade's abolition later in July. Preexisting traditions were grafted onto West Indian emancipation celebrations by black Northerners, including traditions developed during slavery, when holidays like Pinkster and Negro Election Day served as opportunities for symbolic critique and communal self-expression. Drawing on memories of these events, African American communities often observed the First of August with parades, dances, and militia drills.

These practices were often chastised by white abolitionist leaders, and they were also controversial among black abolitionists. On the one hand, African American leaders wanted to attract people to their First of August celebrations to show numerical strength, and parades and dances were certainly attractive. They also wanted to lay claim to public space as political agents, which parades in particular allowed them to do. But on the other hand, many abolitionist leaders, white and black, stressed the need for "moral uplift" and respectability in black communities, and parades and dances were seen by many as unrespectable. Planners for First of August celebrations attempted to balance the values of group unity, effective political action, and adherence to social conventions. Among black abolitionists, the former two values frequently outweighed the latter. Important as decorum was to African American elites, it was often more important to draw on long-standing festive traditions in African American communities and to draw large crowds to First of August events.

W. Caleb McDaniel

See also: American Anti-Slavery Society (AASS); Garrisonians.

Further Readings

Gravely, William B. "The Dialectic of Double-Consciousness in Black American Freedom Celebrations, 1808–1863." *Journal of Negro History* 67, 4 (Winter 1982): 302–317.

Kachun, Mitch. *Festivals of Freedom: Memory and Meaning in African American Emancipation Celebrations, 1808–1915*. Amherst: University of Massachusetts, 2003.

Rael, Patrick. "Besieged by Freedom's Army: Antislavery Celebrations and Black Activism." In *Black Identity & Black Protest in the Antebellum North*. Chapel Hill: University of North Carolina Press, 2002, pp. 54–81.

Whig Party and Antislavery

The Whig Party was an American political party officially formed in 1834 in opposition to Andrew Jackson and the Democratic Party. Political descendants of the National Republican Party, the Whigs advocated for "the American System," a nationalistic economic system that featured tariff protection, federally supported internal improvements, and the continuation of the national bank. Drawing much support from New England Congregationalists, Presbyterians, Quakers, and evangelical Protestants, the Whig Party endorsed a variety of reform movements, believing government should play a role in the moral behavior of Americans and eliminate sin in the United States. Many Northern Whigs supported abolitionism.

Early on in their party's history, Whigs in Congress split sectionally over slavery issues. In 1836, almost all Northern Whigs in the House of Representatives voted along antislavery lines, while nearly all Southern Whigs voted proslavery. Northern Whigs, however, were unique from their Southern colleagues: Southern Whigs and Southern Democrats generally shared the same position on slavery, whereas the antislavery position of Northern Whigs enabled them to present themselves as unique from Northern Democrats on the issue of slavery. Mutual animosity toward the Democratic Party and a nationalist vision kept the Whig party united in spite of divisions over slavery.

By 1840, Northern Whigs grew in strength as they attracted an increasing number of abolitionists, like William Seward. Even with the formation of the abolitionist Liberty Party in 1840, Whigs retained the loyal support of abolitionists. As the Liberty Party gained strength between 1840 and 1844, Northern Whigs increasingly attacked slavery to limit defections. With the onset of the annexation of Texas and the Mexican War, Northern "Conscience" Whigs opposed the expansion of slavery into the West, splintering the party further along sectional lines. That a wing of a large national party associated itself so strongly with antislavery, however, helped legitimize the abolitionist movement.

The nomination and election in 1848 of Zachary Taylor, a war hero from the Mexican War, helped keep the Whigs united. Taylor's election, however, marked a turning point for the Whig Party. The party splintered even further along sectional lines, prefiguring the Civil War. Taylor's effort to avoid the issue of slavery angered some "Conscience" Whigs who joined with members of the Liberty Party to form the Free Soil Party. The defeat of the Whigs in the election of 1852, accompanied by its calls for moderation and union during the struggle over the Compromise of 1850, heralded further defections to the Free Soil Party. Southern Whigs fled to the Democratic Party, which appeared to them much more receptive to slave-holding rights. The defections culminated with the formation of the Republican Party in 1854 when numerous Northern Whigs joined the new party. The Whig Party was in such a beleaguered state by 1856 that at its convention it endorsed former president Millard Fillmore, previously a Whig who was now running as the presidential candidate for the anti-immigrant Know-Nothing Party. In 1860, the small number of remaining Whigs reorganized to form the Constitutional Union Party, but they fared poorly in that portentous election.

Daniel P. Kotzin

See also: Antislavery Evangelical Protestantism; Radical Republicans; Texas, Annexation of (1845).

Further Readings

Holt, Michael F. *The Rise and Fall of the American Whig Party: Jacksonian Politics and the Onset of the Civil War.* New York: Oxford University Press, 1999.

Stewart, James Brewer. "Abolitionists, Insurgents, and Third Parties: Sectionalism and Partisan Politics in Northern Whiggery, 1836–1844." In Alan M. Kraut, ed. *Crusaders and Compromisers: Essays on the Relationship of the Antislavery Struggle to the Antebellum Party System.* Westport, CT: Greenwood Press, 1983, pp. 25–43.

Wilberforce, William

William Wilberforce was a Member of Parliament (MP), an author and Britain's best-known abolitionist. He belonged to one of Kingston-upon-Hull's most affluent merchant families. Wilberforce was gifted intellectually, although his health and eyesight were poor throughout his life. He entered St. John's College, Cambridge, in October 1766 and proved an able and popular student. In 1780, Wilberforce became the MP for his hometown at twenty-one—the minimum age at which one could run—and was later elected in 1784 as MP for the large, prestigious county seat of Yorkshire. From his earliest days, Wilberforce was regarded as an eloquent speaker.

He had a dramatic religious experience in 1785 when he converted to evangelical Christianity. It transformed his life and his politics. In 1787, he founded the Proclamation Society for the reformation of individual and societal morals. At about the same time, Wilberforce met Thomas Clarkson whose research on the Atlantic

In the late eighteenth and early nineteenth centuries, William Wilberforce, an elected member of the British House of Commons, advocated the abolition of the British slave trade and later the abolition of the practice of slavery worldwide. (Library of Congress)

slave trade shocked him. His friend, Prime Minister William Pitt the Younger, also an abolitionist, encouraged Wilberforce to spearhead the issue in the House of Commons. Wilberforce and Clarkson prepared evidence for the Privy Council in 1788. Ill health forced Wilberforce to withdraw temporarily from his political duties, and Pitt presented their findings to Parliament. This resulted in an act that restricted the number of slaves a vessel might carry based on the ship's tonnage. Although popular sentiment continued to mount against the slave trade, George III's mental illness and the resulting Regency Bill Crisis trumped other issues during the winter of 1788–1789. The king's recovery in the spring allowed abolition to return to the agenda.

In 1789, Wilberforce, with Pitt's cooperation, brought a bill forward once again to abolish Great Britain's involvement in the Atlantic slave trade. His speech was praised as being one of the most powerful ever heard in the House. In January 1790, abolition was proving a very time-consuming issue and the matter was given to a Select Committee. By the fall, Wilberforce had 1,400 pages of evidence to present to the House. Many abolitionists argued their case on humanitarian and Christian grounds, but Wilberforce also attempted to destroy the notion that Africans were inferior. He became an ardent supporter of the often troubled Sierra Leone project to repatriate freed blacks to West Africa. He hoped its success would demonstrate that free Africans could establish a well-ordered society.

Wilberforce addressed the Commons on April 18, 1791, but the bill was defeated yet again. He and his fellow abolitionists pressed on, urging more petitions, meetings, pamphlets, sermons, and public education. Their campaign had always been hampered by powerful economic interests that wanted to defeat, or at least delay, abolition. By the early 1790s, the abolitionists lost ground as public and political opinion recoiled from the excesses of the French Revolution and the St. Domingue slave uprising. The issue was revisited in 1792 in the House; Wilberforce received support for gradual abolition but the House of Lords postponed the issue. Once again the "West Indian interest" of powerful planters employed successful delaying tactics.

Despite the downturn in public and political support for abolition, Wilberforce reintroduced the Abolition Bill almost every year in the 1790s. Much to Wilberforce's dismay, even Pitt's enthusiasm cooled during this period. It was not until 1804 that the tide began to turn. Napoleon's hostility to emancipation became known and the cause was helped by the inclusion of new Irish MPs who favored abolition. However, Wilberforce reintroduced the bill in 1804 and 1805 without success. Finally, Parliament voted overwhelmingly in its favor and the Abolition Act received Royal Assent on March 25, 1807. It became illegal to trade in slaves, although stamping out slavery in British colonies would prove far more difficult to effect.

Troubled by multiple health complaints, Wilberforce resigned his seat of Yorkshire in 1812 for the pocket borough of Bramber, Sussex, which he hoped would be a less demanding constituency. He began work on the Slave Registration Bill, which would help monitor slave traffic and ensure compliance with the Abolition Act. Once again, he encountered significant resistance. Despite his failing health, he continued to speak and publish tracts attacking slavery, which led to the founding of the Anti-Slavery Society in 1823 and the campaign to emancipate the slaves in all British colonies. The Society believed in educating and mobilizing popular pressure to overcome remaining opposition. By 1830, it had published half a million tracts.

In 1821, Wilberforce selected his replacement: leadership of the parliamentary campaign passed to Thomas Fowell Buxton. In 1825, Wilberforce resigned from the House of Commons. Despite his lengthy career in politics, he never once enjoyed office. Wilberforce's retirement was spent at Mill Hill, north of London, with his family, although he did suffer significant financial setbacks during this time. His last public appearance was in 1830 at a meeting of the Anti-Slavery Society. Wilberforce lived to see the Emancipation bill gain support and was on his deathbed when it received its final Commons reading on July 26, 1833. He died three days later and is buried in Westminster Abbey.

Wilberforce was involved in many humanitarian causes before Parliament, such as Catholic Emancipation, as well as several causes outside of the House. Although Wilberforce is the best known of the abolitionists, he did not act alone. There were many inside and outside of Parliament who fought for this cause. He found great support from his friends and fellow Christians centered in the village of Clapham, south of London. They were nicknamed the "Saints" by their detractors and later tagged the "Clapham Sect." Nevertheless, Wilberforce was the prime mover of the group and was instrumental in the fight to liberate slaves in Britain and internationally.

Cheryl Fury

See also: Atlantic Slave Trade and British Abolition; British Slavery, Abolition of.

Further Readings

Furneaux, Robin. *William Wilberforce*. London: Hamish Hamilton, 1974.

Lean, Garth. *God's Politician: William Wilberforce's Struggle*. London: Darton, Longman and Todd, 1980.

Pollock, John. *William Wilberforce*. London: Constable, 1977.

Wilberforce, Robert Isaac, and Samuel Wilberforce. *Life of William Wilberforce*, 5 vols. London: John Murray, 1838.

Women's Antislavery Societies

Women's antislavery societies that surfaced in the 1830s played a seminal role in raising women's consciousness about their own lack of political, economic, and other civil rights. They posed the first organized, gender-specific challenge to slavery and racism. Their aggressiveness in the male-controlled public sphere made the societies flashpoints for debates on women's place. Members' experiences fermented a feminist culture that set the stage for the first women's rights convention at Seneca Falls in 1848.

The first female-only, antislavery society comprised a group of black women in Salem, Massachusetts, who organized on February 22, 1832, in response to an invitation in William Lloyd Garrison's the *Liberator*. Later that year, a dozen women organized the racially integrated Boston Female Anti-Slavery Society, followed by the Philadelphia Female Anti-Slavery Society in 1833. Integration between the sexes remained more elusive, and the first of three annual all-female antislavery conventions in 1837 drew eighty-one participants from twelve states. By 1838, at least thirty-three female antislavery societies existed throughout the Northeast.

Members shook off the ridicule and violence that greeted women's entrance into politics. The praise they won for resisting a mob in 1835 emboldened the Boston women to move farther into the public sphere, appearing at political meetings to support antislavery measures. The women sued Southerners who brought slaves to their city and organized fund-raisers for male abolitionists. In 1836, they coordinated an antislavery petition drive across New England that firmly planted women in politics. Female exercise of the constitutional right to petition was a crucial early bridge between the separate spheres that broadened both sexes' conception of women's role as citizens.

The Boston group's boldness appalled many Americans, however, illuminating cultural beliefs about separate spheres so deeply inscribed that even some antislavery women spurned equal rights with men. The clergy also pounced upon the ladies' antislavery societies because their techniques trespassed traditional male prerogatives, most notoriously by the radical act of women speaking in public. The Boston society sponsored the groundbreaking speaking tour of Angelina and Sarah Grimké, for instance, which ignited the famous exchanges between the South Carolina sisters and the Massachusetts clergy on women's place.

The "woman question" split the abolition movement in 1840, when Garrison supporters won control of the American Anti-Slavery Society. Foes of women's expanding role walked out to form their own organization, followed by the Ladies' New York City Anti-Slavery Society. Ironically, although it decried women speaking in public and linking abolition to women's rights, the New York women had hosted the Grimkés' first speaking engagements as abolition agents in "parlor talks" to women only. The ladies' society withdrew to fund-raising and domestic activities such as antislavery needlework.

The female breach into politics nonetheless widened. Lucretia Mott, Lydia Maria Child, and Maria Weston Chapman filled the male defectors' seats on the American Anti-Slavery Society's executive committee. In June 1840, Mott was among female delegates refused recognition because of their sex at the World's Anti-Slavery Convention in London. Her indignation set Mott and sister abolitionist Elizabeth Cady Stanton on the road to Seneca Falls.

Linda J. Lumsden

See also: Garrisonians.

Further Readings

Flexner, Eleanor. *Century of Struggle: The Woman's Rights Movement in the United States.* New York: Atheneum, 1971 (originally published by The Belknap Press of Harvard University Press, 1958).

Yellin, Jean Fagan, and John C. Van Horne, eds. *The Abolitionist Sisterhood: Women's Political Culture in Antebellum America.* Ithaca, NY: Cornell University Press. 1994.

Primary Documents

EXCERPTS FROM *A NARRATIVE OF THE UNCOMMON SUFFERINGS, AND SURPRIZING DELIVERANCE OF BRITON HAMMON*

This is a narrative about the life of an African named Briton Hammon that was written in the style and form of many European writers of the eighteenth century. Hammon was a slave who wrote his memoirs about his experiences after having left his master in Boston in 1747. After having survived a shipwreck on the Florida coast on his way to Jamaica, he was captured by Native Americans. At this point, he was purchased by a Spanish captain and ended up in Havana, Cuba. Thereafter, he was put in a dungeon having run into problems with the law and was confined for five years. After several attempts to escape his captivity by boarding ships bound for Jamaica, he was eventually successful and managed to travel to London. While in London, he was reunited with his former master after thirteen years.

Accounts like Hammon's were rare in eighteenth-century America and Europe because black slaves, former slaves, and free blacks rarely had the opportunity to get an education. The following excerpt offers a glimpse into Hammon's experiences under slavery. (See also Equiano, Olaudah; Slave Narratives.)

A NARRATIVE of the UNCOMMON SUFFERINGS, AND Surprizing DELIVERANCE OF Briton Hammon, A Negro Man,——

Servant to GENERAL WINSLOW, Of Marshfield, in NEW-ENGLAND; Who returned to *Boston*, after having been absent almost Thirteen Years.

CONTAINING An Account of the many Hardships he underwent from the Time he left his Master's House, in the Year 1747, to the Time of his Return to *Boston*.—How he was Cast away in the Capes of Florida;—the horrid Cruelty and inhuman Barbarity of the *Indians* in murdering the whole Ship's Crew;—the Manner of his being carry'd by them into Captivity. Also, An Account of his being

Confined Four Years and Seven Months in a close Dungeon,—And the remarkable Manner in which he met with his good old Master in London; who returned to *New-England*, a Passenger, in the same Ship.

To THE READER,

As my Capacities and Condition of Life are very low, it cannot be expected that I should make those Remarks on the Sufferings I have met with, or the kind Providence of a good GOD for my Preservation, as one in a higher Station; but shall leave that to the Reader as he goes along, and so I shall only relate Matters of Fact as they occur to my Mind—

ON Monday, 25th Day of December, 1747, with the leave of my Master, I went from Marshfield, with an Intention to go a Voyage to Sea, and the next Day, the 26th, got to Plymouth, where I immediately ship'd myself on board of a Sloop, Capt. John Howland, Master, bound to Jamaica and the Bay.—We sailed from Plymouth in a short Time, and after a pleasant Passage of about 30 Days, arrived at Jamaica; we was detain'd at Jamaica only 5 Days, from whence we sailed for the Bay, where we arrived safe in 10 Days. We loaded our Vessel with Logwood, and sailed from the Bay the 25th Day of May following, and the 15th Day of June, we were cast away on Cape-Florida, about 5 Leagues from the Shore; being now destitute of every Help, we knew not what to do or what Course to take in this our sad Condition:—The Captain was advised, intreated, and beg'd on, by every Person on board, to heave over but only 20 Ton of the Wood, and we should get clear, which if he had done, might have sav'd his Vessel and Cargo, and not only so, but his own Life, as well as the Lives of the Mate and Nine Hands, as I shall presently relate.

After being upon this Reef two Days, the Captain order'd the Boat to be hoisted out, and then ask'd who were willing to tarry on board? The whole Crew was for going on Shore at this Time, but as the Boat would not carry 12 Persons at once, and to prevent any Uneasiness, the Captain, a Passenger, and one Hand tarry'd on board, while the Mate, with Seven Hands besides myself, were order'd to go on Shore in the Boat, which as soon as we had reached, one half were to be Landed, and the other four to return to the Sloop, to fetch the Captain and the others on Shore. The Captain order'd us to take with us our Arms, Ammunition, Provisions and Necessaries for Cooking, as also a Sail to make a Tent of, to shelter us from the Weather; after having left the Sloop we stood towards the Shore, and being within Two Leagues of the same, we espy'd a Number of Canoes, which we at first took to be Rocks, but soon found our Mistake, for we perceiv'd they moved towards us; we presently saw an English Colour hoisted in one of the Canoes, at the Sight of which we were not a little rejoiced, but on our advancing yet nearer, we found them, to our very great Surprize, to be Indians of which there were Sixty; being now so near them we could not possibly make our Escape; they soon came up with and boarded us, took away all our Arms Ammunition, and Provision.

The whole Number of CaRoes (being about Twenty,) then made for the Sloop, except Two which they left to guard us, who order'd us to follow on with them; the Eighteen which made for the Sloop, went so much faster than we that they got on board above Three Hours before we came along side, and had kill'd Captain Howland, the Passenger and the other hand; we came to the Larboard side of the Sloop, and they order'd us round to the Starboard, and as we were passing round the Bow, we saw the whole Number of Indians, advancing forward and loading their Guns, upon which the Mate said, "my Lads we are all dead Men," and before we had got round, they discharged their Small Arms upon us, and kill'd Three of our hands, viz. Reuben Young of Cape-Cod, Mate; Joseph Little and Lemuel Doty of Plymouth, upon which I immediately jump'd overboard, chusing rather to be drowned, than to be kill'd by those barbarous and inhuman Savages.

In three or four Minutes after, I heard another Volley which dispatched the other five, viz. John Nowland, and Nathaniel Rich, both belonging to Plymouth, and Elkanah Collymore, and James Webb, Strangers, and Moses Newmock, Molatto. As soon as they had kill'd the whole of the People, one of the Canoes padled after me, and soon came up with me, hawled me into the Canoe, and beat me most terribly with a Cutlass, after that they ty'd me down, then this Canoe stood for the Sloop again and as soon as she came along side, the Indians on board the Sloop betook themselves to their Canoes, then set the Vessel on Fire, making a prodigious shouting and hallowing like so many Devils. As soon as the Vessel was burnt down to the Water's edge, the Indians stood for the Shore, together with our Boat, on board of which they put 5 hands. After we came to the Shore, they led me to their Hutts, where I expected nothing but immediate death, and as they spoke broken English, were often telling me, while coming from the Sloop to the Shore, that they intended to roast me alive. But the Providence of God order'd it otherways, for He appeared for my Help, in this Mount of Difficulty, and they were better to me then my Fears, and soon unbound me, but set a Guard over me every Night. They kept me with them about five Weeks, during which Time they us'd me pretty well, and gave me boil'd Corn, which was what they often eat themselves. The Way I made my Escape from these Villains was this; A Spanish Schooner arriving there from St. Augustine, the Master of which, whose Name was Romond, asked the Indians to let me go on board his Vessel, which they granted. The Way I came to know this Gentleman was, by his being taken last War by an English Privateer, and brought into Jamaica, while I was there knowing me very well, weigh'd Anchor and carry'd me off to the Havanna, and after being there four Days the Indians came after me, and insisted on having me again, as I was their Prisoner;—They made Application to the Governor, and demanded me again from him; in answer to which the Governor told them, that as they had put the whole Crew to Death, they should not have me again, and so paid them Ten Dollars for me, adding, that he would not have them kill any person hereafter, but take as many of them as they could, of those that should be cast away, and bring them to him, for which he would pay them Ten Dollars a-head. At the Havanna I lived with the Governor in the Castle about a Twelve-month, where I was walking thro' the Street, I met with a Press-Gang who immediately prest me, and put me into Goal, and with a Number of others I was confin'd till next Morning, when we were all brought out, and ask'd who would go on board the King's Ships, four of which having been lately built, were bound to Old-Spain, and on my refusing to serve on board, they put me in a close Dungeon, where I was confin'd Four Years and seven months; during which Time I often made application to the Governor, by Persons who came to see the Prisoners, but they never acquainted him with it, nor did he know all this Time what became of me, which was the means of my being confin'd there so long. But kind Providence so order'd it, that after I had been in this Place so long as the Time mention'd above, the Captain of a Merchantman, belonging to Boston, having sprung a Leak was obliged to put into the Havanna to refit, and while he was at Dinner at Mrs. Betty Howard's, she told the Captain of my deplorable Condition, and said she would be glad, if he could by some means or other relieve me; The Captain told Mrs. Howard he would use his best Endeavours for my Relief and Enlargement.

Accordingly, after Dinner, came to the Prison, and ask'd the Keeper if he might see me; upon his Request I was brought out of the Dungeon, and after the Captain had Interrogated me, told me, he would intercede with the Governor for my Relief out of that miserable Place, which he did, and the next Day the Governor sent an Order to release me; I lived with the Governor about a Year after I was delivered from the Dungeon, in which Time I endeavour'd three Times to make my Escape, the last of which proved effectual; the first Time I got on board of Captain Marsh, an English Twenty Gun Ship, with a Number of others, and lay on board conceal'd that Night; and the next Day the Ship being under sail, I thought myself safe, and so made my Appearance upon Deck, but as soon as we were discovered the Captain ordered the Boat out, and sent us all on Shore—I intreated the Captain to let me, in particular, stay on board, begging, and crying to him, to commiserate my unhappy Condition, and added, that I had been confin'd almost five Years in a close Dungeon, but the Captain would not hearken to any Intreaties, for fear of having the Governor's Displeasure, and so was obliged to go on shore, after being on Shore another Twelve month, I endeavour'd to make my Escape the second Time, by trying to get on board of a Sloop bound to Jamaica, and as I was going from the City to the Sloop, was unhappily taken by the Guard, and ordered back to the Castle, and there confined.—However, in a short Time I was set at Liberty, and order'd with a Number of others to carry the He is carried (by Way of Respect) in a large Two-arm Chair; the Chair is lin'd with crimson Velvet, and supported by eight Persons.

Bishop from the Castle, thro' the Country, to confirm the old People, baptize Children, &c. for which he receives large Sums of Money.—I was employ'd in this Service about Seven Months, during which Time I lived very well, and then returned to the Castle again, where I had my Liberty to walk about the City, and do Work for my self;—The Beaver, an English Man of War then lay in the Harbour, and having been informed by some of the Ship's Crew that she was to sail in a few Days, I had nothing now to do, but to seek an Opportunity how I should make my Escape.

Accordingly one Sunday Night the Lieutenant of the Ship with a Number of the Barge Crew were in a Tavern, and Mrs. Howara who had before been a Friend to me, interceded with the Lieutenant to carry me on board: the Lieutenant said he would with all his Heart, and immediately I went on board in the Barge. The next Day the Spaniards came along side the Beaver, and demanded me again, with a Number of others who had made their Escape from them, and got on board the Ship, but just before I did; but the Captain, who was a true Englishman, refus'd them, and said he could not answer it, to deliver up any Englishmen under English Colours.—In a few Days we set Sail for Jamaica, where we arrived safe, after a short and pleasant Passage.

After being at Jamaica a short Time we sail'd for London, as convoy to a Fleet of Merchantmen, who all arrived safe in the Downs, I was turned over to another Ship, the Arcenceil, and there remained about a Month. From this Ship I went on board the Sandwich of 90 Guns; on board the Sandwich, I tarry'd 6 Weeks, and then was order'd on board the Hercules, Capt. John Porter, a 74 Gun Ship, we sail'd on a Cruize, and met with a French 84 Gun Ship, and had a very smart Engagement, A particular Account of this Engagement, has been Publish'd in the Boston News-Papers in which about 70 of our Hands were Kill'd and Wounded, the Captain lost his Leg in the Engagement, and I was Wounded in the Head by a small Shot. We should have taken this Ship, if they had not cut away the most of our Rigging; however, in about three Hours after, a 64 Gun Ship, came up with and took her.—I was discharged from the Hercules the 12th Day of May 1759 (having been on board of that Ship 3 Months) on account of my being disabled in the Arm, and render'd incapable of Service, after being honourably paid the Wages due to me. I was put into the Greenwich Hospital where I stay'd and soon recovered.—I then ship'd myself a Cook on board Captain Martyn, an arm'd Ship in the King's Service. I was on board this Ship almost Two Months, and after being paid my Wages, was discharg'd in the Month of October.—After my discharge from Captain Martyn, I was taken sick in London of a Fever, and was confin'd about 6 Weeks, where I expended all my Money, and left in very poor Circumstances; and unhappy for me I knew nothing of my good Master's being in London at this my very difficult Time. After I got well of my sickness, I ship'd myself on board of a large Ship bound to Guinea, and being in a publick House one Evening,

I overheard a Number of Persons talking about Rigging a Vessel bound to New-England, I ask'd them to what Part of New-England this Vessel was bound? they told me, to Boston; and having ask'd them who was Commander? they told me, Capt. Watt; in a few Minutes after this the Mate of the Ship came in, and I ask'd him if Captain Watt did not want a Cook, who told me he did, and that the Captain would be in, in a few Minutes; and in about half an Hour the Captain came in, and then I ship'd myself at once, after begging off from the Ship bound to Guinea; I work'd on board Captain Watt's Ship almost Three Months, before she sail'd, and one Day being at Work in the Hold, I overheard some Persons on board mention the Name of Winslow, at the Name of which I was very inquisitive, and having ask'd what Winslow they were talking about? They told me it was General Winslow; and that he was one of the Passengers, I ask'd them what General Winslow? For I never knew my good Master, by that Title before; but after enquiring more particularly I found it must be Master, and in a few Days Time the Truth was joyfully verify'd by a happy Sight of his Person, which so overcome me, that I could not speak to him for some Time—My good Master was exceeding glad to see me, telling me that I was like one arose from the Dead, for he thought I had been Dead a great many Years, having heard nothing of me for almost Thirteen Years. I think I have not deviated from Truth, in any particular of this my Narrative, and tho' I have omitted a great many Things, yet what is wrote may suffice to convince the Reader, that I have been most grievously afflicted, and yet thro' the Divine Goodness, as miraculously preserved, and delivered out of many Dangers; of which I desire to retain a grateful Remembrance, as long as I live in the World.

And now, That in the Providence of that GOD, who delivered his Servant David out of the Paw of the Lion and out of the Paw of the Bear, I am freed from a long and dreadful Captivity, among worse Savages than they; And am return'd to my own Native Land, to Shew how Great Things the Lord hoth done for Me; I would call upon all Men, and Say, O Magnifie the Lord with Me, and let us Exalt his Name together!——O that Men would Praise the Lord for His Goodness, and for his Wonderful Works to the Children of Men!

Source: Briton Hammon. *A Narrative of the Uncommon Sufferings, and Surprizing Deliverance of Briton Hammon.* Boston: Printed and Sold by Green & Russell, 1760.

EXCERPT FROM *THE INTERESTING NARRATIVE OF THE LIFE OF OLAUDAH EQUIANO* (1789)

The following selection from Olaudah Equiano's The Interesting Narrative of the Life of Olaudah Equiano (1789) *is a rare account of the experience aboard a slave ship during the Atlantic crossing from the perspective of a slave. It is a sequel to Equiano's story of his enslavement in Africa. This selection, written during the 1780s, describes his experience on the Middle Passage during the mid-1750s. (See also Equiano, Olaudah; Slave Narratives.)*

The first object which saluted my eyes when I arrived on the coast was the sea, and a slave ship which was then riding at anchor and waiting for its cargo. These filled me with astonishment, which was soon converted into terror when I was carried on board. I was immediately handled and tossed up to see if I were sound by some of the crew, and I was now persuaded that I had gotten into a world of bad spirits and that they were going to kill me. . . . Indeed such were the horrors of my views and fears at the moment that, if ten thousand worlds had been my own, I would have freely parted with them all to have exchanged my condition with that of the meanest slave in my own country. When I looked round the ship, too, and saw a large furnace or copper boiling and a multitude of black people of every description chained together, every one of their countenances expressing dejection and sorrow, I no longer doubted of my fate and . . . fainted. When I recovered a little I found some black people about me, who I believed were some of those who had brought me on board and had been receiving their pay; they talked to me in order to cheer me, but all in vain. I asked them if we were not to be eaten by those white men with horrible looks, red faces, and loose hair. They told me I was not, and one of the crew brought me a small portion of spirituous liquor in a wine glass, but being afraid of him I would not take it . . . Soon after this the blacks who brought me on board went off and left me abandoned to despair.

I now saw myself deprived of all chance of returning to my native country or even the least glimpse of hope of gaining the shore . . . and I even wished for my former slavery in preference to my present situation . . . I was soon put down under the decks, and there I received such a salutation in my nostrils as I had never experienced in my life; so that with the loathsomeness of the stench and crying together, I became so sick and low that I was not able to eat, nor had I the least desire to taste anything. . . . [T]wo of the white men offered me eatables, and on my refusing to eat, one of them held me fast by the hands and laid me across I think the windlass, and tied my feet while the other flogged me severely. I had never experienced anything of this kind before, and although, not being used to the water, I naturally feared that element the first time I saw it, yet nevertheless could I have got over the nettings I would . . . have jumped over the side . . . In a little time after, amongst the poor chained men I found some of my own nation, which in a small degree gave ease to my mind. I inquired of these what was to be done with us. [T]hey gave me to understand we were to be carried to these white people's country to work for them. I then was a little revived, and thought if it were no worse than working, my situation was not so desperate. But still I feared I should be put to death, the white people looked and acted, as I thought, in so savage a manner, for I had never seen among my people such instances of brutal cruelty, and this not only shown towards us blacks but also to some of the whites themselves. One white man in particular I saw . . . flogged so unmercifully with a large rope near the foremast that he died in consequence of it; and they tossed him over the side as they would have done a brute. This made me fear these people the more, and I expected nothing less than to be treated in the same manner.

I could not help expressing my fears and apprehensions to some of my countrymen. I asked them if these people had no country but lived in this hollow place (the ship). They told me they did not, but came from a distant one. "Then," said I, "how comes it in all our country we never heard of them?" They told me because they lived so very far off. . . . I asked how the vessel could go? They told me . . . there were cloths put upon the masts by the help of the ropes I saw . . . the white men had some spell or magic they put in the water when they liked in order to stop the vessel. I was exceedingly amazed at this account and really thought they were spirits. . . .

While we stayed on the coast I was mostly on deck, and one day . . . I saw one of these vessels coming in with the sails up. As soon as the whites saw it they gave a great shout, at which we were amazed, and the more so as the vessel appeared larger by approaching nearer. . . . [W]hen the anchor was let go, I and my countrymen who saw it were lost in astonishment to observe the vessel stop, and were now convinced it was done by magic. Soon after this the other ship got her boats out, and they came on board of us, and the people of both ships seemed very glad to see each other. Several of the strangers also shook hands with us black people, and made motions with their hands, signifying I suppose we were to go to their country; but we did not understand them. At last, when the ship we were in had got in all her cargo, they made ready with many fearful noises, and we were all put under deck so that we could not see how they managed the vessel. . . .

The stench of the hold while we were on the coast was so intolerably loathsome that it was dangerous to remain there for any time, and some of us had been permitted to stay on the deck for the fresh air. But now that the whole ship's cargo were confined together it became absolutely pestilential. The closeness of the place and the heat of the climate, added to the number in the ship, which was so crowded that each had scarcely room to turn himself, almost suffocated us. This produced copious perspiration, so that the air soon became unfit for respiration from a variety of loathsome smells and brought on a sickness among the slaves, of which many died . . . This wretched situation was again aggravated by the galling of the chains, now become insupportable, and the filth of the necessary tubs, into which the children often fell and were almost suffocated. The shrieks of the women and the groans of the dying rendered the whole a scene of horror almost inconceivable. Happily perhaps for myself, I was soon reduced so low here that it was thought necessary to keep me almost always on deck, and from my extreme youth I was not put in fetters. In this situation I expected every hour to share the fate of my companions, some of whom were almost daily brought upon deck at the point of death, which I began to hope would soon put an end to my miseries. . . .

One day they had taken a number of fishes, and when they had killed and satisfied themselves with as many as they thought fit, to our astonishment who were on the deck, rather than give any of them to us to eat as we expected, they tossed the remaining fish into the sea again, although we begged and prayed for some as well as we could, but in vain. And some of my countrymen, being pressed by hunger, took an opportunity when they thought no one saw them of trying to get a little privately; but they were discovered, and the attempt procured them some very severe floggings. One day, when we had a smooth sea and moderate wind, two of my wearied countrymen who were chained together . . . preferring death to such a life of misery, somehow made through the nettings and jumped into the sea. Immediately another quite dejected fellow, who on account of his illness was suffered to be out of irons, also followed their example. And I believe many more would very soon have done the same if they had not been prevented by the ship's crew, who were instantly alarmed. . . . Two of the wretches were drowned, but they got the other and afterwards flogged him unmercifully for thus attempting to prefer death to slavery.

In this manner we continued to undergo more hardships . . . Many a time we were near suffocation from the want of fresh air, which we were often without for whole days together. This and the stench of the necessary tubs carried off many. During our passage I first saw flying fishes, which surprised me very much. They used frequently to fly across the ship and many of them fell on the deck. I also now first saw the use of the quadrant. I had often with astonishment seen the mariners make observations with it, and I could not think what it meant. They at last took notice of my surprise, and one of them, willing to increase it as well as to gratify my curiosity, made me one day look through it . . .

Source: Olaudah Equiano. *The Interesting Narrative of the Life of Olaudah Equiano, or Gustavus Vassa, the African, Written by Himself.* New York: W. Durell, 1791.

EXCERPTS FROM *THE CONFESSIONS OF NAT TURNER* (1831)

In 1831, Southampton County in southeastern Virginia was inhabited by approximately 16,000 people, including whites, slaves, and a high proportion of free blacks. Though slavery had been a fixture in the South since the seventeenth *century, there had never been a sustained slave insurrection in the region. Thus, the question remained as to whether a large-scale black revolution could ever occur in the American South. That question was answered during August 21–23, 1831, when Nat Turner and a small group of collaborators (that expanded to more than fifty) launched an insurrection that resulted in the deaths of at least fifty-five white people. Turner himself remained at large before being captured on October 30, 1831. While* The Confessions of Nat Turner *is only one of several accounts of the insurrection that were published at the time, it emerged as the most influential. In the days following his capture, Thomas R. Gray, a white Southern lawyer and slaveholder, asked Turner to provide a firsthand account of his actions and motives. Its details are largely corroborated by unrelated, contemporaneous documentation. For Turner, slavery in the South served as the basis for his holy war. He saw himself as a prophet and Christ-like figure. Turner's narrative indicates the ways in which religious rhetoric used by slaveholders to justify the slave system could be inverted and used to justify violent revolution. Turner was executed by hanging on November 11, 1831. The following are excerpts from* The Confessions of Nat Turner (1831). *(See also* Gabriel's Conspiracy (1800); Vesey's Conspiracy (1822).)*

SIR,—You have asked me to give a history of the motives which induced me to undertake the late insurrection, as you call it—To do so I must go back to the days of my infancy, and even before I was born. I was thirty-one years of age the 2nd of October last, and born the property of Benj. Turner, of this county. In my childhood a circumstance occurred which made an indelible impression on my mind, and laid the groundwork of that enthusiasm, which has terminated so fatally to many, both white and black, and for which I am about to atone at the gallows.

It is here necessary to relate this circumstance—trifling as it may seem, it was the commencement of that belief which has grown with time, and even now, sir, in this dungeon, helpless and forsaken as I am, I cannot divest myself of. Being at play with other children, when three or four years old, I was telling them something, which my mother overhearing, said it had happened before I was born—I stuck to my story, however, and related some things which went, in her opinion, to confirm it—others being called on were greatly astonished, knowing that these things had happened, and caused them to say in my hearing, I surely would be a prophet, as the Lord had shewn me things that had happened before my birth. . . . I was intended for some great purpose . . .

My grandmother, who was very religious . . . noticing the singularity of my manners . . . and my uncommon intelligence for a child, remarked I had too much sense to be raised, and if I was, I would never be of any service to any one as a slave—To a mind like mine, restless, inquisitive and observant of everything that was passing, it is easy to suppose that religion was the subject to which it would be directed. . . .

The manner in which I learned to read and write, not only had great influence on my own mind, as I acquired it with the most perfect ease. . . .

. . . such was the confidence of the negroes in the neighborhood, even at this early period of my life, in my superior judgment, that they would often carry me with them when they were going on any roguery, to plan for them. . . . Having soon discovered to be great, I must appear so, and therefore studiously avoided mixing in society, and wrapped myself in mystery, devoting my time to fasting and prayer. . . .

As I was praying one day at my plough, the Spirit spoke to me. . . . The Spirit that spoke to the prophets in former days—and I was greatly astonished, and for two years prayed continually, whenever my duty would permit—and then again I had the same revelation, which fully confirmed me in the impression that I was ordained for some great purpose in the hands of the Almighty. . . .

I began to direct my attention to this great object, to fulfil the purpose for which, by this time, I felt assured I was intended . . . something was about to happen that would terminate in fulfilling the great promise that had been made to me. . . .

. . . about this time I had a vision—and I saw white spirits and black spirits engaged in battle, and the sun was darkened—the thunder rolled in the Heavens, and blood flowed in streams—and I heard a voice saying, "Such is your luck, such you are called to see, and let it come rough or smooth, you must surely bear it." I now withdrew myself as much as my situation would permit, from the intercourse of my fellow servants, for the avowed purpose of serving the Spirit more fully. . . . And from the first steps of righteousness until the last, was I made perfect; and the Holy Ghost was with me. . . .

. . . while laboring in the field, I discovered drops of blood on the corn as though it were dew from heaven . . . and I then found on the leaves in the woods hieroglyphic characters, and numbers, with the forms of men in different attitudes, portrayed in blood . . . it was plain to me that the Savior was about to lay down the yoke he had borne for the sins of men, and the great day of judgment was at hand. . . .

And on the appearance of the sign, (the eclipse of the sun last February) I should arise and prepare myself, and slay my enemies with their own weapons. And immediately on the sign appearing in the heavens, the seal was removed from my lips, and I communicated the great work laid out for me to do, to four in whom I had the greatest confidence, (Henry, Hark, Nelson, and Sam)—It was intended by us to have begun the work of death on the 4th July last. . . .

Since the commencement of 1830, I had been living with Mr. Joseph Travis, who was to me a kind master, and placed the greatest confidence in me; in fact,

I had no cause to complain of his treatment to me. On Saturday evening, the 20th of August, it was agreed between Henry, Hark and myself, to prepare a dinner the next day for the men we expected, and then to concert a plan. . . .

. . . it was quickly agreed we should commence at home (Mr. J. Travis') on that night, and until we had armed and equipped ourselves, and gathered sufficient force, neither age nor sex was to be spared, (which was invariably adhered to). . . .

On returning to the house, Hark went to the door with an axe, for the purpose of breaking it open, as we knew we were strong enough to murder the family, if they were awaked by the noise; but reflecting that it might create an alarm in the neighborhood, we determined to enter the house secretly, and murder them whilst sleeping. Hark got a ladder and set it against the chimney, on which I ascended, and hoisting a window, entered and came down stairs, unbarred the door, and removed the guns from their places. It was then observed that I must spill the first blood. On which, armed with a hatchet, and accompanied by Will, I entered my master's chamber, it being dark, I could not give a death blow, the hatchet glanced from his head, he sprang from the bed and called his wife, it was his last word, Will laid him dead, with a blow of his axe, and Mrs. Travis shared the same fate, as she lay in bed. The murder of this family, five in number, was the work of a moment, not one of them awoke. . . .

We remained some time at the barn, where we paraded; I formed them in a line as soldiers, and after carrying them through all the manoeuvres I was master of marched them off to Mr. Salathul Francis', about six hundred yards distant. Sam and Will went to the door and knocked. Mr. Francis asked who was there, Sam replied it was him, and he had a letter for him, on which he got up and came to the door; they immediately seized him, and dragging him out a little from the door, he was dispatched by repeated blows on the head; there was no other white person in the family. We started from there for Mrs. Reese's, maintaining the most perfect silence on our march, where finding the door unlocked, we entered, and murdered Mrs. Reese in her bed, while sleeping; her son awoke, but it was only to sleep the sleep of death, he had only time to say who is that, and he was no more.

From Mrs. Reese's we went to Mrs. Turner's, a mile distant, which we reached about sunrise, on Monday morning. Henry, Austin, and Sam, went to the still, where, finding Mr. Peebles, Austin shot him, and the rest of us went to the house; as we approached, the family discovered us, and shut the door. Vain hope! Will, with one stroke of his axe, opened it, and we entered and found Mrs. Turner and Mrs. Newsome in the middle of a room, almost frightened to death. Will immediately killed Mrs. Turner, with one blow of his axe. I took Mrs. Newsome by the hand, and with the sword I had when I was apprehended, I struck her several blows over the head, but not being able to kill her, as the sword was dull. Will turning around and discovering it, despatched her also. A general destruction of property and search for money and ammunition, always succeeded the murders.

By this time my company amounted to fifteen, and nine men mounted, who started for Mrs. Whitehead's, (the other six were to go through a by way to Mr. Bryant's, and rejoin us at Mrs. Whitehead's,) as we approached the house we discovered Mr. Richard Whitehead standing in the cotton patch, near the lane fence; we called him over into the lane, and Will, the executioner, was near at hand, with his fatal axe, to send him to an untimely grave. . . .

I returned to commence the work of death, but they whom I left, had not been idle; all the family were already murdered, but Mrs. Whitehead and her daughter Margaret. As I came round to the door I saw Will pulling Mrs. Whitehead out of the house, and at the step he nearly severed her head from her body, with his broad axe. Miss Margaret, when I discovered her, had concealed herself in the corner, formed by the projection of cellar cap from the house; on my approach she fled, but was soon overtaken, and after repeated blows with a sword, I killed her by a blow on the head, with a fence rail. By this time, the six who had gone by Mr. Bryant's, rejoined us, and informed me they had done the work of death assigned them.

We again divided, part going to Mr. Richard Porter's, and from thence to Nathaniel Francis', the others to Mr. Howell Harris', and Mr. T. Doyles. On my reaching Mr. Porter's, he had escaped with his family. I understood there, that the alarm had already spread, and I immediately returned to bring up those sent to Mr. Doyles, and Mr. Howell Harris'; the party I left going on to Mr. Francis', having told them I would join them in that neighborhood. I met these sent to Mr. Doyles' and Mr. Harris' returning, having met Mr. Doyle on the road and killed him; and learning from some who joined them, that Mr. Harris was from home, I immediately pursued the course taken by the party gone on before; but knowing they would complete the work of death and pillage, at Mr. Francis' before I could get there, I went to Mr. Peter Edwards', expecting to find them there, but they had been here also.

I then went to Mr. John T. Barrow's, they had been here and murdered him. I pursued on their track to Capt. Newit Harris', where I found the greater part mounted, and ready to start; the men now amounting to about forty, shouted and hurraed as I rode up, some were in the yard, loading their guns, others drinking. They said Captain Harris and his family had escaped, the property in the house they destroyed, robbing him of money and other valuables. I ordered them to mount and march instantly, this was about nine or ten o'clock, Monday morning.

I proceeded to Mr. Levi Waller's, two or three miles distant. I took my station in the rear, and as it was my object to carry terror and devastation wherever we went, I placed fifteen or twenty of the best armed and most relied on, in front, who generally approached the houses as fast as their horses could run; this was for two purposes, to prevent escape and strike terror to the inhabitants—on this account I never got to the houses, after leaving Mrs. Whitehead's, until the murders were committed, except in one case.

I sometimes got in sight in time to see the work of death completed, viewed the mangled bodies as they lay, in silent satisfaction, and immediately started in quest of other victims—Having murdered Mrs. Waller and ten children, we started for Mr. William Williams'—having killed him and two little boys that were there; while engaged in this, Mrs. Williams fled and got some distance from the house, but she was pursued, overtaken, and compelled to get up behind one of the company, who brought her back, and after showing her the mangled body of her lifeless husband, she was told to get down and lay by his side, where she was shot dead. I then started for Mr. Jacob Williams, where the family were murdered—Here he found a young man named Drury, who had come on business with Mr. Williams—he was pursued, overtaken and shot.

Mrs. Vaughan was the next place we visited—and after murdering the family here, I determined on starting for Jerusalem—Our number amounted now to fifty or sixty, all mounted and armed with guns, axes, swords and clubs. . . .

. . . on our return we were met by a party of white when, who had pursued our blood-stained track, and who had fired on those at the gate, and dispersed them, which I knew nothing of, not having been at that time rejoined by any of them—Immediately on discovering the whites, I ordered my men to halt and form, as they appeared to be alarmed—The white men, eighteen in number, approached us in about one hundred yards, when one of them fired . . .

. . . I discovered about half of them retreating, I then ordered my men to fire and rush on them; the few remaining stood their ground until we approached within fifty yards, when they fired and retreated. We pursued and overtook some of them who we thought we left dead; (they were not killed) after pursuing them about two hundred yards, and rising a little hill, I discovered they were met by another party, and had halted, and were re-loading their guns . . . on hearing the firing they immediately rushed to the spot and arrived just in time to . . . save the lives of their friends and fellow citizens . . .

As I saw them reloading their guns, and more coming up than I saw at first, and several of my bravest men being wounded, the others became panick struck and squandered over the field; the white men pursued and fired on us several times. Hark had his horse shot under him, and I caught another for him as it was running by me; five or six of my men were wounded, but none left on the field; finding myself defeated here I instantly determined to go through a private way, and cross the Nottoway river at the Cypress Bridge, three miles below Jerusalem, and attack that place in the rear, as I expected they would look for me on the other road, and I had a great desire to get there to procure arms and ammunition.

After going a short distance in this private way, accompanied by about twenty men, I overtook two or three who told me the others were dispersed in every direction. After trying in vain to collect a sufficient force to proceed to Jerusalem, I determined to return, as I was sure they would make back to their old neighborhood, where they would rejoin me, make new recruits, and come down again. On my way back, I called at Mrs. Thomas's, Mrs. Spencer's, and several other places, the white families having fled, we found no more victims to gratify our thirst for blood, we stopped at Majr. Ridley's quarter for the night, and being joined by four of his men, with the recruits made since my defeat, we mustered now about forty strong.

After placing out sentinels, I laid down to sleep, but was quickly roused by a great racket; starting up, I found some mounted, and others in great confusion; one of the sentinels having given the alarm that we were about to be attacked, I ordered some to ride round and reconnoitre, and on their return the others being more alarmed, not knowing who they were, fled in different ways, so that I was reduced to about twenty again; with this I determined to attempt to recruit, and proceed on to rally in the neighborhood . . .

. . . we were immediately fired upon and retreated, leaving several of my men. I do not know what became of them, as I never saw them afterwards. Pursuing our course back and coming in sight of Captain Harris', where we had been the day before, we discovered a party of white men at the house, on which all deserted me but two, (Jacob and Nat), we concealed ourselves in the woods until near night, when I sent them in search of Henry, Sam, Nelson, and Hark, and directed them to rally all they could, at the place we had had our dinner the Sunday before, where they would find me, and I accordingly returned there as soon as it was dark and remained until Wednesday evening, when discovering white men riding around the place as though they were looking for someone, and none of my men joining me, I concluded Jacob and Nat had been taken, and compelled to betray me.

On this I gave up all hope for the present; and on Thursday night after having supplied myself with provisions from Mr. Travis's, I scratched a hole under a pile of fence rails in a field, where I concealed myself for six weeks, never leaving my hiding place but for a few minutes in the dead of night to get water which was very near; thinking by this time I could venture out, I began to go about in the night and eavesdrop the houses in the neighborhood; pursuing this course for about a fortnight and gathering little or no intelligence, afraid of speaking to any human being, and returning every morning to my cave before the dawn of day.

I know not how long I might have led this life, if accident had not betrayed me, a dog in the neighborhood passing by my hiding place one night while I was out, was attracted by some meat I had in my cave, and crawled in and stole it, and was coming out just as I returned. A few nights after, two negroes having started to go hunting with the same dog, and passed that way, the dog came again to the place, and having just gone out to walk about, discovered me and barked, on which thinking myself discovered, I spoke to them to beg concealment.

On making myself known they fled from me. Knowing then they would betray me, I immediately left my hiding place, and was pursued almost incessantly until I was taken a fortnight afterwards by Mr. Benjamin Phipps, in a little hole I had dugout with my sword, for the purpose of concealment, under the top of a fallen tree. On Mr. Phipps' discovering the place of my concealment, he cocked his gun and aimed at me. I requested him not to shoot and I would give up, upon which he demanded my sword. I delivered it to him, and he brought me to prison. During the time I was pursued, I had many hair-breadth escapes, which your time will not permit you to relate. I am here loaded with chains, and willing to suffer the fate that awaits me.

Source: The Confessions of Nat Turner, the Leader of the Late Insurrection. Richmond: Thomas R. Gray, 1832. Rare Book and Special Collections Division, African American Odyssey Collection, Library of Congress.

THE *LIBERATOR* (1831)

On January 1, 1831, reformer William Lloyd Garrison published the first number of his newspaper, the Liberator, *a weekly paper published in Boston that became the mouthpiece for the abolitionist movement of the 1830s. Although antislavery sentiment had existed for several decades in the United States, Garrison revitalized the movement with his call for immediate action to end slavery, abandoning the movement's reliance on a gradualist approach. Although many believed him to be a mentally unbalanced agitator, Garrison inspired dozens of equally diligent abolitionists to challenge the South's peculiar institution. Garrison's dedication to the abolitionist cause never wavered, and he published the paper every week until the end of 1865, after the South had been defeated in the Civil War and Congress had abolished slavery in the United States with the passage of the Thirteenth Amendment. The following is an excerpt of the first number of the* Liberator. *(See also Garrison, William Lloyd; Garrisonians.)*

During my recent tour for the purpose of exciting the minds of the people by a series of discourses on the subject of slavery, every place that I visited gave fresh evidence of the fact that a great revolution in public sentiment was to be effected in the free states—and particularly in New England—than at the South. I find contempt more bitter, opposition more active, detraction more relentless, prejudice more stubborn, and apathy more frozen, than among slaveowners themselves. Of course, there were individual exceptions to the contrary.

This state of things afflicted but did not dishearten me. I determined, at every hazard, to lift up the standard of emancipation in the eyes of the nation, within sight of Bunker Hill and in the birthplace of liberty. That standard is now unfurled; and long may it float, unhurt by the spoliations of time or the missiles of a desperate foe—yea, till every chain be broken, and every bondman set free! Let Southern oppressors tremble—let all the enemies of the persecuted blacks tremble. . . .

Assenting to the "self-evident truth" maintained in the American Declaration of Independence "that all men are created equal, and endowed by their Creator with certain inalienable rights—among which are life, liberty, and the pursuit of happiness," I shall strenuously contend for the immediate enfranchisement of our slave population. . . . In Park Street Church, on the Fourth of July, 1829, in an address on slavery, I unreflectingly assented to the popular but pernicious doctrine of gradual abolition. I seize this opportunity to make a full and unequivocal recantation, and thus publicly to ask pardon of my God, of my country, and of my brethren the poor slaves, for having uttered a sentiment so full of timidity, injustice, and absurdity. . . .

I am aware that many object to the severity of my language; but is there not cause for severity? I will be as harsh as truth, and as uncompromising as justice. On this subject I do not wish to think, or speak, or write, with moderation. No! No! Tell a man whose house is on fire to give a moderate alarm; tell him to moderately rescue his wife from the hands of the ravisher; tell the mother to gradually extricate her babe from the fire into which it has fallen—but urge me not to use moderation in a cause like the present. I am in earnest—I will not equivocate—I will not excuse—I will not retreat in a single inch—and I will be heard. The apathy of the people is enough to make every statue leap from its pedestal, and to hasten the resurrection of the dead.

It is pretended that I am retarding the cause of emancipation by the coarseness of my invective and the precipitancy of my measures. The charge is not true. On this question my influence—humble as it is—is felt at this moment to a considerable extent, and shall be felt in coming years—not perniciously, but beneficially— not as a curse, but as a blessing. And posterity will bear testimony that I was right.

Source: William Lloyd Garrison. "To the Public." *Liberator,* January 1, 1831.

AN APPEAL IN FAVOR OF THAT CLASS OF AMERICANS CALLED AFRICANS (1833)

A tireless abolitionist, Lydia Maria Child was one of the movement's earliest supporters and most brilliant writers. Already a popular author on such topics as domesticity, Child was labeled a radical after she wrote and published her Appeal *in 1833. The book brought tremendous public attention to the horrors of slavery, and Child subsequently published several more on the topic. The following is an excerpt. (See also Child, Lydia Maria.)*

There is among the colored people an increasing desire for information, and laudable ambition to be respectable in manners and appearance. Are we not foolish as well as sinful, in trying to repress a tendency so salutary to themselves, and so beneficial to the community? Several individuals of this class are very desirous to have persons of their own color qualified to teach something more than mere reading and writing. But in the public schools, colored children are subject to many discouragements and difficulties; and into the private schools they cannot gain admission. A very sensible and well-informed colored woman in a neighboring town, whose family have been brought up in a manner that excited universal remark and approbation, has been extremely desirous to obtain for her eldest daughter the advantages of a private school; but she has been resolutely repulsed on account of her complexion. The girl is a very light mulatto, with great modesty and propriety of manners; perhaps no young person in the Commonwealth was less likely to have a bad influence on her associates. The clergyman respected the family, and he remonstrated with the instructer; but while the latter admitted the injustice of the thing, he excused himself by saying such a step would occasion the loss of all his white scholars.

In a town adjoining Boston, a well behaved colored boy was kept out of the public school more than a year, by vote of the trustees. His mother, having some information herself, knew the importance of knowledge, and was anxious to obtain it for her family. She wrote repeatedly and urgently; and the schoolmaster himself told me that the correctness of her spelling, and the neatness of her hand-writing, formed a curious contrast with the notes he received from many white parents. At last, this spirited woman appeared before the committee, and reminded them that her husband, having for many years paid taxes as a citizen, had a right to the privileges of a citizen; and if her claim were refused, or longer postponed, she declared her determination to seek justice from a higher source. The trustees were, of course, obliged to yield to the equality of the laws, with the best grace they could. The boy was admitted, and made good progress in his studies. Had his mother been too ignorant to know her rights, or too abject to demand them, the lad would have had a fair chance to get a living out of the State as the occupant of a workhouse, or penitentiary.

The attempt to establish a school for African girls at Canterbury, Connecticut, has made too much noise to need a detailed account in this volume. I do not know the lady who first formed the project, but I am told that she is a benevolent and religious woman. It certainly is difficult to imagine any other motives than good ones, for an undertaking so arduous and unpopular. Yet had the Pope himself attempted to establish his supremacy over that Commonwealth, he could hardly have been repelled with more determined and angry resistance. Town-meetings were held, the records of which are not highly creditable to the parties concerned. Petitions were sent to the Legislature, beseeching that no African school might be allowed to admit individuals not residing in the town where said school was established; and strange to relate, this law, which makes it impossible to collect a sufficient number of pupils, was sanctioned by the State. A colored girl, who availed herself of this opportunity to gain instruction, was warned out of town, and fined for not complying; and the instructress was imprisoned for persevering in her benevolent plan.

It was said, in excuse, that Canterbury would be inundated with vicious characters, who would corrupt the morals of the young men; that such a school would break down the distinctions between black and white; and that marriages between people of different colors would be the probable result. Yet they assumed the ground that colored people *must* always be an inferior and degraded class—that the prejudice against them *must* be eternal; being deeply founded in the laws of god and nature. Finally, they endeavored to represent the school as one of the *incendiary* proceedings of the Anti-Slavery Society; and they appealed to the Colonization Society, as an aggrieved child is wont to appeal to its parent.

The objection with regard to the introduction of vicious characters into a village, certainly has some force; but are such persons likely to leave cities for a quiet country town, in search of moral and intellectual improvement? Is it not obvious that the *best* portion of the colored class are the very ones to prize such an opportunity for instruction? Grant that a large proportion of these unfortunate people *are* vicious—is it not our duty, and of course our wisest policy, to try to make them otherwise? And what will so effectually elevate their character and condition, as knowledge? I beseech you, my countrymen, think of these things wisely, and in season.

As for intermarriages, if there be such a repugnance between the two races, founded in the laws of *nature,* methinks there is small reason to dread their frequency.

The breaking down of distinctions in society, by means of extended information, is an objection which appropriately belongs to the Emperor of Austria, or the Sultan of Egypt.

I do not know how the affair at Canterbury is *generally* considered: but I have heard individuals of all parties and all opinions speak of it—and never without merriment or indignation. Fifty years hence, the *black* laws of Connecticut will be a greater source of amusement of the antiquarian, than her famous *blue* laws.

A similar, though less violent opposition arose in consequence of the attempt to establish a college for colored people at New-Haven. A young colored man, who tried to obtain education at the Wesleyan college in Middletown, was obliged to relinquish the attempt on account of the persecution of his fellow students. Some collegians from the South objected to a colored associate in their recitations; and those from New-England promptly and zealously joined in the hue and cry. A small but firm party were in favor of giving the colored man a chance to pursue his studies without insult or interruption; and I am told that this manly and disinterested band were all Southerners. As for those individuals, who exerted their influence to exclude an offending fellow-citizen from privileges which ought to be equally open to all, it is to be hoped that age will make them wiser—and that they will learn, before they die, to be ashamed of a step attended with more important results than usually belong to youthful follies.

It happens that these experiments have all been made in Connecticut; but it is no more than justice to that State to remark that a similar spirit would probably have been manifested in Massachusetts, under like circumstances. At our debating clubs and other places of public discussion, the demon of prejudice girds himself for the battle, the moment negro colleges and high schools are alluded to. Alas, while we carry on our lips that religion which teaches us to "love our neighbors as ourselves," how little do we cherish its blessed influence within our hearts! How much republicanism we have to *speak* of, and how little do we practise!

Let us seriously consider what injury a negro college could possibly do us. It is certainly a fair presumption that the scholars would be from the better portion of the colored population; and it is an equally fair presumption that knowledge would improve their characters. There are already many hundreds of colored people in the city of Boston. In the street they generally appear neat and respectable; and in our houses they do not "come between the wind and our nobility." Would the addition of one or two hundred more even be perceived? As for giving offence to the Southerners by allowing such establishments—they have no right to interfere with our internal concerns, any more than we have with theirs. Why should they not give up slavery to please us, by the same rule that we must refrain from educating the negroes to please them? If they are at liberty to do wrong, we certainly ought to be at liberty to do right. They may talk and publish as much about us as they please; and we ask for no other influence over them.

It is a fact not generally known that the brave Kosciusko left a fund for the establishment of a negro college in the United States. Little did he think he had been fighting for a people, who would not grant one rood of their vast territory for the benevolent purpose!

According to present appearances, a college for colored persons will be established in Canada; and thus by means of our foolish and wicked pride, the credit of this philanthropic enterprise will be transferred to our mother country.

The preceding chapters show that it has been no uncommon thing for colored men to be educated at English, German, Portuguese, and Spanish Universities.

In Boston there is an Infant School, three Primary Schools, and a Grammar School. The two last are, I believe, supported by the public; and this fact is highly creditable.

I was much pleased with the late resolution awarding Franklin medals to the colored pupils of the grammar school; and I was still more pleased with the laudable project, originated by Josiah Holbrook, Esq., for the establishment of a colored Lyceum. Surely a better spirit *is* beginning to work in this cause; and when once begun, the good sense and good feeling of the community will bid it go on and prosper. How much this spirit will have to contend with is illustrated by the following fact. When President Jackson entered this city, the white children of all the schools were sent out in uniform, to do him honor. A member of the Committee proposed that the pupils of the African schools should be invited likewise; but he was the only one who voted for it. He then proposed that the yeas and nays should be recorded; upon which, most of the gentlemen walked off, to prevent the question from being taken. Perhaps they felt an awkward consciousness of the incongeniality of such proceedings with our republican institutions. By order of the Committee the vacation of the African schools did not commence until the day after the procession of the white pupils; and a note to the instructer intimated that the pupils were not expected to appear on the Common. The reason given was because "their numbers were so few;" but in private conversation, fears were expressed lest their sable faces should give offence to our slaveholding President. In all probability the sight of the colored children would have been agreeable to General Jackson, and seemed more like home, than any things he witnessed. . . .

If we are not able to contribute to African schools, or do not choose to do so, we can at least refrain from opposing them. If it be disagreeable to allow colored people the same rights and privileges as other citizens, we can do with our prejudice, what most of us often do with better feeling—we can conceal it. . . .

Source: Lydia Maria Francis Child. *An Appeal in Favor of That Class of Americans Called Africans.* Boston: Allen and Ticknor, 1833.

"A POSITIVE GOOD" (1837)

Leaders of the antebellum South, such as John C. Calhoun, considered the potential abolition of slavery not as an issue of human rights, but as a threat to states' rights, the Southern economy and way of life, and Southerners' freedom to maintain that way of life and prevent interference from the federal government. Calhoun, a South Carolina native, was first elected to the U.S. House of Representatives in 1810 and to the U.S. Senate in 1832, after serving as the country's vice president under John Quincy Adams and Andrew Jackson. Over his forty-year career, Calhoun was one of the leading defenders of slavery as "a positive good" and one of Congress's most ardent proponents of states' rights. Following are Calhoun's comments delivered on the Senate floor on February 6, 1837, in which he defends the institution of slavery.

I do not belong, said Mr. C., to the school which holds that aggression is to be met by concession. Mine is the opposite creed, which teaches that encroachments must be met at the beginning, and that those who act on the opposite principle are prepared to become slaves. In this case, in particular. I hold concession or compromise to be fatal. If we concede an inch, concession would follow concession—compromise would follow compromise, until our ranks would be so broken that effectual resistance would be impossible. We must meet the enemy on the frontier, with a fixed determination of maintaining our position at every hazard. Consent to receive these insulting petitions, and the next demand will be that they be referred to a committee in order that they may be deliberated and acted upon. At the last session we were modestly asked to receive them, simply to lay them on the table, without any view to ulterior action. . . . I then said, that the next step would be to refer the petition to a committee, and I already see indications that such is now the intention. If we yield, that will be followed by another, and we will thus proceed, step by step, to the final consummation of the object of these petitions. We are now told that the most effectual mode of arresting the progress of abolition is, to reason it down; and with this view it is urged that the petitions ought to be referred to a committee. That is the very ground which was taken at the last session in the other House, but instead of arresting its progress it has since advanced more rapidly than ever. The most unquestionable right may be rendered doubtful, if once admitted to be a subject of controversy, and that would be the case in the present instance. The subject is beyond the jurisdiction of Congress—they have no right to touch it in any shape or form, or to make it the subject of deliberation or discussion. . . .

As widely as this incendiary spirit has spread, it has not yet infected this body, or the great mass of the intelligent and business portion of the North; but unless it be speedily stopped, it will spread and work upwards till it brings the two great sections of the Union into deadly conflict. This is not a new impression with me. Several years since, in a discussion with one of the Senators from Massachusetts (Mr. Webster), before this fell spirit had showed itself, I then predicted that the doctrine of the proclamation and the Force Bill—that this Government had a right, in the last resort, to determine the extent of its own powers, and enforce its decision at the point of the bayonet, which was so warmly maintained by that Senator, would at no distant day arouse the dormant spirit of abolitionism. I told him that the doctrine was tantamount to the assumption of unlimited power on the part of the Government, and that such would be the impression on the public mind in a large portion of the Union. The consequence would be inevitable.

A large portion of the Northern States believed slavery to be a sin, and would consider it as an obligation of conscience to abolish it if they should feel themselves in any degree responsible for its continuance, and that this doctrine would necessarily lead to the belief of such responsibility. I then predicted that it would commence as it has with this fanatical portion of society, and that they would begin their operations on the ignorant, the weak, the young, and the thoughtless,—and gradually extend upwards till they would become strong enough to obtain political control, when he and others holding the highest stations in society, would, however reluctant, be compelled to yield to their doctrines, or be driven into obscurity. But four years have since elapsed, and all this is already in a course of regular fulfilment.

Standing at the point of time at which we have now arrived, it will not be more difficult to trace the course of future events now than it was then. They who imagine that the spirit now abroad in the North, will die away of itself without a shock or convulsion, have formed a very inadequate conception of its real character; it will continue to rise and spread, unless prompt and efficient measures to stay its progress be adopted. Already it has taken possession of the pulpit, of the schools, and, to a considerable extent, of the press; those great instruments by which the mind of the rising generation will be formed.

However sound the great body of the non-slaveholding States are at present, in the course of a few years they will be succeeded by those who will have been taught to hate the people and institutions of nearly one-half of this Union, with a hatred more deadly than one hostile nation ever entertained towards another.

It is easy to see the end. By the necessary course of events, if left to themselves, we must become, finally, two people. It is impossible under the deadly hatred which must spring up between the two great nations, if the present causes are permitted to operate unchecked, that we should continue under the same political system. The conflicting elements would burst the Union asunder, powerful as are the links which hold it together. Abolition and the Union cannot coexist. As the friend of the Union I openly proclaim it,—and the sooner it is known the better. The former may now be controlled, but in a short time it will be beyond the power of man to arrest the course of events. We of the South will not, cannot, surrender our institutions. To maintain the existing relations between the two races, inhabiting that section of the Union, is indispensable to the peace and happiness of both. It cannot be subverted without drenching the country or the other of the races. . . . But let me not be understood as admitting, even by implication, that the existing relations between the two races in the slaveholding States is an evil:—far otherwise;

I hold it to be a good, as it has thus far proved itself to be to both, and will continue to prove so if not disturbed by the fell spirit of abolition. I appeal to facts. Never before has the black race of Central Africa, from the dawn of history to the present day, attained a condition so civilized and so improved, not only physically, but morally and intellectually.

In the meantime, the white or European race, has not degenerated. It has kept pace with its brethren in other sections of the Union where slavery does not exist. It is odious to make comparison; but I appeal to all sides whether the South is not equal in virtue, intelligence, patriotism, courage, disinterestedness, and all the high qualities which adorn our nature.

But I take higher ground. I hold that in the present state of civilization, where two races of different origin, and distinguished by color, and other physical differences, as well as intellectual, are brought together, the relation now existing in the slaveholding States between the two, is, instead of an evil, a good—a positive good. I feel myself called upon to speak freely upon the subject where the honor and interests of those I represent are involved. I hold then, that there never has yet existed a wealthy and civilized society in which one portion of the community did not, in point of fact, live on the labor of the other.

Broad and general as is this assertion, it is fully borne out by history. This is not the proper occasion, but, if it were, it would not be difficult to trace the various devices by which the wealth of all civilized communities has been so unequally divided, and to show by what means so small a share has been allotted to those by whose labor it was produced, and so large a share given to the non-producing classes. The devices are almost innumerable, from the brute force and gross superstition of ancient times, to the subtle and artful fiscal contrivances of modern. I might well challenge a comparison between them and the more direct, simple, and patriarchal mode by which the labor of the African race is, among us, commanded by the European. I may say with truth, that in few countries so much is left to the share of the laborer, and so little exacted from him, or where there is more kind attention paid to him in sickness or infirmities of age. Compare his condition with the tenants of the poor houses in the more civilized portions of Europe—look at the sick, and the old and infirm slave, on one hand, in the midst of his family and friends, under the kind superintending care of his master and mistress, and compare it with the forlorn and wretched condition of the pauper in the poorhouse.

But I will not dwell on this aspect of the question; I turn to the political; and here I fearlessly assert that the existing relation between the two races in the South, against which these blind fanatics are waging war, forms the most solid and durable foundation on which to rear free and stable political institutions. It is useless to disguise the fact. There is and always has been in an advanced stage of wealth and civilization, a conflict between labor and capital. The condition of society in the South exempts us from the disorders and dangers resulting from this conflict; and which explains why it is that the political condition of the slaveholding States has been so much more stable and quiet than that of the North. . . . Surrounded as the slaveholding States are with such imminent perils, I rejoice to think that our means of defense are ample, if we shall prove to have the intelligence and spirit to see and apply them before it is too late. All we want is concert, to lay aside all party differences and unite with zeal and energy in repelling approaching dangers. Let there be concert of action, and we shall find ample means of security without resorting to secession or disunion. I speak with full knowledge and a thorough examination of the subject, and for one see my way clearly. . . . I dare not hope that anything I can say will arouse the South to a due sense of danger; I fear it is beyond the power of mortal voice to awaken it in time from the fatal security into which it has fallen.

Source: John C. Calhoun. "Slavery a Positive Good." Speech to U.S. Senate, 1837.

EXCERPT FROM *NARRATIVE OF THE LIFE OF FREDERICK DOUGLASS* (1845)

Editor, orator, and abolitionist Frederick Douglass was the foremost African American leader of the nineteenth century in the United States. After escaping from slavery in Baltimore in 1838, Douglass settled in Massachusetts, where he was called on to speak at an abolitionist meeting on the island of Nantucket in 1841. Douglass so impressed abolitionist leader William Lloyd Garrison that Garrison asked him to become an agent for the Massachusetts Anti-Slavery Society, and he soon became one of the abolitionist movement's star orators, traveling throughout the North to lecture to large audiences. Because of his eloquence and poise on the platform, listeners sometimes questioned whether Douglass could have been a slave.

To prove the truth of what he said, Douglass published an account of his experiences in slavery, Narrative of the Life of Frederick Douglass, *in 1845. Together with two later autobiographies,* My Bondage and My Freedom *(1855) and* The Life and Times of Frederick Douglass *(1881), the series is considered one of the best examples of a slave narrative and a classic American autobiography. However, since the narrative contained much factual information, Douglass ran the risk of being captured and returned to slavery after the book was published. To avoid this fate, he embarked on a lecture tour of the British Isles, lasting nearly two years. Following is an excerpt of the book. (See also Douglass, Frederick (1818–1895); Slave Narratives.)*

I now come to that part of my life during which I planned, and finally succeeded in making, my escape from slavery. But before narrating any of the peculiar
circumstances, I deem it proper to make known my intention not to state all the
facts connected with the transaction. My reasons for pursuing this course may
be understood from the following: First, were I to give a minute statement of all
the facts, it is not only possible, but quite probable, that others would thereby be
involved in the most embarrassing difficulties. Secondly, such a statement would
most undoubtedly induce greater vigilance on the part of slaveholders than has
existed heretofore among them; which would, of course, be the means of guarding a door whereby some dear brother bondman might escape his galling chains.
I deeply regret the necessity that impels me to suppress any thing of importance
connected with my experience in slavery. It would afford me great pleasure indeed,
as well as materially add to the interest of my narrative, were I at liberty to gratify a
curiosity, which I know exists in the minds of many, by an accurate statement of all
the facts pertaining to my most fortunate escape. But I must deprive myself of this
pleasure, and the curious of the gratification which such a statement would afford.
I would allow myself to suffer under the greatest imputations which evil-minded
men might suggest, rather than exculpate myself, and thereby run the hazard of
closing the slightest avenue by which a brother slave might clear himself of the
chains and fetters of slavery.

I have never approved of the very public manner in which some of our western
friends have conducted what they call the *underground railroad*. I honor those
good men and women for their noble daring, and applaud them for willingly sub-
jecting themselves to bloody persecution, by openly avowing their participation
in the escape of slaves. I, however, can see very little good resulting from such a
course, either to themselves or the slaves escaping; while, upon the other hand,
I see and feel assured that those open declarations are a positive evil to the slaves
remaining, who are seeking to escape. They do nothing towards enlightening the
slave, whilst they do much towards enlightening the master. They stimulate him to
greater watchfulness, and enhance his power to capture his slave. We owe something to the slave south of the line as well as to those north of it; and in aiding the
latter on their way to freedom, we should be careful to do nothing which would be
likely to hinder the former from escaping from slavery. I would keep the merciless slaveholder profoundly ignorant of the means of flight adopted by the slave.
I would leave him to imagine himself surrounded by myriads of invisible tormen-
tors, ever ready to snatch from his infernal grasp his trembling prey. Let him be left
to feel his way in the dark; let darkness commensurate with his crime hover over
him; and let him feel that at every step he takes, in pursuit of the flying bondman,
he is running the frightful risk of having his hot brains dashed out by an invisible
agency. Let us render the tyrant no aid; let us not hold the light by which he can

trace the footprints of our flying brother. But enough of this. I will now proceed to the statement of those facts, connected with my escape, for which I am alone responsible, and for which no one can be made to suffer but myself.

In the early part of the year 1838, I became quite restless. I could see no reason why I should, at the end of each week, pour the reward of my toil into the purse of my master. When I carried to him my weekly wages, he would, after counting the money, look me in the face with a robber-like fierceness, and ask, "Is that all?" He was satisfied with nothing less than the last cent. He would, however, when I made him six dollars, sometimes give me six cents, to encourage me. It had the opposite effect. I regarded it as a sort of admission of my right to the whole. The fact that he gave me any part of my wages was proof, to my mind, that he believed me entitled to the whole of them. I always felt worse for having received any thing; for I feared that the giving me a few cents would ease his conscience, and make him feel himself to be a pretty honorable sort of robber. My discontent grew upon me. I was ever on the look-out for means of escape; and, finding no direct means, I determined to try to hire my time, with a view of getting money with which to make my escape. He told me I could go nowhere but that he could get me; and that, in the event of my running away, he should spare no pains in his efforts to catch me. He exhorted me to content myself, and be obedient. He told me, if I would be happy, I must lay out no plans for the future. He said, if I behaved myself properly, he would take care of me. Indeed, he advised me to complete thoughtlessness of the future, and taught me to depend solely upon him for happiness. He seemed to see fully the pressing necessity of setting aside my intellectual nature, in order to contentment in slavery. But in spite of him, and even in spite of myself, I continued to think, and to think about the injustice of my enslavement, and the means of escape.

About two months after this, I applied to Master Hugh for the privilege of hiring my time. He was not acquainted with the fact that I had applied to Master Thomas, and had been refused. He too, at first, seemed disposed to refuse; but after some reflection, he granted me the privilege, and proposed the following terms: I was to be allowed all my time, make all contracts with those for whom I worked, and find my own employment; and, in return for this liberty, I was to pay him three dollars at the end of each week; find myself in calking tools, and in board and clothing. My board was two dollars and a half per week. This, with the wear and tear of clothing and calking tools, made my regular expenses about six dollars a week. This amount I was compelled to make up, or relinquish the privilege of hiring my time. Rain or shine, work or no work, at the end of each week the money must be forthcoming, or I must give up my privilege. This arrangement, it will be perceived, was decidedly in my master's favor. It relieved him of all need of looking after me. His money was sure. He received all the benefits of slaveholding without its evils; while I endured all the evils of a slave, and suffered all the care and anxiety of a freeman. I found it a hard bargain. But, hard as it was, I thought it better than the old mode of getting along. It was a step towards freedom to be allowed to bear the responsibilities of a freeman, and I was determined to hold on upon it. I bent myself to the work of making money. I was ready to work at night as well as day, and by the most untiring perseverance and industry, I made enough to meet my expenses, and lay up a little money every week. I went on thus from May till August. Master Hugh then refused to allow me to hire my time longer. The ground for his refusal was a failure on my part, one Saturday night, to pay him for my week's time. This failure was occasioned by my attending a camp meeting about ten miles from Baltimore. During the week, I had entered into an engagement with a number of young friends to start from Baltimore to the camp ground early Saturday evening; and being detained by my employer, I was unable to get down to Master Hugh's without disappointing the company. I knew that Master Hugh was in no special need of the money that night. I therefore decided to go to camp meeting, and upon my return pay him the three dollars. I stayed at the camp meeting one day longer than I intended when I left. But as soon as I returned, I called upon him to pay him what he considered his due. I found him very angry; he could scarce restrain his wrath. He said he had a great mind to give me a severe whipping. He wished to know how I dared go out of the city without asking his permission. I told him I hired my time, and while I paid him the price which he asked for it, I did not know that I was bound to ask him when and where I should go. This reply troubled him; and, after reflecting a few moments, he turned to me, and said I should hire my time no longer; that the next thing he should know of, I would be running away. Upon the same plea, he told me to bring my tools and clothing from home forthwith. I did so; but instead of seeking work, as I had been accustomed to do previously to hiring my time, I spent the whole week without the performance of a single stroke of work. I did this in retaliation. Saturday night, he called upon me as usual for my week's wages. I told him I had no wages; I had done no work that week. Here we were upon the point of coming to blows. He raved, and swore his determination to get hold of me. I did not allow myself a single word; but was resolved, if he laid the weight of his hand upon me, it should be blow for blow. He did not strike me, but told me that he would find me in constant employment in the future. I thought the matter over during the next day, Sunday, and finally resolved upon the third day of September, as the day upon which I would make a second attempt to secure my freedom. I now had three weeks during which to prepare for my journey. Early on Monday morning, before Master Hugh had time to make any engagement for me, I went out and got employment of Mr. Butler, at his ship-yard near the drawbridge, upon what is called the City Block, thus making it unnecessary for him to seek employment for me. At the end of the week, I brought him between eight and nine dollars. He seemed very well pleased, and asked why I did not do the same the week before. He little knew what my plans were. My object in working steadily was to remove any suspicion he might entertain of my intent to run away; and in this I succeeded admirably. I suppose he thought I was never better satisfied with my condition that at the very time during which I was planning my escape. The second week passed, and again I carried him my full wages; and so well pleased was he, that he gave me twenty-five cents, (quite a large sum for a slaveholder to give a slave,) and bade me to make a good use of it. I told him I would.

Things went on without very smoothly indeed, but within there was trouble. It is impossible for me to describe my feelings as the time of my contemplated start drew near. I had a number of warm-hearted friends in Baltimore,—friends that I loved almost as I did my life,—and the thought of being separated from them forever was painful beyond expression. It is my opinion that thousands would escape from slavery, who now remain, but for the strong cords of affection that bind them to their friends. The thought of leaving my friends was decidedly the most painful thought with which I had to contend. The love of them was my tender point, and shook my decision more than all things else. Besides the pain of separation, the dread and apprehension of a failure exceeded what I had experienced at my first attempt. The appalling defeat I then sustained returned to torment me. I felt assured that, if I failed in this attempt, my case would be a hopeless one—it would seal my fate as a slave forever. I could not hope to get off with any thing less than the severest punishment, and being placed beyond the means of escape. It required no very vivid imagination to depict the most frightful scenes through which I should have to pass, in case I failed. The wretchedness of slavery, and the blessedness of freedom, were perpetually before me. It was life and death with me. But I remained firm, and, according to my resolution, on the third day of September, 1838, I left my chains, and succeeded in reaching New York without the slightest interruption of any kind. How I did so,—what means I adopted,—what direction I traveled, and by what mode of conveyance,—I must leave unexplained, for the reasons before mentioned.

I have been frequently asked how I felt when I found myself in a free State. I have never been able to answer the question with any satisfaction to myself. It was a moment of the highest excitement I ever experienced. I suppose I felt as one may imagine the unarmed mariner to feel when he is rescued by a friendly man-of-war from the pursuit of a pirate. In writing to a dear friend, immediately after my arrival at New York, I said I felt like one who had escaped a den of hungry lions. This state of mind, however, very soon subsided; and I was again seized with a feeling of great insecurity and loneliness. I was yet liable to be taken back, and subjected to all the tortures of slavery. This in itself was enough to damp the ardor of my enthusiasm. But the loneliness overcame me. There I was in the midst of thousands, and yet a perfect stranger; without home and without friends, in the midst of thousands of my own brethren—children to a common Father, and yet I dared not to unfold to any of them my sad condition. I was afraid to speak to any one for fear of speaking to the wrong one, and thereby falling into the hands of money-loving kidnappers, whose business it was to lie in wait for the panting fugitive, as the ferocious beasts of the forest lie in wait for their prey. The motto which I adopted when I started from slavery was this—"Trust no man!" I saw in every white man an enemy, and in almost every colored man cause for distrust. It was a most painful situation; and, to understand it, one must needs experience it, or imagine himself in similar circumstances. Let him be a fugitive slave in a strange land—a land given up to be the hunting-ground for slaveholders—whose inhabitants are legalized kidnappers—where he is every moment subjected to the terrible liability of being seized upon by his fellowmen, as the hideous crocodile seizes upon his prey!— I say, let him place himself in my situation—without home or friends—without money or credit—wanting shelter, and no one to give it—wanting bread, and no money to buy it,—and at the same time let him feel that he is pursued by merciless men-hunters, and in total darkness as to what to do, where to go, or where to stay,—perfectly helpless both as to the means of defense and means of escape,—in the midst of plenty, yet suffering the terrible gnawings of hunger,—in the midst of houses, yet having no home,—among fellow-men, yet feeling as if in the midst of wild beasts, whose greediness to swallow up the trembling and half-famished fugitive is only equaled by that with which the monsters of the deep swallow up the helpless fish upon which they subsist,—I say, let him be placed in this most trying situation,—the situation in which I was placed,—then, and not till then, will he fully appreciate the hardships of, and know how to sympathize with, the toil-worn and whip-scarred fugitive slave.

Source: Frederick Douglas. *Narrative of the Life of Frederick Douglass, an American Slave, Written by Himself.* Boston: The Anti-Slavery Office, 1845.

EXCERPT FROM *UNCLE TOM'S CABIN* (1852)

The first book by an American author to have as its hero an African American, Uncle Tom's Cabin *was published serially in the* National Era, *an antislavery paper in Washington, D.C., in 1851 and 1852 and in book form later in 1852. By turns sentimental and realistic, the novel appealed strongly to nineteenth-century readers, and because the book presented the horrors of slavery in vivid human terms, it had a powerful impact. While fueling antislavery sentiment in the North,* Uncle Tom's Cabin *infuriated Southerners, who charged that author Harriet Beecher Stowe knew nothing about plantation life and grossly misrepresented it.*

In response to her critics, Stowe published A Key to Uncle Tom *(1853), a non-fiction work containing documentary evidence that supported her indictment of slavery in the novel. Though no one expected* Uncle Tom's Cabin *to be popular or successful, more than 300,000 copies were sold within the first year. The book was several times adapted for the stage and was ultimately translated into fifty-five languages. President Abraham Lincoln only slightly exaggerated when upon meeting Stowe in 1863, he said, "So you're the little woman who wrote the book that made this big war." The following is an excerpt of the book. (See also Literature and Abolition.)*

"And now," said Legree, "come here, you Tom. You see, I telled ye I didn't buy ye jest for the common work. I mean to promote ye, and make a driver of ye; and tonight ye may jest as well begin to get ye hand in. Now, ye jest take this yer gal and flog her; ye've seen enough on't to know how." "I beg Mas'r' pardon," said Tom; "hopes Mas'r won't set me at that. It's what I an't used to—never did—and can't do, no way possible."

"Ye'll larn a pretty smart chance of things ye never did know, before I've done with ye!" said Legree, taking up a cowhide and striking Tom a heavy blow across the cheek, and following up the infliction by a shower of blows.

"There!" he said, as he stopped to rest; "now, will ye tell me ye can't do it?"

"Yes, Mas'r," said Tom, putting up his hand, to wipe the blood that trickled down his face. "I'm willin' to work, night and day, and work while there's life and breath in me. But this yer thing I can't feel it right to do; and, Mas'r, I never shall do it—never!"

Tom had a remarkably smooth, soft voice, and a habitually respectful manner that had given Legree an idea that he would be cowardly and easily subdued. When he spoke these last words, a thrill of amazement went through everyone. The poor woman clasped her hands and said, "O Lord!" and everyone involuntarily looked at each other and drew in their breath, as if to prepare for the storm that was about to burst.

Legree looked stupefied and confounded; but at last burst forth: "What! Ye blasted black beast! Tell me ye don't think it right to do what I tell ye! What have any of you cussed cattle to do with thinking what's right? I'll put a stop to it! Why, what do ye think ye are? May be ye think ye're a gentleman, master Tom, to be a telling your master what's right, and what an't! So you pretend it's wrong to flog the gal!"

"I think so, Mas'r," said Tom; "the poor crittur's sick and feeble; 'twould be downright cruel, and it's what I never will do, nor begin to. Mas'r, if you mean to kill me, kill me; but, as to my raising my hand again any one here, I never shall— I'll die first!"

Tom spoke in a mild voice, but with a decision that could not be mistaken. Legree shook with anger; his greenish eyes glared fiercely, and his very whiskers seemed to curl with passion. But, like some ferocious beast, that plays with its victim before he devours it, he kept back his strong impulse to proceed to immediate violence, and broke out into bitterly raillery.

"Well, here's a pious dog, at last, let down among us sinners—a saint, a gentleman, and no less, to talk to us sinners about our sins! Powerful holy crittur, he must be! Here, you rascal, you make believe to be so pious—didn't you never hear, out of yer Bible, 'Servants, obey yer masters'? An't I yer master? Didn't I pay down twelve hundred dollars, cash, for all there is inside yer old cussed black shell? An't yer mine, now, body and soul?" he said, giving Tom a violent kick with his heavy boot; "tell me!"

In the very depth of physical suffering, bowed by brutal oppression, this question shot a gleam of joy an triumph through Tom's soul. He suddenly stretched himself up, and, looking earnestly to heaven, while the tears and blood that flowed down his face mingled, he exclaimed, "No! no! no! my soul an't yours, Mas'r! You haven't bought it—ye can't buy it! It's been bought and paid for by One that is able to keep it. No matter, no matter, you can't harm me!"

"I can't!" said Legree, with a sneer; "we'll see—we'll see! Here Sambo, Quimbo, give this dog such a breakin' in as he won't get over this month!"

The two gigantic Negroes that now laid hold of Tom, with fiendish exultation in their faces, might have formed no unapt personification of powers of darkness. The poor woman screamed with apprehension, and all rose, as by a general impulse, while they dragged him unresisting from the place.

Source: Harriet Beecher Stowe. *Uncle Tom's Cabin; Or, Life among the Lowly.* Boston: John P. Jewett & Company, 1852, 61–64.

EXCERPTS FROM *CANNIBALS ALL! OR SLAVES WITHOUT MASTERS* (1857)

As antislavery sentiment spread throughout the North, spurred by the vocal activities of abolitionists, proponents of slavery in the South felt increasing pressure to defend their cherished institution. One of their most eloquent spokesmen was George Fitzhugh, who published Cannibals All! or Slaves without Masters *in 1857. Fitzhugh argued that slavery was a "positive good" for African Americans, whom he maintained were incapable of taking care of themselves. Fitzhugh also maintained that the slave labor system was economically indispensable for the South. An excerpt of the book appears next. (See also Fitzhugh, George.)*

The Blessings of Slavery

The negro slaves of the South are the happiest, and in some sense, the freest people in the world. The children and the aged and infirm work not at all, and yet have all the comforts and necessaries of life provided for them. They enjoy liberty, because they are oppressed neither by care or labor. The women do little hard work, and are protected from the despotism of their husbands by their masters. The negro men and stout boys work, on the average, in good weather, no more than nine hours a day. The balance of their time is spent in perfect abandon. Besides, they have their Sabbaths and holidays. White men, with som muh of license and abandon, would die of ennui; but negroes luxuriate in corporeal and mental repose. With their faces upturned to the sun, they can sleep at any hour; and quiet sleep is the gretest of human enjoyments. "Blessed be the man who invented sleep." 'Tis happiness in itself-and results from contentment in the present, and confident assurance of the future. We do not know whether free laborers ever sleep. They are fools to do so; for, whilst they sleep, the wily and watchful capitalist is devising means to ensnare and exploit them. The free laborer must work or starve. He is more of a slave than the negro, because he works longer and harder for less allowance than the slave, and has no holiday, because the cares of life with him begin when its labors end. He has no liberty and not a single right. . . .

Until the lands of America are appropriated by a few, population becomes dense, competition among laborers active, employment uncertain, and wages low, the personal liberty of all the whites will continue to be a blessing. We have vast unsettled territories; population may cease to increase slowly, as in most countries, and many centuries may elapse before the question will be practically suggested, whether slavery to capital be preferable to slavery to human masters. But the negro has neither energy nor enterprise, and, even in our sparser populations, finds with his improvident habits, that his liberty is a curse to himself, and a greater curse to the society around him. These considerations, and others equally obvious, have induced the South to attempt to defend negro slavery as an exceptional institution, admitting, nay asserting, that slavery, in the general or in the abstract, is morally wrong, and against common right. With singular inconsistency, after making this admission, which admits away the authority of the Bible, of profane history, and of the almost universal practice of mankind—they turn around and attempt to bolster up the cause of negro slavery by these very exploded authorities. If we mean not to repudiate all divine, and almost all human authority in favor of slavery, we must vindicate that institution in the abstract.

To insist that a status of society, which has been almost universal, and which is expressly and continually justified by Holy Writ, is its natural, normal, and necessary status, under the ordinary circumstances, is on its face a plausible and probable proposition. To insist on less, is to yield our cause, and to give up our religion; for if white slavery be morally wrong, be a violation of natural rights, the Bible cannot be true. Human and divine authority do seem in the general to concur, in establishing the expediency of having masters and slaves of different races. In very many nations of antiquity, and in some of modern times, the law has permitted the native citizens to become slaves to each other. But few take advantage of such laws; and the infrequency of the practice establishes the general truth that master and slave should be of different national descent. In some respects the wider the difference the better, as the slave will feel less mortified by his position. In other respects, it may be that too wide a difference hardens the hearts and brutalizes the feeling of both master and slave. The civilized man hates the savage, and the savage returns the hatred with interest. Hence West India slavery of newly caught negroes is not a very humane, affectionate, or civilizing institution. Virginia negroes have become moral and intelligent. They love their master and his family, and the attachment is reciprocated. Still, we like the idle, but intelligent house-servants, better than the hard-used, but stupid outhands; and we like the mulatto better than the negro; yet the negro is generally more affectionate, contented, and faithful.

The world at large looks on negro slavery as much the worst form of slavery; because it is only acquainted with West India slavery. But our Southern slavery has become a benign and protective institution, and our negroes are confessedly better off than any free laboring population in the world. How can we contend that white slavery is wrong, whilst all the great body of free laborers are starving; and slaves, white or black, throughout the world, are enjoying comfort? . . .

The aversion to negroes, the antipathy of race, is much greater at the North than at the South; and it is very probable that this antipathy to the person of the negro, is confounded with or generates hatred of the institution with which he is usually connected. Hatred to slavery is very generally little more than hatred of negroes.

There is one strong argument in favor of negro slavery over all other slavery; that he, being unfitted for the mechanic arts, for trade, and all skillful pursuits, leaves those pursuits to be carried on by the whites; and does not bring all industry into disrepute, as in Greece and Rome, where the slaves were not only the artists and mechanics, but also the merchants.

Whilst, as a general and abstract question, negro slavery has no other claims over other forms of slavery, except that from inferiority, or rather peculiarity, of race, almost all negroes require masters, whilst only the children, the women, and the very weak, poor, and ignorant, &c., among the whites, need some protective and governing relation of this kind; yet as a subject of temporary, but worldwide importance, negro slavery has become the most necessary of all human institutions.

The African slave trade to America commenced three centuries and a half since. By the time of the American Revolution, the supply of slaves had exceeded the demand for slave labor, and the slaveholders, to get rid of a burden, and to prevent the increase of a nuisance, became violent opponents of the slave trade, and many of them abolitionists. New England, Bristol, and Liverpool, who reaped the profits of the trade, without suffering from the nuisance, stood out for a long time against its abolition. Finally, laws and treaties were made, and fleets fitted out to abolish it; and after a while, the slaves of most of South America, of the West Indies, and of Mexico were liberated. In the meantime, cotton, rice, sugar, coffee, tobacco, and other products of slave labor, came into universal use as necessaries of life. The population of Western Europe, sustained and stimulated by those products, was trebled, and that of the North increased tenfold. The products of slave labor became scarce and dear, and famines frequent. Now, it is obvious, that to emancipate all the negroes would be to starve Western Europe and our North. Not to extend and increase negro slavery, pari passu, with the extension and multiplication of free society, will produce much suffering. If all South America, Mexico, the West Indies, and our Union south of Mason and Dixon's line, of the Ohio and Missouri, were slaveholding, slave products would be abundant and cheap in free society; and their market for their merchandise, manufactures, commerce, &c., illimitable. Free white laborers might live in comfort and luxury on light work, but for the exacting and greedy landlords, bosses, and other capitalists.

We must confess, that overstock the world as you will with comforts and with luxuries, we do not see how to make capital relax its monopoly—how to do aught but tantalize the hireling. Capital, irresponsible capital, begets, and ever will beget, the immedicabile vulnus of so-called Free Society. It invades every recess of domestic life, infects its food, its clothing, its drink, its very atmosphere, and pursues the hireling, from the hovel to the poor-house, the prison and the grave. Do what he will, go where he will, capital pursues and persecutes him. "Haeret lateri lethalis arundo!"

Capital supports and protects the domestic slave; taxes, oppresses, and persecutes the free laborer.

Source: George Fitzhugh. *Cannibals All!, or, Slaves without Masters.* Richmond, VA: A. Morris, Publisher, 1857.

EXCERPT FROM *THE IMPENDING CRISIS* (1857)

In an unusual indictment of slavery, North Carolinian Hinton Helper published this book in 1857, arguing that slavery was the source of all poverty, crime, and despair in the South, for both whites and blacks. His main goal was not to alleviate the condition of slaves but rather to focus on how the presence of slavery deprived poor white Southern farmers of the opportunity to better themselves, because slaves were perpetually too expensive for them and thus prevented them from rising in society. Slavery also denied the lowest laboring classes in the South work opportunities. Hinton was loudly denounced among his fellow Southerners for publishing the book, while Northerners believed that the work confirmed all their suspicions of life in the South. The following is an excerpt of the work.

Inscribed on the banner which we herewith unfurl to the world, with the full and fixed determination to stand by it or die by it, unless one of more virtuous efficacy shall be presented, are the mottoes which, in substance, embody the principles, as we conceive, that should govern us in our patriotic warfare against the most subtle and insidious foe that ever menaced the inalienable rights and liberties and dearest interests of America:

    1st. Thorough Organization and Independent Political Action on the part of the Non-Slaveholding whites of the South.

    2nd. Ineligibility of Slaveholders—Never another vote to the Trafficker in Human Flesh.

    3rd. No Co-operation with Slaveholders in Politics—No Fellowship with them in Religion—No Affiliation with them in Society.

    4th. No Patronage to Slaveholding Merchants—No Guestship in Slave-waiting Hotels—No Fees to Slaveholding Lawyers—No Employment of Slaveholding Physicians—No Audience to Slaveholding Parsons.

    5th. No Recognition of Pro-slavery Men, except as Ruffians, Outlaws, and Criminals.

    6th. Abrupt Discontinuance of Subscription to Pro-slavery Newspapers.

    7th. The Greatest Possible Encouragement to Free White Labor.

    8th. No more Hiring of Slaves by Non-slaveholders.

    9th. Immediate Death to Slavery, or if not immediate, unqualified Proscription of its Advocates during the Period of its Existence.

    10th. A Tax of Sixty Dollars on every Slaveholder for each and every Negro in his Possession at the present time, or at any intermediate time between now and the 4th of July, 1863—said Money to be Applied to the transportation of the Blacks to Liberia, to their Colonization in Central or South America, or to their Comfortable Settlement within the Boundaries of the United States.

    11th. An additional Tax of Forty Dollars per annum to be levied annually, on every Slaveholder for each and every Negro found in his possession after the 4th of July, 1863—said Money to be paid into the hands of the Negroes so held in Slavery, or, in cases of death, to their next of kin, and to be used by them at their own option.

This, then, is the outline of our scheme for the abolition of slavery in the Southern States. Let it be acted upon with due promptitude, and, as certain as truth is mightier than error, fifteen years will not elapse before every foot of territory, from the mouth of the Delaware to the emboguing of the Rio Grande, will glitter with the jewels of freedom. Some time during this year, next, or the year following, let there be a general convention of non-slaveholders from every slave State in the Union, to deliberate on the momentous issues now pending. First, let them adopt measures for holding in restraint the diabolical excesses of the oligarchy; secondly, in order to cast off the thraldom which the infamous slave-power has fastened upon them, and, as the first step necessary to be taken to regain the inalienable rights and liberties with which they were invested by Nature, but of which they have been divested by the accursed dealers in human flesh, let them devise ways and means for the complete annihilation of slavery; thirdly, let them put forth an equitable and comprehensive platform, fully defining their position, and inviting the active sympathy and co-operation of the millions of down-trodden non-slaveholders throughout the Southern and Southwestern States. Let all these things be done, not too hastily, but with calmness, deliberation, prudence, and circumspection; if need be, let the delegates to the convention continue in session one or two weeks; only let their labors be wisely and thoroughly performed; let them, on Wednesday morning, present to the poor white of the South, a well-digested scheme for the reclamation of their ancient rights and prerogatives, and, on the Thursday following, slavery in the United States will be worth absolutely less than nothing; for then, besides being so vile and precarious that nobody will want it, it will be a lasting reproach to those in whose hands it is lodged.

From the abstract of our plan for the abolition of slavery, it will be perceived that, so far from allowing slaveholders any compensation for their slaves, we are, and we think justly, in favor of imposing on them a tax of sixty dollars for each and every negro now in their possession, as also for each and every one that shall be born to them between now and the 4th of July, 1863; after which time, we propose that they shall be taxed forty dollars per annum, annually, for every person by them held in slavery, without regard to age, sex, color, or condition—the money, in both instances, to be used for the sole advantage of the slaves. As an addendum to this proposition, we would say that, in our opinion, if slavery is not totally abolished by the year 1869, the annual tax ought to be increased from forty to one hundred dollars; and furthermore, that if the institution does not then almost immediately disappear under the onus of this increased taxation, the tax ought in the course of one or two years thereafter, to be augmented to such a degree as will, in harmony with other measures, prove an infallible deathblow to slavery on or before the 4th of July, 1876.

At once let the good and true men of this country, the patriot sons of the patriot fathers, determine that the sun which rises to celebrate the centennial anniversary of our national independence, shall not set on the head of any slave within the limits of our Republic. Will not the non-slaveholders of the North, of the South, of the East, and of the West, heartily, unanimously sanction this proposition? Will it not be cheerfully indorsed by many of the slaveholders themselves? Will any *respectable* man enter a protest against it? On the 4th of July, 1876—sooner, if we can—let us make good, at least so far as we are concerned, the Declaration of Independence, which was proclaimed in Philadelphia on the 4th of July, 1776—that "all men are endowed by their Creator with certain inalienable rights; that among these, are life, liberty, and the pursuit of happiness; that to secure these rights, governments are instituted among men, deriving their just powers from the consent of the governed; that whenever any form of government becomes destructive of these ends, it is the right of the people to alter or to abolish it, and to institute a new government, laying its foundation on such principles, and organizing its powers in such form, as to them shall seem most likely to effect their safety and happiness." In purging our land of the iniquity of negro slavery, we will only be carrying on the great work that was so successfully commenced by our noble sires of the Revolution; some future generation may possibly complete the work by annulling the last and least form of oppression.

To turn the slaves away from their present homes—away from all the property and means of support which their labor has mainly produced, would be unpardonably cruel—exceedingly unjust. Still more cruel and unjust would it be, however, to the non-slaveholding whites no less than to the negroes, to grant further toleration to the existence of slavery. In any event, come what will, transpire what may, the institution must be abolished. The evils, if any, which are to result from its abolition, cannot, by any manner of means, be half as great as the evils which are certain to overtake us in case of its continuance. The perpetuation of slavery is the climax of iniquity. . . .

Source: Hinton Rowan Helper. *The Impending Crisis of the South.* New York: Burdick Brothers, 1857, 24–33.

EMANCIPATION PROCLAMATION (1863)

A war measure signed by President Abraham Lincoln on September 22, 1862, to take effect on January 1, 1863, the Emancipation Proclamation freed the slaves in all areas rebelling against the Union at that point. Technically, therefore, the proclamation did not free any slaves, as slaves from conquered Confederate territory had already been freed under a series of Confiscation Acts regarding captured contraband. Slaves in areas still within the control of the Confederacy were obviously not affected by the proclamation, nor were slaves residing in the border states that had remained loyal to the Union. Despite the limited practical impact of the proclamation, however, it had an enormous psychological impact, elevating the abolition of slavery to one of the North's stated war aims and leading the way for the adoption of the Thirteenth Amendment after the war ended in Union victory in 1865. (See also Lincoln, Abraham; Washington, D.C., Compensated Emancipation in.)

Whereas on the 22nd day of September, A.D. 1862, a proclamation was issued by the President of the United States, containing, among other things, the following, to wit:

"That on the 1st day of January, A.D. 1863, all persons held as slaves within any State or designated part of a State the people whereof shall then be in rebellion against the United States shall be then, thenceforward, and forever free; and the executive government of the United States, including the military and naval authority thereof, will recognize and maintain the freedom of such persons and will do no act or acts to repress such persons, or any of them, in any efforts they may make for their actual freedom.

"That the executive will on the 1st day of January aforesaid, by proclamation, designate the States and parts of States, if any, in which the people thereof, respectively, shall then be in rebellion against the United States; and the fact that any State or the people thereof shall on that day be in good faith represented in the Congress of the United States by members chosen thereto at elections wherein a majority of the qualified voters of such States shall have participated shall, in the absence of strong countervailing testimony, be deemed conclusive evidence that such State and the people thereof are not then in rebellion against the United States."

Now, therefore, I, Abraham Lincoln, President of the United States, by virtue of the power in me vested as Commander-In-Chief of the Army and Navy of the United States in time of actual armed rebellion against the authority and government of the United States, and as a fit and necessary war measure for suppressing said rebellion, do, on this 1st day of January, A.D. 1863, and in accordance with my purpose so to do, publicly proclaimed for the full period of one hundred days from the first day above mentioned, order and designate as the States and parts of States wherein the people thereof, respectively, are this day in rebellion against the United States the following, to wit:

Arkansas, Texas, Louisiana (except the parishes of St. Bernard, Palquemines, Jefferson, St. John, St. Charles, St. James, Ascension, Assumption, Terrebone, Lafourche, St. Mary, St. Martin, and Orleans, including the city of New Orleans), Mississippi, Alabama, Florida, Georgia, South Carolina, North Carolina, and Virginia (except the forty-eight counties designated as West Virginia, and also the counties of Berkeley, Accomac, Morthhampton, Elizabeth City, York, Princess Anne, and Norfolk, including the cities of Norfolk and Portsmouth), and which excepted parts are for the present left precisely as if this proclamation were not issued.

And by virtue of the power and for the purpose aforesaid, I do order and declare that all persons held as slaves within said designated States and parts of States are, and henceforward shall be, free; and that the Executive Government of the United States, including the military and naval authorities thereof, will recognize and maintain the freedom of said persons.

And I hereby enjoin upon the people so declared to be free to abstain from all violence, unless in necessary self-defence; and I recommend to them that, in all case when allowed, they labor faithfully for reasonable wages.

And I further declare and make known that such persons of suitable condition will be received into the armed service of the United States to garrison forts, positions, stations, and other places, and to man vessels of all sorts in said service.

And upon this act, sincerely believed to be an act of justice, warranted by the Constitution upon military necessity, I invoke the considerate judgment of mankind and the gracious favor of Almighty God.

Source: Abraham Lincoln. *Emancipation Proclamation, January 1, 1863.* Presidential Proclamations, 1791–1991, Record Group 11, General Records of the United States Government, National Archives.

THIRTEENTH AMENDMENT (1865)

The first of three Reconstruction Amendments enacted in the years immediately following the Civil War, the Thirteenth Amendment officially prohibited slavery in the United States and its territories. Originally proposed by Senator John Henderson in January 1865 and almost immediately adopted by the U.S. Congress, although not without considerable debate, the amendment received the requisite number of state endorsements on December 18, 1865.

Section 1. Neither slavery nor involuntary servitude, except as a punishment for crime whereof the party shall have been duly convicted, shall exist within the United States, or any place subject to their jurisdiction.

Section 2. Congress shall have power to enforce this article by appropriate legislation.

Source: The House Joint Resolution proposing the 13th amendment to the Constitution, January 31, 1865. Enrolled Acts and Resolutions of Congress, 1789–1999, General Records of the United States Government, Record Group 11, National Archives.

Selected Bibliography

Anstey, Roger. *The Atlantic Slave Trade and British Abolition 1766–1810*. Atlantic Highlands, NJ: Humanities Press, 1975.

Aptheker, Herbert. *American Negro Slave Revolts*. 5th ed. New York: Columbia University Press, 1987.

Bennett, Michael. *Democratic Discourses: The Radical Abolition Movement and Antebellum American Literature*. New Brunswick, NJ: Rutgers University Press, 2005.

Berlin, Ira, et al. *Slaves No More: Three Essays on Emancipation and the Civil War*. Cambridge: Cambridge University Press, 1992.

Blackburn, Robin. *The American Crucible: Slavery, Emancipation and Human Rights*. London: Verso, 2011.

Blackburn, Robin. *The Overthrow of Colonial Slavery, 1776–1848*. London: Verso Press, 1988.

Blue, Frederick J. *No Taint of Compromise: Crusaders in Antebellum Politics*. Baton Rouge: Louisiana State University Press, 2005.

Bolt, Christine, and Seymour Drescher, eds. *Anti-Slavery, Religion, and Reform: Essays in Memory of Roger Anstey*. Hamden, CT: Archon Press, 1980.

Bordewich, Fergus M. *Bound for Canaan: The Underground Railroad and the War for the Soul of America*. New York: Amistad, 2005.

Carretta, Vincent, ed. *Unchained Voices: An Anthology of Black Authors in the English-Speaking World of the Eighteenth Century*. Lexington: University of Kentucky Press, 1996.

Conforti, Joseph A. *Samuel Hopkins and the New Divinity Movement: Calvinism, the Congregational Ministry, and Reform in New England between the Great Awakenings*. Grand Rapids, MI: Wm. B. Eerdmans Publishing Company, 1981.

Cover, Robert M. *Justice Accused: Antislavery and the Judicial Process*. New Haven, CT: Yale University Press, 1975.

Cumbler, John T. *From Abolition to Rights for All: The Making of a Reform Community in the Nineteenth Century.* Philadelphia: University of Pennsylvania Press, 2008.

Davis, David Brion. "The Emergence of Immediatism in British and American Antislavery Thought." *Mississippi Valley Historical Review* 49 (September 1962): 209–230.

Davis, David Brion. *The Problem of Slavery in the Age of Emancipation.* New York: Alfred A. Knopf, 2014.

Davis, David Brion. *The Problem of Slavery in the Age of Revolution, 1770–1823.* 2nd ed. Oxford: Oxford University Press, 1999.

Davis, David Brion. *The Problem of Slavery in Western Culture.* New York: Oxford University Press, 1966.

Delbanco, Andrew. *The Abolitionist Imagination.* Cambridge, MA: Harvard University Press, 2013.

Dillon, Merton L. *Abolitionists: The Growth of a Dissenting Minority.* DeKalb: Northern Illinois University Press, 1974.

Drescher, Seymour. *Abolition: A History of Slavery and Antislavery.* New York: Cambridge University Press, 2009.

Drescher, Seymour. *Capitalism and Antislavery: British Mobilisation in Comparative Perspective.* Oxford: Oxford University Press, 1986.

Drescher, Seymour. *Econocide: British Slavery and the Slave Trade in the Era of Abolition.* Pittsburgh: University of Pittsburgh Press, 1977.

Drescher, Seymour. *The Mighty Experiment: Free Labor versus Slavery in British Emancipation.* Oxford: Oxford University Press, 2002.

DuBois, Laurent. *A Colony of Citizens: Revolution & Slave Emancipation in the French Caribbean, 1787–1804.* Chapel Hill: University of North Carolina Press, 2004.

Egerton, Douglas R. *Gabriel's Rebellion: The Virginia Slave Conspiracies of 1800 and 1802.* Chapel Hill: University of North Carolina Press, 1993.

Egerton, Douglas R. *He Shall Go Out Free: The Lives of Denmark Vesey.* Madison: Madison House, 1999.

Fehrenbacher, Don E. *The Slaveholding Republic: An Account of the United States Government's Relations to Slavery.* Completed and edited by Ward M. McAfee. New York: Oxford University Press, 2001.

Finkelman, Paul. *An Imperfect Union.* Chapel Hill: University of North Carolina Press, 1981.

Finkelman, Paul. *Slavery and the Founders: Race and Liberty in the Age of Jefferson.* 2nd ed. Armonk, NY: M.E. Sharpe, 2001.

Fladeland, Betty. *Men and Brothers: Anglo-American Anti-Slavery Cooperation.* Urbana: University of Illinois Press, 1972.

Foner, Eric. *The Fiery Trial: Abraham Lincoln and American Slavery*. New York: W.W. Norton, 2010.

Foner, Eric. *Free Soil, Free Labor, Free Men*. New York: Oxford University Press, 1970.

Foner, Eric. *Reconstruction: America's Unfinished Revolution, 1863–1877*. New York: Harper & Row, Publishers, 1988.

Gara, Larry. *The Liberty Line: The Legend of the Underground Railroad*. Lexington: University Press of Kentucky, 1961.

Gellman, David Nathaniel. *Emancipating New York: The Politics of Slavery and Freedom, 1777–1827*. Baton Rouge: Louisiana State University Press, 2006.

Genovese, Eugene. *From Rebellion to Revolution: Afro-American Slave Revolts in the Making of the Modern World*. Baton Rouge: Louisiana State University Press, 1979.

Grover, Kathryn. *The Fugitive's Gibraltar: Escaping Slaves and Abolitionism in New Bedford, Massachusetts*. Amherst: University of Massachusetts Press, 2001.

Harrold, Stanley. *The Abolitionists and the South, 1831–1861*. Lexington: University of Kentucky Press, 1995.

Harrold, Stanley. *American Abolitionists*. Harlow, Eng.: Longman Publishers, 2001.

Harrold, Stanley. *Border Wars: Fighting over Slavery before the Civil War*. Chapel Hill: University of North Carolina Press, 2010.

Hinks, Peter P. *To Awaken My Afflicted Brethren: David Walker and the Problem of Antebellum Slave Resistance*. University Park: Pennsylvania State University Press, 1997.

Hodges, Graham Russell. *David Ruggles: A Black Radical Abolitionist and the Underground Railroad in New York City*. Chapel Hill: University of North Carolina Press, 2010.

Husband, Julie. *Antislavery Discourse and Nineteenth-Century American Literature: Incendiary Pictures*. New York: Palgrave Macmillan, 2010.

Huzzey, Richard. *Freedom Burning: Anti-Slavery and Empire in Victorian Britain*. Ithaca, NY: Cornell University Press, 2012.

Jackson, Maurice. *Let This Voice Be Heard: Anthony Benezet, Father of Atlantic Abolitionism*. Philadelphia: University of Pennsylvania Press, 2009.

Jacobs, Donald M., ed. *Courage and Conscience: Black and White Abolitionists in Boston*. Bloomington: Indiana University Press, 1993.

James, C.L.R. *The Black Jacobins: Toussaint L'Ouverture and the San Domingo Revolution*. 2nd ed. New York: Vintage, 1963. Originally published 1938.

Jeffrey, Julie Roy. *Abolitionists Remember: Antislavery Autobiographies and the Unfinished Work of Emancipation*. Chapel Hill: University of North Carolina Press, 2008.

Jeffrey, Julie Roy. *The Great Silent Army of Abolitionism: Ordinary Women in the Antislavery Movement*. Chapel Hill: University of North Carolina, 1998.

Jennings, Lawrence C. *French Anti-Slavery. The Movement for the Abolition of Slavery in France, 1802–1848*. Cambridge: Cambridge University Press, 2000.

Jones, Howard. *Mutiny on the* Amistad. New York: Oxford University Press, 1987.

Jordan, Ryan P. *Slavery and the Meetinghouse: The Quakers and the Abolitionist Dilemma, 1820–1865*. Bloomington: Indiana University Press, 2007.

Kachun, Mitch. *Festivals of Freedom: Memory and Meaning in African American Emancipation Celebrations, 1808–1915*. Amherst: University of Massachusetts, 2003.

Klingberg, Frank J. *The Anti-Slavery Movement in England*. New Haven, CT: Yale University Press, 1926.

Kraut, Alan M., ed. *Crusaders and Compromisers: Essays on the Relationship of the Antislavery Struggle to the Antebellum Party System*. Westport, CT: Greenwood Press, 1983.

Laurie, Bruce. *Beyond Garrison: Antislavery and Social Reform*. New York: Cambridge University Press, 2005.

Locke, Mary Staughton. *Anti-Slavery in America from the Introduction of African Slaves to the Prohibition of the Slave-Trade*. Boston: Ginn and Company, 1901; reprint, Johnson Reprint Corporation, 1968.

Loveland, Anne C. "Evangelicalism and 'Immediate Emancipation' in American Antislavery Thought." *Journal of Southern History* 32 (1966): 172–188.

Mayer, Henry. *All on Fire: William Lloyd Garrison and the Abolition of Slavery*. New York: St. Martin's Griffin, 1998.

McCalman, Iain. "Anti-Slavery and Ultra Radicalism in Early Nineteenth Century England." *Slavery and Abolition* 7 (September 1986): 99–117.

McDaniel, W. Caleb. *The Problem of Democracy in the Age of Slavery: Garrisonian Abolitionism & Transatlantic Reform*. Baton Rouge: Louisiana State University Press, 2013.

McGinty, Brian. *John Brown's Trial*. Cambridge, MA: Harvard University Press, 2009.

McGlone, Robert E. *John Brown's War against Slavery*. New York: Cambridge University Press, 2009.

McInerney, Daniel J. *The Fortunate Heirs of Freedom: Abolition and Republican Thought*. Lincoln: University of Nebraska Press, 1994.

McInnes, Maurice Dee. *Slaves Waiting for Sale: Abolitionist Art and the American Slave Trade*. Chicago: University of Chicago Press, 2011.

McKivigan, John R. *The War against Proslavery Religion: Abolitionism and the Northern Churches*. Ithaca, NY: Cornell University Press, 1984.

McKivigan, John R., and Stanley Harrold. *Antislavery Violence: Sectional, Racial, and Cultural Conflict in Antebellum America*. Knoxville: University of Tennessee Press, 1999.

McPherson, James. *The Negro's Civil War: How American Negroes Felt and Acted during the War for the Union*. Champagne-Urbana: University of Illinois Press, 1982.

McPherson, James. *The Struggle for Equality, Abolitionists and the Negro in the Civil War and Reconstruction*. Princeton, NJ: Princeton University Press, 1964.

Midgley, Clare. *Women against Slavery: The British Campaigns, 1780–1870*. New York: Routledge, 1992.

Miller, William Lee. *Arguing about Slavery: The Great Battle in the United States Congress*. New York: Alfred A. Knopf, 1995.

Minkema, Kenneth. "Jonathan Edwards's Defense of Slavery." *Massachusetts Historical Review* 4 (2002): 23–59.

Mitchell, Thomas G. *Anti-Slavery Politics in Antebellum and Civil War America*. Westport, CT: Praeger Publishers, 2007.

Nash, Gary B. *Race and Revolution*. Madison, WI: Madison House, 1990.

Nash, Gary, and Jean Soderlund. *Freedom by Degrees: Emancipation and Its Aftermath in Pennsylvania*. New York: Oxford University Press, 1991.

Newman, Richard S. *The Transformation of American Abolitionism: Fighting Slavery in the Early Republic*. Chapel Hill: University of North Carolina Press, 2002.

Nuremberger, Ruth Ketring. *The Free Produce Movement: A Quaker Protest against Slavery*. Durham, NC: Duke University Press, 1942.

Oakes, James. *The Radical and the Republican: Frederick Douglass, Abraham Lincoln, and the Triumph of Antislavery Politics*. New York: W.W. Norton, 2007.

Oubre, Claude F. *Forty Acres and a Mule: The Freedmen's Bureau and Black Land Ownership*. Baton Rouge: Louisiana State University Press, 1978.

Painter, Nell Irvin. *Exodusters: Black Migration to Kansas after Reconstruction*. New York: W.W. Norton & Co., 1992.

Painter, Nell Irvin. *Sojourner Truth: A Life, A Symbol*. New York: W.W. Norton & Co., 1996.

Patterson, Orlando. *Slavery and Social Death: A Comparative Study*. Cambridge, MA: Harvard University Press, 1982.

Pease, Jane, and William Pease. *Bound with Them in Chains: A Biographical History of the Antislavery Movement*. Westport, CT: Greenwood Press, 1972.

Perry, Lewis. *Radical Abolitionism: Anarchy and the Government of God in Antislavery Thought*. Ithaca, NY: Cornell University Press, 1973.

Perry, Lewis, and Michael Fellman, eds. *Antislavery Reconsidered.* Baton Rouge: Louisiana State University Press, 1979.

Quarles, Benjamin. *Black Abolitionists.* New York: Oxford University Press, 1969.

Rabinowitz, Howard N. *Race Relations in the Urban South, 1865–1890.* Athens: University of Georgia Press, 1996.

Rediker, Marcus. *The Amistad Rebellion: A Transatlantic Odyssey of Slavery and Freedom.* New York: Viking, 2012.

Reynolds, Davis S. *John Brown, Abolitionist: The Man Who Killed Slavery, Sparked the Civil War, and Seeded Civil Rights.* New York: Alfred A. Knopf, 2005.

Rice, C. Duncan. *The Scots Abolitionists, 1833–1861.* Baton Rouge: Louisiana State University Press, 1981.

Richards, Leonard L. *Gentlemen of Property and Standing: Anti-Abolition Mobs in Jacksonian America.* New York: Oxford University Press, 1970.

Ripley, C. Peter, ed. *The Black Abolitionist Papers.* 5 vols. Chapel Hill: University of North Carolina Press, 1985.

Robertson, Stacey M. *Hearts Beating for Liberty: Women Abolitionists in the Old Northwest.* Chapel Hill: University of North Carolina Press, 2010.

Roediger, David. *The Wages of Whiteness: Race and the Making of the American Working Class.* New York: Verso, 1999.

Rose, Willie Lee. *Rehearsal for Reconstruction: The Port Royal Experiment.* New York: Oxford University Press, 1964.

Roth, Sarah M. *Gender and Race in Antebellum Popular Culture.* New York: Cambridge University Press, 2014.

Saillant, John. *Black Puritan, Black Republican: The Life and Thought of Lemuel Haynes, 1753–1833.* New York: Oxford University Press, 2003.

Salerno, Beth A. *Sister Societies: Women's Antislavery Organizations in Antebellum America.* DeKalb: Northern Illinois University Press, 2005.

Schmidt-Nowara, Christopher. *Empire and Anti-Slavery: Spain, Cuba and Puerto Rico, 1833–1874.* Pittsburgh: Pittsburgh University Press, 1999.

Scott, Rebecca. *Slave Emancipation in Cuba* Princeton, NJ: Princeton University Press, 1985.

Scully, Pamela, and Diana Paton, eds. *Gender and Slave Emancipation in the Atlantic World.* Durham, NC: Duke University Press, 2005.

Sewell, Richard H. *Ballots for Freedom: Antislavery Politics in the United States, 1837–1860.* New York: Oxford University Press, 1976.

Soderlund, Jean. *Quakers and Slavery: A Divided Spirit.* Princeton, NJ: Princeton University Press, 1985.

Solow, Barbara L., and Stanley L. Engerman, eds. *British Capitalism and Caribbean Slavery: The Legacy of Eric Williams.* Cambridge: Cambridge University Press, 1987.

Staudenraus, Philip J. *The African Colonization Movement, 1816–1865*. New York: Columbia University Press, 1961.

Stauffer, John. *The Black Hearts of Men: Radical Abolitionists and the Transformation of Race*. Cambridge, MA: Harvard University Press, 2002.

Stauffer, John. *Giants: The Parallel Lives of Frederick Douglass & Abraham Lincoln*. New York: Twelve, 2008.

Stewart, James Brewer. *Holy Warriors: The Abolitionists and American Slavery*. New York: Hill and Wang, 1996.

Swift, David E. *Black Prophets of Justice: Activist Clergy before the Civil War*. Baton Rouge: Louisiana State University Press, 1989.

Temperley, Howard. *British Antislavery, 1833–1870*. London: Longman, 1972.

Upchurch, Thomas Adams. *Abolition Movement*. Santa Barbara, CA: Greenwood, 2011.

Van Horne, John C., ed. *Religious Philanthropy and Colonial Slavery: The American Correspondence of the Associates of Dr. Bray, 1717–1777*. Chicago: University of Illinois Press, 1985.

Vorenberg, Michael. *Final Freedom: The Civil War, the Abolition of Slavery, and the Thirteenth Amendment*. Cambridge: Cambridge University Press, 2001.

Walker, James W. St. G. *The Black Loyalists: The Search for a Promised Land in Nova Scotia and Sierra Leone, 1783–1870*. 2nd ed. Toronto: University of Toronto Press, 1992.

Walters, Ronald G. *The Antislavery Appeal: American Abolitionism after 1830*. New York: W.W. Norton & Co., 1984; Baltimore: Johns Hopkins University Press, 1978.

Walvin, James. *England, Slaves and Freedom 1776–1838*. Oxford: University Press of Mississippi, 1987.

Walvin, James, ed. *Slavery and British Society, 1776–1846*. Baton Rouge: Louisiana State University Press, 1982.

Whitman, T. Stephen. *The Price of Freedom: Slavery and Manumission in Baltimore in Early National Maryland*. Lexington: University Press of Kentucky, 1997.

Whyte, Iain. *Scotland and the Abolition of Black Slavery 1756–1838*. Edinburgh: University Press, 2006.

Wiecek, William M. *The Sources of Antislavery Constitutionalism in America, 1760–1848*. Ithaca, NY: Cornell University Press, 1977.

Williams, Eric. *Capitalism and Slavery*. Chapel Hill: University of North Carolina Press, 1944.

Wyatt-Brown, Bertram. *Lewis Tappan and the Evangelical War against Slavery*. Cleveland: Case Western Reserve University Press, 1969.

Yarema, Allen E. *American Colonization Society: An Avenue to Freedom?* Lanham, MD. University Press of America, 2006.

Yellin, Jean Fagan. *Women and Sisters: The Antislavery Feminists in American Culture.* New Haven, CT: Yale University Press, 1989.

Zilversmit, Arthur. *The First Emancipation: The Abolition of Slavery in the North.* Chicago: University of Chicago Press, 1967.

Index

Note: Page numbers in *italics* indicate photos; page numbers in **bold** indicate main encyclopedia entries.

AASS. *See* American Anti-Slavery Society (AASS)

Abolition newspapers. *See* Antislavery journalism in the United States and Great Britain

Abolition of Slavery Bill (1833), 66

Abolitionist magazine, 239

Abolitionist women, **1–3.** *See also* Women's antislavery societies; individual abolitionist women

Adams, John Quincy, **3–4;** belief in Slave Power conspiracy, 4; delay of Texas annexation, 218; legal representation for *Amistad* captives, 4, 20; Lundy's influence on, 4, 218; open sympathy to antislavery, 331–32; opposition to annexation of Texas, 308; stance against Gag Rule, 13; troubled by debates about slavery, 3–4

Advocate of Peace and Universal Brotherhood newsletter, 71

AFASS. *See* American and Foreign Anti-Slavery Society

Africa Squadron, **5–7,** 44

African America evangelicalism, 27–28

African American communities, **7–8**

African American newspapers. *See* Antislavery newspapers; individual newspapers

African Civilization Society, 132, 148

African Free School, 242, 290

African Freemasonry, 173–75, 358

African Methodist Episcopal (AME) Church, 9, 27–28, 84, 126, 345, 357–58

African Methodist Episcopal Zion (AMEZ) Church, 28, 84, 126

African Repository magazine (ACS), 14

African School for Blacks, 49

Albany Anti-Slavery Society, 248

Allan, William T., 202

Allen, Ephraim, 149

Allen, Richard, **9–10,** 126, 327–28

AMA. *See* American Missionary Association

American Abolition Society, 11, 52, 307

American and Foreign Anti-Slavery Society (AFASS), **10–12,** 147; activism, 333; dissolution of, 334; formation of, 11, 35, 147, 153,

306, 307, 331; merger with Liberty Party, 11–12; multi-pronged attack on slavery, 333; rejection of slavery-focused causes, 331; representation of fugitive slaves, 334

American Anti-Slavery Society (AASS), 11, **12–13,** 253, 255, 350; "Appeal to the Christian Women of the South," 168; commemoration of Elijah Lovejoy, 216; Congregationalist opposition to, 94; Declaration of Sentiments, 12, 151, 349; dissolution of, 336; formation of, 25, 33, 151, 170, 184, 185, 235, 250, 274, 303, 306; Foster's lectures for, 94; Garrisonian's role with, 94, 151–53, 330; Grimké sisters activism, 26; intra-AASS conflicts, 13, 112, 153, 235, 371; leading speakers for, 331; legal help for fugitive slaves, 330–31; multi-pronged attack on slavery, 333; NEASS auxiliary role, 242; nonviolent strategies, 350; opposition to, 94; Phillips executive committee role, 253; postal campaign, 12–13, 255–57, 256; promotion of immediate emancipation, 12; Quaker members, 12; Smith's departure from, 291; Tappan brothers work for, 304, 306

American Baptist Free Mission Society, 84

American Board of Commissioners for Foreign Missions (ABCFM), 93

American Civil Liberties Union (ACLU), 326

American Colonization Society (ACS), **13–15,** 185, 250, 301; AASS condemnation of, 12;

Abbey Foster's meeting leadership, 13; Allen's condemnation of, 328; Birney's involvement with, 52; Clay's support for, 83; Congregationalist support for, 93; consequences and expansion of, 250; Delany's opposition to, 108; description, 329–30; early leaders, 327; evangelical Protestant support, 26; Federalists and, 120–21; founding of Liberia, 13, 14, 15, 201; free people of color's opposition to, 120; Garrison's opposition of, 15, 151, 328–29; Henry Clay's support for, 201, 327; mission of, 150; NEASS struggles with, 240; negative opinion of blacks toward, 327–28; Paul's opposition to, 249; Walker's condemnation of, 328

American Convention of Abolition Societies, **16–17,** 24, 162, 242, 249, 277

American Friends Service Committee, 264

American Home Missionary Society (AHMS), 93

American Missionary Association (AMA), 11, **17–19,** 94, 307, 350

American Peace Society, 71

American Revolution, 14, 22–23, 31, 51, 137, 139–40, 163, 172, 173, 177, 197–98, 247, 261, 272, 281, 323, 324, 341, 352, 406–7

American Slavery as It Is: Testimony of a Thousand Witnesses (Weld, Grimké, Grimké), 168, 189, 298, 363

American Society for Colonizing the Free People of Color. *See* American Colonization Society

Amistad, **19–20**; Adams as council for captives, 4, 20; Committee formation, 19; Judson's ruling on the captives, 20; Lewis Tappan's involvement, 303, 305, 307; post-trial aid to captives, 17; USS *Washington* discovery of, 19

An Antidote for the Furious Combination (Ruggles), 276

Andry, Manuel, 155, 156

Anglican Church, 21, 60, 126

Anglo-African Magazine, 291

Anthony, Susan B., 2, 100, 130, 263

Anti-Corn Law League, 37

Anti-Masonic Party (NY), 140

Anti-Slavery Advocate newspaper, 32

The Antislavery Bugle newspaper, 32, 130

Anti-Slavery Catechism (Child), 78

Anti-Slavery Convention of American Women, 235

Antislavery evangelical Protestantism, **20–30**; African American evangelicalism, 27–28; early tactics, 24–25; intraparty divisions, 25–27; origins, 21–23; political action, 28–29; rise of immediatism, 23–24

Antislavery journalism in the United States and Great Britain, **30–36**; *Anti-Slavery Advocate,* 32; *Anti-Slavery Reporter,* 31, 32; *The Antislavery Bugle,* 32, 130; *Colored American,* 7, 32, 241, 248, 276; *Emancipator,* 12, 29, 167, 216, 217, 275, 306, 341; *Frederick Douglass' Paper,* 7, 31, 32, 35, 112, 291; *Freedom's Journal,* 7, 275, 358; *Genius of Universal Emancipation,* 32, 33, 150, 183, 211, 217–18, 262; *Instigator,* 32; *National Era,* 47, 48, 307, 317, *318*; *The Northern Star and Freeman's Advocate,* 237; *True American,* 80, 342. See also *Liberator*

Anti-Slavery Reporter abolition newspaper, 31, 32

Anti-Slavery Society, 24, 32, **36–38,** 85

Anti-Slavery Society of Canada, 74, 334

Antislavery songs, **38–40**

An Appeal in Favor of That Class of Americans Called Africans (Child) (1833), 78, 212, 389–93

An Appeal to the Colored Citizens of the World (Walker), 239, 327–28

Appeal to the Christian Women of the South (Grimké), 212

Appeal to the Colored Citizens of the World, but in Particular, and Very Expressly, to Those of the United States (Walker), 188, 349, 358

Articles of Confederation, 243

Atlantic slave trade and British abolition, **41–45**; Benezet's writings on, 42–43, 49; Clarkson's opposition to, 43, 56–57; Congressional debate on ending, 95–97; Denmark's antislavery legislation, 43–44; growth of, 41–42; pre-Napoleonic war history, 56; Sharp's writing on, 43; slaving voyages, 42. *See also* Africa Squadron; British slavery, abolition of

"Auld Lang Syne" song, 40

Authors critical of slaveholders, 126–27

"Away to Canada" song (Simpson), 39

Bacon, John, 102

Bailey, Gamaliel, **47–49,** 175, 307

Baker, Hilary, 325

Baldwin, James, 299

Baldwin, Roger S., 20

Baptists, 25, 27, 57, 60–61, 65, 84, 100–101, 126, 149, 247, 248

Barkers, George R., 241

"Battle Hymn of the Republic" (Howe), 281

Battle of Bunker Hill, 281

Baumford, Isabella. *See* Truth, Sojourner

Beecher, Lyman: immediatism work, 26; Lane Seminary presidency, 26; missionary work, 23, 186; promotion of Christian abolitionism, 306

Bellamy, Joseph, 22

Benezet, Anthony, **49–51,** 260; antibondage consciousness-raising essays, 249; call for meeting of Society for the Relief of Free Negroes Unlawfully Held in Bondage, 261; correspondence with Sharp, 50–51; schools for blacks founded by, 49, 260; support for Free Produce Movement, 131; Wilberforce's quoting of, 51; writings on Atlantic slave trade, 42–43, 49–51

Bennett, Rolla, 346

Bennett, Thomas, 345

Bill of Rights, 177–78

Birney, James Gillespie (1792–1857), **52–53**; Chase's legal defense of, 75; cofounding of AFASS, 331; as come-outer, 84–85; Liberty Party presidency, 153; role in AASS formation, 25

Black Codes, 270

Black Freemasons, 173–75, 358

Black Republicans, 280

Blake (Delany), 213

Bleeding Kansas, **53–55**

Bonaparte, Napoleon, 22, 44, 56, 171–72, 232, 369

The Book and Slavery Irreconcilable (Heyrick), 185

Boston Female Anti-Slavery Society, 85, 251, 329, 330, 370–71

Boston Vigilance Committee, 253

Bourne, George, 185–86, 188

Boyer, Jean-Pierre, 345–46

Bradley, James, 200

Brazil: abolition memorialization in, 228; antislavery treaties, 44; belief in gradual emancipation, 160, 165; deep roots of slavery in, 165; gradual emancipation in, 160; illegal slave traffic, 5; manumission in, 221–25; plantation slavery, 41; slave revolts, 58

Brisbane, William, 255

British and Foreign Anti-Slavery Society, 31

British Quakers, 21, 31

British slavery, abolition of, **56–67**; Abolition of Slavery Bill, 66; abolition petitions, 57; abolitionist publications, 65; Africa Squadron, 5–7, 44; Anti-Slavery Society, 24, 32, 36–38, 85; antislavery journalism in, 30–36; antislavery sentiment, 21, 22; ban on slavery, 5; belief in gradual emancipation, 160; Bussa's rebellion, 58, 59, 62; capture of slave ships, 7; Caribbean preoccupation, 57; Christian missionaries, 57, 60, 62, 66; colonial needs for slaves, 61; daily violence against slaves, 59; Demerara slave revolt, 62–63, 65; efforts of Clarkson, 56–57; Emancipation Act, 24, 25;

emergence of antislavery evangelical Protestantism, 20–21; gradual emancipation and, 163; League of Universal Brotherhood, 71; revived abolitionist campaign, 63–64; revolts by slaves, 58, 59; "Sketch of a Negro Code," 60–61; slave registration data, 58, 63; Society for the Amelioration and Gradual Abolition of Slavery, 64; *Somerset* legal decision, 59; support for Garrison, 32; Treaty of Amiens, 44; violent treatment of slaves, 62–63

Brom and Bett v. Ashley (1782), 137

The Brotherhood of Thieves, or A True Picture of the American Church (Foster), 94

Brown, John, 32, 47, 55, 79, 108, 112–13, 154, 179, 229, 253, 263, 279, 280–82, *348. See also* Harpers Ferry raid

Brown, Morris, 347

Brown, William Wells, 153, 213

Brown v. Topeka Board of Education (1953), 101

Buffum, Arnold, 263

Bureau of Refugees, Freedmen, and Abandoned Lands (Freedmen's Bureau), 123

Burke, Edmund, 60–61

Burned-Over District, **67–68,** 124, 288

Burns, Anthony, **69–70,** 143, 282, 320, 323, 335, 353

Burritt, Elihu, **70–71**

Bush, George H. W., 313

Bussa's rebellion (1816), 58, 59, 62

Butler, Benjamin, 97–98, 253

Buxton, Thomas, 151, 261

Calhoun, John C., 106, 109, 178, 393–97

Calvinists, 22, 124

Campbell, Bernard, 360

Can Abolitionists Vote or Take Office under the United States Constitution? (Phillips), 252, 338–39

Canada, antislavery in, **73–75**; belief in gradual emancipation, 160; black migrations to Sierra Leone, 127; gradual progress, 73–74; natural death through attrition, 74; origins of movement, 73; second phase of activism, 74–75

Canadian Anti-Slavery Society, 334

Canadian Quakers, 73

Cannibals All! Or Slaves without Masters (Fitzhugh) (1857), 128–29, 404–7

Caribbean. *See* West Indies

Carter, Robert, III, 193

Cass, Lewis, 54

Chandler, Elizabeth Margaret, 262

Channing, William Henry, 322–23

Chapman, Maria Weston, 38, 85–86, 152, 322. *See also* Women's antislavery societies

Chase, Salmon P., **75–77,** *76;* argument about Constitution and slavery, 100, 109, 339; enjoyment of Helper's books, 176; political influence of, 109, 176; promotion of rights for free black men, 231; repeal of Ohio's black laws, 333

Chavannes, Jean-Baptiste, 172

Child, Lydia Maria, **77–79**; abolitionist pamphlets of, 212; antislavery writings, 48, 78–79; *An Appeal in Favor of That Class of Americans Called Africans,* 78, 212, 389–93;

in song lyrics, 39. *See also* Women's antislavery societies
Choate, Rufus, 85, 86
Christianity: Allen and belief in, 9; black preachers, 60–61; conversions of slaves, 57; "democratic egalitarianism" of, 208; dominance in slave quarters, 57, 61, 65; Edmundson's view on, 259; Equiano's devotion to, 116; Free Produce Movement and, 132; Hopkins and, 93; immediate emancipation and, 166, 348; Mott's belief in value of, 235; practices of Garrisonians, 152; representation in antislavery songs, 38; Republicanism and, 272; slave narratives and, 283; Union Missionary Society, 17–18. *See also* Antislavery evangelical Protestantism; Baptists; Methodists; Presbyterians; Puritans
Christophe, Henri, 172
Church Anti-Slavery Society, 12
Civil Code of the State of Louisiana, 138
Civil Rights Act (1866), 310–11
Civil War: AFASS and, 35; AMA foreign and home missions, 18; antislavery evangelical Protestantism, 29; Boston memorial, 228–29; as challenge for Quakers, 263; Chase's role in North-South peace convention, 76–77; Child's agitation for immediate abolition, 79; Confiscation Acts passage, 90; contrabands, 97–99, *98*; Crandall's distribution of abolitionist pamphlets, 101; Delany's recruitment of blacks, 108; Douglass's rise to prominence, 113; Field Order No. 15, 122–23; Freedmen's Aid Societies, 133–34;

Freedmen's Bureau, 123, 129, 133, 134–36, 254–55; Freemasonry and, 175; heroism of abolitionist women, 3; Higginson's leadership of black soldiers, 281; illegal slave trade controversy, 189; influence of Nat Turner's Rebellion, 33, 209, 210, 314–15, 341, 382; Massachusetts Anti-Slavery Society activism, 240, 251; North's immediate freedom for slaves, 87; Radical Republicans and, 269; secessionist activities, 35; Smith's radical reform efforts, 286, 288; Thirteenth Amendment and, 309; 33rd U.S. Colored Volunteers, 255; Tubman's fund-raising efforts, 313
"Civilization" (J. Smith), 292
Claiborne, William, 154–57
Clarkson, Thomas, 248; cofounding of Society for the Abandonment of the Slave Trade, 31, 37; opposition to Atlantic slave trade, 43, 56–57; support for Free Produce Movement, 131
Clay, Cassius, **79–81**, *80*; freeing of family's slaves, 80; lectures against slavery, 81; Mexican War volunteer for service, 80; publishing of *True American* newspaper, 80, 342; support for gradual emancipation, 80
Clay, Henry, 14, **82–83**; attitude toward free blacks, 14; defense of Cassius Clay, 81; Liberty Party candidacy, 204; opposition to Texas annexation, 83; political career of, 82–83, 204, 233, 332; reputation as "great compromiser," 89; support for American Colonization Society, 201, 327

Clotelle: or The Colored Heroine (Wells), 213
Cockburn, Francis, 102
Coffin, Catherine White, 100
Coffin, Levi, 100, 246, 263
Colonial Slavery Abolition Act (1833), 74
Colored American, African American newspaper, 7, 32, 241, 248, 276
Colored Free Produce Society of Pennsylvania, 131–32
Come-outerism, **83–85**
Committee for the Relief of the Black Poor, 116
Committee for West India Missions, 18
Commonwealth of Massachusetts v. Jennison. See Quock Walker decision
Commonwealth v. Aves (1836), **85–87,** 138, 139, 329, 330
Compensated emancipation, 47, 48, 52–53, 161, 184, 262, 288, 359–61. *See also* Washington, D.C., compensated emancipation in
Compensated Emancipation Convention (Cleveland), 70–71
Compensated Emancipation Society, 71
Compromise of 1850, **87–90**; Chase's opposition to, 76; and evangelical Protestantism, 29; events leading to, 88; Fugitive Slave Law comparison, 88–90, 142; Henry Clay's problem-solving efforts, 89; successes of, 89–90
The Confessions of Nat Turner (Gray) (1831), 210, 381–88
Confiscation Acts (1861, 1862), **90–91**
Congregationalism and antislavery, **92–94**; Edwards's influence on his

pupils, 92–93; inconsistent opposition, 93–94; opposition to the AASS, 94; tolerance of slavery by Congregationalists, 92
Congress of Vienna (1815), 44, 57
Congressional debate on ending U.S. Atlantic slave trade, **95–97**
Connecticut Federalism, 119
Connecticut Society for the Promotion of Freedom, 93
Constitution. *See* U.S. Constitution and slavery
The Constitution—A Proslavery Document (Phillips), 252
Contrabands, **97–99,** *98*
Cornish, Samuel, 18, 247
Corse, Barney, 276
Crandall, Prudence, **99–101**; boarding schools for black girls, 330; departure from the Quakers, 263; distribution of abolitionist literature, 101; preparation of black women as teachers, 100; Quaker background, 99–100; temperance and women's rights advocacy, 101; threats against Crandall's Academy, 100–101
Creole affair (1841), **102–4,** 352
Cugoano, Quobna Ottobah, 50, 126, 283
Curtis, Benjamin Robbins, 85
Cushing, William, 265–66

Danish West Indies, 160
Davis, Henry Winter, 269–70
Declaration of Independence (1776), **105–7,** 177, 178, 191, 209, 217, 274, 299, 325, 328, 352, 389, 410
Declaration of Sentiments, 12, 151, 349

A Defense for Fugitive Slaves
(Spooner), 295–96
Delany, Martin Robinson (1812–1885),
107–8, 148, 213; black Freemasonry
member, 175; Brown's reaching out
to, 108; Civil War service, 107; pub-
lisher of *Pittsburgh Mystery,* 108;
recruitment of blacks during Civil
War, 108
Demerara slave revolt, 62–63, 65
Democratic Party and antislavery,
109–10
Deslondes, Charles, 156
Dessalines, Jean-Jacques, 172
District of Columbia Emancipation
Act, 359–61
Douai, Adolph, 342
Douglas, Sarah, 2
Douglas, Stephen, 54, 107, 109,
191–92
Douglass, Frederick (1818–1895),
2, **111–14**; antislavery newspaper
ownership, 7, 31, 32, 35, 112;
autobiography of, *111,* 112,
210–11, 397–402; books written by, 112–14; condemnation of
speech by Garnet, 148; early life,
111; entrance into abolitionist
movement, 112; escape from slavery, 111–12; high opinion of James
Smith, 291; invitation to Delany,
108; Massachusetts Anti-Slavery
Society agent, 331; memorial
statue, Massachusetts, 228; orator skills of, 237; preaching against
slavery, 12–13; Tremont Temple
rally, *325*; view of the Constitution,
339; Walker's association with,
359. See also *North Star,* African
American newspaper

*Dred: A Tale of the Great Dismal
Swamp* (Stowe), 301
Dred Scott v. Sandford (1857), 77, 85,
110, 121, 138, 139, 143, 191–92,
274, 285, 296
Duane, James, 325
Dutch Quakers, 259
Dwight, Timothy, 119

Early, Peter, 95–96
Eaton, Clement, 181
Edmundson, William, 259
Edwards, Jonathan: antislavery senti-
ment, 22; apologist for the Great
Awakening, 92; influence on
pupils, 92–93; revival meetings,
126
Edwards, Jonathan, Jr., 22, 93
Electoral College, 119
Elevator newspaper, 237
Emancipation Act (1833, Britain), 24,
25
Emancipation Day memorial, 228
Emancipation Proclamation (Lincoln)
(1863), 35, 81, 151–52, 255, 310,
410–12
Emancipator antislavery newspaper,
12, 29, 167, 216, 217, 275, 306,
341
Embargo Act (1807), 149
England: abolition movement origins,
31; Anti-Slavery Society, 24;
Board of Baptist Ministers In and
Near London, 25; Foreign Slave
Trade Bill, 3131; London Quaker
Abolition Committee, 31. *See also*
British slavery, abolition of
English Society for Effecting the
Abolition of the Slave Trade, *56*
Ensor, Robert, 102

Equiano, Olaudah, **115–16,** 198; autobiographic account of, 115, *212*; childhood kidnapping of, 50, 209; criticism of slaveholders, 126; First Great Awakening and, 126; *The Interesting Narrative of Olaudah Equiano or Gustavus Vassa, the African,* 115, 209, *212,* 378–81; *The Narrative* editions of, 115–16

Essex County Antislavery Society, 335

Excerpt from *The Impending Crisis of the South and How to Meet It* (Helper) (1857), 407–10

Excerpt from *The Interesting Narrative of Olaudah Equiano* (Equiano), 378–81

Excerpt from *Narrative of the Life of Frederick Douglass* (Douglass) (1845), 397–402

Excerpt from *Uncle Tom's Cabin* (Stowe) (1852), 402–4

Excerpts from *Cannibals All! Or Slaves Without Masters* (Fitzhugh) (1857), 404–7

Excerpts from *The Confessions of Nat Turner* (Gray) (1831), 381–88

Excerpts from *A Narrative of the Uncommon Sufferings, and Surprising Deliverance of Briton Hammon* (Hammon), 373–78

Extinguisher Extinguished . . . Or David M. Reese, M.D. Used Up (Ruggles), 276

Fayerweather, George, 100

Federalists and antislavery, **119–21,** 146, 338; creation of colonizationists, 120–21; influence on abolitionists, 120; Massachusetts Federalists, 121; New England Federalism, 119, 120

Fee, John G., 18

Field Order No. 15, **122–23**

Fifteenth Amendment (Constitution), 2, 13, 253

Finney, Charles Grandison, **124–25;** higher law arguments of, 178, 179, 186; influence on Arthur Tappan, 304; influence on Oneida students, 199; missionary work, 23; moral perfectionism ideas, 199; New Measures of, 68; Oberlin College presidency, 178; religious revivals of, 23, 24, 68, 124–25

First Confiscation Act, 90–91

First Great Awakening and antislavery, **125–27**

Fisk, Wilbur, 18

Fitzhugh, George, **128–29;** belief that slavery was good, 128; *Cannibals All! Or Slaves without Masters,* 128–29, 404–7; employment at Freedmen's Bureau, 129; proslavery booklets by, 128–29

Foreign Slave Trade Bill (1806), 3131

Fortress Monroe, 97–98

Foster, Abby Kelley (1811–1887), **130,** 263; departure from the Quakers, 263; role at ACS meetings, 13; role in spreading gospel of antislavery ideas, 331; Western Antislavery Society role, 130

Fourteenth Amendment, 270, 271

Fox, George, 158, 259

France: belief in gradual emancipation, 160; emancipation of slaves, 172; Treaty of Amiens, 44

Franckean Evangelical Lutheran Synod, 84

Franklin, Benjamin: Declaration of Independence and, 105; "On the Slave Trade" editorial, 209; role in Pennsylvania Abolition Society, 249; support for abolition, 325, 326

Frederick Douglass' Monthly antislavery newspaper, 31, 32, 35

Frederick Douglass' Paper, African American newspaper, 7, 31, 32, 35, 112, 291

Free African School, 49

Free Colored School (Albany, NY), 237

Free Presbyterian Church, 84

Free Produce Movement, 10, **130–32**; Allen's advocacy for, 9; Grimké sisters' participation, 167; impracticality of, 132; Quaker support for, 131

Free Produce Society of Pennsylvania, 131

Free Soil Party, 28, 29, 47, 55, 204, 230, 332–33; Mexican War and, 230

The Freedman's Book (Child), 79

Freedman's Journal, 247

Freedmen's Aid Societies, **133–34**

Freedmen's Bureau (Bureau of Refugees, Freedmen, and Abandoned Lands), 123, **134–36,** 254–55; Fitzhugh's employment at, 129; formation of, *135*; Johnson's support for, 135–36; Lincoln's support for, 134; post–Civil War school construction, 133

Freedom suits in North America, **136–39**

"Freedom's Call" song (Simpson), 39

Freedom's Journal, African American newspaper, 7, 275, 358

Freemasonry and antislavery, **139–40**; black Freemasonry, 173–75, 358; claims of nondiscrimination, 140; foundations of Freemasonry, 139–40; Hall's involvement with, 173, 174; tenets of universal fellowship, 173

French, Mansfield, 255

French National Convention, 172

French Revolution, 172

Friends Foreign Mission Association, 263

Fugitive Slave Law (1850), 84, **141–43,** 274, 282; Burritt and, 69–70; Compromise of 1850 comparison, 88–90, 89–90, 142; Cushing's enforcement of, 121; description, 29, 148; Douglass and, 112; escape of slaves from Maryland, *141*; and higher law, 177; influence in Canada, 74; Loguen and Payne's opposition to, 84; postpassage vigilance committee formation, 333; reaction of Northerners to, 143. *See also* Burns, Anthony

Furnas, J. C., 299, 300

Gabriel's conspiracy (1800), **145–47**; amendment of Manumission Act, 147; branding and incarceration, 146; charges against Gabriel, 145–46

Gag Rule (1836), 4, 13, 190, 330, 351, 363

Gannet, Ezra Stiles, 323

Garnet, Henry Highland (1815–1882), 34, 100, **147–48**; Douglass's condemnation of speech by, 148; establishment of AFASS, 147; establishment of African Civilization Society, 132; praise of Gerrit Smith, 290; Walker's association with, 359

Garrett, Thomas, 263

Garrison, William Lloyd, 11, **149–52,** *149*, 248; Angelina Grimké's letter to, 167; antislavery newspapers, 31, 32, 33, 78; antislavery sentiment, 25; attack on American Colonization Society, 15, 151; British groups in support of, 32; campaign for women's rights, 330; coediting of *Genius of Universal Emancipation,* 150; cofounding of NEASS, 151, 184, 329; Declaration of Sentiments authorship, 12; defense of Emancipation Proclamation, 151–52; denunciation of Constitution, 178–79; departure from the AASS, 94, 152; Fitzhugh's interest in the works of, 128; formation of AASS, 33, 151, 185; founding of New England Anti-Slavery Society, 151; *Free Press* editorial role, 149; immersion in Federalist politics, 120; influence on Lewis Tappan, 306; meeting with Wilberforce, 151; memorial statue, Boston, 227; National Liberty Party membership, 112; opposition to colonization, 328–29; Phillips as confidant of, 252; Quaker pietism influence on, 179; support for disunionism, 89; support for immediate emancipation, 183, 187; Tremont Temple rally, *325.* See also *Liberator* abolitionist newspaper

Garrison Literary and Benevolent Association, 275

Garrisonians, 11, 26, 28, 84, 121, **152–54,** 194, 250, 306, 321, 330, 335, 336, 338–39, 350

Gates, Seth, 331–32

Gay, Sydney Howard, 320

Gell, Monday, 345, 346

Genius of Universal Emancipation newspaper, 32, 33, 150, 183, 211, 217–18, 262

George III, King of England, 105

German Coast (Louisiana) Insurrection (1811), **154–57**

German Moravians, 60

Germantown antislavery petition (1688), **157–59**

"Get off the Track" song (Hutchinson), 39–40

Giddings, Joshua, 331–32

Gilbert, Oliver, 312

Goodbye to Uncle Tom (Furnas), 299

Gordon, Thomas, 272

Gradual emancipation, **159–65;** call for immediate *vs.,* 150; Clay's support for, 80; Connecticut laws, 161; countries with belief in, 160; Great Britain and, 163; and Moret's Law, 164; New Hampshire laws, 160–61; New Jersey laws, 161–62; Pennsylvania laws, 160; Rhode Island laws, 161; slaveholders opposition to, 162; slavery opponents' belief in, 24; in the West Indies, 160, 163

Graef, Abraham op de, 157

Graef, Derick op de, 157

Gray, Thomas R., 210, 381–88

Great Awakening, 92, 125. *See also* First Great Awakening and antislavery

Great Britain. *See* British slavery, abolition of; England

Greene, Ann Terry, 251

Grimké, Angelina, 1, 13, *166,* **166–69;** AASS activism, 13, 26; *American*

Slavery as It Is: Testimony of a Thousand Witnesses, 168, 189, 298, 363; departure from the Quakers, 263; Free Produce Movement participation, 167; letter to Garrison, 167; marriage to Theodore Weld, 84, 168; Quaker affiliation, 166–67; speaking out against slavery, 166, 167–68; witness to suffering of slaves, 2; women's rights activism, 1, 168–69

Grimké, Charlotte Forten, **169–70**

Grimké, Sarah, 263; AASS activism, 13, 26; *American Slavery as It Is: Testimony of a Thousand Witnesses,* 168, 189, 298, 363; departure from the Quakers, 263; Free Produce Movement participation, 167; Quaker affiliation, 166–67; speaking out against slavery, 166, 167–68

Gronniosaw, James Albert Ukasaw, 126

Haitian Revolution, 58, 59, **171–73**

Hall, Prince, 126, 140, **173–75**

Hamilton, Alexander, 242, 325

Hammet, Benjamin, 346

Hammon, Briton, 373–78

Hammon, Jupiter, 126

Harper, Elizabeth, 2

Harpers Ferry raid (1859), 79, 112–13, 179, 229, 253, 279, 280–81, 286, 288–89, 296, 323, 334–35, *348,* 355

Harrington, James, 272

Haviland, Laura, 263

Hayden, Lewis, 8, 153, 175

Haynes, Lemuel, 22, 126–27, 209

Helper, Hinton, **175–76,** 342, 407–10

Hendericks, Gerret, 157

The Heroic Slave (Douglass), 112

Heyrick, Elizabeth, 184–86, 188, 218, 262

Hicks, Elias, 100, 131, 235, 263

Higginbotham, A. Leon, 266–67

Higgins, James W., 241

Higginson, Thomas Wentworth, 280, 282, 323, 335

Higher law and antislavery, **177–79**; arguments of Finney, 178, 179, 186; arguments of Seward, 178, 186; Bill of Rights and, 177–78; evangelical Protestantism and, 29; Fugitive Slave Law and, 177; gradual emancipation and, 161

Hilton, John T., 153, 175

Hiring-out and challenges to slavery, **180–82**

His Promised Land (Parker), 245–46

Homestead Act (1866), 123

Hopkins, Samuel, 22, 93

Hopper, Isaac, 263, 276

Howard, Oliver Otis, 134–35. *See also* Freedmen's Bureau

Howe, Julia Ward, 281

Howe, Samuel Gridley, 281

Hughes, Benjamin, 175

Human Rights serial, 256

Hutchinson Family, 39–40

Immediate, Not Gradual Emancipation (Heyrick), 184–85, 218, 262

Immediate emancipation, **183–88**; AASS support for, 12, 25; Agency Committee's support for, 65; Beecher's conversion efforts, 26; Bermuda and Antigua's support for, 66; Child's support for, 78; emergence of, 23–24, 328–31;

Garrison's support for, 183, 187; Methodist support for, 24; post-1830 demand for, 20–21, 24; Quakers and, 262; Republicanism and, 273–74; Sturge and, 202; Weld's support for, 26

The Impending Crisis of the South and How to Meet It (Helper) (1857), 176, 342, 407–10

Incidents in the Life of a Slave Girl (Jacobs), 79, 189–90, 211

Indiana Meeting of Anti-Slavery Friends, 263

Instigator abolition newspaper, 32

The Interesting Narrative of Olaudah Equiano or Gustavus Vassa, the African (Equiano) (1789), 115, 209, *212,* 378–81

Internal slave trade and antislavery, **189–90**

Iowa Quakers, 263

Jackson v. Bulloch (1837), 87

Jacobs, Harriet, 79, 189–90, 211

Jamaican slave revolt, 65, 163

Jay, John, 325

Jefferson, Thomas, and antislavery, **191–93,** 272; ban on foreign slave trade, 97; Claiborne's letter to, 154–55; *Dred Scott* decision and, 192–93; Gabriel's conspiracy and, 146; lifelong slaveholder history, 193; Louisiana Purchase authorized by, 232; *Notes on the State of Virginia,* 192, 209; paradoxical role of, 191; signatory to ban on slavery, 97. *See also* Declaration of Independence

Jerry Rescue, **193–95,** 353

Jim Crow laws, 114

Jocelyn, Simeon S., 18, 19

Johnson, Andrew, 77, 122–23, 135–36

Johnson, Oliver, 320

Johnston, William, 241

Jones, Absalom, 9

Jones, Richard Allenand Absalom, 250

Jones v. Mayer (1968), 311

Justice and Expediency (Whittier), 211

Kansas Aid Committee, 335

Kansas Emigrant Society, 335

Kansas-Nebraska Act (1854), 29, 35, 53–54, 76, 109, 143, 282, 353–54

Keith, George, 260

Kendall, Amos, 256

Key, Francis Scott, 40

King, Boston, **197–98,** 209, 283

King, Rufus, 325

Ladies' New York City Anti-Slavery Society, 371

The Land of Gold (Helper), 175, 342

Lane Seminary Debates (1834), **199–200**

Latin America, 163–65, 172

Lay, Benjamin, 260

League of Universal Brotherhood, 71

Leavitt, Joshua, 19, 25, 28, 151, 203, 306

Letter to a Clergyman Urging Him to Set Free a Black Girl He Held in Slavery (MacGregor), 73

Letters from New York (Child), 78

Letters of the Late Ignatius Sancho, an African (Sancho), 209

Liberator abolitionist newspaper (1831), 2, 31–35, 33, 34, 38, 100, 101, 112, 150–53, 152, 167, 170,

178, 184, 185, 187–88, 211–12, 218, 239, 250, 328, 349, 370, 388–89

Liberia, **201–3**; ACS's creation of, 13, 14, 201; Afro-Liberians rulership of, 202–3; antislavery songs in, 39; black emigration to, 15, 38, 162, 202; Delany's travels to, 108; Garnet as resident minister to, 148; Vey town, Monrovia, *201*

Liberty Party, **203–4**; AFASS endorsement of, 11; Bailey's organizing for, 48; Birney's presidency, 52–53, 153; *Christian Citizen* newspaper sympathy with, 71; consideration of antislavery opinions, 332; evangelical Protestants and, 28–29; founders of, 28, 203; Free Soil Party replacement of, 204; Garrison's membership, 112; Lewis Tappan's support for, 307; membership of Chase, 75–76; merger with AFASS, 11; Mexican War and, 204; support of antislavery candidates, 28

Life and Times of Frederick Douglass (Douglass), *111*

Lincoln, Abraham, 110, **205–7**; announcement of preliminary Emancipation Proclamation, 206; Cooper Institute antislavery speech, 206; debate on meaning of Declaration of Independence, 107; early political career background, 205; efforts for antislavery constitutional amendment, 207; Emancipation Proclamation, 35, 81, 151–52, 255, 310, 410–12; enjoyment of Helper's books, 176; Garrisonian's proslavery interpretation of, 335;

Gerrit Smith's support for, 288–89; pocket-veto of Reconstruction Act, 270; preferences for no new slaves, 205; Radical Republicans' prodding of, 269; secession crisis, 35, 89, 91, 96, 143, 213, 229, 233, 274, 279–80; signing First Confiscation Act, 90; signing the District of Columbia Emancipation Act, 359, 360; slavery-related interpretation of the Constitution, 339, 354; support for Freedmen's Bureau, 134; support for Thirteenth Amendment, 309. *See also* Emancipation Proclamation

Literature and abolition, **207–14**; *American Slavery as It Is: Testimony of a Thousand Witnesses* (Weld, Grimké, Grimké), 168, 189, 298, 363; Child's abolitionist pamphlets, 212; early eighteenth century, 208; early nineteenth century, 209–10; Founding Fathers, 209; mid-eighteenth century to early nineteenth century, 208–9; radical abolitionists, 211; social reformers, 210–11; work of Brown, 213; work of Douglass, *111*, 112, 210–11, 397–402; work of Equiano, 209; work of Garrison, 211; work of Grimké, Angelina, 168, 189, 212, 298, 363; work of Grimké, Sarah, 168, 189, 212, 298, 363; work of Harper, 213; work of Jacobs, 79, 189–90, 211; work of James McCune Smith, 291–92; work of Rush, 50, 277; work of Smith, James McCune, 291–92; work of Sojourner Truth, 213; work of Spooner, 295–96; work

of Stowe, 35, 143, 190, 212–13, 317–18, *318,* 352–53, 363
Livingstone, Robert, 105
Locke, John, 106
Loguen, Jermain, 8, 28, 84, 194, 320, 353
London Quaker Abolition Committee, 31
Lord Dunmore's Proclamation, **214–15**
Louisiana Purchase (1803), 171, 232
L'Ouverture, Toussaint, 172, 349, 352
Lovejoy, Elijah, 31, 120
Lovejoy, Elijah (1802–1837), **216,** 322; abolitionist weekly publication, 33, *34;* death from proslavery mob, 351; hero reputation of, 216; Lincoln's reaction to murder of, 205; murder of, 330; New England Federalism roots, 120
Lundy, Benjamin, 4, 32, 120, **217–19,** 262; antislavery newspaper of, 32, 33, 150, 183, 211, 217; opposition to Texas annexation, 308; support for Free Produce Movement, 131; support for immediate emancipation, 183. See also *Genius of Universal Emancipation* newspaper
Lynchings, 114, 146, 216, 299, 330, 349, 382

Mabee, Carlton, 350
Macaulay, Zachary, 31
MacGregor, James, 73
Machiavelli, Niccolo, 272
Magnalia Christi Americana (Mather), 208
Manifest Destiny, 53–54

Manumission, **221–26**; AMA and, 17; description, 221; as familial endeavor, 223; freedom *vs.* independence conferred by, 225–26; as gendered experience, 222–23; gradual emancipation and, 161; hiring-out and, 181; Liberia and, 202; Lundy and, 217; slaveholders and, 222, 223–24, 223–25; social processes of, 222; statues, 225; variability of societal rates, 221–22. *See also* New York Manumission Society
Manumission Act (1782), 147
Marrant, John, 126–27, 208
Mason, James, 142
Mason Committee, 281
Massachusetts Abolition Society, 11
Massachusetts Anti-Slavery Society (MASS), 240, 251
Massachusetts Federalists, 121
Massachusetts General Colored Association, 358
Mather, Cotton, 208
May, Samuel Joseph, 100, 152, 153, 187, 194
McKim, J. Miller, 320, 335–36
Memoirs of the Life of Boston King, a Black Preacher (King), 283
Memorialization of antislavery and abolition, **227–30,** 228; Emancipation Day, January 1, 228; Monument Park, Michigan, 227; Robert Gould Shaw Memorial, 228–29; slave memorial, Mount Vernon, 228; Sojourner Truth Memorial Statue, 227; Stowe Library and Museum, 227–28; Underground Railroad memorial, 228; West

Indies Emancipation Day Celebration, 39, 363–65; William Garrison statue, Boston, 227
Mendi Committee, 17
Mennonites, 158
Mesmerism, 68
Methodists, 21, 24, 27, 60, 126, 197–98
Mexican War and antislavery, **230–31**; Adams opposition to, 4; Clay's volunteer for service, 80; come-outerism and, 83; Liberty Party and, 204; sectional compromise, 88; Wilmot Proviso and, 109, 163, 231
Mirror of Liberty black magazine, 241, 276
Missionaries and missionary organizations: American Home Missionary Society, 93; American Missionary Association, 11, 17–19, 94, 307, 350; Beecher's work, 23, 186; Committee for West India Missions, 18; Finney's work, 23; Lewis Tappan's support of, 307; New England missionary organization, 68; Union Missionary Society, 17, 27; Western Evangelical Missionary Association, 18
"Missionary Hymn" song, 40
Missouri Compromise (1820), 29, 54, **232–34**; boundary lines, 89; Compromise of 1850 comparison, 88; House of Representatives deliberation, 232; Kansas-Nebraska Act overturning of, 282; Massachusetts legislature role, 233; Mexican War and, 231; Sixteenth Congress deliberation, 232–33; slavery prohibition clause, 109; unpopularity in the North, 233–34

Missouri Crisis (1819–1821), 232
Monroe, James, 14, 22, 146, 147
Monument Park, Michigan, 227
Moret's Law (1870), 164
Morgan, Lynda, 181
Mormonism, 68
Mott, James, 262
Mott, Lucretia Coffin, **234–36,** 262; belief in nonviolent doctrine of nonresistance, 236; fight for Fifteenth Amendment, 2; Free Produce Movement participation, 132, 167, 235; plans for relocating slaves back to Africa, 2; role in founding the AASS, 151, 235; Seneca Falls Convention attendance, 235–36, 263, 370, 371; women's rights activism, 235, 336; World Anti-Slavery Convention participation, 235. *See also* Women's antislavery societies
My Bondage and Freedom (Douglass), *111*, 112
Myers, Harriet (1807–1865), **236–38**
Myers, Stephen (1800–1870), 8, **236–38**

NAACP Legal Defense Fund, 326
Napoleon. *See* Bonaparte, Napoleon
The Narrative of Sojourner Truth: A Northern Slave (Truth and Gilbert), 312
Narrative of Sojourner Truth (Sojourner Truth), 1
Narrative of the Life of Frederick Douglass, An American Slave, Written by Himself (Douglass) (1845), *111*, 112, 210–11, 397–402

A *Narrative of the Uncommon Sufferings, and Surprising Deliverance of Briton Hammon,* excerpts (Hammon), 373–78
Nat Turner's Confessions (Gray), 315
Nat Turner's Rebellion, 33, 209, 210, 314–15, 341, 382
National Anti-Slavery Standard newspaper, 32, 33, 78
National Association for the Advancement of Colored People (NAACP), 169, 326
National Convention of Colored Citizens (1843), 147, 275
National Convention of the Women's League, 168–69
National Era antislavery newspaper, 47, 48, 307, 317, *318*
NEASS. *See* New England Antislavery Society
Negro Seamen Act (1822), 347
The Negroes in Negroland (Helper), 176
New Divinity Movement, 22, 92, 93
New England Antislavery Society (NEASS), **239–40**; activist stance of, 239–40; Garrison's cofounding of, 151, 184, 329; immediatism doctrine, 184, 239; renaming as Massachusetts Anti-Slavery Society, 240; struggles with ACS members, 240
New England Emigrant Aid Company (NEEAC), 54
New England Federalists, 119, 120
New Philadelphia, black community, 8
New York Anti-Slavery Society, 349
New York City Abolition Society, 291
New York Committee of Vigilance, **240–41,** 276, 333

New York Manumission Society (NYMS), 16, 161, 184, 241, **242–43**
New York Temperance Society, 275
Newman, Henry S., 263–64
Newspapers. *See* Antislavery journalism in the United States and Great Britain
Nojoque, a Question for a Continent (Helper), 176
Nonresistance Society, 350
Nonviolence, 49, 263, 348, 349–51, 353
North Star, African American newspaper, 7, 35, 106, 281
The Northern Star and Freeman's Advocate newspaper, 237
The Northern Star Association, 237
Northwest Ordinance (1787), **243–44**
Norton, Andrews, 323
Notes on the State of Virginia (Jefferson), 192, 209
Noyes, John Humphrey, 68
Nullification Controversy (1832), South Carolina, 279

O'Connell, Daniel, 151
Ohio Anti-Slavery Society, 32
Ohio Black Laws, 246
"Old Liberia Is Not the Place for Me" song (Simpson), 39
"On the Fourteenth Query of Thomas Jefferson's Notes on Virginia" (J. Smith), 292
"On the Slave Trade" (Franklin), 209
Oneida Community, 68
Original Anti-Slavery Songs (Simpson), 40
Otis, James, 325

Paine, Thomas, 325

Parker, John Percial, **245–46**

Parker, Theodore, 69, 179, 281, 323, 355

Pastorius, Francis Daniel, 157–59

Paul, Benjamin, 247–48

Paul, Nathaniel, **247–48**

Paul, Thomas, 175

Pemberton, James, 325

Penn, Will, 158

Pennsylvania Abolition Society (PAS), **248–51,** 326; abolition leadership role, 16; American Convention of Abolition Society meetings, 16; early history, 239, 249; formation of, 238, 324; founding of, 248; gradualist tone of, 162; immediate emancipation and, 184; importance to American abolitionism, 250–51; joint abolition work of, 242; membership of Rush, 277; preference for legal, political venues, 249; Quaker role in formation of, 23; relationship with free black community, 250; Revolutionary War lapse of activities, 248–49

Pennsylvania Freeman, 32

Pennsylvania Gradual Abolition Act (1780), 324

Perry, Matthew Calbraith, 6

Philadelphia Female Anti-Slavery Society, 235, 370

Philadelphia Institute for Colored Youth, 2

Philadelphia Port Royal Relief Committee, 335

Philadelphia Quarterly Meeting (Quakers), 261

Philadelphia Yearly Meeting of Friends, 235

Phillips, Wendell, **251–53**; antislavery pamphlets of, 252; arrest for role in riot, 70; Boston abolition leadership, 69; Garrisonian membership, 152; marriage to Ann Terry Greene, 251; oratorical skills of, 252; quest for political equality for blacks, 152; radical Republican beliefs of, 253; social reform activism, 253; World Anti-Slavery Convention attendance, 252

Phoenix Society of New York, 275

Phrenology, 68

Pillsbury, Parker, 152, 355

Pinckney, Charles Cotesworth, 338

Pinckney's Treaty (1795), 19

Pitkin, Timothy, 96

A Plan for the Abolition of Slavery (and) to the Non-Slaveholders of the South (Spooner), 296

A Plan of Brotherly Co-Partnership of the North and South for the Peaceful Extinction of Slavery (Burritt), 70–71

Pointe Coupée Rebellion (1795), 155, 156

Polk, James K., 204, 230–31

Pomeroy, Samuel, 360

Port Royal (South Carolina), **254–55,** 335

"A Positive Good" (Calhoun) (1837), 393–97

Postal campaign (1835), 12–13, **255–57**

Poyas, Peter, 345, 346

Presbyterians, 25, 27, 33, 52, 68, 73, 74, 84, 93, 132, 147–48, 166, 168

Pritchard, "Gullah" Jack, 345–46

Protestants/Protestantism. *See* Antislavery evangelical Protestantism
Puritans, 67, 208, 216, 259
Purvis, Robert, 320

Quaker Loyalist community (Canada), 73
Quakers and antislavery, **259–64**; AASS members, 12; abolitionists at odds with, 263; American Friends Service Committee, 264; antislavery sentiment, 1, 21, 31; Atlantic slave trade opposition, 43; Benezet's writing on, 49; Canadian Quakers, 73; discouragement of African Americans from joining, 262–63; doctrine against stolen goods, 159; Dutch Quakers, 259; early antislavery history, 21–23, 31; Fox's founding of, 158, 259; Free Produce Movement and, 131–32; Friends Foreign Mission Association, 263; Garrisonians membership, 152; German Antislavery Petition and, 157–59; Germantown antislavery petition, 157–59; gradual emancipation and, 160; immediatism and, 262; Indiana Meeting of Anti-Slavery Friends, 263; influence on Garrison, 179; Iowa Quakers, 263; London Quaker Abolition Committee, 31; opposition to Atlantic slave trade, 43; organization of worship for blacks, 208; Philadelphia Quakers, 33, 48, 151; post–WW I antislavery agitation, 264; role in abolition societies formation, 23; role with the NYMS, 242; slave power argument and, 263; support for Free Produce

Movement, 131; support for immediate emancipation, 184–85; work for Underground Railroad, 263. *See also* individual Quakers
Quok Walker decision (1783), **265–67**

Radical Abolition Party, 291
Radical Republicans, **269–70**; Confiscation Acts, 91, 123; prodding of Lincoln, 269; reconstruction ideas of, 269, 271; support for plantation confiscation, 123; views on slavery, 81
Rael, Patrick, 242
Ramsey, James, 43
Randolph, Edmond, 338
Randolph, John, 96
Rankin, John, 246
Reconstruction Acts in the United States (1867–1868), 270, **271–72**; First Reconstruction Act, 271; Fourth Reconstruction Act, 272; Second Reconstruction Act, 271; Third Reconstruction Act, 272
Remond, Charles Lenox, 153
A Representation of the Injustice and Dangerous Tendency of Tolerating Slaver (Sharp), 43
Republicanism and antislavery, **272–75**, 358, 392; embrace of Renaissance theorists, 272; enjoyment of liberty at the core of, 273; immediatism and, 273–74
Rigaud, André, 172
Robert Gould Shaw Memorial to the Fifty-Fourth and Fifty-Fifth Colored Regiments, 228–29
Roberts v. Boston (1850), 333
Ruggles, David, 241, **275–77**; African American bookstore ownership,

275–76; articles in *Mirror of Liberty* magazine, 276; employment of freed slaves, 275; hydrotherapy clinic of, 276–77; New York Committee of Vigilance secretary, 241, 333; pamphlets written by, 276; support for schools for blacks, 100; work with Underground Railroad, 276

Rush, Benjamin, **277–78**; antislavery writings of, 50, 277; Declaration of Independence signatory, 325; Pennsylvania Abolition Society activism, 249, 277; support for abolition, 325

Safe houses of the Underground Railroad, 7, 194, 320

Sanborn, Franklin, 281

Sancho, Ignatius, 209

Sandiford, Ralph, 249, 260

Scott, Orange, 27

Secession crisis and abolitionists, 35, 89, 91, 96, 143, 213, 229, 233, 274, **279–80**

Second Confiscation Act, 90–91

Second Great Awakening, 67–68, 186

Secret Six, **280–82,** 323, 335. *See also* Harpers Ferry raid; Higginson, Thomas Wentworth; Howe, Samuel Gridley; Parker, Theodore; Sanborn, Franklin; Smith, Gerrit; Stearns, George Luther

The Selling of Joseph (Sewall), 92, 208

Seneca Falls Convention (1848), 235–36, 263, 370, 371

Sewall, Samuel, 92

Seward, William Henry: higher law arguments of, 178, 186; influence on Oneida students, 199; sympathy toward antislavery, 332

Sewell, Samuel, 208

Sharp, Granville, 21; challenge of British slavery, 42, 43; cofounding of Society for the Abandonment of the Slave Trade, 31, 37; correspondence with Benezet, 50–51

Sherman, John, 176

Sherman, Roger, 105; Declaration of Independence and, 105

Sherman, William T.: issuance of Field Order No. 15, 122–23

A Short Account of That Part of Africa, Inhabited by the Negroes (Benezet), 42–43

A Short Account of the People Called Quakers (Benezet), 49

Sidney, Algernon, 272

Silver Bluff Church (South Caroline), 126

Simpson, Joshua, 39, 40

"Sketch of a Negro Code" (Burke), 60–61

Slade, William, 331–32

Slave narratives, **283–84**; of Allen, 10; of Brown, 213; of Cugoano, 283; of Douglass, 210–11, 283; of Equiano, 283; of Garnet, 211; initial circulation of, 209; of Jacobs, 211, 283; of King, 198, 283; of Sojourner Truth, 213; of Venture Smith, 283

Slave Power argument, 4, **284–85**; Adams and, 4, 284–85; Bailey's attack on, 48; Democrats and, 110; Douglass and, 112; Fitzhugh and, 129; Fugitive Slave Law and, 143; Quakers and, 263; Republicans and, 110, 274; Secret Six and, 282; Wilmot Proviso and, 285

Slaveholders: Allen's condemnation of, 9; authors critical of, 126–27;

Canadian ban of, 48; come-outerism and, 84; Compromise of 1850 and, 88; evangelicals view of, 22, 27; federal government policy on, 48, 97–98; Fugitive Slave Law and, 141; Garrison's beliefs about, 25; impact of Haitian Revolution for, 171; manumission and, 222, 223–25; occasional turn to abolition, 8; opinion of American Colonization Society, 327; opinions of free blacks, 14; opposition to gradual emancipation, 162; property rights of, 98; resentment of antislavery pronouncements, 15

Slavery (Channing), 323

Sloan, James, 95

Smalls, Robert, 255

Smeathmen, Henry, 116

Smilie, John, 96

Smith, Gerrit, **285–90**, *286*; armed rescue of Jerry McHenry, 282; efforts at reforming nonsectarian free churches, 84; elder statesman role, 289; Garnet's praise of, 290; James Smith's criticism of, 289–90; Liberty Party leadership, 11, 194, 203, 204; philanthropic work of, 237; racial reform efforts of, 287–88; religious vision of, 287; revival enthusiasm of, 28; Secret Six membership, 280–82; support for Compensated Emancipation Convention, 70–71; support for Lincoln administration, 288–89; uniqueness among white reformers, 285–86; upstate NY African American community, 8; use of politics to fight slavery, 34. *See also* Liberty Party

Smith, James McCune, 287, **290–92**; criticism of Gerrit Smith, 289–90; Douglass's high opinion of, 291; New York City Abolition Society cofounder, 291; reputation as black intellectual, 290–91; writings of, 291–92

Smith, Joseph, 68

Société des Amis des Noirs (Paris), 51

Society for the Abandonment of the Slave Trade, 31

Society for the Abolition of the Slave Trade, 43

Society for the Amelioration and Gradual Abolition of Slavery, 64

Society for the Relief of Free Negroes Unlawfully Held in Bondage, 51, 261. *See also* Pennsylvania Abolition Society

"Some Considerations on the Keeping of Negroes" (Woolman), 208

Somerset, James, 43

Somerset decision (1772), 31, 36, 43, 51, 59, 86–87, 137, **293–94**

Songs of the Free, and Hymns of Christian Freedom (Chapman), 38

South Carolina Nullification Controversy (1832), 279

Southern Homestead Act (1866), 123

Spooner, Lysander, **295–96**

Stanton, Elizabeth Cady, 2, 336, 371. *See also* Women's antislavery societies

Stanton, Henry B., 26

"The Star Spangled Banner" (Key), 40

Stearns, George Luther, 281, 282

Stevens, Thaddeus, 140, 270

Stewart, Maria, 359

Still, William, 8, 320

Stone, Lucy, 130
Story, Joseph, 20
Stowe, Harriet Beecher, 35, 143, 190, 211–12, *212*, 227–28, **297–301**, *297*. See also *Dred: A Tale of the Great Dismal Swamp* (Stowe); *Uncle Tom's Cabin*
Stowe Library and Museum, Connecticut, 227–28
Strader v. Graham (1851), 87
Sturge, Joseph, 202
Sumner, Charles, 270
Sunderland, La Roy, 27
Supplemental Act, District of Columbia Emancipation Act (1862), 361
Swedenborgianism, 68
Syracuse, NY, abolitionists, 195

Tallmadge, James, 232
Tallmadge Amendment, 232, 285
Taney, Roger Brooke, 77, 110, 139, 191–92. See also *Dred Scott v. Sandford*
Tappan, Arthur, **303–5**; American Tract Society cofounding, 304; *Amistad* Committee membership, 19; antislavery newspaper, 28–29, 304; bailing Garrison out of jail, 150; cofounding of AFASS, 13, 35, 331; contributions to American Sunday School Union, 304; financial assistance for Crandall, 100; Finney's influence on, 304; founding of Oberlin College, 26; gun distribution defensive violence strategy, 351; New York Anti-Slavery Society meetings, 124–25; opposition to colonization, 328; reluctance for full support of

abolitionists, 305; role with the AASS, 12, 26, 303, 304, 306; teenage business experiences, 303–4; Weld's influence on, 306
Tappan, Lewis, 11, **305–7**; AMA membership, 18; *Amistad* case involvement, 303, 305, 307; antislavery newspaper, 28–29, 304; antislavery sentiment, 24; bailing Garrison out of jail, 150; cofounding of AFASS, 13, 35, 331; *Evangelist* newspaper, 306; founding of AASS, 303; founding of *Journal of Commerce,* 307; founding of Oberlin College, 26; Garrison's influence on, 306; launch of *Emancipator,* 306; New York Anti-Slavery Society meetings, 124–25; opposition to colonization, 328; postal campaign announcement, 255–56; role with the AASS, 12, 26, 303, 304, 306; role with the AFASS, 13, 35, 306–7; support for Liberty Party, 307; support of American Missionary Association, 307; Weld's influence on, 306
Taylor, Richardson, 146
Taylor, Zachary, 89
Texas, annexation of (1845), **308–9**; Adams's delay of, 218; Calhoun's support for, 230; Clay's opposition to, 83; Lundy's opposition to, 308; Tyler's success in achieving, 309; Whig party and, 366
Thirteenth Amendment (1865), 35, 99, 162, 169, 207, 289, 295, **309–11,** 324, 336, 340, 412
33rd U.S. Colored (First Regiment of South Carolina Volunteers), 255

Thompson, George, 151, 248

Thompson, Henry, 199

Thompson, Smith, 20

Thoughts on African Colonization (Garrison), 151

Thoughts upon Slavery (Wesley), 50

Three-fifths clause, U.S. Constitution, 233, 284, 337, 339

Tompkins, Daniel D., 325

Tourist antislavery newspaper, 32

The Tragic Prelude (Curry), *348*

Transatlantic slave trade, 5

Transcontinental railroad, 54

Treaty of Amiens (1802), 44

Treaty of Guadalupe Hidalgo, 88

Tremont Temple rally (Boston, 1860), *325*

Trenchard, John, 272

True American antislavery newspaper, 80, 342

Truth, Sojourner, **311–12**; "Aren't I a Woman" speech, 312; background, 1–2, 211, 227, 311–12; memorials to, 227; published memoirs of, 312; Rush's hydrotherapy cure for, 277; Stowe's story about, 213

Tubman, Harriet, 263, **312–13**; background, 2–3, 312–13; Garrett's support of, 263; Underground Railroad work, 313

Turner, Nat, 33, 209–10, **314–15**. *See also* Nat Turner's Rebellion

Tyler, John, 102, 328

Uncle Tom's Cabin (Stowe) (1852), **317–18**, *318,* 352, 363; depiction of cruelties of slave life, 190, 212; excerpt from, 402–4; Furnas's criticism of, 299; global success of, 298, 317; importance to the cause

of abolition, 35, 143, 297; *National Era* serialization of, 317, *318*; Northern and Southern criticism of, 318; Southern racist popularizations, 300

The Unconstitutionality of Slavery (Spooner), 295, 296

Underground Railroad, 1, 7, 84, 142, **319–20**; fugitive slave laws *vs.,* 352–53; Harriet Myers fund-raising support for, 238; memorial to, 228; methods of travel, 319–20; National Park Service's Network to Freedom definition, 319; New York State Committee as safe harbor for, 241; Parker's career with, 245; Quaker involvement, 263; Ruggles's work with, 276; safe house network, 7, 194, 320; Stephen Myers leadership of, 236–37; Still's notes on, 320; trust issues of, 246; Tubman's work with, 313

The Underground Railroad (Stills), 320

Union League of Philadelphia, 335

Union Missionary Society, 17, 27

Unitarianism and antislavery, **321–23**; Garrisonians involvement with, 152, 321; Lewis Tappan's brief embrace of, 306; ministry of Samuel Joseph May, 100, 187, 194; ministry of Theodore Parker, 179, 281, 323; ministry of William Channing, 322–23

United States, antislavery in, **324–36**; American Colonization Society, 327–28; *Commonwealth v. Aves,* 85–87, 138, 139, 329, 330; early abolition societies, 324–27; efforts at improving social conditions for blacks, 326–27; emergence of immediatism, 328–31; Founding Fathers support for, 325; mainstream politics and the end of slavery, 334–36; New England abolition societies, 326; New Jersey gradual abolition act, 327; New York City Abolition Society, 291, 324; Northern abolition societies, 325–26; Pennsylvania Gradual Abolition Act, 324; political antislavery, 331–34; Virginia Abolition Society, 325; women's antislavery activism, 329–30. *See also* individual antislavery societies

Upshur, Abel, 6, 328

U.S. Constitution and slavery, 29, **337–40**; abolishment of Atlantic slave trade, 95; Articles of Confederation, 243; Chase's arguments about, 100, 339; Crandall and, 100; Democrat's proslavery interpretation, 100; Douglass's opinion of, 339; Fifteenth Amendment, 2, 13, 253; Fifth Amendment, 184; Fourteenth Amendment, 270, 271; on fugitives from justice, 141; Garrisonians' proslavery interpretation of, 153, 338; Garrison's denunciation of, 35, 120, 178–79, 252, 291, 338; Higginson's opinion of, 281; higher law and, 177–79; immediate emancipation and, 186; immediatists on, 186–87; internal slave trade and, 186; Lincoln's slavery-related interpretation, 354; Phillips's opinion of, 252, 338–39; regulation of slavery, 86; Spooner's opinion of, 295; Thirteenth Amendment ending of, 35, 99, 162, 169, 207, 289,
295, 309–11, 324, 336, 340, 412; three-fifths clause, 141, 233, 284, 337, 339

U.S. South, antislavery in, **340–42**; folklore depicting daily life, 340–41; funny songs, 340–41; Nat Turner's Rebellion, 33, 209, 210, 314–15, 341, 382; Northern antislavery campaign, 341–42; religious antislavery support, 341; trickster tales, 340; Underground Railroad operations, 342

Van Buren, Martin, 332–33
Van Rensellaer, Thomas, 241
Vesey, Denmark, 345–47
Vesey, Robert, 346
Vesey, Sandy, 346
Vesey's Conspiracy, 10, **345–47**
Vigilance Committees, 7
Violence and nonviolence in American abolitionism, **347–56**; black antislavery violence, 348–49; defensive violence, 351; Garrison and, 349–50; hanging of Turner, 349; Kansas-Nebraska Act, 353–54; lynchings, 114, 146, 216, 299, 330, 349, 382; nonviolence, 49, 263, 348, 349–51, 353; Northern abolitionists and slave revolt, 354–56; slave rebels and a revolutionary heritage, 351–52; Smith and, 347–48; Underground Railroad *vs.* fugitive slave laws, 352–53; Walker and, 348
Virginia Abolition Society, 325

Wade, Benjamin F., 269–70
Wade, Richard, 181
Walker, David, 175, 188, 239, 327–28, 348, **357–59**

Walker v. Jennison (1781–1783), 137, 265

War of 1812, 119

Ward, Samuel Ringgold, 18

Washington, D.C., compensated emancipation in, **359–61**

Washington, George, 193, 285, 326

Webster, Daniel, 102

Webster-Ashburton Treaty (1842), 5, 103

Wedgwood, Josiah, 56, *56*

Weekly Anglo-African magazine, 291

Weld, Theodore Dwight, 120, **362–63**; *American Slavery as It Is: Testimony of a Thousand Witnesses,* 168, 189, 298, 363; editorial role for the *Emancipator,* 167; embrace of abolitionism, 25; government researcher and lobbyist, 363; influence in the AASS, 12, 25; influence on Northerners, 3335; influence on Tappan brothers, 306; marriage to Angelina Grimké, 84, 168; opposition to colonization plan, 26; organization of Lane Seminary debates, 199, 362–63; study on American slavery, 168; vision of training antislavery reformers, 125; withdrawal from Lane Seminary, 202

Wesley, John, 21, 50

West Africa Squadron, 6

West Indies: AMA foreign missions to, 18; antislavery evangelical Christianity in, 24, 126; gradual emancipation in, 160, 163; harassment of Catholic slaves, 63; *Liberator* antislavery newspaper circulation in, 35; monitoring of newly freed slaves, 37; slave trade, 57–58, 174; slave unrest, 57; sugar plantation slavery, 41, 74

West Indies Emancipation Day Celebration, 39, **363–65**

Western Antislavery Society, 130

Western Evangelical Missionary Association, 18

Wheatley, Phillis, 126

Whig Party and antislavery, **366–67**; alliance with the Liberty Party, 204; antislavery strategies, 273; "Appeal of Independent Democrats" by, 109; Birney's abolitionist stance, 203–4; effort "crush out" agitation of the slavery issue, 353; intra-party split over slavery, 366–67; Lincoln's Illinois Whig leadership, 205; members open to antislavery, 331–32; Northern Whigs, 366; President Taylor's ownership of slaves, 89, 366–67; Seward's abolitionist stance, 178, 333; Southern Whigs, 367; Stevens abolitionist stance, 334

Whitefield, George, 50, 92, 125, 126, 127. *See also* First Great Awakening and antislavery

Whittier, John Greenléaf, 149, 211, 262

Wilberforce, William, **367–70,** *368*; effort at ending Atlantic slave trade, 21–22, 31, 43–44, 261, 367–69; Garrison's meeting with, 151; Pitt's collaboration with, 37, 368; Proclamation Society founder, 367–68; quoting of Benezet by, 51; seeking of support from British, 151; support for Catholic Emancipation, 369–70; support for Sierra Leone repatriation project, 368; Wesley's letter to, 21

William and Mary Quarterly, 208–9

Williams, Peter, Jr., 247

Wilmot, David, 84, 109

Wilmot Proviso, 4, 84, 109, 163, 231

Wilson, George, 346

Wilson, Henry, 360

Winny v. Whitesides (1824), 138

Women's antislavery societies, **370–71**; Boston Female Anti-Slavery Society, 85, 251, 329, 330, 370–71; Ladies' New York City Anti-Slavery Society, 371; Massachusetts societies, 370; New England, 370–71; Philadelphia Female Anti-Slavery Society, 235, 370

Women's Social and Political Union, 37

Woolman, John, 131, 208, 260–61

World Anti-Slavery Convention (1840), 34, 235, 252, 262, 371

Worth, Daniel, 18

Wright, Elizur, Jr., 24–26, 28, 256–58, 306

Wright, Henry C., 152, 350

Wright, Theodore, 8, 18

Zong massacre (1781), 59

About the Editors

PETER HINKS is authority on African American history and the early American antislavery movement. He is the author of *To Awaken My Afflicted Brethren: David Walker and the Problem of Antebellum Slave Resistance* (1997).

JOHN MCKIVIGAN is the Mary O'Brien Gibson Professor of History and the editor of *the Frederick Douglass Papers* at Indiana University-Purdue University Indianapolis and the author of numerous books on abolitionism.